Communications in Computer and Information Science 2629

Series Editors

Rationale

The CCIS series is devoted to the publication of proceedings of computer science conferences. Its aim is to efficiently disseminate original research results in informatics in printed and electronic form. While the focus is on publication of peer-reviewed full papers presenting mature work, inclusion of reviewed short papers reporting on work in progress is welcome, too. Besides globally relevant meetings with internationally representative program committees guaranteeing a strict peer-reviewing and paper selection process, conferences run by societies or of high regional or national relevance are also considered for publication.

Topics

The topical scope of CCIS spans the entire spectrum of informatics ranging from foundational topics in the theory of computing to information and communications science and technology and a broad variety of interdisciplinary application fields.

Information for Volume Editors and Authors

Publication in CCIS is free of charge. No royalties are paid, however, we offer registered conference participants temporary free access to the online version of the conference proceedings on SpringerLink (http://link.springer.com) by means of an http referrer from the conference website and/or a number of complimentary printed copies, as specified in the official acceptance email of the event.

CCIS proceedings can be published in time for distribution at conferences or as post-proceedings, and delivered in the form of printed books and/or electronically as USBs and/or e-content licenses for accessing proceedings at SpringerLink. Furthermore, CCIS proceedings are included in the CCIS electronic book series hosted in the SpringerLink digital library at http://link.springer.com/bookseries/7899. Conferences publishing in CCIS are allowed to use our online conference service (Meteor) for managing the whole proceedings lifecycle (from submission and reviewing to preparing for publication) free of charge.

Publication process

The language of publication is exclusively English. Authors publishing in CCIS have to sign the Springer CCIS copyright transfer form, however, they are free to use their material published in CCIS for substantially changed, more elaborate subsequent publications elsewhere. For the preparation of the camera-ready papers/files, authors have to strictly adhere to the Springer CCIS Authors' Instructions and are strongly encouraged to use the CCIS LaTeX style files or templates.

Abstracting/Indexing

CCIS is abstracted/indexed in DBLP, Google Scholar, EI-Compendex, Mathematical Reviews, SCImago, Scopus. CCIS volumes are also submitted for the inclusion in ISI Proceedings.

How to start

To start the evaluation of your proposal for inclusion in the CCIS series, please send an e-mail to ccis@springer.com

Juha Röning · Joaquim Filipe
Editors

Robotics, Computer Vision and Intelligent Systems

5th International Conference, ROBOVIS 2025
Porto, Portugal, February 25–27, 2025
Proceedings

Springer

Editors
Juha Röning
University of Oulu
Oulu, Finland

Joaquim Filipe
Polytechnic Institute of Setubal/INSTICC
Setubal, Portugal

ISSN 1865-0929 ISSN 1865-0937 (electronic)
Communications in Computer and Information Science
ISBN 978-3-032-00985-2 ISBN 978-3-032-00986-9 (eBook)
https://doi.org/10.1007/978-3-032-00986-9

This Springer imprint is published by the registered company Springer Nature Switzerland AG
The registered company address is: Gewerbestrasse 11, 6330 Cham, Switzerland

Preface

This book contains the proceedings of the 5th International Conference on Robotics, Computer Vision and Intelligent Systems. This year, ROBOVIS was held in Porto, Portugal, on February 25–27, 2025. It was sponsored by the Institute for Systems and Technologies of Information, Control and Communication (INSTICC) and endorsed by the International Association for Pattern Recognition. ROBOVIS 2025 was also organized in cooperation with the ACM Special Interest Group on Artificial Intelligence and the Portuguese Association for Artificial Intelligence.

Robotics is a field that is closely connected to Computer Vision and Intelligent Systems. Research and development of robots require technologies originating from the other two areas; research work in Computer Vision has often been driven by needs in Robotics; Intelligent Systems models and software have often been developed aiming at applications in the areas of physical agents, i.e. robots, or in domains related to scene understanding, video and image processing, and many other aspects of computer vision. There is a need for a venue where these three research communities, often isolated, meet and discuss innovation possibilities driven by the intersection of these highly synergetic fields.

ROBOVIS 2025 received 43 paper submissions from 20 countries, of which nine (20.93%) were accepted and published as full papers. A double-blind paper review was performed for each submission by at least 2, but usually 3 or more, members of the International Program Committee, which was composed of established researchers and domain experts.

The high quality of the ROBOVIS 2025 program was enhanced by the keynote lectures delivered by distinguished speakers who are renowned experts in their fields: Luís Paulo Reis (University of Porto, Portugal), Honghai Liu (University of Portsmouth, UK) and Roland Siegwart (ETH Zürich, Switzerland).

All presented papers will be submitted for indexing by DBLP, Google Scholar, EI-Compendex, INSPEC, Japanese Science and Technology Agency (JST), Norwegian Register for Scientific Journals and Series, Mathematical Reviews, SCImago, Scopus, zbMATH and Web of Science / Conference Proceedings Citation Index.

Several awards, based on the combined marks of paper reviewing, as assessed by the Program Committee, and the quality of the presentation, as assessed by session chairs at the conference venue, were conferred at the conference's closing session as recognition for the best contributions.

The program for this conference required the dedicated effort of many people. Firstly, we must thank the authors, whose research efforts are reported here. Next, we thank the members of the Program Committee and the auxiliary reviewers for their diligent and professional reviewing. We would also like to deeply thank the invited speakers for their invaluable contribution and for taking the time to prepare their talks. Finally, a word of appreciation for the hard work of the INSTICC team; organizing a conference of this level is a task that can only be achieved by the collaborative effort of a dedicated and highly competent team.

We hope you all had an exciting and inspiring conference. We hope to have contributed to the development of our research community, and we look forward to having additional research results presented at the next edition of ROBOVIS, details of which are available at https://robovis.scitevents.org.

February 2025

Juha Röning
Joaquim Filipe

Organization

Conference Chair

Joaquim Filipe	Polytechnic Institute of Setubal/INSTICC, Portugal

Program Chair

Juha Röning	University of Oulu, Finland

Program Committee

Hussein Abdullah	University of Guelph, Canada
Mohd Ashraf Ahmad	University Malaysia Pahang, Malaysia
Yannick Aoustin	LS2N, France
Juan Augusto	Middlesex University London, UK
Sofiane Boucenna	ENSEA Graduate School, France
Ivan Buzurovic	Harvard University, USA
Ratchatin Chanchareon	Chulalongkorn University, Thailand
Liming Chen	Centrale Lyon, France
William Cockshott	Glasgow University, UK
Raymond H. Cuijpers	Eindhoven University of Technology, Netherlands
Partha Das	Independent Researcher, India
František Duchon	Slovak University of Technology in Bratislava, Slovak Republic
Nils Einecke	Honda Research Institute Europe GmbH, Germany
Ahmed El-Sayed	University of Bridgeport, USA
Daniele Fontanelli	Università degli Studi di Trento, Italy
Luigi Freda	Independent Researcher, Italy
Udo Frese	University Bremen, Germany
Ismael García-Varea	University of Castilla-La Mancha, Spain
Yakup Genç	Gebze Technical University, Turkey
Mahmoud Hassaballah	South Valley University, Egypt
Jamshed Iqbal	University of Hull, UK
Michael Jenkin	York University, Canada

Additional Reviewers

M. Eduarda Andrada	Institute of Systems and Robotics, University of Coimbra, Portugal
Afonso Eloi Carvalho	CMU Portugal/University of Coimbra, Portugal
Thomas Röfer	Independent Researcher, Germany
Debarshi Sanyal	Indian Association for the Cultivation of Science, India

Invited Speakers

Roland Siegwart	ETH Zurich, Switzerland
Luís Paulo Reis	University of Porto, Portugal
Honghai Liu	University of Portsmouth, UK

Invited Talks

Aerial Robots – From Omnidirectional Flight to Physical Interaction at Height

Roland Siegwart

ETH Zuerich, Switzerland

Abstract. In the last 20 years, flying robots have evolved from fascinating lab prototypes to extremely useful tools for aerial imaging, search and rescue, and inspections at height. However, the limited flight capabilities, as well as the restricted computing power of drones renders autonomous operations quite challenging. This talk will focus on the design and autonomous navigation of arial robots capable of physical interactions. These omnidirectional flying robots enable physical work at height, thus opening totally new challenges and applications.

FC Portugal: Tri-World Champions in RoboCup 3D Humanoid Soccer Simulation

Luís Paulo Reis

Faculty of Engineering, University of Porto, Porto, Portugal

Abstract. This talk presents an overview of FC Portugal, a tri-world champion team (2022–2024) from the Universities of Porto and Aveiro in the RoboCup 3D Simulation League. We explore the team's advanced methods for developing individual and collective skills, such as humanoid running, kicking, and dribbling, as well as coordinated team strategies like joint moves, setplays, tactics, and strategies. Central to this is TSAL (Team Strategy Abstraction Language), a novel framework that combines deep symbolic reinforcement learning with human knowledge to optimize high-level team tactics. In addressing the challenges of reinforcement learning in robotics, such as sample efficiency, intertask coordination, and stability, we have developed a symmetryenriched learning framework using Skill-Set Primitives—a hierarchical structure that simplifies transitions and reduces the policy to a shallow neural network. This enables us to improve sample efficiency, stability, and accelerate agent skill training by over 100 times compared to traditional approaches, facilitating the rapid learning of complex and robust humanoid behaviors such as omnidirectional walking with push-recovery, running, sprinting, kicking, and dribbling skills.

Multi-modal Sensing and Understanding for Human Machine Systems

Honghai Liu

School of Computing, University of Portsmouth, UK

Abstract. The talk first presents the state of the art in multimodal sensing and understanding for human machine systems with focuses on neuroprosthetics and afterstroke rehabilitation. It then discusses principles of individual sensing modalities, their combination and their pathways to motor cortex for representing motor capability. Next the talk focuses on wearable sonomyography for neuroprosthetic control and corticomuscular coherence based assessment for afterstroke rehabilitation. The talk is concluded with future directions and challenges.

Contents

Predicting Sources of High Vertical Acceleration on the Road by Preceding Vehicle Observation 1
Petr Jahoda, Jan Cech, Jan Svancar, and Tomas Hanis

Deep Learning-Based Object Recognition for Automated Dissolution Monitoring 15
Simon-Johannes Burgdorf, Md Rezwanul Karim, and Kerstin Thurow

Automating 3D Dataset Generation with Neural Radiance Fields 28
Paul Schulz, Thorsten Hempel, and Ayoub Al-Hamadi

Cut-and-Splat: Leveraging Gaussian Splatting for Synthetic Data Generation 44
Bram Vanhele, Brent Zoomers, Jeroen Put, Frank Van Reeth, and Nick Michiels

LiCAR: Pseudo-RGB LiDAR Image for CAR Segmentation 63
Ignacio de Loyola Páez-Ubieta, Edison P. Velasco-Sánchez, and Santiago T. Puente

Toward Truly Intelligent Autonomous Systems: A Taxonomy of LLM Integration for Everyday Automation 74
Magnus Jung, Thorsten Hempel, Basheer Al-Tawil, Qiaoyue Yang, Sven Wachsmuth, and Ayoub Al-Hamadi

Robot Vision System for Retail Shelf Monitoring 92
Abhishek V. Latha, Mohammad Rahimipour, and Adel Merabet

Integrating Vision-Based AI and Large Language Models for Real-Time Aquaculture Net Pens Inspection 103
Waseem Akram, Muhayy Ud Din, Lakmal Seneviratne, and Irfan Hussain

Shadow-Robust Autonomous Navigation with Traversability Judgement Using Stereo Camera 115
Motonobu Omori, Kota Hyashi, Hiroshi Yoshitake, and Motoki Shino

Error Modification of Robot Motion Generation by LLM Based on Parts Function and Physical Features of Robot 130
Takahiro Suzuki and Manabu Hashimoto

Hybrid Neural Network-Based Indoor Localisation System for Mobile Robots Using CSI Data in a Robotics Simulator ... 148
Javier Ballesteros-Jerez, Jesus Martínez-Gómez, Ismael García-Varea, Luis Orozco-Barbosa, and Manuel Castillo-Cara

Towards a Reliable Multimodal AI Monitoring System for Pain Detection and Quantification ... 164
Huibin Wang, Sören Nienaber, Laslo Dinges, Magnus Jung, and Ayoub Al-Hamadi

Automatic Comparison of Ecuadorian Facial Features with Marquardt Beauty Mask ... 182
Jesús Ormaza, Paulina Morillo, and Diego Vallejo-Huanga

Online Collaborative UAV Path Planning for Mapping and Spraying Missions ... 193
Ali Moltajaei Farid and Malek Mouhoub

Statistically Consistent Total Least-Squares Estimation of Object Scales ... 208
Arne Hasselbring and Udo Frese

Silent Speech Interface Based on Surface Electromyography Using Arduino and Ensemble Learning ... 228
William Kyle Deveza, Joseph Bryan Ibarra, and Marloun Sejera

PENet: A Joint Panoptic Edge Detection Network ... 250
Yang Zhou and Giuseppe Loianno

Norm-Based Stability Conditions for Neutral Systems with Discrete Delays ... 265
Ozlem Faydasicok and Sabri Arik

Evaluating Pose Awareness and 3D Consistency in Semantic Matching ... 275
Paolo Sebeto, Jean-Baptiste Weibel, Christian Hartl-Nesic, and Markus Vincze

Detection, Characterization, and Localization of Oranges and Their Stems Using RGB-D Camera and Image Processing ... 294
Alaeddin Bani Milhim, Colton Cunningham, and The Leo Nguyen

Scene-Aware Prediction of Diverse Human Movement Goals ... 312
Qiaoyue Yang, Amadeus Weber, Magnus Jung, Ayoub Al-Hamadi, and Sven Wachsmuth

Explainable Detection of Logical and Structural Anomalies Based on Multimodal Large Language Models 328
Noeko Fujii and Tetsuya Sakai

Learn Where I Can Walk: Auto-labeling of Walked Areas Using Monocular Camera Trajectory 348
Helmut Engelhardt, Matthias Kalenberg, Jörg Franke, and Sina Martin

Material Classification Using Visio-Tactile Sensor for Haptic Feedback Generation 364
Md Golam Rabby Shuvo, Sonya Coleman, Dermot Kerr, and Justin Quinn

Pipeline Inspection a Case Study for Human Cognition Inspired Condition Management System 383
Hariom Dhungana

Active Closure: Symbolic Active Contour for Spatial Automated Reasoning ... 397
J. I. Olszewska

Synth it Like KITTI: Synthetic Data Generation for Object Detection in Driving Scenarios 414
Richard Marcus, Christian Vogel, Inga Jatzkowski, Niklas Knoop, and Marc Stamminger

NAUTICAL: Navigation Aid Using U-Net and *Theta** with Integrated Collision Avoidance and Landmarking 433
Yashwardhan Deshmukh, Martin J.-D. Otis, and Salick Diagne

Entropy-Guided Self-regulated Learning Without Forgetting for Distribution-Shift Continual Learning with Blurred Task Boundaries 454
Rui Yang, Matthieu Grard, Emmanuel Dellandréa, and Liming Chen

Objects Detection on the Water Surface Using Satellite Imagery, Drones and Vessel-Based Imaging Applied for Logistics 469
Iheb Ben Salah, Martin J.-D. Otis, Remy Rahem, and Mahassen Ardhaoui

A Flexible Output Distribution for Regression-Based Probabilistic Long-Term Human Trajectory Prediction 488
Ronny Hug, Stefan Becker, Wolfgang Hübner, Michael Arens, and Jürgen Beyerer

Is an Object-Centric Representation Beneficial for Robotic Manipulation? 510
Alexandre Chapin, Emmanuel Dellandréa, and Liming Chen

Outdoor Robot Geo-Localization Using Vision Technics 524
Hasinarivo Marie Berthis Ramanana, Jean-Pierre Jessel, Tahiry Filamatra Andriamarozakaniaina, and Hagamalala Santatra Bernardin

Improving Stability and Precision of Bird Tracking in Stereo Vision Systems 535
Grzegorz Madejski, Aleksy Stocki, Dawid Gradolewski, Włodzimierz Kaoka, and Wlodek J. Kulesza

Author Index 557

Predicting Sources of High Vertical Acceleration on the Road by Preceding Vehicle Observation

Petr Jahoda(✉), Jan Cech, Jan Svancar, and Tomas Hanis

Faculty of Electrical Engineering, Czech Technical University, Prague, Czech Republic
jahodpet@cvut.cz

Abstract. We propose a novel method that detects sources of high vertical acceleration on the road by visual tracking of a preceding vehicle. The method is general, predicting any kind of road anomalies, such as potholes, bumps, debris, etc., unlike direct observation methods that rely on training visual detectors of those cases. The method works in poor visibility or when the preceding vehicle occludes the road anomaly. The approach is validated on our dataset that includes anomalies collected in both controlled settings and real-world scenarios captured in normal traffic conditions. The experiment confirms a strong correlation between a signal measured by a visual tracker, which estimates a vertical displacement of the preceding vehicle, and the IMU signal from the ego vehicle. We demonstrate that our system detects road surface anomalies with high accuracy, achieving AUC 0.969. The method is computationally cheap and runs in real-time on consumer hardware.

1 Introduction

Road safety and comfort are key concerns in the modern transportation. The detection of sources of unexpected vertical acceleration on the road, which we refer to as anomalies in this paper, such as potholes, bumps, rutting, expansion joints, and debris, is significant for ensuring the safety of vehicle occupants, enhancing driving comfort, and minimizing wear and tear on tires, wheels, or vehicle suspension components.

Particularly important are forward-looking systems that identify such irregularities before the vehicle encounters them, allowing for timely alerts to human or autonomous drivers, or providing additional predictive information enabling appropriate response of chassis subsystems like suspension, traction, and braking systems.

The predictive systems, which often rely on cameras to directly recognize surface anomalies with clear visibility in front of a vehicle, face challenges. Visibility of road irregularities can be severely compromised due to weather conditions, time of day, or often due to obstruction by other traffic participants.

This paper proposes a system that leverages indirect detection of road surface irregularities by monitoring the movement of a vehicle ahead. Our method automatically detects typical motion patterns indicative of surface anomalies, akin to an experienced driver being able to recognize a problem by observing sudden jolts of the preceding vehicle, even without direct sight of the cause on the road. See Fig. 1 for an illustration of the proposed approach.

J. Röning and J. Filipe (Eds.): ROBOVIS 2025, CCIS 2629, pp. 1–14, 2026.
https://doi.org/10.1007/978-3-032-00986-9_1

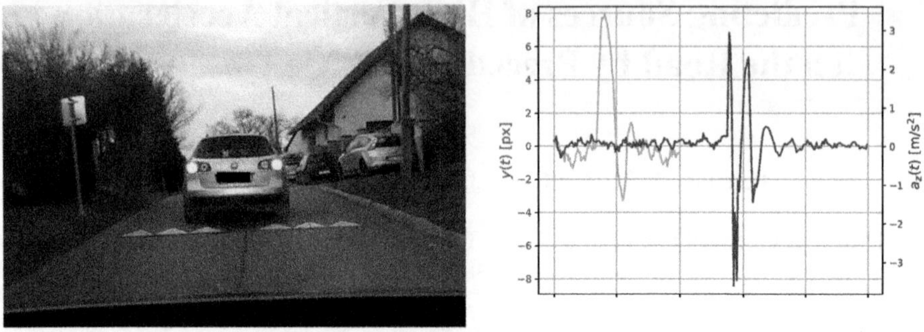

Fig. 1. The idea of the approach is to detect road surface anomalies by visually tracking a preceding vehicle, e.g., a preceding vehicle going over a speed bump (left). Vertical tracking signal from the ego-camera (in red) provides information that there is a source of high vertical acceleration ahead. The effect on the ego vehicle is then confirmed by accelerometer recording (in blue). The method proposes a statistic to determine whether the visual acceleration is excessive, thereby detecting the anomaly and providing a timely alert along with the predicted time and distance to the contact with the anomaly.

The method is robust to visibility challenges, as car rears are designed on purpose to be well visible in any time/weather condition. Thus even for common anomalies, the method can provide early detection before the vehicle approaches close enough to detect them directly.

Our contributions are summarized as follows:

1. **Novel Method for Road Surface Anomaly Detection.** We introduce a new method for detecting road surface irregularities by observing the motion of a vehicle traveling ahead. This indirect approach circumvents the limitations of direct road surface observation and offers a novel perspective on anomaly detection.
2. **Dataset of Surface Anomalies Traversed by a Preceding Vehicle.** We collected a dataset, called SVAR (Sources of Vertical Acceleration on the Road), of videos in which a preceding vehicle traverses surface anomalies on the road. The dataset consists of two subsets. The first subset comprises a controlled experiment utilizing two instrumented vehicles to capture a traversal over speed bumps. The second subset pertains to an "in-the-wild" scenario, derived from recordings in standard traffic conditions.
3. **Correlation Analysis.** We confirmed a high correlation between the visual signals obtained from observing the preceding vehicle and the IMU signals recorded when traversing the same anomaly by the ego vehicle. This correlation validates the effectiveness of our visual observation technique as a reliable proxy for direct measurements.
4. **High-Accuracy in Road Surface Anomaly Detection.** The study shows that the visual signal enables the detection of road surface irregularities with high accuracy. By analyzing the motion patterns of the vehicle ahead, our system can accurately identify the anomalies.

These contributions underscore the potential of our proposed system to enhance predictive road safety mechanisms and support the development of advanced driver-assistance systems (ADAS) and autonomous driving technologies.

The remainder of the paper is structured as follows. Related work is reviewed in Sect. 2. The proposed method is described in Sect. 3. Experiments are given in Sect. 4. Finally, Sect. 5 concludes the paper.

2 Related Work

The detection of anomalies on road surfaces has been addressed in the literature through multiple approaches. There are two main principles: (1) Effect-based methods, where a road surface defect is identified ex-post by traversing over, usually detected by accelerometers [13]. (2) Predictive methods, where anomalies are spotted a priori before a vehicle encounters them, typically using a camera [6] or a lidar [18].

These methods include detection of potholes [8], speed bumps [1], or general pavement distress [4]. For a more detailed taxonomy of these methods, we refer to a recent survey [15].

Recent vision-based methods rely on machine learning and deep models, utilizing supervised training with datasets of manually annotated images [9]. An alternative approach to manual labeling is self-supervised learning, where a training label for images is supplied by an accelerometer, and then image-only model is used for deployment [2]. Another approach is to treat anomalies as unpredictable off-distribution samples [19].

An example of a predictive commercial system is “Magic Body Control” by Mercedes-Benz [11], which relies on a forward-looking stereo-camera to monitor road-surface disturbances as, e.g., speed bumps, and communicates with the suspension controller to adjust real-time response to mitigate effects on the vehicle body.

Cooperative techniques to collect and share road-surface hazards have been considered for a fleet of vehicles [5] or in a vehicle-to-vehicle scenario [14, 17, 20].

Our work aims to predictively detect road surface anomalies using the perception system of the ego vehicle, which indirectly infers anomalies from the motion pattern of the preceding vehicle using a camera. This system is complementary to direct sensing methods and can be advantageous in adverse conditions, such as poor visibility, or where the preceding vehicle obscures a road anomaly, which is frequent in urban traffic.

The closest work to our approach is [10] which adopts a control engineering perspective. It focuses on solving an inverse problem of estimating the road profile by modeling the vehicle’s vertical dynamics and employing a Kalman filter. However, their experiment does not demonstrate detection of anomalies from a perspective of an ego vehicle, but uses a static camera observing several vehicles from the side as they drive over a single pothole, which is not our target scenario.

3 Method

The proposed method detects a preceding vehicle in the image of a front-looking camera and visually tracks it over time. Surface anomalies are found by detecting excessive deviations of the trajectory around the mean location.

Fig. 2. Flowchart of the proposed method. It employs instance segmentation to isolate a preceding car in the initial frame followed by continuous tracking by CoTracker [7].

The pipeline of the algorithm is sketched in Fig. 2. First, all vehicles are found by instance segmentation. We use Mask2Former [3] which delivers instance segmentation mask for all vehicles in the frame. The target vehicle is found to be the closest to the center of the image. Then the vehicle is tracked by CoTracker [7], which jointly tracks a grid of points. We set N points equidistantly distributed over the instance mask. The tracker returns respective horizontal, and vertical locations $x_i(t), y_i(t)$ for every grid point i in frame t. Since we are only interested in vertical motion, we aggregated over vertical locations of tracked points $y(t) = \frac{1}{N}\sum_{i=1}^{N} y_i(t)$. Then the signal indicating excessive displacement is calculated as standard deviation in a short window of T frames

$$s(t) = \sqrt{\frac{1}{T}\sum_{\tau=t-T+1}^{t} \left(y(\tau) - \bar{y}\right)^2}, \tag{1}$$

where $\bar{y} = \frac{1}{T}\sum_{\tau=t-T+1}^{t} y(\tau)$ is the mean location. Signal $s(t)$ is finally thresholded (with non-maximum suppression) to detect anomalies on the road surface and to distinguish them from a normal background.

In all experiments, we set temporal window $T = 30$ frames, which represent one second in our setup. Points tracked by CoTracker were equidistantly distributed over the instance masks, by 6 pixels vertically and horizontally by default. We limit the maximum number of points to $N = 400$ to fit in GPU memory.

Discussion: Note that the anomaly is detected by thresholding the signal $s(t)$ in Eq. (1), relying on tracking in the image plane (in pixels). In principle, it is possible to convert the displacements into the scene based on the vehicle distance and set the threshold in meters. However, accuracy of the displacement estimate in the scene obviously depends on the distance, which would need to be taken into account, see our analysis in Sect. 4.3. Otherwise, false detection would easily occur at a distance. This is not a problem when the thresholding is done in pixels, as the displacement in pixels is naturally small for a distant target.

The presented method does not compensate for the camera ego-motion. This is usually not a problem, unless the camera of the ego vehicle rotates significantly. This could happen for instance if the ego vehicle traverses over a surface anomaly too. The vibration causing camera motion (especially rotation) disrupts the signal $s(t)$ and would cause false detections. However, this is not a concern because our typical scenario involves a flat road and sudden irregularity. When the ego-vehicle is passing over an unevenness, or the road is of such poor quality that it leads to excessive vibrations, it is not worthwhile to perform any measurement. Therefore, we exclude all cases where the ego vehicle undergoes significant vertical acceleration, based on the IMU in the ego vehicle. In principle, it is possible to estimate and compensate for the camera's own movement using the IMU or visual odometry, but that exceeds the scope of this paper.

Another simplification we made is that we do not model the vehicle suspension. Clearly, the vehicle body motion response to the excitation coming from road anomalies is not linearly proportional to the depth or height of the road irregularity. It is a complex function dependent on many factors, such as axle and suspension kinematics, tuning of the vehicle suspension, vehicle body dynamics, etc. The simplification is justified because we target urban traffic situations, which typically occur at lower speeds where excitation signals exhibit dominant low-frequency spectra, making anomalies clearly detectable in vehicle body motions. We frame the problem as a binary classification: the positive class represents surface anomalies, while the negative class corresponds to the natural background.

4 Experiments

Fig. 3. Examples of anomalies, sources of high-vertical acceleration, on the road surface in our SVAR dataset (in-the-wild subset). Note that except for the leftmost column, the road surface anomalies are not visible to a human observer, but are detectable by observing the preceding vehicle. See supplementary videos at https://youtu.be/FM7T88Rdmqg for better illustration.

4.1 Datasets

We collected a dataset called SVAR (Sources of Vertical Acceleration on the Road), consisting of two subsets. The first subset is acquired for a controlled experiment, using two instrumented cars and well-defined road surface anomaly and traversing scenarios. The second subset was acquired in normal traffic, where the ego car was lightly instrumented with the camera and IMU, usually of a smartphone.

Dataset for Controlled Experiment. We used two cars that were instrumented in the same way. In particular, ZED2 camera was mounted behind the windscreen, and IMU was attached to the floor of the trunk. Finally, an automotive-grade GPS (with an external antenna on the roof) was installed. Each instrument was connected to the computer that recorded the data. The synchronization of the recordings between the cars was done using GPS time stamps.

Two cars repeatedly crossed three same speed bumps (of dimensions $2 \times 1.78 \times 0.06$ meters, both approaching and exiting edge of 7°, see Fig. 1) in various mutual distances from about 3 to 40 m. The speed of the traversal was about 20 km/h.

Synchronized GPS units give us precise measurements of the distance between the cars. The IMU in the preceding vehicle provides automatic annotation of the event, when it travels over the speed bump.

In-the-Wild Dataset. We collected anomalies on the road surface in normal traffic conditions. In this case, a single car was instrumented with a camera and the accelerometer. The first part of the dataset was captured using consumer smartphones, the second part with a more advanced test vehicle, but only a standard automotive camera and an accelerometer were used.

The annotation process was semi-automatic. When an excessive vertical acceleration was found, we checked whether a car detector [3] spots a vehicle in front. If so, we manually inspected whether the preceding vehicle went over the same surface anomaly and annotated the apex frame of the event. Note that the events, when the ego-vehicle simultaneously encounters other road surface anomaly, which is detected by accelerometer, are not considered in the following experiments, as discussed above.

In total, we collected 65 events when a preceding car encountered road surface anomalies. Short video clips were cut out of long recordings, 5 s prior and 5 s post the apex frame. The anomalies are of various nature, e.g., speed bumps, potholes, or other road depressions, unaligned surface levels when road segments connects, or "wavy" road surfaces. Sometimes the anomalies are hardly or not at all visible directly, and the only indication of the problem is the motion pattern of the preceding vehicle. Several examples are shown in Fig. 3 and in our supplementary videos at https://youtu.be/FM7T88Rdmqg.

These events are relatively rare. In particular, 65 events were found in about 15 h long recordings. The occurrence depends on the road quality and traffic density, since a preceding vehicle indicating the anomaly is needed. We got most of the events for urban driving in rush hours and very few for rural roads.

The distance distribution to the preceding vehicle in our dataset is presented in Fig. 4 together with the traversal speed distribution for the events in the dataset. The distance is visually estimated from the perspective camera by $d = f\frac{W}{w}$, where W is the average width of a car (in meters), w is the width of the instance masks of the rear of the car in the image (in pixels) and f is the focal length (in pixels).

4.2 Correlation Analysis

In Fig. 5, we demonstrate an example of raw signals from the accelerometer and the camera around a road surface anomaly, the vertical acceleration $a_z(t)$ and the location

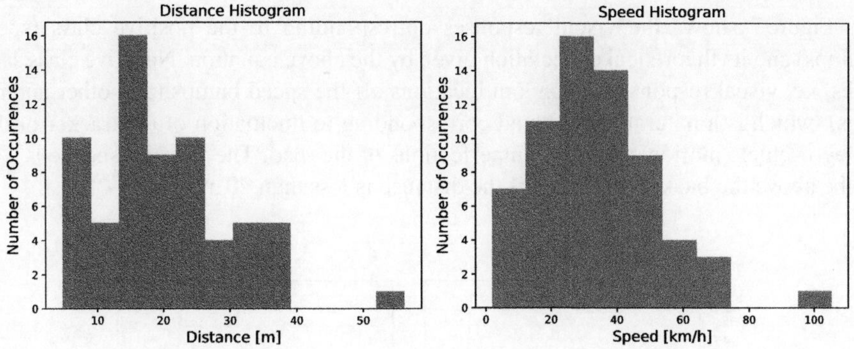

Fig. 4. Histogram of distances to a preceding vehicle and histogram of speeds for the events in our "in-the-wild" dataset.

of the car $y(t)$ found by the visual tracker. The figure shows the normalized cross-correlation over time between velocities computed by differentiating $y(t)$ and integrating $a_z(t)$. The position of the highest correlation corresponds to the temporal delay between the cars that cross over the same anomaly on the road surface. We can see that the correlation is high despite the signals originating from different sensors. On average, the peak correlation for the events in our "in-the-wild" dataset is 0.62 with standard deviation 0.08. The distributions of peak correlations is depicted in Fig. 6. Sometimes low correlation may occur, which is usually due to cars passed slightly different trajectories, as a driver of the ego vehicle tried to mitigate the impact of the anomaly.

4.3 Visual Signal Strength as a Function of the Vehicle Distance

In the following experiment, we measured, on the controlled dataset described in Sect. 4.1, how the strength of the signal depends on the distance to the preceding car. In Fig. 7, we show the visual response $s(t)$ in Eq.(1), computed at the time of traversal over the speed bump for various distances. Obviously, the response is stronger the closer the two vehicles are.

Let us assume that due to a speed bump, a vehicle moves in the scene vertically by displacement δ (in meters). In theory, observing the vehicle from behind by perspective fronto-parallel camera, with focal length f (in pixels) in distance d (in meters), then the displacement in the image plane (in pixels) is given by $\Delta y = f\frac{\delta}{d}$. Theoretical visual response $s(t)$, which we measure in Eq. (1), is sum of two processes – the excitation due to the anomaly and due to the natural background. That is

$$\hat{s}(d) = \alpha f \frac{\delta}{d} + \beta. \tag{2}$$

The camera captures Full-HD 1920×1080 image, vertical field of view is $54°$, which means $f = 1066$ pixels. We set $\delta = 0.06$ m, a height of the speed bump. Parameters α and β are fit in the least square sense.

Figure 7 shows the visual responses corresponding to the positive class (speed bumps) and its theoretical expectation given by the above equation. Negative class samples, i.e. visual responses of random locations off the speed bumps (and other anomalies), which is a natural background corresponding to fluctuation of the tracker or due to ego vehicle motion caused by imperfections of the road. The visual response is seen to be above the background level if the distance is less than 20 m.

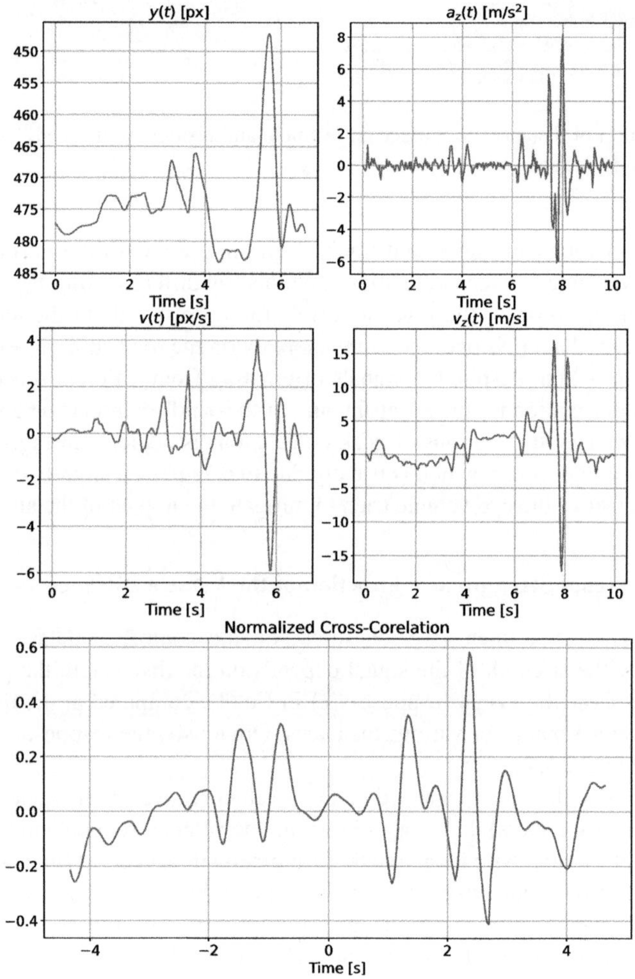

Fig. 5. Visual-IMU signal cross-correlation: raw visual location signal found by CoTracker (top-left), raw accelerometer data (top-right), velocity data (middle) and their temporal cross-correlation (bottom). The highest correlation peak occurs at time 2.3 s, which is exactly the delay between the preceding and ego vehicle encountering the anomaly.

4.4 Accuracy of the Road Surface Anomaly Detector

In this section, we evaluate the accuracy of our proposed road surface anomaly detector. To the best of our knowledge, there is no similar approach to compare with. Therefore, we compare with the following two baselines, where the CoTracker [7] is replaced by simpler estimators. The rest of the pipeline remains the same.

Lucas-Kanade: Interest points, "Good features to track" [16], are detected within the bounding box of the vehicle and are tracked between subsequent frames using Lucas-Kanade tracker [12]. We used OpenCV implementation. Vertical displacements from all the interests points are averaged to provide vertical location $y(t)$.

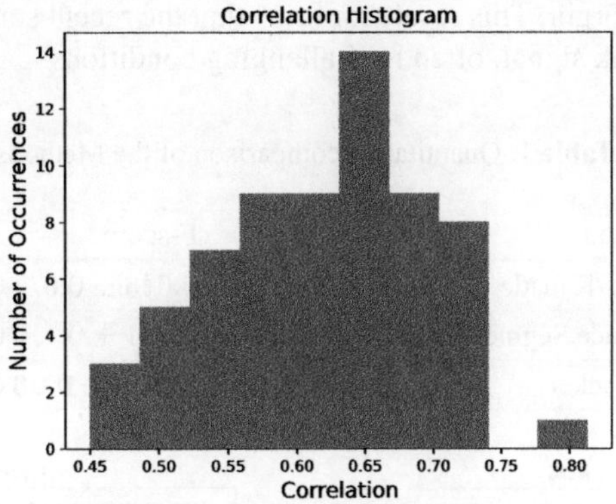

Fig. 6. Histogram of peak cross-modal correlations (Visual-IMU) for anomalies of the "in-the-wild" dataset.

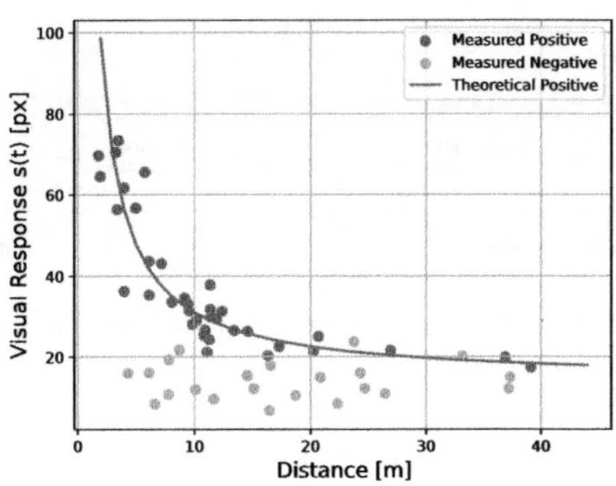

Fig. 7. Visual responses $s(t)$ estimated by Eq. (1) vs. car distances for the controlled experiment. Plot shows positive class samples (speed bumps), negative class samples (natural background), and the theoretical expectation given by our model in Eq. (2).

Instance Segmentation: Vehicle is simply tracked by the center of gravity of the instance mask found by Mask2Former [3]. Vertical component is the location $y(t)$.

The following results are calculated on the challenging in-the-wild dataset. We added the same number of random background events to the dataset of road surface anomalies, in order to have samples of both positive and negative classes.

The quantitative comparison is shown in Table 1. To compare Accuracy and F-score, the threshold of visual response in Eq. (1) that separates the positive (road surface anomaly) and negative (background) classes is set to maximize the F-score for each one of the methods. This is done in a cross-validation setup. The optimum threshold is estimated on the training set and tested on the unseen subset. The results are averaged and standard deviation over the five-fold cross-validation is shown in Table 1. AUC is the area under the ROC curve. It is seen that the full method using CoTracker performs the best by a large margin. This result confirms that the recent state-of-the-art tracker is able to recover a weak signal, often in challenging conditions.

Table 1. Quantitative comparison of the Methods.

Method	Accuracy↑	F-score↑	AUC↑
Lucas-Kanade	0.722 ± 0.06	0.643 ± 0.07	0.836
Instance Segmentation	0.842 ± 0.11	0.821 ± 0.11	0.919
CoTracker	$\mathbf{0.915 \pm 0.05}$	$\mathbf{0.903 \pm 0.06}$	**0.969**

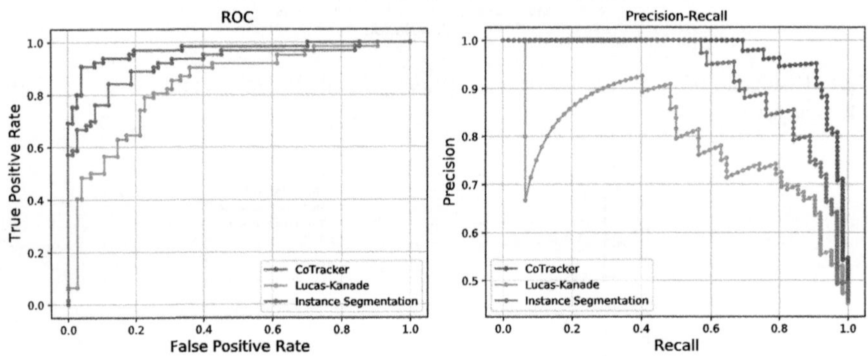

Fig. 8. ROC and Precision-Recall curves for the tested methods. CoTracker [7] outperforms the other baselines.

To provide further insight, we show ROC and precision-recall curves in Fig. 8. The CoTracker outperforms the baselines, for all thresholds. It has a higher or equal true positive rate, lower false negative rate and higher precision and recall than the baselines.

Finally for the CoTracker, we show precision as a function of the threshold in Fig. 9. We can see that precision is one (no false positives occurred) for threshold higher than 24. This result suggests that the threshold can be set very conservatively when the system is deployed to detect the strongest road surface anomalies while minimizing false detections.

4.5 Predicting Time and Distance to Contact

The previous experiment evaluates the detection accuracy of the anomalies. In addition, the following experiment evaluates preciseness of their temporal and spatial localization. This is done by time and distance to the contact. We define the time to contact as the elapsed time between the preceding and ego vehicles encountering the anomaly. The distance to contact is the distance between the preceding and ego vehicle at the moment when the preceding vehicle encounters the anomaly.

The quantities are evaluated in both subsets of SVAR dataset. For the controlled-experiment subset, times t_1 and t_2 when vehicles traverse anomalies are found from their IMUs. The elapsed time between the traverses $t_2 - t_1$ is the ground-truth time to contact, the GPS-based distance between the cars at time t_1 is the ground-truth distance to contact.

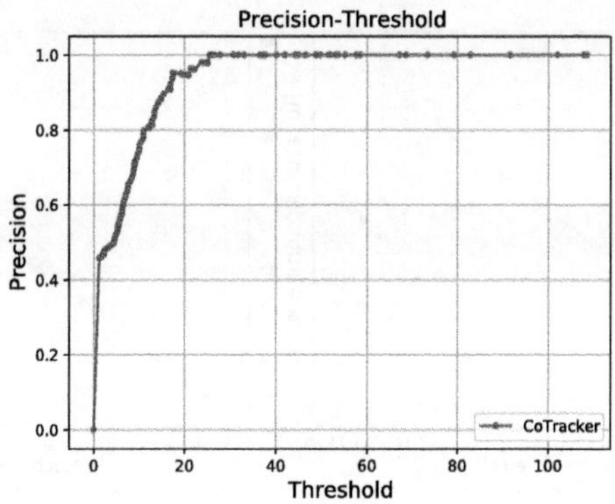

Fig. 9. Precision vs. threshold on the visual response using CoTracker.

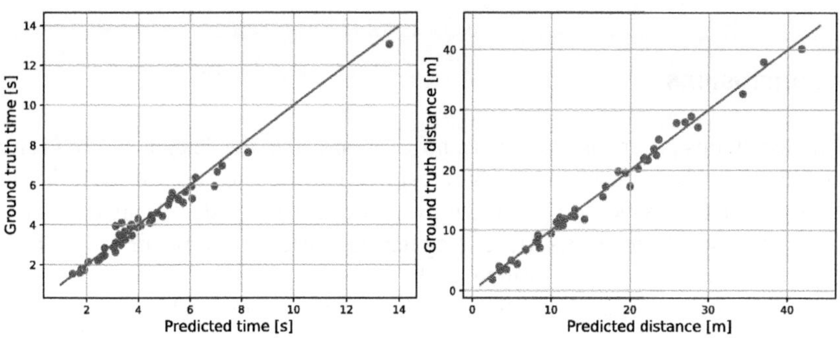

Fig. 10. Time and distance to contact for the controlled setup subset – scatter plots.

For the in-the-wild subset, we have no data from preceding vehicles. Therefore, we manually annotate time t_1 on the video stream, time t_2 is found the same from the ego IMU as above. The ground-truth distance is found from the perspective camera with known focal length, the width of the car in the image and average real-world width of a car as in Sect. 4.3.

The predictions are found by estimating the time $\hat{t}_1$ by the method, see Sect. 3. Distance to contact $\hat{d}$ is estimated from the perspective camera. Time to contact is estimated by $\frac{\hat{d}}{v(\hat{t}_1)}$, as we assume that the vehicle speed after time $\hat{t}_1$ remains constant.

The results are shown as scatter plots in Fig. 10 and Fig. 11 for the controlled and in-the-wild subsets, respectively. Mean absolute/relative errors are 0.28 [s] / 7%, 0.80 [m] / 7% for the first subset, and 0.21 [s] / 11%, 0.35 [m] / 3% for the latter.

The error is small, allowing for a timely alert. The distance to the car is estimated using average car width, but could be estimated more precisely by other sensors. For the time to contact, a constant speed is assumed, which might not have occurred in the data.

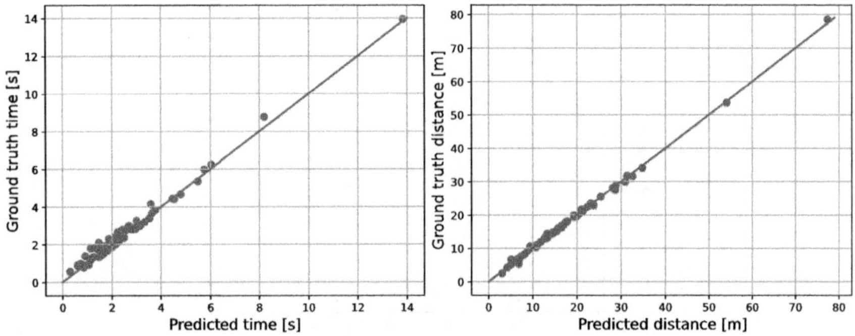

Fig. 11. Time and distance to contact for the "in-the-wild" subset – scatter plots.

5 Conclusions

In conclusion, this paper has presented a novel approach to the detection of road surface anomalies of any kind that cause a significant vertical acceleration through the observation of preceding vehicles. Our system, which operates by identifying characteristic motion patterns indicative of surface irregularities, offers a promising solution to the limitations faced by direct observation methods.

We showed that visual signal from tracking the preceding vehicle correlates with the signal measured from accelerometer of the ego vehicle. The high accuracy of our road surface anomaly detection system demonstrates the viability of using visual cues from preceding vehicles as a dependable indicator of road conditions. In our SVAR datasets, we have instances where a road surface anomaly is not perceivable on the road surface from the driver point of view, but the system detects it from the motion of the preceding vehicle. The method is computationally efficient and operates in real-time on consumer-grade hardware.

A limitation of our current proof-of-concept method is that it does not compensate for the camera ego motion. Our future research will include tracking the vehicle in 3D using IMU and visual odometry. This should extend the applicability of the method for cases where the ego vehicle traverses over another road distress or poor road surfaces that may cause vibrations and a camera rotation. Nevertheless, we see this is not a major weakness, as the target and the most important scenario is a flat road and a sudden road surface anomaly.

Acknowledgment. The research was supported by Toyota Motor Europe, and by CTU student grant under project SGS23/173/OHK3/3T/13.

References

1. Aishwarya, P.V., Reddy, D.S., Sonkar, D.K., Koundinya, P.N., Rajalakshmi, P.: Robust deep learning based speed bump detection for autonomous vehicles in Indian scenarios. In: 2023 IEEE 26th International Symposium on Real-Time Distributed Computing (ISORC), pp. 201–206. IEEE (2023)
2. Cech, J., et al.: Self-supervised learning of camera-based drivable surface roughness. In: 2021 IEEE Intelligent Vehicles Symposium (IV), pp. 1319–1325. IEEE (2021)
3. Cheng, B., Misra, I., Schwing, A.G., Kirillov, A., Girdhar, R.: Masked-attention mask transformer for universal image segmentation. CVPR (2022)
4. Du, Z., Yuan, J., Xiao, F., Hettiarachchi, C.: Application of image technology on pavement distress detection: a review. Measurement **184**, 109900 (2021)
5. Jaguar Land Rover: Pothole detection technology research announced by jaguar land rover (2020). https://www.landrover.com/experiences/news/pothole-detection.html
6. Jakubec, M., Lieskovská, E., Bučko, B., Zábovská, K.: Comparison of CNN-based models for pothole detection in real-world adverse conditions: overview and evaluation. Appl. Sci. **13**(9), 5810 (2023)
7. Karaev, N., Rocco, I., Graham, B., Neverova, N., Vedaldi, A., Rupprecht, C.: CoTracker: it is better to track together (2023)
8. Kim, Y.M.: Review of recent automated pothole-detection methods. Appl. Sci. **12**(11), 5320 (2022)
9. Kulambayev, B., et al.: Real-time road surface damage detection framework based on mask R-CNN model. Int. J. Adv. Comput. Sci. Appl. **14**(9) (2023)
10. Li, D., Xiao, B., Pan, H.: Estimating severe irregularities of road ahead based on preceding vehicle responses. Control. Eng. Pract. **127**, 105300 (2022)
11. Loeber Motors blog: What is Mercedes-Benz Magic Body Control? (2015). https://www.loebermotors.com/blog/mercedes-benz-magic-body-control/
12. Lucas, B.D., Kanade, T.: An iterative image registration technique with an application to stereo vision. In: IJCAI'81: 7th international joint conference on Artificial intelligence, vol. 2, pp. 674–679 (1981)
13. Martinez-Ríos, E.A., Bustamante-Bello, M.R., Arce-Sáenz, L.A.: A review of road surface anomaly detection and classification systems based on vibration-based techniques. Appl. Sci. **12**(19), 9413 (2022)
14. Rahman, M., Rideout, G.: Using the lead vehicle as preview sensor in convoy vehicle active suspension control. Veh. Syst. Dyn. **50**(12), 1923–1948 (2012)
15. Rathee, M., Bačić, B., Doborjeh, M.: Automated road defect and anomaly detection for traffic safety: a systematic review. Sensors **23**(12), 5656 (2023)

16. Shi, J., et al.: Good features to track. In: 1994 Proceedings of IEEE conference on computer vision and pattern recognition, pp. 593–600. IEEE (1994)
17. Stone, S.: Connected, autonomous cars: passive pothole patrollers. IEEE Potentials **39**(1), 52–58 (2019)
18. Talha, S.A., Manasreh, D., Nazzal, M.D.: The use of lidar and artificial intelligence algorithms for detection and size estimation of potholes. Buildings **14**(4), 1078 (2024)
19. Vojíř, T., Matas, J.: Image-consistent detection of road anomalies as unpredictable patches. In: Proceedings of the IEEE/CVF Winter Conference on Applications of Computer Vision, pp. 5491–5500 (2023)
20. Zhu, X., Kundu, S.K.: Road anomaly detection and localization for connected vehicle applications. Technical report, SAE Technical Paper (2023)

Deep Learning-Based Object Recognition for Automated Dissolution Monitoring

Simon-Johannes Burgdorf(✉), Md Rezwanul Karim, and Kerstin Thurow

Center for Life Science Automation, University of Rostock, 18119 Rostock, Germany
simon-johannes.burgdorf@uni-rostock.de

Abstract. Chemical and biological processes often involve the dissolution of substances in a solvent. In this work, we describe a possibility for automation to monitor such dissolution processes to increase the efficiency of the overall process. A Faster Region-based Convolutional Neural Network with a ResNet50 backbone was trained to monitor and automate the dissolution process of particles in various solutions. A dataset was created, containing four different solutions that show the dissolution process at various stages. The results demonstrate that the model is capable of detecting medium to large particles, especially those with no or minimal overlap with other particles. Additionally, the model was able to monitor colored solutions, such as potassium permanganate solution. The model demonstrates strengths in detecting medium to large particles. By expanding the dataset, the detection performance for smaller particles can be improved, leading to an overall enhancement of the model's capabilities. Automating this process is a crucial step toward fully autonomous laboratories.

Keywords: Laboratory automation · Faster-RCNN · Particle detection · Overfitting · Generalization

1 Introduction

The continuous advancement in artificial intelligence, particularly in computer vision (CV), allows machines to take over tasks that previously required human vision. In laboratory automation, scientific staff often have to monitor monotonous and time-consuming processes or repeat simple tasks in large quantities. A common task in laboratories is the dissolution of solids in solvents. Lab technicians are required to promote the dissolution of solids through mechanical actions such as stirring or shaking. The solution is repeatedly visually inspected to assess the dissolution progress, and the process continues until all solids are fully dissolved. However, process errors can occur, such as the oversaturation of the solution, where the dissolution stagnates. This process is performed daily in many laboratories worldwide and represents a critical subprocess that could be automated through CV. This would significantly increase throughput and reduce manual effort.

The goal of automation is the detection of solids and the measurement of the solution's turbidity. Spectroscopic methods, particularly UV-VIS and infrared spectroscopy,

J. Röning and J. Filipe (Eds.): ROBOVIS 2025, CCIS 2629, pp. 15–27, 2026.
https://doi.org/10.1007/978-3-032-00986-9_2

are employed for real-time measurements, providing insights into the progress of the dissolution process [1, 2]. In all methods, turbidity caused by macroscopic or microscopic particles in the solvent is measured to determine the dissolution endpoint. Depending on the method used, turbidity is expressed in nephelometric turbidity units or formazin nephelometric units.

Two additional optical methods used to measure turbidity are nephelometry and turbidimetry. Both techniques are based on the absorption and scattering of a light beam passed through a sample. The principle of nephelometry is based on the Tyndall effect. In this method, a light source sends a beam through the sample, where it is scattered by the particles in the solution. The scattered light is directly related to the number and size of the particles in the solution. This method is especially suitable for solutions with low particle density, as higher concentrations make scattering measurements less precise [3].

In contrast to nephelometry, turbidimetry measures the attenuation of light passing through the solution. A light beam is directed through the sample, and a detector on the opposite side measures the intensity of the transmitted light. This principle is based on the Beer-Lambert law, which states that light intensity decreases as particle concentration increases. This method is particularly suitable for solutions with higher particle densities [3]. In summary, the choice of measurement method depends on the solution's density, particle size, and desired measurement accuracy. Turbidimetry more easily correlates particle concentration with the measured value than nephelometry, as it measures light absorption rather than scattering. Additionally, measurement accuracy is influenced by other factors, such as particle concentration, geometry, incident light wavelength, and the refractive index difference between the particles and the fluid [4].

With advancements in computing power and continuous improvements in CV, these methods have been adopted across various fields [5, 6]. The authors, Zhou C. et al., explored the challenge of turbidity measurement and incorporated the consideration of ambient lighting conditions in their approach [7]. One of the greatest challenges in turbidity measurement is ambient light, as most methods rely on light scattering or attenuation. Zhou et al. introduce predictive networks that enable turbidity measurements with over 95% accuracy across different lighting scenarios.

Mullins et al. described an image processing-based system for turbidity measurement in domestic and industrial wastewater. Their method, Camera Estimated Turbidity, scans multiple images to determine the turbidity of the liquid. The experimental setup includes an infrared light source, a CMOS camera, and a glass container [8]. A stirrer ensures an even distribution of turbidity in the sample. The camera is controlled via MATLAB, and the light intensity for each image is measured and then averaged to reduce error.

A notable finding from the research into various turbidity measurement methods and systems is that most are based on traditional techniques. In contrast, this work aims to explore solutions that detect undissolved particles using a camera. The key advantage of detecting the dissolution state of a solution via camera is its flexibility and insensitivity to ambient light conditions. Unlike traditional methods that can be affected by external lighting, camera-based systems offer reliable results regardless of the environment. Additionally, the experimental setup is easy to replicate, and the neural network can quickly adapt to different solvents, making this approach highly versatile and efficient in various laboratory settings. This detection is achieved through an object detector that has been trained in advance with an appropriate dataset. The following chapters describe the measurement system that captures the images used for training and is also employed in the actual process. Additionally, the model, training process, and the adapted hyperparameters are explained. Finally, the training is evaluated, and an outlook on the next steps is provided.

2 Materials and Methods

2.1 Hardware

Measuring System. A universal optical measurement system (Visual Analyzer Unit VAU, amplius GmbH, Rostock, Germany) is used to capture the macroscopic images. This device was designed for use in automated systems handling liquids but can also operate in standalone mode. The measurement system is housed in an enclosure to prevent external influences such as unwanted light or particle and dust accumulation. Samples to be analyzed can be transported into the enclosure via a sled mounted on a translational rail (LEFB25NM1S-300, SMC Pneumatics, Los Angeles, USA). The optical system, consisting of a camera (UI-3880CP-C-HQ Rev.2, IDS Imaging Development Systems GmbH, Obersulm, Germany) and lighting technology, captures one or more images of the sample once inside. The sample is illuminated by an underlying lighting system (HI-LIGHT-100/140 RGB, Büchner Lichtsysteme GmbH, Welden, Germany) (Fig. 1).

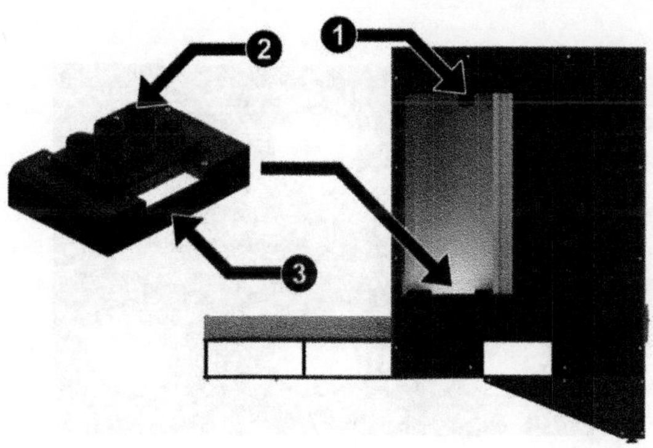

Fig. 1. Visual Analyzer Unit (side view) with open side door: 1. Camera; 2. a rack for holding sample containers; 3. sled with an illumination unit.

The underlying lighting is adjusted to emit a neutral tone. The illumination from below makes the outlines of undissolved particles clearly visible, enhancing contrast. For the specific application, up to six samples can be examined simultaneously. For this purpose, the vials are placed in designated positions within the rack and mounted on the sled.

Computing Environment. Training neural networks is a computationally intensive process that requires a significant amount of memory. For this purpose, a workstation equipped with the latest technology and a powerful graphics card with 24 GB of VRAM.

This is particularly advantageous for large datasets, as all data can be stored in memory without needing to be constantly reloaded during training.

The exact components are listed in Table 1.

Table 1. Technical specifications of the workstation used for training neural networks.

Component	Description
CPU	Intel Core i9-13900K, 8 × 3.0 GHz, 16 × E, 36 MB L3 Cache
GPU	NVIDIA GeForce RTX 4090, 24 GB
RAM	64 GB (2 × 32 GB Kit) DDR5–5200 CL40
SSD	2 TB Samsung 980 Pro, M.2 PCIe 4.0

2.2 Dataset

For training the neural network, a dataset consisting of real sample images is required. This involves capturing various images that display a wide range of variations. Different substances were dissolved in solvents, and this process was recorded in a series of images using the measurement system.

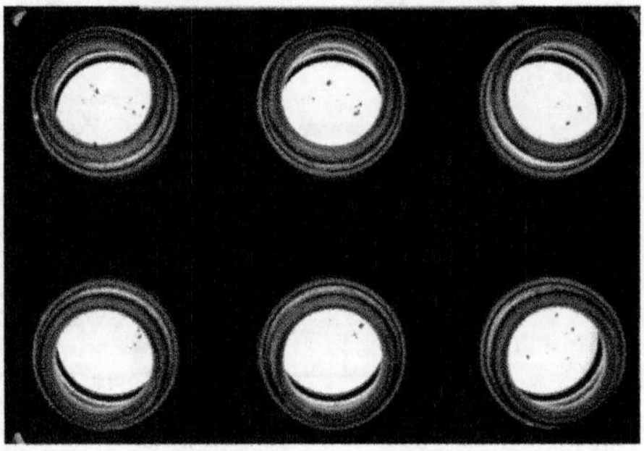

Fig. 2. The output image from the measurement system, capturing six vials from a top-down perspective, which will be used as part of the dataset for training the neural network.

The images created by the measurement system are rectangular and show the six vials from above (see Fig. 2). To prepare these images for the dataset, the vials are rectangular cropped from all the images. The next step involves further processing the images by removing the necks of the vials so that only the inside of the vials is visible. The final step includes squaring the images and scaling them to a uniform size. Figure 3 visually illustrates the steps for image preparation.

After preparing the images, they need further processing for training. For object detection, in this case, the detection of undissolved particles of a substance in a solvent,

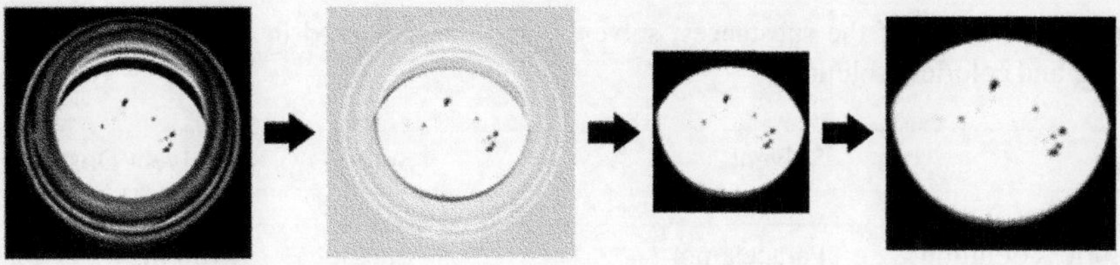

Fig. 3. Illustration of the steps for image preparation. The vials are first cropped to remove unnecessary areas, such as the necks, leaving only the inside visible. The images are then squared, and the final step involves scaling them to a uniform size for consistency in the dataset.

these particles have to be marked with bounding boxes. These boxes serve as the foundation for training the neural networks. Therefore, each image and each particle within it is enclosed by a box that determines the exact position and the corresponding class.

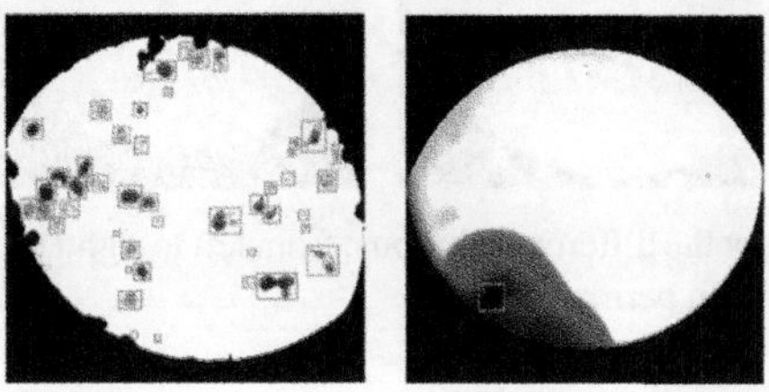

Fig. 4. Two sample images from the dataset. Unresolved particles are highlighted with green bounding boxes, indicating the areas where particles have been detected.

Figure 4 shows two examples from the dataset. In these examples, the undissolved particles are marked by a green box, indicating the particles. After processing all images, the dataset is divided into three subsets, each with a specific purpose. The first and largest subset, containing 70% (2688 images) of the images, is used to train the neural model. The second subset, comprising 20% (256 images) of the images, is used to validate the performance during training. The final and smallest subset, making up 10% (128 images) of the dataset, is used for testing and final performance evaluation.

2.3 Chemicals

In this study, four different solutions were examined, which can be categorized into two types: colored and colorless solutions. Table 2 presents the substances used, the quantities, and the solvent employed.

The dissolution of paracetamol in water and sodium acetate results in colorless solutions, where particles of different sizes can be detected. In contrast, copper sulfate and potassium permanganate form colored solutions in water. Copper sulfate turns the water bluish, without significantly affecting illumination. However, the dissolution of potassium permanganate gives the water an intense purple color, which greatly impacts lighting conditions. Figure 5 shows an example image for each of these solutions.

Table 2. Overview of the substances, solvents, and dosages used in the experiment for both colored and colorless solutions.

Type	Solvent	Solute	Solvent Dosage [mg/ml]
Colorless Solution	Paracetamol	Ethanol	100 mg
	Sodium acetate	Water	150 mg
Colored Solution	Copper sulfate	Water	258 mg
	Potassium permanganate	Water	10 mg

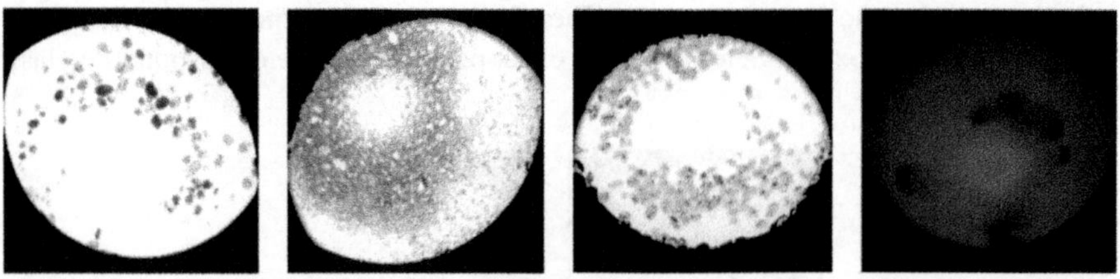

Fig. 5. Example images for the different solutions, from left to right: sodium acetate, paracetamol, copper sulfate, and potassium permanganate.

2.4 Software

For object detection in images, there are various libraries that provide comprehensive functionality to train neural networks. In this study, the open-source library TensorFlow 2 Object Detection API, developed by Google, was used. This interface offers pre-configured neural networks that can either be used directly by the user or adapted to specific tasks. The models are divided into two categories: speed and accuracy. Additionally, each model includes pre-trained neurons trained on the COCO dataset, which can be utilized for transfer learning, allowing the model to be adapted to specific tasks. To further optimize the training, hyperparameters can be adjusted, directly impacting the training process. Moreover, real-time evaluation is possible to monitor the model's performance during training.

Faster Region-based Convolutional Neural Network ResNet50 V1 Model. A Faster Region-based Convolutional Neural Network (Faster R-CNN) model is used for detecting undissolved particles in solutions. This model is a two-stage object detection method. In the first step, region proposals are generated regions that potentially contain one or more objects. In the second step, these predictions are classified, and the positions of the bounding boxes are refined.

The backbone of this model is ResNet50, a deep convolutional neural network with 50 layers, used for feature extraction. The input size for this model is 640×640 pixels. The larger input image size captures more details, which can positively affect detection performance while maintaining high speed. In total, 41 models are available, with the Faster R-CNN achieving a detection speed of 53 ms, below the average of 95 ms.

However, the mean accuracy of the Faster R-CNN model mean average precision (mAP) is 29.3%, compared to the average across all available networks, which is 36%. The lower detection performance on the COCO dataset indicates that the Faster R-CNN model is less complex [9]. This lower complexity allows the model to efficiently learn less complex data. For this reason, Faster R-CNN was chosen for this study, as it offers a good balance between speed and accuracy and is well-suited for the specific requirements of this analysis.

Hyperparameter. Hyperparameters are essential for training and must be adapted to the specific dataset. One key hyperparameter is the number of classes represented by the dataset. This parameter also affects the model architecture, specifically the final layers of the model. Another important hyperparameter relates to the model input, including the size of the input images. Due to transfer learning, the same image size that was used to train the pre-trained neurons is applied here, which is 640 × 640 pixels.

As previously mentioned, this is a Faster R-CNN model that performs detection in two stages. The generation of potential image regions in the first step, particularly their size, can be controlled by specifying ratios relative to the image size and aspect ratios. A profound understanding of the dataset is required for this. In the first step, the aspect ratios of the bounding boxes are calculated from the ground truth values and represented in a histogram. The arithmetic mean is then calculated, followed by the standard deviation. The results are shown in Fig. 6.

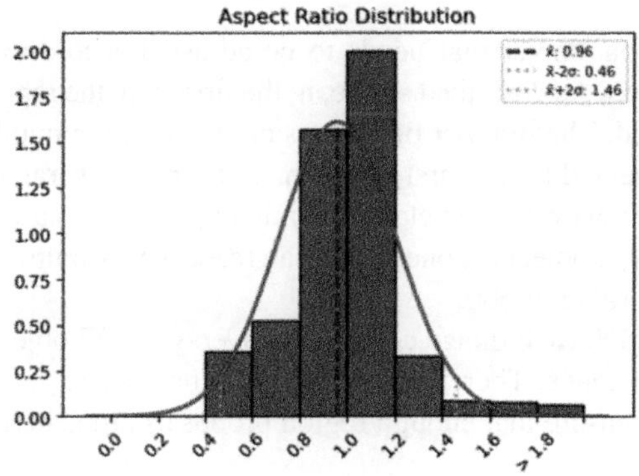

Fig. 6. Histogram of aspect ratios of bounding boxes from an object detection model, with the normal distribution (Gaussian curve), mean (blue), and standard deviation (orange) intervals. Values above 1.8 are grouped together.

A similar approach is taken with the aspect ratios, as well as the heights and widths of the bounding boxes. All values are combined, and the arithmetic mean and standard deviation are calculated to determine the optimal values for the configuration file.

For the aspect ratios, the arithmetic mean is 0.96, and the standard deviation is 0.258. Accordingly, the following values are used for the aspect_ratios parameter: 0.46, 0.71, 0.96, 1.22, and 1.46. For the heights and widths, the arithmetic mean is 0.0267, and the standard deviation is 0.0134. The following values are used for the scales parameter:

0.000041, 0.013484, 0.026927, 0.040369, and 0.053812. The histogram of the data distribution and the density function are shown in Fig. 7.

By adapting the scales and aspect_ratios parameters to the dataset, more accurate predictions of potential objects can be achieved in the first step. The values for height_stride and width_stride remain at 16.

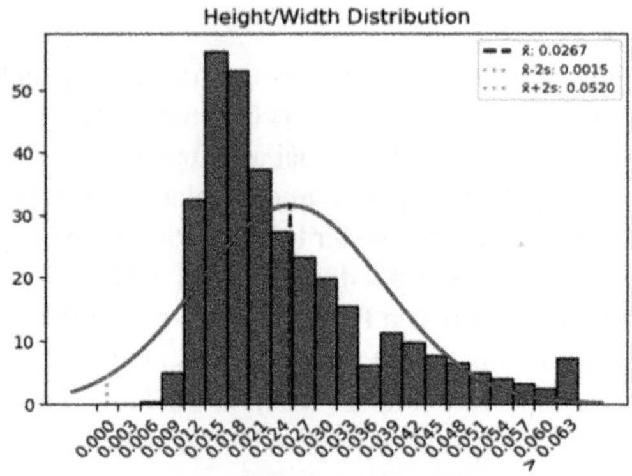

Fig. 7. Histogram of the heights and widths of bounding boxes from an object detection model, with the normal distribution (Gaussian curve), mean (blue), and standard deviation (orange) intervals. Values above 0.063 are grouped together.

The next hyperparameter that needs to be adjusted according to the dataset also relates to the first step. As described above, in the first step, the regions that may contain an object are defined. The number of regions depends on the number of objects in the image and is represented by the first_stage_max_proposals parameter. By default, this value is set to 300. However, upon closer examination of the dataset, as shown in Fig. 8, the possible number of objects in one image can reach a maximum of around 390, which exceeds the default value of 300.

As shown in Fig. 8, each image contains an average of 87 objects, with a maximum of 389 boxes in one image. Therefore, the value for first_stage_max_proposals must be increased to 650 to ensure that enough region proposals are generated in the first stage during training.

Additionally, further settings are adjusted in the second stage. A total of three parameters were modified: dropout_keep_probability, max_detections_per_class, and max_total_detections. The first parameter, dropout_keep_probability, controls the probability that neuron weights are randomly disabled during training. This value was set to 0.5 to prevent overfitting the training data too quickly. The second parameter, max_detections_per_class, defines how many detections are allowed per class. The third parameter, max_total_detections, determines the maximum number of objects that can be detected in one image. Both parameters were set to 400 to allow a sufficient number of detections per image.

In addition to the changes made to the model itself, the parameters for training and real-time validation were also adjusted. Due to the image size of 640 $\times$ 640 pixels and the three color channels, a significant amount of data is required for training. With a total

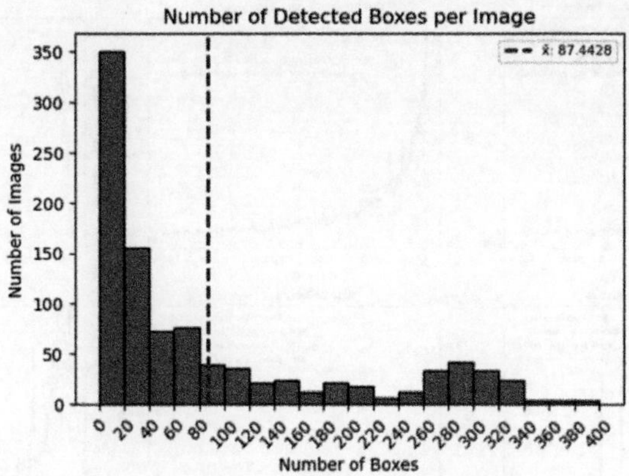

Fig. 8. Distribution of detected object boxes per image, with a mean of 87.44 boxes per image, indicated by the dashed line.

of 1,153 images (1,053 from the training dataset and 100 from the validation dataset) and the neural network used, about 24 GB of memory is consumed during training. Increasing the number of images further would result in program parts being swapped to RAM, which could lead to a decrease in performance.

The model is trained for a total of 100,000 steps, with the learning rate gradually decreasing throughout the training following an annealing schedule. The maximum learning rate of 0.04 is reached after a warm-up phase of 2,000 steps. A momentum optimizer is used for this process.

This training is based on transfer learning, where pre-trained neurons are loaded to increase training stability. Since the network already can recognize basic structures, this can positively impact the final result. To configure transfer learning correctly, the paths for the pre-trained weights must be specified, and the fine_tune_checkpoint_type parameter must be set to detection. Additionally, an augmentation step was integrated: random horizontal flipping of the images. This technique artificially expands the dataset and improves the model's generalization capability. Moreover, the max_number_of_boxes parameter was set to 400 to ensure that a sufficient number of boxes can be processed per image.

3 Results

This section presents the training process and the corresponding curves. A total of six loss metrics are used, providing a comprehensive view of the training process:

classification loss, localization loss, regularization loss, Region Proposal Networks (RPN) localization loss, RPN object loss, and total loss. The training curves are shown in Fig. 9.

Starting with the classification loss, shown in the first graph of the overview, it can be observed that the model fits perfectly with the training data throughout the entire training process. However, the validation curve begins to rise after step 10,000. This suggests that

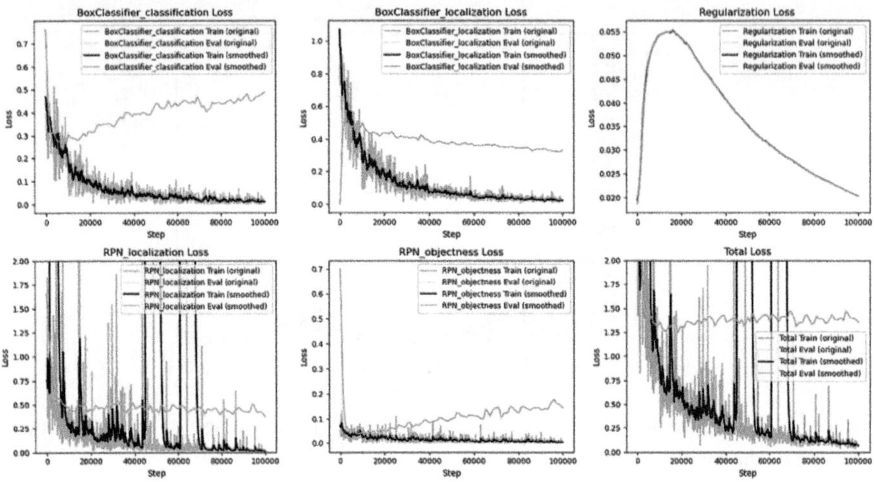

Fig. 9. Comparison of Training and Evaluation Losses for Different Components of the Model, including Box Classifier (Classification and Localization), Regularization, RPN (Localization and Objectness), and Total Loss. Smoothed loss values are shown alongside the original values to highlight trends. The model exhibits lower training losses compared to evaluation losses, potentially indicating overfitting.

the model captures the training data well but struggles to generalize the learned features to the validation data. Additional regularization techniques, such as using dropout or data augmentation, could be beneficial in addressing this issue. This loss function indicates how well the model can assign objects within the boxes to the correct class. The second graph displays the localization loss, which evaluates the accuracy of the detection's bounding boxes. It is evident that the loss for the training data decreases over time, as does the loss for the validation data.

The third graph shows the regularization loss, which is intended to limit the complexity of the model. This approach helps prevent overfitting by penalizing large weights in the model. The curve shows that the regularization loss increases until around step 20,000 and then flattens out for the remainder of the training. The decrease in the regularization loss after 40,000 steps could indicate that the model is under-regularized. This suggests that stronger regularization could help counteract overfitting and thereby improve the model's generalization ability. The next two graphs show the RPN localization loss and the RPN object loss. Both loss functions relate to the first stage of the network, where potential regions for object detection are proposed. The RPN localization loss indicates how well the model localizes the proposed regions. In contrast, the RPN object loss evaluates how well the model can identify regions where objects are actually present. The two graphs suggest that the dataset is not sufficiently representative, resulting in a lack of generalization. Expanding the dataset and revising the annotations could improve the overall model performance. The total loss is the sum of all the loss components described above and provides a rough overview of the model's overall performance. The graphs indicate that overfitting occurred during training, as seen in the evaluation curves, which rise in contrast to the training curves, which remain at the same level or continue to decrease.

3.1 COCO Evaluation Metrics

COCO metrics are calculated during training using the validation dataset to evaluate the model's performance.

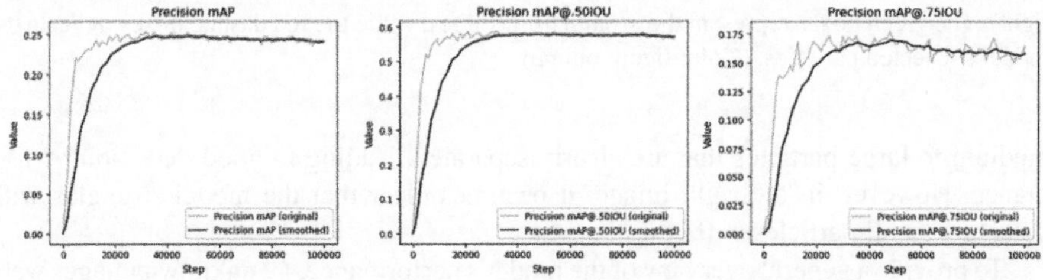

Fig. 10. Precision metrics during training for object detection. The graphs display precision mAP, mAP@0.50IOU, and mAP@0.75IOU, with original (blue) and smoothed (light blue) values across training steps. (Color figure online)

Figure 10 shows the mAP as well as the precision at confidence thresholds of 0.5 and 0.75. All three curves rise sharply at the beginning of the training and stabilize around step 40,000 at different levels. Precision indicates how well the model distinguishes between true positives and false positives. The first graph shows the mAP on the validation set, which reaches 0.253, slightly lower than the 0.293 on the COCO dataset. The other graphs show the precision at thresholds of 0.5 and 0.75, which specify when detection is considered successful.

At a threshold of 0.5, the model achieves a maximum precision of 0.58, while at 0.75, precision drops to 0.177. This indicates that while the model detects objects, its confidence in the accuracy of detections decreases at higher thresholds, meaning the model becomes less reliable when stricter alignment between predicted and actual boxes is required.

3.2 Detection Example

This chapter presents three detection examples that provide insight into the model's performance. Three unknown images were evaluated by the model to demonstrate the generalization capability learned during training. Figure 11 shows the three results: on the left, a sample of potassium permanganate, and on the right, a sample of sodium acetate. The green boxes represent the ground truth values, while the red dashed boxes indicate the particles detected by the model.

The potassium permanganate sample contains 5 ground truth values, while the model detected a total of 6 particles. The detection is accurate and demonstrates the model's capabilities. In contrast, the sodium acetate sample shows significant differences, mainly due to the higher number of particles in the image. The middle image in Fig. 11 shows

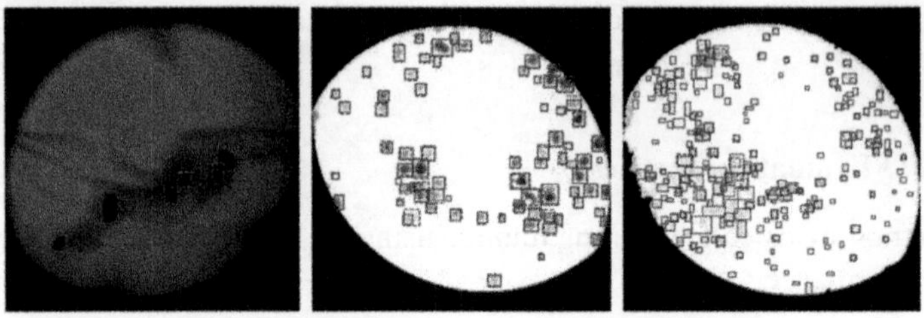

Fig. 11. Detection results for potassium permanganate (left) and sodium acetate (middle and right). The green boxes represent the ground truth values, while the red dashed boxes indicate the model's detected particles. (Color figure online)

medium to large particles that are clearly separated, leading to good detection performance. However, in the right image, it becomes clear that the model struggles with detecting small particles with low contrast.

To provide a general overview of the model's performance, 49 unknown images were evaluated by the model, and the mAP at IoU = 0.50:0.95 as well as the mean average recall (mAR) at IoU = 0.50:0.95 were calculated. The model's average precision on the test dataset is 0.06, while the average recall is 0.398.

4 Discussion and Conclusion

In this study, a Faster-RCNN model with a ResNet50 backbone was trained to monitor the dissolution process of particles. Four different solutions were prepared, their dissolution processes were documented photographically, and the images were then annotated and categorized into three groups for training the Faster-RCNN network. During training, overfitting was observed on the validation data, which was also reflected in the test dataset. The model successfully detected medium to large, clearly separated particles but struggled with small particles or those with low contrast.

To improve the model's detection performance in the future, a significantly larger dataset is required, with special attention to precise data annotation. Accurate annotations are essential to avoid impairing the model's detection capabilities. Additionally, less complex models should be considered to further reduce overfitting and improve the model's generalization ability.

Nevertheless, research in this area, particularly the automated monitoring of dissolution processes, remains a crucial step in laboratory automation. We are confident that the measures mentioned above will significantly enhance the model's detection performance, and in the future, it will be possible to fully automate this subprocess.

Acknowledgments. The authors would like to thank B.Sc. Anne Reichelt for her invaluable support in conducting the experiments.

Disclosure of Interests. The authors have no conflicts of interest to declare that are relevant to the content of this article.

References

1. Skoog, D.A., West, D.M., Holler, J.F., Crouch, S.R.: Fundamentals of Analytical Chemistry. Thomson-Brooks/Cole, Belmont (2004)
2. Harris, D.C.: Lehrbuch der Quantitativen Analyse, 8th edn. Springer, Heidelberg (2014)
3. Matos, T., Martins, M.S., Henriques, R., Goncalves, L.M.: 2214-7144, **64**, 105624 (2024)
4. Ahluwalia, V.K.: Instrumental Methods of Chemical Analysis, 1st edn. Springer, Cham (2023)
5. Galbally, J., Marcel, S., Fierrez, J.: IEEE Trans. Image Process. **23**(2), 710–724 (2014). https://doi.org/10.1109/TIP.2013.2292332
6. Chong-Yi, L., Ji-Chang, G., Run-Min, C., Yan-Wei, P., Bo, W.: IEEE Trans. Image Process. **25**(12), 5664–5677 (2016). https://doi.org/10.1109/TIP.2016.2612882
7. Zhou, C., et al.: IEEE Trans. Instrum. Meas. **71**, 1–13 (2022). https://doi.org/10.1109/TIM.2022.3146521
8. Mullins, D., Coburn, D., Hannon, L., Jones, E., Clifford, E., Glavin, M.: Water science and technology a journal of the International Association on Water. Pollut. Res. **77**(5–6), 1469–1482 (2018). https://doi.org/10.2166/wst.2018.030
9. https://github.com/tensorflow/models/blob/master/research/object_detection/g3doc/tf2_detection_zoo.md. Accessed 23 Sept 2024

Automating 3D Dataset Generation with Neural Radiance Fields

Paul Schulz(✉), Thorsten Hempel, and Ayoub Al-Hamadi

Otto von Guericke University, Universitätsplatz 1, 39104 Magdeburg, Germany
paul.schulz@ovgu.de

Abstract. 3D detection is a critical task to understand spatial characteristics of the environment and is used in a variety of applications including robotics, augmented reality, and image retrieval. Training performant detection models require diverse, precisely annotated, and large scale datasets that involve complex and expensive creation processes. Hence, there are only few public 3D datasets that are additionally limited in their range of classes. In this work, we propose a pipeline for automatic generation of 3D datasets for arbitrary objects. By utilizing the universal 3D representation and rendering capabilities of Radiance Fields, our pipeline generates high quality 3D models for arbitrary objects. These 3D models serve as input for a synthetic dataset generator. Our pipeline is fast, easy to use and has a high degree of automation. Our experiments demonstrate, that 3D pose estimation networks, trained with our generated datasets, archive strong performance in typical application scenarios.

Keywords: Dataset generation · Radiance fields · 3D Pose estimation

1 Introduction

3D scene perception and manipulation is a fundamental task in various fields where autonomous agents interact with their environment. Applications in autonomous driving, mobile robotics, medicine or manufacturing [1,5,7,11] and intuitive human-robot interaction systems [21,22] rely on this capability.

To effectively perform scene manipulation, an agent has to estimate the pose of relevant objects within its environment. State-of-the-art pose estimation methods utilize neural networks that require large, diverse and precisely annotated 3D datasets for training. However, generating this data is a significant challenge, because collecting and annotating 3D datasets is labor-intensive and expensive, particularly when tailored datasets are required for specific applications.

Recent works proposed approaches to automate 3D dataset generation, by incorporating 3D models of the objects of interest [8,10,11,13,27,30,32]. These methods either generate real or synthetic datasets. Automating real world dataset generation requires dedicated equipment and is limited in its field of application [10,30,32]. Synthetic dataset generation does not have these limitations, because it only requires 3D modeling software and the workflow can be easily adapted [8,11,13,27].

However, real-world and synthetic approaches assume that 3D models of the target objects are available. Creating these models with traditional methods, like 3D scanning

J. Röning and J. Filipe (Eds.): ROBOVIS 2025, CCIS 2629, pp. 28–43, 2026.
https://doi.org/10.1007/978-3-032-00986-9_3

Fig. 1. Automated dataset generation with our pipeline. The process start with capturing images of an object, continues with 3D model creation and finishes with 3D dataset generation.

or 3D modeling, is expensive and requires expert knowledge. Generating even a single high quality model for an individual target object may require, a textureless CAD model 3D scanning equipment and model refinement [26] (Fig. 1).

We address these limitations by proposing a pipeline, which incorporates 3D model creation into the dataset generation process. To archive this, our pipeline creates 3D models from 2D images of target objects by utilizing Radiance Fields. Afterward, our pipeline incorporates these models in a state-of-the-art dataset generation workflow.

In contrast to previous works, our pipeline generates datasets for the pose estimation of arbitrary objects without requiring 3D models. To verify our approach, we applied our pipeline to six objects of varying complexity and trained a 3D pose estimation model on our generated datasets. Furthermore, we tested the trained networks for two tasks: in-hand pose estimation and tabletop pose estimation. In summary, our contribution is an end-to-end dataset generation pipeline, which begins with arbitrary objects and ends with diverse, precisely annotated 3D datasets for these objects.

2 Related Works

To the best of our knowledge, our method is the first to automate dataset generation by utilizing Radiance Fields for 3D model creation. Most similarly, Wong et al. [31] introduced a synthetic dataset generation pipeline, but in contrast to us, they use photogrammetry to create 3D models from 2D images. In the following, we provide an overview of synthetic dataset generation methods and Radiance Field frameworks that could potentially be integrated into our pipeline.

2.1 Automated Generation of Synthetic 3D Datasets

Dataset Generation Methods. Synthetic dataset generation takes place in virtual 3D environments, like game engines [27] or general 3D modeling software [8]. The dataset generation workflow, proposed by state-of-the-art publications, can be divided in two phases: scene composition and rendering + annotation. Scene composition constructs 3D scenes by placing objects in a virtual environment. These objects include target objects and additional content like distractors. The subsequent rendering + annotation process generates RGB images from the scenes, by applying 3D rendering software.

Since all parameters of the 3D scene are known, the step also performs automated annotation [11,27,31].

Recent works can be divided in general and specific generation methods. General methods can be applied to arbitrary domains, specific method incorporate domain restrictions and are therefore applied in specific domains.

Hodan et al. [8] created a general generator for the BOP challenge. Tremblay et al. [27] developed another general method for the pose estimation of arbitrary household objects. Both methods are suitable for arbitrary target objects, because they do not incorporate domain restrictions. In contrast to that, Sun et al. [23] developed a specific method, which creates datasets for the autonomous driving domain. Their framework incorporates special domain shifts for autonomous driving, like changing weather conditions. Other specific methods [11,13] tackle industrial tasks, like bin packing. These methods apply domain restrictions in the form of special industrial environment. Furthermore, McCormac et al. [14] applied a specific dataset generator to create a benchmark dataset for household scenes.

Dataset Generation Frameworks. Recent works also introduced dedicated frameworks to develop customized dataset generators [4,6,17]. These frameworks incorporate measurements to approach a central limitation of synthetic dataset generation, which is known as the simulation to reality gap (Sim2Real gap). The Sim2Real gap causes a performance drop, when networks trained on synthetic data are applied in the real world. The gap can be divided into the appearance gap and the content gap. The appearance gap is caused by differences in detailed, pixel-level scene appearances, resulting from a lack of realism [9,12]. The content gap is related to the context of simulated scenes. It appears when the scene content does not reflect the variety of objects and environments found in the real world [9,12,19]. Dataset generation frameworks incorporate photorealistic rendering and domain randomization to reduce the Sim2Real gap. Photorealistic rendering reduces the appearance gap by making objects and environments appear more realistic. Domain randomization reduces the content gap by randomizing the texture of objects of interest and/or the 3D environment [4,17].

2.2 Radiance Fields

In 2020, Mildenhall et al. [15] introduced Neural Radiance Fields (NeRF) for novel view synthesis. NeRFs combine the function approximation capability of multi layer perceptrons (MLP) with principles of volume rendering. NeRFs learn an unrestricted volumetric 3D representation and the view dependent appearance of an object or a scene from 2D images. Furthermore, they utilize volume rendering principles like ray marching to render photorealistic views from this representation [15,25].

Dataset generators require 3D models of the object in the form of meshes or pointclouds. Extracting such representations is straight forward: In the first step one applies a volume sampling algorithm like Marching Cubes to transfer the volume in a mesh, afterward, one projects the color of the images onto the mesh surface. However, applying this approach, leads to a significant fidelity drop. Despite a tendency to learn smooth volumes [35], NeRFs learn unrestricted volumes. Therefore, the surfaces extracted from

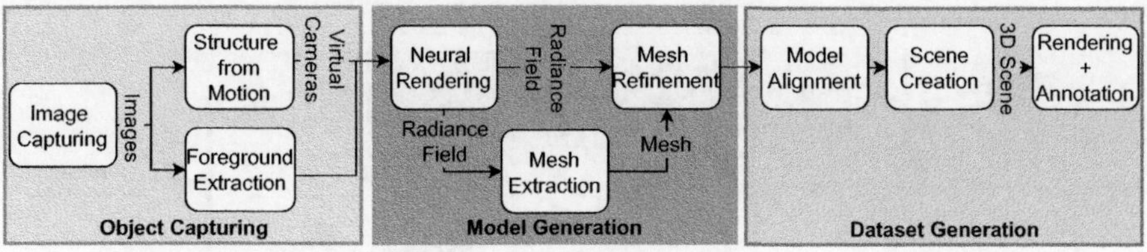

Fig. 2. Automated dataset generation pipeline, each block is depicted with its corresponding phases.

the volume may not resemble the actual surface of the scene. [24,29,34] We will refer to this problem as unconstrained surface issue. Recent works approach this problem by regularizing NeRF to resemble surfaces [18,29,33]. Wang et al. [29] and Yariv et al. [33] approximate the zero level set of the SDF with volume rendering. Oechsle et al. [18] unify volume and surface rendering by learning an occupancy field. 3D models exported from these representations have a more accurate surface than 3D model exported from standard NeRF models.

NeRFs model view dependent effects as part of the appearance. With the goal of high quality mesh export in mind, this feature can lead to difficulties, since view dependency might be baked into the mesh texture. A way to migrate this problem, is to decompose the appearance in reflectance and illumination [3].

Tang et al. [24] present a pipeline for textured mesh generation, which addresses this weakness. They optimize a NeRF and utilize two MLPs for color rendering to separate view-dependent colors into diffuse and specular components. Afterward, they apply a mesh refinement strategy, which adjusts mesh vertices and faces. The diffuse color is baked in a diffuse texture. Combined with the refined mesh, it can be used in traditional 3D modeling software.

3 Methodical Approach

Our goal was to create a reliable, fast and easily adaptable synthetic dataset generation pipeline for 3D Pose Estimation. The pipeline should work for arbitrary objects, without requiring 3D models of the target objects. We propose a pipeline that expands a state-of-the-art synthetic dataset generator with a neural rendering framework, specialized on 3D model creation.[1] The design of this pipeline is illustrated in Fig. 2. In the following, we will introduce each component of the pipeline in detail.

3.1 Object Capturing

Object Capturing is the first block of our pipeline. It captures 2D images of a target object and prepares them to be used to train a Radiance Field. The design of our Object Capturing process is depicted in Fig. 3.

[1] The implementation of our pipeline is available under: https://github.com/PaulSK98/Nerf2Dataset.git.

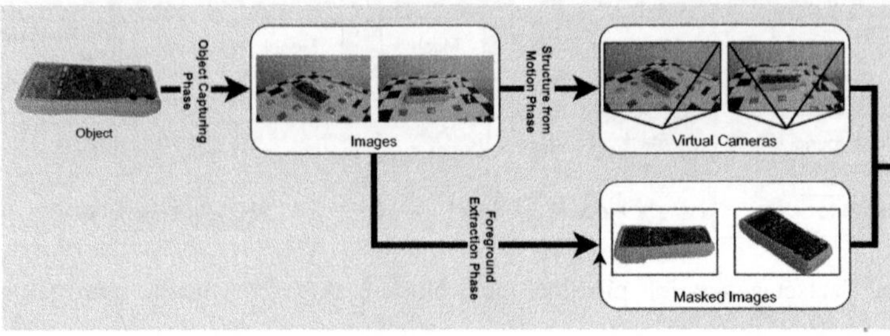

Fig. 3. Design of our Object Capturing block, each capturing phase is displayed with its in- and output. The process begins with image capturing. Structure from Motion and Foreground Extraction perform post-processing on the captured images.

The process begins with capturing images of the object of interest. Our setup to perform this task is shown in Fig. 4. Radiance Fields work well when maintaining a constant camera-to-object distance, varying distances may lead to rendering artifacts [2]. Additionally, Object Capturing should include many perspectives to prevent overfitting to specific views. To ensure both aspects, we captured the object in a 360-degree circular trajectory, with the object placed on a rotating plate and the camera kept static. We masked the static scene parts of the background during this process. We chose this setup because it is easily reproducible by others, as it only requires a fixed camera and a plate to rotate the object. Radiance Fields assume a static object of interest, a static light source and a moving camera. To reduce additional view-depended effects which might be introduced by hurting this assumption, we use diffuse background light during capturing.

Applying Structure-from-Motion (SfM) is the first of two post-processing steps after image capturing. Neural rendering frameworks utilize SfM pipelines like COLMAP [20] to estimate camera poses for real-world images. Since COL-MAP is the de-facto standard for this step, we applied COLMAP as well. COLMAP relies on a sufficient number of 2D features and 2D-to-3D correspondences to estimate camera positions. To support this process for objects with fewer features, we used a plane with tags as the background during object capturing. Foreground extraction is the second post-processing step, applied during Object Capturing. It ensures that the Radiance Field learns the target object rather than the background. We applied an off-the-shelf foreground extractor to perform this task.

3.2 Model Generation

Model Generation is the second stage of our pipeline. It takes the output from the previous block (virtual cameras and masked images) as input and creates high-quality textured meshes. To achieve this, we integrated a NeuS implementation[2] of the Nerf2Mesh framework by Hoang et al. [24] into the design of the Model Generation Block. The block design is displayed in Fig. 5. As mentioned in the previous section, Radiance

[2] The implementation is available under: https://github.com/ashawkey/nerf2mesh.

Fig. 4. Object capturing set up, we placed the object on a rotating plate and captured it with a static camera.

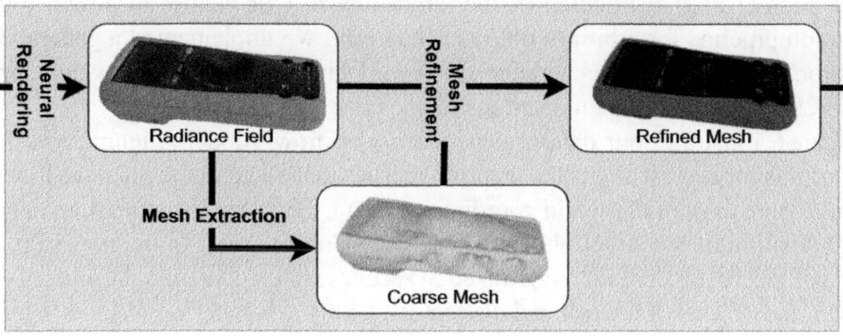

Fig. 5. Design of our Model Generation block, it receives the output of the previous block as input and generates a textured 3D model.

Fields struggle with poor texture mapping. Volumetric representations additionally suffer from the unconstrained surface issue. The NeuS-based Nerf2Mesh implementation migrates both of these issues by incorporating a neural surface and by separating the texture into a diffuse and a specular branch. Neural Rendering is the first step in the Model Generation process. It trains a NeuS-based Radiance Field using the virtual cameras and masked images, provided by the Object Capturing process. Furthermore, Neural Rendering applies a Multiresolution Hash Encoding [16] to speed up the training process. Afterward, the Marching Cubes algorithm extracts a coarse mesh from the Radiance Field. In the last step of Model Generation, Mesh Refinement optimizes the mesh geometry and appearance through differentiable rendering and non-differentiable face adjustment. In the end, a textured mesh is exported, by mapping the texture on the refined mesh.

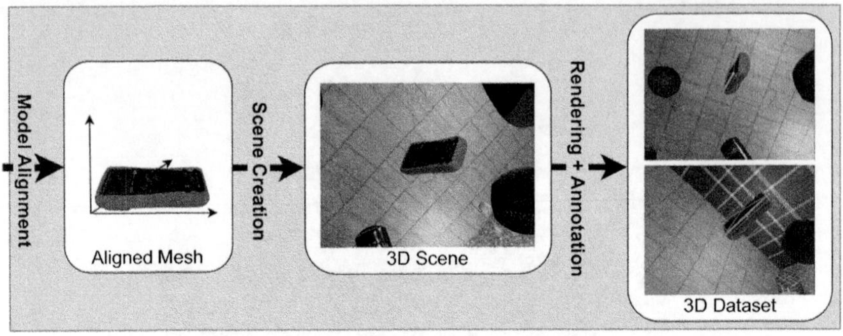

Fig. 6. Design of our Dataset Generation block, based on the textured meshes of the subsequent block, it generates a 3D Dataset in automated fashion.

3.3 Dataset Generation

Dataset Generation is the third and final step of our pipeline. It creates a synthetic 3D dataset for 6D Pose Estimation of the target object. Our goal is to design a dataset generation pipeline for arbitrary objects. Therefore, we implemented a general dataset generator. Because dataset generation frameworks integrate measures, which approach the Sim2Real gap, we implemented the block via BlenderProc [4].

Figure 6 illustrates our dataset generation workflow. Model Alignment is the first phase of this process. It aligns the textured meshes generated in the previous block with the coordinate axes of the world coordinate system. This step is required, to determine the 3D position of the target objects after Scene Composition. In the next step, Scene Composition creates domain randomized 3D scenes which contain light sources, virtual cameras, the objects of interest and distractors. Lastly, a Rendering + Annotation phase renders images from the virtual cameras and annotates the target objects present in the image. It utilizes BlenderProc's photorealistic rendering capabilities to approach the appearance gap.

4 Experiments

We chose six objects with varying texture complexity to test our pipeline. All six objects are displayed in Table 1. We assigned each of these objects to a complexity category. We defined the categories according to the complexity of view dependent effects, caused by the objects. Simple objects like the elephant have a matte surface, therefore they less likely trigger view dependent effects. Complex objects like the controller have large smooth areas combined with concave and convex geometries, leading to intricate view-dependent effects.

We tested Object Capturing and Model Generation for all these objects. Dataset Generation was tested for one object per category. All experiments were conducted with an NVIDIA Quadro RTX 8000 graphics card.

Table 1. Target objects, categorized according to complexity.

Simple	 Baseball	 Elephant
Intermediate	 Cup	 Remote
Complex	 Controller	 Multimeter

4.1 Object Capturing

Table 2 displays qualitative results for three of six objects. During Object Capturing, we took 105 images per object, similar to the perspectives shown in the first column of Table 2. Structure from Motion derived camera poses for all six objects of interest. The trajectories for these objects are similar to the trajectories displayed in the second row.

4.2 Model Generation

Object Capturing successfully processed all six objects, enabling Model Generation to create textured meshes for each object. Table 3 summarizes the qualitative performance of this process. In the beginning, Neural Rendering trained a NeuS-based Radiance Field for all objects. The first column of Table 3 shows views rendered from three of the six Radiance Fields. The remaining Radiance Fields produce similar results. All Radiance Fields generated novel views of high quality. Minor artifacts are present in challenging areas, such as the central wheel of the multimeter. This qualitative results indicate that the Radiance Fields learned accurate 3D representations, enabling photo-realistic view synthesis.

Table 4 presents quantitative performance metrics of our Radiance Fields on real world test images. Other Radiance Field frameworks [15, 16, 24] achieve similar results on synthetic and real-world datasets of comparable complexity. Therefore, the quantitative results indicate successful 3D representation learning as well. Mesh Export extracted triangular meshes for all six target objects. Due to the NeuS-based Radiance Fields avoiding the unconstrained surface issue, the meshes exhibit relatively high surface quality. However, stronger rendering errors persist in the coarse mesh, for example in the central area of the multimeter. During Mesh Refinement, the coarse meshes were optimized, and the diffuse texture of the appearance model was exported for each object.

Table 2. Object Capturing for three target objects (elephant, remote, multimeter).

Image Capturing	Structure from Motion	Foreground Extraction
	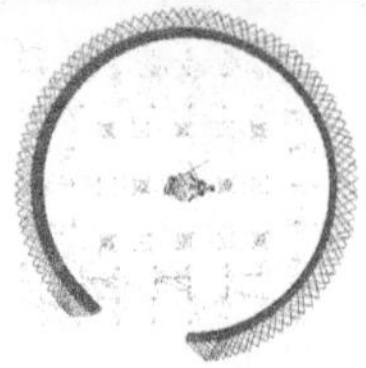	

	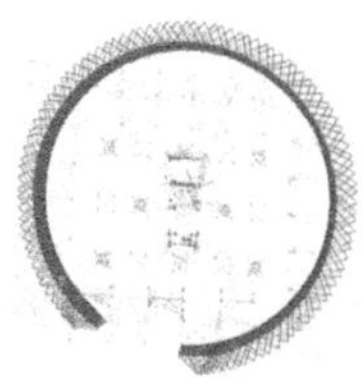	

Mesh refinement improved vertex positions and mesh faces, correcting minor flaws in the coarse meshes, such as the holes in the elephant's ear. The textured meshes are displayed in the third row of Table 3. The diffuse mesh textures appear darker than the rendered meshes from the previous phase because they do not account for the lighting conditions during capture. Overall, the meshes demonstrate high fidelity, comparable to the rendered views of the Radiance Fields.

4.3 Dataset Generation

Our Dataset Generation process created a dataset for the elephant, the remote, and the multimeter. It aligned each mesh with Blender's internal coordinate system in the first step. Afterward, it applied Scene Composition and Rendering + Annotation to create a synthetic dataset. Figure 7 displays annotated and unannotated images of the elephant dataset, which were generated with this workflow. The first row of Fig. 7 demonstrates measurements to approach the content gap. The first row shows how domain randomization creates diverse backgrounds. Additionally, the second row demonstrates the photo-realistic rendering capabilities of BlenderProc.

Table 3. Model Generation for three target objects (elephant, remote, multimeter).

Neural Rendering	**Mesh Extraction**	**Mesh Refinement**

Table 4. Peak Signal to Noise Ratio (PSNR), Learned Perceptual Image Patch Similarity (LPIPS) and Structural Similarity Index Measure (SSIM) for the Radiance Fields, generated during the Neural Rendering Phase.

	PSNR [dB]	LPIPS	SSIM
Elephant	35.09	0.0105	0.994
Cup	32.52	0.0349	0.983
Baseball	38.61	0.0103	0.996
Remote	32.72	0.0191	0.990
Controller	32.70	0.0317	0.982
Multimeter	34.58	0.0370	0.982
Average	32.88	0.0239	0.9878

4.4 Pipeline Validation

We trained and tested a pose estimation network on three generated datasets to verify our pipeline. The pose estimation model is based on the DOPE (Deep Object Pose Estimation) [28] approach that predicts keypoint belief maps and their corresponding affinity maps. DOPE has to be trained per object, therefore we trained 3 different models. Each DOPE network was trained for 100 epochs, with a learning rate of 0.0001 and a batch size of 64.

To verify our pipeline in practical scenarios, we tested the DOPE models for two scenarios: tabletop pose estimation and in-hand pose estimation. Since we generated datasets for custom objects, no public datasets are available to apply these scenarios. Furthermore, a real world test set is not attainable, without significant effort, due to the

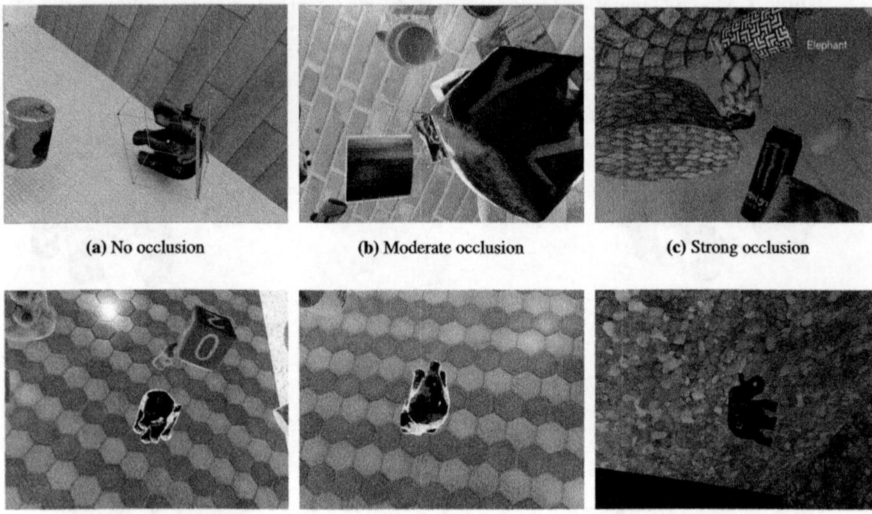

(a) No occlusion **(b)** Moderate occlusion **(c)** Strong occlusion

(d) Camera on top **(e)** Camera behind **(f)** No direct light

Fig. 7. Images, sampled from the elephant dataset, demonstrating, occlusion aware annotation (a, b, c) and photorealistic rendering (d, e, f).

complex annotation process. To still assess the model's performance, we recorded test sequences for both tasks and performed a qualitative evaluation.

Tabletop Pose Estimation. To test our networks on tabletop pose estimation, we created a scene which contains the target objects and some distractors. All three networks were tested on this sequence, qualitative results of this process are displayed in Fig. 8. The results for the multimeter and the remote indicate successful pose estimation with correct bounding box locations. However, the performance of the DOPE network trained on the elephant dataset was notably worse. Unlike the other two objects, the elephant was evaluated against a complex background. This complexity may have contributed to the detection challenges. To address this issue, we created a test sequence, which solely focuses on the elephant was Fig. 9 shows four frames of this sequence. The DOPE model performed significantly better, showing strong performance.

In-Hand Pose Estimation. We recorded a human, holding the target object in different angles, in front of a camera, to derive the test sequences for in-hand pose estimation. The six frames, depicted in Fig. 10 showcases the performance of our the three models. The multimeter and remote networks achieved a performance similar to that of the tabletop scenario. The elephant network produced more accurate bounding boxes compared to the previous scenario. However, the performance of the elephant network was still worse than the performance of the remaining two networks.

Fig. 8. Tabletop pose estimation with elephant (first column), remote (second column), and multimeter (third column) as target objects.

Fig. 9. Table-top pose estimation for the elephant in a simpler scenario.

4.5 Limitations

Our pipeline has some limitations related to the general concept and specific pipeline blocks. The pipeline is limited to the front side of the target objects, it cannot reconstruct the back side of objects, since these parts are not present during Radiance Field training. Subsequently, the back side can neither be meshed nor detected. Furthermore, the generated meshes show high fidelity but contain small errors in ambiguous regions, like the central regions of the multimeter. These errors are introduced during Neural Rendering and inherited in the subsequent phases. This limitation might restrict our pipeline to objects of lower complexity.

Fig. 10. Qualitative results during in-hand detection for the three target objects.

5 Conclusion and Future Work

In this work, we proposed a pipeline that utilizes Radiance Fields to automatically generate datasets for the 3D pose estimation of arbitrary objects. In contrast to previous works, our pipeline does not require 3D models of the object of interest to generate datasets. Our experiments demonstrated that our pipeline can generate high-quality textured meshes for objects of varying complexity. We also showed that the pipeline is sufficient to train 3D pose estimation models that work in practical scenarios. Our pipeline only involves two manual steps: placing the target objects on the turntable and aligning the model with Blender's internal coordinate system. Based on these results, we conclude that Radiance Fields can provide 3D models which are sufficient to generate high-quality synthetic datasets in an automated fashion.

Future works will address the conceptual weakness of our pipeline by expanding the model generation to full object reconstruction. Generating two models per object and fusing them is an approach we might pursue in upcoming publications to archive this. Expanding the pipeline to stereo 3D datasets is another promising research direction, we might approach in future works. This could be realized by creating and leveraging stereo images to improve object detection accuracy and enable depth perception. Furthermore, we will expand our qualitative evaluation with a quantitative evaluation. We will apply our pipeline to a benchmark dataset, which contains 3D models and a real world test set, is a way to approach this goal.

Acknowledgments. This work is funded and supported by the Federal Ministry of Education and Research of Germany (BMBF) (AutoKoWAT-3DMAt under grant No. 13N16336), German Research Foundation (DFG) (SEMIAC under grant number No. 502483052) and by the European Regional Development Fund (ERDF) (ENABLING under grant No. ZS/2023/12/182056) and (RoboLab under grant No. ZS/2023/12/182065).

Disclosure of Interests. The authors have no competing interests to declare that are relevant to the content of this article.

References

1. Barragan, J.A., Zhang, J., Zhou, H., Munawar, A., Kazanzides, P.: Realistic data generation for 6d pose estimation of surgical instruments. In: 2024 IEEE International Conference on Robotics and Automation (ICRA), pp. 13347–13353 (2024). https://api.semanticscholar.org/CorpusID:270380244
2. Barron, J.T., et al.: Mip-NeRF: a multiscale representation for anti-aliasing neural radiance fields. In: 2021 IEEE/CVF International Conference on Computer Vision (ICCV), pp. 5835–5844 (2021). https://api.semanticscholar.org/CorpusID:232352655
3. Boss, M., et al.: NeRD: neural reflectance decomposition from image collections. In: 2021 IEEE/CVF International Conference on Computer Vision (ICCV), pp. 12664–12674 (2020). https://api.semanticscholar.org/CorpusID:227351877
4. Denninger, M., et al.: Blenderproc2: a procedural pipeline for photorealistic rendering. J. Open Source Softw. **8**, 4901 (2023). https://api.semanticscholar.org/CorpusID:257066198
5. Dosovitskiy, A., Ros, G., Codevilla, F., López, A.M., Koltun, V.: Carla: An open urban driving simulator. In: Conference on Robot Learning (2017). https://api.semanticscholar.org/CorpusID:5550767
6. Greff, K., et al.: Kubric: a scalable dataset generator. In: 2022 IEEE/CVF Conference on Computer Vision and Pattern Recognition (CVPR), pp. 3739–3751 (2022). https://api.semanticscholar.org/CorpusID:247291749
7. Hempel, T., Al-Hamadi, A.: An online semantic mapping system for extending and enhancing visual slam. Eng. Appl. Artif. Intell. **111**, 104830 (2022). https://api.semanticscholar.org/CorpusID:247315020
8. Hodan, T., et al.: Bop challenge 2020 on 6d object localization. ArXiv **abs/2009.07378** (2020). https://api.semanticscholar.org/CorpusID:221738833
9. Kar, A., et al.: Meta-Sim: learning to generate synthetic datasets. In: 2019 IEEE/CVF International Conference on Computer Vision (ICCV), pp. 4550–4559 (2019). https://api.semanticscholar.org/CorpusID:135465355
10. Kaskman, R., Zakharov, S., Shugurov, I.S., Ilic, S.: Homebreweddb: RGB-d dataset for 6d pose estimation of 3D objects. In: 2019 IEEE/CVF International Conference on Computer Vision Workshop (ICCVW), pp. 2767–2776 (2019). https://api.semanticscholar.org/CorpusID:102351850
11. Kleeberger, K., Landgraf, C., Huber, M.F.: Large-scale 6d object pose estimation dataset for industrial bin-picking. In: 2019 IEEE/RSJ International Conference on Intelligent Robots and Systems (IROS), pp. 2573–2578 (2019). https://api.semanticscholar.org/CorpusID:209500613
12. Kshitiz Gupta, N.W.: Closing the sim2real gap with nvidia isaac sim and NVIDIA ISAAC replicator (2022). https://developer.nvidia.com/blog/closing-the-sim2real-gap-with-nvidia-isaac-sim-and-nvidia-isaac-replicator/ Accessed 05 Mar 2024
13. Li, X., et al.: A sim-to-real object recognition and localization framework for industrial robotic bin picking. IEEE Robot. Autom. Lett. **7**, 3961–3968 (2022). https://api.semanticscholar.org/CorpusID:246663752
14. McCormac, J., Handa, A., Leutenegger, S., Davison, A.J.: Scenenet RGB-D: 5m photorealistic images of synthetic indoor trajectories with ground truth. ArXiv **abs/1612.05079** (2016). https://api.semanticscholar.org/CorpusID:1434190

15. Mildenhall, B., et al.: NeRF: representing scenes as neural radiance fields for view synthesis. In: Vedaldi, A., Bischof, H., Brox, T., Frahm, J.-M. (eds.) ECCV 2020. LNCS, vol. 12346, pp. 405–421. Springer, Cham (2020). https://doi.org/10.1007/978-3-030-58452-8_24
16. Müller, T., Evans, A., Schied, C., Keller, A.: Instant neural graphics primitives with a multiresolution hash encoding. ACM Trans. Graph. (TOG) **41**, 1 – 15 (2022). https://api.semanticscholar.org/CorpusID:246016186
17. NVIDIA: Replicator (2022). https://docs.omniverse.nvidia.com Accessed: 11 Sep 2024
18. Oechsle, M., Peng, S., Geiger, A.: UNISURF: unifying neural implicit surfaces and radiance fields for multi-view reconstruction. In: 2021 IEEE/CVF International Conference on Computer Vision (ICCV), pp. 5569–5579 (2021). https://api.semanticscholar.org/CorpusID:233307004
19. Prakash, A., et al.: Structured domain randomization: bridging the reality gap by context-aware synthetic data. In: 2019 International Conference on Robotics and Automation (ICRA), pp. 7249–7255 (2018). https://api.semanticscholar.org/CorpusID:53085592
20. Schönberger, J.L., Frahm, J.M.: Structure-from-motion revisited. In: 2016 IEEE Conference on Computer Vision and Pattern Recognition (CVPR), pp. 4104–4113 (2016). https://api.semanticscholar.org/CorpusID:1728538
21. Strazdas, D., Hintz, J., Felßberg, A.M., Al-Hamadi, A.: Robots and wizards: an investigation into natural human–robot interaction. IEEE Access **8**, 207635–207642 (2020). https://api.semanticscholar.org/CorpusID:227220375
22. Strazdas, D., et al.: Robot system assistant (ROSA): towards intuitive multi-modal and multi-device human-robot interaction. Sensors **22** (2022). https://api.semanticscholar.org/CorpusID:246318849
23. Sun, T., et al.: Shift: a synthetic driving dataset for continuous multi-task domain adaptation. In: 2022 IEEE/CVF Conference on Computer Vision and Pattern Recognition (CVPR), pp. 21339–21350 (2022). https://api.semanticscholar.org/CorpusID:249712110
24. Tang, J., et al.: Delicate textured mesh recovery from nerf via adaptive surface refinement. In: 2023 IEEE/CVF International Conference on Computer Vision (ICCV), pp. 17693–17703 (2023). https://api.semanticscholar.org/CorpusID:257353528
25. Tewari, A., et al.: Advances in neural rendering. Comput. Graph. Forum **41** (2021). https://api.semanticscholar.org/CorpusID:236162433
26. Tran, Q.H., Choate, J.A., Taylor, C.N., Nykl, S.L., Curtis, D.H.: Monocular vision and machine learning for pose estimation. In: 2023 IEEE/ION Position, Location and Navigation Symposium (PLANS), pp. 128–136 (2023). https://api.semanticscholar.org/CorpusID:259123291
27. Tremblay, J., To, T., Birchfield, S.: Falling things: a synthetic dataset for 3D object detection and pose estimation. In: 2018 IEEE/CVF Conference on Computer Vision and Pattern Recognition Workshops (CVPRW), pp. 2119–21193 (2018). https://api.semanticscholar.org/CorpusID:4945743
28. Tremblay, J., et al.: Deep object pose estimation for semantic robotic grasping of household objects. ArXiv **abs/1809.10790** (2018). https://api.semanticscholar.org/CorpusID:52893770
29. Wang, P., et al.: NeuS: learning neural implicit surfaces by volume rendering for multi-view reconstruction. ArXiv **abs/2106.10689** (2021). https://api.semanticscholar.org/CorpusID:235490453
30. Wang, P., et al.: Phocal: a multi-modal dataset for category-level object pose estimation with photometrically challenging objects. In: 2022 IEEE/CVF Conference on Computer Vision and Pattern Recognition (CVPR), pp. 21190–21199 (2022). https://api.semanticscholar.org/CorpusID:248863254
31. Wong, M.Z., et al.: Synthetic dataset generation for object-to-model deep learning in industrial applications. PeerJ Comput. Sci. **5** (2019). https://api.semanticscholar.org/CorpusID:202734374

32. Xiang, Y., Schmidt, T., Narayanan, V., Fox, D.: PoseCNN: A convolutional neural network for 6D object pose estimation in cluttered scenes. ArXiv **abs/1711.00199** (2017). https://api.semanticscholar.org/CorpusID:3440950
33. Yariv, L., Gu, J., Kasten, Y., Lipman, Y.: Volume rendering of neural implicit surfaces. ArXiv **abs/2106.12052** (2021). https://api.semanticscholar.org/CorpusID:235605960
34. Yariv, L., et al.: BakedSDF: meshing neural SDFs for real-time view synthesis. In: ACM SIGGRAPH 2023 Conference Proceedings (2023). https://api.semanticscholar.org/CorpusID:257232921
35. Zhang, K., Riegler, G., Snavely, N., Koltun, V.: NeRF++: analyzing and improving neural radiance fields. ArXiv **abs/2010.07492** (2020). https://api.semanticscholar.org/CorpusID:222380037

Cut-and-Splat: Leveraging Gaussian Splatting for Synthetic Data Generation

Bram Vanhele(✉), Brent Zoomers, Jeroen Put, Frank Van Reeth, and Nick Michiels

Hasselt University, Flanders Make, Digital Future Lab, Wetenschapspark 2, 3590 Diepenbeek, Belgium
{bram.vanhele,brent.zoomers,jeroen.put,frankvan.reeth, nick.michiels}@uhasselt.be

Abstract. Generating synthetic images is a useful method for cheaply obtaining labeled data for training computer vision models. However, obtaining accurate 3D models of relevant objects is necessary, and the resulting images often have a gap in realism due to challenges in simulating lighting effects and camera artifacts. We propose using the novel view synthesis method called Gaussian Splatting to address these challenges. We have developed a synthetic data pipeline for generating high-quality context-aware instance segmentation training data for specific objects. This process is fully automated, requiring only a video of the target object. We train a Gaussian Splatting model of the target object and automatically extract the object from the video. Leveraging Gaussian Splatting, we then render the object on a random background image, and monocular depth estimation is employed to place the object in a believable pose. We introduce a novel dataset to validate our approach and show superior performance over other data generation approaches, such as Cut-and-Paste and Diffusion model-based generation.

Keywords: Synthetic data · Deep learning · Object detection · Instance segmentation · Gaussian splatting

1 Introduction

Deep neural networks are capable of solving complex computer vision problems. However, to do so, these models require a large number of annotated images specific to the problem they are solving. While obtaining numerous photos for a given problem is usually relatively straightforward, manually annotating these images is a very costly process. Certain annotation types, like semantic segmentation, can take humans dozens of minutes, while others, such as depth estimation and pose estimation, are complicated to do manually. Additionally, human-generated annotations may contain errors, biases, and inconsistencies, leading to a model performing poorly.

Using synthetic data alleviates some of these problems. Images are generated from a description of a scene. This description is then used to get the annotations

J. Röning and J. Filipe (Eds.): ROBOVIS 2025, CCIS 2629, pp. 44–62, 2026.
https://doi.org/10.1007/978-3-032-00986-9_4

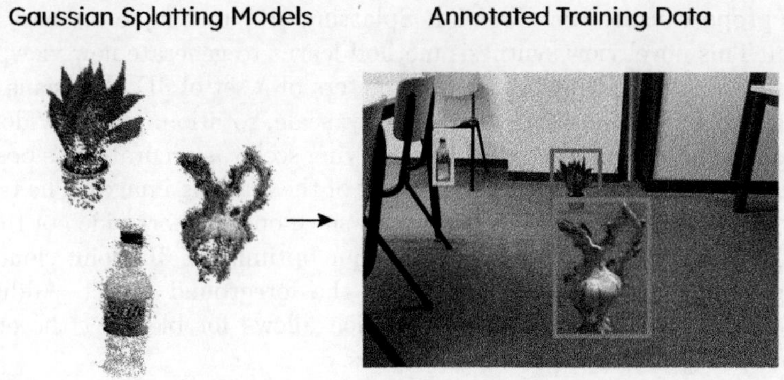

Fig. 1. Our approach extracts foreground objects from trained Gaussian Splatting models and places them in plausible positions in background images to create high-quality synthetic images for training instance segmentation models.

for those images. The most common method for generating data is using 3D rendering engines such as Blender or Unity [3,14,24,30]. A 3D scene composition containing the target objects is randomly created and rendered using a rendering technique such as rasterization or ray casting. This way, training data can be generated relatively quickly with pixel-perfect annotations. A downside of this technique is that the generated images can look quite different from the actual images due to the difficulty of accurately simulating light transport and camera sensor behavior. To keep this domain gap as small as possible, much information about the rendered scene is needed. Accurately textured 3D models are required for the target objects, and the target environment needs to be modeled as close as possible to the actual problem.

Synthetic data can also be generated using generative models, such as a GAN [21], Diffusion Model [2,31], or using novel view synthesis techniques such as NeRF [12]. These learning-based approaches have the benefit that no textured 3D model is needed, and often, the domain gap is smaller as these models are trained to produce images based on the actual photographs. However, it is more difficult to control what is rendered since these techniques do not base their rendering on a 3D scene representation. Additionally, training data is needed to train these models, and artifacts can still be generated in the images.

This work focuses on creating synthetic datasets for detecting and segmenting specific objects in cases where a physical copy of the object is available for creating a dataset. The aim is to detect instances of that particular object or objects that are very similar. Hence, we do not consider very broad classes of objects such as *dog*, *tree*, or *car*. This problem is more constrained but still has many valuable applications. Consider, for example, computer vision in a supermarket setting. They sell many different products, but all products of one type look largely the same. We strive to make the whole dataset creation process as convenient as possible by keeping the amount of manual work at a minimum. Our experiments focus on common household objects in natural settings.

We propose using the Gaussian Splatting [19] technique for easy dataset creation. This novel view synthesis method learns to generate new viewpoints of a specific scene by optimizing the parameters of a set of 3D Gaussians. During training, these Gaussians' position, opacity, scale, rotation, and view-dependent color are optimized to represent the underlying scene as accurately as possible by minimizing a visual loss over the rendering of the training images. The technique lends itself well to creating synthetic data since only a short video of the target object is needed. Furthermore, the technique optimizes a 3D point cloud during training, which can be used to segment the foreground object. Additionally, each Gaussian has an opacity value, which allows for blending the extracted foreground object with background images.

Our proposed method, called *Cut-and-Splat*, uses the Gaussian Splatting method to generate context-aware synthetic data automatically. First, we capture a short video of a target object on a flat surface. We then train a Gaussian Splatting model for this object and automatically extract the Gaussians that make up the foreground object from the model. Next, we select a random background image and identify plausible support surfaces for the target objects in this image to ensure a logical scene composition. We use monocular depth estimation to find structure in the background image. The Gaussian Splatting model for the foreground object is then used to render it as if placed on that surface, resulting in a rendered image of the foreground object and an opacity map. This map is used to blend the foreground objects and background and to create object detection and instance segmentation annotations. The depth of the background is also used to ensure proper occlusions. You can see an example of some Gaussian Splatting models and an image created by our method in Fig. 1.

To evaluate our approach, we introduce a custom dataset specifically for evaluating image-based synthetic data generation approaches. Such a dataset is currently lacking in this field. It contains novel view synthesis input videos and two different validation sets taken from different cameras. Using this dataset, we perform an ablation that shows our approach can generate data that can serve to train good-performing instance segmentation models. We benchmarked our approach against other image-based data generation methods, such as Cut-and-Paste [7] and a Diffusion model [18]. Our code and dataset are available at https://github.com/EDM-Research/cut-and-splat.

2 Related Work

Early forms of synthetic data generation use existing images of the target objects to generate new annotated images for object detection and instance segmentation. Cut, Paste, and Learn [7] uses a neural network to segment the foreground object from the existing images. We will refer to this work as Cut-and-Paste in this paper. These foregrounds are randomly transformed and placed on a random background image. Multiple blending modes are used so the network does not overfit on composition artifacts. Similarly, Ghiasi et al. [13] propose to generate additional samples by copying and pasting objects from one image to another using their existing segmentation masks. These methods allow for simple but effective data synthesis. Only a segmentation mask is needed for the foreground object, which can be done more efficiently using modern techniques such as Segment Anything [20]. A downside of these approaches is that the generated images look unrealistic as implausible compositions are made, and artifacts could be introduced. Recent work has attempted to solve this by training a synthesizer network using a discriminator [29] or finding plausible locations to paste objects to [6,9]. These methods are still limited by the existing viewpoints of the foreground objects, so they cannot be rendered in context correctly.

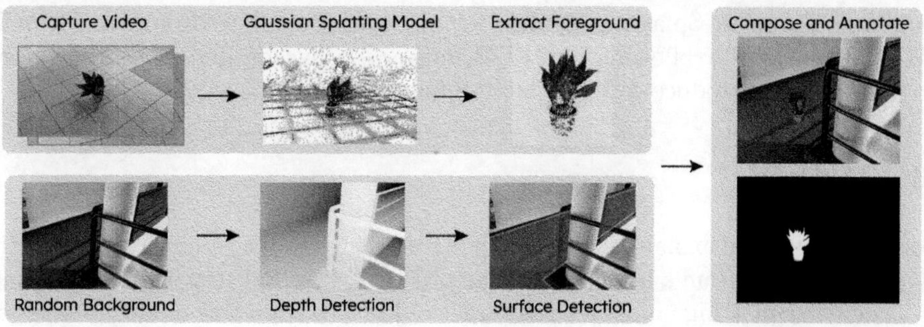

Fig. 2. An overview of our method for easily creating realistic synthetic data. First, a Gaussian Splatting model is trained on a simple input video. The model representing the foreground is extracted. Second, an arbitrary background image is taken, and the depth is detected to find feasible placement positions. The Gaussian Splatting model is used to render the foreground object in a plausible pose.

Another approach to synthetic data is using a rendering engine, such as Unity [3,24] or Blender [14]. Some solutions use less advanced rendering, such as OpenGL [17]. Generating data this way gives complete control over all the parameters, making it a very flexible option for generating diverse training data. Objects can be rendered from all viewpoints. A significant downside is that textured 3D models are needed and that the often complex environments of the target data must also be modeled in 3D to achieve a small domain gap. Due to the difficulty of simulating the physical properties of light, it is challenging to render photorealistic images. This causes the domain gap to be more significant, which can negatively impact downstream performance. To overcome this, techniques such as Domain Randomization [28] and Domain Adaptation [25] have been applied.

This paper presents a synthetic data generation technique that includes the benefits of both approaches. We can generate foreground objects at all possible viewpoints by leveraging the novel view synthesis method of Gaussian Splatting, creating highly varied training data. A Gaussian Splatting model can be made from a video of a target object. Hence, no textured 3D model is needed.

The novel view synthesis method can generate a highly accurate image representation of the object, leading to a smaller domain gap compared to render engines. Research has shown that object detectors use context when detecting and classifying objects [5]. Our approach ensures plausible object context by finding logical surfaces in background images and leveraging novel view synthesis to correctly render the object in that position. When creating data with a graphics engine, the environment in which the objects are placed must also be modeled, which can add more complexity. Our approach can use any RGB image as an environment by using depth estimation to find structure.

PEGASUS [23] is another approach that leverages Gaussian Splatting for synthetic data generation. They focus on 6DoF pose estimation for robotics and use Gaussian Splatting models for the background environment as well. We differentiate by allowing any RGB image as a background, making it more convenient to introduce different environments in the datasets.

3 Method

In this section, we explain our method for creating a realistic and varied synthetic training dataset from a basic video of an object. The initial step involves training a Gaussian Splatting model for the target object. To train this model, a series of images of the target scene, along with their calibrated camera positions and an initial sparse point cloud, are required. These inputs can be easily obtained by recording a brief video of the object and using a structure-from-motion algorithm such as COLMAP [27]. A video of about one minute is sufficient, and this is the only manual action required to create a dataset with our approach.

The Gaussian Splatting models trained for each object still contain Gaussians representing the background scene, which do not belong to the target object. This is undesirable, as we only want to generate training data containing the foreground object. Therefore, we automatically extract the Gaussians relevant to the target object from the complete model. A training image for the downstream task is created by selecting a random image from a set of background images and rendering the foreground object in this image. This is done by finding support surfaces in the background image and ensuring the correct perspective for the foreground objects to create realistic images. Realism is further improved by taking depth into account. Figure 2 shows an overview of our proposed method.

3.1 Foreground Object Extraction

After optimization, the object is defined by a set of 3D Gaussians. Each Gaussian is centered around a mean μ, representing a location in 3D space. To separate the foreground object from the trained model, we make the assumption that the object is situated on a flat surface, like the floor or a table. This assumption enables us to identify the foreground object by filtering out the ground plane. We apply Random Sample Consensus (RANSAC) [10] to the point cloud defined by the μ values. Specifically, we select three random points from the point cloud and count the number of points that lie close to the plane defined by those three points. This is repeated for several iterations, and the plane with the most inliers is considered the ground plane. This results in a set of points that belong to the ground plane.

The Gaussians corresponding to the points on the plane are removed from the model. The internal point cloud of the Gaussian Splatting model is not geometrically perfect. Some points belonging to the ground plane are thus not marked as such since they deviate too much from the detected plane. These points are very sparse, so we can filter them out using a statistical filter that removes points further away from their neighbors compared to the average for the point cloud. For this, we consider 50 neighbors and keep points less than 0.1 standard deviations away from their neighbors. Decreasing the ratio makes the filter more aggressive and will remove more noise. The geometry of the target object is robust to this filter, as it has many dense points since it is the focus of the Gaussian Splatting model.

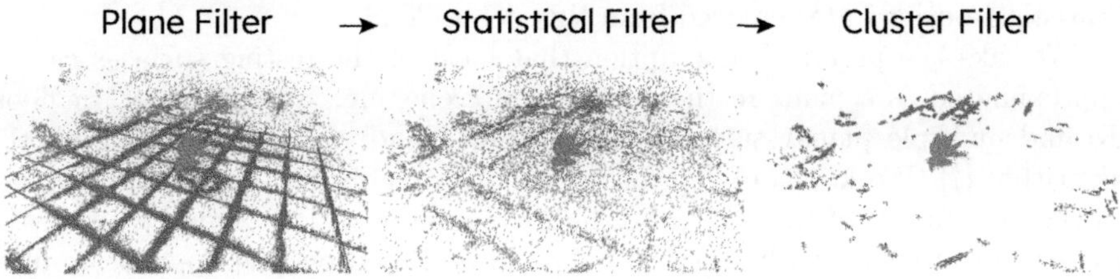

Fig. 3. A subsequent plane filter, statistical filter, and cluster filter are used to extract the plant object from the point cloud representation of the trained Gaussian Splatting model. Red illustrates points that are selected for removal. (Color figure online)

After separating the foreground object from the resting plane, a halo of points around the target object that the statistical filtering algorithm did not successfully remove can remain. These background points exist because they are outside of the focus of the input video. Hence, there are not many observations of these points, and the Gaussian Splatting representation is noisy. We filter out these background points by applying the DBSCAN [8] clustering algorithm to the point cloud. Assuming that the target object is roughly at the center of the point cloud, we keep the cluster closest to the middle. The middle is the average of all points. For DBSCAN, we use an ϵ value of 0.5 and a minimum of 100 points. Since the previous filtering step created a large gap between the target object and the halo of noise, the parameters of this step are not sensitive. Figure 3 contains an illustration of the three filtering steps that are done to extract a foreground object.

3.2 Object Placement

Existing synthetic data generators often paste the object over a random selection of background images with no regard for the physical plausibility of the resulting scene configuration. This can result in awkward images of objects completely out of place, objects floating in the air, or objects scaled too large or small to fit into the background scene. Previous methods do not consider the background image's perspective and ignore that objects are most often in a resting position when photographed. Research has shown that context can be important when training object detection models [6].

Therefore, we make sure that the foreground objects are placed in more realistic scene configurations. We achieve this by using the monocular depth estimation technique called Depth Anything [32] to generate depth maps for the background images. This approach allows us to use any collection of RGB images from the internet as backgrounds. It also enables users to capture relevant images for their specific problem domain. As a result, the synthetic data produced more closely matches the real-world conditions, bridging the domain gap even further.

The depth map of the background image is converted to a point cloud using an estimation of the intrinsic matrix by assuming an FOV of 55°C and a central principal point. While not perfectly accurate, this leads to visually good results. Statistical outliers are removed from this point cloud.

We take the practical assumption that most of the resting surfaces can be approximated as a plane in the background scene, e.g., a table, chair, or floor. To find multiple planar surfaces in the point cloud, we use a statistics-based algorithm [1]. We keep only surfaces that are roughly horizontal with respect to the orientation of the scene. We find the up-axis of the scene based on the PCA [11] of the convex hull of the point cloud. Based on this up-axis, we filter out planes that are not horizontal to avoid placement on, for example, walls. Additionally, horizontal planes that are too close to the top of the scene are also removed. When picking a random plane to place an object on, the probability each plane is selected is based on its surface area. For computations on point clouds, we use Open3D [33]. We assume resting surfaces are horizontal, but this assumption can easily be relaxed. The normals of the detected planes will later be used to align the target object to the surface. Figure 4 illustrates some potential object placement positions found by our approach.

Fig. 4. Illustration of possible object placements in the background images computed by our approach. For each image, we show 1000 possible placement positions, indicated by colored dots. A different color indicates a different plane.

3.3 Scene Composition

To generate a new scene composition, we select a foreground object and one of the approximately horizontal surfaces in the background to place it on. A random point on that surface is chosen as a final destination for the object. We position the foreground object in the scene by taking into account the surface normal of the fitted plane and rotating the object to its upright resting position. The resting configuration for objects is chosen by aligning its normal in the foreground point cloud data with the surface normal of the resting plane. The normal of the foreground object is the normal of the filtered-out plane from the Gaussian Splatting model. This process ensures depth-dependent scaling and perspective-correct placement. To increase variation in the representations of the object in the dataset, we rotate the object randomly around its local up axis. There is no mechanism that ensures correct inter-object scaling.

Once the foreground object's position, orientation, and scaling are determined, the Gaussian Splatting model is evaluated with those parameters, and the foreground object is rendered from the appropriate viewpoint. The rendering is done once to obtain the color values and then again with the splat color set to white to obtain the opacity map. Next, the opacity values are filtered by considering the background scene's depth values to have realistic occlusions. A median filter is applied to the background depth map to prevent noisy occlusions. Figure 5 shows an example of how the depth is used to simulate occlusion. The final opacity map is then used to blend the foreground object realistically into the background scene.

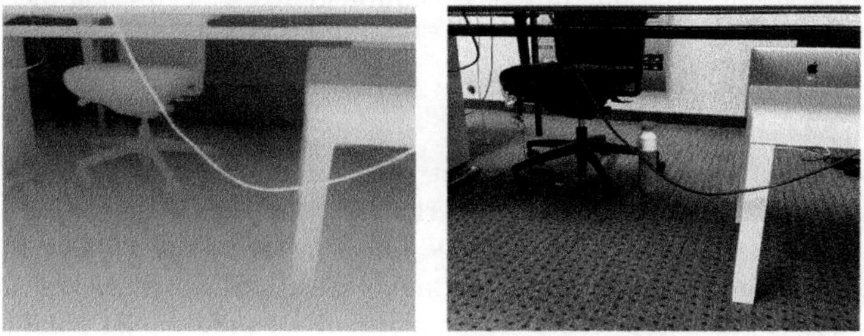

Fig. 5. The red bottle is rendered on the floor in the background (right). The depth map (left) computed by Depth Anything is used to realistically occlude the object behind the cable. (Color figure online)

The lighting is not adapted to the background scene when placing the Gaussian Splatting renders in the background images. Due to this, the object's appearance is limited to the lighting conditions from the captured video. This could cause the model to overfit this visual representation of the object and not generalize to other lighting conditions. To avoid this, we augment the object's appearance in two ways. Firstly, when rendering the Gaussians for the foreground, we use a random vector to calculate the spherical harmonics instead of the actual camera position. This changes the object's appearance even when the camera angle remains the same, introducing more variations. This is illustrated in Fig. 6. Additionally, we apply pixel-level augmentations such as blurring, color adjustments, noise addition, and random tone curves. While these augmentations may not simulate realistic lighting, they introduce additional variation to help the model adapt to different lighting conditions in the test data.

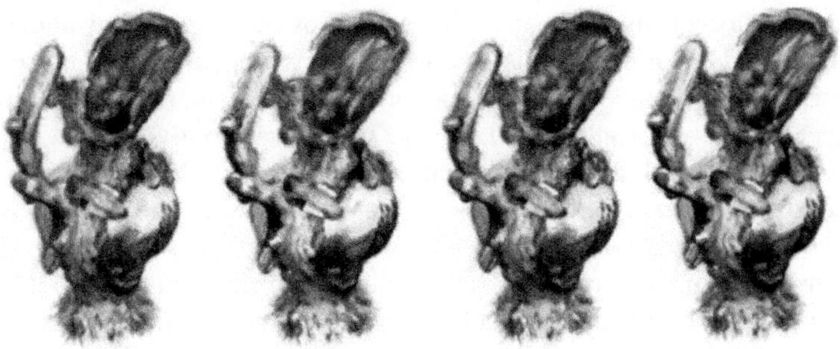

Fig. 6. By varying the angle at which the spherical harmonics are evaluated with respect to the camera, we introduce subtle variations.

After rendering, the opacity maps of the foreground objects are used to export annotations that can be used to train detection models on the created images. These annotations are bounding boxes and instance segmentation masks.

4 Results

In this section, we demonstrate that our approach can efficiently generate datasets suitable for training high-performing instance segmentation models. We use our method to create multiple datasets for training such models and evaluate their performance using real annotated data. To show the individual importance of the components of our method, we perform an ablation. Next, we compare our approach to two other image-based synthetic data generation approaches. Cut-and-Paste [7] is an approach that is often used due to its effectiveness and simplicity. Since Diffusion models [18] have the ability to generate very realistic-looking images, we also include an experiment comparing our approach to synthetic data generated by a Diffusion model. We do not compare our approach to NeRF-based data generation since the foreground object is more difficult to extract from these models. This could have a large impact on the results.

In all experiments, we train a Mask R-CNN [15] model with a ResNet50 [16] backbone. The model is trained for 100 epochs, with 1000 images for each epoch. The model backbone is initialized with weights trained on ImageNet [4], and some basic image augmentations are used during training. We compute the mean average precision (mAP) over the 0.5 to 0.95 overlap threshold range as a validation metric. This computation is done over the predicted bounding boxes. When training Gaussian Splatting models, we use the standard Gaussian Splatting version and implementation [19] with all the default parameters.

4.1 IBSYD Dataset

Leveraging novel view synthesis for synthetic data generation is a relatively new domain. To thoroughly test our approach, we, therefore, introduce a custom dataset. The *Image Based Synthetic Data (IBSYD)* dataset. The dataset describes several challenging and diverse objects: a bottle of eyedrops, a plant, a semi-transparent bottle of soda, a water bottle, and a colorful vase with a handle. These objects are illustrated in Fig. 7. For each object, a video is provided that can serve as input for a novel view synthesis method such as ours. Each object was placed on the floor separately, and a one-minute video was recorded with a smartphone. This process takes only a few minutes in total and is the only manual action needed.

Fig. 7. We introduce the Image Based Synthetic Data (IBSYD) dataset, which contains five challenging and varied objects.

Additionally, the dataset includes a test set of real images to validate whether the generated images can be used to train detection models. We manually took several photographs, each containing one to three objects. The objects are placed naturally, i.e., on a tabletop or the floor, and have occlusions. Photographs are taken from a wide variety of indoor scenes. We used two different cameras to create these photographs. 50 photographs were taken with the same iPhone used to create the input videos, and 50 were taken with a Canon 500D camera. This allows us to investigate if the generated datasets are overfitted to the camera used to train the Gaussian Splatting model. The images from the Canon camera differ significantly from those from the smartphone as the camera has a different lens and sensor, the objects are sometimes out of focus, and in some cases, the flash was used. The distribution of object occurrences and combinations is the same between the two validation sets. Figure 8 shows an example from both datasets.

Fig. 8. The IBSYD dataset contains two validation datasets. One taken with an iPhone camera (example on the left) and one taken with a Canon camera (example on the right).

4.2 Ablation

First, we perform an ablation to highlight the abilities of our approach and to show the importance of the different components proposed in our pipeline. Namely, we investigate the impact of the smart placement technique and augmentation of the representation of the foreground object. For this reason, we generate three different datasets with our *Cut-and-Splat* approach using the input videos of the aforementioned IBSYD dataset. One using the full approach, one without augmentation, and one without smart placement. For the latter, objects are rendered from a random camera angle and placed in a random position on the screen. We train an instance segmentation model on each of these datasets and test it on the two different test sets. The background images are taken from the COCO dataset [22]. Each rendered dataset contains 5000 images, and each image has one to three objects. Some visualizations of the Gaussian Splatting models trained for our objects are shown in Fig. 9. Figure 10 shows several images created by our dataset. We observe that objects are placed on surfaces with plausible poses.

Fig. 9. Objects rendered by Gaussian Splatting after segmenting the foreground objects.

Fig. 10. Some examples of images rendered by our approach.

Table 1. Performance of instance segmentation models trained on datasets generated by different variations of our method.

Dataset	mAP_{iPhone}	mAP_{Canon}
Cut-and-Splat	**81.21**	**79.68**
no augmentation	71.17	73.71
no smart placement	52.05	53.51

The results in Table 1 show that a model trained on a dataset generated by *Cut-and-Splat* delivers very good results, scoring around 80 mAP. This holds true for both the iPhone and Canon validation datasets. This indicates that the trained model does not overfit on the camera used to capture the Gaussian Splatting model. Furthermore, we observe a significant decrease in performance when no augmentation is used when rendering the foreground images. This highlights its importance in overcoming the lack of realistic lighting on the rendered objects. Finally, when objects are rendered in random positions, we see a very large drop in performance to almost 50 mAP. This shows the benefit of realistically placing objects in the background scenes. Thanks to this, the training data is more similar to the target domain, leading to a large increase in performance. Some successful detections made by the model trained on the full *Cut-and-Splat* dataset are shown in Fig. 11.

Fig. 11. Some successful detections on the iPhone test set made by an instance segmentation model trained on a dataset generated by *Cut-and-Splat*.

4.3 Versus Cut-and-Paste

In the Cut-and-Paste approach, foreground objects are cropped from a limited set of input images and placed on background images following a random transformation. The downsides are that only a limited amount of viewpoints are considered and that objects are placed without considering context. However, this approach does not suffer from artifacts introduced by Gaussian Splatting like our approach.

We create a Cut-and-Paste dataset of the IBSYD dataset following the same specifications as in our previous experiment, i.e., COCO backgrounds, 5000 images, and up to three objects per photo. For each object, we select ten frames from the input video and manually extract the foreground mask using Segment Anything [20]. The frames are taken from widely varying camera positions to ensure a good representation of the object. Some examples of this dataset are shown in Fig. 12.

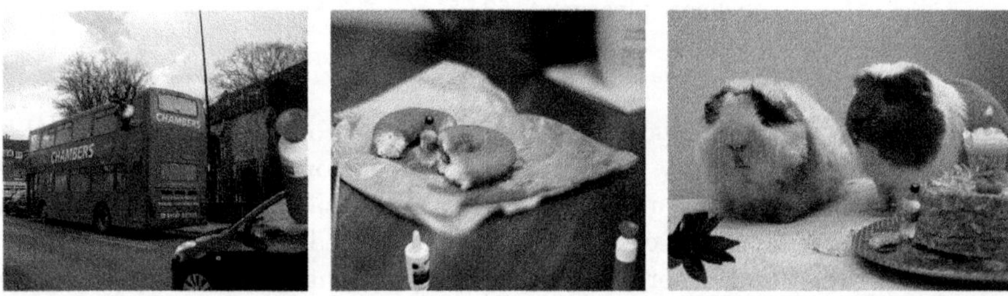

Fig. 12. Some examples of images generated using the Cut-and-Paste approach.

The COCO images we used as backgrounds for generating data do not match the target domain well. This often leads to strange-looking images, even when we use our method for realistic scene composition. For this reason, we introduce a set of relevant background images for this experiment. We took 80 photographs in the same rooms where the test set was recorded. The objects of the test set do not occur in these photographs. The same camera as in the iPhone test set is used, and the photographs are taken from random poses that do not match the test set. Using these backgrounds, we create a second dataset using the Cut-and-Paste approach. As a comparison, we also create a *Cut-and-Splat* dataset using these backgrounds.

For both our approach and the Cut-and-Paste method, we create two datasets. One with unrelated background images and one with in-domain background images. An instance segmentation model is trained on each of these datasets and tested on the iPhone test set. This way, we compare the performance of *Cut-and-Splat* to that of Cut-and-Paste approach, and we research whether using in-domain backgrounds leads to higher-quality synthetic data.

The results in Fig. 13 show that models trained on datasets generated by our approach outperform those trained on Cut-and-Paste datasets. This shows that the plausible object context and increase in viewpoint variation in our method leads to better datasets. We observe that for *Cut-and-Splat*, the in-domain backgrounds lead to a small increase in performance. For Cut-and-Paste, using in-domain backgrounds gives a much larger boost in performance. This indicates that our approach is more robust to out-of-domain backgrounds. Hence, less effort needs to be spent collecting background data.

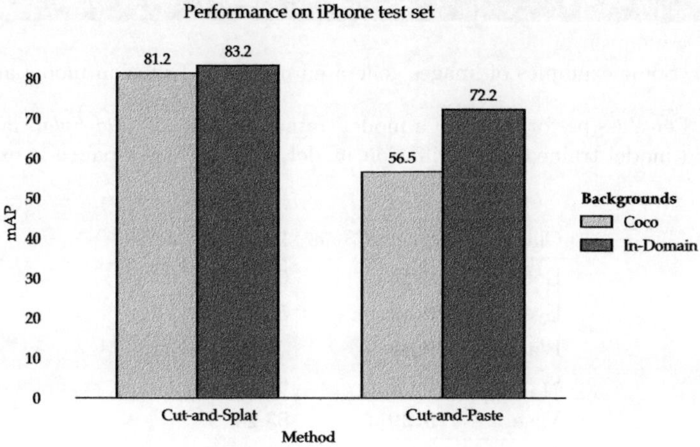

Fig. 13. The performance of instance segmentation models trained on data generated by *Cut-and-Splat* versus Cut-and-Paste. We consider using both unrelated COCO backgrounds and domain-relevant background images.

4.4 Versus Diffusion Model

There are multiple different ways to use a Diffusion model to generate synthetic data. To avoid training or fine-tuning a Diffusion model, we use an approach similar to Cut-and-Paste. We randomly place the foreground objects on an image and use Stable Diffusion XL [26] inpainting to generate a background. This has the benefit that the background is generated to fit the foreground images to create a realistic-looking image. Additionally, the foreground images are slightly adapted to the generated background, creating even more realism. We use ChatGPT to generate random prompts that ask the Diffusion model to place the objects in indoor environments.

Using this approach, we generate a 5000-image synthetic dataset for the IBSYD objects. Some samples of this dataset are shown in Fig. 14. An instance segmentation model is trained on that dataset and tested on the iPhone test set.

Fig. 14. Some examples of images generated using the Diffusion model approach.

Table 2. Per-class performance of a model trained on the *Cut-and-Splat* dataset compared to a model trained on a Diffusion model dataset. Performance is expressed in mAP.

Class	*Cut-and-Splat*	Diffusion Model
Bottle	**88.44**	66.67
Eyedrops	**79.39**	51.67
Plant	**69.89**	4.72
Sprite	**93.07**	62.40
Vase	**75.29**	53.20
Total	**81.21**	48.86

From the results in Fig. 2, we observe that our approach also outperforms the Diffusion model-based data generation by a large margin. This holds true for all classes. Although the images generated by the Diffusion model look very realistic, the model sometimes significantly deforms the objects to make them fit better in the background. This can warp the representation of the downstream model for those objects, causing worse performance. Data generation approaches based on Diffusion models that are specifically designed for synthetic data should lead to better performance.

5 Future Work and Limitations

There still are limitations to our approach that could inspire future work. Some of these limitations are inherent to the current state of Gaussian Splatting. These models do not support complex lighting features, such as relighting and refractions. Transparent objects are also often not represented correctly. In this study, we used data augmentation to simulate different lighting effects. However, this is not realistic. Direct relighting of the spherical harmonics of the Gaussian Splatting model based on the background image could result in better-quality images. Additionally, the effects of the placed object on the background representation, such as shadows and ambient lighting, are not considered.

Our approach limits itself to generating synthetic data of objects standing upright on flat surfaces. While much of the demand for synthetic data falls under this category, other scenarios could benefit from synthetic data that are not supported by our method. For example, a bin-picking scenario where objects are tossed randomly in a box.

Finally, our approach does not consider the side of the object that is on the floor during the recording of the input video. Similarly, artifacts are sometimes visible in the rendered images due to the bottom of objects being removed by the plane filter. This can be an issue for objects that are not very tall or have a large contact surface with the floor. Future work can avoid this by recording the object in multiple poses and merging the Gaussian Splatting models together. Additionally, a learned point cloud segmentation approach could be used to extract the foreground object with fewer artifacts.

6 Conclusion

In this work, we proposed an approach for generating synthetic data that tries to overcome the limitations of current approaches. Cut-and-Paste methods are hindered by the limited amount of variation in viewpoints of the foreground object and the general lack of realism. Rendering-based approaches require an accurate textured object model and a 3D representation of the background scene. Generative AI models, on the other hand, require fine-tuning or retraining to generate specific objects.

Our approach leverages Gaussian Splatting to avoid the need for textured 3D models while introducing many variations in the representation of the target objects at a high level of realism. Our approach is very convenient as the only manual effort required is a video of the target object.

To evaluate our approach and other future image-based synthetic data generation approaches, we introduced the IBSYD dataset. From experiments on this dataset, we have concluded that instance segmentation models trained on data generated by our method achieve good performance. Additionally, we have shown that the smart placement employed by our technique leads to better-performing models as the generated data is plausible. As a benchmark, we have compared our approach to two alternative image-based synthetic data generation approaches. This comparison has shown that the added viewpoint variation and plausible object placement lead to better results compared to Cut-and-Paste. Additionally, we have shown that the consistency with the original object representation in our method gives us a significant edge over the Diffusion model-based approach.

Acknowledgments. This study was supported by the Special Research Fund (BOF20OWB24) of Hasselt University and by the FWO fellowship grant (1SHDZ24N). The research was carried out within the framework of the NORM. AI SBO project (Natural Objects Rendering for Economic AI Models), funded by Flanders Make, the strategic research centre for the Manufacturing Industry in Belgium. This work was made possible with support from MAXVR-INFRA, a scalable and flexible infrastructure that facilitates the transition to digital-physical work environments.

References

1. Araújo, A.M., Oliveira, M.M.: A robust statistics approach for plane detection in unorganized point clouds. Pattern Recogn. **100**, 107115 (2020). https://doi.org/10.1016/j.patcog.2019.107115
2. Azizi, S., Kornblith, S., Saharia, C., Norouzi, M., Fleet, D.J.: Synthetic data from diffusion models improves imagenet classification. Trans. Mach. Learn. Res. (2023), https://openreview.net/forum?id=DlRsoxjyPm
3. Borkman, S., et al.: Unity perception: generate synthetic data for computer vision (2021). https://arxiv.org/abs/2107.04259
4. Deng, J., Dong, W., Socher, R., Li, L.J., Li, K., Fei-Fei, L.: Imagenet: a large-scale hierarchical image database. In: 2009 IEEE Conference on Computer Vision and Pattern Recognition, pp. 248–255 (2009).https://doi.org/10.1109/CVPR.2009.5206848
5. Divvala, S.K., Hoiem, D., Hays, J.H., Efros, A.A., Hebert, M.: Empirical Study Context Object Detect. (2009). https://doi.org/10.1109/CVPR.2009.5206532
6. Dvornik, N., Mairal, J., Schmid, C.: Modeling visual context is key to augmenting object detection datasets. In: Proceedings of the European Conference on Computer Vision, pp. 364–380 (2018)
7. Dwibedi, D., Misra, I., Hebert, M.: Cut, paste and learn: surprisingly easy synthesis for instance detection. In: Proceedings of the IEEE/CVF International Conference on Computer Vision, pp. 1310–1319. IEEE Computer Society, Los Alamitos, CA, USA (2017).https://doi.org/10.1109/ICCV.2017.146
8. Ester, M., Kriegel, H.P., Sander, J., Xu, X.: A density-based algorithm for discovering clusters in large spatial databases with noise. In: Proceedings of the Second International Conference on Knowledge Discovery and Data Mining, pp. 226–231. KDD'96, AAAI Press (1996)
9. Fang, H.S., Sun, J., Wang, R., Gou, M., Li, Y.L., Lu, C.: Instaboost: boosting instance segmentation via probability map guided copy-pasting. In: Proceedings of the IEEE/CVF international conference on computer vision, pp. 682–691 (2019)
10. Fischler, M.A., Bolles, R.C.: Random sample consensus: a paradigm for model fitting with applications to image analysis and automated cartography. Commun. ACM **24**(6),pp. 381–395 (1981).https://doi.org/10.1145/358669.358692, https://doi.org/10.1145/358669.358692
11. F.R.S., K.P.: Liii. on lines and planes of closest fit to systems of points in space. Lond. Edinb. Dublin Philos. Mag. J. Sci. **2**(11),pp. 559–572 (1901).https://doi.org/10.1080/14786440109462720
12. Ge, Y., et al.: Neural-sim: learning to generate training data with nerf (2022)
13. Ghiasi, G., et al.: Simple copy-paste is a strong data augmentation method for instance segmentation. In: Proceedings of the IEEE/CVF Conference on Computer Vision and Pattern Recognition, pp. 2918–2928 (2021)
14. Greff, K., et al.: Kubric: a scalable dataset generator. In: Proceedings of the IEEE/CVF Conference on Computer Vision and Pattern Recognition (2022)
15. He, K., Gkioxari, G., Dollár, P., Girshick, R.: Mask r-CNN. In: 2017 IEEE International Conference on Computer Vision (ICCV), pp. 2980–2988 (2017).https://doi.org/10.1109/ICCV.2017.322

16. He, K., Zhang, X., Ren, S., Sun, J.: Deep residual learning for image recognition. In: 2016 IEEE Conference on Computer Vision and Pattern Recognition (CVPR), pp. 770–778 (2015). https://api.semanticscholar.org/CorpusID:206594692
17. Hinterstoisser, S., Pauly, O., Heibel, H., Martina, M., Bokeloh, M.: An annotation saved is an annotation earned: using fully synthetic training for object detection . In: Proceedings of the IEEE/CVF International Conference on Computer Vision Workshops, pp. 2787–2796 (2019).https://doi.org/10.1109/ICCVW.2019.00340, https://doi.ieeecomputersociety.org/10.1109/ICCVW.2019.00340
18. Ho, J., Jain, A., Abbeel, P.: Denoising diffusion probabilistic models. In: Larochelle, H., Ranzato, M., Hadsell, R., Balcan, M., Lin, H. (eds.) Advances in Neural Information Processing Systems, vol. 33, pp. 6840–6851. Curran Associates, Inc. (2020). https://proceedings.neurips.cc/paper_files/paper/2020/file/4c5bcfec8584af0d967f1ab10179ca4b-Paper.pdf
19. Kerbl, B., Kopanas, G., Leimkühler, T., Drettakis, G.: 3d gaussian splatting for real-time radiance field rendering. ACM Trans. Graph. **42**(4) (2023). https://repo-sam.inria.fr/fungraph/3d-gaussian-splatting/
20. Kirillov, A., et al.: Segment anything. In: Proceedings of the IEEE/CVF International Conference on Computer Vision, pp. 4015–4026 (2023)
21. Li, D., Ling, H., Kim, S.W., Kreis, K., Fidler, S., Torralba, A.: Bigdatasetgan: synthesizing imagenet with pixel-wise annotations. In: Proceedings of the IEEE/CVF Conference on Computer Vision and Pattern Recognition, pp. 21298–21308 (2022)
22. Lin, T.-Y., et al.: Microsoft COCO: common Objects in Context. In: Fleet, D., Pajdla, T., Schiele, B., Tuytelaars, T. (eds.) ECCV 2014. LNCS, vol. 8693, pp. 740–755. Springer, Cham (2014). https://doi.org/10.1007/978-3-319-10602-1_48
23. Meyer, L., Erich, F., Yoshiyasu, Y., Stamminger, M., Ando, N., Domae, Y.: Pegasus: physical enhanced gaussian splatting simulation system for 6dof object pose dataset generation. In: Proceedings of the International Conference on Intelligent Robots and Systems (2024). https://meyerls.github.io/pegasus_web
24. Moonen, S., Vanherle, B., de Hoog, J., Bourgana, T., Bey-Temsamani, A., Michiels, N.: Cad2render: A modular toolkit for GPU-accelerated photorealistic synthetic data generation for the manufacturing industry. In: Proceedings of the IEEE Winter Conference on Applications of Computer Vision Workshops, pp. 583–592 (2023)
25. Oza, P., Sindagi, V.A., Sharmini, V.V., Patel, V.M.: Unsupervised domain adaptation of object detectors: a survey. In: IEEE Transactions on Pattern Analysis and Machine Intelligence ,pp. 1–24 (2023).https://doi.org/10.1109/TPAMI.2022.3217046
26. Podell, D., et al.: SDXL: improving latent diffusion models for high-resolution image synthesis. In: Proceedings of the International Conference on Learning Representations (2024). https://openreview.net/forum?id=di52zR8xgf
27. Schönberger, J.L., Frahm, J.M.: Structure-from-motion revisited. In: Proceedings of the IEEE/CVF Conference on Computer Vision and Pattern Recognition, pp. 4104–4113 (2016).https://doi.org/10.1109/CVPR.2016.445
28. Tremblay, J., et al.: Training deep networks with synthetic data: Bridging the reality gap by domain randomization. In: Proceedings of the IEEE/CVF Conference on Computer Vision and Pattern Recognition Workshops (2018)
29. Tripathi, S., Chandra, S., Agrawal, A., Tyagi, A., Rehg, J.M., Chari, V.: Learning to generate synthetic data via compositing. In: Proceedings of the IEEE/CVF Conference on Computer Vision and Pattern Recognition, pp. 461–470. IEEE Computer Society, Los Alamitos, CA, USA (2019).https://doi.org/10.1109/CVPR.2019.00055, https://doi.ieeecomputersociety.org/10.1109/CVPR.2019.00055

30. Wood, E., Baltrušaitis, T., Hewitt, C., Dziadzio, S., Cashman, T.J., Shotton, J.: Fake it till you make it: face analysis in the wild using synthetic data alone. In: Proceedings of the IEEE/CVF International Conference on Computer Vision, pp. 3681–3691 (2021)
31. Wu, W., Zhao, Y., Shou, M.Z., Zhou, H., Shen, C.: Diffumask: synthesizing images with pixel-level annotations for semantic segmentation using diffusion models. In: Proceedings of the IEEE/CVF International Conference on Computer Vision, pp. 1206–1217 (2023). https://api.semanticscholar.org/CorpusID:257636752
32. Yang, L., Kang, B., Huang, Z., Xu, X., Feng, J., Zhao, H.: Depth anything: unleashing the power of large-scale unlabeled data. In: Proceedings of the IEEE/CVF Conference on Computer Vision and Pattern Recognition (2024)
33. Zhou, Q.Y., Park, J., Koltun, V.: Open3D: a modern library for 3D data processing. arXiv:1801.09847 (2018)

LiCAR: Pseudo-RGB LiDAR Image for CAR Segmentation

Ignacio de Loyola Páez-Ubieta(✉), Edison P. Velasco-Sánchez, and Santiago T. Puente

AUtomatics, RObotics, and Artificial Vision Lab, IUII: University Institute for Computer Research, University of Alicante, Crta. San Vicente s/n, San Vicente del Raspeig, 03690 Alicante, Spain
{ignacio.paez,edison.velasco,santiago.puente}@ua.es

Abstract. With the advancement of computing resources, an increasing number of Neural Networks (NNs) are appearing for image detection and segmentation. However, these methods usually accept as input a RGB 2D image. On the other side, Light Detection And Ranging (LiDAR) sensors present a different number of horizontal layers, making those with a large number more expensive, but able to obtain data that is similar to that obtained by traditional low-resolution RGB cameras. With the purpose of whether or not is possible to perform object segmentation on pseudo-RGB images obtained from a large number of horizontal layer LiDAR sensor, a new dataset has been generated. This dataset combines the information given by the LiDAR sensor into a Spherical Range Image (SRI), concretely the reflectivity, near infrared and signal intensity 2D images. These images are then fed into instance segmentation NNs. These NNs segment the cars that appear in these images, having as a result Bounding Box (BB) and mask precision of 88% and 81.5% respectively with You Only Look Once (YOLO)-v8 large. By using this segmentation NN, some trackers have been applied so as to follow each car segmented instance along a video feed, having great performance in real world experiments. Results show that even with a small dataset, NNs are able to learn how to segment cars in pseudo-RGB images, leaving only the pending task of providing more samples so as to improve accuracy.

Keywords: Artificial intelligence · Mobile robots · Neural networks · Instance segmentation · LiDAR · YOLO

1 Introduction

The first Artificial Intelligence (AI) models date back to 1943 [9]. Initially, the goal was to simulate the function of a single neuron. Since then, several advances have led to the development of more complex structures, the most recent of which are data storage [6] and Graphics Processing Units(GPUs) [3], in 2006 and 2010 respectively.

J. Röning and J. Filipe (Eds.): ROBOVIS 2025, CCIS 2629, pp. 63–73, 2026.
https://doi.org/10.1007/978-3-032-00986-9_5

Regarding object detection and segmentation methods, there are three different approaches; single, two and multi-stage methods [5]. Among them, the first one is the one that receives more attention, since they are usually faster [14], allowing to have inference times close to realtime. Some examples of these single-stage methods are You Only Look Once (YOLO) or Single Shot DetectorSSD [8].

Normally, these methods require a RGB image as input. However, variations have been introduced in recent years that allow the input of pseudo-RGB images generated from Light Detection And Ranging (LiDAR) sensors. For example, [4] uses a combination of RGB and LiDAR images to perform object detection by first identifying regions of interest in the LiDAR point cloud. Using these regions, a RGB image is extracted from the original RGB image and used as input to a YOLO Neural Network (NN), which finally detects the cars. Although this method gives good results, it requires the handling of LiDAR and RGB images and does not detect objects accurately. Other papers, such as [10], generate a pseudo-RGB image from a LiDAR sensor. This is used to detect and track pedestrians across the image. To do this, they slide the Bounding Box(BB) in 5 parts to build the descriptor. However, it only performs object detection, not segmentation, using an old YOLO distribution, since at the time of submission new YOLO distributions had appeared. Finally, [20] demonstrates the generation of a pseudo-RGB image from a LiDAR sensor in a process that is comparable to the aforementioned method. By using detection and segmentation methods, they are able to achieve good results in both indoor and outdoor environments. However, the preliminary processing of the image from 2048×128 to 1000×300 is necessary due to the limitations of the selected NN, which is not fully capable of handling high-distortion images. Therefore, a denoising and interpolation process is required to enhance the image quality. Furthermore, the limited number of images and instances in the dataset raises questions about the quality of the results. By contrast, generating pseudo-RGB images and using the latest State Of The Art (sota) detection and segmentation methods enable us to eliminate this pre-processing step.

In this work, we perform the segmentation of car instances on Spherical Range Images (SRIs), obtained by combining three different channels from a LiDAR sensor, with several single-stage methods from the YOLO family.

The main contributions of this work are:

- A new dataset for segmenting cars in pseudo-RGB 2D images has been generated. These images are SRIs obtained by combining several channels from a LiDAR sensor.
- The aforementioned dataset has been used to train several SOTA NNs for instance detection and segmentation. As a result, it has been validated that it is possible to successfully detect and segment objects in images generated from LiDAR sensors.
- Once the best instance segmentation method was obtained, a tracker was incorporated, achieving excellent results without affecting real-time inference.

This paper is organised as follows: Sect. 2 introduces both the image generation process and the segmentation NNs used, Sect. 3 shows the experimental setup of the system, Sect. 4 shows the results obtained on the test set and also on completely new real world scenarios and Sect. 5 summarises the results of the paper, as well as introduces the main lines of future works.

2 Methodology

In this Section, the process used to generate the SRIs and the segmentation NNs that were used in Sect. 3 are presented.

2.1 Image Generation

The generation of images from a LiDAR sensor is a two-step process. Initially, a point cloud is created, comprising the reflectance, intensity and illumination of each point derived from the data provided by the LiDAR. Subsequently, this point cloud is transformed into a SRI, which represents the XYZ point cloud in polar coordinates.

In the initial process, data is obtained from the LiDAR sensor. The used sensor provides 4 different 2D images:

- Range (Rg): depth is expressed in mm and discretised to the nearest 1 mm, with a maximum range of 524 m, in accordance with the specifications outlined in the sensor manual.
- Calibrated reflectivity (Rf): the measurements on the signal photons are scaled based on measured range and sensor sensitivity at that range, providing an indication of target reflectivity.
- Signal photons (It): intensity of the photons in the signal returned.
- Near infrared photons (If): Near InfraRed (NIR) photons associated with the natural environmental illumination.

A pseudo-RGB point cloud is generated, in which each point is characterised by a 3D position and a set of luminance factors. The former is obtained from Rg, whereas the latter is the consequence of a value combination, resulting in the formation of pseudo-RGB images in the format $[Rf, If, It]$.

The generated point cloud is then transformed into a SRI. This method was initially presented in [17] and subsequently elaborated by [18]. In general terms, each layer of the LiDAR is transformed into a row, with the horizontal viewing angle of the LiDAR becoming each column (in this case, 360°). An example of the process of combining the LiDAR channels to produce the final pseudo-RGB SRI is shown on Fig. 1. The images have been cropped in order to facilitate closer examination.

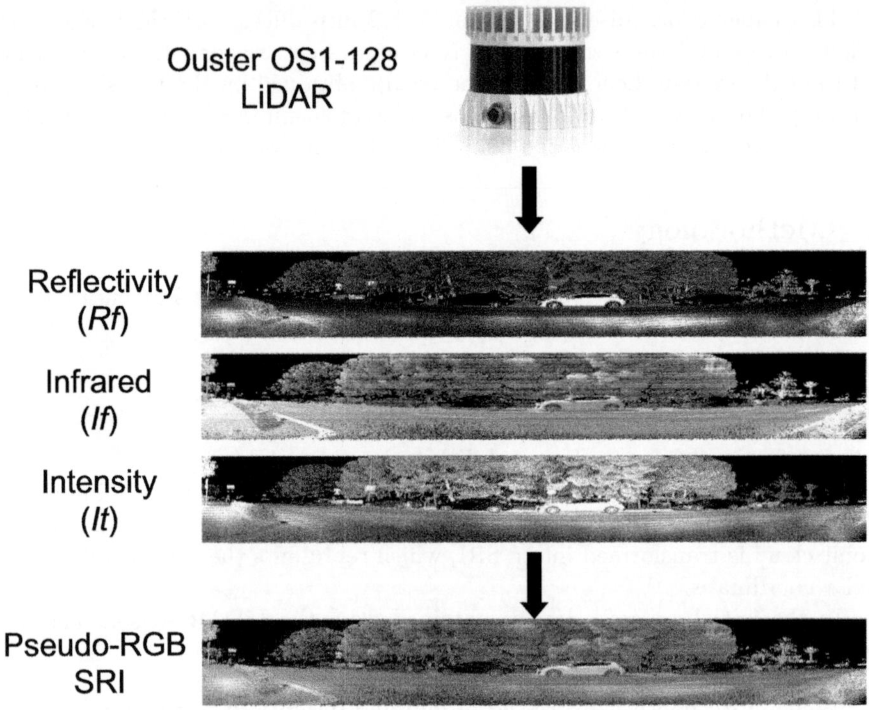

Fig. 1. Partial view of the combination of LiDAR channels for generating the pseudo-RGB SRI.

2.2 Segmentation NNs

A fast but accurate method is required to perform instance segmentation. For this purpose, single-stage SOTA methods such as YOLO-v5 [7], YOLO-v7 [19] and YOLO-v8 [16] were chosen.

YOLO-v5 appeared online on 2020. This model was the first in the YOLO NNs family to support instance segmentation, as well as being released by a private company. There is not much hindsight on this model, as no official paper was published. But it seems that the anchor box selection process was built into the model, allowing it to automatically learn the most appropriate size for each dataset [21].

YOLO-v7 appeared online on 2022, but the paper was published in 2023. They introduced a trainable bag-of-freebies, a new reparametrization module, and a composite scaling method. All these features were used to achieve an improvement in the loss function, label assignment, support for multiple architectures, or a good trade-off between network parameters, computation, inference speed, and accuracy.

YOLO-v8 also appeared online on 2022, but later than YOLO-v7, having its paper publication in 2024. To improve on previous versions, a new loss function called focal loss, a new data enhancement method called mixup [22], and a new evaluation metric called Average Precision Across Scale (APAS) were introduced. These allow to focus on complex images instead of simple ones, to improve the generalisation and strength of the model by merging images and labels, and to ensure the accuracy of the model over different scales.

3 Experiments

In this Section, the elements used for the execution of the experiments are presented, as well as details from the generated dataset. The NNs training procedure and the results obtained are shown in Sect. 4.

3.1 Setup

The Ouster OS1-128 3D-LiDAR was used to obtain the dataset. This sensor is mounted on roBot for Localization in Unstructured Environments (BLUE), a mobile robotic platform [12,13] which is still being updated today [2]. The NNs were trained on a computer with a NVIDIA DGX-A100 Tensor Core GPU with 40 GB of RAM. For data acquisition and inference, an on-board computer with an AMD Ryzen 7 5700G as Central Processing Unit (CPU), a NVIDIA RTX 3060 with 12 GB as GPU and 32 GB of Random-Access Memory(RAM) was used. The BLUE robot with the Ouster OS1-128 3D-LiDAR and the on-board computer is shown in Fig. 2.

Fig. 2. BLUE robot with both the Ouster OS1-128 3D-LiDAR and the on-board computer.

3.2 Dataset

After obtaining the data from the LiDAR sensor and converting it to SRIs, 400 images were obtained, each with approximately 14 car instances. These images contain different outdoor environments from the University of Alicante and have a resolution of 2048 × 128 pixels. The cars appearing in the images were labelled using the LabelMe [15] tool.

The generated dataset has been divided into training/validation/test sets according to the 85/10/5 ratio. A summary of the generated dataset can be found in Table 1. This dataset is available online at LICAR dataset[1]

Table 1. Generated dataset specifications.

Set	Images	Instances
Train	340	4784
Validation	40	569
Test	20	299

3.3 NN Training

All trainings were performed using transfer learning from previously trained models provided by each NN model, as it has shown to improve model accuracy while training the models in [11].

YOLO-v5 was trained for 300 epochs with a batch size of 128 and 8 workers, using a single channel rectangular image with an image size of 2048 pixels as the longest side. YOLO-v7 was trained for 100 epochs with a batch size of 64 and only 1 worker, also using single channel rectangular images of 2048 pixels. YOLO-v8 was trained for 100 epochs with a batch size of 256, again using single channel rectangular 2048 pixel rectangular images.

The rest of the parameters used are the default ones, provided by each model as recommended for performing instance segmentation task.

4 Results

This section presents the results obtained after training the previously mentioned NNs with the generated dataset.

4.1 Test Set

After training the aforementioned models using the training and validation sets, the final results are obtained. The test set contained 20 images with 299 instances. However, in order to have a fair comparison, some parameters of the

[1] https://www.iuii.ua.es/licar/index.html

used NNs are given in Table 2, as well as the computation times per image (executed in the on-board BLUE computer with a NVIDIA RTX 3060 GPU). These computation times are expressed as the sum of three values, which consist of the time spent during preprocess, inference and postprocess steps. So, for example, YOLO-v7 has a similar number of layers to YOLO-v8 medium, but is between YOLO-v8 medium and YOLO-v8 large in terms of number of parameters. Another example is YOLO-v5, which has fewer layers than YOLO-v8 nano, but is between YOLO-v8 small and YOLO-v8 medium in terms of number of parameters.

Table 2. Some NN specifications.

NN	Speed (ms)	Number of layers	Number of parameters
YOLO-v8 nano	0.3+6.5+0.5	261	3263811
YOLO-v8 small	0.3+8.3+0.5	261	11790483
YOLO-v8 medium	0.3+18.2+0.6	331	27240227
YOLO-v8 large	0.3+28.7+0.5	401	45912659
YOLO-v7	0.9+23.7+0.7	325	37842476
YOLO-v5 medium	0.9+15.9+0.7	220	21652358

The results for BB detection and mask segmentation are shown in Tables 3 and 4, respectively. In terms of BB detection, YOLO-v8 medium and large have very close results, with the precision being higher for the YOLO-v8 large model. However, when moving to the mask segmentation task, YOLO-v8 is the model with the best results in 3 of the 4 metrics evaluated.

Also, all the trained models fall within the real-time specification, as their computation time should be between 33.3 and 66.6 ms for 30 and 15 Frames Per Second (FPS). So our final choice is YOLO-v8 large.

Table 3. Results in BB detection.

NN	Precision	Recall	mAP @0.5	mAP@0.5-0.95
YOLO-v8 nano	0.858	0.756	0.85	0.589
YOLO-v8 small	0.836	0.832	0.871	0.633
YOLO-v8 medium	0.824	0.832	**0.888**	**0.654**
YOLO-v8 large	**0.88**	0.811	0.881	0.649
YOLO-v7	0.81	0.823	0.87	0.62
YOLO-v5 medium	0.783	**0.835**	0.849	0.587

Table 4. Results in mask segmentation.

NN	Precision	Recall	mAP @0.5	mAP@0.5-0.95
YOLO-v8 nano	0.795	0.676	0.758	0.448
YOLO-v8 small	0.77	0.749	0.803	0.471
YOLO-v8 medium	0.782	0.732	0.807	0.477
YOLO-v8 large	0.815	**0.751**	**0.826**	**0.509**
YOLO-v7	0.803	0.679	0.769	0.474
YOLO-v5 medium	**0.831**	0.605	0.732	0.431

Some images of the test subset segmented by YOLO-v8 large can be seen in Fig. 3. As can be seen, cars are correctly segmented in both near and far distance in all images, representing the 360° of the LiDAR sensor Field Of View (FOV).

Fig. 3. Some partial view samples from test set segmented by YOLO-v8 large.

4.2 Real Experiments

Once the best segmentation method was found, it was tested in a completely new and unseen environment. Also some trackers like BoT-SORT [1] and ByteTrack [23] were added to keep the position of different segmented instances across a video. Figure 4 illustrates a subset of frames cropped for clarity from a sample video[2] using the BoT-SORT tracker.

This tracker was chosen over ByteTrack because it represents an evolution, including some improvements such as a camera compensation based feature tracker and a suitable Kalman filter. BoT-SORT was used with 0.7 as the threshold for first and second association, 0.75 as the threshold for initialising a new track if the detection does not match any previous track, 20 as the buffer size for removing tracks and 0.8 as the threshold for matching tracks.

[2] https://youtu.be/FNemm0QZXo4

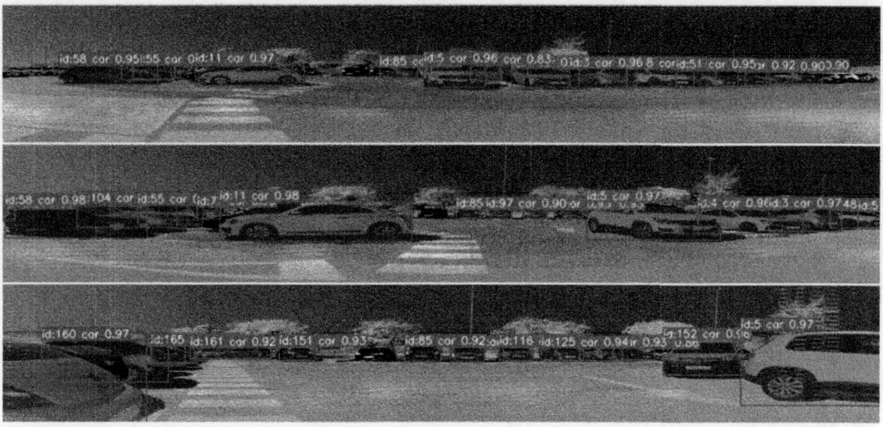

Fig. 4. Several partial view frames running YOLO-v8 large using BoT-SORT as tracker.

As shown in Fig. 4, the detection and tracking of cars is generally successful across frames, with the tracker ID remaining consistent. It should be noted that some cars present problems, such as the black vehicle located in the central left portion of the image. Additionally, some segmentations are not entirely accurate, as evidenced by the white car that appears in the left portion of the final frame. Nevertheless, the issue could be addressed by labelling a greater number of samples across a wider range of images, thereby demonstrating that it is feasible to segment cars on a pseudo-RGB image obtained from a LiDAR sensor.

5 Conclusion

This paper presents the segmentation of instances in SRIs using several single-step methods such as YOLO-v5, YOLO-v6 and YOLO-v8. Specifically, the aim was to detect cars in pseudo-RGB images obtained from a LiDAR sensor by combining the different channels available. The results have shown that it is possible to perform instance segmentation in a LiDAR image using YOLO-v8 large, having a precision of 81.5%. This model provided the best accuracy in mask segmentation, allowing real-time inference on BLUE's on-board computer and the mobile robot to segment cars in outdoor environments. The augmentation of the dataset with a greater number of images and a more diverse range of scenarios will enhance the overall performance of this method, which has already proven to be effective and opens the way for the use of LiDAR object detection and segmentation.

Future work will consist of using the designed system to segment different types of objects, as well as designing a new method for calibrating LiDAR and the camera using the segmented masks obtained with this method.

Acknowledgments. Research work was funded by grant PID2021-122685OB-I00 funded by MICIU/AEI/10.13039/501100011033 and ERDF/EU and grant PRE2019-088069 funded by MICIU/AEI/10.13039/501100011033 and ESF Investing in your future. The computer facilities were provided through the IDIFEFER/2020/003 project.

Disclosure of Interests. The authors have no competing interests to declare that are relevant to the content of this article.

References

1. Aharon, N., Orfaig, R., Bobrovsky, B.Z.: Bot-sort: Robust associations multi-pedestrian tracking. arXiv preprint (2022). https://doi.org/10.48550/arXiv.2206.14651
2. Castaño Amorós, J., et al.: Desarrollos en blue para manipulación móvil en entornos exteriores no estructurado. In: XLIII Jornadas de Automática (JA), pp. 851–857 (2022). https://doi.org/10.17979/spudc.9788497498418.0851
3. Cireşan, D.C., Meier, U., Gambardella, L.M., Schmidhuber, J.: Deep, big, simple neural nets for handwritten digit recognition. Neural Comput. **22**(12), 3207–3220 (2010). https://doi.org/10.1162/NECO_a_00052
4. Fan, Y.C., Yelamandala, C.M., Chen, T.W., Huang, C.J.: Real-time object detection for lidar based on ls-r-yolov4 neural network. J. Sens. **2021**(1), 5576262 (2021). https://doi.org/10.1155/2021/5576262
5. Gu, W., Bai, S., Kong, L.: A review on 2d instance segmentation based on deep neural networks. Image Vis. Comput. **120**, 104401 (2022). https://doi.org/10.1016/j.imavis.2022.104401
6. Hinton, G.E., Osindero, S., Teh, Y.W.: A fast learning algorithm for deep belief nets. Neural Comput. **18**(7), 1527–1554 (2006). https://doi.org/10.1162/neco.2006.18.7.1527
7. Jocher, G., et al.: ultralytics/yolov5: v6.2 - yolov5 classification models, apple m1, reproducibility, clearml and deci.ai integrations (2022). https://doi.org/10.5281/zenodo.7002879
8. Liu, W., et al.: SSD: Single shot multibox detector. In: Computer Vision–ECCV 2016: 14th European Conference, Amsterdam, The Netherlands, October 11–14, 2016, Proceedings, Part I 14, pp. 21–37. Springer (2016). https://doi.org/10.1007/978-3-319-46448-0_2
9. McCulloch, W.S., Pitts, W.: A logical calculus of the ideas immanent in nervous activity. Bull. Math. Biophys. **5**, 115–133 (1943). https://doi.org/10.1007/BF02478259
10. Olivas, A., Munoz-Banón, M.A., Velasco, E., Torres, F.: Robust single object tracking and following by fusion strategy. In: 2023 International Conference on Informatics in Control, Automation and Robotics (ICINCO), vol. 1, pp. 624–631 (2023). https://doi.org/10.5220/0012178900003543
11. Páez-Ubieta, I.d.L., Castaño-Amorós, J., Puente, S.T., Gil, P.: Vision and tactile robotic system to grasp litter in outdoor environments. J. Intell. Robot. Syst. **109**(2), 36 (2023). https://doi.org/10.1007/s10846-023-01930-2
12. Del Pino, I., Cova, S., Contreras, M.Á., Candelas, F.A., Torres, F.: Presenting blue: a robot for localization in unstructured environments. In: 2018 IEEE International Conference on Autonomous Robot Systems and Competitions (ICARSC), pp. 130–135 (2018). https://doi.org/10.1109/ICARSC.2018.8374172

13. Del Pino, I., Muñoz-Bañon, M.Á., Cova-Rocamora, S., Contreras, M.Á., Candelas, F.A., Torres, F.: Deeper in BLUE. J. Intell. Robot. Syst. **98**(1), 207–225 (2019). https://doi.org/10.1007/s10846-019-00983-6
14. Sultana, F., Sufian, A., Dutta, P.: A review of object detection models based on convolutional neural network. Intell. comput. image process. based appl. pp. 1–16 (2020). https://doi.org/10.1007/978-981-15-4288-6_1
15. Torralba, A., Russell, B.C., Yuen, J.: LabelMe: online image annotation and applications. Proc. IEEE **98**(8), 1467–1484 (2010). https://doi.org/10.1109/JPROC.2010.2050290
16. Varghese, R., M., S.: Yolov8: A novel object detection algorithm with enhanced performance and robustness. In: 2024 International Conference on Advances in Data Engineering and Intelligent Computing Systems (ADICS), pp. 1–6 (2024). https://doi.org/10.1109/ADICS58448.2024.10533619
17. Velasco-Sánchez, E., de Loyola Páez-Ubieta, I., Candelas, F.A., Puente, S.T.: Lidar data augmentation by interpolation on spherical range image. In: 2023 IEEE 28th International Conference on Emerging Technologies and Factory Automation (ETFA), pp. 1–4. IEEE (2023). https://doi.org/10.1109/ETFA54631.2023.10275512
18. Velasco-Sánchez, E.P., Muñoz-Bañón, M.Á., Candelas, F.A., Puente, S.T., Torres, F.: Lilo: lightweight and low-bias lidar odometry method based on spherical range image filtering. arXiv preprint (2023). https://doi.org/10.48550/arXiv.2311.07291
19. Wang, C.Y., Bochkovskiy, A., Liao, H.Y.M.: Yolov7: trainable bag-of-freebies sets new state-of-the-art for real-time object detectors. In: 2023 IEEE/CVF Conference on Computer Vision and Pattern Recognition (CVPR), pp. 7464–7475 (2023). https://doi.org/10.1109/CVPR52729.2023.00721
20. Yu, X., Salimpour, S., Queralta, J.P., Westerlund, T.: General-purpose deep learning detection and segmentation models for images from a lidar-based camera sensor. Sensors **23**(6), 2936 (2023). https://doi.org/10.3390/s23062936
21. Zaidi, S.S.A., Ansari, M.S., Aslam, A., Kanwal, N., Asghar, M., Lee, B.: A survey of modern deep learning based object detection models. Digit. Sig. Process. **126**, 103514 (2022). https://doi.org/10.1016/j.dsp.2022.103514
22. Zhang, H., Cisse, M., Dauphin, Y.N., Lopez-Paz, D.: mixup: beyond empirical risk minimization. In: Sixth International Conference on Learning Representations (ICLR) (2018). https://doi.org/10.48550/arXiv.1710.09412
23. Zhang, Y., et al.: Bytetrack: multi-object tracking by associating every detection box. In: Proceedings of the European Conference on Computer Vision (ECCV), pp. 1–21. Springer Nature Switzerland (2022). https://doi.org/10.1007/978-3-031-20047-2_1

Toward Truly Intelligent Autonomous Systems: A Taxonomy of LLM Integration for Everyday Automation

Magnus Jung[1(✉)], Thorsten Hempel[1], Basheer Al-Tawil[1], Qiaoyue Yang[2], Sven Wachsmuth[2], and Ayoub Al-Hamadi[1]

[1] Otto-von-Guericke University, Universitätspl. 2, 39106 Magdeburg, Germany
magnus.jung@ovgu.de
[2] University Bielefeld, Universitätsstr. 25, 33615 Bielefeld, Germany
https://www.ovgu.de/, https://www.uni-bielefeld.de/

Abstract. With the rapid development of large language models (LLMs), their integration into autonomous systems has become essential. This integration significantly increases the flexibility and adaptability of the system. In this paper, we propose a categorization of LLM integration into three levels: open-loop, closed-loop, and autonomous systems fully driven by robotic LLMs. They are analyzed through existing literature, real experiments with the humanoid robot TIAGo, and simulations with models such as ChatGPT-4 and Vicuna 13b-v1.5-16k. We demonstrate the potential of LLMs to enhance the flexibility and adaptability of autonomous systems, particularly in dynamic environments where conventional finite state machines may prove inadequate. Closed-loop systems effectively handle unexpected situations with human-like problem solving. Integrating LLMs with autonomous systems enables new real-world applications by enhancing their ability to adapt, reason, and respond intelligently in dynamic environments.

Keywords: Large Language Models · Autonomous Systems · State Machines

1 Introduction

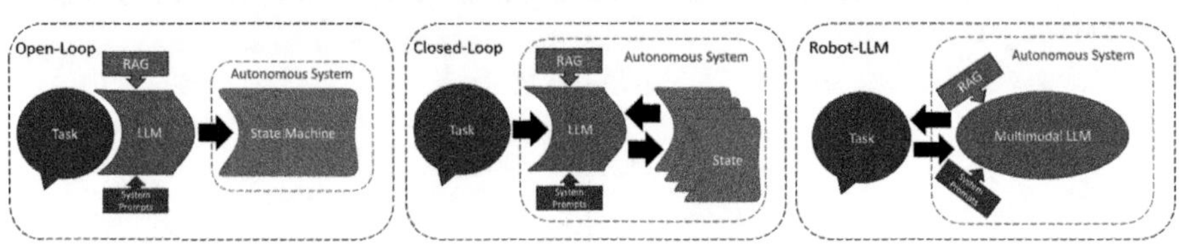

Fig. 1. Schematic representation of the three levels of LLM integration for autonomous systems (open-loop, closed-loop and robotic LLM systems).

Intelligent systems (e.g., intelligent robots or assistive systems) are central to many futuristic applications, yet society's expectations often exceed the current state of the

J. Röning and J. Filipe (Eds.): ROBOVIS 2025, CCIS 2629, pp. 74–91, 2026.
https://doi.org/10.1007/978-3-032-00986-9_6

art [32]. While research continues to advance individual capabilities and AI-powered modules for autonomous systems such as robots, assistive systems, software systems, smart home systems, autonomous vehicles, etc., these systems still fall short of being intuitive or truly intelligent [43]. For example, humanoid robots equipped with modules such as emotion recognition, gaze direction estimation, and engagement detection may struggle to exhibit appropriate social behavior. For instance, while they may be able to recognize a smiling user, they often rely on predefined scripts to respond and lack the ability to adapt their interactions based on context [40]. Another example is state driven workflows for adaptive control systems. SQL queries and Bash commands often rely on rigid, predefined rules, making it difficult to detect errors and resolve problems dynamically [66]. This lack of adaptability leads to lower success rates and efficiency compared to systems that could seamlessly connect the various modules dynamically through contextual knowledge.

Open problems in autonomous systems are often addressed by breaking them down into sub-goals; this approach increases the challenge of bringing the solutions together. Despite the increasing use of AI to tackle specific tasks, the overall integration and adaptability of these modules remains limited, preventing intelligent systems from meeting human-level expectations [31]. The challenge for intelligent action is not in the individual modules, but in how they interact with the environment and align with the system's goals. It is the thoughtful and adaptive interaction between these modules that builds competence and ultimately enables natural and intelligent behavior in autonomous systems.

The rapid development of large language models (LLMs) in recent years has made natural language processing possible. By incorporating LLMs and their knowledge processing capabilities, natural interaction becomes possible, and task planning can be automated at a low- or no-code level.

This paper explores three levels of LLM integration - open-loop, closed-loop, and robotic LLM systems - into autonomous systems, using the TIAGo robot from Pal Robotics as a demonstrator (see Fig. 2) to evaluate the advantages and disadvantages of each approach. In the open-loop configuration, a state machine with predefined states and transitions is generated and then executed on the autonomous system. In the closed-loop configuration, an LLM dynamically selects the next state and its parameters in real time, adapting based on the previous states of the system and the current task requirements. At the third level of integration, predefined states are completely removed and the MLLM (a multimodal LLM) directly controls the autonomous system by processing multiple input modalities and generating corresponding actions without relying on a predefined state structure. In the following sections, these levels are explained, analyzed, simulated, and implemented (see Fig. 1). There are significant differences between these systems in terms of flexibility, security, and hardware requirements, as shown in Fig. 3 and detailed in Table 1. It is shown that the closed-loop system shows a significant increase in performance compared to previous systems in dynamic environments with disturbances and that it is (currently) superior to other LLM integration depths in terms of feasibility, safety and precision.

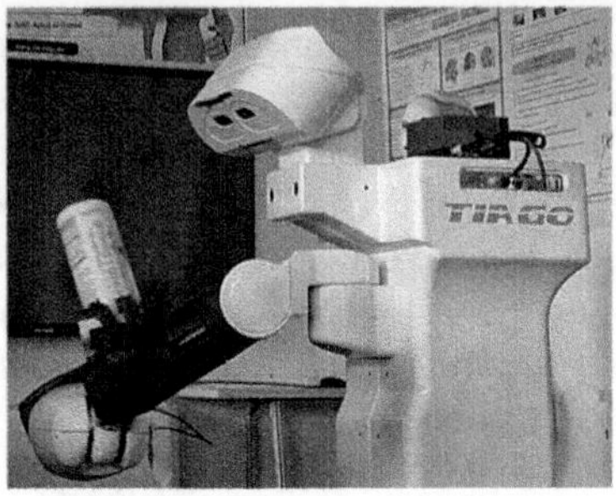

Fig. 2. Humanoid robot TIAGo from Pal Robotics performing a pick-and-place task autonomously using closed-loop LLM integration.

2 Related Works

The creation of a variety of discrete actions for tackling independent problems leads to a variety of atomic actions that can be stored in a library as functions with input variables and parameters [44]. These actions can be combined to perform previously unknown tasks [44] that can be achieved through the use of finite state machines. Most current systems operate in an open-loop configuration, meaning that once the task and motion plan have been generated, they cannot troubleshoot or adapt to unexpected changes in the environment [12,22].

2.1 State Machines

Since the 2000s, there has been minimal change in how individual capabilities are combined to enable machines to autonomously solve tasks and pursue goals [10,42]. Rule-based systems, typically implemented as finite state machines, remain the dominant approach [19]. In these systems, the precise sequence and order of actions are critical to success [22].

State machines model systems with finite states and transitions, where actions occur within states and transitions move between them [20]. This paper focuses on actions performed within states and logically arranged by transition conditions. State machines are often used to model and control the behavior of systems in robotics, software engineering, and automation [19,34]. The states and their transition conditions are (manually) predefined, leading to deterministic behavior in static environments (without random transition selection) [49]. They have evolved through fuzzy logic (1960s) [67], behavior-based robotics (1980s) [9], and probabilistic systems (1990s) [26]. In the 2000s, these systems were further enhanced with machine learning and artificial intelligence [8], although these approaches offer limited flexibility and only predefined possible outcomes.

Today, autonomous systems include a wide range of scientifically validated skills (modules) [43], spanning actuation (e.g., movement [53], speech output [5]) and input processing (e.g. image processing for pose estimation [15], gaze recognition [1,21], social information [2], SLAM [3], speech recognition [4], etc.).

However, the interaction between actuation and sensor processing is very inflexible due to a lack of common sense [12]. Specifically, the lack of independent assessment of situations using logical reasoning, experiential knowledge, practical judgment and social understanding. This gap can now be filled by LLMs.

2.2 Large Language Models

Large Language Models (LLMs) have attracted considerable attention in recent years. They are transformer-based models that acquire strong language processing and generation capabilities by learning statistical relationships from large amounts of text during a self-supervised and semi-supervised training process [7]. Based on these large amounts of text during training, they can reflect the common sense of society in inference [12]. Further, they are able to process additional knowledge from supplementary information during inference [50].

In conjunction with processed sensor inputs such as object recognition [46], face recognition [29], emotion recognition [13], body pose estimation [15], gaze recognition [1,21], speech processing [4], VLMs (vision-language models) [72], etc. , these systems can flexibly respond to environmental changes and unexpected situations [12]. In this context, the output of the LLM is not predefined, non-deterministic, but determined by the specific interplay of task and environmental influences.

Training custom LLMs is not feasible for most institutions due to hardware requirements [37,50]. However, pre-trained LLMs exhibit human-like common sense influenced by their training data, and vary in speed, size, comprehension, and memory [45]. In addition, there are various methods for adapting existing LLMs to specific requirements, including hidden or system prompts [30] and Retrieval-Augmented Generation (RAG) [18].

System Prompts. Using system prompts, some set before interaction with the LLM begins and some appended to each prompt (sometimes before and sometimes after the prompt), the output of the LLM can be directed [30]. This includes positioning the LLM in a specific role with defined behavioral instructions [61]. The format of the response can also be specified, allowing further processing of the free text response [6]. By imposing strict rules within the system prompts, the LLM is prepared for use within a more complex system, and disruptive properties of the LLM are suppressed.

Retrieval Augmented Generation. RAG in the context of LLMs is a technique that aims to improve the generative performance of these models by integrating retrieved information from external knowledge sources [73]. LLMs have impressive text generation capabilities; however, they are limited to the knowledge available during their training [68]. This knowledge is static and may become outdated or incomplete. In addition, it is biased due to the distribution of the training data [17], which limits its effectiveness in applications for autonomous systems. Through RAG, user prompts are enhanced by dynamically adding relevant retrieved data in context [18]. This includes conveying the characteristics and capabilities of the system, as well as providing example applications of the system, or recording past applications to gain knowledge and insight for future tasks.

This paper examines the integrability of LLMs in autonomous systems and classifies their depth of integration using a three-level taxonomy and compares it with the current state. It provides an outlook on the possibilities of future applications, as well as their validation and risks. Simulations of simple situations are used to demonstrate the strengths of these approaches.

3 Taxonomy of LLM Integration

The integration of the LLM into autonomous systems takes place on several levels. Here the LLM assesses problems and supports task planning while maintaining compatibility with existing solutions.

A brief overview of the strengths and weaknesses of the three integration levels is given in the Table 1. Depending on the architecture of the system, combinatorial applications of the integration levels are also possible. As LLMs are easily distracted by unnecessary information [55], the decision about necessary sensor inputs (information acquisition) is left to the LLMs. This ensures that only necessary information is processed and that the LLM remains focused. All three levels use system prompts and RAG. System prompts are used to define the output format and interpret the task from the perspective of an autonomous system. RAG provides the LLM with system information, state definitions, background information, hints, example tasks, and their results from previous applications. This enables the generation of new solutions based on specific experience and prior knowledge.

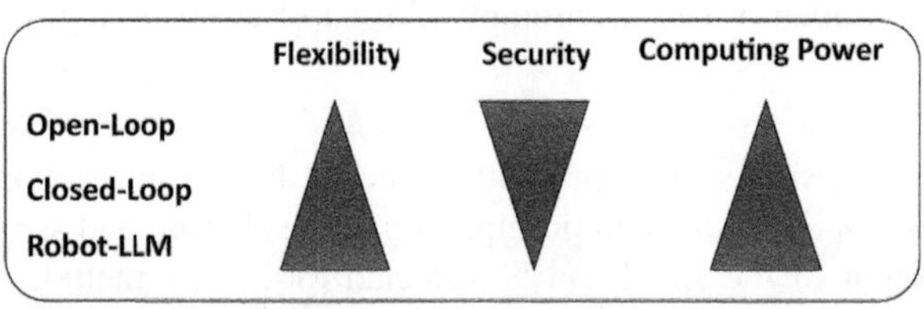

Fig. 3. Overview of the main comparison criteria for the three levels of integration of LLM in autonomous systems.

3.1 Level 1: Open-Loop Systems

The development of autonomous systems often involves the manual creation of state machines to define tasks and ensure safety [47]. However, this can cause the state machine to stop in dynamic environments, making full task execution unreliable [12]. The manual creation process is time-consuming and complex, as even simple tasks can result in large, unwieldy machines [22]. While prebuilt substate machines improve clarity, they limit flexibility and cannot respond to unexpected events due to their predetermined, open-loop structure.

A promising alternative to manually created state machines is the use of LLMs that can generate a concrete state machine from a free-form task description (see Fig. 4). Guided by system prompts and RAG, these models produce high-quality state machines

Table 1. Comparison of the three LLM integration levels, using 'xx' (very applicable), 'x' (applicable), and '(x)' (partially applicable).

Criterion	Open-Loop	Closed-Loop	Robot-LLM
Flexibility		x	xx
Free Task Formulation	xx	xx	xx
Complex Task Definition		x	x
Common Sense	(x)	x	xx
Learnable (RAG)	x	x	x
Dialog Capability		x	x
Skills	x	x	xx
Safety	xx	x	
Verifiability	xx	x	
Traceability	x	x	
Repeatability	xx	x	
Deterministic	x		
Reliability of Skills	xx	xx	
Task Focus Maintenance	xx	x	
Minimization of LLM Hallucination Risk	xx	x	xx
Minimization of LLM Hacking Risk		x	xx
Computing Power	xx	x	
Real-Time Capability	xx	x	
Offline Capability	xx	x	(x)

comparable to manually generated ones [28]. The advantage is that the user doesn't need any specific prior knowledge, and the generated state machine is deterministic, verifiable, and adjustable via graphical interfaces without programming skills [24].

Regarding the three criteria security, flexibility, and computational power, it is evident that this LLM-based state machine development (open-loop) offers high security, since the end user does not have direct access to the LLM, thus preventing problems like prompt injection [41]. Task verifiability is ensured by graphically examining the generated state machine, with individual states designed to remain safe regardless of combinations. In addition, state machine generation can be offloaded as it does not require real-time execution on the device, allowing the use of powerful LLMs. The flexibility of the approach lies in the natural task descriptions and their automatic interpretation by the LLM. However, the flexibility of the task execution is limited, as no adaptation to unexpected events is possible.

Several approaches have been proposed to use LLMs in state machine generation. One innovative method uses LLMs as task planners, decomposing natural language descriptions into sub-goals, which are then translated into robot actions [22,23]. Another approach uses the code-writing capabilities of LLMs to generate robot programs, with "code-as-policies" defining robot-centric programs in Python that invoke

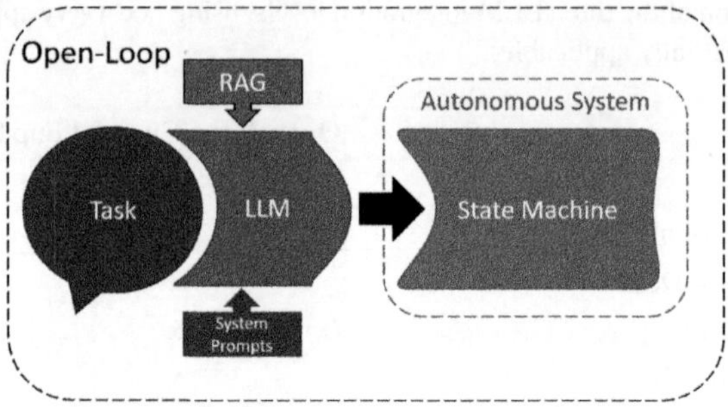

Fig. 4. Schematic of the first level of LLM integration for autonomous systems: the open-loop. In this configuration, a state machine is first generated and then executed on the autonomous system.

parameterized primitives [22,38]. However, these methods have mainly addressed smaller subtasks, leaving full state machine generation for autonomous system control unrealized. The Alchemist system allows end-users to create and execute robotic applications using natural language input, bypassing the need for specialized programming knowledge [11,51]. Despite its utility, Alchemist faces challenges in debugging the generated code, highlighting the difficulties of open-loop programming [28,59]. The PROGPROMPT project uses LLMs to build executable programs based on specifications of available actions and objects [58]. While traditional high-level planning in robotics involves searching a predefined space [16,25], PROGPROMPT directly generates a complete program with predefined action primitives [58]. However, its linear execution avoids loops and does not adapt to errors, limiting flexibility for new tasks. Another open-loop concept is CODEBOTLER [22], an open-source tool designed to simplify service robot programming using LLMs and a user-friendly web interface. It generates LMPs that can be executed via ROS Actionlib on different robot platforms. However, CODEBOTLER lacks support for low-level behaviors, such as the instruction "follow Alice to her office" [22], and linear execution prevents it from responding to dynamic changes or unforeseen events [22]. Another model, the Foundation Model-based Open Vocabulary Task Planning and Executive System for General Service Robots [47], focuses on task execution in the RoboCup@Home competition. It uses ROS with SMACH, but is limited to linear processes with sub-state machines, which hinders flexibility and responsiveness to dynamic environmental changes or task uncertainties [47].

An important area where LLMs are used as planning aids in the open-loop method is navigation. For example, a cobot navigation approach in human-centered smart manufacturing can interpret natural language commands and generate Python code for navigation actions [63]. The Pathfinder algorithm performs path planning, enabling the Autonomous Transport System (ATS) to interpret complex voice commands for task completion [63]. For effective navigation, the LLM is given scene semantics, allowing it to generate simple instructions such as "Go to object XY". From this point on, the path planner takes over the execution of the instruction [63].

The SMART-LLM study [27] shows that LLMs can control multi-agent systems by breaking down high-level tasks into subtasks for robot coordination, demonstrating their role in both planning and multi-robot management.

These open-loop systems can be enhanced by improving the knowledge base of LLMs. Appropriate collaboration between humans and autonomous machines can improve the system through hints and enhancements provided by humans [39]. The improved functions/processes are stored for reuse in subsequent processes.

The lack of error detection in open-loop systems is a major limitation, especially in complex environments. Initial attempts use uncertainties from multimodal LLMs (MLLMs), but these only restart the open loop without dynamically responding to changes [70]. Hybrid systems with step-by-step instructions offer more granular planning, but still face the same problem of restarting the process instead of adapting to errors or changes [57]. In addition, generating long executable code or large state machines with LLMs is challenging [62]. To address these issues, a shift to a closed-loop system is needed, where the LLM incrementally solves problems at runtime.

3.2 Level 2: Closed-Loop Systems

A closed-loop approach requires the ad hoc execution of the LLM (on the autonomous device) to determine the next action module (state) during task execution. This makes the real-time capability of the LLM, and therefore its size, relevant. This level of integration also uses existing and pre-defined states and transitions, leveraging the accumulated experience to solve specific tasks. The LLM acts as the master of the system, deciding after each state based on the information from the transition and the parameters collected during the execution of the previous actions (see Fig. 5). To increase speed, pre-defined routines or sub-state machines can also be considered as states.

The system has access to a wide range of reliable functions, enabling it to respond directly to dynamic environments and unexpected situations. The LLM determines the next required state, including not only action states but also states for gathering additional information. Using RAG, the LLM learns from examples and its own experience by storing state sequences.

The closed-loop system balances safety, flexibility, and computational power. It is safe as actions occur only through predefined states, but the combination of these states increases the demands on their integrity. To avoid errors, system prompts and RAG must be optimized to prevent the LLM's output from exceeding the system's framework. In terms of flexibility, the system is limited only by the number of available states; more states allow for greater creativity and tailored solutions, making actions more human-like. The system can be trained and optimized by RAG using past trajectories to improve its task performance. In terms of computational power, running the LLM on the autonomous device requires careful selection to avoid performance degradation during decision pauses.

Especially in path planning, simple closed-loop systems are already in use [14,33, 54,56]. One example is the 3P-LLM [33], which allows probabilistic path planning using LLMs. It demonstrates that models such as GPT-3.5-turbo can provide real-time feedback for path planning and outperform their more powerful counterparts. The system receives user instructions in natural language describing the destination within the environment and dynamically updates the path when an obstacle is detected [33].

In addition, studies on object-based navigation have shown that LLMs can not only support navigation, but also improve object recognition. A study on zero-shot object navigation [14] emphasizes that humans do not adhere to predefined class labels, but

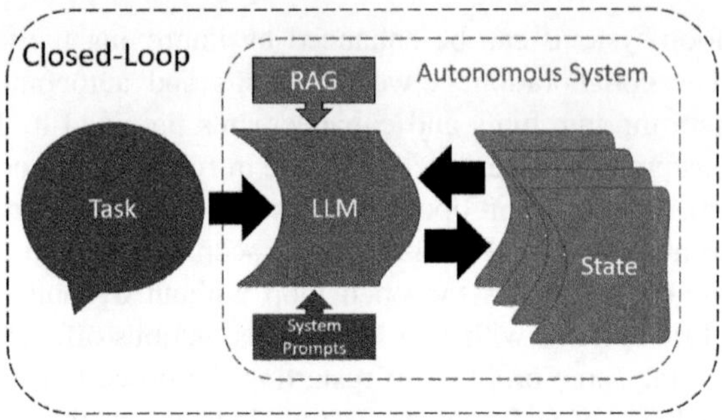

Fig. 5. Schematic representation of the second level of LLM integration for autonomous systems: the closed-loop. In this configuration an LLM runs continuously on the system and selects the next state and its parameters in real time on the autonomous system based on previous states and transitions and the task at hand.

describe objects in free, natural language. The system synthesizes prompts for the LLM using extracted object labels. Pre-trained models such as CLIP [52] and GLIP [36] are used to perform zero-shot target anchoring of open vocabulary in the wild [14]. The LLM controls the navigation process by generating an output from the object list that tells the agent in which direction to move. When the target object is located, the decision process is complete and the agent navigates directly to it [14]. This iterative approach highlights the flexibility of LLMs to respond to dynamic environments. The LFENav system [56] also uses LLMs for semantic navigation. The emergence of LLMs provides new avenues for semantic understanding, allowing them to analyze user instructions, select sub-goals, and generate action instructions.

As an alternative to state machines, the concept of LLM-BT [71], which combines LLMs with behavior trees, represents a promising solution. This method allows the addition of new actions based on changes in the environment and assigns appropriate priorities for the execution of these actions, thereby increasing the adaptability of the system [71].

Finally, cooperative agents, as seen in CAMON [64], have shown that LLMs have remarkable capabilities for planning and communication in a closed-loop context. These systems enable multiple agents to communicate efficiently, share tasks and collaborate through a dynamic leadership organisation, further enhancing navigation efficiency in complex environments [64].

Collectively, these approaches illustrate how LLMs in closed-loop systems not only extend existing capabilities, but also create new opportunities for autonomous navigation and interaction with dynamic environments. They not only promote flexibility and creativity in problem solving, but also enhance contextual understanding and common sense, which are critical to the success of autonomous systems. These advances in LLM technology and their application to autonomous systems can be seen as a fundamental step towards smarter and more adaptive robots capable of successfully tackling complex tasks in dynamic environments.

3.3 Level 3: Robot-LLM

In a fully integrated LLM within the autonomous system, no states are used. There is minimal pre-processing of sensor data (e.g., image data by VLMs) and hardware-level outputs are used for system control. It is possible to have a specific MLLM optimized for the specific input and output channels [65], thus forming a robot LLM (see Fig. 6). This allows the system to achieve maximum flexibility, but also requires it to manage its capabilities autonomously. There is no prior knowledge of its capabilities. As a result, the reliability of the execution of specific tasks is reduced [35]. In addition to the LLM, powerful VLMs are needed to process the input and convert it into linguistically understandable information. It is critical that the information conveyed is relevant at the time. This can be achieved by MLLMs.

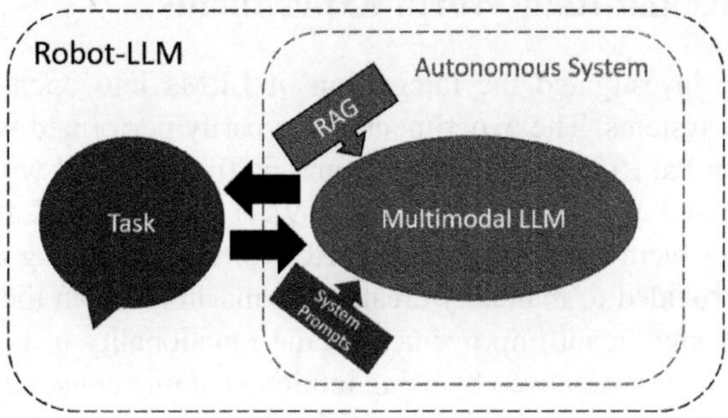

Fig. 6. Schematic representation of the third level of LLM integration for autonomous systems: the robot LLM. In this configuration, the use of predefined states is eliminated and the MLLM takes direct control of the autonomous system, receiving all inputs and controlling all outputs.

Considering the three criteria of security, flexibility and computational power, robot-LLM represents a very promising scenario for flexibility, provided that the LLM can develop a complete understanding of the system and gain full control over all components. This is challenging and makes existing models and methods obsolete. It raises the capabilities of the system to a level where natural and intuitive behavior of the autonomous system becomes possible. However, there is a concern that accuracy may decrease, making this variant attractive for Human-Robot Interaction (HRI), but still requiring separate modules for tasks that require precision. In terms of computing power, Level 3 relies heavily on high computational power to process complex multimodal inputs in real time and generate solutions. In terms of security, this system is also much more vulnerable to LLM hacking. The different modalities can influence the LLM and cause undesired behavior. Furthermore, the high level of flexibility increases the risk of unintended and erroneous actions, as there is no safety net provided by inherently secure and verifiable states. This system has not yet been implemented.

3.4 Risks of LLM Integration

The use of LLMs presents both significant opportunities and certain risks. On the one hand, the advantage of incorporating common sense also brings a disadvantage, as it can reduce the precision and accuracy of executions. This can be mitigated by using states with specific actions, such as dedicated AI models for specific tasks. On the other hand, LLMs are prone to hallucination, resulting in responses that do not match the desired output format for further processing. This problem is exacerbated by the fact that LLMs, originally designed as open dialog systems, are now being repurposed to control autonomous systems.

There is also the risk of LLM hacking. In open-loop systems, only authorized individuals have access to the inputs provided to the LLM. In closed-loop systems, however, the LLM can be manipulated during speech processing and parameter passing. This problem is even more pronounced in robotic LLMs, where any external input can be passed directly to the multimodal LLM, potentially leading to system manipulation.

4 Simulations and Real-World Experiments

In this study, we investigated the integration of LLMs into open-loop and closed-loop autonomous systems. The experiments were partly performed with the humanoid robot TIAGo from Pal Robotics (see Fig. 2) and partly simulated with different LLMs (ChatGPT-4 [48] and Vicuna 13b-v1.5-16k [69], a fine-tuned LLaMA model [60]). The state machines were implemented using ROS SMACH, and a graphical user interface (GUI) was provided to manually create state machines from the predefined states and transitions. A significant improvement in the functionality of both open-loop and closed-loop systems was achieved by using intuitive naming conventions for individual states. When the function was clearly identifiable from the state name, even the smaller LLM could work more effectively with these states.

The states, their descriptions, and example state machines were made available to the LLMs through the RAG. The LLMs either acted as generators of state machines (open-loop) or as masters determining the next state in the sequence (closed-loop). At level 1, the system was characterized as a generator of autonomous systems, with a predefined output format that included the states and their transitions. At level 2, the system was optimized to select the next state based on the transitions and parameters of the previous state, without parallelization (only one subsequent state). The output format at level 1 consisted of two lists - states with parameters and transitions - while at level 2 only the next state with parameters was generated (see Fig. 2). If the LLM produced an invalid format, the task was repeated with more explicit instructions about the desired format.

A variety of example tasks from the field of autonomous mobile assistance systems were used to evaluate the possibilities and challenges of open and closed-loop systems. These experiments included fine-grained states as well as experiments combining single states into larger sub-state machines. The tasks were always presented to the LLM in free-form language.

4.1 Open-Loop

Creating state machines manually, even with the help of a GUI, became increasingly time-consuming as their complexity increased. In contrast, LLMs significantly streamlined the process in an open-loop system. For simpler tasks, where larger sub-state

Table 2. Comparison of output formats for open-loop and closed-loop systems. The output generated by the LLM in the open-loop system is significantly longer and more complex. This increased length and complexity correlates with a higher failure rate.

Open-Loop System

```
[
    {
        "nodeA": {
            "id": <...>,
            "state": "{
                'state': '<...>',
                'parameters': {
                    '<...>': '<...>',
                    ...
                }
            }"
        },
        "nodeB": {
            "id": <...>,
            "state": "{
                'state': '<...>',
                'parameters': {
                '<...>':'<...>',
                ...
                }
            }"
        },
        "transition": "<...>"
    },
    ...
]
```

Closed-Loop System

```
state: <...>
parameters: {
                 '<...>':'<...>',
                 ...
                 }
```

machines could be used as modular building blocks, all of the LLMs tested produced results identical to those created manually. However, for more complex tasks requiring specialized knowledge, such as working with AprilTags, smaller models such as Vicuna 13b-v1.5-16k struggled due to their limited understanding and began to hallucinate. While RAG improved the performance of these smaller models, the reliability of their results remained inconsistent. ChatGPT-4, on the other hand, consistently completed tasks effectively. However, as task complexity increased, error rates increased for both small and large LLMs. The main sources of error were incorrect output formats and hallucinations. The error rate also depended on the task and task formulation, but could be described qualitatively as an exponential increase.

The complexity of state machines is further limited by the token limits of LLMs. This also affects the ability to process additional information via RAG, where iterative approaches helped but posed challenges in maintaining coherence over multiple iterations. Real-world applications typically require more complex state machines with a large number of states and transitions. Without decomposing tasks into smaller sub-state machines, practical applicability remains uncertain.

4.2 Closed-Loop

Closed-loop systems offer a significant advantage in their ability to respond flexibly to disturbances because the LLM can dynamically respond to unexpected events. This can exceed the performance of predefined open-loop state machines.In addition, the closed-loop system only needs to generate very short outputs consisting of the next state and its parameters, unlike open-loop methods where complete state machines are generated in advance. This simplified output facilitates automatic validation of the LLM's response and reduces the risk of hallucination, allowing immediate correction. In addition, the token limit has much less impact on the complexity of the resulting state machine.

As with the open-loop system, performance varied according to the technical knowledge of the LLM. ChatGPT-4 consistently provided better state suggestions due to its broader understanding of technical concepts. In environments with minimal perturbations - where only perturbations accounted for in manually created state machines occurred - both large and small LLMs were able to mimic complex state machines and produce sequences identical to those created manually. However, smaller models such as Vicuna 13b-v1.5-16k were more likely to encounter problems with states that required specific technical knowledge (these states were often skipped, resulting in certain tasks becoming unexecutable). Improving the RAG integration reduced the error rate, suggesting that optimizing the RAG process could address these issues in the future. ChatGPT-4, on the other hand, did not encounter these problems because it already had the necessary specific technical knowledge without relying on RAG.

In addition, especially with the smaller LLM Vicuna 13b-v1.5-16k, it became apparent that the focus on the task and previously performed actions would drift away after a certain period of time. While repeated task delivery and the history of previously traversed states led to improvements, the problem could not be completely resolved.

When tested in more dynamic scenarios, the closed-loop system showed creative but reasonable responses to unforeseen events. For example, if an object was not found in the expected location, the system searched other areas of the room. If the object was still not found, it interacted with people to inquire about the object. If a particular person could not be found to hand over the object, the system tried to locate the person by calling out. If this failed, the system either gave the object to another person, specifying who it was for, or kept the object and waited for it to be picked up. These experiments highlight the problem-solving approach of a closed-loop system, where state machines become more complex as perturbations and task complexity increase. However, since the LLM only needs to determine the next step, the error rate - especially with ChatGPT-4 - remained close to zero after optimizing the RAG and well-chosen system prompts and demonstrating human-like problem solving strategies.

The behavior of the system varied depending on the contextual information included in the free-form task description. For example, when an object was described as "critical," the LLM refused to release it to unauthorized persons. This demonstrates that level-2 closed-loop systems can mirror human decision-making behavior and respond flexibly to perturbations.

In addition, several simulations were run to analyze the extent to which the prior knowledge provided by the RAG led to better results. In addition to the available states and their definitions, the LLM was provided with state sequences and associated transitions from previous tasks. This was illustrated by the following simulation: A level 2 system was initially tasked with navigating to a specific room using only basic motion commands ("move forward" (to the next door/into the room), "turn 90° left", "turn 90°

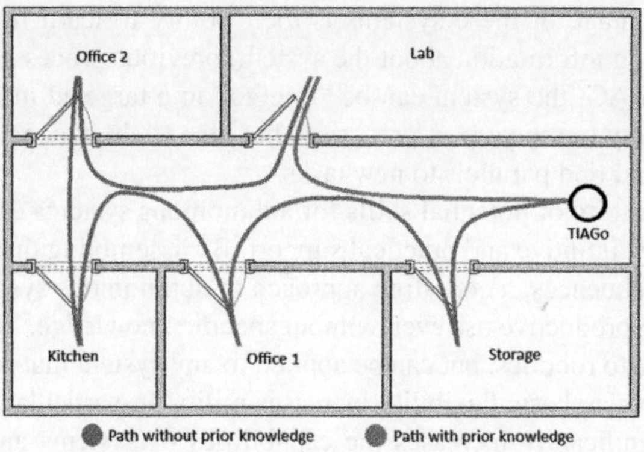

Fig. 7. Illustration of the route planning of a simulated closed-loop system. The goal is to navigate to the laboratory. Without prior knowledge (blue path) the system needs 13 steps. With the knowledge gained from the first run without prior knowledge (via RAG), it was able to find the shortest path (green) and took only two steps. (Color figure online)

right", and "where am I?"). The floor plan is shown in Fig. 7. As prior knowledge, the system was given information about the number of doors on the left and right. Without any other prior knowledge, the system tried to search the rooms one by one until it found the corresponding room. In contrast, the system that had this sequence as prior knowledge went directly to the desired room and also found the shortest routes to the previously discovered rooms. This demonstrates the ability of LLMs to optimize task performance through experience, which can be transferred via RAG.

It can be observed that LLMs in closed-loop systems are significantly more robust in proposing meaningful next states, with fewer hallucinations and output format errors. These systems are capable of solving more complex tasks and are more flexible in responding to and communicating with their environment.

5 Conclusion

This paper presents a taxonomy for autonomous systems with integrated LLMs. First tests already show the capabilities as well as the advantages and disadvantages of such systems. It is shown that with existing resources, systems can be realized that use LLMs to control state machines in closed-loop operation. This leads to a significant increase in intuitiveness of use and interaction, as well as improved adaptation to unexpected disturbances and creative solutions.

A key advantage of these systems is their natural and intuitive operation. The use of LLMs significantly improves situational understanding and adaptability, enabling the successful completion of more complex tasks that require greater flexibility and are subject to more disturbances. In addition, LLMs have been shown to be easier to integrate into closed-loop systems and significantly less prone to error, particularly due to shorter outputs and better situational understanding. This also makes it easier to create more complex, less linear processes.

Another advantage of these systems is their ability to learn from previous situations. By providing information about the system, previous processes, and background information via RAG, the system can be "briefed" in a targeted manner. This enables the system not only to repeat past processes, but also to draw conclusions from them, optimize them, and find parallels to new tasks.

The vast repertoire of potential skills for autonomous systems can be extended and used for everyday, intuitive and practical support. By assembling these capabilities into states and their sequences, a code-free approach to autonomous systems can be implemented, allowing productive use even without specific knowledge. The field of application is not limited to robotics, but can be applied to any system that can be described by state machines, where basic flexibility increases utility. In particular, the use of closed-loop systems significantly increases the capabilities of systems and enables human-centered applications.

Future work will test these systems in complex scenarios, including multi-robot collaboration, and explore applications in domains such as smart homes, manufacturing, and healthcare to demonstrate their versatility. A more comprehensive comparison with other state-of-the-art automation techniques will also be conducted to deeply evaluate their respective strengths and limitations in practical use cases.

Acknowledgments. This work is funded and supported by the German Research Foundation (DFG) (SEMIAC under grant number No. 502483052), by the Federal Ministry of Education and Research of Germany (BMBF) (AutoKoWAT-3DMAt under grant No. 13N16336) and by the European Regional Development Fund (ERDF) (ENABLING under grant No. ZS/2023/12/182056 and RoboLab under grant No. ZS/2023/12/182065).

Disclosure of Interests. The authors have no competing interests to declare that are relevant to the content of this article.

References

1. Abdelrahman, A.A., Hempel, T., Khalifa, A., Al-Hamadi, A., Dinges, L.: L2CS-Net: fine-grained gaze estimation in unconstrained environments. In: 2023 8th International Conference on Frontiers of Signal Processing (ICFSP), pp. 98–102. IEEE (2023)
2. Abdelrahman, A.A., Strazdas, D., Khalifa, A., Hintz, J., Hempel, T., Al-Hamadi, A.: Multimodal engagement prediction in multiperson human-robot interaction. IEEE Access **10**, 61980–61991 (2022)
3. Al-Tawil, B., Hempel, T., Abdelrahman, A., Al-Hamadi, A.: A review of visual slam for robotics: evolution, properties, and future applications. Front. Robot. AI **11**, 1347985 (2024)
4. Alharbi, S., et al.: Automatic speech recognition: systematic literature review. IEEE Access **9**, 131858–131876 (2021)
5. Alonso Martin, F., Malfaz, M., Castro-González, Á., Castillo, J.C., Salichs, M.Á.: Four-features evaluation of text to speech systems for three social robots. Electronics **9**(2), 267 (2020)
6. Beurer-Kellner, L., Fischer, M., Vechev, M.: Guiding LLMS the right way: fast, non-invasive constrained generation. arXiv preprint: arXiv:2403.06988 (2024)
7. Bharathi Mohan, G., et al.: An analysis of large language models: their impact and potential applications. Knowl. Inf. Syst., 1–24 (2024)

8. Bishop, C.M., Nasrabadi, N.M.: Pattern Recognition and Machine Learning, vol. 4. Springer (2006)
9. Brooks, R.: A robust layered control system for a mobile robot. IEEE J. Robot. Autom. **2**(1), 14–23 (1986)
10. Chen, J., Abbod, M., Shieh, J.S.: Integrations between autonomous systems and modern computing techniques: a mini review. Sensors **19**(18), 3897 (2019)
11. Cobbe, K., et al.: Training verifiers to solve math word problems. arXiv preprint: arXiv:2110.14168 (2021)
12. Ding, Y., Zhang, X., Paxton, C., Zhang, S.: Task and motion planning with large language models for object rearrangement. In: 2023 IEEE/RSJ International Conference on Intelligent Robots and Systems (IROS), pp. 2086–2092. IEEE (2023)
13. Dinges, L., Al-Hamadi, A., Hempel, T., Al Aghbari, Z.: Using facial action recognition to evaluate user perception in aggravated HRC scenarios. In: 2021 12th International Symposium on Image and Signal Processing and Analysis (ISPA), pp. 195–199. IEEE (2021)
14. Dorbala, V.S., Mullen Jr, J.F., Manocha, D.: Can an embodied agent find your "cat-shaped mug"? LLM-based zero-shot object navigation. IEEE Robot. Autom. Lett. (2023)
15. Fang, H.S., et al.: AlphaPose: whole-body regional multi-person pose estimation and tracking in real-time. IEEE Trans. Pattern Anal. Mach. Intell. **45**(6), 7157–7173 (2022)
16. Fikes, R.E., Nilsson, N.J.: STRIPS: a new approach to the application of theorem proving to problem solving. Artif. Intell. **2**(3–4), 189–208 (1971)
17. Gallegos, I.O., et al.: Bias and fairness in large language models: a survey. Comput. Linguist., 1–79 (2024)
18. Gao, Y., et al.: Retrieval-augmented generation for large language models: a survey. arXiv preprint: arXiv:2312.10997 (2023)
19. Ghzouli, R., Berger, T., Johnsen, E.B., Wasowski, A., Dragule, S.: Behavior trees and state machines in robotics applications. IEEE Trans. Software Eng. **49**(9), 4243–4267 (2023)
20. Grieskamp, W., Gurevich, Y., Schulte, W., Veanes, M.: Generating finite state machines from abstract state machines. In: Proceedings of the 2002 ACM SIGSOFT international symposium on Software Testing and Analysis, pp. 112–122 (2002)
21. Hempel, T., Jung, M., Abdelrahman, A.A., Al-Hamadi, A.: NITEC: versatile hand-annotated eye contact dataset for ego-vision interaction. In: Proceedings of the IEEE/CVF Winter Conference on Applications of Computer Vision, pp. 4437–4446 (2024)
22. Hu, Z., et al.: Deploying and evaluating LLMS to program service mobile robots. IEEE Robot. Autom. Lett. (2024)
23. Huang, W., Abbeel, P., Pathak, D., Mordatch, I.: Language models as zero-shot planners: extracting actionable knowledge for embodied agents. In: International Conference on Machine Learning, pp. 9118–9147. PMLR (2022)
24. Hugel, V., Amouroux, G., Costis, T., Bonnin, P., Blazevic, P.: Specifications and design of graphical interface for hierarchical finite state machines. In: RoboCup 2005: Robot Soccer World Cup IX 9, pp. 648–655. Springer (2006)
25. Jiang, Y.Q., Zhang, S.Q., Khandelwal, P., Stone, P.: Task planning in robotics: an empirical comparison of PDDL-and asp-based systems. Front. Inf. Technol. Electr. Eng. **20**, 363–373 (2019)
26. Kaelbling, L.P., Littman, M.L., Cassandra, A.R.: Planning and acting in partially observable stochastic domains. Artif. Intell. **101**(1–2), 99–134 (1998)
27. Kannan, S.S., Venkatesh, V.L., Min, B.C.: Smart-LLM: smart multi-agent robot task planning using large language models. arXiv preprint: arXiv:2309.10062 (2023)
28. Karli, U.B., Chen, J.T., Antony, V.N., Huang, C.M.: Alchemist: LLM-aided end-user development of robot applications. In: Proceedings of the 2024 ACM/IEEE International Conference on Human-Robot Interaction, pp. 361–370 (2024)

29. Khalifa, A., Abdelrahman, A.A., Strazdas, D., Hintz, J., Hempel, T., Al-Hamadi, A.: Face recognition and tracking framework for human-robot interaction. Appl. Sci. **12**(11), 5568 (2022)
30. Kong, X., Zhang, W., Hong, J., Braunl, T.: Embodied AI in mobile robots: coverage path planning with large language models. arXiv preprint: arXiv:2407.02220 (2024)
31. Korteling, J.H., van de Boer-Visschedijk, G.C., Blankendaal, R.A., Boonekamp, R.C., Eikelboom, A.R.: Human-versus artificial intelligence. Front. Artif. Intell. **4**, 622364 (2021)
32. Kwon, M., Jung, M.F., Knepper, R.A.: Human expectations of social robots. In: 2016 11th ACM/IEEE International Conference on Human-Robot Interaction (HRI), pp. 463–464. IEEE (2016)
33. Latif, E.: 3P-LLM: probabilistic path planning using large language model for autonomous robot navigation. arXiv preprint: arXiv:2403.18778 (2024)
34. Lee, D., Yannakakis, M.: Principles and methods of testing finite state machines-a survey. Proc. IEEE **84**(8), 1090–1123 (1996)
35. Lewis, P., et al.: Retrieval-augmented generation for knowledge-intensive NLP tasks. In: Advances in Neural Information Processing Systems, vol. 33, 9459–9474 (2020)
36. Li, L.H., et al.: Grounded language-image pre-training. In: Proceedings of the IEEE/CVF Conference on Computer Vision and Pattern Recognition, pp. 10965–10975 (2022)
37. Li, X., et al.: FLM-101B: An open LLM and how to train it with $100 K budget. arXiv preprint: arXiv:2309.03852 (2023)
38. Liang, J., et al.: Code as policies: language model programs for embodied control. In: 2023 IEEE International Conference on Robotics and Automation (ICRA), pp. 9493–9500. IEEE (2023)
39. Liu, H., et al.: Enhancing the LLM-based robot manipulation through human-robot collaboration. arXiv preprint: arXiv:2406.14097 (2024)
40. Liu, P., Orru, Y., Paxton, C., Shafiullah, N.M.M., Pinto, L.: Ok-robot: What really matters in integrating open-knowledge models for robotics. arXiv preprint: arXiv:2401.12202 (2024)
41. Liu, Y., et al.: Prompt injection attack against LLM-integrated applications. arXiv preprint: arXiv:2306.05499 (2023)
42. Madani, K., Rinaldi, A.M., Russo, C., Tommasino, C.: A combined approach for improving humanoid robots autonomous cognitive capabilities. Knowl. Inf. Syst. **65**(8), 3197–3221 (2023)
43. Maslej, N., et al.: Artificial intelligence index report 2023. arXiv preprint: arXiv:2310.03715 (2023)
44. Mower, C.E., et al.: ROS-LLM: A ROS framework for embodied AI with task feedback and structured reasoning. arXiv preprint: arXiv:2406.19741 (2024)
45. Naveed, H., et al.: A comprehensive overview of large language models. arXiv preprint: arXiv:2307.06435 (2023)
46. Nazir, A., Wani, M.A.: You only look once-object detection models: a review. In: 2023 10th International Conference on Computing for Sustainable Global Development (INDIACom), pp. 1088–1095. IEEE (2023)
47. Obinata, Y., et al.: Foundation model based open vocabulary task planning and executive system for general purpose service robots. arXiv preprint: arXiv:2308.03357 (2023)
48. OpenAI, Achiam, J., et al.: GPT-4 technical report. arXiv preprint: arXiv:2303.08774 (2024)
49. O'Regan, G., O'Regan, G.: Automata theory. guide to discrete mathematics: an accessible introduction to the history, theory, logic and applications, pp. 121–131 (2021)
50. Ouyang, A.: Understanding the performance of transformer inference. Ph.D. thesis, Massachusetts Institute of Technology (2023)
51. Ouyang, L., et al.: Training language models to follow instructions with human feedback. In: Advances in Neural Information Processing Systems, vol. 35, pp. 27730–27744 (2022)

52. Radford, A., et al.: Learning transferable visual models from natural language supervision. In: International Conference on Machine Learning, pp. 8748–8763. PMLR (2021)
53. Saveriano, M., Abu-Dakka, F.J., Kramberger, A., Peternel, L.: Dynamic movement primitives in robotics: a tutorial survey. Int. J. Robot. Res. **42**(13), 1133–1184 (2023)
54. Schumann, R., Zhu, W., Feng, W., Fu, T.J., Riezler, S., Wang, W.Y.: VELMA: verbalization embodiment of LLM agents for vision and language navigation in street view. In: Proceedings of the AAAI Conference on Artificial Intelligence, vol. 38, pp. 18924–18933 (2024)
55. Shi, F., et al.: Large language models can be easily distracted by irrelevant context. In: International Conference on Machine Learning, pp. 31210–31227. PMLR (2023)
56. Shi, Y., Liu, J., Zheng, X.: LFENav: LLM-based frontiers exploration for visual semantic navigation. In: IFIP International Conference on Artificial Intelligence Applications and Innovations, pp. 375–388. Springer (2024)
57. Sikorski, P., et al.: Deployment of NLP and LLM techniques to control mobile robots at the edge: a case study using GPT-4-turbo and LLaMA 2. arXiv preprint: arXiv:2405.17670 (2024)
58. Singh, I., et al.: ProgPrompt: generating situated robot task plans using large language models. In: 2023 IEEE International Conference on Robotics and Automation (ICRA), pp. 11523–11530. IEEE (2023)
59. Tian, L., Ellis, K., Kryven, M., Tenenbaum, J.: Learning abstract structure for drawing by efficient motor program induction. In: Advances in Neural Information Processing Systems, vol. 33, 2686–2697 (2020)
60. Touvron, H., et al.: LLaMA: open and efficient foundation language models. arXiv preprint: arXiv:2302.13971 (2023)
61. Tseng, Y.M., et al.: Two tales of persona in LLMS: a survey of role-playing and personalization. arXiv preprint: arXiv:2406.01171 (2024)
62. Wang, R., Yang, Z., Zhao, Z., Tong, X., Hong, Z., Qian, K.: LLM-based robot task planning with exceptional handling for general purpose service robots. arXiv preprint: arXiv:2405.15646 (2024)
63. Wang, T., Fan, J., Zheng, P.: An LLM-based vision and language cobot navigation approach for human-centric smart manufacturing. J. Manuf. Syst. (2024)
64. Wu, P., Mu, Y., Zhou, K., Ma, J., Chen, J., Liu, C.: CAMON: cooperative agents for multi-object navigation with LLM-based conversations. arXiv preprint: arXiv:2407.00632 (2024)
65. Wu, S., Fei, H., Qu, L., Ji, W., Chua, T.S.: Next-GPT: any-to-any multimodal LLM. arXiv preprint: arXiv:2309.05519 (2023)
66. Wu, Y., Yue, T., Zhang, S., Wang, C., Wu, Q.: StateFlow: enhancing LLM task-solving through state-driven workflows. arXiv preprint: arXiv:2403.11322 (2024)
67. Zadeh, L.A.: Fuzzy sets. Inf. Control **8**(3), 338–353 (1965)
68. Zhang, Z., Fang, M., Chen, L., Namazi-Rad, M.R., Wang, J.: How do large language models capture the ever-changing world knowledge? a review of recent advances. arXiv preprint: arXiv:2310.07343 (2023)
69. Zheng, L., et al.: Judging LLM-as-a-judge with MT-bench and chatbot arena. In: Advances in Neural Information Processing Systems, vol. 36, pp. 46595–46623 (2023)
70. Zheng, Z., Feng, Q., Li, H., Knoll, A., Feng, J.: Evaluating uncertainty-based failure detection for closed-loop LLM planners. arXiv preprint: arXiv:2406.00430 (2024)
71. Zhou, H., Lin, Y., Yan, L., Zhu, J., Min, H.: LLM-BT: performing robotic adaptive tasks based on large language models and behavior trees. arXiv preprint: arxiv:2404.05134 (2024)
72. Zhou, P., et al.: A survey on generative AI and LLM for video generation, understanding, and streaming. arXiv preprint: arXiv:2404.16038 (2024)
73. Zhu, Y., et al.: Large language models for information retrieval: a survey. arXiv preprint: arXiv:2308.07107 (2023)

Robot Vision System for Retail Shelf Monitoring

Abhishek V. Latha[1,2], Mohammad Rahimipour[1], and Adel Merabet[1](✉)

[1] Division of Engineering, Saint Mary's University, Halifax, NS B3N 3C3, Canada
adel.merabet@smu.ca

[2] Computing and Data Analytics, Saint Mary's University, Halifax, NS B3N 3C3, Canada

Abstract. In this paper, automated retail shelf monitoring, that includes tag verification and on-shelf availability checking, is proposed using a robot vision system. The mobile robot platform with camera vision extracts images of the products and tags on the shelves. The tags images are processed using computer vision tools such as YOLOv5 and EasyOCR to detect the tags and extract all information to be compared with a database for compliance. The extracted images of the products are used to reconstruct the entire shelving unit, the YOLOv5 is used for object detection, and the depth estimation MiDas model is used to build the depth map image of the shelving unit. This combined method, based on object detection and depth estimation, is used to check on-shelf availability of the products. Experimentation is conducted using a small shelving unit. It has been found that the proposed procedure can verify products, tags and availability and insure on time shelf monitoring by the robot vision system.

Keywords: Robot · Image · Deep learning · Depth estimation · Tag · On-shelf availability · Retail

1 Introduction

Shelf monitoring for retail stores can reduce lost sales opportunities. Key factors to improve customer satisfaction and profit are insuring on-shelf availability of the products and their information on the tag, especially the price, is accurate and reflects any update at the management level. Manual checking for on-shelf availability and tag update is a labor-intensive that reduces productivity. For an effective maintain of the high on-shelf availability and tag correctness, a solution is required to automatically detect the changes in the products quantity on the front of the shelves and the tags pricing update to advice the store personnel to make adequate actions such as refill products and change tags.

One solution for automated shelf monitoring in retail stores is the combination of mobile robotics and computer vision for real time monitoring. A mobile robot, equipped with multiple cameras, can frequently navigate between the store aisles to check the shelves by taking images of products on the shelves, then processing those images for on-shelf availability and tag accuracy. The recent advances in deep learning tools for computer vision and image processing allowed the establishment of sophisticated models for object detection, classification and depth estimation [1–4]. Deep learning tool YOLO

J. Röning and J. Filipe (Eds.): ROBOVIS 2025, CCIS 2629, pp. 92–102, 2026.
https://doi.org/10.1007/978-3-032-00986-9_7

(You Only Look Once) is a popular object detection model due to its high speed and accuracy. It uses conventional neural networks (CNN) structure and provides the object classes and bounding boxes with high confidence scores [5]. Deep learning techniques have been investigated in retail stores applications for object detection related to the products and their arrangements in shelves [6–9].

Depth estimation is a technique that can be used to check on-shelf availability. If a product is available at the front of the shelf, it can be assumed a high availability for that product or low availability otherwise. Monocular depth estimation with MiDaS neural networks are powerful tools for depth estimation that can be used in shelf monitoring. MiDaS estimates the depth map of an input image, which is a 2D image where each pixel value represents the distance of the corresponding point in the scene from the camera [10–12]. The depth map can be combined with the detection of products on the shelf to analyze the depth estimation of each product and decide about the availability rate.

In this work, the automated shelf monitoring includes verification of the information of the tags and products and their locations on the shelfing unit using a robot vision system. Section 2 describes the physical parts of the robot vision system. Section 3 provides the steps to detect, classify and verify the tags on the shelves. Section 4 explains the on-shelf availability process using the concepts of depth estimation and object detection. Section 5 presents the experimental results using a small scale shelving unit followed by conclusions and future works.

2 Robot Vision System

The robot vision system includes a robot mobile platform, to navigate between the shelves in the aisles of a retail store, and a vision tower, of three cameras, to capture images of the products on shelves as illustrated in Fig. 1. In this work, a small scale of two shelves with three rows on each shelf is used to test the robot vision system. Twenty-eight (28) grocery products and others are arranged on the two shelves.

2.1 Robot Mobile Platform

The robot mobile platform is composed of the robot operating system (ROS) based mobile robot TurtleBot3, shown in Fig. 2. (*a*), equipped by Raspberry Pi 3 to run the ROS and uses *OpenCR* control board to run the motors of the wheels. Autonomous navigation is achieved using NVIDIA Jetson TX2 to execute ROS for mapping and movement toward the target.

2.2 Camera Vision Platform

The vision tower includes three cameras, See3CAM_30–3.4 MP autofocus USB camera with liquid lens shown in Fig. 2.(*b*), and NVIDIA Jetson Nano to capture images from the video streams of the three cameras and wirelessly transfer them to a host computer for image processing.

Fig. 1. Robot vision system and shelves.

(*a*) (*b*)

Fig. 2. Essential parts of the robot vision system. (*a*) TurtleBot3 Waffle Pi. (*b*) See3CAM_30–3.4 MP USB 3.0 Camera with liquid lens.

3 Tag Detection, Classification and Verification

The detection and classification of the products' tags include different procedures such as building a database of tags related to the products on the shelves and their locations, detecting the tags from the images extracted by the robot cameras, extracting the information on the tags, and finally verify if that information is compatible with the one available from the database.

3.1 Tag Database

The tag includes the necessary information about the product such as the name, the identification (ID) number and the price. This information and the tag location in the store, such as class label, shelf number, row number and column number, are recorded in database tables, maintained in Microsoft SQL server, as illustrated in Fig. 3. Furthermore, images of the tags are collected and stored in a folder to be used in the training and testing of the object detection algorithm. These images are annotated with class labels, providing the necessary training data for the object detection model.

	A	B	C	D	E	F	G	H
1	Id	Name	Price	Descriptio	Class_labe	Shelf_no	Row_no	Column_no
2	6.9E+09	Ritz Low S	17.99	Ritz Low S	0	1	1	1
3	6.9E+09	Ritz Chees	18.42	Ritz Chees	1	1	1	2
4	8.92E+09	Great Valu	7.65	Coconut L	2	1	1	3
5	7.92E+09	Bear Paws	23.41	Bear Paws	3	1	1	4
6	1.51E+09	President	16.33	President	4	1	1	5

Fig. 3. Tag Database with samples of products.

3.2 Image Extraction

The robot navigates through the shelves and the cameras provide video streams of 30 images per second. One (01) image per 180 images is extracted to avoid redundancy in extracted images. These images are stored in a folder and wirelessly transferred to a host computer for image processing.

3.3 Tag Detection

The tag detection is carried out using the object detection model YOLOv5 [13]. For object detection, YOLOv5 structure is composed of multiple convolutional layers and predicts the object class, bounding box location, and the confidence score for each object in the input image. Tag images are extracted from images collected from the video streams of the cameras installed on the robot.

3.4 Image Resolution Enhancement

The extraction of all information from the tag image, to be carried out by optical character recognition (OCR) tools, requires high images resolution. Enhanced deep residual neural networks (EDSR) tool is an advanced tool to increase image resolution [14]. In this work, the EDSR architecture uses a scaling factor of 2 for the resolution enhancement of the tag images.

3.5 Information Extraction

Optical character recognition (OCR) is a tool to extract text from images. In the case of tags, this information is required to check the accuracy of the data from the tag image and the one from the database. In this work, the package *EasyOCR*, implemented using Python and the *PyTorch* library, is used for extracting texts from tag images.

3.6 Tag Verification

The detected tags, extracted from the images of the tags on the shelves, by the YOLOv5 are collected in a sequence to be compared with the one of the database to verify the matching between the two sequences.

The case of missing tags is verified if the length of the YOLOv5 output sequence is different than the length of the database sequence. The missing tags can be determined by finding the class labels present in the database sequence and not in the detected sequence of the YOLOv5 output. The missed class labels provide the locations of missed tags on the shelves.

The case of misplaced tags is verified by comparing element by element the detected sequence and the database sequence. If at any index, a violation is detected it means that the tag, located at that index of the detected sequence, is misplaced and its real location is found in the database sequence through using its class label.

The next step is verifying the tag content for any inaccuracy especially related to the price. The extracted information (name and price) of two sequences, detected and database, are compared to determine any anomaly.

Finally, results of verification for missed, misplaced and incorrect tags are provided in a generated report.

4 Depth Estimation for On-Shelf Availability

On-shelf availability indicates the quantity of products available at a given location and time. In this work, the on-shelf availability is achieved using the depth estimation concept. The depth map of an input image is estimated using the MiDaS tool. The depth map is a 2D image where each pixel value represents the distance of the corresponding point in the scene from the camera [10–12]. The objective of the application is to detect and identify products on the shelf and check if a particular object location is empty or not. Information about depth estimation can be used to identify whether the quantity of products in a specific location is high or low.

The application loads the MiDaS model and applies input transforms to the shelf image for resizing and normalization. Then, it extracts the depth map of the image. The depth map is a 2D array of the same size as the input image, where each pixel value represents the distance of the corresponding point in the scene from the camera. Next, the actual image is processed by YOLOv5 object detection tool to detect the products on the shelf and their bounding boxes with the corresponding coordinates. Using the coordinates of the bounding boxes of the objects in the actual image, the centre point of the bounding box of each object in the image is calculated. Then, using the coordinates of the center points of all products, points with same coordinates are located on the depth map image and their depth values are collected and compared to a threshold value. If the depth value of the object, specified by its center point, is less than the threshold, the application considers its quantity to be low and the product on-shelf availability is low; otherwise, the product is available on the shelf. The application stores the names and locations of the products with low availability in a list.

5 Experimental Results

In a laboratory environment, the robot vision system navigates in front of a retail shelving unit, of two shelves, that display 28 grocery products and others as shown in Fig. 1. Each shelf has three racks (rows). The camera vision tower has three cameras (one camera per rack). During the navigation, each camera records a video and the extracted images for the products are stored in folders (one folder per rack). An example of stored images for the upper rack (row number one) is shown in Fig. 4. Furthermore, the extracted images for the tags are stored in folders, one folder per rack, as shown in Fig. 5.

The reconstruction of the image of the entire shelving unit includes the following image processing procedures: (1) Stitching the individual images of the same rack to create a panoramic image using the function *cv2.stitcher* from the *OpenCV* library. (2) A vertical concatenation of the three racks images, using the function *vconcat*, to create the entire image of the shelving unit as illustrated in Fig. 6.

5.1 Tag Detection, Classification and Verification

For the tag detection, the object detection model YOLOv5 is used where its network is trained using the annotated images of the tags and the database of Fig. 3. The network outputs are the bounding boxes of the tags, and the object classes tabulated in a sequence. Examples of the output images are provided in Fig. 7, where the tags are detected with their bounding boxes with names and confidence scores. Other information on the tag, such as name, ID number and price, are detected by the *EasyOCR* model. The generated sequence, that includes the information of the product, is compared to the original sequence, built from the database, and it is found that both sequences are similar. Therefore, the arrangement of the tags, in the shelving unit, and their contents comply with the information provided in the database.

Fig. 4. Stored images for the upper rack of the shelving unit.

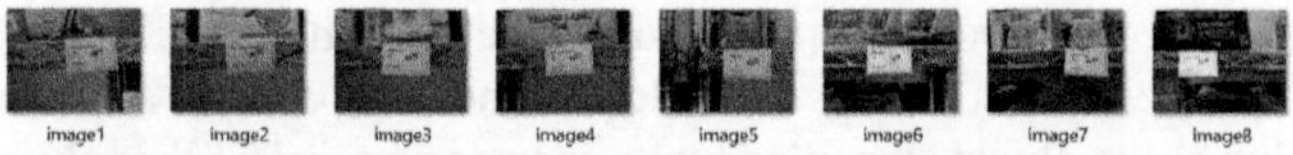

Fig. 5. Stored images of product tags in the shelving unit.

Fig. 6. Reconstructed shelving unit with products.

Fig. 7. Tag detection result using YOLOv5.

5.2 On-Shelf Availability

The MiDaS DPT-Large model is used for monocular depth estimation, which is the most accurate but also the slowest model. The model is loaded using the *torch.hub* library, which provides easy access to pre-trained models. The shelving unit image, shown in Fig. 6, is fed to the MiDaS model and the output is the depth estimation map image illustrated in Fig. 8. The detection of the products on the shelving unit is conducted using YOLOv5 and the result is illustrated in Fig. 9, where it can be observed that all products are detected within their bounding boxes. Furthermore, the coordinates of the bounding boxes are provided by the YOLOv5 model. Using these coordinates, the center point of the bounding boxes is calculated and located in the depth estimation map image. As both images (shelving unit image and depth estimation map image) are equal in size, the location of the center point on the depth estimation image represents the same product on the shelving unit image. At the center points of all products, the depth estimation value of each product is collected and compared to the threshold value of 8. The result is shown in Fig. 10, where it can be observed that the product (Object3) has a depth value of 7.537998 (less than 8) which means that this product is not at the front of the shelf and can be considered as less available on the shelf. Whereas the other products have depth values greater than 8 which means that these products are located at the front of the shelf assuming that other products are behind the one in the front. It can be concluded that these products are available on the shelf. In this experiment, only the product (Object3), located in shelf 1, row 1 and column 4, has low availability as shown in the numerical result of Fig. 10.(*a*) and marked in the image of Fig. 10.(*b*).

Fig. 8. Depth estimation map of the shelving unit.

Zooms on the images, for the shelving unit and the depth estimation map at the location (shelf 1, and row 1), are provided in Fig. 11 to show how the depth estimation can evaluate the availability of the product on the shelf. It can be observed that the product (Object3) is not available in high quantity.

Fig. 9. Results of product detection using YOLOv5.

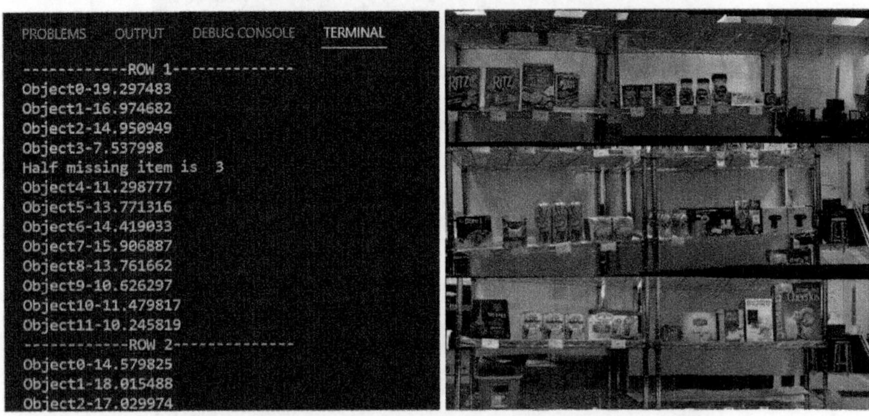

(*a*) (*b*)

Fig. 10. On-shelf availability results. (*a*) textual result. (*b*) Visual result.

Fig. 11. Original image and equivalent depth estimation image (zoom).

6 Conclusions

Retail shelf monitoring is automated using a robot vision system. Images of the products and tags are extracted and processed to conduct tag verification and on-shelf availability. Deep learning based object detection YOLOv5 is used to detect the products and tags by extracting class labels and bounding boxes. This output provides information about the products and tags related to the ones available on the database. Deep learning based MiDaS is used to build the depth estimation map of the products on the shelving unit and the calculated depth value provides information about the on-shelf availability of the products. The experimentation, conducted on a small scale shelving unit, has shown that the robot vision system and the deep learning tools provide accurate results for shelf monitoring. Future works include the assessment of the proposed solution in a real retail store with multiple shelves.

Acknowledgment. This work is financially supported in part by the David Sobey Retailing Centre (DSC) at Saint Mary's University.

References

1. Gül, V., Kuzu, R.S.: Toward retail product recognition on grocery shelves. In: Proceedings of the 6th International Conference on Graphic and Image Processing (ICGIP 2014), vol. 9443, pp. 1–7. SPIE, Beijing, China (2015)
2. Wang, J., Huang, C., Zhao, L., Li, Z.: Lightweight identification of retail products based on improved convolutional neural network. Multimedia Tools Appl. **81**, 31313–31328 (2022)
3. Wei, Y., Tran, S., Xu, S., Kang, B., Springer, M.: Deep learning for retail product recognition: challenges and techniques. Comput. Intell. Neurosci. **2020**, 1–23 (2020)
4. Wajire, P., Angadi, S., Nagar, L.: Image classification for retail. In: 2020 International Conference on Industry 4.0 Technology, pp. 23–28, Pune, India (2020)
5. Redmon, J., Divvala, S., Girshick, R., Farhadi, A: You only look once: unified, real-time object detection. In: Proceedings of the 2016 IEEE Conference on Computer Vision and Pattern Recognition, Las Vegas, NV, USA, (2016)
6. Youzi Xiao, Y., et al.: A review of object detection based on deep learning. Multimedia Tools Appl. **79**, 23729–23791 (2020)
7. Zhao, Z.Q., Zheng, P., Xu, S.T., Wu, X.: Object detection with deep learning: a review. IEEE Trans. Neural Netw. Learn. Syst. **30**(11), 3212–3232 (2019)
8. Higa, K., Kota Iwamoto, K.: Robust shelf monitoring using supervised learning for improving on-shelf availability in retail stores. Sensors **19**, 2722 (2019)
9. Saqlain, M., Rubab, S., Khan, M.M., Ali, N., Shahzeb, A.: Hybrid approach for shelf monitoring and planogram compliance (Hyb-SMPC) in retails using deep learning and computer vision. Math. Probl. Eng. **2022**, 1–18 (2022)
10. Ranftl, R., Lasinger, K., Hafner, D., Schindler, K., Koltun, V.: Towards robust monocular depth estimation: Mixing datasets for zero-shot cross-dataset transfer. IEEE Trans. Pattern Anal. Mach. Intell. **44**(3), 1623–1637 (2022)
11. Polasek, T., Čadík, M., Keller, Y., Benes, B.: Vision UFormer: long-range monocular absolute depth estimation. Comput. Graph. **111**, 180–189 (2023)
12. Ming, Y., Meng, X., Fan, C., Yu, H: Deep learning for monocular depth estimation: a review. Neurocomputing **438**, 14–33 (2021)

13. Object detection algorithm — YOLOv5 architecture Homepage. https://medium.com/analytics-vidhya/object-detection-algorithm-yolo-v5-architecture-89e0a35472ef. Accessed 26 May 2023
14. Lim, B., Son, S., Kim, H., Nah, S, Lee, K.M.: Enhanced deep residual networks for single image super-resolution. In: 2017 IEEE Conference on Computer Vision and Pattern Recognition Workshops (CVPRW), Honolulu, HI, USA (2017)

Integrating Vision-Based AI and Large Language Models for Real-Time Aquaculture Net Pens Inspection

Waseem Akram, Muhayy Ud Din, Lakmal Seneviratne, and Irfan Hussain(✉)

Khalifa University Center for Autonomous Robotic Systems (KUCARS), Khalifa University, Abu Dhabi, UAE
{waseem.akram,muhayyuddin.ahmed,lakmal.seneviratne,irfan.hussain}@ku.ac.ae

Abstract. This paper presents a novel approach for real-time aquaculture net pen monitoring by integrating vision-based AI with large language models. Traditional monitoring methods, which rely heavily on manual inspection and semi-autonomous systems, are often labor-intensive and inefficient. This work uses advanced AI techniques, combining YOLO-based deep learning model for detecting net defects such as biofouling, vegetation, and net holes, with large language model ChatGPT-4 to interpret and summarize inspection results in real-time. The proposed approach provides a real-time aqua-net inspection that enhances the accuracy and speed of net inspections while minimizing human intervention. Experimental results demonstrate significant improvements in detection precision resulting in mAP score of 0.9701 on our custom aqua-net dataset, operational efficiency, and automated report generation, highlighting the potential of this integrated approach to transform aquaculture management and promote sustainability.

Keywords: Aquaculture · Net defect detection · Marine vehicle · Deep learning Large language model

1 Introduction

Aquaculture plays an increasingly vital role in global food production, contributing significantly to the world's seafood supply [23]. As traditional fisheries face growing pressures from overfishing, environmental changes, and sustainability concerns, aquaculture has emerged as a critical industry for meeting global demand [10]. Among various aquaculture practices, net pen farming—where fish are farmed in submerged enclosures—has gained prominence due to its scalability and efficiency. However, this method also introduces significant challenges, particularly in maintaining the structural integrity of the nets and ensuring the health and safety of the farmed fish in marine dynamic environment [18].

One of the primary challenges in fish farming is the degradation of nets, which can lead to fish escapes, biofouling, and aquatic plant growth on the net surface [6,27]. Additionally, monitoring the water quality within the net pens, including parameters such as temperature, salinity, and dissolved oxygen, is crucial for ensuring optimal fish

J. Röning and J. Filipe (Eds.): ROBOVIS 2025, CCIS 2629, pp. 103–114, 2026.
https://doi.org/10.1007/978-3-032-00986-9_8

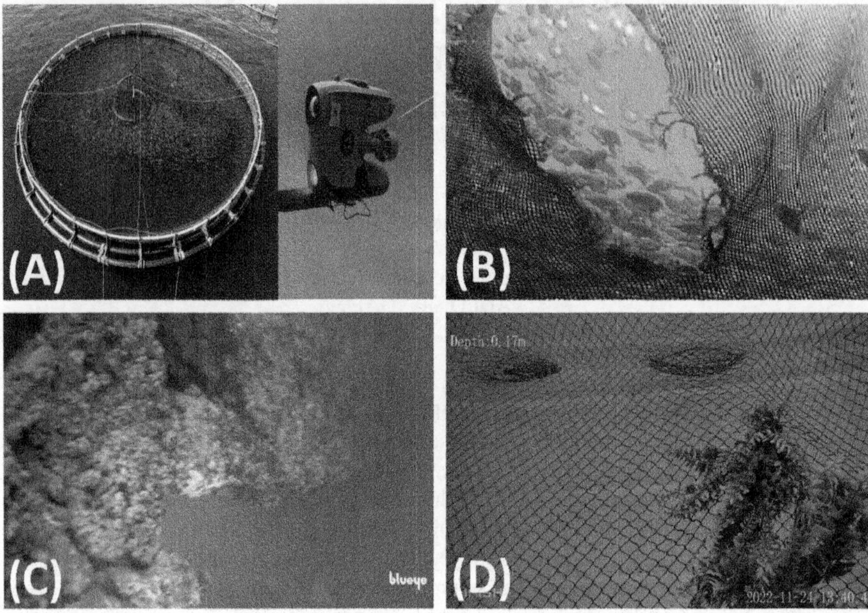

Fig. 1. Autonomous aquaculture inspection using an ROV: (A) displays the ROV conducting an inspection of aquaculture net pens, (B) illustrates a hole in the net, (C) presents biofouling growth on the surface of the net, and (d) depicts vegetation growth on the net. Image courtesy of [5,22].

health. These factors make continuous inspection and maintenance a necessity. However, current monitoring techniques are labor-intensive and inefficient, often relying on manual inspection by divers or semi-autonomous Remotely Operated Vehicles (ROVs) [4,5] (see Fig. 1). While ROVs reduce some of the manual workload [9], they still require significant human oversight and struggle to provide real-time, comprehensive analysis [29].

To address these limitations, there is a growing interest in using AI technologies for automating and enhancing aquaculture monitoring processes [2,19]. Vision-based AI models, which excel at tasks such as image segmentation and object detection [13,21], offer the potential to autonomously detect net defects, fish health issues [3,14], and environmental changes [15]. For instance, Zhang et al. [29] proposed the use of Mask-RCNN [11] for net hole detection problems in a laboratory setup, achieving an impressive Average Precision score of 94.48%. Likewise, Liao et al. [15] proposed a MobileNet-SSD network model for hole detection in open-sea fish cages. They achieved a commendable average precision score of 88.5% by combining MobileNet with the SSD network model for net hole detection. Tao et al. [24], applied deep learning to detect net holes using the YOLOV1 (You Only Look Once) algorithm on images captured under controlled lab conditions. In contrast, Madshaven et al. [16], employed a combination of classical computer vision and image processing techniques for tracking, alongside neural networks for segmenting the net structure and classifying scene content, including the detection of irregularities caused by fish or seaweed. Furthermore, Qiu et al. [20], utilized image-enhancing methods for net structure analysis and marine growth segmentation in their work [7].

However, these models generate vast amounts of data, which can overwhelm operators, making real-time decision-making difficult. Moreover, while detection models excel at identifying visual patterns, they lack the capability to provide context, prioritize critical information, or generate actionable insights. The integration of Large Language Models (LLMs) [8], such as GPT-based architectures, brings transformative capabilities to this scenario. LLMs, with their ability to understand and generate human-like language, can interpret the complex data produced by vision-based AI, generating concise summaries, flagging anomalies, and producing actionable reports in real time [17]. This integration provides a fully automated, end-to-end solution for monitoring and decision-making tasks [1,28].

The primary motivation of this paper is to explore how integrating vision-based AI with LLMs can streamline aquaculture net pen monitoring, making it more efficient, reducing reliance on manual interventions, and enhancing the accuracy and speed of real-time decisions. The proposed system performs real-time analysis of visual data, detecting net defects such as biofouling, vegetation, and net holes in a custom aquired dataset within aquaculture setup. The detection is performed via a recently developed YOLOV10 and YOLOV11 models, integrated with the LLM based ChatGPT-4 model for automatically generating reports that summarize key findings and offer recommendations for corrective actions.

The main contributions of this paper include:

- A real-time aquaculture monitoring system that integrates vision-based AI with LLMs to improve detection accuracy and reporting efficiency.
- The YOLOV11 model is utilized for detecting net defects, reducing the need for manual inspections, boosting operational efficiency, and providing better decision-making support.
- Detection results are integrated with ChatGPT-4 through customized prompts to generate concise, context-aware reports and recommendations regarding net conditions.

Through these contributions, we aim to provide a solution that not only enhances the aquaculture monitoring process but also promotes sustainable aquaculture practices by ensuring early detection of issues that could otherwise lead to significant economic and environmental losses.

2 Methodology

In this section, we discuss the methodology used for real-time aquaculture inspection, which integrates a vision-based anomaly detection model with LLM for report generation. An overview of the framework is shown in Fig. 2. The system uses an ROV equipped with a camera to capture real-time underwater images of net pens, using the YOLO-based detection model to identify net defects including biofouling, vegetation, and net holes. These results are then processed by an LLM Chatgpt-4 model, which generates comprehensive summaries and reports based on the detected issues and the current state of the net.

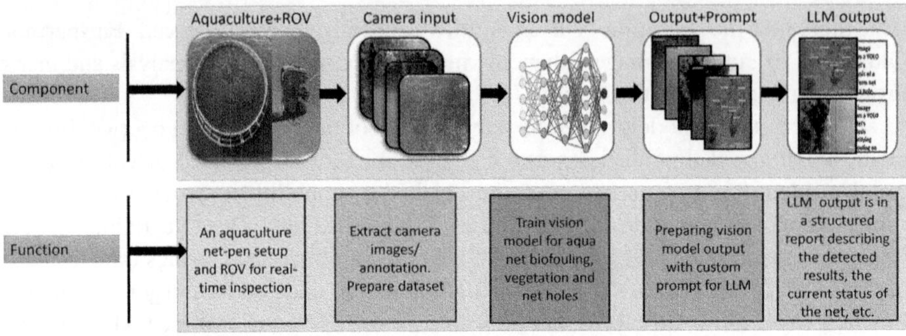

Fig. 2. Overview of the workflow for aquaculture net pen inspection.

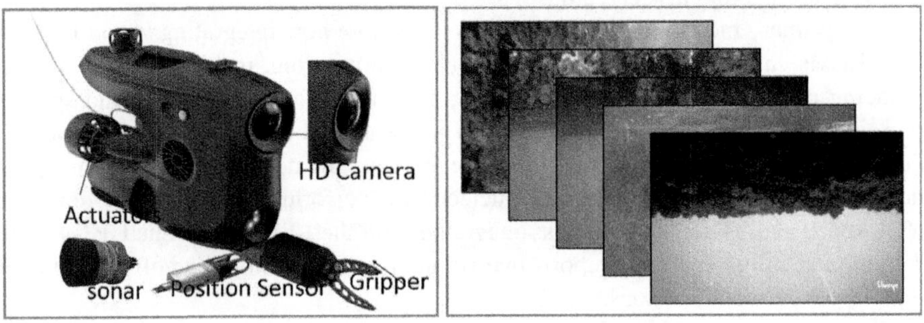

Fig. 3. Aquaculture data collection. The left side displays Blueye Pro X, while the right side shows their corresponding camera images, capturing real-time underwater inspection data.

2.1 ROV-Based Data Acquisition

The inspection process begins with an ROV deployed into the aquaculture net pens. The ROV is equipped with an underwater camera capable of capturing high-resolution real-time images of the nets and surrounding environment. The ROV is navigated to various sections of the net pens to ensure thorough coverage, with the camera continuously streaming visual data to the processing system. The primary aim is to detect net defects (e.g., biofouling, vegetation and net holes). The ROV, depicted in Fig. 3, is equipped with six thrusters and a Doppler Velocity Log (DVL), Inertial Measurement Unit (IMU), and a camera sensor. It is capable of operating in saltwater, brackish water, or freshwater environments for up to 2 h on a single charge and can dive to depths of 300 m while tethered by a 400-meter cable. Additionally, it is equipped with a forward-facing camera that captures video at 25–30 frames per second (fps) in full HD resolution, enabling the production of high-quality video streams of the surrounding area. Subsequently, these camera images are used in the detection steps. Samples of the dataset used for training are shown in Fig. 4.

Fig. 4. Examples of images from the dataset. (A) shows varying sizes of different classes, (B) shows the texture and color similarities between biofouling and fish, (c) shows a class under low visibility conditions, (D) and (E) show classes with distinct textures and colors, and (F) shows the challenge of distinguishing the class from the background.

2.2 Detection Using YOLO Model

The images captured by the ROV are processed in real-time using the YOLOV10 and YOLOV11 object detection model, which has been specifically fine-tuned for aquaculture applications using our custom aqua-net dataset [26]. This dataset includes images of biofouling, vegetation, and net holes. YOLOV10 and YOLOV11, state-of-the-art deep learning models, are designed for efficient, real-time object detection.

YOLOv10 [25] is a recent version of the YOLO (You Only Look Once) object detection model series, designed to improve upon its predecessors by offering greater accuracy and efficiency in real-time detection tasks. Built with an enhanced architecture, YOLOv10 uses updated CSPDarknet architecture to deliver faster inference times while maintaining high precision in detecting small objects and complex patterns. This version integrates deeper feature extraction layers, attention mechanisms, and improved anchor-free mechanisms, allowing it to better handle dense environments like aquaculture setups. YOLOv11 [12], a new variant enhanced features and improvements to increase performance and flexibility. It is built for speed, accuracy, and ease of use, making it an ideal option for various tasks, including object detection and tracking, instance segmentation, image classification, and pose estimation. These models are well-suited for identifying multiple anomalies in a single image, such as net holes, biofouling, and vegetation growth, even in challenging underwater conditions where lighting and clarity may vary. Its ability to detect fine-grained details with high confidence makes it

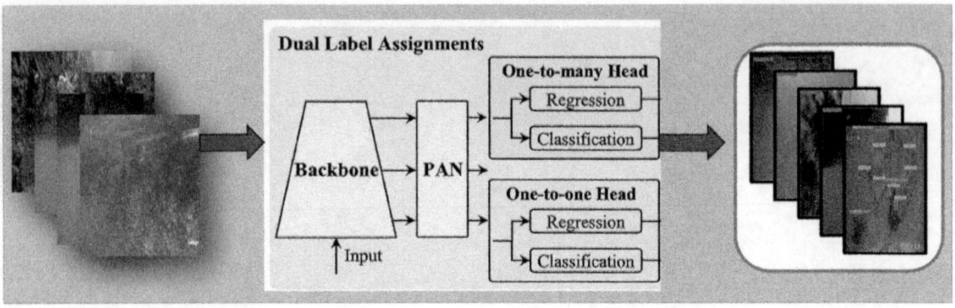

Fig. 5. Aqua-net input scan to YOLOV10 vision-based model.

Table 1. Steps for YOLO+ChatGPT-4 to perform the aqua-net inspection tasks.

Steps	Description
Load model	Fine-tuned YOLO model is deployed for the detection tasks
Load image	The input image is loaded and passed to the model
Detection	The detection task is applied on the input image
Display results	The results form YOLOV10 and YOLOV11 models are visualized
Create Prompt	The detection results are integrated with the custom prompt
Display output	The detection results with ChatGPT response are integrated and visualized

an ideal tool for aquaculture monitoring, enabling proactive maintenance and intervention. An architectural diagram of YOLOV10 model is shown in Fig. 5. The detection model outputs bounding boxes around detected object, along with classification labels and confidence scores, which are critical for identifying areas that require immediate attention or maintenance.

The YOLOV10 and YOLOV11 models were trained on our custom aqua-net dataset, which contains labeled images of biofouling, vegetation, and net holes encountered in net pen structures. In total, the dataset contains 7194 images along with bounding boxes for each object class and divided into a 80% for training and 20% for testing. The training process used a transfer learning approach, initializing the model with pre-trained weights from a generic object detection dataset, which were then fine-tuned on the aqua-net dataset to specialize in detecting aquaculture-specific anomalies. Additionally, the model underwent training for 60 epochs, with each epoch consisting of 512 iterations. This rigorous training process resulted in a highly accurate and efficient detection model capable of operating in real-time during underwater inspections (Table 1).

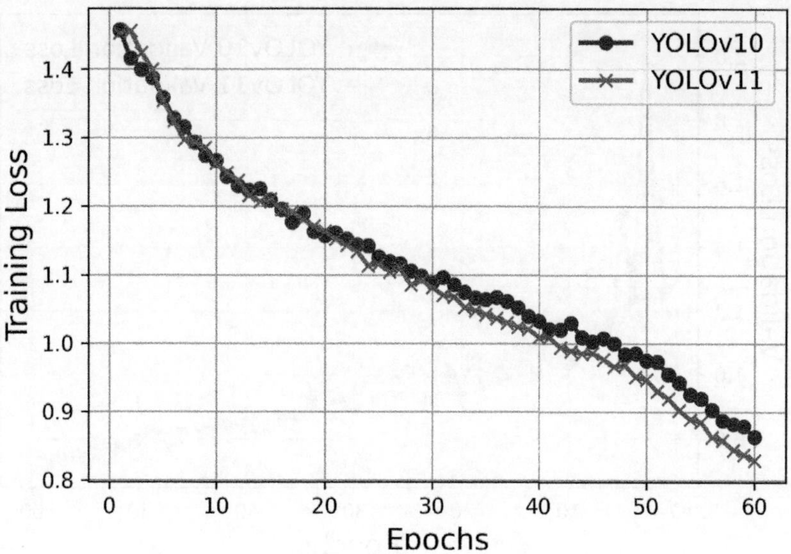

Fig. 6. Training loss over epochs for YOLOV10 and YOLOV11.

2.3 Integration with Large Language Model

The integration of a YOLO-based vision model with an LLM forms the core of the system's development. This is achieved by designing and structuring prompts for the LLM. The YOLOV model detects defects such as net holes, biofouling, and vegetation in the net, providing details on the type, location, and confidence score of each detected object. These results are then formatted into a customized prompt for ChatGPT-4 using the OpenAI API. The LLM interprets the prompt, generating natural language summaries. These customized prompts are critical for integrating the vision and language models, as they are designed to produce structured information based on the detected defects in the aqua-net.

The input prompt provided to ChatGPT-4 includes structured data from the YOLO model, reflecting the detection results. Objects detected by the YOLOV10 model are stored in a string variable named "detClass", which is incorporated into the custom prompt, where they request brief definitions of the detected objects, along with their location in the image, confidence score, severity levels, potential impact, and the recommendation actions required promptly.

ChatGPT-4 processes this information, summarizing the inspection results into a clear, easy-to-understand report. This report includes a detailed description of the detected anomalies, their potential impact on fish health or net integrity, and suggested corrective actions. The structure of the prompt influences the report's detail—short prompts yield concise summaries, while more detailed prompts provide in-depth analysis. The system's final output is an automatically generated inspection report, seamlessly blending the vision model's detection results with the LLM's interpretations. By integrating vision-based AI with an LLM, the system enables fast, accurate, and auto-

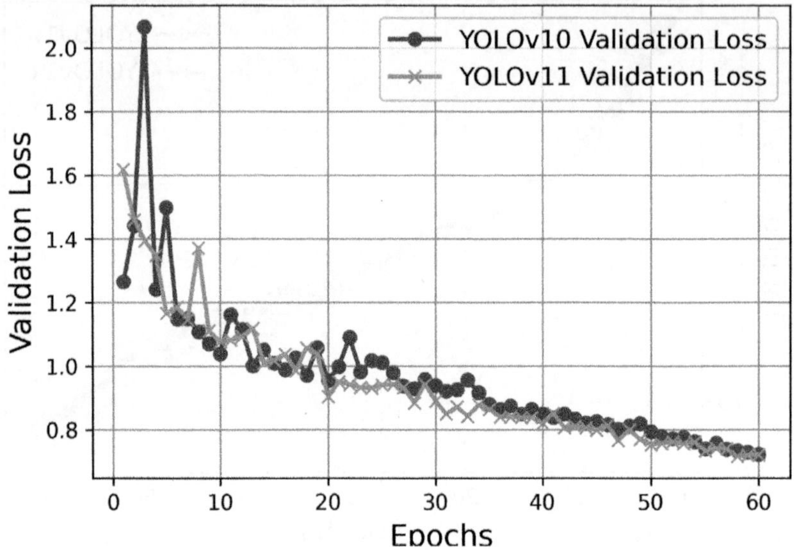

Fig. 7. Validation loss over epochs for YOLOV10 and YOLOV11.

mated reporting, significantly reducing the time and effort required for monitoring and maintenance.

3 Results and Discussion

In this section, we discuss the implementation results. We employed two YOLO variants named YOLOV10 and YOLOV11 for our experiments. During the training process, we analyzed both the training loss and validation loss to assess the model's learning progress and generalization ability. The training loss (see Fig. 6), which reflects how well the model fits the training data, showed a steady decline as the training epochs progressed. This indicates that both YOLOV10 and YOLOV11 effectively learned to minimize errors on the training set. YOLOV11 exhibited a faster convergence rate, while YOLOV10 took a few more epochs to stabilize, potentially due to a more complex architecture or additional layers that required more time to adjust their parameters. In contrast, the validation loss, which measures how well the model generalizes to unseen data is shown in Fig. 7. The results showed a sharp decrease in the first few epochs. However, as training continued, the validation loss for both models began to plateau. YOLOV11 maintained a relatively low validation loss, suggesting a good balance between fitting the training data and generalizing to new examples. On the other hand, YOLOV10 showed a slight increase in validation loss after a certain point, hinting at potential overfitting, where the model became too specialized on the training data and less capable of handling unseen data.

Figure 8, compares the performance of YOLOV10 and YOLOV11 using three key metrics: Precision, Recall, and Mean Average Precision (mAP). Both models exhibit

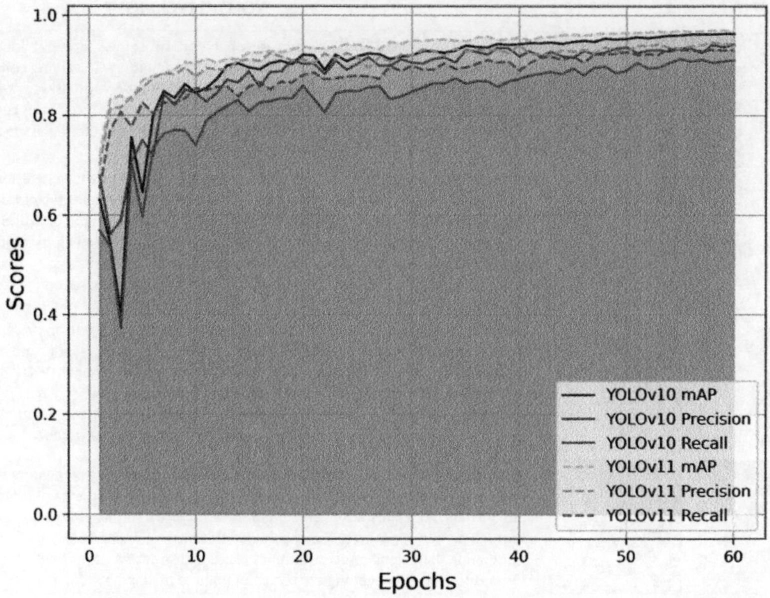

Fig. 8. Performance metrics (mAP, Precision, and Recall) evaluation on YOLOV10 and YOLOV11.

significant improvements across all metrics as training progresses. YOLOV10 shows a strong increase in precision from 0.6786 to 0.9417 and recall from 0.5681 to 0.9105, highlighting its capability to accurately detect objects. However, YOLOV11 outperforms slightly, with precision rising from 0.6983 to 0.9425 and recall improving from 0.6523 to 0.9307. The mAP results further confirm YOLOV11's superior performance, with a final score of 0.9701 compared to YOLOV10's 0.9634, indicating that YOLOV11 achieves a better balance between precision and recall, making it the more accurate model overall.

Figure 9 showcases the results of YOLO object detection integrated with textual descriptions generated by the ChatGPT-4. In this blended approach, YOLOV10 and YOLOV11 accurately identifies and localizes objects within the image, while ChatGPT provides relevant textual information based on the detected objects. The combination of visual detection and natural language processing enhances the interpretability of the results, with YOLO focusing on precise object identification and ChatGPT generating contextual descriptions, explanations, or summaries related to the detected net defects. This allows a more informative output, combining the strengths of both models—YOLO's visual precision and ChatGPT's language understanding—to improve interaction, understanding, and usability in real-world applications for autonomous aquaculture net inspection.

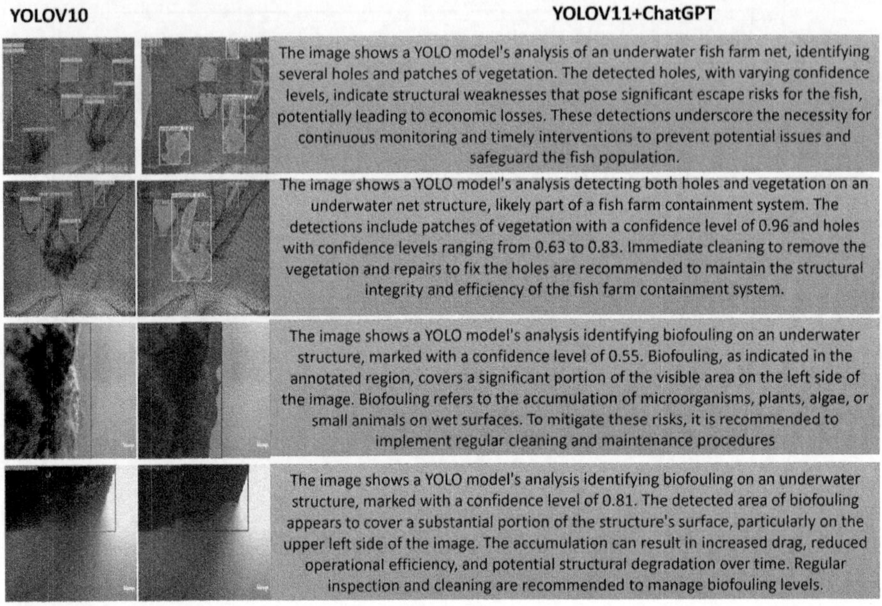

Fig. 9. Showcasing qualitative results through YOLOV10 and YOLOV11+ChatGPT.

4 Conclusion

In this work, we integrated YOLO-based object detection with the ChatGPT language model to enhance aquaculture monitoring. Our findings showed that YOLOV11 slightly outperformed YOLOV10 in terms of precision, recall, and mAP. This combined system improves real-time monitoring by detecting aquatic species and generating contextual descriptions, aiding better decision-making and sustainability in aquaculture. Future work will focus on scaling the system for larger farms, adapting it for tasks like water quality monitoring and disease detection, and optimizing real-time performance for broader applications.

Acknowledgements. This work is supported by the Khalifa University under Award No. RC1-2018-KUCARS-8474000136, CIRA-2021-085, MBZIRC-8434000194, KU-BIT-Joint-Lab-8434000534.

Declaration. During the preparation of this work the author(s) used ChatGPT-4 in order to improve language and readability. After using this tool/service, the author(s) reviewed and edited the content as needed and take(s) full responsibility for the content of the publication.

References

1. Ahmed, M., et al.: Vision-based autonomous navigation for unmanned surface vessel in extreme marine conditions. In: 2023 IEEE/RSJ International Conference on Intelligent Robots and Systems (IROS), pp. 7097–7103. IEEE (2023)

2. Akram, W., Ahmed, M., Saoud, L.S., Seneviratne, L., Hussain, I.: Autonomous underwater robotic system for aquaculture applications. arXiv preprint: arXiv:2308.14762 (2023)
3. Akram, W., Ahmed, M., Seneviratne, L., Hussain, I.: Evaluating deep learning assisted automated aquaculture net pens inspection using ROV. arXiv preprint: arXiv:2308.13826 (2023)
4. Akram, W., Casavola, A.: A visual control scheme for AUV underwater pipeline tracking. In: 2021 IEEE International Conference on Autonomous Systems (ICAS), pp. 1–5. IEEE (2021)
5. Akram, W., Casavola, A., Kapetanović, N., Miškovic, N.: A visual servoing scheme for autonomous aquaculture net pens inspection using ROV. Sensors **22**(9), 3525 (2022)
6. Akram, W., et al.: Aquaculture defects recognition via multi-scale semantic segmentation. Expert Syst. Appl. **237**, 121197 (2024)
7. Bakht, A.B., et al.: MuLA-GAN: multi-level attention GAN for enhanced underwater visibility. arXiv preprint: arXiv:2312.15633 (2023)
8. Chang, Y., et al.: A survey on evaluation of large language models. ACM Trans. Intell. Syst. Technol. **15**(3), 1–45 (2024)
9. Din, M.U., et al.: Marine X: design and implementation of unmanned surface vessel for vision guided navigation. In: 2023 21st International Conference on Advanced Robotics (ICAR), pp. 226–231. IEEE (2023)
10. Gui, F., Zhu, H., Feng, D.: Research progress on hydrodynamic characteristics of marine aquaculture netting. Fish. Mod **46**, 9–14 (2019)
11. He, K., Gkioxari, G., Dollar, P., Girshick, R.: Mask R-CNN. In: IEEE International Conference on Computer Vision (ICCV) (2017)
12. Jocher, G., Chaurasia, A., Qiu, J.: YOLO by ultralytics. https://github.com/ultralytics/ultralytics. Accessed 07 Oct 2024
13. Jocher, G., et al.: ultralytics/YOLOv5: v7.0 - YOLOv5 SOTA realtime instance segmentation (2022). https://doi.org/10.5281/zenodo.7347926
14. Li, D., Du, L.: Recent advances of deep learning algorithms for aquacultural machine vision systems with emphasis on fish. Artif. Intell. Rev. **55**(5), 4077–4116 (2022)
15. Liao, W., Zhang, S., Wu, Y., An, D., Wei, Y.: Research on intelligent damage detection of far-sea cage based on machine vision and deep learning. Aquacult. Eng. **96**, 102219 (2022)
16. Madshaven, A., Schellewald, C., Stahl, A.: Hole detection in aquaculture net cages from video footage. In: Fourteenth International Conference on Machine Vision (ICMV 2021), vol. 12084, pp. 258–267. SPIE (2022)
17. Minaee, S., et al.: Large language models: a survey. arXiv preprint: arXiv:2402.06196 (2024)
18. Noakes, D.J.: Environmental impacts of salmon net pen farming. Salmon: Biology, Environmental Impact and Economic Importance, Nova Science Inc., New York, NY, pp. 239–256 (2014)
19. Paspalakis, S., Moirogiorgou, K., Papandroulakis, N., Giakos, G., Zervakis, M.: Automated fish cage net inspection using image processing techniques. IET Image Proc. **14**(10), 2028–2034 (2020)
20. Qiu, W., Pakrashi, V., Ghosh, B.: Fishing net health state estimation using underwater imaging. J. Mar. Sci. Eng. **8**(9), 707 (2020)
21. Ren, S., He, K., Girshick, R., Sun, J.: Faster R-CNN: towards real-time object detection with region proposal networks. In: Advances in Neural Information Processing Systems (NIPS) (2015)
22. Roboflow: Net Defect Detection Dataset-v1 (2022). Accessed 14 Dec 2022
23. Subasinghe, R., Soto, D., Jia, J.: Global aquaculture and its role in sustainable development. Rev. Aquac. **1**(1), 2–9 (2009)
24. Tao, Q., Huang, K., Qin, C., Guo, B., Lam, R., Zhang, F.: Omnidirectional surface vehicle for fish cage inspection. In: OCEANS 2018 MTS/IEEE Charleston, pp. 1–6. IEEE (2018)

25. Wang, A., et al.: YOLOv10: real-time end-to-end object detection. arXiv preprint: arXiv:2405.14458 (2024)
26. Waseem, A.: Aqua_net dataset (2024). https://universe.roboflow.com/aqua-lzsrt/aqua_net-2. Accessed 07 Oct 2024
27. Yan, G., Ni, X., Mo, J.: Research status and development tendency of deep sea aquaculture equipments: a review. J. Dalian Ocean Univ. **33**(1), 123–129 (2018)
28. Yang, X., Zhang, S., Liu, J., Gao, Q., Dong, S., Zhou, C.: Deep learning for smart fish farming: applications, opportunities and challenges. Rev. Aquac. **13**(1), 66–90 (2021)
29. Zhang, Z., Gui, F., Qu, X., Feng, D.: Netting damage detection for marine aquaculture facilities based on improved mask R-CNN. J. Mar. Sci. Eng. **10**(7), 996 (2022)

Shadow-Robust Autonomous Navigation with Traversability Judgement Using Stereo Camera

Motonobu Omori[1(✉)], Kota Hyashi[1], Hiroshi Yoshitake[2], and Motoki Shino[2]

[1] Department of Human and Engineered Environmental Studies, Graduate School of Frontier Sciences, The University of Tokyo, Chiba, Japan
momori@edu.k.u-tokyo.ac.jp

[2] Department of Mechanical Engineering, School of Engineering, Institute of Science Tokyo, Tokyo, Japan

Abstract. There are high expectations for autonomous personal mobility vehicles (PMVs) in outdoor environments to support the daily lives of older people. These autonomous PMVs are required to adhere to traffic rules and exhibit safe obstacle avoidance. Existing methods extract regions recommended for travel based on stereo camera images with semantic segmentation and navigate through them to meet the requirements. Currently, there is a problem where the recommended area is incorrectly extracted due to changes in surface brightness caused by shadows, leading to failures in autonomous navigation. Therefore, this study focused on 3D point clouds obtained with a stereo camera and proposed a robust autonomous navigation method that addresses shadows. Finally, the effectiveness of the proposed method was evaluated through autonomous navigation experiments conducted in environments that include shadows.

Keywords: Personal mobility vehicle · Autonomous navigation · Outdoor environment · Shadow · Traversability

1 Introduction

In recent years, new transportation services capable of transporting users from their departure points to their destinations and supporting older people's daily travel by combining multiple mobilities are highly expected [1]. While existing public transportation can be used in such services, there is a demand for first and last-mile transportation services connecting places without existing public transportation, such as sections between the departure point and the nearest bus stop. Therefore, personal mobility vehicles (PMVs), capable of traveling inside outdoor pedestrian spaces, are expected to be automated.

Autonomous PMVs are required to reach the destination, adhere to traffic rules, and avoid obstacles. In previous studies, to meet these requirements, methods using cameras [2–4], LiDARs [5], or combinations of both sensors [6] for environmental perception have been proposed. These methods detect areas recommended for travel

J. Röning and J. Filipe (Eds.): ROBOVIS 2025, CCIS 2629, pp. 115–129, 2026.
https://doi.org/10.1007/978-3-032-00986-9_9

based on camera images acquired from sensors installed on the vehicle and generate paths within the recommended areas. In particular, the existing method with a stereo camera [4] can avoid obstacles and adhere to traffic rules using computer vision, without integrating additional expensive sensors such as LiDARs for surrounding environment perception. In this autonomous navigation system shown in Fig. 1, global path planning is performed using position obtained with GNSS and a topological map. Subsequently, this method applies semantic segmentation to the images from the stereo camera to detect the traversable regions that should be traveled according to traffic rules. Based on the coordinate data of each image pixel, a Driving Recommendation Map (DRM) is generated. Local path planning is then performed based on the DRM, and autonomous navigation is executed by outputting control commands for speed and steering angle to follow the path.

However, in the existing methods using computer vision, there are challenges regarding the robustness to changes in road surface brightness due to shadows [7]. As shown in Fig. 2, the system [4] determined traversable areas as non-traversable due to shadows, failing to reach the destination. Therefore, this study aims to develop a local path planning method that robustly determines traversability and executes autonomous navigation in the presence of road surface brightness changes caused by shadows.

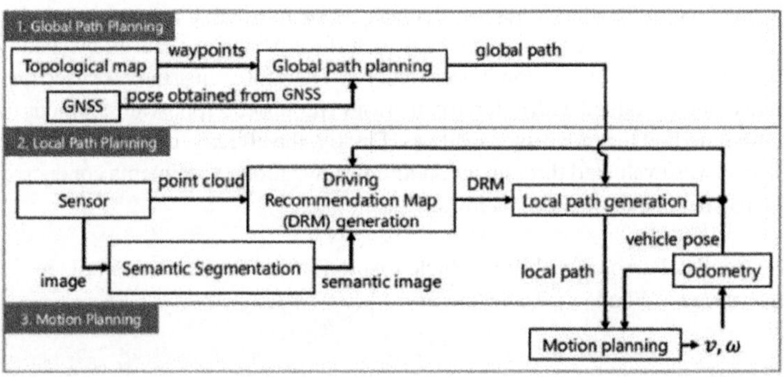

Fig. 1. System architecture of autonomous navigation system [4].

2 Related Works

As approaches for robust autonomous navigation against road surface brightness changes, there are methods that improve semantic segmentation by considering the effects of brightness changes. Additionally, sensor fusion techniques that incorporate sensor data robust to brightness changes are also considered.

2.1 Shadow-Robust Semantic Segmentation

Several methods have been proposed to achieve robust semantic segmentation against brightness changes. Firstly, previous studies [8, 9] proposed machine learning methods

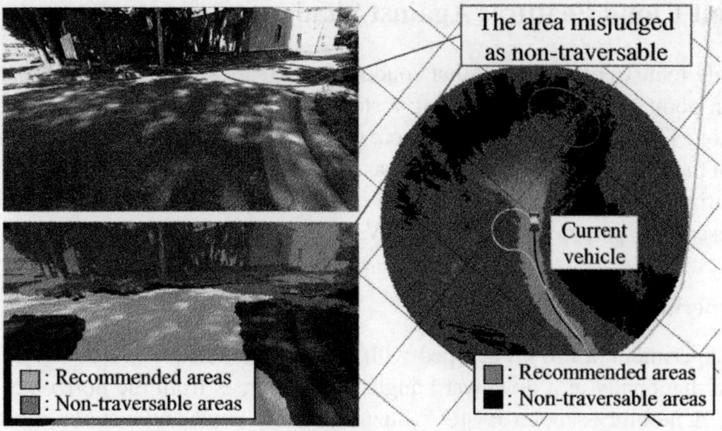

Fig. 2. System architecture of autonomous navigation system [4].

to detect and remove shadows from the camera images, enabling pre-removal of shadows for semantic segmentation. Some methods collect annotated training images containing shadows to provide the semantic segmentation model with knowledge about shadows [10, 11]. A method to transfer shadow knowledge from existing datasets to the model, known as transfer learning, has also been proposed [7]. Although several methods are improving semantic segmentation through machine learning, preparing training data to deal with shadows of various shapes in diverse environments is challenging, and non-robust situations still exist.

2.2 Utilization of Shadow Robust Sensor Data

Some autonomous navigation methods utilize sensor data, such as from LiDAR and radar [12, 13], which are robust to the brightness changes. For example, the position data of point clouds from LiDAR represent physical information without color information and can be used for robust traversability judgement. Existing methods [14, 15] generate voxel maps from LiDAR-acquired point clouds and determine whether all four wheels of the vehicle can make contact with the ground [16] or whether the tires can roll [17] at a certain area. However, these sensors are expensive, and it is important to achieve robust autonomous navigation cost-effectively without increasing the number of sensors used in the system.

This study focused on the ability of the stereo camera to obtain 3D point cloud data based on the disparity between right and left images within the existing system [4]. However, for reliable local path generation based on road surface traversability using the point clouds, it is essential to understand and consider the characteristics of the acquisition rate of point clouds and how positional errors in the point cloud data occur, especially in the presence of road surface brightness changes. 3D point cloud data can be used under conditions that ensure a sufficiently high acquisition rate and positional accuracy to determine whether the vehicle can traverse the area.

3 Point Cloud Features Against Shadows

This study focuses on a method that conducts traversability judgement of road surfaces based on point clouds acquired using a stereo camera for shadow-robust autonomous navigation. The point cloud features were examined to ensure stable autonomous navigation of the PMV, even in shadowed areas. The features were investigated, with respect to the horizontal distance between the sensor and the targeted points, which was selected as an observable parameter from the PMV.

3.1 Experimental Method

In this experiment, a PMV equipped with a stereo camera was used. The camera was mounted diagonally at a downward angle of 25 degrees from the horizontal direction in front. A mobility scooter ET4D7 (Suzuki Motor Corp.) and a stereo camera ZED2 (Stereolabs Inc.) were used in this experiment. Table 1 shows the specifications and settings of the camera. This sensor is designed to capture depth information up to a range of 20 m, but stereo cameras commonly have the limitation that depth accuracy decreases in proportion to the square of the distance.

Table 1. Specifications of ZED 2.

Name	Value
Resolution	1,280 × 720 pixels
Frame per second	15 fps
Baseline	120 mm
Maximum field of view	120° (D) × 110°(H) × 70° (V)
Depth range	0.2–20 m

Point clouds were acquired in 6 scenes, a combination of 3 different asphalt roads and the presence of shadows, as illustrated in Fig. 3, to understand the features concerning the presence of shadows. This study focused on the distance from the sensor to the point cloud as a critical factor affecting point cloud acquisition and position data. Additionally, environmental information within a minimum distance of 5 m must be acquired to avoid obstacles detected in front of the PMV when the vehicle has a maximum speed of 6 km/h and a maximum steering angle of 35 degrees. Thus, the positional information of the point clouds in the height and depth directions, as shown in Fig. 3, were measured at positions ranging from 1.0 to 10.0 m ahead of the vehicle with intervals of 0.5 m. Placing two marker boxes at each position using a tape measure, point data for N_{obtain} pixels in the center among the pixels located between them on the image were measured.

The point cloud acquisition rates r were calculated with Eq. 1. Here, n_{valid} denotes the number of pixels with valid data. Additionally, the height and depth errors ε_z and ε_x with respect to the true value were calculated with Eqs. 2 and 3, respectively.

$$r = n_{valid}/N_{obtain} \tag{1}$$

$$\varepsilon_z = \frac{1}{N_{valid}} \sum_{i=1}^{N_{valid}} (z_i - \mu_z) \tag{2}$$

$$\varepsilon_x = \frac{1}{N_{valid}} \sum_{i=1}^{N_{valid}} (x_i - \mu_x) \tag{3}$$

Here, the true height μ_z was set to be 0, with the assumption that the road surface is flat. The true depth μ_x was set to be the position in the depth direction where the boxes exist (1.0 m to 10.0 m, in increments of 0.5 m). Then, the measured depth and height values are denoted as x_i and z_i, and N_{obtain} and N_{error} were set to 100 and 10, respectively.

Fig. 3. Experimental scenes without shadows (left) and with shadows (right).

3.2 Experimental Results

There was a tendency for the acquisition rates r to decrease under conditions with shadows (Fig. 4). However, as shown in Fig. 4, the reduction was not significant and r was consistently obtained at a rate over 60%, even with shadows.

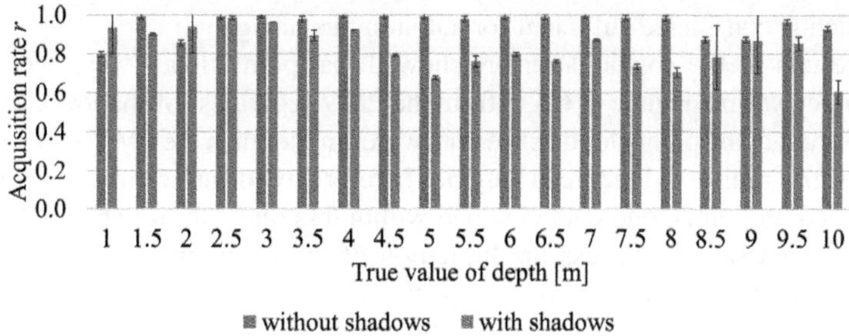

Fig. 4. Point cloud acquisition rates.

Regarding the depth and height errors of the point cloud data, as illustrated in Figs. 5 and 6, the errors and variations tend to increase with greater distances. At distances of 6.5 m or less, the variation in the height direction was smaller than the PMV's tire radius (0.128 m), and both the error and variation in the depth direction were smaller than the tread length (0.57 m).

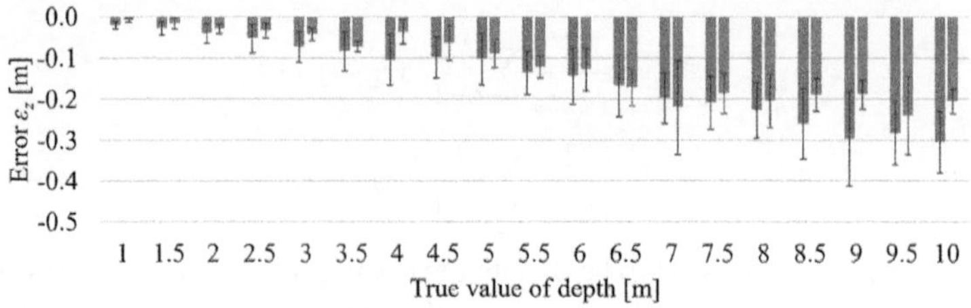

Fig. 5. Point cloud height errors.

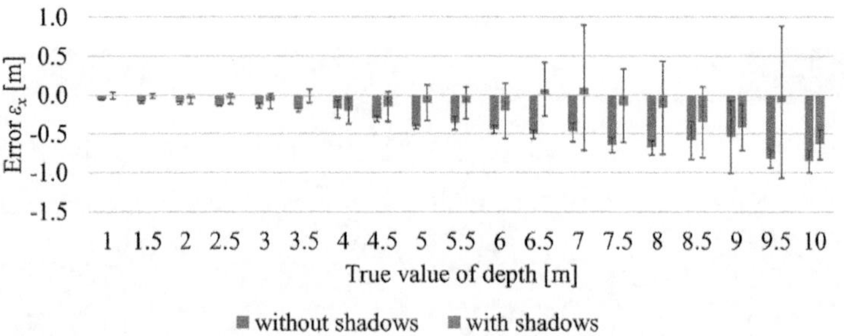

Fig. 6. Point cloud depth errors.

3.3 Discussion

The results showed a tendency for the acquisition rates r to decrease under conditions with shadows (Fig. 4). As shown in Fig. 7, it was found that point clouds are difficult to obtain at the edge regions where areas of high and low brightness meet. This is likely because the pixels at these boundary regions fail to capture RGB information accurately, leading to stereo-matching failures between the left and right camera images. However, the acquisition rate consistently exceeded 60% under conditions ranging from 1.0 to 10 m, which is considered sufficient for autonomous navigation.

The results of the positional errors showed that point clouds were acquired with high accuracy within a range of 6.5 m from the PMV regardless of shadows. In addition, within this range, the point cloud data errors were smaller than the PMV's specifications, such as the tire radius and the tread length. Therefore, road surface traversability can be judged based on point cloud data obtained within this range for reliable path planning. Then, it is necessary to discuss the limitation of the environment in which the path planning method functions effectively to generate a path from the current location to the waypoint within the region determined as traversable.

An error of 0.5 m in the depth direction may occur, and the vehicle width is approximately 1 m. This error may lead to an underestimation of the traversable area, resulting in the system incorrectly recognizing that the road is narrower and impassable on narrow roads with a width of 2 m or narrower, as shown in Fig. 8. Even on sufficiently wide roads, uneven road surfaces may cause the height difference to be overestimated due to errors in the height direction. Additionally, significant vibration of the PMV during travel can increase the likelihood of point cloud data errors, leading to incorrect traversability

Fig. 7. Failure to acquire point clouds at edge regions.

judgements and a higher risk of failure in autonomous navigation. Therefore, flat and sufficiently wide roads are set as the target environment.

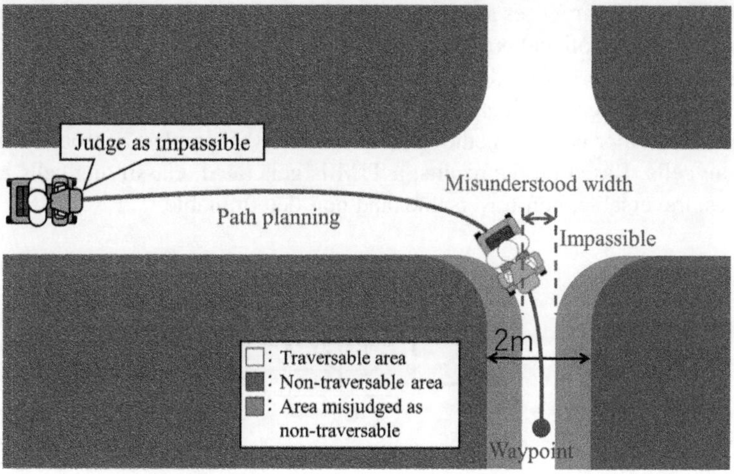

Fig. 8. Failure to extract traversable areas.

4 Proposed Method

This study proposes a shadow-robust path planning method with physical traversability judgement based on point cloud positional information, without the color information, which is susceptible to road surface brightness changes. This method uses the point clouds within a range where the data can be obtained with sufficient accuracy for autonomous navigation. It generates a Traversability Judgement Map (TJM) by creating a Digital Elevation Map (DEM) from the point clouds of a stereo camera and determines traversability for each cell in the DEM. Then, the method generates a local path by exploring paths based on the TJM.

4.1 Digital Elevation Map Generation

To refer to the road surface height around the PMV, a DEM is generated in a circular shape by dividing the road surface within a distance of d_{th} from the PMV into a mesh grid and recording the height information for each cell. Initially, among the point clouds acquired in each frame, those with a height less than the z_{th} are selected. Subsequently, they are transformed into the road surface coordinate system with the vehicle as the origin. The average height of the point cloud data within each cell of the DEM is stored and updated in real time. Herein, in this study, areas with low point cloud density are considered to be areas with uncertain traversability, and DEM records heights only for cells where at least n_{filter} or more points are obtained.

4.2 Traversability Judgement Map Generation

For each cell of the DEM, a physical traversability judgement is conducted to generate the TJM. This study proposes a traversability assessment method based on determining whether the tire can roll and proceed using height information [13]. This method examines the traversability in four directions in the target cell, as shown in Fig. 9. In reality, the direction in which the tires roll within the target area is not limited to these four directions. This approximate method was adopted as the simplest approach when using the square cells. Based on the results, a TJM is generated, classifying cells into three categories: traversable, non-traversable, and non-determinable.

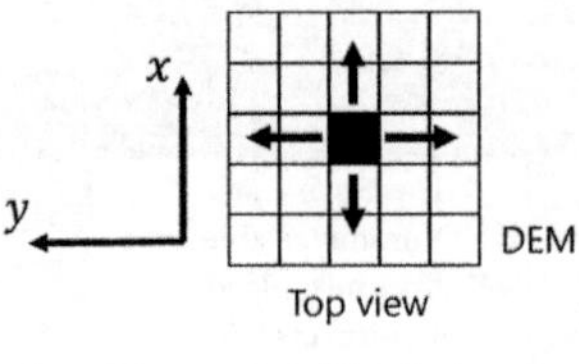

Fig. 9. The rolling direction of traversability judgement at each cell of a DEM.

Determine Contact Points. In one of the four directions, the tire is rolled, as shown in Fig. 10, and two points where the tire makes contact with the ground are calculated. In this process, the point p_0 of the cell being evaluated and the points $p_1, p_2, p_3, \ldots$, located within a distance of up to the tire diameter 2 r from p_0 along the rolling direction, where contact is possible, are sequentially examined, as illustrated in Fig. 11. If the height of p_n is neither much higher nor lower than p_0, compared to the threshold, a circle passing through the two points is considered. Then, the contact points are determined by checking whether any of the points $p_{n+1}, p_{n+2}, \ldots$ lie inside or above this circle. This process is repeated until two contact points are determined, labeling each point as P and P', respectively.

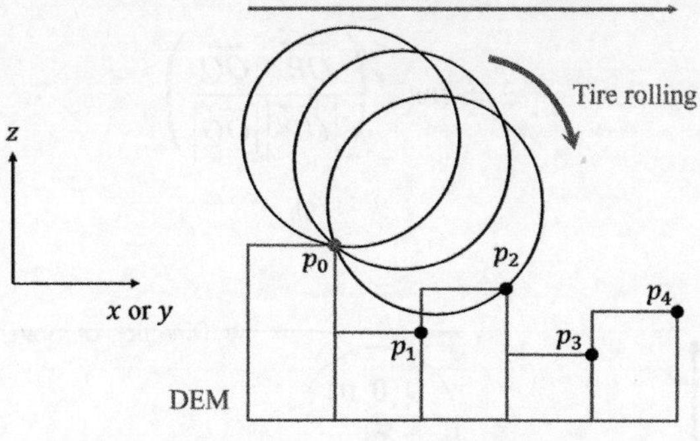

Fig. 10. Schematic diagram of contact points determination.

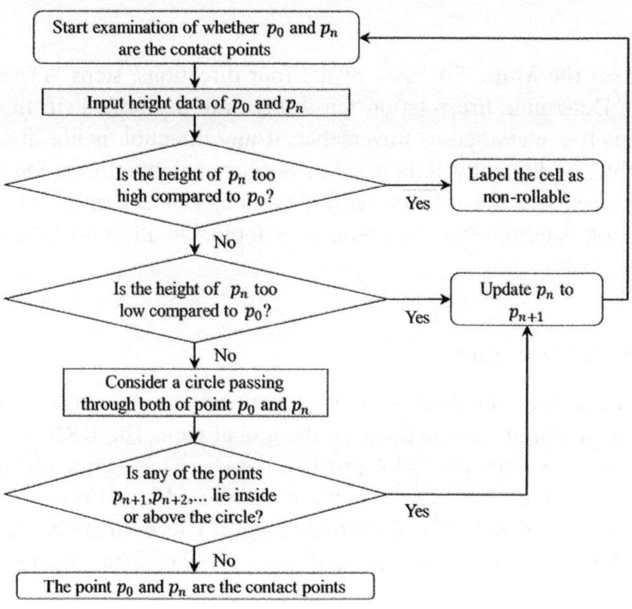

Fig. 11. Flowchart of contact points determination.

Determine Tire Rotation Feasibility. As shown in Fig. 12, with two points P and P' placed as described, the center of the tire is set as the origin O, and the point of the tire directly below point O in the vertical direction is set as Q. The angle θ formed by OP' and OQ is calculated using Eq. 4. Then, θ_{th} is compared to a threshold value θ_{th}. If it satisfies Eq. 5, the direction is classified as rollable; otherwise, it is classified as non-rollable.

$$\theta = \cos^{-1}\left(\frac{\overrightarrow{OP'} \cdot \overrightarrow{OQ}}{\left|\overrightarrow{OP'}\right|\left|\overrightarrow{OQ}\right|}\right) \tag{4}$$

$$\theta < \theta_{th} \tag{5}$$

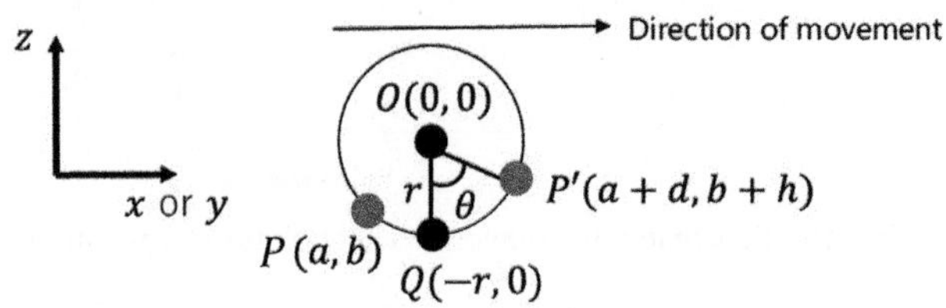

Fig. 12. Parameters for determination of tire rotation feasibility.

Label Cells on the Map. For each of the four directions, steps "Determine contact points" and "Determine tire rotation feasibility" are performed. If all directions are rollable, the cell is classified as traversable; if any direction is not, it is classified as non-traversable. Additionally, if there are cells where height information is not recorded during this process and tire rotation feasibility cannot be determined, the target cell is classified as non-determinable. This process is applied to all cells of the DEM to create a TJM.

4.3 Local Path Generation

Similarly to the existing method [4], in local path planning, a global target point is set towards the direction of the waypoint on the global path. The DRM is also generated within a range of d_{th} from the PMV, just like the DEM. Subsequently, paths from the current location to the global target point are evaluated based on the driving recommendation degree on the DRM and the route length. This evaluation aims to generate a path passing through regions with shorter distances to the global target point and higher driving recommendation degrees.

In the existing method, cells in the DRM with driving recommendation degree below the threshold p_{th} were designated as non-path-search areas. In contrast, in this proposed method, cells classified as non-traversable in the TJM were considered non-path-search areas. This setting realizes autonomous navigation with robust traversability judgement in the presence of changes in road surface brightness.

5 Validation of Proposed Method

To evaluate the physical traversability determination based on point cloud positional information in environments with significant road surface brightness changes, the proposed method is compared with the existing method that determines traversability based on image recognition. The proposed method is verified whether it can determine road surface traversability more robustly against the brightness changes and generate a stable path compared to the existing method. Autonomous navigation was conducted in environments with shadows using both methods to examine the impact of surface brightness changes on navigation, and the effectiveness of the proposed method.

5.1 Experimental Method

The experimental vehicle described in Sect. 3 was used. Autonomous navigation experiments involving right and left turns and straight-through movement were conducted at outdoor intersections under sunny conditions where shadows were present, using the existing method [4] and the proposed method. The intersection has the shape shown in Fig. 13, and the vehicle starts from the origin of the road surface coordinate system. The global target points were set as (20, −25) for the right turn, (20, 20) for the left turn, and (40, 0) for the straight-through movement. The vehicle was driven until it crossed the goal line. The environment consisted of three intersections with different surrounding environments and shadow shapes, resulting in nine conditions for combinations of intersections and destinations. The DEM, TJM, and DRM parameters were set as shown in Table 2. In the proposed method, considering the point cloud features, d_{th} was set to 6 m. Additionally, experiments were conducted with d_{th} = 8 m and d_{th} = 10 m to examine the effect of data errors on autonomous navigation due to farther point clouds.

The criterion for successful autonomous navigation was defined as the PMV passing the goal line in the intended direction without contacting the curb. The success rates of both methods were compared over the nine trials with a fixed d_{th}. To minimize the impact of time-dependent shadow variations, autonomous navigation using both the existing and proposed method under identical conditions was performed consecutively.

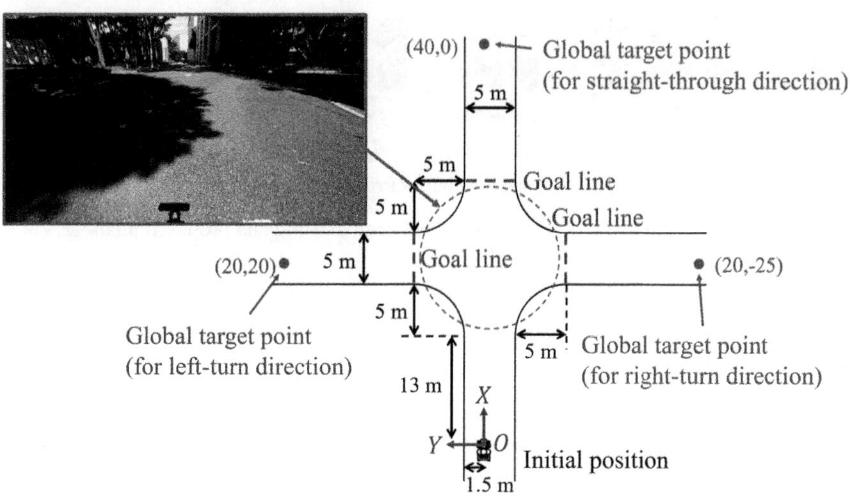

Fig. 13. Overview of experimental intersection.

Table 2. Parameters for DEM, TJM, and DRM generation.

Parameter	Value
Grid size	0.1×0.1 m
d_{th}	6,8 or 10 m
z_{th}	0.075 m
θ_{th}	40°
n_{filter}	100

5.2 Experimental Results

The existing method detected a non-traversable area in the shadowed region, which is traversable, failing to pass through. In contrast, the area was judged as passable when path planning was performed using the proposed method for the same scenario. Consequently, while the existing method failed to generate a path toward the destination, leading to sharp turns and failure in autonomous navigation, the proposed method successfully generates a path toward the destination in some cases. Additionally, since the proposed method recognizes curbs as non-traversable, it prevents the PMV from entering non-traversable areas. As shown in Fig. 14, the success rate of the proposed method is significantly higher compared to the existing method for all conditions of d_{th}, achieving more robust autonomous navigation.

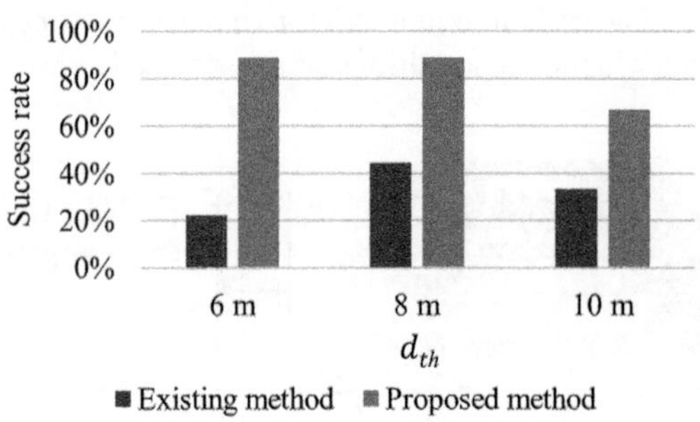

Fig. 14. Comparison of success rates between existing and proposed methods.

5.3 Discussion

The results indicate that a shadow-robust traversability judgement can be achieved based on the point cloud positional information without the color information, even in environments where significant road surface brightness variations adversely affect semantic segmentation. Additionally, adjusting the map size can achieve more robust traversability judgement and autonomous navigation. However, there was an instance where the proposed method failed in autonomous navigation even under the condition of $d_{th} = 6$

m. In this case, shortly after the PMV started to travel, the system incorrectly identified a non-traversable area, where a curb is present, as traversable and generated a path leading into that area, as shown by the red circle in Fig. 15 (left). Although a 14 cm curb was present, the DEM only detected a height difference of approximately 5 cm. This suggests that the point cloud data obtained by the stereo camera is affected by various factors, including the pixel coordinates on the image, the PMV's speed, acceleration, etc., in addition to the characteristics identified in Sect. 3. Although the non-traversable area was recognized afterward, there was not enough time to update the path and avoid the area based on the updated path.

When path planning is performed with $d_{th} = 8$ m in the same moment, as shown in Fig. 15 (right), a non-traversable area is detected in the outer region marked by the yellow circle, allowing the PMV to move forward toward the intersection and generate a path for a right turn. This suggests that expanding the range for traversability judgement can prevent this failure. However, as mentioned in the previous section, the impact of errors of distant point clouds becomes more significant. Therefore, with the current sensor accuracy, it is considered challenging to eliminate areas where traversability is misjudged within the TJM, regardless of the d_{th}. Accordingly, a strategy is required to prevent the failure due to the areas of uncertain traversability, such as generating paths that would allow enough time to avoid areas initially uncertain but later recognized as non-traversable.

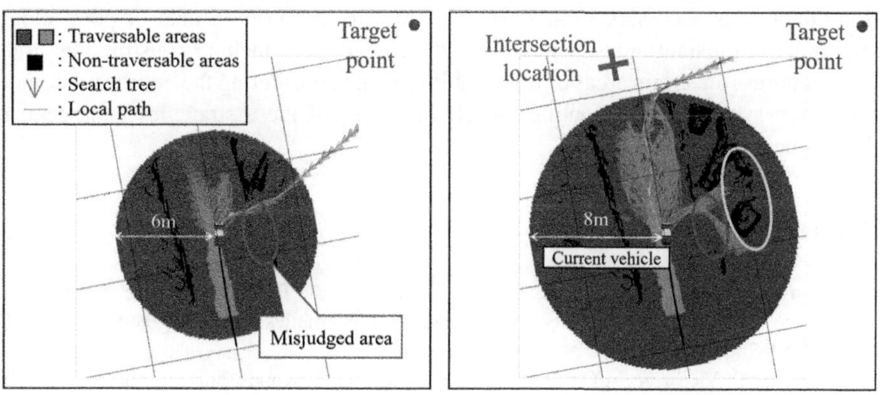

Fig. 15. Path planning scenes in left turning with the smaller DEM (left) and the larger DEM (right).

6 Conclusions

This study aimed to develop a robust local path planning method for autonomous PMV navigation in environments with road surface brightness changes due to shadows. To this end, we focused on determining physical traversability based on 3D point cloud positional information for an existing autonomous navigation system using a stereo camera. The point cloud features in environments with road surface brightness changes were analyzed, and a path planning method considering the features to judge road surface traversability was proposed. Autonomous navigation using the proposed method was performed on flat and wide roads, and it was confirmed that the method improves robustness against road surface brightness changes, which affect the semantic segmentation, demonstrating its effectiveness. As a result of the above, the following findings were obtained.

- The stereo camera can acquire point cloud data from the road surface with a high acquisition rate and accuracy, regardless of the bright changes caused by shadows.
- For road surfaces covered by shadows that are deemed non-traversable by semantic segmentation, traversability judgement based on the point cloud information without color information can identify them as traversable.
- Traversability judgement based on the point clouds can detect height differences, such as curbs, preventing the PMV from entering non-traversable.

In this study, autonomous navigation was conducted within a limited scope of right turns, left turns, and straight movements at intersections to evaluate local path planning using the proposed method. However, for social implementation, it is necessary to conduct validation experiments in large-scale environments, including scenarios with varying weather conditions and road geometries, considering global path planning and motion planning. In addition, for autonomous navigation especially on narrow, uneven roads or to achieve stable autonomous navigation that considers a wider range of point cloud data, it is necessary to address the errors in the position data of point clouds acquired from distant areas. Therefore, future challenges include constructing strategies to address uncertain areas of traversability while considering the entire autonomous navigation system and evaluating the effectiveness of these strategies in large-scale environments.

References

1. Chong, Z.J., et al.: Autonomous personal vehicle for the first and last-mile transportation services. In: IEEE 5th International Conference on Cybernetics and Intelligent Systems (CIS), pp. 253–260 (2011)
2. Neto, A.M., Victorino, A.C., Fantoni, I., Zampieri, D.E.: Robust horizon finding algorithm for real-time autonomous navigation based on monocular vision. In: 14th International IEEE Conference on Intelligent Transportation Systems (ITSC), pp. 532–537 (2011)
3. Yu, C., Cherfaoui, V., Bonnifait, P.: Semantic evidential lane grids with prior maps for autonomous navigation. In: IEEE 19th International Conference on Intelligent Transportation Systems (ITSC), pp. 1875–1881 (2016)
4. Onozuka, Y., Matsumi, R., Shino, M.: Autonomous mobile robot navigation independent of road boundary using driving recommendation map. In: IEEE/RSJ International Conference on Intelligent Robots and Systems (IROS), pp. 4501–4508 (2021)
5. Caltagirone, L., Bellone, M., Svensson, L., Wahde, M.: LIDAR-based driving path generation using fully convolutional neural networks. In: IEEE 20th International Conference on Intelligent Transportation Systems (ITSC), pp. 1–6 (2017)
6. Jiao, J., et al.: Real-time metric-semantic mapping for autonomous navigation in outdoor environments. IEEE Trans. Autom. Sci. Eng. (2024)

7. Hayashi, K., Nakamichi, H., Yoshitake, H., Shino, M.: Shadow-robust semantic segmentation for autonomous navigation in walking space. In: IEEE/SICE International Symposium on System Integration (SII), pp. 965–971 (2024)
8. Le, H., Samaras, D.: Shadow removal via shadow image decomposition. In: IEEE/CVF International Conference on Computer Vision (ICCV), pp. 8577–8586 (2019)
9. Wang, J., Li, X., Yang, J.: Stacked conditional generative adversarial networks for jointly learning shadow detection and shadow removal. In: IEEE/CVF Conference on Computer Vision and Pattern Recognition, pp. 1788–1797 (2018)
10. Onozuka, Y., Matsumi, R., Shino, M.: Weakly-supervised recommended traversable area segmentation using automatically labeled images for autonomous driving in pedestrian environment with no edges. Sensors **21**(2), 437 (2021)
11. Zhou, W., Berrio, J.S., Worrall, S., Nebot, E.: Automated evaluation of semantic segmentation robustness for autonomous driving. IEEE Trans. Intell. Transp. Syst. **21**(5), 1951–1963 (2020)
12. Dickmann, J., et al.: Automotive radar: the key technology for autonomous driving: From detection and ranging to environmental understanding. In: IEEE Radar Conference (RadarConf), pp. 1–6 (2016)
13. Kahn, G., Abbeel, P., Levine, S.: BADGR: an autonomous self-supervised learning-based navigation system. IEEE Robot.Autom. Lett. **6**(2), 1312–1319 (2021)
14. Shino, M., Ota, S., Ishikawa, T., Matsumi, R.: Driving assistance method for mobility scooters based on determining traversable area considering characteristics of road surface information. In: The Transportation and Logistics Conference, vol. 26, p. 1203 (2017)
15. Imai, Y., Hayashi, R., Matsumi, R.: Detection of traversable area for personal mobility vehicles in pedestrian environment using a stereo camera. In: The Proceedings of JSME Annual Conference on Robotics and Mechatronics (Robomech), vol. 2015, p. 1A1-H02 (2015)

Error Modification of Robot Motion Generation by LLM Based on Parts Function and Physical Features of Robot

Takahiro Suzuki(✉) and Manabu Hashimoto

Chukyo University, Yagoto-honmachi 101-2, Showa-ku, Nagoya, Aichi, Japan
{suzuki,mana}@isl.sist.chukyo-u.ac.jp

Abstract. We propose a method for generating robot motions based on simple commands given by humans. Large language models (LLMs) are generic models that can be used to generate robot motion procedures for various tasks. However, they often output errors, such as specifying inappropriate procedures or tools, or they select tools that are difficult for robots to grasp. For example, the LLM suggests using a spoon or a whisk when scooping hot water. In this study, we address these problems by setting the function of tools, such as "scoop" or "stir," and by utilizing the robot's physical features. We also generate a robot motion trajectory based on a motion template. A comparison between the proposed method and a method that does not take into account the physical features of the robot confirmed that our method had a higher task success rate and was able to select tools that were easier for the robot to operate.

Keywords: Error modification · Robot motion generation · LLM · Part function · Physical features of robot

1 Introduction

Life-support robots are expected to execute actions based on simple commands such as "Please make a hot coffee." To develop such robots, it is necessary to generate motion procedures such as "1. Put coffee powder into the cup," "2. Add hot water," and "3. Stir" from instructions given by the user. It is also necessary to determine the appropriate tools and methods for executing each task.

Zhou et al. proposed a method for tool recognition [1], and various other methods have been developed for determining how to use the tools [2,3]. Several studies have examined how to determine which motion procedures and tools to use, many of them taking advantage of the recent rapid advancements in large language models (LLMs) [4,5]. However, the motion procedures and tools generated by LLMs are sometimes logically incorrect or inconsistent with the actual usage scene [6–8]. To resolve this issue, Suzuki et al. came up with a method to evaluate the appropriateness of the motion procedures and tools generated by LLMs and then modify them if necessary [9]. However, LLMs have difficulty considering the physical constraints of robots [7]. Therefore, it is necessary to modify the tool while considering this constraint.

J. Röning and J. Filipe (Eds.): ROBOVIS 2025, CCIS 2629, pp. 130–147, 2026.
https://doi.org/10.1007/978-3-032-00986-9_10

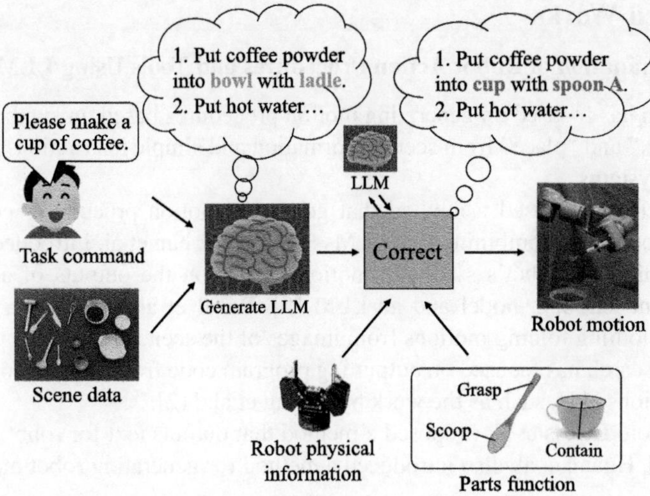

Fig. 1. Outline of proposed method for generating robot motion trajectory from task command. Candidates for motion procedures and tools are generated by LLM. Our method can detect and modify errors in the motion procedures and tools based on the parts function and physical information of robot. Finally, robot motion is generated on the basis of the motion procedures and tools.

Our purpose in this study is to detect and modify errors in the motion procedures and tools generated by LLMs. In addition, we aim to generate robot motion trajectories for executing tasks using the specified procedures and tools (Fig. 1).

LLMs do not always determine appropriate motion procedures and tools. For example, an LLM might suggest a "natsume," a tea caddy used in traditional Japanese tea ceremony, to scoop coffee powder, or propose pouring it into a bowl. Furthermore, when there are multiple tools of the same type in a scene, the LLM may not select the tool that is easiest for the robot to operate. In our method, these erroneous outputs from LLMs are detected and modified to ensure the appropriate procedures and tools.

Motion procedure and tool errors are detected and modified by functional constraints. For selecting tools that are easier for the robot to operate, each tool is evaluated based on factors such as ease of grasping and ease of task execution. The tool is then modified by considering both the evaluation results and the appropriateness suggested by the LLM.

The contributions of this research are as follows.

1. We proposed a method that enables the generation of robot motions from simple language instructions.
2. The proposed method allows for the detection and modification of errors in robot motions generated by LLMs.
3. We demonstrate the necessity of modifying tools while considering the robot's physical features.

2 Related Works

2.1 Determination of Robot Action Procedures and Tools Using LLM

Past research has focused on generating motion procedures based on symbolic motions such as "pick" and "place" from scene information and simple instructions provided by humans or systems.

Huang et al. proposed a method that generates motion procedures composed of symbolic motions by combining two LLMs [4], and Brohan et al. introduced a method for determining the robot's symbolic motions based on the outputs of a pre-trained reinforcement learning model and an LLM [5]. Raval et al. proposed a method for generating clothing folding motions from images of the scene [10].

Other research has focused on outputting program code from scene information and task instructions [11], such as the work by Huang et al. [12].

In addition, Driess et al. proposed a method that outputs text for robot motion procedures [13]. Huang et al. also introduced a method for generating robot motion trajectories [8].

However, prior studies have reported that if the motion procedures or tools generated by the LLM contain errors, there is a risk of executing tasks incorrectly [6–8]. In other words, the robot may not be able to execute motions in accordance with the task instructions given by the user. Therefore, it is necessary to verify whether the motion procedures and tools output by the LLM contain errors, and if they do, to modify them.

2.2 Modification of Robot Action Generated by LLM

There are various methods for modifying errors in the motion generation results produced by LLMs.

Lin et al. proposed a method that evaluates the correctness and feasibility of generated procedures before the robot executes them, and modifies them when the feasibility is deemed low [14]. Park et al. introduced a technique for LLMs to determine whether instructions from users are feasible, and if not, to modify the robot's motions by contacting a human [15]. In a related study, Abugurain et al. proposed a method for modifying motions according to human preferences [16]. Song et al. proposed a method for robot interaction with an LLM during task execution to modify its motions [17]. Shirai et al. developed a method [6] for outputting robot motion plans in a PDDL format [18, 19], which involves inputting the generated motion plans into a motion planner. If an error occurs during motion generation, the system provide feedback on the error message to the LLM. It allowing for the modification of the robot motion plan. Zhi et al. proposed a method that involves inputting images when errors occur into the LLM, resulting in the output of improved program code [20].

However, these methods do not modify motion procedures and tools while considering the physical features of the robot. Generally, some tools are easy for a robot to grasp or operate, while others are more difficult. For example, tools that have a significant overlapping area with the robot's hand, or where the surfaces between the hand and tool are in close contact, are likely easier to grasp. Thus, it is essential to consider the physical features of the robot when generating motion procedures and tools. Unfortunately, LLMs are unable to do this.

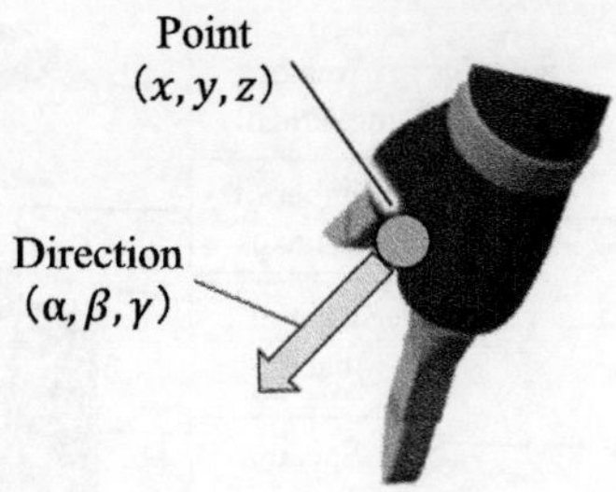

Fig. 2. Position and direction of robot. A robot motion trajectory contains multiple points, each consisting of x, y, and z, which indicate the position in 3D space, and α, β, and γ, which are the grasping directions.

In this study, we aim to detect and modify errors in the motion procedures and tools generated by LLMs while taking the physical features of the robot into account.

3 Problem Formulation

3.1 Definition

Given RGB image and point cloud data of a scene, a string of simple instructions (e.g., meal name), a pre-defined motion template, point cloud data of the robot's hand, and the goal is to generate which indicate the position and direction in 3D space. A robot motion trajectory contains multiple points, each consisting of x, y, and z, which indicate the position in 3D space, and α, β, and γ, which are the grasping directions (Fig. 2). The system uses the point cloud of the gripper as input data in order to facilitate the implementation of the proposed method.

3.2 Assumptions

The following assumptions are taken in this study.

1. The task is making a meal.
2. Symbol motions such as "put" and "stir" that the robot can execute, along with their functional constraints, are set as motion templates.
3. Tools are stably placed, and they do not touch each other.
4. The correspondence between the ingredients and the tools and the names of the tools is known
5. The robot has parallel two fingers.

4 Physical Features of Robot

When automating tasks using robots, motions performed by humans are not always appropriate for robots. For example, when humans handle tools, they often grasp parts with complex shapes to ensure stability. However, since a robot assumed in this method

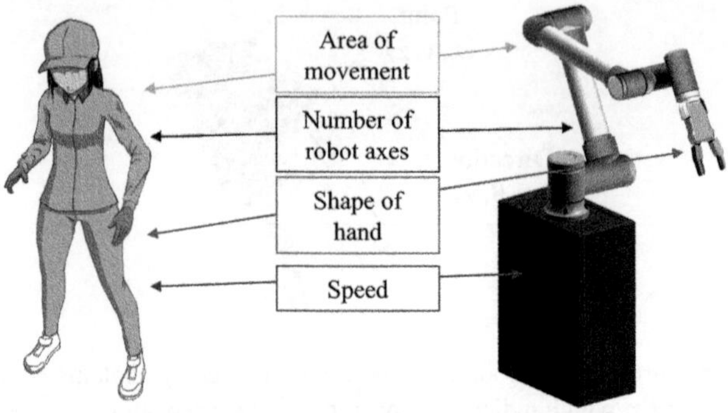

Fig. 3. Examples of physical feature differences between humans and robots. Due to this difference in physical features, the optimal motion for a human is not necessarily the same for a robot. This means that the motions and robot parameters (such as grasping point) must be determined by taking into account the physical features of the robot.

has parallel two-finger grippers, it often grasps parts with flat surfaces. Figure 3 shows examples of the physical feature differences between humans and robots. Since robots have their own unique physical characteristics, directly transferring human motions to robots, or generating robot motions and parameters based on human subjectivity, is usually inappropriate [21]. Therefore, robot motions must be generated while taking consideration of the robot's physical features.

For these reasons, it is also necessary to modify the tools to those that are easier for the robot to operate (i.e., tools that consider the robot's physical features). Among the various physical features of robots, we focus on hand shape in this study, as it directly contacts the tools and is closely related to the robot's motions.

5 Method

5.1 Overview of Proposed Method

The flow of the proposed method is shown in Fig. 4. We use GPT-4 (referred to as GPT) as the LLM.

First, motion procedure and candidate tools are determined by GPT from the tool information and the given commands (Generate procedure, Determine tool). However, these candidates may include incorrect procedures or tools. Next, the system checks for errors (Check tool), and if any are detected, it modifies them to appropriate tools. At this stage, however, there is no guarantee that the selected tools are optimal or easy for the robot to operate. To address this, the system uses the robot's physical features and information about the tools generated by GPT to select tools that are easier for the robot to operate (Modify optimal tool). In addition, the overall procedure and tool are evaluated, and if they are judged inappropriate, the LLM modifies them (Check overall optimality, Modify procedures and tools). Finally, the motion trajectory of the robot is generated from the language-level procedure and tool information (Generate robot trajectory).

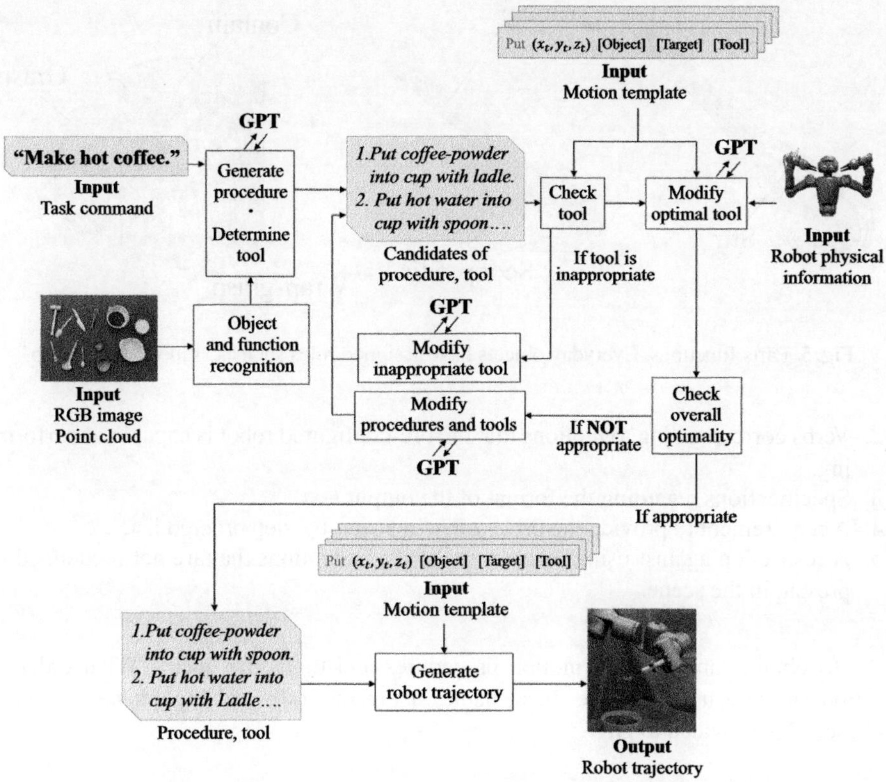

Fig. 4. Flow of proposed method. Inputs are task command, RGB image, point cloud data, robot's physical information (point cloud data of hand), and motion template. Output is robot motion trajectory. The part marked "GPT" is the module that interacts with the GPT.

5.2 Generating Candidates for Robot Motion

In this module, a candidate set of motion procedures and tools is generated (Generate procedure, Determine tool). The motion procedure is composed of pre-defined symbol motions such as "put" and "stir" that the robot can execute. In this study, the "put" motion is the action of scooping the ingredient and pouring it into a other tool.

First, the names of the tools in the scene are recognized from an RGB image using an object recognition method [22] (Object recognition). The point cloud is segmented into functional labels using a deep learning model [23] (Function recognition). Details of the functional information are provided in the next section.

Next, the candidates of motion procedures and tools are generated from the scene information using GPT. GPT outputs an answer in the form of text when provided with a query. Prior knowledge can also be supplied to guide the generation of responses.

The following prior knowledge is supplied to GPT.

1. The names of ingredients and tools in the scene.

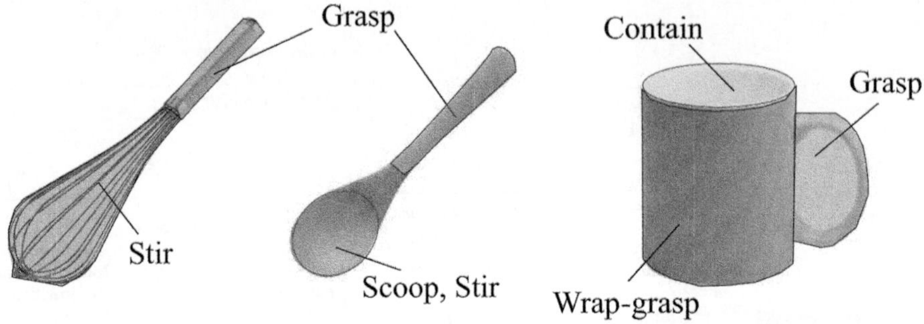

Fig. 5. Parts functions. Everyday objects have assigned roles such as "scoop" and "grasp."

2. Verbs corresponding to motions that the pre-configured robot is capable of performing.
3. Specifications regarding the format of the output text.
4. A requirement to provide the procedures in a step-by-step ordered list.
5. A restriction against using ingredients, tools, or motions that are not predefined or present in the scene.

To obtain candidates of motion procedures and tools, the query "What order of action can you take to make (meal name) using the tools and ingredients you have chosen?" is provided to GPT.

5.3 Parts Function and Motion Template

Parts Function. Following the definition by Myer et al. [24], everyday objects have assigned roles such as "scoop" and "grasp." These roles are referred to as functions. Figure 5 shows an example of the functions of a whisk, spoon, and cup.

For example, when using a whisk to stir, the user often mixes the ingredients with the stir function while grasping the whisk with the grasp function. This highlights the fact that tools utilized to accomplish a motion must have specific functionalities. In other words, there are strong constraints between function and motion. There are also strong constraints between tool and function, such as "the spoon has a scoop and contain function." The proposed method judges the appropriateness of tools based on the constraints between function, motion, and tool. If the tool is inappropriate, it modifies to the appropriate tool.

Motion Template. In this study, we improve the motion template originally proposed by Tsusaka et al. [25] Fig. 6 shows the improved motion template. It maps the name of a motion to the trajectory of the motion in a certain region of function corresponding to that motion. In the case of the "put" motion such as scooping and pouring a liquid into another container, the motion can be completed when the region of the scoop function moves in a certain way, regardless of the type of tool. In addition, the positional relationship between the grasp and scoop function is constant. In other words, the motion trajectory of the robot hand can be generated from the motion of the scoop function.

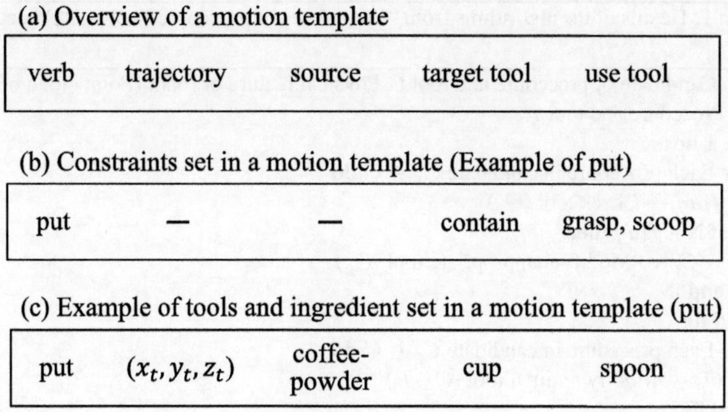

Fig. 6. Motion template, which corresponds to a verb indicating the motion, motion trajectory, and functional constraint of each tool.

In this study, we use the common motion trajectory model [26] as the motion trajectory set in the motion template.

However, note that a "put" motion cannot be completed with only a motion name and a motion trajectory. Information on "which ingredient to scoop (source ingredient)", "where to pour the scooped ingredient (target tool)", and "which tool to use (use tool)" is necessary. Therefore, the source, target tool, and use tool terms are added to the motion template.

Furthermore, the tools must satisfy functional constraints. In the case of a "put" motion, the target tool must be able to contain ingredients. The use tool must have a grasp function that can be grasped by the robot and a scoop function for scooping ingredients. Thus, the tools set as target tool and use tool have functional constraints. Therefore, we set functional constraints for the target tool and use tool for each motion template.

5.4 Modification of Motion Procedures and Tools

Our method checks the appropriateness of the motion procedure and tools, and modifies them if they are inappropriate. In addition, it modifies the tool to make it easier to operate. The procedure is shown in Algorithm 1. This is the details of the algorithms from "Candidates of procedure, tool" to "Procedure, tool" in Fig. 4.

Check Tool. First, check the tool for each procedure(C_p) in C. GPT judges whether the tools set as target tool and use tool satisfy the functional constraints according to the motion template. The function takes C_p as input and outputs $True$ if the tool is appropriate and $False$ if it is inappropriate.

Modify Inappropriate Tool. If the output of the Check tool is $False$, GPT extracts tools that satisfy the constraints, and selects an appropriate tool from among them.

Algorithm 1: Details of the algorithms from "Candidates of procedure, tool" to "Procedure, tool" in Fig. 4.

Require: Candidate of procedure and tool C Physical feature of robot (Point cloud of hand) R
Ensure: Procedure and tool P

while 1 **do**
  for Each procedure in candidate $C_p \in C$ **do**
    $flag \leftarrow$ Check tool (C_p)
    if Not $flag$ **then**
      $C_p \leftarrow$ Modify inappropriate tool (C_p)
    end if
  end for
  for Each procedure in candidate $C_p \in C$ **do**
    $C_p \leftarrow$ Modify optimal tool (C_p, R)
  end for
  $flag \leftarrow$ Check overall optimality (C)
  if $flag$ **then**
    break
  end if
  $C \leftarrow$ Modify procedures and tools (C)
end while
$P \leftarrow C$

Modify Optimal Tool. Using the physical feature and tool information, the tool of C_p is modified to one that is suitable for the task and easy for the robot to operate.

Since the target tool is not operated by the robot, it is not necessary to consider the physical features of the robot. Therefore, GPT is presented with all tools that satisfy the functional constraints. GPT selects the appropriate tool from among them.

In contrast, since the use tool is operated by the robot, it is necessary to consider the physical features. The proposed method enumerates all tools t in the scene that satisfy the functional constraints. Then, each tool t_n is evaluated using Eq. 1 to determine the tool T with the minimum output value. T is then set as the use tool. The lowest value output by Eq. 1 means that t_n is a tool that is easy for the robot to operate and appropriate for the operation.

$$T = \underset{t_n}{\operatorname{argmin}}\{w_1 Gr(t_n) + w_2 Rc(t_n) + w_3 Ra(t_n) + w_4 Rf(t_n)\} \tag{1}$$

Here, w1, w2, w3, and w4 denote weight, and $Gr(t_n)$ denotes the priority value of a use tool for a particular motion. As an example, take spoons A, B, and C, ladle A, a coffee powder brush, and a cup in the scene, where the motion is "put" (scoop and pour into another container). The brush is excluded in advance because it does not satisfy the functional constraints. If the GPT prioritizes as "spoon, ladle", the output is 1.0 if t_n is spoon A, B or C, and 2.0 if t_n is ladle A.

$Rc(t_n)$, $Ra(t_n)$, and $Rf(t_n)$ denote values for the physical features of the robot. These values are calculated from the grasping point and direction of each tool and from the information of the robot hand, using designated criteria for each term. $Rc(t_n)$,

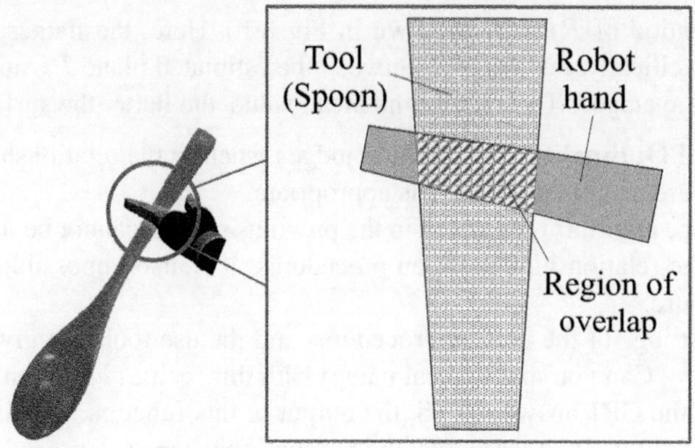

Fig. 7. $Rc(t_n)$ calculation method.

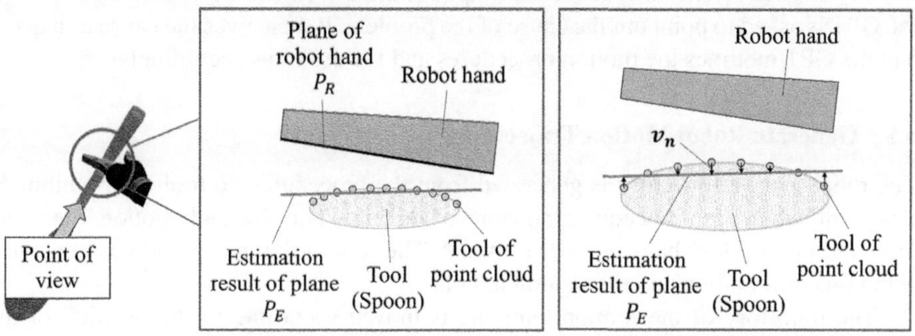

(a) R_a (b) R_f

Fig. 8. (a) $Ra(t_n)$ and (b) $Rf(t_n)$ calculation methods.

$Ra(t_n)$, and $Rf(t_n)$ output the ranking of the tools in order of their value. Our method for estimating the grasping point and direction is the same as Ando et al.'s [26].

The calculation method is designed based on the idea that the larger the overlap area between the robot hand and the tool, the easier it is to grasp the tool (higher possibility of grasping). The calculation method of $Rc(t_n)$ is shown in Fig. 7. Here, the number of points in the overlap region is counted.

Next, the calculation method for $Ra(t_n)$ is designed based on the idea that the greater the adherence of the robot hand to the tool, the less likely the tool is to move when the robot grasps it.

The calculation of $Ra(t_n)$ is shown in Fig. 8(a). The method is subject to the condition that the robot hand has two parallel fingers. Therefore, the more parallel the robot hand is to the tool, the less likely the tool is to move when the robot grasps it. We calculate the parallelism between the plane P_R of the robot hand and the tool P_E.

The cost value of $Rf(t_n)$ is designed based on the idea that the more planar the tool surface is, the greater the contact surface between the robot hand and the part, and thus the more stable the motion.

The calculation of $Rf(t_n)$ is shown in Fig. 8(b). Here, the flatness of the tool is calculated. Specifically, the distance between the estimated plane P_E and each point is calculated and averaged. The smaller the mean value, the flatter the surface of the tool.

Check Overall Optimality. This module judges whether the relationship between the overall procedure and the use tool C is appropriate.

Note that the algorithm discussed in the previous section cannot be modified to take into account the relationships between procedures. It is also impossible to modify the motion procedure.

First, the strings of the motion procedures and the use tools are given to the GPT. Then, the query "Can you make (meal name) with this recipe?" is given and an answer is obtained. If the GPT answers YES, the output of this function is $True$. It then exits from the infinite loop. In other words, the motions between each procedure and the use tools are appropriate. If the GPT answers NO, the output of this function is $False$.

Modify Procedures and Tools. If the output of the Check overall optimality is $False$, the GPT is asked to point out the cause of the problem. It then gives the cause as a query and the GPT modifies the motion procedures and the use tools accordingly.

5.5 Generate Robot Motion Trajectory

The robot motion trajectory is generated from the procedure and tool information. At this point, the motion procedure, the name of the ingredient for each motion, the target tool, and the use tool have been determined. The robot motion trajectory is generated using this information and the motion template.

The trajectory of the motion template is moved according to the position of the tool for each motion. Finally, the trajectories are concatenated according to the motion procedure. In other words, the concatenated motion trajectories become a robot motion trajectory for making a specific meal.

6 Experiment

6.1 Determining the Motion Procedure and Tool Using Virtual Data

Setup. We experimentally investigated whether it is possible to determine appropriate motion procedures and use tools from scene information and simple instruction given by a user.

In this experiment, we assumed that the perceptions and functions of the tools and the ingredients were already known. The tools were a spoon, natsume (Japanese tea caddy), chawan(Japanese cup), whisk, chagama(Japanese pot), ladle, cup, plate, bowl, hammer, knife, rice scoop, pot, rice cooker, and cutting board. The ingredients were matcha powder ($\subset$natsume, meaning that matcha powder is contained in the natsume), hot water ($\subset$chagama, pot), water ($\subset$bowl), curry roux ($\subset$pot), salt ($\subset$bowl), sugar ($\subset$bowl), coffee powder ($\subset$bowl), rice ($\subset$rice-cooker), pineapple ($\subset$cutting-board), chocolate ($\subset$bowl), miso ($\subset$bowl), and dried vegetables ($\subset$bowl). The functions were cut, contain, scoop, grasp, wrap-grasp, stir, pound, paint, and none. The motion templates were put, stir, pound, and cut. The "put" motion is the action of scooping the ingredient and pouring it into a other tool.

The instructions given by the user were tasks to make matcha, coffee, curry rice, and instant miso soup. Fifty trials were conducted for each task and the results were evaluated by a human. Success was judged if the output motion procedure and the use tools satisfied all of the following elements.

- Common criteria for all tasks
  1. The target tool in the motions in criteria 1 and 2 of each task must be the same tool.
- Task of making matcha
  1. "Put matcha powder into (chawan or cup) with spoon" must be included in the procedure.
  2. "Put hot water into (chawan or cup) with ladle" must be included in the procedure.
  3. After steps 1 and 2, the procedure must include stirring the matcha powder or hot water with a whisk or spoon.
  4. The procedure must not include the addition of ingredients other than matcha powder, hot water, and sugar to the target tool of steps 1 and 2.
- Task of making coffee
  1. "Put coffee powder into (chawan or cup) with spoon" must be included in the procedure.
  2. "Put hot water into (chawan or cup) with ladle" must be included in the procedure.
  3. After steps 1 and 2, the procedure must include stirring the coffee powder or hot water with a spoon.
  4. The procedure must not include the addition of ingredients other than coffee powder, hot water, and sugar to the target tool of steps 1 and 2.
- Task of making curry
  1. "Put curry roux into (chawan or plate) with ladle" must be included in the procedure.
  2. "Put cooked rice into (chawan or plate) with rice scoop" must be included in the procedure.
  3. The procedure must not include the addition of ingredients other than rice and curry roux to the target tool of steps 1 and 2.
- Task of making miso soup
  1. "Put miso into (chawan or cup) with (ladle or spoon)" must be included in the procedure.
  2. "Put hot water into (chawan or cup) with ladle" must be included in the procedure.
  3. After steps 1 and 2, the procedure must include stirring the miso or hot water with a whisk or spoon.
  4. The procedure must not include the addition of ingredients other than miso, hot water, and dried vegetables to the target tool of steps 1 and 2.

Table 1. Successes (types A and B) and failures (types C and D) for each meal (50 trials per task).

Product	No. of successes		No. of failures		Success rate
	Type A	Type B	Type C	Type D	
Hot matcha	25	21	2	2	92%
Hot coffee	10	36	1	3	92%
Curry rice	0	40	0	10	80%
Miso soup	6	32	1	11	76%

Motion sequences and tools initially generated by GPT

```
1. Put instant coffee into cup with spoon.
2. Put sugar into cup with spoon.
3. Put hot water into cup with spoon.
4. Stir instant coffee in cup with spoon.
```

Check consistency and result of correcting tools (sequence 2)
・・・ Consistency: OK, correcting not required

```
INPUT:  Put sugar into cup with spoon.
  SYSTEM: Consistency of target tool -> OK
          (Cup has contain function)
  SYSTEM: Consistency of use tool -> OK
          (Spoon has scoop, stir, grasp functions)
  SYSTEM: You have selected the cup.
          Is it the best selection?
          Other tools with the same functionality
          are chawan, plate, bowl.
  GPT:    Cup.
  SYSTEM: You have selected the spoon.
          Is it the best selection?
          Other tools with the same functionality
          are ladle, rice-scoop.
  GPT:    Spoon.
OUTPUT: Put sugar into cup with spoon.
```

Check consistency and result of correcting tools (sequence 3)
・・・ Consistency: OK, correcting required

```
INPUT:  Put hot water into cup with spoon.
  SYSTEM: Consistency of target tool -> OK
          (Cup has contain function)
  SYSTEM: Consistency of use tool -> OK
          (Spoon has scoop, stir, grasp functions)
  SYSTEM: You have selected the cup.
          Is it the best selection?
          Other tools with the same functionality
          are chawan, plate, bowl.
  GPT:    You should put hot water in a cup.
  SYSTEM: You have selected the spoon.
          Is it the best selection?
          Other tools with the same functionality
          are ladle, rice-scoop.
  GPT:    Ladle.
OUTPUT:  Put hot water into cup with ladle.
```

Final output

```
1.  Put instant coffee into cup with spoon.
2.  Put sugar into cup with spoon.
3.  Put hot water into cup with ladle.
4.  Stir instant coffee in cup with spoon.
```

(a) Modify the tools

```
INPUT: 1. Put hot water into chagama with ladle.
       2. Put matcha powder into chawan with natsume.
       3. Stir hot water in chawan with whisk.

  # ~~Check and modify tools~~

  SYSTEM: 1. Put hot water into cup with ladle.
          2. Put matcha powder into chawan with spoon.
          3. Stir hot water in chawan with whisk.

  # ~~Check overall optimality~~
  SYSTEM: Can you make hot matcha with this recipe?
  GPT:    No.
  SYSTEM: Why can't you make hot matcha with this recipe?
  GPT:    The process of the recipe is incorrect. After
          putting the matcha powder in the chawan, you
          should then pour the hot water over it, not
          stirring the hot water alone in the chawan.
  SYSTEM: On the basis of those, please improve the
          procedure and tool for making hot matcha.
  GPT:    1. Put matcha powder into chawan with spoon.
          2. Put hot water into chawan with ladle.
          3. Stir matcha powder and hot water in chawan
             with whisk.

  # ~~Check and modify tools~~
  SYSTEM: 1. Put matcha powder into chawan with spoon.
          2. Put hot water into chawan with ladle.
          3. Stir matcha powder and hot water in chawan
             with whisk.

  # ~~Check overall optimality~~
  SYSTEM: Can you make hot matcha with this recipe?
  GPT:    YES.
```

(b) Check overall optimality

Fig. 9. Example of actual system and GPT response in the task of making matcha. (a) Modify the tools. In the blue box, the tool is modified to be the optimal tool for adding hot water. (b) Check overall optimality. In the blue box, the system asks GPT if the first procedure can be used to make matcha, and GPT responds that it cannot. Next, GPT points out the inappropriate part of the procedure. Finally, GPT improves the procedure and use tool candidates based on the items pointed out. (Color figure online)

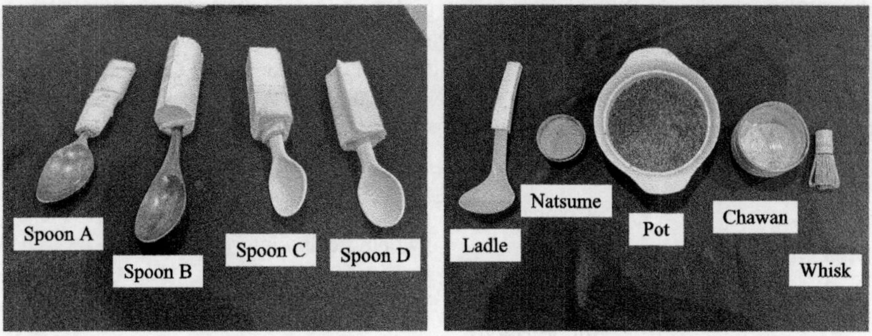

Fig. 10. Tools and ingredients used in experiment.

Results. The experimental results are shown in Table 1. If the GPT outputs the correct candidates of motion procedure and use tool, and if the procedure and tools are not modified by the proposed method, the result is classified as Type A. If the GPT outputs incorrect candidates and the procedure and tools are then modified, the result is classified as Type B. It is the added value of the proposed method. In other words, both types A and B can be judged as a success. If the output of the GPT is correct but the proposed method modifies it to the wrong procedure or tool, it is classified as type C. It is the error coming from the proposed method. If the output of the GPT is incorrect and it is not modified, it is classified as type D. Both types C and D are judged as a failure.

The success rate of determining the appropriate motion procedure and use tool was 85%. These results demonstrate that the proposed method was able to modify the candidates output by the GPT to the correct motion procedure and use tool. With the proposed method, the success count is the sum of types A and B. Without the proposed method, the success count is the sum of types A and C. When the results with and without the proposed method are compared, it can be confirmed that the proposed method is effective.

For the task of making miso soup, which had a particularly low success rate, the tools used to pour the ingredients were often very different. In this task, the GPT tended to initially determine a bowl as the pouring destination for miso and hot water, but the proposed method was able to modify the pouring destination to a cup or a chawan in many cases. However, only the pouring destination for miso was sometimes modified. GPTs are considered to be operational if specific ingredients are used, even if the pouring destination is different. Therefore, an error occurs.

Figure 9(a) shows an example of the actual response of the system and GPT when modifying the tools in the task of making matcha and (b) shows an example of the actual response of the system and GPT during the Check overall optimality process.

6.2 Task Execution by Actual Robot

Setup. Next, we experimentally investigated whether a robot could execute a task according to the instructions. In this case, note that it is also necessary to take into account the physical features of the robot.

Table 2. Success rate with different spoons (ten trials per column). With the comparison method, the robot succeeded in the task more often when spoon A was used, but less often with the other spoons. This means that spoon A is considered an easier tool for the robot to operate. The proposed method had the same number of successes with spoon A, and it selected spoon A more often. In other words, the proposed method was able to select a tool that is easy for the robot to operate.

Method	Comparison method (w/o physicality information)				Proposed method (w/ physicality information)
Type of spoon	A	B	C	D	A, B, C, D
No. of successes	8	3	1	3	7

In this experiment, we used Torobo (Tokyo Robotics) as the robot and Realsense SR305 (Intel) as the sensor. The actual tools and ingredients used are shown in Fig. 10. Sponges and 3D-printed objects were utilized to shape the handles of the spoon and ladle.

The motion templates and functions used were the same as in the previous experiment. It was making matcha. The task was judged successful when the robot could actually pour matcha powder and hot water into a chawan and then stir it with a whisk.

We compared the proposed method with a method that does not take into account the physical features of the robot. In our method, all tools were set up in the scene and the robot executed the task in this state. The experiment was run for ten trials.

The method that did not use the physical features of the robot utilized only the GPT output $(Cr(t_n))$ in the Modify optimal tool process to select the appropriate use tool. If a spoon was selected, a pre-determined spoon was used. To create this situation, we set one type of spoon in the scene and then conducted an experiment in which all types of spoons were set up. Ten trials were conducted for each spoon, for a total of 40 trials.

Results. The experimental results for the comparison and proposed methods are shown in Table 2. SpoonA, B, C and D in this table are the same as the tools shown in Fig. 10.

For the comparison method, the number of successful tasks was higher when spoon A was used, but it was lower for the other spoons. In addition, all failures in this experiment were caused by the robot motion, not by the GPT.

Figure 11 shows the grasping of each spoon by the robot. Spoon A was grasped stably, but the other spoons were grasped in a state where the position changed or the spoon could not scoop ingredients. This is the reason for the failure of the task. From these results, we can conclude that spoon A is an easy operating tool for the robot, and that the other tools are difficult to operate.

As shown in Table 2, the proposed method had the same number of successes when spoon A was used. This can be attributed to spoon A being selected in all cases where a spoon was chosen to be used. The proposed method can take into account the physical

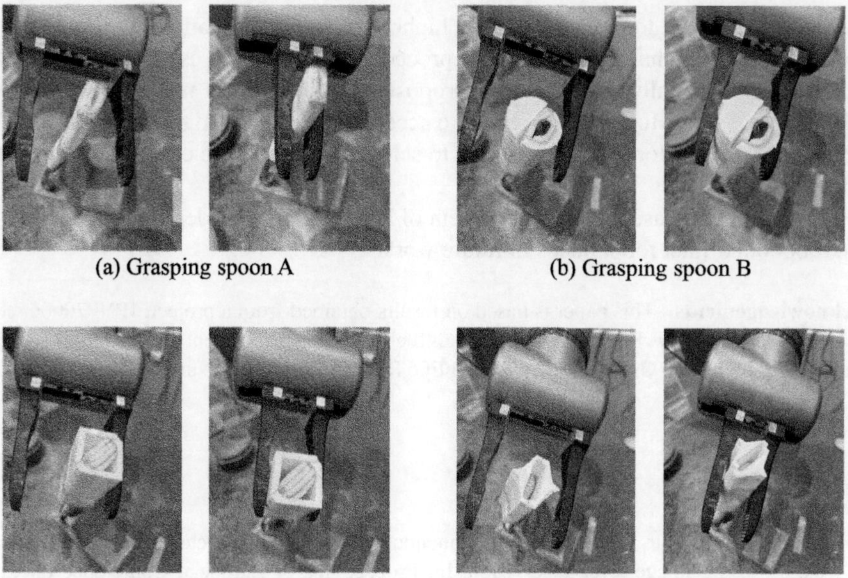

(a) Grasping spoon A

(b) Grasping spoon B

(c) Grasping spoon C

(d) Grasping spoon D

Fig. 11. The robot grasping each spoon. The left figure shows each spoon just before grasping and the right figure shows each spoon just after grasping. For spoon A, the position of the spoon did not change before and after grasping. However, the positions of the other spoons changed, and they were grasped in a state in which they could not scoop the ingredients. Therefore, they failed in the task.

features of the robot, so that spoon A is selected which is easy for the robot to operate. In other words, this result demonstrates that it is necessary to take into account the physical features of the robot.

One example of the proposed method failing is when the ladle was selected three times as the use tool for putting the matcha powder. As shown in Fig. 8, the ladle could not scoop the ingredient inside the natsume due to the size of the tool. This failure presumably occurred because the proposed method cannot take the size of the tool into account.

7 Conclusion

In this work, we proposed a method to detect and modify errors in motion procedures and use tools generated by GPT, along with a method to generate a robot motion trajectory.

In the proposed method, the appropriateness of the tools is judged based on the functional constraints and then modified if necessary. Next, among the tools satisfying the functional constraints, each tool is evaluated from the two perspectives of the numerical results of the physical features of robot and the appropriateness output by the

LLM, and modified to the tool with the highest evaluation. Finally, GPT evaluates the appropriateness of the entire movement procedure and the tools used.

We experimentally compared the proposed method with a method that does not take the physical features of the robot into account and confirmed that ours had a higher task success rate. Moreover, it was able to select tools that were easier for the robot to operate.

We aim to increase the number of item of Eq. 1 and to consider physical features of the robot other than robot hands in future work.

Acknowledgements. This paper is based on results obtained from a project, JPNP20006, commissioned by the New Energy and Industrial Technology Development Organization (NEDO) and JSPS KAKENHI, Grant-in-Aid for Scientific Research(C), Grant Number 21K03984.

References

1. Zhou, X., Girdhar, R., Joulin, A., Krahenbuhl, P., Misra, I.: Detecting twenty-thousand classes using image-level supervision. In: Proceedings of European Conference on Computer Vision, Israel, pp. 350–368 (2022)
2. Qin, Z., Fang, K., Zhu, Y., Fei-Fei, L., Savarese, S.: KETO: learning keypoint representations for tool manipulation. In: Proceedings of IEEE International Conference on Robotics and Automation, pp. 7278–7285 (2020)
3. Turpin, D., Wang, L., Tsogkas, S., Dickinson, S., Garg, A.: GIFT: generalizable interaction-aware functional tool affordances without labels. In: Proceedings of Robotics:Science and Systems (2021)
4. Huang, W., Abbeel, P., Pathak, D., Mordatch, I.: Language models as zero-shot planners: extracting actionable knowledge for embodied agents. In: Proceedings of International conference on machine learning, USA, pp. 9118–9147 (2022)
5. Brohan, A., et al.: Do As I Can, Not As I Say: grounding language in robotic affordances. In: Proceedings of the Conference on Robot Learning, New Zealand, pp. 9118–9147 (2022)
6. Shirai, K., et al.: Vision-language interpreter for robot task planning. In: Proceedings of IEEE International Conference on Robotics and Automation, Japan, pp. 2051–2058 (2024)
7. Jin, Y., et al.: RobotGPT: robot manipulation learning from ChatGPT. IEEE Robot. Autom. Lett. **9**(3), 2543–2550 (2024)
8. Huang, W., Wang, C., Zhang, R., Li, Y., Wu, J., Fei-Fei, L.: VoxPoser: composable 3D value maps for robotic manipulation with language models. In: Proceedings of the Conference on Robot Learning, USA (2023)
9. Suzuki, T., Ando, Y., Hashimoto, M,.: Automatic error correction of GPT-based robot motion generation by partial affordance of tool. In: Proceedings of International Conference on Computer Vision Theory and Applications, Italy, vol. 4, pp. 314–323 (2024)
10. Raval, V., Zhao, E., Zhang, H., Nikolaidis, S., Seita, D.: GPT-fabric: folding and smoothing fabric by leveraging pre-trained foundation models. arXiv preprint: arXiv:2406.09640 (2024)
11. Liang, J., et al.: Code as policies: language model programs for embodied control. In: Proceedings of International Conference on Robotics and Automation, UK, pp. 9493–9500 (2023)
12. Huang, S., Jiang, Z., Dong, H., Qiao, Y., Gao, P., Li, H.: Instruct2Act: mapping multi-modality instructions to robotic actions with large language model. arXiv preprint: arXiv:2305.11176 (2024)

13. Driess, D., et al.: PaLM-E: an embodied multimodal language model. In: Proceedings of the International Conference on Machine Learning, USA, pp. 8469–8488 (2023)
14. Lin, K., Agia, C., Migimatsu, T., Pavone, M., Bohg, J.: Text2Motion: from natural language instructions to feasible plans. Autonom. Robots **47**(8), 1345–1365 (2023)
15. Park, J., et al.: CLARA: classifying and disambiguating user commands for reliable interactive robotic agents. IEEE Robot. Autom. Lett. **9**(2), 1059–1066 (2024)
16. Abugurain, M., Park, S.: Integrating disambiguation and user preferences into large language models for robot motion planning. arXiv preprint: arXiv:2404.14547 (2024)
17. Song, C.H., Wu, J., Washington, C., Sadler, B.M., Chao, W.-L., Su, Y.: LLM-planner: few-shot grounded planning for embodied agents with large language models. In: Proceedings of International Conference on Computer Vision, France, pp. 2998–3009 (2023)
18. Haslum, P., Lipovetzky, N., Magazzeni, D., Muise, C.: An introduction to the planning domain definition language. Synth. Lect. Artif. Intell. Mach. Learn. **13**(2), 1–187 (2019)
19. Fox, M., Long, D.: PDDL2.1: an extension to PDDL for expressing temporal planning domains. J. Artif. Intell. Res. **20**, 61–124 (2003)
20. Zhi, P., et al.: Closed-loop open-vocabulary mobile manipulation with GPT-4V. arXiv preprint: arXiv:2404.10220 (2024)
21. Suzuki, T., Hashimoto, M.: Generation method of robot assembly motion considering physicality gap between humans and robots. In: Proceedings of International Symposium on Visual Computing, USA, vol. 2, pp. 385–396 (2023)
22. Redmon, J., Divvala, S., Girshick, R., Farhadi, A.: You only look once: unified, real-time object detection. In: Proceeding of Conference on Computer Vision and Pattern Recognition, USA, pp. 779–788 (2016)
23. Qi, C. R., Yi, L., Su, H., Guibas, L.J.: PointNet++: deep hierarchical feature learning on point sets in a metric space. In: Proceedings of International Conference on Neural Information Processing Systems, USA, pp. 5105–5114 (2017)
24. Myers, A., Teo, C. L., Fermuller, C., Aloimonos, Y.: Affordance detection of tool parts from geometric features. In: Proceedings of International Conference on Robotics and Automation, USA, pp. 1374–1381 (2015)
25. Tsusaka, Y., Okazaki, Y., Komatsu, M., Yokokohji, Y.: Development of in-situ robot motion modification method by hand-guiding instruction. Trans. Jpn Soc. Mech. Eng. **78**(791), 2450–2461 (2012)
26. Ando, Y., Suzuki, T., Akizuki, S., Hashimoto, M.: A method of generating robot motion using common motion trajectory model and function information of tools. IEEJ Trans. Electron., Inf. Syst. **143**(9), 877–884 (2023)

Hybrid Neural Network-Based Indoor Localisation System for Mobile Robots Using CSI Data in a Robotics Simulator

Javier Ballesteros-Jerez[1(✉)], Jesus Martínez-Gómez[1], Ismael García-Varea[1], Luis Orozco-Barbosa[1], and Manuel Castillo-Cara[2]

[1] Computing Systems Department, Universidad de Castilla-La Mancha, Albacete, Spain
{javier.ballesteros,jesus.martinez,ismael.garcia,luis.orozco}@uclm.es

[2] Artificial Intelligence Department, Universidad Nacional de Educación a Distancia, Madrid, Spain
manuelcastillo@dia.uned.es

Abstract. We present a hybrid neural network model for inferring the position of mobile robots using Channel State Information (CSI) data from a Massive MIMO system. By leveraging an existing CSI dataset, our approach integrates a Convolutional Neural Network (CNN) with a Multilayer Perceptron (MLP) to form a Hybrid Neural Network (HyNN) that estimates 2D robot positions. CSI readings are converted into synthetic images using the TINTO tool. The localisation solution is integrated with a robotics simulator, and the Robot Operating System (ROS), which facilitates its evaluation through heterogeneous test cases, and the adoption of state estimators like Kalman filters. Our contributions illustrate the potential of our HyNN model in achieving precise indoor localisation and navigation for mobile robots in complex environments. The study follows, and proposes, a generalisable procedure applicable beyond the specific use case studied, making it adaptable to different scenarios and datasets.

Keywords: Indoor localisation · Positioning · Deep learning · Hybrid neural network · Robotics simulation

1 Introduction

Mobile robots are increasingly becoming integrated into various areas of our daily lives, including industrial tasks, medical assistance, and space exploration. Critical to their autonomous operation in these environments is the ability to accurately locate themselves. Without precise localisation, mobile robots face difficulties in basic tasks such as autonomous navigation, operational decision-making, and interaction with objects or people [1]. Therefore, knowing the exact position of the robot at each instant is essential to determine the subsequent actions to be performed.

Recent advancements in robot localisation have significantly improved their autonomous capabilities, particularly through the innovative use of wireless signals. Using technologies such as Wi-Fi, Bluetooth, or ultra-wideband (UWB), researchers

J. Röning and J. Filipe (Eds.): ROBOVIS 2025, CCIS 2629, pp. 148–163, 2026.
https://doi.org/10.1007/978-3-032-00986-9_11

have developed more precise and reliable localisation systems, proposing an alternative to traditional methods of robotic localisation [2,3]. Wireless signals enable mobile robots to accurately determine their position in scenarios where traditional methods (e.g. GPS or visual SLAM) are ineffective. By leveraging wireless signals, robots can safely navigate complex indoor spaces, and interact with their surroundings in environments such as warehouses, hospitals, and offices.

In recent years, significant advancements have been made in using Channel State Information (CSI) signals within Massive MIMO (Multiple-Input, Multiple Output) systems for indoor localisation [4]. The combination of CSI with fingerprinting techniques has emerged as a highly effective approach, leveraging the spatial diversity and multipath propagation characteristics inherent in MIMO systems. These advancements are primarily driven by the application of deep learning methodologies [5], which allows for the direct use of signal readings to determine user locations with high precision, even centimetre-level accuracy in indoor environments [6].

Nevertheless, assessing localisation systems in real environments with these techniques presents numerous challenges, including the high costs in infrastructure, time, and human resources required for fingerprinting data collection [7,8]. To mitigate these problems, existing datasets containing wireless signal readings are useful knowledge sources. In addition, robotics simulators offer an effective solution for evaluating the effectiveness of localisation systems in mobile robots [9].

The goal of this paper is, therefore, to develop and evaluate robust localisation systems for mobile robots based on wireless CSI readings. Our proposal involves CSI data coming from existing datasets, which are transformed using the TINTO tool [10,11] to feed a hybrid neural network (HyNN) composed of a Convolutional neural network (CNN) branch with a multilayer perceptron (MLP) branch. The evaluation is performed using a robotics simulator, namely Webots[1], which eases the design and development of different test cases. Although we have focused on the existing dataset created in [12], this proposal holds potential for broader applications. The main contributions of this paper are:

- The development of a HyNN fed from transformed CSI data, which combines a CNN branch with a MLP, and is used to perform robot localisation.
- The use of robotics simulators to recreate real scenarios and integrate the localisation solution with the operation of the mobile robot.
- The integration of the HyNN outputs, namely the robot position, with state estimators (e.g. Kalman filters) to analyse their value in the development of robust and accurate robot localisation systems.

The rest of this paper is organised as follows: in Sect. 2, we delve into the related work and review research in indoor localisation using wireless signals, deep learning-based approaches, and robotics simulation tools. Section 3 presents the proposal and analyses how to develop a localisation model from CSI readings. The experimental design is discussed in Sect. 4, where we also present the obtained results. Finally, Sect. 5 outlines the conclusions and future work.

[1] https://cyberbotics.com/.

2 Related Work

2.1 Measurement of Wireless Signals for Indoor Localisation

Recent advancements in indoor localisation employ wireless signal measurements, particularly those associated with Bluetooth, Wi-Fi, and UWB technologies [13]. Wi-Fi-based localisation is a popular method due to its widespread availability and ease of deployment, typically using Received Signal Strength (RSS). Although RSS methods are simple and cost-effective, they are susceptible to inaccuracies due to environmental variations and signal fluctuations [14]. To overcome these limitations, researchers have explored MIMO systems [4], which can simultaneously transmit and receive multiple data streams, through the use of multiple transmission and reception antennas. This feature enhances the robustness and reliability of wireless communication, and highlight MIMO systems as a promising tool for accurate localisation.

A significant advancement in indoor localisation is the use of CSI. CSI provides detailed information on signal propagation, capturing amplitude and phase information for each subcarrier, thereby enabling more precise localisation than RSS methods. Represented as a matrix of complex numbers, CSI leverages the spatial diversity of MIMO systems to create a comprehensive environment profile, thus facilitating high-accuracy indoor localisation [15].

2.2 Fingerprinting

Fingerprinting is a scene analysis technique that generates environment maps using wireless signal measurements from access points. It involves an offline phase, where reference measurements (e.g., RSS or CSI values) are collected at known locations to build a signal map, and an online phase, where real-time measurements are matched against this map to determine the device position. By leveraging the spatial and multipath propagation characteristics of CSI and MIMO systems, fingerprinting enhances the accuracy and reliability of indoor localisation.

2.3 Deep Learning for Position Estimation

Deep learning has emerged as a powerful tool for enhancing indoor position estimation by leveraging the detailed signal characteristics captured by MIMO and CSI. By integrating deep learning techniques with the fingerprinting method, researchers can develop models that learn complex patterns and spatial relationships from the rich dataset of wireless signals, significantly improving the accuracy of indoor localisation systems. CNN and MLP are two types of neural networks effectively used in this context. CNNs are particularly well-suited for processing and extracting features from synthetic images, as they can learn spatial hierarchies and patterns within the data. MLPs are useful for combining these extracted features and performing precise position predictions [16].

In [6], the authors explored the integration of CSI and deep learning for indoor positioning within a MIMO system. A CNN was designed to estimate user positions using the fingerprint of the CSI data collected from 64 antennas over an indoor area of

2.5 by 2.5 m. The study showed that the proposed system can achieve high accuracy in indoor localisation with the proposed method, reporting a mean error of under 6 cm in the estimations. The favourable outcomes obtained in these works aimed us to explore their use in the development of robust mobile robot localisation systems.

2.4 Simulation Tools

The process of developing (and validating) robotic localisation algorithms is characterised by its high cost and complexity. This point commonly reduces the range of test cases and limits the evaluation procedure. Robotic simulators are perfect for overcoming these problems, and they enable agile and powerful simulated test scenarios generation, obviating the costs and complexity associated with real-worlds experiments. One of the most interesting simulation engines is Webots, fully integrated with the Robot Operating System (ROS), and with an extensive set of simulated robots and world definitions. Webots programming capabilities are essential for its integration in higher-level applications used, for instance, to evaluate the performance of localisation solutions [17].

3 Localisation from CSI Readings

3.1 Data Preprocessing

Our proposal starts with the preprocessing of CSI data, which is initially presented as the matrix of complex numbers $M \in \mathbb{C}^{A \times S}$, where A represents the number of antennas and S denotes the number of subcarriers. The complex data is then converted to polar coordinates, resulting in modulus and argument (in radians) values. This transformation creates the dataset, with each measurement position represented by rows and the converted polar values forming the columns. Each row includes the X and Y positions as dependent variables of the CSI readings. Table 1 shows the format of the dataset.

Table 1. Example of the dataset format. *A* is the antenna, *S* is the subcarrier, m is the modulus, ϕ is the argument, *PosX* is the position X, and *PosY* is the position Y.

A1S1-m	A1S1-ϕ	A1S2-m	A1S2$-\phi$	$\cdots$	PosX	PosY
0.234	0.643	0.275	0.631	$\cdots$	302	2391
$\cdots$	$\cdots$	$\cdots$	$\cdots$	$\cdots$	$\cdots$	$\cdots$
0.180	-1.989	0.152	-1.961	$\cdots$	-1215	1221

3.2 Images Generation from Data

For the input data of the CNN, the TINTO tool is used to transform CSI readings into synthetic images. This process, detailed in [11], involves applying a dimensionality reduction algorithm to the CSI data, followed by translating and scaling the coordinates to generate 2D images that represent the locations of characteristic pixels. Furthermore, TINTO includes a blurring technique, which adds more ordered information to the images, improving the regression task in the CNN. In our proposal, all generated images have been created with dimensions of 35×35 pixels, using the blurring technique.

3.3 Model Training

For our proposal, a HyNN has been developed. The HyNN model is capable of reading images on the CNN branch, and data on the MLP branch, enhancing the model ability to learn spatial feature. Each branch consists of two sub-branches. The CNN processes images with convolution, max pooling, and average pooling layers. The MLP processes the CSI data through dense layers with normalisation and dropout for regularisation. These branches are integrated through final dense and concatenation layers, leading to the output layer. Figure 1 illustrates a simplified schematic of the HyNN architecture.

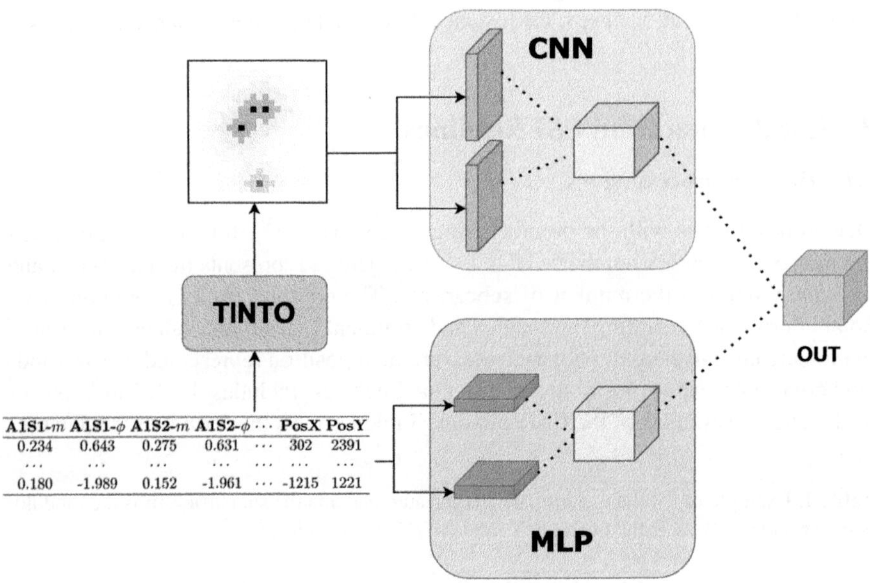

Fig. 1. Simplified architecture of the Hybrid Neural Network.

The dataset contains X and Y positions as target variables, which requires two models for each scenario: one to predict X and the other to predict Y. We used an 85% train, 10% validation, and 5% test split for training, implemented with Keras and TensorFlow.

3.4 Integration Into a Simulation Procedure

To evaluate our proposed localisation system in a robotics simulator, the following steps are necessary. By following these steps, we can assess the performance of the localization algorithm in a controlled, simulated environment:

1. Scenario reconstruction. Reconstruct the real scenario in the simulator, maintaining the Cartesian coordinates used in the real environment.
2. Positions of the route. Start the simulation to obtain the actual robot position along the pre-defined path.
3. CSI data of route positions. Associate the CSI readings from the preprocessed dataset with the route positions. For this association, calculate the mean of the CSI data from at least nine of the closest positions (with CSI data) to the actual robot position. This ensures that the data used for the evaluation closely approximate the actual conditions while preventing reuse of the training data.
4. Subsampling. Subsample the route positions to match the model prediction rate in a real-world scenario, adjusting for predictions/frames per second.
5. Noise application. Apply Gaussian noise to the route CSI readings, adjusting for modulus and argument ranges. Scenarios with no noise, low (10%), medium (20%) and high (30%) noise levels are generated by setting the standard deviation as a percentage of each data range. Adding noise to the CSI data emulates the interference and fluctuations typical of real-world environments, ensuring the system is tested under conditions representative of practical, real-time operation.
6. Model prediction and evaluation. Launch the simulation, loading the models to predict the new CSI readings for each route position. This simulates real-world operation and allows for evaluating and comparing the average error between the actual position and the estimated position by the model.

4 Experiments and Results

4.1 Dataset

For this research, the existing dataset created in [12] was used, which contains extensive raw CSI samples collected via 64 antennas. Using a pilot signal of 100 subcarriers, the CSI is determined, resulting in a matrix of $[64 \times 100]$ dimensions for each position. The dataset was created in a small, flat interior space, with dimensions illustrated in Fig. 2. CSI readings were obtained at 5-mm intervals across the entire area, yielding measurements at 252,004 positions.

Data was collected for three different antenna configurations: Uniform Rectangular Array (URA), Uniform Linear Array (ULA), and Distributed (DIS), as shown in Fig. 2. For our evaluation, we selected the ULA dataset to integrate into the robotics simulator. This choice is based on its practicality and ease of replication in real-world environments, making it a suitable example for this study. Moreover, we created additional datasets with varying numbers of antennas: 8, 16, 32, and 64. This allows us to study the accuracy based on the number of deployed antennas. Table 2 shows the Mean Error (ME) results in function of the used antennas for ULA scenario. ME is calculated as:

$$ME(mm) = \mathbb{E}\{|p - \hat{p}|\}, \tag{1}$$

where p is the real position and $\hat{p}$ is the estimated position.

Table 2. ME, in millimetres, of the ULA scenario for the HyNN models, in the test partition results.

ULA	8 antennas	16 antennas	32 antennas	64 antennas
HyNN ME	164.98	137.37	104.53	**49.66**

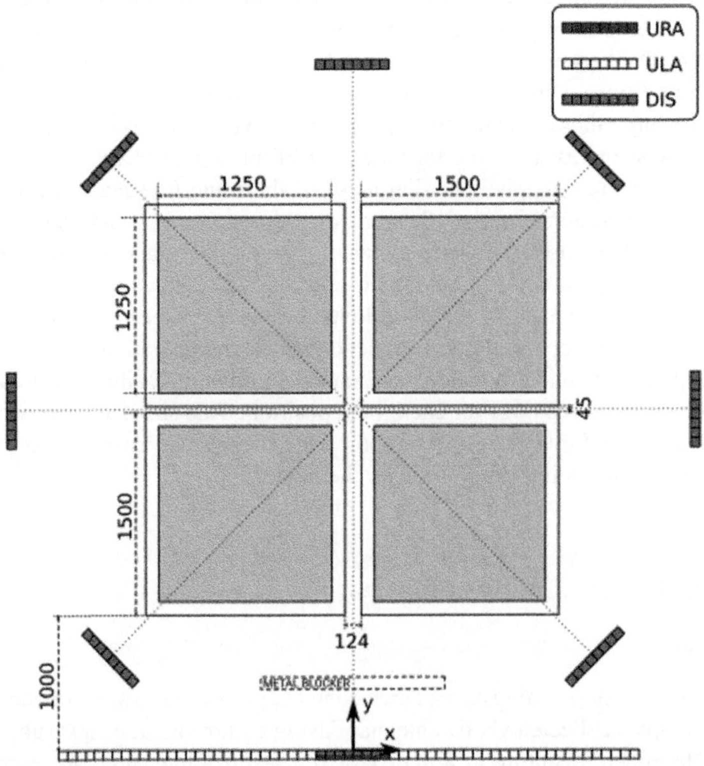

Fig. 2. Scenario configuration. The antennas are spaced around a scenario where yellow zones represent CSI readings positions. All measurements in the figure are in millimetres (Figure obtained from [12] (Color figure online)).

The inclusion of a 64-antenna configuration allows for capturing a higher level of spatial diversity and multipath propagation characteristics inherent in MIMO systems, resulting in improved localisation accuracy. This configuration provides a theoretical reference for the model's performance under optimal conditions, while additional experiments with fewer antennas demonstrate the system's adaptability to scenarios with limited resources.

4.2 Experimentation

To proceed with the experimentation in Webots, the actual scenario was initially reconstructed in the simulator, adhering to the coordinates delineated in the dataset, as shown in Fig. 3. By employing the Webots Supervisor node, it is possible to determine the position of the robot in relation to the dataset (second step defined in Sect. 3.4). The robot selected for experimentation is the e-puck2[2] robot, mainly due to its small size (7.5 cm in diameter), and its compatibility with Wi-Fi through a built-in microcontroller, which allows it to read CSI signals and use the developed localisation system. The efficacy of the proposed solution will be assessed based on its capacity to address various navigation problems, focusing on the system performance in estimating the robot position along a given route.

Fig. 3. Reconstruction of the scenario in Webots.

To improve and optimise the HyNN predictions, a simple implementation of a Kalman filter has been performed. By incorporating a two-dimensional Kalman filter, which state is represented by the X and Y position coordinates and the velocity in each axis, we can combine the measurements from the HyNN with the state predictions of the filter. Although the state transition matrix is simplified to account only for the effect of velocity on position at each simulator time step, assuming constant velocity, the Kalman filter still provides valuable information about the robot velocity and helps to smooth out the estimations. This implementation allows us to predict future locations and behaviours based on the current and previous positions and velocities, contributing to the overall effectiveness of the localisation system. This implementation can be easily adapted to other scenarios and conditions, as it does not require performing a definition of the robot motion model.

Once the integration of our proposal to the dataset has been done (Sect. 3.4), we aim to demonstrate its effectiveness and reliability in practical applications by evaluating the

[2] https://www.cyberbotics.com/doc/guide/epuck?version=cyberbotics:R2019a.

system through specific test cases or experiments. The system will be evaluated in terms of:

- **Number of Antennas.** The number of antennas used to collect and measure the CSI data. The results obtained for 8, 16, 32 and 64 antennas will be studied.
- **Noise Level.** Indicates the amount of interference or randomness present in the data. The impact of noise on the CSI data will be evaluated, considering low, medium, high and no noise scenarios.
- **Kalman Filter.** Algorithm used to estimate the system state from noisy measurements, with the objective of reducing the error. In this case, the measurements are those predicted by HyNN. The results will be studied when applying or not applying the Kalman filter.

The source code for the research is available in a public repository on GitHub[3].

Prediction Times. Prior to initiating the experimental procedures, it is essential to measure the prediction times of the models in accordance with the number of antennas used. By analysing the prediction times, it will be possible to define the frames per seconds (FPS) at which to work, thus performing a sampling for each model corresponding to

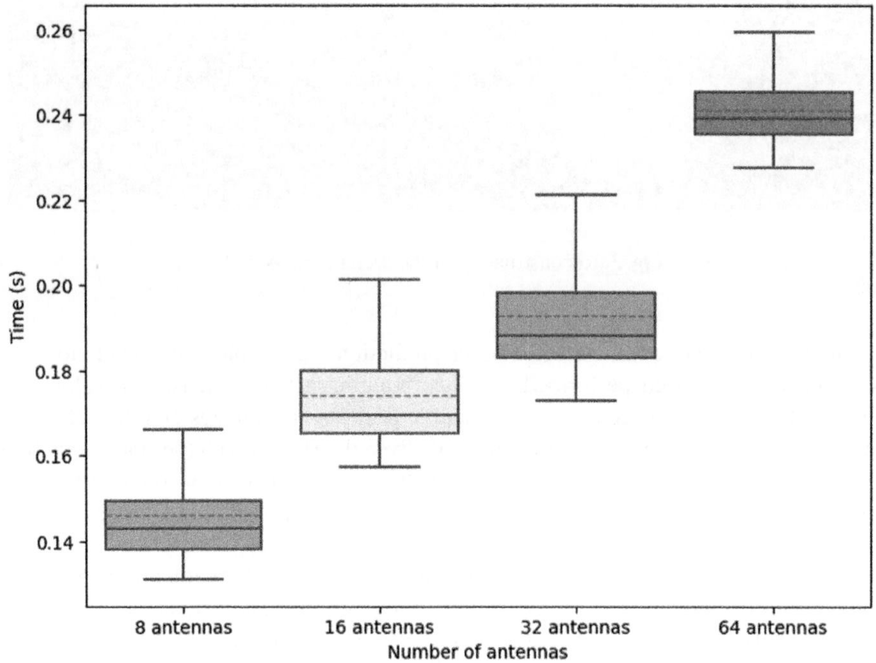

Fig. 4. Box plot of the prediction times in seconds of the models as a function of the number of antennas.

[3] https://github.com/Javierbj02/HyNN-Robot-Positioning.

the prediction rate in real conditions. Figure 4 presents a box plot that provides a comprehensive illustration of the variation in HyNN model prediction time as a function of the number of antennas used. Consequently, each box represents the distribution of prediction times for a specific number of antennas. It is evident that there is a direct correlation between the number of antennas and the prediction time. As the number of antennas increases, the prediction time also increases, which is to be expected given that the use of a larger number of antennas implies the processing of a greater quantity of data.

Following this analysis, it can be concluded that for datasets comprising 8, 16, 32, and 64 antennas, the models are capable of performing 5, 4, 4, and 3 predictions per second, respectively. These FPS will be used to sample the data for evaluation of the system, as outlined in Sect. 3.4.

Experiment 1: Position Estimation During Uniform Motion. The objective of this experiment is to validate an entire procedure and to analyse whether the mean error ranges, documented in Sect. 4.1, are in line with those observed in the course of this experiment. For this purpose, the robot follows a straight-line path with a length of 1429 mm at a constant velocity.

Table 3 shows the Mean Error in millimetres obtained in the first experiment, for each noise level and number of antennas, with a comparison of the results with and without the Kalman filter. Figure 5 shows a plot of the results of the predictive models with and without the Kalman filter, with the mean across all noise levels plotted for each number of antennas. The dashed lines represent the HyNN predictions, while the solid lines illustrate the results of integrating the Kalman filter. The blue line depicts the actual trajectory of the robot, starting at point 1 and concluding at point 2.

Table 3. Mean Error Results in millimetres obtained in Experiment 1.

Noise level	Kalman Filter	Number of antennas			
		8	16	32	64
None	No	162.32	128.71	82.12	40.75
	Yes	124.64	95.76	59.12	**31.90**
Low	No	179.73	133.99	80.89	37.68
	Yes	106.71	93.02	54.68	**26.15**
Medium	No	247.50	169.53	85.10	42.18
	Yes	126.00	109.15	62.02	**24.81**
High	No	381.23	186.51	96.47	45.20
	Yes	272.25	108.90	76.46	**25.80**

After this experiment, it can be stated that the results obtained are in alignment with those achieved during training. Furthermore, it can be concluded that the scenarios with 8 and 16 are insufficient and will not be included in the subsequent plots. However, they will be studied in the same way.

Although it is not the main objective of this experiment, we can highlight how the Kalman filter significantly improves all the results in a straight path at constant speed. This improvement is especially evident the higher the noise in the measurements, demonstrating its effectiveness in filtering noise, significantly increasing the robustness of the localisation algorithm.

Experiment 2: Position Estimation During Obstacle Avoidance. The objective of this experiment is to evaluate the effectiveness of a state estimator that operates on time-series data, such as the Kalman filter, in order to improve the accuracy of the position estimation provided by the HyNN. In addition, it is intended to study the influence of noise on the results. To this end, a route of 1880 mm with obstacles is defined, being necessary to avoid them in order to progress.

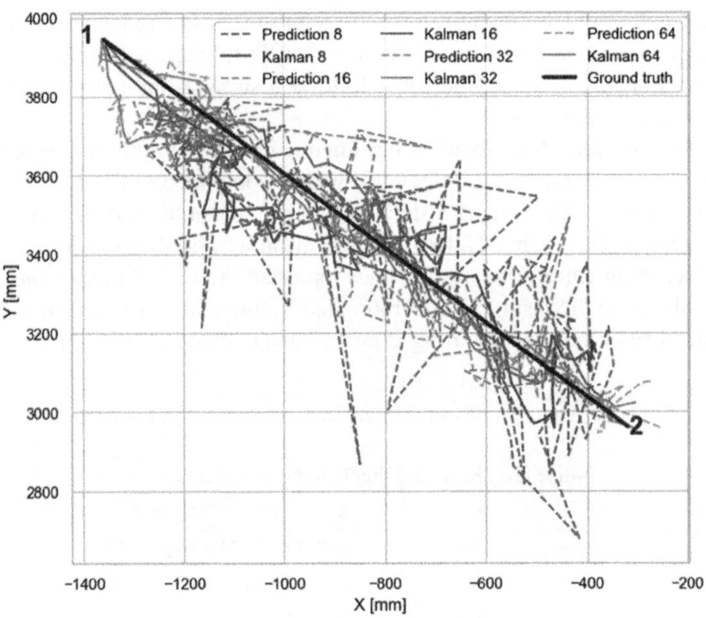

Fig. 5. Results of predictions obtained in Experiment 1.

Table 4 illustrates the Mean Error in millimetres obtained in Experiment 2 for each noise level and number of antennas, comparing also the use or not of the Kalman filter. Figure 6 depicts a comparison of the prediction outcomes with and without the Kalman filter. For the 32 and 64 antenna configurations, the averaged outcomes across all noise levels have been plotted. The dashed lines correspond to the HyNN predictions, whereas the solid lines illustrate the integrated Kalman filter results. The blue line represents the actual robot trajectory, beginning at point 1 and ending at point 7.

Table 4. Mean Error Results in millimetres obtained in Experiment 2.

Noise level	Kalman Filter	Number of antennas			
		8	16	32	64
None	No	150.27	114.05	83.10	**42.91**
	Yes	131.29	109.45	83.37	49.91
Low	No	171.45	128.37	81.86	**46.51**
	Yes	124.64	113.34	80.84	52.06
Medium	No	317.36	169.10	79.68	**48.66**
	Yes	230.48	125.45	77.19	51.37
High	No	376.77	221.48	91.70	57.88
	Yes	279.60	173.77	86.66	**53.05**

Upon examination of the results, it becomes evident that in most cases the application of the Kalman filter significantly reduces the mean error, which becomes especially evident in the presence of elevated noise levels. This integration demonstrates its efficacy in environments with noise present, providing a more accurate estimation and enhancing the location algorithm's reliability in such contexts. Conversely, in scenarios where noise is minimal, the use of Kalman filter may even prove to be suboptimal, potentially due to the time required for stabilisation. Moreover, it can be observed that

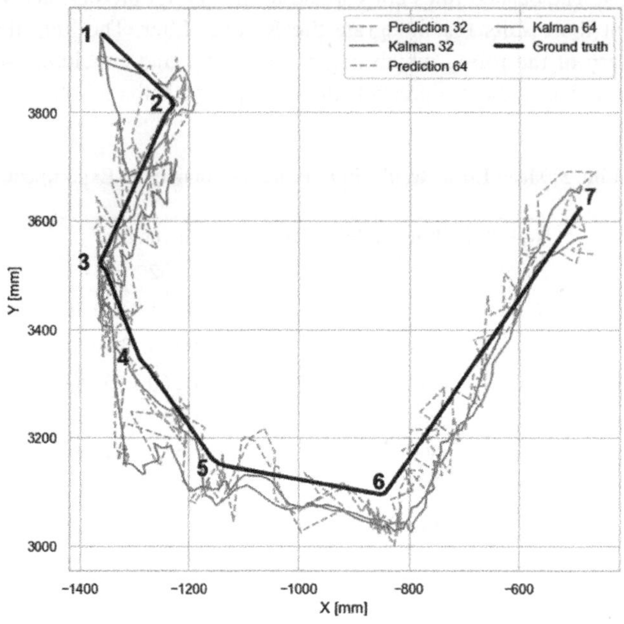

Fig. 6. Results of predictions obtained in Experiment 2.

when 64 antennas are employed, thereby enabling the HyNN to perform more accurate predictions, the Kalman filter performs less well in the majority of cases, due to the simplified Kalman filter model.

While the efficacy of the Kalman filter could be enhanced by employing a parameterisation and motion model according to each robot, the objective has been to develop a straightforward implementation without defining specific motion models to facilitate adaptation to other problems. This explains why it performs better on a path such as that in Experiment 1, where the velocity remains constant throughout, whereas in Experiment 2 the robot adjusts its speed as it progresses to avoid obstacles.

Experiment 3: Position Estimation in Robot Kidnapping Problem. In the context of robotics, the kidnapped robot problem refers to the loss of knowledge of a robot about its position due to a forced and unexpected displacement by external agents.

The aim of this experiment is to analyse the performance of the developed system in a scenario that can occur in real robots, such as the kidnapped problem, in order to measure the position recovery factor under these conditions. This experiment is similar to Experiment 2, since the robot has to avoid obstacles. However, at some point in the simulation, the robot is abruptly moved to a different position. The path length is 1779 mm.

Table 5 shows the Mean Error in millimetres obtained in Experiment 3, for each noise level and number of antennas, with a comparison of the results with and without the Kalman filter. Figure 7 depicts the predictive outcomes with and without the Kalman filter, with the results for the 32 and 64 antenna configurations averaged across all noise levels. The dashed lines correspond to the HyNN predictions, while the solid lines represent the results that integrate the Kalman filter. The blue line depicts the actual trajectory of the robot, which begins at point 1 and concludes at point 8. The jump between points 4 and 5 represents the kidnapping of the robot.

Table 5. Mean Error Results in millimetres obtained in Experiment 3.

Noise level	Kalman Filter	Number of antennas			
		8	16	32	64
None	No	156.40	112.08	61.94	**35.56**
	Yes	146.55	109.69	65.43	49.44
Low	No	204.78	133.62	60.72	**37.84**
	Yes	144.82	104.60	61.09	51.19
Medium	No	360.67	166.89	66.14	**41.46**
	Yes	226.89	131.77	59.42	53.19
High	No	387.21	198.17	81.60	**46.75**
	Yes	236.75	121.70	66.76	51.01

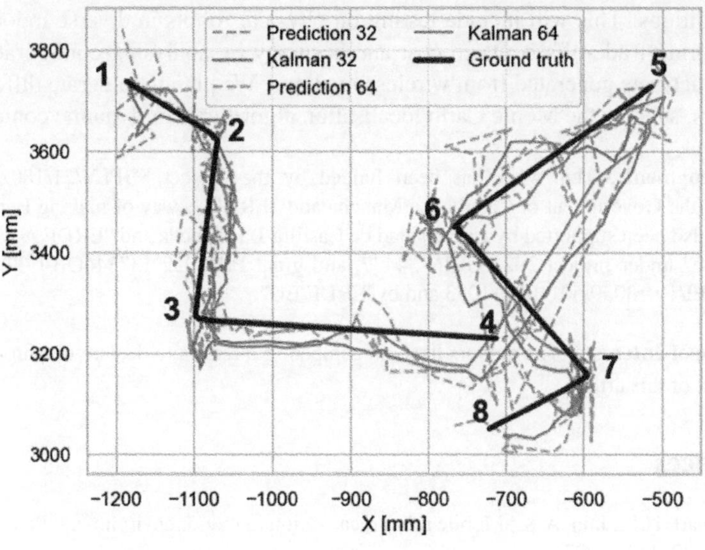

Fig. 7. Results of predictions obtained in Experiment 3.

In this experiment, it is observed that when the initial estimates are accurate (64-antenna setup), the Kalman filter demonstrates a systematic decline in performance. In contrast, in the presence of substantial noise, with an initial error exceeding 70 mm, the Kalman filter demonstrates a consistent improvement. Furthermore, it is crucial to note that in a kidnapping situation, the robot motion becomes highly nonlinear. This renders the Kalman filter unable to accurately estimate the new robot position after the kidnapping, resulting in a prolonged convergence period to the new actual position. This phenomenon elucidates the inferior performance observed in the 32- and 64-antenna scenarios when employing the Kalman filter, where the HyNN already obtains high prediction accuracy.

5 Conclusions and Future Work

We have presented a procedure to integrate a position estimation algorithm, fed by CSI data and based on a Hybrid Neural Network approach, into a higher-level solution that includes a robotic operating system, simulation capabilities, and the Kalman filter localisation algorithm. This proposal allows for flexible design and development of test cases, enabling in-depth analysis of the position estimation algorithm. The cornerstone of the proposal is the synthetic generation of CSI readings based on an existing dataset. Based on the obtained results, we can conclude that the position estimator is suitable for real-world robotic scenarios, even in the presence of noise. Specifically, using 32 or 64 antennas ensures an average error of approximately 10 cm or less (135% of the robot's diameter).

Future work will focus on validating the system in real-world environments to address the limitations of simulation-based evaluation and assess robustness under practical conditions. This will include testing on physical robots in diverse indoor scenarios, exploring trade-offs between cost and accuracy by analysing configurations with different datasets generated from wireless readings. We plan to integrate different state estimators, such as the Monte Carlo localisation algorithm, for dynamic contexts.

Acknowledgments. This work has been funded by the project SBPLY/21/180225/000062 funded by the Government of Castilla-La Mancha and "ERDF A way of making Europe". This work has also been supported by Universidad de Castilla-La Mancha and "ERDF A way of making Europe" under project 2023-GRIN-34437, and grant PID2022-137344OB-C33 funded by MICIU/AEI/10.13039/501100011033 and by"ERDF/EU".

Disclosure of Interests. The authors have no competing interests to declare that are relevant to the content of this article.

References

1. Dulimart, H.S., Jain, A.K.: Mobile robot localization in indoor environment. Pattern Recogn. **30**(1), 99–111 (1997)
2. Singh, A., Emam, M., Al Mtawa, Y.: Comparative analysis of indoor localization across various wireless technologies. Eng **4**(3), 2293–2308 (2023)
3. Yassin, A., et al.: Recent advances in indoor localization: a survey on theoretical approaches and applications. IEEE Commun. Surv. Tutorials **19**(2), 1327–1346 (2017)
4. Larsson, E.G., Edfors, O., Tufvesson, F., Marzetta, T.L.: Massive MIMO for next generation wireless systems. IEEE Commun. Mag. **52**(2), 186–195 (2014)
5. Vieira, J., Leitinger, E., Sarajlic, M., Li, X., Tufvesson, F.: Deep convolutional neural networks for massive MIMO fingerprint-based positioning. In: 2017 IEEE 28th Annual International Symposium on Personal, Indoor, and Mobile Radio Communications (PIMRC), pp. 1–6. Montreal (2017)
6. Bast, S.D., Guevara, A.P., Pollin, S.: CSI-based Positioning in Massive MIMO systems using convolutional neural networks. In: 2020 IEEE 91st Vehicular Technology Conference (VTC2020-Spring), Antwerp, Belgium, pp. 1–5 (2020)
7. Zhu, X., Qu, W., Qiu, T., Zhao, L., Atiquzzaman, M., Wu, D.O.: Indoor intelligent fingerprint-based localization: principles, approaches and challenges. IEEE Commun. Surv. Tutorials **22**(4), 2634–2657 (2020)
8. Pérez-Navarro, A., et al.: 1 - challenges of fingerprinting in indoor positioning and navigation. In: Intelligent Data-Centric Systems, Geographical and Fingerprinting Data to Create Systems for Indoor Positioning and Indoor/Outdoor Navigation, pp. 1–20. Academic Press (2019)
9. Žlajpah, L.: Simulation in robotics. Math. Comput. Simul. **79**(4), 879–897 (2008)
10. Castillo-Cara, M., Talla-Chumpitaz, R., García-Castro, R., Orozco-Barbosa, L.: TINTO: converting tidy data into image for classification with 2-Dimensional convolutional neural networks. In: SoftwareX, vol. 22, p. 101391 (2023)
11. Talla-Chumpitaz, R., Castillo-Cara, M., Orozco-Barbosa, L., García-Castro, R.: A novel deep learning approach using blurring image techniques for Bluetooth-based indoor localisation. Inf. Fusion **91**, 173–186 (2023)
12. De Bast, S., Pollin, S.: Ultra dense indoor MaMIMO CSI dataset. IEEE Dataport (2021). https://doi.org/10.21227/nr6k-8r78
13. Zafari, F., Gkelias, A., Leung, K.K.: A survey of indoor localization systems and technologies. IEEE Commun. Surv. Tutorials **21**(3), 2568–2599 (2019)

14. Dong, Q., Dargie, W.: Evaluation of the reliability of RSSI for indoor localization. In: 2012 International Conference on Wireless Communications in Underground and Confined Areas, Clermont Ferrand, pp. 1–6 (2012)
15. Chapre, Y., Ignjatovic, A., Seneviratne, A., Jha, S.: CSI-MIMO: an efficient Wi-Fi fingerprinting using channel state information with MIMO. Pervasive Mob. Comput. **23**, 89–103 (2015)
16. Gardner, M.W., Dorling, S.R.: Artificial neural networks (the multilayer perceptron)–a review of applications in the atmospheric sciences. Atmos. Environ. **32**(14–15), 2627–2636 (1998)
17. Michel, O.: Cyberbotics Ltd., Webots™: Professional Mobile Robot Simulation. Int. J. Adv. Rob. Syst. **1**, 5 (2004)

Towards a Reliable Multimodal AI Monitoring System for Pain Detection and Quantification

Huibin Wang(✉), Sören Nienaber, Laslo Dinges, Magnus Jung, and Ayoub Al-Hamadi

Neuro-Information Technology Group, Institute for Information Technology and Communications, Otto-von-Guericke University Magdeburg, 39106 Magdeburg, Germany
huibin.wang@ovgu.de
https://www.nit.ovgu.de/

Abstract. Accurate and robust pain intensity detection has significant implications for patient monitoring and rehabilitation, especially in personalized treatment and management. Benefiting from the complementarity of multiple modalities, multimodal fusion-based methods for pain intensity classification have garnered widespread attention. In this study, we propose an novel Bi-Modal Fusion framework based on Electrodermal Activity (EDA) and Electromyography (EMG) for pain classification. This framework combines LSTM with an attention module in a unified block to learn complex dynamic features from biosignals, effectively capturing both global and local patterns. Meanwhile, focal loss is used as the loss function to mitigate the impact of class imbalance during model training. Through extensive experiments, our method achieves an average accuracy improvement of 3.31% compared to SOTA across 11 sub-datasets of X-ITE pain database, with a notable improvement of 7.20% on the Reduced Electrical Tonic sub-dataset (RETD). Our research not only validates the effectiveness of the proposed method but also highlights its robustness across different modalities and sub-datasets. These findings lay a solid foundation for our long-term goal of developing an accurate and robust clinical multimodal AI monitoring system for pain detection and quantification.

Keywords: Pain intensity classification · Bi-modal fusion · LSTM · Attention mechanism · Focal loss · EDA · EMG

1 Introduction

Pain is one of the most complex and subjective experiences that humans encounter, encompassing multiple physiological and psychological dimensions. It not only affects patients' daily lives but also has profound implications for overall health. Chronic pain, in particular, has a significant impact on patients' quality of life and mental health. Therefore, the objective and accurate assessment of pain intensity has become a critical challenge in clinical diagnosis and treatment [17,34]. Traditional pain assessment methods typically rely on self-reports from patients, such as the Visual Analog Scale (VAS) and the Numerical Rating Scale (NRS) [6,16,22]. This however is rather inaccurate as both the self perceived pain is reliant on factors like personal experiences,

J. Röning and J. Filipe (Eds.): ROBOVIS 2025, CCIS 2629, pp. 164–181, 2026.
https://doi.org/10.1007/978-3-032-00986-9_12

influences like pain medication or other personal biases [4,5,24]. On the other hand, expert reports are also based on visual clues that experience heavy bias by the reporting expert. Thus, this work is motivated by two key factors:

1. The necessity to support medical staff in patient care. On the one hand, it is not feasible to have personnel care for a single patient around the clock. On the other hand, some hospitals are also understaffed, which even increases problems concerning manual pain monitoring and hampers their realizability.
2. Patients that are unable to communicate their pain effectively, may suffer further from incorrectly administered analgesics, thus experiencing more pain or other long term impairments from the experienced pain. Examples of such patients range from patients in a coma over non-verbal patients to patients with mental impairments like Alzheimer's [1].

Thus, improving a real-time, automated pain detection would benefit patients experiences and improve the work of medical practitioners.

Recent research has shown that behavioral cues and physiological signals are highly effective for pain detection [29]. Meanwhile, data-driven machine learning models have demonstrated strong predictive capabilities. Consequently, there has been growing interest in recent years in utilizing machine learning models for automated pain detection based on these various behavioral and physiological indicators [21].

Among these indicators, facial expressions and audio signals are commonly used as behavioral cues, while heart rate variability (ECG), muscle activity (EMG), and skin conductance (EDA) serve as physiological signals [20]. Electroencephalogram (EEG) can effectively capture an individual's stress and anxiety states [26]. However, due to the high cost of data acquisition, sensitivity to artifacts, and the complexity of experimental conditions, research on pain detection algorithms based on EEG signals remains relatively limited [7]. Research has shown that the EDA modality generally outperforms other single modalities in accurate pain detection, with EMG being the second best modality [21,32]. Due to the complementarity between these two modalities, their fusion can significantly enhance classification performance, highlighting the immense potential of multimodal fusion algorithms. Therefore, this study selects these two modalities for an in-depth investigation of the Bi-Modal Fusion model for pain intensity detection.

Despite some progress in fusion algorithms for biological signals related to pain detection, several limitations still exist [11,21,32]: (1) Datasets are often highly imbalanced due to their class distribution, causing the model to overly focus on the majority classes while neglecting the minority classes, thereby impairing classification performance. (2) Many approaches have low model complexities, resulting in weak feature extraction capabilities. Thus, we focus on addressing these two issues by proposing a novel LSTM-Attention-based Bi-Modal Fusion framework for pain intensity classification, which significantly improves the model's performance.

This work is part of a series of projects and research works that focus on the automated detection of pain in clinical patients. Most notably, our work includes a dataset that recorded video data and bio signals of subjects exposed to heat pain. Further, it includes a more recently captured electrical and heat pain dataset. Our work also serves as a preparation for a new clinical study that captures multi-modal data in a clinical Intensive Care Unit (ICU) setting from patients shortly after an abdominal surgery.

Contributions

1. We propose a novel Bi-Modal Fusion framework that combines LSTM and Attention mechanism for the pain classification task, enhancing the model's ability to capture both global and local features.
2. To address the issue of class imbalance in biological signals (EDA and EMG), we employ focal loss as the loss function to mitigate the impact of imbalanced data during model training.
3. Extensive experiments demonstrate not only improved pain classification performance but also the framework's robustness across different modalities and subdatasets of the X-ITE pain database.

2 Related Work

Uni-Modal Pain Intensity Classification. Behavioral cues and physiological signals play a crucial role in pain detection. Common behavioral indicators include facial expressions and audio signals, while physiological indicators encompass heart rate variability (ECG), muscle activity (EMG), and skin conductance (EDA) [20]. Due to advantages such as ease of data collection and lower computational and algorithmic complexity, many studies focus on uni-modal pain intensity classification [9,15,19,23,30,33,36]. For instance, a ECG-based method [9] applied a multi-task neural network and found that adding auxiliary tasks, such as patient age and gender classification, notably improved pain classification accuracy. A study on audio signals [30] used handcrafted features and spectrograms combined with CNN, LSTM, and expert knowledge to enhance classification performance. A video-based method [36] proposed a local perception module comprising feature and attention branches, coupled with a multi-task identity-aware module, achieving superior pain assessment performance.

Multi-modal Pain Intensity Classification. The complementarity of different modalities significantly aids in enhancing information richness and improving the accuracy and robustness of classification models [20]. Consequently, pain classification models based on multi-modal fusion are rapidly advancing [2,8,10,20,21,25,28,31]. For instance, Wang et al. integrated EDA, EMG, and ECG signals, utilizing both handcrafted features and temporal dynamic features extracted by Bi-LSTM to enhance pain intensity classification performance [31]. Thiam et al. also focused on EDA, EMG, and ECG signals, employing deep denoising convolutional autoencoders to reconstruct the signals of each modality, thereby learning the inherent complex dynamic features. They further employed a gating layer to achieve adaptive weighting of different modality features, optimizing feature-level fusion [28]. Additionally, Rojas et al. conducted pain analysis using Support Vector Machine (SVM), Decision Tree (DT), and Linear Discriminant Analysis (LDA) on three physiological signals: Electrodermal Activity (EDA), Photoplethysmography (PPG), and Respiration (RESP). The results indicate

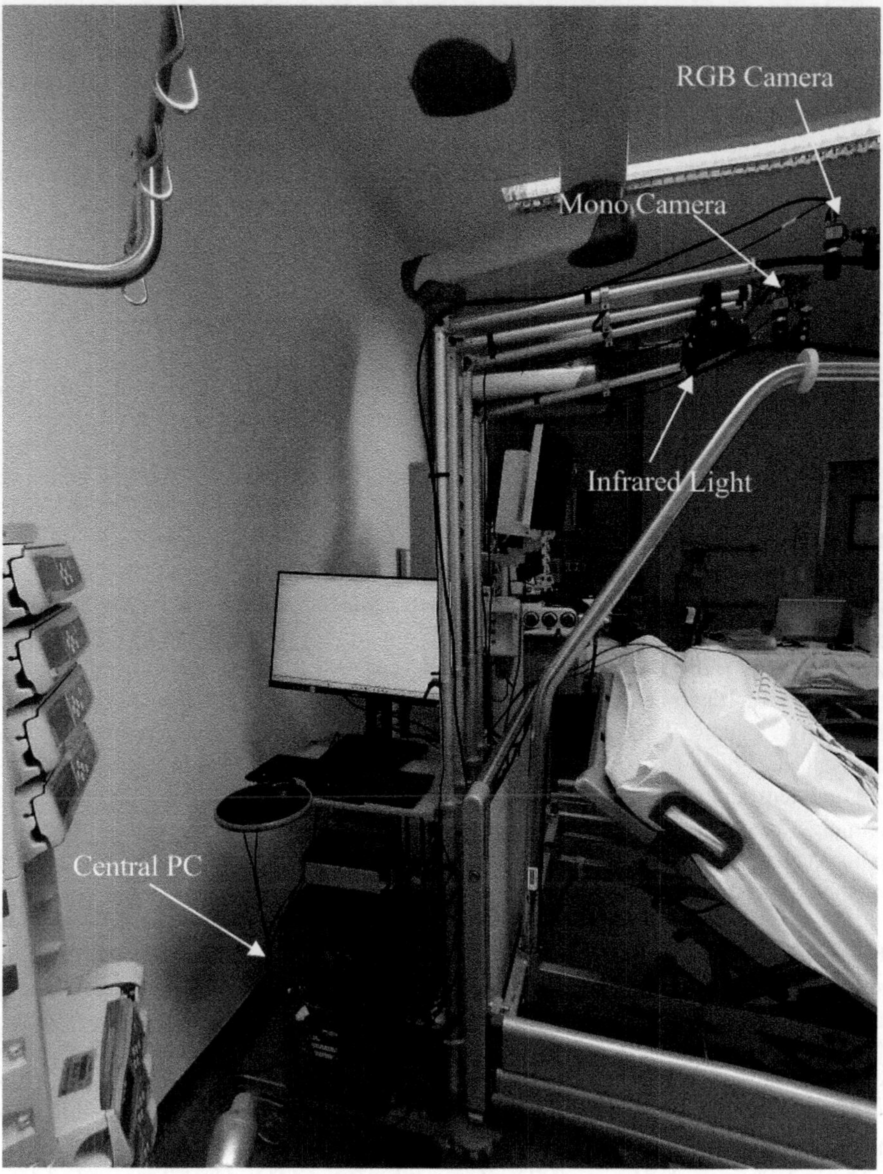

Fig. 1. Setup of our multimodal AI monitoring system for pain detection at the University Hospital of Ulm to capture data from postoperative ICU patients.

that EDA is the best single modality, and SVM is the most effective method [8]. Ehsan et al. conducted a comprehensive analysis of pain intensity detection using five modalities: facial expressions, audio, ECG, EMG, and EDA. They employed LSTM and sample-weighted LSTM for the analysis of uni-modal, bi-modal, and multi-modal fusion approaches. Their findings revealed that EDA and EMG are the two best-performing single modalities, with multi-modal fusion significantly outperforming either modality alone [21]. However, to the best of our knowledge, fusion algorithms based on these two modalities have not been sufficiently studied, primarily due to two notable issues: class imbalance issue within the dataset and relatively simplistic model structures. Therefore, our research focuses on addressing these two challenges to enhance fusion algorithm performance for pain intensity classification leveraging the optimal modalities of EDA and EMG.

3 Multi-modal AI Monitoring System for Pain Detection

In this section, we provide a detailed description of the used dataset, the employed preprocessing techniques, and the proposed Bi-Modal Fusion framework.

3.1 Dataset X-ITE Pain Database

Electrical and Heat Pain Dataset. The electrical & heat pain dataset was captured in a basic test environment at the University Hospital of Ulm. In this study, we captured multi-modal data from 134 healthy participants aged between 18 and 50. These participants were subjected to two types of pain stimuli (thermal and electrical), with three intensity levels (low, medium, and high) and two stimulus durations (phasic and tonic). For each participant eight modalities were recorded: RGB frontal video of the face, audio signals, RGB body video, RGB side video of the face and a thermal video of the face. For the biosignals the EDA, ECG and EMG for the muscles trapezius, zygomaticus and corrugator were recorded. Lastly, the onset and duration of the pain stimulus were recorded to allow for synchronisation of the data. For details about this pain database, including the quantification of pain stimulus intensity, data collection methods, and the used equipments, please refer to [12].

According to the studies [21,32], EDA and EMG have shown to be the best-performing single modalities. To ensure a fair comparison, we selected the same subset of 127 participants and their corresponding EDA and EMG data [12]. Due to the significant class imbalance issue within the dataset (77% of the signals representing No-Pain level), Othman et al. [21] adopted a reduction strategy, reducing some No-Pain samples prior to each pain intensity sequence while preserving different numbers of No-Pain samples directly adjacent to each pain intensity sequence. Therefore, in addition to the original six sub-datasets: Phasic sub-dataset (PD), Heat Phasic sub-dataset (HPD), Electrical Phasic sub-dataset (EPD), Tonic sub-dataset (TD), Heat Tonic sub-dataset (HTD), and Electrical Tonic sub-dataset (ETD), five additional 'Reduced sub-datasets' were created. HTD was not reduced as it is nearly balanced.

Postoperative ICU Dataset. In a novel upcoming study, we employed the knowledge from the previous datasets to create a realistic environment in the ICU of the University Hospital of Ulm. For this, we constructed a small, mobile rig that is placed behind a standard hospital bed. An image of the rig placed behind a bed can be seen in Fig. 1. The rig contains a PC, which serves as the central hub for all programs, as well as the main data saving device. Further, two cameras were mounted above the patient's head using extendable arms. One camera is a standard RGB camera. The second camera is a mono camera with a near infrared filter on the lens, which allows only infrared light to be captured by the camera. Additionally, an infrared light was mounted next to the camera. This camera is necessary to allow a constant video recording independent of the lighting conditions in the patient's room, especially at night, when the room must remain dark to avoid impeding the patient's sleep. To capture the bio signals, the patients are wired to a central recording nexus. The recorded biosignals still consists of ECG, EDA and EMG, the same as used in the laboratory datasets. For the EMG however, only the frontalis muscle is recorded as it correlates strongly with the corrugator [33]. One of the main focus of this dataset is to verify a robust pain detection system in a realistic clinical trial.

3.2 Data Preprocessing

Our study focuses on the design of model's architecture, without making improvements at the data level. To ensure a fair comparison with SOTA [21], we used the same data preprocessing methods.

EDA. EDA signals are used to assess sweat activity and are a measure of skin conductance. The specific preprocessing steps are as follows:

1. The raw 1-dimensional EDA signals were sampled at a frame rate of 25 frames per second (fps) without additional filtering.
2. The temporal descriptor for each second of the signal includes four statistics: minimum, maximum, mean, and standard deviation, calculated from both the signal itself and its first and second derivatives.
3. To highlight within-subject response variations while reducing the influence of differences between subjects, person-specific standardization [33] was applied. Specifically, the mean and standard deviation were first calculated for each subject. Each feature value was then normalized by subtracting the corresponding mean and dividing by the standard deviation.
4. The sliding window method was employed, combining data from ten seconds ago to predict the next time step's pain intensity level. Data from the first ten seconds cannot be matched to any predictions due to the lack of prior observations.

Ultimately, a 12×1-dimensional descriptor for the EDA signals was obtained.

EMG. The 3-channel EMG signals are used to measure the activity of three muscles: the corrugator supercilii (close to the eyebrows), the zygomaticus major (at the cheeks), and the trapezius (neck/shoulder). The following are the specific preprocessing steps:

1. The raw 3-channel EMG signals were sampled at a frame rate of 25 fps and subsequently underwent a zero-phase 3rd-order Butterworth band-pass filter [21] with cut-off frequencies of 20 and 250 Hz.

2. The temporal descriptor for each second of the signal includes four statistics: minimum, maximum, mean, and standard deviation, calculated from both the signal itself and its first and second derivatives.
3. To highlight within-subject response variations while reducing the influence of differences between subjects, person-specific standardization [33] was applied. Specifically, the mean and standard deviation were first calculated for each subject. Each feature value was then normalized by subtracting the corresponding mean and dividing by the standard deviation.
4. The sliding window method was employed, combining data from ten seconds ago to predict the next time step's pain intensity level. Data from the first ten seconds cannot be matched to any predictions due to the lack of prior observations.

A 12×3-dimensional descriptor for the EMG signals was ultimately derived.

3.3 The Overall Framework

We propose a novel Bi-Modal Fusion framework based on EDA and EMG signals for pain classification, shown as Fig. 2. This framework integrates LSTM and attention mechanism, specifically designed for feature extraction from time-series data. The model consists of multiple LSTM-attention blocks, each containing one LSTM layer and an attention module. Through this design, we enhance the model's ability to capture both global and local features. The extracted features from the two modalities are then fused at the feature level for classification. Additionally, to address the class imbalance issue within the dataset, we adopted focal loss as the loss function to mitigate the impact of imbalanced data during model training, ultimately improving pain intensity classification performance.

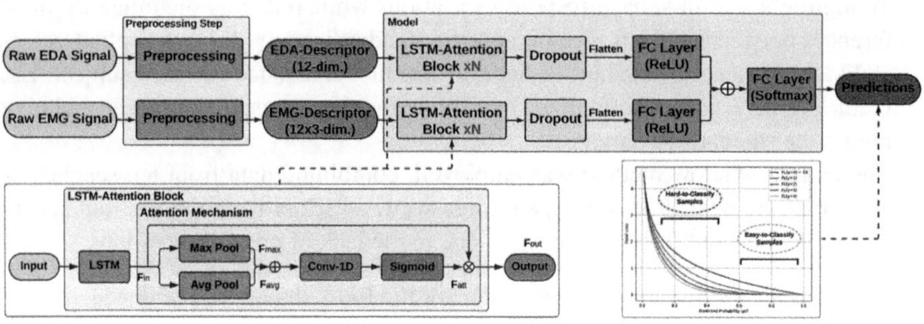

Fig. 2. Multimodal AI monitoring system for pain detection - Architecture of our proposed Bi-Modal Fusion (EDA + EMG) framework. This framework utilizes handcrafted statistical features derived from raw biosignals as input, enhances the extraction of both local and global features through multiple LSTM-Attention blocks, and employs focal loss to address class imbalance issue within the dataset.

LSTM-Attention Block. Firstly, LSTM [14] serves as the foundational module of the model, designed to handle long-term dependencies in time series data. By introducing learnable gating mechanisms, LSTM effectively alleviates the vanishing gradient problem, allowing it to capture short-term dynamic changes in the sequence while retaining long-term information. Secondly, the attention module [35] utilizes learnable weights to adjust the importance of input features, thereby emphasizing regions most relevant to the specific task. This enhances the model's selectivity for key feature regions and enables it to adaptively identify and highlight task-relevant information. The formula is as follows:

$$\mathbf{F}_{\text{out}} = \textit{sigmoid}\,(\textit{CNN-1D}\,(\textit{cat}\,(\textit{MaxPool}(\mathbf{F}_{\text{in}}),\, \textit{AvgPool}(\mathbf{F}_{\text{in}})))) \odot \mathbf{F}_{\text{in}} \quad (1)$$

Specifically, the input features $\mathbf{F}_{\text{in}}$ undergo both max pooling and average pooling operations along the channel axis to extract extreme values $\mathbf{F}_{\text{max}}$ and mean values $\mathbf{F}_{\text{avg}}$. These two results are then concatenated and passed into a 1D convolutional layer to extract local correlations of the features. Finally, a sigmoid activation function is used to generate the attention weights $\mathbf{F}_{\text{att}}$, reflecting the importance of features across different time steps. The input features and the attention weights are then multiplied element-wise to produce the attention-weighted features $\mathbf{F}_{\text{out}}$. To enhance the model's feature extraction capability, we stack multiple LSTM-attention blocks to enable the model to progressively capture deep dependencies within complex time series signals.

Focal Loss. Due to the class imbalance issue presents in the dataset, models often excessively focus on the majority classes while neglecting the minority classes, leading to a decline in classification performance. To address this problem, we chose to use focal loss [18] as the loss function. Focal loss dynamically controls the reduction of sample loss by adjusting the parameter γ. Due to the limited number of minority class samples, the model often struggles to learn sufficient effective features, resulting in a lower predicted probability. As shown in Fig. 2, as the value of γ increases, the loss for minority class samples remains relatively high, while the loss for majority class samples approaches zero. This adjustment mechanism effectively reduces the model's focus on the majority classes while enhancing its learning capability for the minority classes, thereby improving the model's robustness in handling imbalanced datasets. The specific formula is as follows:

$$\text{FL}(p_t) = -\alpha_t(1 - p_t)^{\gamma} \log(p_t) \quad (2)$$

where p_t is the predicted probability of class t by the model, α_t is the parameter used to balance the weights of different classes, which we set to 1 in this study, γ is the focusing parameter that controls the degree to which the sample loss is reduced. Fine-tuning is conducted in Sect. 4.4, as γ is a critical hyperparameter.

Model-Level Fusion. The features output from multiple LSTM-attention blocks are processed through dropout, flatten, and fully connected layers before being concatenated. Finally, the concatenated features are fed into the classifier and trained using focal loss. The specific parameter settings are shown in Table 1.

Table 1. Key hyperparameters of different model configurations for Uni-Modal and Bi-Modal Fusion. BM, FL, Att, CE, LR, and FT represent Base Model, Focal Loss, Attention, Cross Entropy, Learning Rate, and Fine Tuning respectively. *8* and *64* for Hidden Size and Neurons (FC-layer) were used for Uni-Modal. Num Layers and *Num Blocks* refer to LSTM and LSTM-Attention block. All methods were trained for 300 Epochs using the Adam optimizer.

Method	Batch Size	Hidden Size	Num Layers /*Num Blocks*	Dropout Rate	Kernel Size (Conv-1D)	Neurons (FC-layer)	LR	Loss
BM [21]	512	4/*8*	1	0.5	–	128/*64*	1×10^{-6}	CE
BM + FL ($\gamma = 2$)	512	4/*8*	1	0.5	–	128/*64*	1×10^{-6}	FL
BM + Att	512	4/*8*	1	0.5	3	128/*64*	1×10^{-6}	CE
BM + FL + Att ($\gamma = 2$)	512	4/*8*	1	0.5	3	128/*64*	1×10^{-6}	FL
BM + FL + Att ($\gamma = 0$, FT)	128	8	*3*	0.5	7	256	2.11×10^{-5}	FL
BM + FL + Att ($\gamma = 1$, FT)	128	4	*2*	0.2	3	256	2.24×10^{-5}	FL
BM + FL + Att ($\gamma = 2$, FT)	128	4	*2*	0.1	5	128	3.41×10^{-5}	FL
BM + FL + Att ($\gamma = 3$, FT)	256	4	*2*	0.4	5	32	8.77×10^{-5}	FL

4 Experiments

4.1 Implementation Details

Based on the EDA and EMG biosignals from the novel multimodal pain dataset [12], we conducted classification tasks for both seven and four classes of pain intensity. Specifically, we considered two durations of pain stimuli: phasic (P, 5 s) and tonic (T, 1 min) for each stimulus type: heat (H) and electrical (E). The stimuli were presented at three intensity levels: low (1), medium (2), and high (3).

For the 7-class classification task, we defined the following classes:

- Phasic pain (PD, RPD sub-datasets): No-Pain (NP), HP1, HP2, HP3, EP1, EP2, and EP3.
- Tonic pain (TD, RTD sub-datasets): NP, HT1, HT2, HT3, ET1, ET2, and ET3.

In the 4-class classification task, we focused on one type of pain stimulus (P or T) for one modality (H or E) at the same intensity levels, resulting in the following classes:

- Heat phasic pain (HPD, RHPD sub-datasets): NP, HP1, HP2, HP3.
- Electrical phasic pain (EPD, REPD sub-datasets): NP, EP1, EP2, EP3.
- Heat tonic pain (HTD sub-dataset): NP, HT1, HT2, HT3.
- Electrical tonic pain (ETD, RETD sub-datasets): NP, ET1, ET2, ET3.

The important hyperparameters for the model and training are detailed shown in Table 1. We utilized PyTorch 2.4.0 with CUDA support, along with an NVIDIA GeForce RTX 2080 Ti GPU with 11 GB of memory. The classification performance was measured using accuracy, and comprehensive hyperparameter optimization was performed using Weights & Biases [3].

4.2 Effectiveness Analysis

The RETD sub-dataset (4-class) was used to validate the effectiveness of our proposed framework, we also used the reproduced SOTA model [21] as the baseline for a fair comparison.

Table 2. Results for Uni-Modal (EMG, EDA) and Bi-Modal Fusion (EDA + EMG) on the RETD sub-dataset (4-class). FT represents the Fine Tuning of γ in Focal Loss. Tables 2, 3 and 4 present the results (Accuracy %) of each experiment after three runs, showing the calculated mean and standard deviation.

Method	Uni-Modal: EMG	Uni-Modal: EDA	Bi-Modal Fusion: EDA + EMG
Random Guess	25.00	25.00	25.00
Trivial Classifier	48.94	48.94	48.94
Base Model [21]	48.89 ± 0.18	54.52 ± 0.65	52.02 ± 0.52
Base Model + Focal Loss	49.62 ± 0.71	55.54 ± 0.51	55.86 ± 0.74
Base Model + Attention	50.56 ± 0.86	55.25 ± 0.13	55.61 ± 0.49
Base Model + Focal Loss + Attention	51.14 ± 0.50	56.02 ± 0.05	56.84 ± 0.59
Base Model + Focal Loss + Attention (FT)	$\mathbf{52.33} \pm 0.21$	$\mathbf{56.50} \pm 0.03$	$\mathbf{59.22} \pm 0.39$

As shown in Table 2, this is a 4-class classification task (NP, ET1, ET2, ET3), with the proportions of the four classes being 48.94%, 14.44%, 18.77%, and 17.85%, respectively. Therefore, the probability of correct prediction for Random Guess is 25.00%, while 48.94% for Trivial Classifier.

As illustrated in Table 2 and Fig. 3, for Bi-Modal Fusion, the individual use of focal loss and attention mechanism achieves improvements of 3.84% and 3.59%, respectively, highlighting the effectiveness of these two approaches. When both methods are used simultaneously with fine tuning of γ, our model outperforms the base model by 7.20%, further emphasizing their complementarity. In the case of single modality, the independent application of focal loss and attention mechanism also demonstrated positive effects: an enhancement of 1.02% and 0.73% for EDA, and 0.73% and 1.67% for EMG, respectively. The combination of focal loss and attention mechanism, along with fine-tuning of γ, resulted in performance improvements of 1.98% and 3.44% for EDA and EMG, respectively, compared to the base model, displaying a similar growth trend as observed in bi-modal fusion, which also indicates the robustness of the proposed method across different modalities.

Interestingly, for the base model, the performance of single modality EDA surpassed that of bi-modal fusion. However, after applying our proposed method, the performance of bi-modal fusion consistently outperformed that of any single modality. This phenomenon can be attributed to the significantly enhanced quality of feature extraction from single modality when utilizing focal loss or attention mechanism, thus resulting in a synergistic effect where the fusion of two modalities achieves greater performance than the sum of their individual contributions. Moreover, as the quality of extracted single modality features increases, the superiority of bi-modal fusion over each individual modality becomes more pronounced.

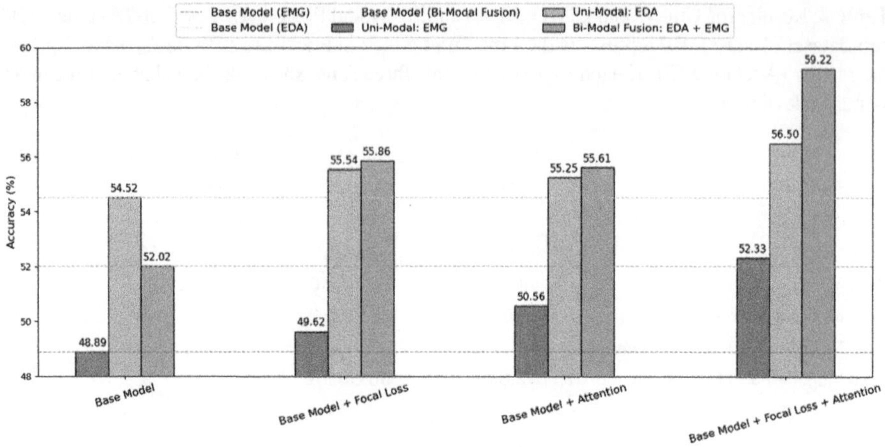

Fig. 3. Effectiveness analysis: Performance of different model configurations for Uni-Modal (EMG, EDA) and Bi-Modal Fusion (EDA + EMG) on the RETD sub-dataset (4-Class). Notable results demonstrate the effectiveness of using Focal Loss and Attention mechanism.

4.3 Robustness Analysis

To analyze the robustness of the proposed method across different sub-datasets, we evaluated the performance of the optimal model based on the RETD sub-dataset on the remaining 10 sub-datasets (without further fine-tuning). As shown in Fig. 4, an improvement in performance was observed across each sub-dataset (average improvement of 3.31%), particularly notable in the reduced sub-datasets. This is mainly due to the reduction strategy adopted in [21], which effectively reduces the data from No-Pain signals, ensuring that the resulting sub-datasets are relatively balanced. Consequently, the model can learn the effective features of the minority classes sufficiently rather than being limited to the majority classes. This has led to a significant improvement in the performance of our proposed method on these sub-datasets.

4.4 Focal Loss Tuning

Using focal loss as the loss function can effectively mitigate the class imbalance issue within the dataset. The key parameter γ, controls the reduction in loss for different samples, which is crucial for reducing the model's overemphasis on majority classes and improving its ability to learn effective features from minority classes. Thus, we performed fine-tuning of γ for the Bi-Modal Fusion model.

As shown in Table 3, when γ is 1, the model achieves the best performance, striking a balance between the loss reduction for both majority and minority classes. When applying the fine-tuned model to Uni-Modal experiments, it can be observed that for the EDA modality, $\gamma = 1$ also produces the best result, while for the EMG modality, $\gamma = 3$ yields the best performance, with $\gamma = 1$ being the second best. Therefore, considering all aspects, the model parameters tuned with $\gamma = 1$ show relatively optimal performance on the RETD sub-dataset.

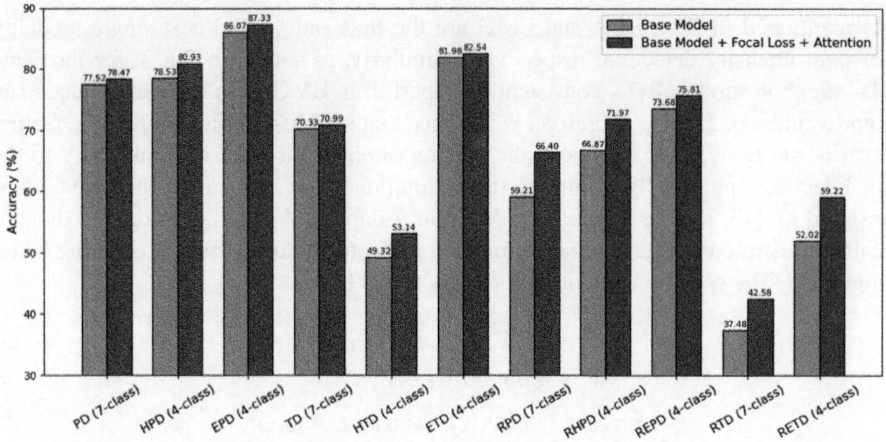

Fig. 4. Robustness analysis: Performance comparison between the base model [21] and our proposed model across 11 sub-datasets.

Table 3. Results of models fine-tuned with different γ values for Uni-Modal (EMG, EDA) and Bi-Modal Fusion (EDA + EMG).

Method	Uni-Modal: EMG	Uni-Modal: EDA	Bi-Modal Fusion: EDA + EMG
Base Model + Focal Loss + Attention ($\gamma = 0$)	51.52 ± 0.09	55.99 ± 0.06	57.88 ± 0.11
Base Model + Focal Loss + Attention ($\gamma = 1$)	51.90 ± 0.12	$\mathbf{56.50} \pm 0.03$	$\mathbf{59.22} \pm 0.39$
Base Model + Focal Loss + Attention ($\gamma = 2$)	51.73 ± 0.19	56.04 ± 0.26	58.58 ± 0.28
Base Model + Focal Loss + Attention ($\gamma = 3$)	$\mathbf{52.33} \pm 0.21$	55.95 ± 0.26	58.05 ± 0.40

In the Robustness Analysis 4.3, we directly used the optimal model with $\gamma = 1$ (without further fine-tuning) on the remaining 10 sub-datasets, demonstrating the model's robustness across different sub-datasets.

4.5 Fusion Strategy Comparison

Table 4. Performance of the optimized Bi-modal Fusion model fine-tuned based on different γ values under various feature fusion strategies. *: The best performance obtained across different fine-tuned γ values and fusion strategies.

Method	Directly Cat	Adaptive Sum	Adaptive Cat
Base Model + Focal Loss + Attention ($\gamma = 0$)	57.88 ± 0.11	57.97 ± 0.72	$\mathbf{58.02} \pm 0.83$
Base Model + Focal Loss + Attention ($\gamma = 1$)	59.22 ± 0.39	58.81 ± 0.41	$\mathbf{59.25} \pm 0.43$
Base Model + Focal Loss + Attention ($\gamma = 2$)	58.58 ± 0.28	59.02 ± 0.68	$\mathbf{59.37}^{*} \pm 0.85$
Base Model + Focal Loss + Attention ($\gamma = 3$)	58.05 ± 0.40	58.31 ± 0.72	$\mathbf{58.55} \pm 0.79$

As mentioned in [21], EDA and EMG are the first and second best single modality for pain intensity detection, respectively. Similarly, as shown in Fig. 3, for the same classification model, EDA consistently outperforms EMG with an average accuracy improvement of 5.10%. Therefore, we believe that simple concatenation at the feature level is too basic, as it overlooks the different contributions of each modality to the final decision, potentially disrupting the optimal matching pattern between modalities. Inspired by [13,28], we further introduced an Adaptive Weighting Module to dynamically adjust the importance of each modality's features during fusion, ensuring better alignment. The specific calculation formulas are as follows:

$$\mathbf{F}_{\text{cat}} = cat(\mathbf{F}_{\text{modal1}}, \mathbf{F}_{\text{modal2}}) \tag{3}$$

$$\mathbf{w} = softmax\,(MLP(\mathbf{F}_{\text{cat}})) \tag{4}$$

$$\mathbf{F}_{\text{fused}} = cat\,(w_1 \cdot \mathbf{F}_{\text{modal1}}, w_2 \cdot \mathbf{F}_{\text{modal2}}) \tag{5}$$

Specifically, as depicted in Fig. 5, we first concatenate the two modality features and then apply a Multi-Layer Perceptron (MLP) to the concatenated features, generating two weights. These weights are multiplied by their respective features to obtain the weighted features. Finally, the two weighted features are either summed or concatenated to produce the final fused feature. Since the weights are generated by the MLP from the concatenated features, they inherently capture the global interaction between the two modalities. Additionally, the tanh activation function used in the MLP maps the input between −1 and 1, emphasizing the positive or negative correlations between the features. Therefore, the two learnable weights can be interpreted as reflecting the relative importance of each modality's features.

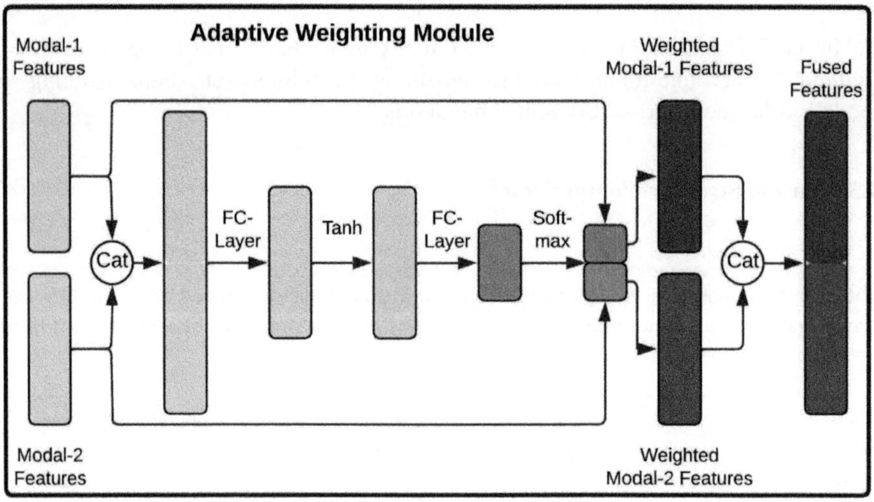

Fig. 5. Flowchart of the Adaptive Weighting Module for assigning learnable weights to different modality features.

As shown in Table 4, we conducted experiments on the optimal models (without further fine-tuning) obtained through different γ values to compare different fusion strategies for the weighted features. The results demonstrate that using concatenation for weighted features consistently yields the best performance, outperforming both summation and direct concatenation without weighting. Furthermore, the optimal model based on $\gamma = 2$, when using the adaptive concatenation fusion strategy (without further fine-tuning), achieved a result of 59.37%, which still surpassed the fine-tuned optimal model with $\gamma = 1$ (59.22%), highlighting the effectiveness of the adaptive weighting module combined with the concatenation strategy.

5 Discussion

This work focuses on enhancing the pain classification performance of the Bi-Modal Fusion algorithm based on EDA and EMG signals. Through our analysis of the SOTA method [21], we identified two key problems: (1) class imbalance issue within the dataset, and (2) limited feature extraction capabilities due to the use of only a single LSTM layer. To address these challenges, we proposed an improved model that integrates LSTM with an attention module, enhancing its ability to capture both global and local features. Additionally, we apply focal loss to effectively mitigate the class imbalance issue during training. Extensive experiments demonstrate that the incorporation of focal loss and the attention mechanism contributes positively to classification performance. When both techniques are combined, we observe a significant performance improvement of 7.20% on the RETD sub-dataset, highlighting the effectiveness of the proposed method. Furthermore, the framework shows a trend of performance improvement across different modalities and sub-datasets, further underscoring the robustness of our approach. Therefore, we believe that the proposed LSTM-Attention based Bi-Modal Fusion framework based on EDA and EMG signals holds significant potential for clinical pain detection.

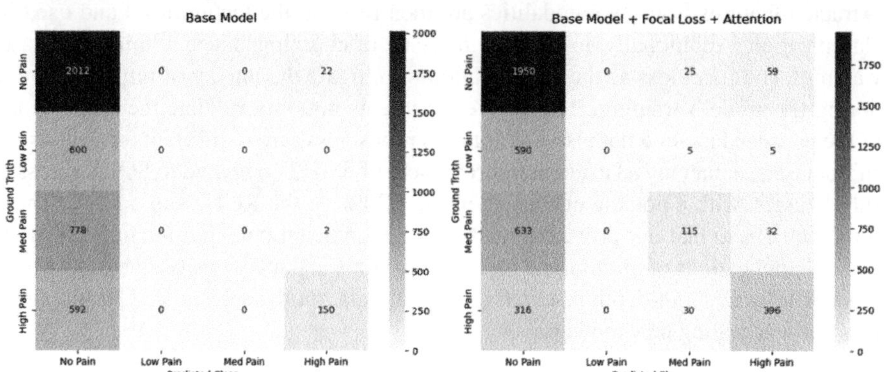

Fig. 6. Confusion matrices for the RETD sub-dataset (4-class): base model [21] (left) and proposed model (right), demonstrating notable improvement in minority classes.

However, we found that although the model's performance has improved on minority classes, there remains significant room for enhancement in the Low-Pain and Medium-Pain levels, as illustrated in Fig. 6. Therefore, in our future work, we will focus on the following aspects:

1. Input Data: The handcrafted statistical features currently utilized capture only basic statistical properties and overlook the complex dynamic relationships inherent in raw biological signals. This limitation may result in similar handcrafted features for minority classes, making it challenging for the model to differentiate between them. Thus, we believe that combining LSTM-based feature extraction from denoised biosignals with experience-based handcrafted features represents a meaningful research direction [31].
2. Feature-Level Fusion: The EDA and EMG signals corresponding to a pain stimulus are inherently related, however, the current model lacks effective information interaction. Therefore, employing cross-attention mechanism could facilitate interaction between two modalities, thereby enhancing the fusion effect [27].
3. New Modalities: Facial expressions, vocal cues, and body posture are effective indicators of a patient's pain state [11]. The complementary nature of various modalities can enhance a system's robustness. Therefore, our next step is to integrate video and audio data from patients to further improve the accuracy and robustness of our framework.

Ultimately, our goal is to develop a reliable multimodal fusion framework for pain intensity detection in clinical applications, particularly for improving patient care in postoperative settings.

6 Conclusion

This study proposes an effective Bi-Modal Fusion framework for pain classification based on EDA and EMG signals, which integrates LSTM and attention mechanism, demonstrating strong capabilities for capturing both global and local features. The extracted features from two modalities are then fused at the feature level and used for classification. Additionally, to address the issue of class imbalance within the dataset, we employed focal loss as the loss function to mitigate the impact of imbalanced data during the model's training. Extensive experiments not only validate the effectiveness of the proposed method but also highlight its robustness across different modalities and sub-datasets, achieving an average improvement of 3.31% compared to SOTA across 11 sub-datasets, with a notable enhancement of 7.20% on the RETD sub-dataset. Therefore, we believe that our proposed method has significant potential for facilitating the clinical applications of multimodal fusion algorithms in pain intensity detection. Future work will focus on in-depth research into input data, more sophisticated fusion strategies and integrating new modalities.

Acknowledgments. This work was supported by DFG Projects (Pain analysis AL 638/20-1, AL 638/19-1 and Vitalkam AL 638/14-1) and EFRE-Project (Orakel, Nr. 40 3704 1002).

Competing Interests. The authors declare no competing interests.

References

1. Aust, M.P.: Pain Assessment in Nonverbal Patients. Am. J. Crit. Care **22**(3), 256–256 (2013). https://doi.org/10.4037/ajcc2013701
2. Badura, A., Masłowska, A., Myśliwiec, A., Piętka, E.: Multimodal signal analysis for pain recognition in physiotherapy using wavelet scattering transform. Sensors **21**(4) (2021). https://doi.org/10.3390/s21041311, https://www.mdpi.com/1424-8220/21/4/1311
3. Biewald, L.: Experiment tracking with weights and biases (2020). https://www.wandb.com/. software available from wandb.com
4. Boring, B.L., Ng, B.W., Nanavaty, N., Mathur, V.A.: Over-rating pain is overrated: a fundamental self-other bias in pain reporting behavior. J. Pain **23**(10), 1779–1789 (2022). https://doi.org/10.1016/j.jpain.2022.06.002
5. Bouajram, R.H., Sebat, C.M., Love, D., Louie, E.L., Wilson, M.D., Duby, J.J.: Comparison of self-reported and behavioral pain assessment tools in critically ill patients. J. Intensive Care Med. **35**(5), 453–460 (2020). https://doi.org/10.1177/0885066618757450. pMID: 29448873
6. Chapman, C.R., Casey, K.L., Dubner, R., Foley, K.M., Gracely, R.H., Reading, A.E.: Pain measurement: an overview. Pain **22**(1), 1–31 (1985). https://doi.org/10.1016/0304-3959(85)90145-9. https://www.sciencedirect.com/science/article/pii/0304395985901459
7. Chen, D., et al.: Scalp EEG-based pain detection using convolutional neural network. IEEE Trans. Neural Syst. Rehabil. Eng. **30**, 274–285 (2022). https://doi.org/10.1109/TNSRE.2022.3147673
8. Fernandez Rojas, R., et al.: Multimodal physiological sensing for the assessment of acute pain. Front. Pain Res. **4** (2023). https://doi.org/10.3389/fpain.2023.1150264
9. Gkikas, S., Chatzaki, C., Tsiknakis, M.: Multi-task neural networks for pain intensity estimation using electrocardiogram and demographic factors. In: Maciaszek, L.A., Mulvenna, M.D., Ziefle, M. (eds.) ICT4AWE ICT4AWE 2021 2022. CCIS, vol. 1856, pp. 324–337. Springer, Cham (2023). https://doi.org/10.1007/978-3-031-37496-8_17
10. Gkikas, S., et al.: Multimodal automatic assessment of acute pain through facial videos and heart rate signals utilizing transformer-based architectures. Front. Pain Res. (Lausanne, Switzerland), **5**, 1372814 (2024). https://doi.org/10.3389/fpain.2024.1372814
11. Gkikas, S., Tsiknakis, M.: Automatic assessment of pain based on deep learning methods: a systematic review. Comput. Methods Programs Biomed. **231**, 107365 (2023). https://doi.org/10.1016/j.cmpb.2023.107365, https://www.sciencedirect.com/science/article/pii/S0169260723000329
12. Gruss, S., et al.: Multi-modal signals for analyzing pain responses to thermal and electrical stimuli. J. Visualized Exp. **146**, e59057 (2019). https://doi.org/10.3791/59057
13. Gu, X., Wang, Z., Jin, I., Wu, Z.: Advancing multimodal data fusion in pain recognition: a strategy leveraging statistical correlation and human-centered perspectives (2024). https://arxiv.org/abs/2404.00320
14. Hochreiter, S., Schmidhuber, J.: Long short-term memory. Neural Comput. **9**(8), 1735–1780 (1997)
15. Huang, Y., Qing, L., Xu, S., Wang, L., Peng, Y.: HybNet: a hybrid network structure for pain intensity estimation. Vis. Comput. **38**(3), 871–882 (2022). https://doi.org/10.1007/s00371-021-02056-y
16. Jensen, M.P.: The validity and reliability of pain measures in adults with cancer. J. Pain **4**(1), 2–21 (2003). https://doi.org/10.1054/jpai.2003.1, https://www.sciencedirect.com/science/article/pii/S1526590002650011
17. Kunz, M., Lautenbacher, S., LeBlanc, N., Rainville, P.: Are both the sensory and the affective dimensions of pain encoded in the face? Pain **153**(2), 350–358 (2012)

18. Lin, T.Y., Goyal, P., Girshick, R., He, K., Dollár, P.: Focal loss for dense object detection (2018). https://arxiv.org/abs/1708.02002
19. Nakanishi, T., Fujiwara, K., Sobue, K.: Prediction model of postoperative pain exacerbation using a wearable electrocardiogram sensor. In: 2023 Asia Pacific Signal and Information Processing Association Annual Summit and Conference (APSIPA ASC), pp. 195–198 (2023). https://doi.org/10.1109/APSIPAASC58517.2023.10317498
20. Othman, E., Werner, P., Saxen, F., Al-Hamadi, A., Gruss, S., Walter, S.: Automated electrodermal activity and facial expression analysis for continuous pain intensity monitoring on the x-ite pain database. Life **13**(9) (2023). https://doi.org/10.3390/life13091828, https://www.mdpi.com/2075-1729/13/9/1828
21. Othman, E., Werner, P., Saxen, F., Fiedler, M.A., Al-Hamadi, A.: An automatic system for continuous pain intensity monitoring based on analyzing data from uni-, bi-, and multi-modality. Sensors **22**(13) (2022). https://doi.org/10.3390/s22134992, https://www.mdpi.com/1424-8220/22/13/4992
22. Payen, J.F., et al.: Assessing pain in critically ill sedated patients by using a behavioral pain scale. Crit. Care Med. **12**, 2258–2263 (2001)
23. Pouromran, F., Radhakrishnan, S., Kamarthi, S.: Exploration of physiological sensors, features, and machine learning models for pain intensity estimation. PLoS ONE **16**(7), e0254108 (2021)
24. Robinson, M.E., Myers, C.D., Sadler, I.J., Riley, J.L.I., Kvaal, S.A., Geisser, M.E.: Bias effects in three common self-report pain assessment measures. Clin. J. Pain **13**, 74–81 (1997)
25. Salekin, M.S., et al.: Multimodal neonatal procedural and postoperative pain assessment dataset. Data Brief **35**, 106796 (2021)
26. Segning, C.M., da Silva, R.A., Ngomo, S.: An innovative EEG-based pain identification and quantification: a pilot study. Sensors **24**(12) (2024). https://doi.org/10.3390/s24123873, https://www.mdpi.com/1424-8220/24/12/3873
27. Shetty, S., V S, A., AJIT, M.: Comprehensive review of multimodal medical data analysis: Open issues and future research directions. Acta Informatica Pragensia **11**, 423–457 (2022). https://doi.org/10.18267/j.aip.202
28. Thiam, P., Kestler, H., Schwenker, F.: Multimodal deep denoising convolutional autoencoders for pain intensity classification based on physiological signals. In: ICPRAM 2020: Proceedings of the 9th International Conference on Pattern Recognition Applications and Methods, 2020, pp. 289–296 (2020). https://doi.org/10.5220/0008896102890296
29. Thiam, P., Kestler, H.A., Schwenker, F.: Multimodal deep denoising convolutional autoencoders for pain intensity classification based on physiological signals. In: ICPRAM, pp. 289–296 (2020)
30. Thiam, P., Schwenker, F.: Combining deep and hand-crafted features for audio-based pain intensity classification. In: Schwenker, F., Scherer, S. (eds.) MPRSS 2018. LNCS (LNAI), vol. 11377, pp. 49–58. Springer, Cham (2019). https://doi.org/10.1007/978-3-030-20984-1_5
31. Wang, R., Xu, K., Feng, H., Chen, W.: Hybrid RNN-ANN based deep physiological network for pain recognition. In: 2020 42nd Annual International Conference of the IEEE Engineering in Medicine & Biology Society (EMBC), vol. 2020, pp. 5584–5587 (2020). https://doi.org/10.1109/EMBC44109.2020.9175247
32. Werner, P., Al-Hamadi, A., Gruss, S., Walter, S.: Twofold-multimodal pain recognition with the x-ite pain database. In: 2019 8th International Conference on Affective Computing and Intelligent Interaction Workshops and Demos (ACIIW), pp. 290–296 (2019). https://doi.org/10.1109/ACIIW.2019.8925061
33. Werner, P., Al-Hamadi, A., Limbrecht-Ecklundt, K., Walter, S., Gruss, S., Traue, H.C.: Automatic pain assessment with facial activity descriptors. IEEE Trans. Affect. Comput. **8**(3), 286–299 (2016)

34. Williams, A.C.D.C.: Facial expression of pain: an evolutionary account. Behav. Brain Sci. **25**(4), 439–455 (2002). https://doi.org/10.1017/S0140525X02000080
35. Woo, S., Park, J., Lee, J.Y., Kweon, I.S.: CBAM: convolutional block attention module (2018). https://arxiv.org/abs/1807.06521
36. Xin, X., Li, X., Yang, S., Lin, X., Zheng, X.: Pain expression assessment based on a locality and identity aware network. IET Image Process. **15**(12), 2948–58 (2021). https://doi.org/10.1049/ipr2.12282

Automatic Comparison of Ecuadorian Facial Features with Marquardt Beauty Mask

Jesús Ormaza[1,2], Paulina Morillo[1,3(✉)], and Diego Vallejo-Huanga[1,3]

[1] Department of Computer Science, Universidad Politécnica Salesiana, Quito, Ecuador
pmorillo@ups.edu.ec

[2] School of Computing and Mathematical Sciences, University of Leicester, Leicester, UK

[3] Universidad Politécnica Salesiana, IDEIAGEOCA Research Group, Quito, Ecuador

Abstract. Surgical specialists use facial analysis tools to evaluate human beauty, particularly in the context of reconstructive procedures. Among the tools used to perform facial analysis is the Marquardt Beauty Mask, a mask developed by Stephen Marquardt that represents the perfect proportions a face should have. This article shows the implementation of a web tool that uses computer vision to extract the differences between the proportions of the mask, considered an ideal model of beauty, and a facial photograph of a person. In addition, we performed a statistical analysis of the differences found between the features of 432 facial photographs of Ecuadorians and the mask. The results reveal that Ecuadorian faces, across all ethnicities and genders, show significant deviations in three of the four key distances used to evaluate the mask's suitability. Only one distance aligns closely with the ideal proportions defined by the mask, with over 90% of individuals meeting this criterion. According to the results, the measures calculated on the faces differ considerably from those in the Marquardt Beauty mask. These differences show that Ecuadorians have faces that are wider and longer than the mask. Therefore, the widespread use of tools built for a single archetype of people could be inaccurate in evaluating the harmony and symmetry of a face.

Keywords: Image processing · Face detection · Golden ratio · Ethnic groups

1 Introduction

Although a person's beauty is not an absolute concept, in most cultures, it is defined by the harmony and symmetry of the face. Scientists, thinkers, and artists have been interested in beauty throughout history since it is related, in turn, to physical attractiveness, which has influence and connotations within society, from biological processes such as choosing a partner to social processes such as obtaining status, being selected for a job, etc. [19]. Some studies have demonstrated a correlation between facial symmetry and beauty, health, and personality traits. In [6] conducted experiments involving 55 volunteers who evaluated photographs of 20 women based on these attributes. The findings revealed that faces with greater symmetry were perceived as more attractive, healthier,

This work was supported by the IDEIAGEOCA Research Group of the Universidad Politécnica Salesiana in Quito, Ecuador.

J. Röning and J. Filipe (Eds.): ROBOVIS 2025, CCIS 2629, pp. 182–192, 2026.
https://doi.org/10.1007/978-3-032-00986-9_13

and associated with positive personality traits. Conversely, faces with lower symmetry were often judged less attractive and more likely to exhibit anxious traits. Some authors consider it a social phenomenon because beauty is a perception, often influenced by the media that imposes standards and models of beauty [16]. Several mathematical proportions are proposed to evaluate facial symmetry and beauty, such as the 1:1 ratio and axial division into thirds. However, the number ϕ, also known as the golden ratio, appears to be the most effective for assessing facial symmetry and beauty, as it is found in a wide variety of entities, ranging from man-made structures to living organisms [17]. This number appears recurrently in nature and is associated with harmony. Its value is equivalent to 1.1618, resulting from the ratio between two segments considered as the proportion of golden beauty.

Dr. Stephen R. Marquardt, a specialist in oral and maxillofacial surgery, explored facial proportions using the mathematical properties of the ϕ number (golden ratio) applied to geometry. He designed a geometric figure known as the "golden decagon," consisting of one primary decagon and 42 secondary decagons [1]. According to Dr. Marquardt, the golden decagon is applicable in various contexts, including the analysis of human facial beauty. Building on this concept, he developed the "Marquardt mask" or "golden mask," a tool representing the ideal proportions of the human face. This mask serves as a benchmark for evaluating facial beauty by assessing how closely a face aligns with its proportions [14]. The Marquardt mask has found applications across multiple disciplines, including dentistry and surgery. For instance, in [7], the mask was used to analyze photographs of dental patients to determine whether individuals with proper occlusion and perceived attractiveness exhibit the golden ratio in their facial structure. Similarly, in [15], the mask was proposed as an alternative technique for planning facial feminization surgeries.

In computing, the mask served as an instrument to evaluate the beauty of 30 female finalists in beauty contests [18], using MATLAB tools, features were extracted from the face photographs and compared to the mask to obtain a numerical score. Other works do not directly use the mask, but the number ϕ and the golden ratio concept to develop machine learning models [8, 13]. A common aspect in most works is that the mask is adjusted manually. In contrast, the proposed tool automatically adjusts the mask and calculates the distances based on facial landmarks detected by a face detection algorithm. This approach reduces human error and increases the accuracy of the fitting process by relying on mathematical calculations rather than subjective visual assessment.

In general terms, the mask has been developed based on a single type of individual: Caucasians. Although there are variations, Asian and African, there may be groups of people for whom the mask is unsuitable, as shown [20] in this study with people from South India. Applying the mask to 150 photographs of faces and taking distances over different points, the distances of the faces were compared with those of the mask using statistical methods. Finally, they concluded that the mask was inadequate for their population.

This work proposes the development of a web tool that allows users to submit a facial image, select the gender, and automatically process the image to adjust it to Marquardt's mask. The tool provides the image with the mask applied and calculates four key distances to evaluate the face's alignment with the mask. These distances can be used to assess differences in specific face areas, such as width and height, to study potential malformations or aesthetic enhancements. In addition, a comparative analysis is presented between Ecuadorians' facial harmony and symmetry versus the beauty standard based on the proportions of the Marquardt mask based on Caucasian features.

2 Methodology

2.1 Application Architecture

A web application was developed to facilitate the use of the mask in digital facial photographs, which processes an image, adjusts it to the mask according to the face's gender, and calculates the facial metrics. The application architecture follows the diagram in Fig. 1. Using an architecture based on APIs allows you to distribute the load and choose the appropriate technology in each module. In this way, the application is decomposed into small modules that communicate with each other, optimizing the use of the resources available on the platform.

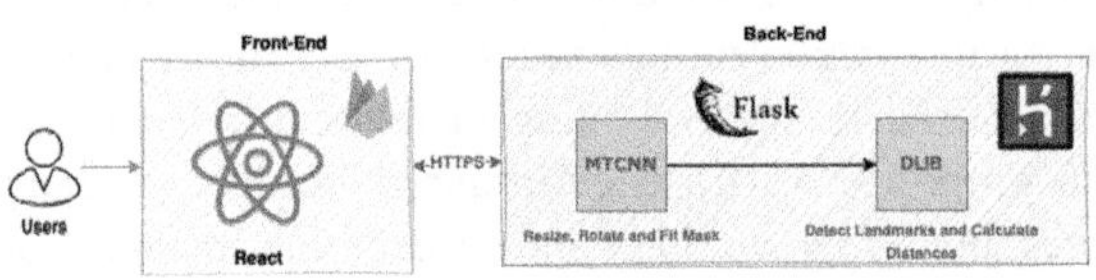

Fig. 1. *Full-stack* diagram of the application architecture.

First, React is used to develop the part of *front-end* because it is a light framework that allows reusability of the components and easy maintenance of the code and hosted on *Firebase*, a platform developed by Google that offers free hosting service. Then, the Python programming language is used with the Flask web development framework to build face detection services. This language has many libraries specialized in computer vision that facilitate image processing. The part of *back-end* is hosted on the *Heroku* platform, allowing us to easily host and manage Flask-based applications.

2.2 Mask Fitting and Feature Extraction

Figure 2 outlines the steps for processing each image. The mask images were obtained from Marquardt's official website, where two variants are available: a female version (MF) and a male version (MM), with original dimensions of 567 × 705 pixels and 500 × 711 pixels, respectively, as detailed in [2]. The mask images underwent preprocessing to ensure compatibility with the facial images. They were edited to make the background transparent and cropped so that the edges of the photos aligned precisely with the mask's borders. This step was crucial for achieving accurate overlay during superimposition, as it removed any gaps between the mask's borders and the image edges. The resulting dimensions are 441 × 599 pixels (MF) and 500 × 711 pixels (MM).

Then, face detection is performed using a pre-trained model based on the Multitask Convolutional Neural Network (MTCNN) [21]. The MTCNN model operates in three main stages, each utilizing a neural network. The first network, *P-Net*, identifies numerous candidate regions likely to contain a face within the image. These candidate regions are then passed to the second network, *R-Net*, a refinement layer that eliminates most false positives—regions that do not correspond to a face or its parts. Finally, the output is processed by the third network, *O-Net*, which performs a final refinement to confirm face regions and generates the coordinates of five key facial landmarks [9]: the eyes, nose, and corners of the lips, as illustrated in Fig. 2. The coordinates provided by the model are used to adjust the mask, adhering to the guidelines established by Marquardt in [2].

For the later phase of adjustment of the mask, it is sought that the face has a vertical position, in which when joining the pupils of the eyes with a line, its slope is equal to zero. Therefore, each image is rotated by an angle θ using the coordinates of each eye as a reference, with notation X_i and Y_i. The value of the angle of rotation is calculated with the Equation with the arctangent of the relationship between the difference of (Y_2-Y_1) and the difference (X_2-X_1).

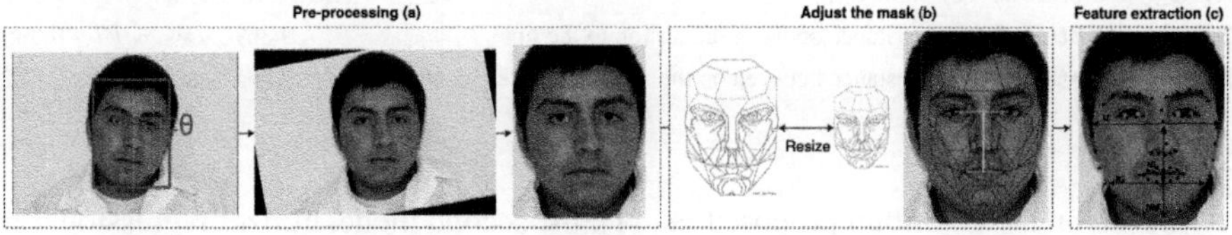

Fig. 2. Steps for processing an image of the dataset.

The next step is to crop the rotated photo using the box that frames the face. To position the mask on the face, reference lines are drawn on both photographs, the face and the mask: i) a horizontal line between the pupils, ii) a horizontal line between the extreme parts of the lips, and iii) a vertical line between the intermediate parts of i) and ii). The lines on the mask must match their corresponding lines on the face image.

The vertical lines of the face and the mask must be the same length to fit together. To calculate the vertical line on the face, the midpoint of each horizontal line is calculated, taking each line as a two-dimensional vector. The value of the vertical line is calculated as the module of the resulting vector between the coordinates of the midpoints.

The vertical line of the mask is obtained using a ratio based on the image of the female mask. The length of the image (LI) is equal to 599px, and its vertical line (LV_M) equals 225px, so the aspect ratio λ between the vertical line of the mask and the total length of the mask is equal to 2.662. The width of the image (AM) is 441px, maintaining consistency with its aspect ratio. Then, to resize the image simply multiply λ with LV_M. When resizing the mask, its morphology is not lost since the proportion between the length of the resized image and the vertical line is the same regardless of its dimensions.

To evaluate the facial characteristics of an individual, four key distances were analyzed: Inter-Zygomatic (IZ), Inter-Gonial (IG), NasioNLip (NL), and NasioNMenton (NM) [20]. These distances, commonly used in facial bone analysis, are traditionally calculated on facial radiographs to ensure precision. In this study, the distances were computed using frontal facial images. The calculation of these distances relies on 68 key facial landmarks, which were extracted using two pre-trained models embedded in the DLIB library [12]. DLIB, implemented in C++, is accessible through other programming languages like Python.

The first model detects faces in an image by combining two algorithms: the Histogram of Oriented Gradients (HOG) feature descriptor [5] and the Support Vector Machine (SVM) classification algorithm [10]. The HOG descriptor divides the image into sub-regions (cells) to compute histograms of gradient orientations, normalize them, and generate a feature set. These features are then fed into the SVM classifier, determining whether a specific region contains a face.

Table 1. Calculation of distances on the face and mask.

	Face	Description	Man mask	Woman mask
IZ	$d_{1R} = dist(P1, P17)$	Face width	$d_{1M} = AM$	$d_{1M} = AM$
IG	$d_{2R} = dist(P5, P13)$	Jaw width	$d_{2M} = AM * 0.717$	$d_{2M} = AM * 0.709$
NL	$d_{3R} = dist(P28, P52)$	Distance between the nasion to the lips	$d_{3M} = LI * 0.367$	$d_{3M} = LI * 0.368$
NM	$d_{4R} = dist(P28, P52)$	Distance between on the nation and the chin	$d_{4M} = LI * 0.565$	$d_{4M} = LI * 0.571$

Based on the algorithm proposed in [11], the second model utilizes regression trees enhanced through gradient boosting to identify the 68 key facial points. This model takes the bounding box enclosing the face as input, as provided by the first model. To achieve high precision in detecting landmarks, the bounding box generated by the HOG-based model serves as the input. Once the 68 key points are identified, the Euclidean distances between specific landmark pairs are calculated, representing the modules of the resulting vectors. Additionally, the distances on the mask are computed as proportional measures based on the resized dimensions of the mask, as detailed in Table 1.

2.3 Analysis of Facial Symmetry in Images of Ecuadorian People

This study uses a dataset of facial images of Ecuadorian individuals, publicly available at [3]. The dataset is categorized into four of the most representative ethnic groups in Ecuador: Afro-Ecuadorian (50 instances), European descendants (50 instances), Indigenous (50 instances), and Mestizo (280 instances). Each ethnic group features distinct cardinalities for female ($|F|$) and male ($|M|$) instances. The Indigenous group has $|F| = 11$ and $|M| = 39$, while the European-descendant group consists of $|F| = 9$ and $|M| = 41$. The Mestizo group, the largest category, includes $|F| = 61$ and $|M| = 219$. Finally, the Afro-Ecuadorian group contains $|F| = 11$ and $|M| = 39$. This distribution highlights the varying representation of ethnicities and genders within the dataset, providing a comprehensive basis for the analysis.

To analyze the similarity of a face with the mask, two key concepts used to define beauty are employed: symmetry and facial harmony. Symmetry in the context of facial analysis refers to the resemblance between the right and left sides of the face. In the case of the mask, its left side is identical to its right side. If, when superimposing the mask on the image of the face, the right and left parts fit perfectly, the face is symmetrical. On the other hand, facial harmony relates to the balance between the proportions of different parts of the face and its symmetry. Given that the mask adheres to the golden ratio when calculating the ratio between each distance from the face, d_{iR}, and its corresponding distance in the mask, d_{iM}, a value close to one indicates harmony in the face.

The statistical analysis begins by grouping the data by gender and ethnicity. The Shapiro-Wilk test and Q-Q plot are used to assess data normality. As noted in [4], the Shapiro-Wilk test is particularly sensitive to deviations from normality in datasets with fewer than 50 instances. In contrast, the Q-Q plot visually assesses normality and is recommended for larger datasets. Once the normality of the data is demonstrated, parametric tests are applied to measure the differences between the actual measurements of the face and those of the mask.

Finally, each distance from the face d_{iR} is divided by its corresponding in the mask d_{iM}, i.e. $r = d_{iR}/d_{iM}$. Where a $r = 1$ implies that the mask fits perfectly on the face. However, when $r \neq 1$, each individual is grouped into three groups based on the value of r: Group 1 for $r < 0.9$, Group 2 for $0.9 \leq r \leq 1.1$, and Group 3 for $r > 1.1$. The grouping criteria were established because there is no mathematically defined standard for assessing whether a face adapts to the mask. Instead, the evaluation is typically visual. To provide a more systematic and quantifiable approach, these groups were defined to categorize the level of fit. In this way, if r belongs to group one, it means that $d_{iR} < d_{iM}$, if r belongs to group two, then $d_{iR} = d_{iM}$, otherwise $d_{iR} > d_{iM}$.

3 Results and Discussion

The final result of the web application is available at https://mrd-mask.web.app/. Figure 3 shows the application interface, where the user can enter a photograph and choose its gender. With these input data, the processing is performed to obtain an image of the face with the Marquardt mask superimposed and adjusted. The ratios between the distances from the original face and the corresponding distances from the mask are also shown. To improve the application's performance, the face's image must be a max-

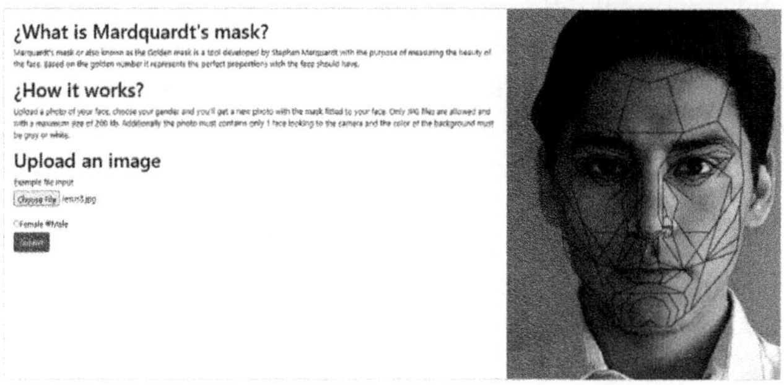

Fig. 3. Marquardt Mask Superimposition Interface.

imum of 200 KB and be in JPG format. In addition, it is recommended that the face is centered, looking at the camera, and the background color is white or gray.

The dataset of facial images of Ecuadorian people [3], consisting of 432 photographs, was used to carry out the experiments. The *dataset* is a compilation of snapshots taken of the faces of Ecuadorian people with their respective biometric metadata. The average dimensions of the images are 1920×1280 pixels. The normality of the distances for each ethnicity and gender was assessed using the statistical tests detailed in Table 2, with a significance level of $\alpha = 0.01$. These results indicate that the distributions of all distances follow a normal trend, as all values exceed the alpha value. Consequently, the t-student test was employed to evaluate the differences between the distances from the face and those from the mask.

Table 2. Shapiro-Wilks test for IZ, IG, NL, and NM distances.

Sex	Ethnicity	p-value			
		IZ	IG	NL	NM
Men	Indigenous	0.5180	0.1559	0.0323	0.9403
	European	0.1398	0.2048	0.8785	0.4085
	Afro-Ecuadorian	0.9018	0.8380	0.4196	0.5949
Women	Indigenous	0.4445	0.1330	0.7135	0.7980
	European	0.1398	0.2048	0.8785	0.4085
	Afro-Ecuadorian	0.9031	0.5873	0.9887	0.4210

In the experimental process, each image was processed, including mask adjustment to the face, feature extraction, and distance calculation. The mean and standard deviation (SD) of the distances for each ethnic group are summarized in Table 3. The t-Student test, performed with a significance level of $\alpha = 0.05$, tested the null hypothesis $H_0 : \mu_{d_{iM}} = \mu_{d_{iR}}$ against the alternative hypothesis $H_a : \mu_{d_{iM}} \neq \mu_{d_{iR}}$. The results indicate that, for all ethnic groups, the IZ, IG, and NM distances show significant differences compared to their corresponding mask distances. In contrast, the NL distance does not exhibit significant differences.

In most cases, the *p-values* were below the significance level α, leading to the rejection of the null hypothesis. This implies that most individuals in each group do not have distances comparable to those of the mask. The data were grouped based on their r value and visualized in Fig. 4 to further analyze the distances by ethnicity and the total population.

Additionally, box plots were used to observe the data distribution and compare statistics such as the mean and inter-quartile range. As illustrated in Fig. 5, although the mask was designed based on European models, it is the Afro-Ecuadorian ethnic group that exhibits the closest alignment to the ideal proportions. Their IZ, IG, and NL distances are the closest to the mask's mean. In contrast, other ethnic groups show significant deviations from these distances, which may be attributed to the self-identification process described in the *dataset*, where each individual was categorized into an ethnic group based on their self-perception and the group they considered to belong to.

European women show the most extended interquartile range within the female gender for the IZ, NL, and NM distances, on the other hand, the interquartile range of European men in the NM distance also shows the longest. The reason for the dispersion of data on European ethnicity may be due to self-naming in the *dataset*, so, having characteristics that seem evident to European people, such as skin color, is not enough to affirm that an individual has European ancestry. The group with the most atypical points is European men, in which at least one atypical point is shown in each distance, which shows that the people who called themselves European descendants do not have a relationship with the ideal metrics of this ethnic group. Furthermore, some individuals could call themselves Europeans based solely on characteristics such as skin or eye color.

Table 3. t-student test for face vs. mask distances.

		Women					Men				
		Photography		Mask		p-value	Photography		Mask		p-value
		Mean	SD	Mean	SD		Mean	SD	Mean	SD	
Indigenous	IZ	424.27	36.95	368.73	26.95	7.68e-04	416.74	35.27	375.36	31.74	6.22e-07
	IG	353.31	31.93	261.43	19.11	3.51e-07	351.41	34.53	269.13	22.75	2.20e-16
	NL	177.53	13.21	182.43	13.36	3.98e-01	192.12	20.34	196.29	16.54	3.25e-01
	NM	338.94	31.14	283.06	20.72	1.13e-04	355.40	35.26	302.19	25.47	9.04e-11
European- Descendant	IZ	427.27	40.46	368.56	39.03	6.43e-03	417.86	36.08	362.30	32.52	1.75e-10
	IG	356.02	29.34	261.31	27.67	2.83e-06	357.40	34.51	259.76	23.32	2.20e-16
	NL	177.29	21.38	182.41	19.26	6.01e-01	187.96	18.61	189.49	16.70	6.98e-01
	NM	342.67	40.14	283.03	29.88	2.82e-03	351.74	32.22	291.72	26.12	3.81e-14
Mestizo	IZ	417.66	35.60	374.05	39.06	2.58e-09	421.16	37.71	371.68	33.82	2.20e-16
	IG	344.87	31.24	265.20	27.70	2.20e-16	360.00	36.02	266.5	24.25	2.20e-16
	NL	179.93	18.95	185.09	19.28	1.39e-01	189.82	19.11	194.39	17.67	9.74e-03
	NM	343.02	32.99	287.18	29.91	2.20e-16	355.88	32.09	299.26	29.91	2.20e-16
Afro- Ecuadorian	IZ	398.15	36.35	378.27	44.91	2.68e-01	398.15	31.05	368.44	40.50	5.19e-04
	IG	330.04	31.98	268.20	31.84	1.97e-04	332.92	28.83	264.17	29.04	2.20e-16
	NL	186.65	19.82	187.21	22.20	9.50e-01	190.12	22.08	192.67	21.15	6.05e-01
	NM	344.35	34.62	290.48	34.45	1.56e-03	348.80	37.88	296.61	32.56	7.34e-09

In Fig. 4, for the IG and NM distances, the dominant group is Group 3, indicating that the population tends to have faces that are wider and more elongated compared to the ideal measurements of the mask. Similar to findings in a study conducted in [20] on South Indians, individuals in Ecuador show wider faces relative to the mask, suggesting differences in facial characteristics between the Ecuadorian population and those on whom the mask was modeled. Over 90% of Ecuadorian facial images, across both genders, belong to Group 2 for the NL distance; this implies that for most of the population, the distance between the nasion and the lips is considered ideal. In the IZ distance, more than 35% of individuals from both sexes fall into Group 1, meaning many have faces that are narrower than the mask's ideal width. The distribution of these groups is similar across both genders for all distances.

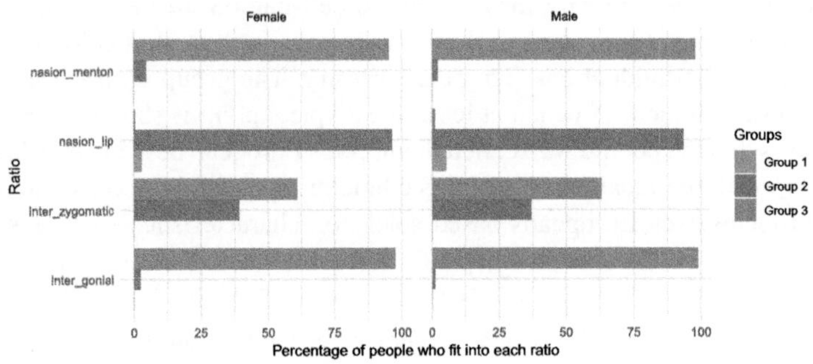

Fig. 4. Data Distribution according to the ratio r of each distance.

A comparison between the characteristics of men and women shows that for vertical distances, men show lengths greater than women, that is, longer faces. On the other hand, the horizontal distances are similar for men and women, except for the mestizo population in the IG distance; then, the female faces are as wide as the male ones. As there are differences between the facial characteristics of men and women, we can say that their beauty should be measured separately using different masks.

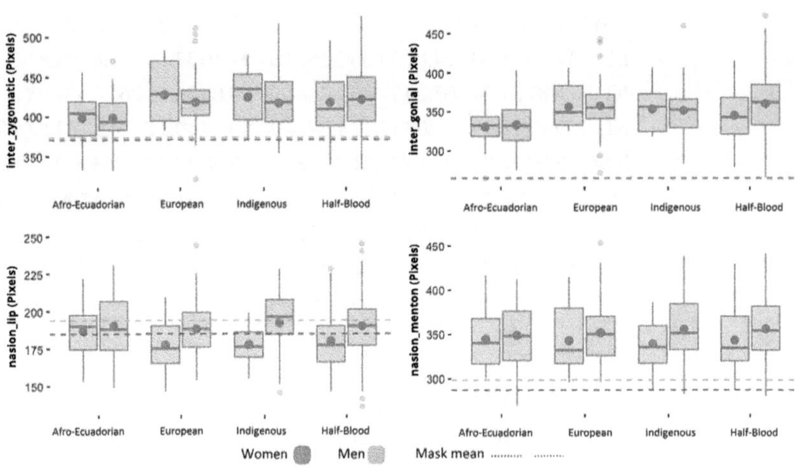

Fig. 5. Box plots of each distance in pixels differentiated by ethnicity and sex.

4 Conclusions and Limitations

This article introduces a web tool that automatically compares an individual's facial features with the Marquardt mask using a frontal photograph. The application of computer vision algorithms for extracting and analyzing facial metrics offers significant advantages over manual methods traditionally used by surgeons, such as automated measurements and reduced human error. Normality tests were employed to select appropriate statistical methods for comparing the facial metrics of the Ecuadorian population with those of the Marquardt mask.

The results revealed significant differences in all measured distances except for the NL distance. Overall, the analyzed faces were broader and longer than the mask, indicating that their dimensions do not conform to the golden ratio and, therefore, lack harmony according to this standard. Since no variant of the mask exists for the South American population, it is evident that the beauty standard represented by the Marquardt mask does not align with the diverse and multicultural characteristics of the Ecuadorian population. While the limited sample size constrained the analysis of specific female ethnic groups (European-descendant, Mestizo, and Afro-Ecuadorian), the dataset provided a valuable overview of the Ecuadorian population.

References

1. Making the mask. https://www.beautyanalysis.com/research/our-research/making-mask/. Accessed 13 Mar 2021
2. Repose frontal mask application. https://www.beautyanalysis.com/beauty-and-you/you-and-the-mask/repose-frontal-mask-application/. Accessed 13 Mar 2021
3. Avilés, J., Toapanta, H., Morillo, P., Vallejo-Huanga, D.: Dataset of ethnic facial images of ecuadorian people (2019). https://doi.org/10.6084/m9.figshare.8266730.v3
4. Avram, C., Măruşteri, M.: Normality assessment, few paradigms and use cases. Revista Romana de Medicina de Laborator **30**, 251–260 (2022). https://doi.org/10.2478/rrlm-2022-0030
5. Dalal, N., Triggs, B.: Histograms of oriented gradients for human detection. In: IEEE Conference on Computer Vision and Pattern Recognition (CVPR 2005), vol. 2 (2005)
6. Fink, B., Neave, N., Manning, J.T., Grammer, K.: Facial symmetry and judgements of attractiveness, health and personality. Personality Individ. Differ. **41**(3), 491–499 (2006). https://doi.org/10.1016/j.paid.2006.01.017, https://www.sciencedirect.com/science/article/pii/S0191886906000973
7. González, L., Zárate, H., Rosales, M.: Relationship between facial golden ratio and malocclusion in Mexican patients who attended the orthodontics clinic at facultad de odontología de la universidad tecnológica de méxico during 2009 with facial aesthetics criteria evaluated with marquardt mask. Revista Mexicana de Ortodoncia **2**, e9–e17 (2014). https://doi.org/10.1016/S2395-9215(16)30124-6
8. Gunes, H., Piccardi, M.: Assessing facial beauty through proportion analysis by image processing and supervised learning. Int. J. Hum. Comput. Stud. **64**, 1184–1199 (2006). https://doi.org/10.1016/j.ijhcs.2006.07.004
9. Hassaballah, M., Salem, E., Ali, A.M.M., Mahmoud, M.M.: Deep recurrent regression with a heatmap coupling module for facial landmarks detection. Cogn. Comput. **16**(4), 1964–1978 (2024). https://doi.org/10.1007/s12559-022-10065-9

10. Hearst, M., Dumais, S., Osuna, E., Platt, J., Scholkopf, B.: Support vector machines. IEEE Intell. Syst. Appl. **13**(4), 18–28 (1998). https://doi.org/10.1109/5254.708428
11. Kazemi, V., Sullivan, J.: One millisecond face alignment with an ensemble of regression trees. In: Proceedings of the IEEE Conference on Computer Vision and Pattern Recognition, pp. 1867–1874 (2014)
12. King, D.E.: Dlib-ml: a machine learning toolkit. J. Mach. Learn. Res. **10**, 1755–1758 (2009)
13. Mao, H., Jin, L., Du, M.: Automatic classification of Chinese female facial beauty using support vector machine, pp. 4842–4846 (2009). https://doi.org/10.1109/ICSMC.2009.5346057
14. Marquardt, S.: Dr. stephen r. marquardt on the golden decagon and human facial beauty. interview by dr. gottlieb. J. Clin. Orthod. JCO **36**, 339–47 (2002)
15. Mullins, K.D.: Does the marquardt mask serve as a helpful guide for facial feminization surgery (2016). https://hdl.handle.net/2144/19492
16. Naini, F.: Leslie g. farkas: pioneer of modern craniofacial anthropometry. Arch. Facial Plast. Surgery **12**, 141–2 (2010). https://doi.org/10.1001/archfacial.2010.29
17. Prokopakis, E.P., et al.: The golden ratio in facial symmetry. Rhinology **51**(1), 18–21 (2013). https://doi.org/10.4193/Rhino12.111
18. Rizvi, Q.M., Karawia, A.A., Kumar, S.: Female facial beauty analysis for assesment of facial attractivness. In: 2013 2nd International Conference on Information Management in the Knowledge Economy, pp. 156–160 (2013)
19. Thornhill, R., Gangestad, S.: Human facial beauty - averageness, symmetry, and parasite resistance. Hum. Nat. (Hawthorne, N.Y.) **4**, 237–269 (1993). https://doi.org/10.1007/BF02692201
20. Veerala, G., et al.: Marquardt's facial golden decagon mask and its fitness with south Indian facial traits. J. Clin. Diagn. Res. JCDR **10**, ZC49–ZC52 (2016). https://doi.org/10.7860/JCDR/2016/16791.7593
21. Zhang, K., Zhang, Z., Li, Z., Qiao, Y.: Joint face detection and alignment using multitask cascaded convolutional networks. IEEE Signal Process. Lett. **23** (2016). https://doi.org/10.1109/LSP.2016.2603342

Online Collaborative UAV Path Planning for Mapping and Spraying Missions

Ali Moltajaei Farid and Malek Mouhoub(✉)

Department of Computer Science, University of Regina, Regina, Canada
{afarid,mouhoubm}@uregina.ca

Abstract. Mapping and spraying play a crucial role in precision agriculture. In some technologies, companies employ an offline approach to plan paths for a swarm of UAVs. However, in real-world scenarios, unforeseen challenges often arise during missions, necessitating adaptive path adjustments. Currently, human intervention remains common to address these issues as they occur. In this regard, greater autonomy will likely be essential. To address these dynamic and uncertain situations, this paper introduces a novel online planner designed to enable UAVs to make slight adjustments to their pre-planned paths in real time until issues are resolved. This proposed approach facilitates autonomous online path planning that seamlessly integrates both pre-planned and dynamically adjusted routes. Primary planning is carried out offline, with the online planner activated to handle unexpected challenges as they arise. Depending on the circumstances, UAVs can collaborate to resolve issues while adhering to specified constraints to achieve their objectives.

Keywords: Unmanned Aerial Vehicles (UAVs) · Multiple-UAV path planning

1 Introduction

Agriculture is one of the largest and most significant markets in the world. The agritech companies are investing heavily in the field to improve the effectiveness of precision agriculture. Most of these technologies require mapping and spraying, which is very challenging [32]. In mapping and spraying missions, spraying with UAVs has a lot of crucial parameters [22] that should be set and controlled correctly, such as the number of spray nozzles, the shape of the spray, the optimal speed for the sprayer, binary or non-binary spray type, the spray model in wind, the accuracy of the weed positioning, the relationship of spray quality and temperature, the minimum safety distance from obstacles or peers, or the maximum volume of the spraying liquid. In addition to these design parameters, according to the regulations in most countries [20], we require a human in the loop who can take control of the mission in unknown issues. In the future, we will require a degree of autonomy.

UAVs are attracting more and more attention from companies around the world. This is because they are agile, fast and less destructive in mapping or spraying in precision agriculture [28]. However, there are several limitations of UAVs, including limited payload, energy, communication link, and computational resources [17]. This will also

J. Röning and J. Filipe (Eds.): ROBOVIS 2025, CCIS 2629, pp. 193–207, 2026.
https://doi.org/10.1007/978-3-032-00986-9_14

be extended to having no access to stable cloud computing in the area of precision farming. This is because the location of farms can be very far from the cities and companies are looking for product that can work in any farm. However edge computing [26] still is seen a valid option by AgTech companies for enabling fast off-board processing [4].

UAVs have a number of significant configurations, including multi-rotor, fixed-wing, VTOL fixed-wing, and helicopters (see Fig. 2). Multi-rotors, perhaps, are the cheapest way of mapping and spraying with most companies worldwide. Still, the frequency of required recharging cycles slows down the task accomplishment, so fixed-wing will be another option. This type can have a heavier payload, fewer recharging cycles, and a larger number of sensors. at the cost of more complex control and requirement of fly runs. Combining both advantages of fixed-wing and multi-rotor, VTOL fixed-wing was born. VTOL fixed-wing takes off and lands like a multi-rotor and, at other times, performs as a fixed-wing. Finally, helicopters are one of the most expensive UAVs that are not economical for small farms and only have value for large farms.

There are many reasons to apply UAVs in precision agriculture. These are not limited, but include mapping [27], spraying [12], checking the quality of the harvest [10], checking the quality of soil [29], helping other robots find and pick raped fruits [18], helping ground robots maneuver, seeding, spraying, etc. Each part of this application contains algorithm design, image processing, finding the proper location of targets, actuator designs, electronic design, and mechanical design. However, in this paper, we will only focus on mapping and spraying, which have most of the UAV applications in the sector.

Precision farming systems can be online, offline, and hybrid systems. Although offline planners might be seen as an excellent strategy to overcome on-board limitations, they cannot cover the whole mission safely. For instance, real-world scenarios always have many unforeseen complexities, such as collisions, weather changes, UAV malfunction, etc. For this reason, the online planner plays a vital role in mapping and spraying. Hybrid systems have been developed to combine the advantages of online and offline planners.

In recent years, there has been a growing emphasis on developing collaborative systems that allow multiple UAVs to work together autonomously to complete tasks efficiently and reliably. The main parts include communication [16] and control methods [23], such as centralized, decentralized, and hybrid.

In mapping when we are using multiple UAVs there is a need to manage these UAVs to avoid collision, in addition, there might be a malfunction of UAVs that need an urgent automatic re-planing to finalize the mission by the time, so the online planner should find the best alternative and re-plan the mission in an effective way. Finally, in weather changes, the fleet should make appropriate safe decisions to avoid any hazard.

In spraying there are further risks. Since we are using an aerosol, it will be hazardous for wrong spraying. In addition, weather conditions can cause the spraying liquid to go to a place that is not supposed to be. For this reason in addition to the above online mapping requirements, we require to manage the spraying UAV to keep safety of the farm.

Online path-planning can be accomplished through a number of methods, such as graph search. Perhaps A* is one of the most important graph-based approaches that

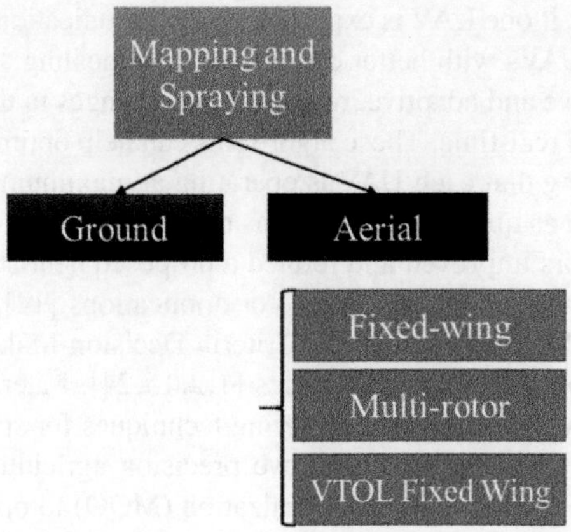

Fig. 1. The mapping-spraying UAV options.

also requires high computational power. An evolutionary algorithm, such as a genetic algorithm, is another time-efficient approach that will require a proper definition of the objectives. There are also some reactive methods, such as dynamic window and velocity obstacles. Finally, the potential field as a virtual field approach is another approach that could trap in local minima if this approach is used as a local planner.

The Traveling Salesman Problem (TSP) and other similar approaches [19,31] are used for the planning of the path [9]. The TSP is a classic optimization problem that involves finding the shortest possible route by visiting all cities exactly once and returning to the starting city. A tour in a TSP is a sequence of cities that represents a potential solution to the problem. The tour starts at the first city, visits each of the other cities exactly once, and returns to the starting city. The goal is to find a tour with the minimum total distance traveled.

The Model Predictive Control (MPC) is a rigorous optimal control approach. It is often used to modify path planning, but is computationally intensive. Furthermore, finding a suitable value for a large number of parameters is another challenge that might be difficult to set in all problems [36] (Fig. 1).

Using reinforcement learning is another option [25]. The suitable outcome of this approach has a tight relation with proper training of the model for deriving the best policy. In addition, online reinforcement learning can be complex if there are many variations in the environment. Finally, without a realistic simulator, it will be so difficult to derive a proper policy for complex actions such as spraying [5].

Re-healing in the swarm UAVs refers to the process of redistributing tasks among swarm UAVs to optimize their performance and ensure efficient completion of the mission [30]. In a swarm, each UAV has limited resources, such as battery life, communication range, and processing power. Therefore, it is important to distribute the workload evenly among the UAVs to prevent any one UAV from becoming overloaded or running out of resources prematurely. Re-healing involves dynamically assigning tasks to different UAVs based on their current status and workload. For example, if one UAV's battery is running low, its tasks can be redistributed to other UAVs with more battery life remaining. Similarly, if one UAV is experiencing communication issues, its tasks can be reassigned to other UAVs with better connectivity. Re-healing algorithms are typically designed to be reactive and adaptive, responding to changes in the environment and the status of the UAVs in real-time. These algorithms can help optimize the performance of the swarm by ensuring that each UAV is operating at maximum efficiency and that the mission is completed as quickly and safely as possible.

In [15], the authors improved and refined a proposed heuristic approach, originally designed as an offline planner for multirotor applications [14], extending it to fixed-wing systems. We also combined Multi-Criteria Decision-Making (MCDM) with the offline planner to optimize user preferences [1,2,15,24]. Later, the authors improved the offline planner by incorporating clustering techniques for spraying applications, as detailed in [15]. As mentioned, to improve precision agriculture autonomy, we will need a proper online multi-objective optimization (MOO) to optimize spray and mapping missions in farms with uncertainty. Since there are a lot of complexities in this context, in this paper, we elaborate more on different issues in precise agriculture and show how the system can act and decide autonomously on unknown issues. Rehealing is one of the major contributions of this paper in improving our previously designed system. Wind is a disturbance factor that affects the performance of the UAV in spraying. In [21], CNN is used to learn the control policy of the UAV in response to wind disturbances. The wind disturbance model provides a way to simulate the wind environment and the effects of wind on the UAV. The DNN is trained on these simulated data to learn how to adjust the UAV's control inputs in response to wind disturbances, in order to maintain the desired trajectory. The main issue with this design is the requirement of a large dataset and very high processing power for the training phase of the proposed off-policy RL. In addition, the article did not consider untrained issues that might occur in practice. In [14,15], the authors did not investigate unknown issues such as wind, low energy UAVs, or obstacles. We mainly focused on off-line planning which might not be suitable for precision agriculture where we are dealing with a lot of uncertainties. Furthermore, in [15], the authors addressed the issue of wind by considering a combination of approaches, such as clustering and Voronoi cells, to tackle the challenges posed by wind. However, in this paper, our aim is to further advance our multi-UAV approach by incorporating an online planning feature into the multi-objective path planner. Note that we do not utilize MCDM into the proposed strategies and online planner.

2 Problem Formulation

Consider a set of n UAVs $A = \{a_1, a_2, \ldots, a_i, \ldots, a_n\}$. The three-dimensional position of each UAV a_i at instant t is denoted by $p_i(t)$. Each a_i comes with a limited field of view (FOV) and a limited camera range (R). The UAV a_i can cover the area $S(p_i(t)) = qw$ at time t, where q is the diagonal field of view and w the horizontal field of view. Consequently, the area covered by the set A, at time t, is $Ar(t) = \cup_{1 \leq i \leq n} S(p_i(t))$. Obviously, $Ar(t)$ can be much smaller than the area of interest (AoI) S. By setting ov_1 and ov_2 overlaps on the images taken by the drone, we ensure adequate mapping without loss of information. Each a_i will be placed in a 3D space with a defined height. Each UAV a_i has a limited communication range (R_c) with its peers $\{a_{i1}, ..., a_{ik}\}$.

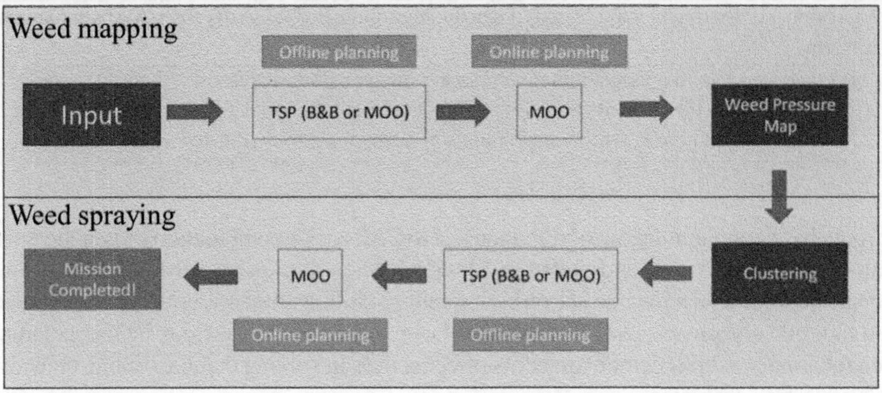

Fig. 2. The previous proposed planning [13,15] combined with online MOO planning.

In mapping, the AoI S is divided into a set of n subareas $Z_1, Z_2, \ldots, Z_i, \ldots, Z_n$ using the K-means clustering [35]. On the other hand, for spraying, the user (farmer) first chooses how many percent of total detected weeds should be covered. On some occasions, the user might neglect the small areas that contain weeds and focus on larger areas to save aerosol. After this choice, we again use the K-mean clustering to divide the area into subareas. Each subarea Z_i is assigned to a UAV a_i and is divided into $H_i = \frac{Z_i}{S(p_i(t))}$ cells. For a given UAV a_i, a feasible path consists of a sequence of λ_i cells that cover the mapping or spraying of the entire sub-area Z_i, with each cell visited exactly once. The main objective of the planner is to find the set of n optimal paths for the UAVs that cover the entire area $S = \cup_{1 \leq i \leq n} Z_i$ while optimizing the previously planned mission based on real-time unknown issues. This might be wind, or existing obstacles in either dynamic or static nature in the planned mission.

3 Multi-objective Optimizers

Multi-objective optimization is a technique used to optimize multiple objectives simultaneously. In this approach, instead of optimizing a single objective, multiple objectives are taken into account, and the goal is to find the best trade-off between them. The main challenge in multi-objective optimization is to find a set of solutions that are optimal with respect to all objectives. This requires balancing the trade-offs between the objectives and finding a set of solutions that are non-dominated, meaning that no other solution is better in all objectives. Multi-objective optimization algorithms use various techniques to find these non-dominated solutions, including particle swarm optimization (MPSO) [8], non-dominated sorting genetic algorithm version 2 (NSGA2) [7], and multi-objective evolutionary algorithm based on decomposition (MOAE/D) [34].

In this paper we will apply NSGA2 as MOO planner. NSGA2 is a popular multi-objective optimization algorithm that was developed by Deb [7]. NSGA2 is an extension of the original NSGA algorithm and is based on the concept of non-dominated sorting, which involves dividing the population of candidate solutions into different levels or

Algorithm 1: Non-Dominated Sorting Genetic Algorithm II (NSGA-II) for UAV path planning problems.

1) Generate an initial population of solutions using a random search
2) Evaluate the objective functions (o_1 to o_5) of each solution to determine the Pareto front
3) Sort the population based on the Pareto front using the non-dominated sorting algorithm

fronts based on their degree of dominance. NSGA2 uses a combination of genetic operators such as crossover and mutation, along with non-dominated sorting and crowding distance to evolve a diverse set of high-quality solutions that are optimal with respect to multiple objectives. The algorithm has been widely used in various fields, including engineering, and has demonstrated its effectiveness in solving complex multi-objective optimization problems.

Multi-objective optimizers can be either online or offline. Since these algorithms are processing hungry, especially when we are dealing with high amount of data, we break down our proposed system into two layers: offline and online layers. In the first layer, since we know enough about the agriculture field that we are interested to map or spray, we can translate this information to the designed simulator, then the algorithm can effectively plan the proper trajectory planning for the UAVs. In this process, the ground station processor can run the simulation and generate the waypoints and pass it to each UAV. In the next layer, we modified the MOO algorithm in a way that it can be implemented in the UAV to use on-board processor to change the offline trajectory planning in case of unknown issue is detected.

3.1 Offline Planning

In offline planning, the planner receives the inputs from the user including the map [14] and the preferences [15]. Next, it will use the K-means clustering to divide the map to equal divisions, which is based on the total area coverage of UAV (either mapping or spraying as shown in Fig. 3) at the certain altitude. Then it will optimize the objectives using multi-objective optimize including the distance, energy, and risks [15]. Recently, we used travelling salesman problem (TSP) to solve this multi-objective problem. In this way, the traveling salesman will find the best tour of waypoint to optimize the whole objectives. Each waypint can be passed once. For more details you may refer to for mapping [15] for spraying.

3.2 Online Planning

Online planning can be achieved either using the-on-board processor or edge-computing. on-board UAV processor (i.e., NVIDIA Jestson [3]) and edge computing have their advantages and disadvantages. The choice between the two depends on the specific application and requirements of the UAV system. The on-board processor offers high-performance computing capabilities, while edge computing brings computation closer to the source of data and can reduce latency. On the other hand, edge computing is a distributed computing paradigm that brings computation and data storage closer to the sources of data, such as sensors and IoT devices, to reduce latency and improve

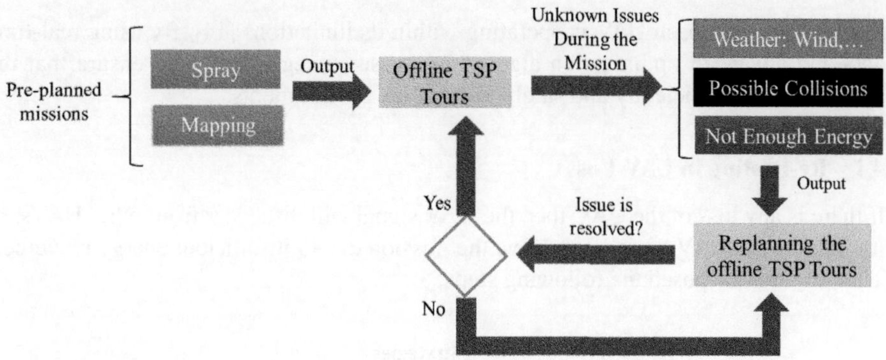

Fig. 3. The proposed UAV planning system.

efficiency. In recent years, there has been a growing interest in using edge computing to support the swarm of UAVs (Unmanned Aerial Vehicles) for various applications, including surveillance, search and rescue, and package delivery. This approach enables the UAVs to communicate and collaborate with each other, share data, and optimize their performance based on multiple objectives such as energy consumption, flight time, and safety.

Ultimately, the choice between the two will depend on factors such as the size of the UAV, the amount of data being processed, and the desired level of real-time decision-making capabilities. In both contexts, online fast multi-objective optimization algorithms can play a crucial role in enabling efficient and effective swarm-based UAV systems.

In this paper, we combined off-line and online planners. As shown in Fig. 4, in either spray or mapping, we first use TSP path planning based on the objectives introduced in [15]. The objectives of the UAV mission include minimizing the use of energy and time for mapping, while maximizing safety (that is, minimizing risk). Furthermore, for the spraying phase, the UAV should reduce its aerosol consumption, energy and time usage, and risk to ensure both its own safety and that of its surroundings. Normally, the mission is planned offline and in case of an emergency situation, the offline plan will be reviewed to solve the issue by the online planner. Both the offline and online planner uses the multi-objective optimizer with the proposed strategies (see Fig. 5). The only difference is that in the online planner we use continuous MOO while in the offline planner we use discrete system in some cases, such as collision avoidance system.

4 Proposed Strategies

As mentioned in both spray and mapping missions there are a few challenges, such as low-energy UAVs, wind, and obstacles. To address these challenges, all proposed strategies are used on collision avoidance multi-objective path planning to enable real-time path planning of a swarm of UAVs. These strategies consider multiple systems. goals, such as minimizing the risk of collisions, maximizing the efficiency of the swarm, and ensuring that each UAV is operating within its limitations [14]. By using real-time data and advanced optimization algorithms, these strategies can help ensure that the swarm operates efficiently and safely in complex environments.

4.1 Re-healing in UAV Loss

If there is any loss of the UAV, then the UAV signal will disappear from other UAVs, or it might be the UAV decision to leave the mission due to insufficient energy resources. This way, we proposed the following steps:

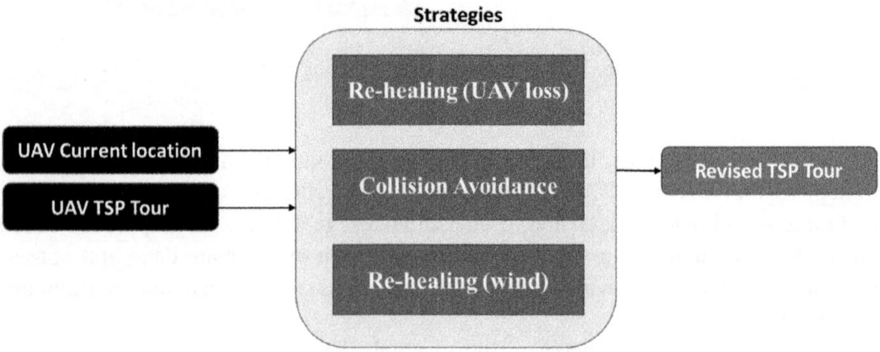

Fig. 4. Activated online planner procedure with the proposed strategies.

1) The remained tour will be communicated within the swarm using a gossip-based approach.
2) All other UAVs will estimate the time required to complete their task and their current energy status.
3) The UAV that will end sooner-if it has enough energy-will take on the remaining tours.
4) If other UAVs also complete their tasks, they will join the remaining tours if they have enough energy. The UAV, which takes on the task sooner, will act as a leader and divide the area into smaller subareas if other UAVs also want to help, and then will communicate the tour locations with other members.

4.2 Re-healing in Wind

If there is a wind during the mission, the UAVs can collaboratively determine parts of the farm that remained unsprayed. We assume that the UAVs can determine the areas that remained unsprayed in each waypoint (or city). Since we assume that there are enough reliable data in the field about the current wind speed and direction, each UAV can estimate the areas that are not or weakly sprayed. In this way, the UAVs produce a map of unsprayed areas that were planned to be sprayed. The map will be shared among all UAVs using gossip-based communication [6], next each UAV will plan to cover the areas that are closer to it. In this scenario, the system has two options:

1) Redefine the path planing once the system determines the unsprayed area,
2) Finish the offline planned coverage first and then cover those unsprayed area.

4.3 Pause the Mission and Landing

In case of any unexpected wind or gust, the swarm will land in the area, and will restart the mission after resolving the harsh weather.

4.4 Multiple Take-Off

When starting the mission, UAVs might collide to each other. In this regard, we have designed an online take-off controller similar to the one reported in [11]. Assuming there are n UAVs, first, UAV a_2 waits for UAV a_1 to take-off and reach a specific preset altitude h_t. Then, the Euclidean distance d_t is computed between $p_1(t)$ and $p_2(t)$. a_2 will take-off if and only if $d_t \geq d_{safe}$, where d_{safe} is a predefined safety distance.

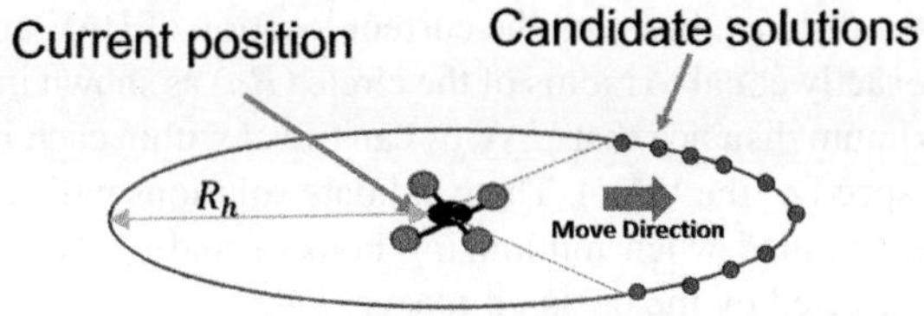

Fig. 5. The set of candidate solutions to consider for obstacle avoidance.

4.5 Online Collision Avoidance

Online planner has been developed for both mapping and spraying. In both cases as the sensors detect any obstacles in the pre-planned offline route, the online collision avoidance system will be activated. We use the following objectives (o_1 to o_5) to keep the optimality of the path.

1) Minimize the distance between the planned path and obstacles in the environment:

$$minimize\ o_1 = \sum \|p_i(t) - o_j(t)\| \tag{1}$$

where p_i is a point on the planned path and o_j is an obstacle in the environment.
2) Maximize the clearance between the planned path and obstacles:

$$maximize\ o_2 = \sum clearance(p_i, o_j) \tag{2}$$

where clearance(p_i, o_j) is a function that returns the minimum distance between point p_i and obstacle o_j. For clearance we used the Matlab function named *clearance*.

3) Maximize the smoothness of the path to minimize sudden changes in direction or velocity:

$$minimize\ o_3 = \sum curvature(p_i, p_{i+1}, p_{i+2}) \tag{3}$$

where curvature(p_i, p_{i+1}, p_{i+2}) is a function that measures the curvature of the path between points p_i, p_{i+1}, and p_{i+2}. For curvature we used *smoothness* function. This function, valuates the smoothness of the planned path. Values close to 0 indicate a smoother path. Straight-line paths return a value of 0. There are similar functions in the literature such as [33].
4) Minimize the time taken to reach the goal while avoiding collisions: minimize $o_4 = time$.
5) Minimize the energy expended by the robot while avoiding collisions: minimize $o_5 = energy$. Energy consumption during the planning path is computed based on [15].

Since the altitude of UAVs is assumed to be always steady (unlike in [14]), instead of a dispersing the initial candidate solutions inside the circle, we will only have candidate locations where the distance between the current location of UAV and the initial candidate locations is exactly equal to radius of the circle (R_h) as shown in Fig. 6. Also, R_h is based on the maximum distance that UAV a_i can travel within each iteration (according to the maximum speed of the UAV). The candidate solutions will correspond to Pareto optimal solutions obtained when minimizing both o_1 and o_5. One of these candidate positions will be selected by the decision-maker [14].

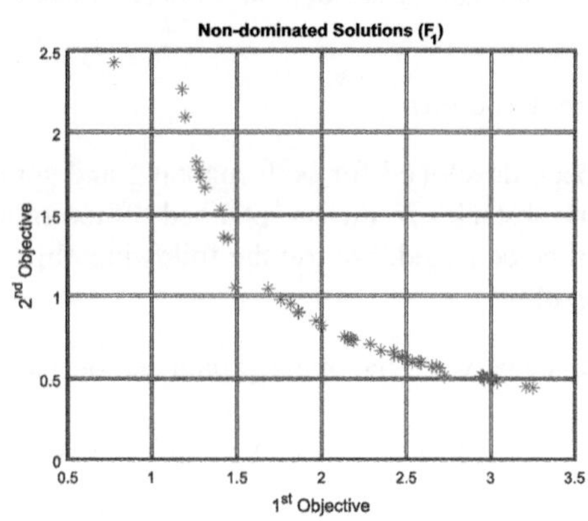

Fig. 6. A sample pareto front in collision avoidance based on first and second objectives (for better view we did not consider the rest of objectives).

5 Technical Issues

There are some technical issues in the above-mentioned design. One of the main drawbacks is the simultaneous reaction of the algorithm to deal with new inputs. This might not be a good outcome if the update of the previous step's output is far away from the new step's output. So, to avoid fluctuation, we have a control system to preserve the stability of the swarm. Additionally, to preserve the system against the fluctuating outputs, we limited the speed of update to T_s.

Also, to make the NSGA2 a fast program, we only set up the NSGA2 max iteration into 5 iterations. However, there are some improvements in higher max iterations, we tried to keep the computation to a minimum as well as we could.

6 Simulation Results

We constructed our simulator using MathWorks Matlab running on a laptop with an Intel Core i7 processor and 8GB RAM. The simulation includes various metrics for evaluating the performance of the multi-objective path planning strategy, such as the number of collisions avoided, the time taken to complete the mission and the fuel consumption of the UAVs. The parameters for the NSGA2 algorithm are listed in Table 1.

6.1 Simulation with Obstacles

When the UAV sees an obstacle in its FOV, it will activate the collision avoidance system, In this way, the online planner as shown in Fig. 7 uses the Pareto front to find the best optimal change in the route to perform the mission. Figure 8 shows an example scenario in which the UAV detects a static obstacle using its onboard sensors, then

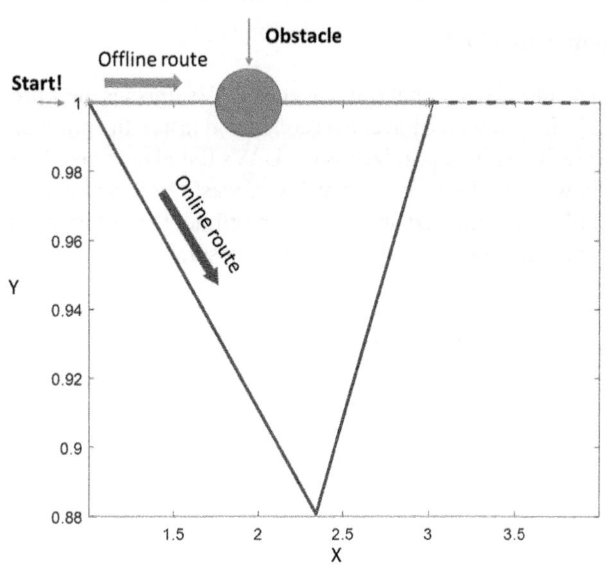

Fig. 7. A sample scenario where the UAV detects the static obstacle and revises the route; after collision avoidance, it will continue the offline route.

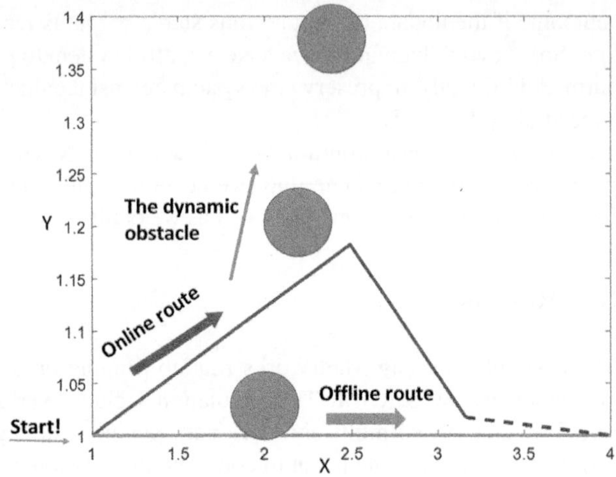

Fig. 8. A sample scenario where the UAV detects the dynamic obstacle (obstacle goes from the bottom to top) and revises the route; after collision avoidance, it will continue the offline route.

re-plans the route and finds the new optimal path and after passing the obstacles it resumes the pre-planned offline path planning route. In this simulation, we considered a multi-rotor and can be easily extended to fixed-wing using Dubin's rotation [15]. Additionally in Fig. 8, also, we tested the system performance in dynamic obstacles, and it successfully passed the obstacle without any collision.

6.2 Simulation with Wind

The simulation results showed that if the fleet of UAVs finishes their pre-planned offline routes (option 2), the spray mission can be conducted faster. In option 2, when we set the system to activate the online optimizer as the UAVs found unsprayed areas instantly, the UAVs might show some fluctuations which can waste time and energy. Instead, when UAVs first complete the planned spray mission offline, the online planner can produce a new set of waypoints to recover the remaining unsprayed area.

Table 1. The Parameters of NSGA2.

Algorithm	Parameter	Value
$NSGA2$	Mutation Rate	0.02
	Cross-over percentage	0.7
	Mutation percentage	0.4
	Mutation Step Size	0.3

7 Conclusion and Future Work

In this paper, we considered an online planner on top of the proposed offline planner in [14]. Both planners are working with multiple objective optimizations. The difference might be based on continuous or discrete optimization. In the offline planner, since we are using TSP for proper path planning, we used a discrete optimizer. In contrast, in an online planner, we might need to revise the route slightly which can be done with a continuous planner. We proposed four strategies, including, re-healing, collision avoidance, pausing the mission, and multiple take-off collision avoidance systems. In the future, it will be interesting to check the overall time of processing in benchmark processors such as NVIDIA Jetson. In addition, we used a very simple model of spray and mapping, in the novel UAVs we might have several patterns of spray and a number of spraying nozzles as well as cameras that can complicate the current design, and we will leave it as a future work.

References

1. Ahmed, S., Mouhoub, M.: Conditional preference networks with user's genuine decisions. Comput. Intell. **36**(3), 1414–1442 (2020)
2. Alanazi, E., Mouhoub, M.: Variable ordering and constraint propagation for constrained CP-nets. Appl. Intell. **44**, 437–448 (2016)
3. Ayoub, N., Schneider-Kamp, P.: Real-time on-board deep learning fault detection for autonomous UAV inspections. Electronics **10**(9), 1091 (2021)
4. Canning, J.: Australian AgTech: a commentary on the report of the Agri-Tech expert working group June 2021. J. Telecommun. Digital Econ. **10**(1), 34–49 (2022)
5. Chen, G., Lu, Y., Yang, X., Hu, H.: Reinforcement learning control for the swimming motions of a beaver-like, single-legged robot based on biological inspiration. Robot. Auton. Syst. **154**, 104116 (2022)
6. Dasgupta, P.: A multiagent swarming system for distributed automatic target recognition using unmanned aerial vehicles. IEEE Trans. Syst. Man Cybern. Part A Syst. Hum. **38**(3), 549–563 (2008)
7. Deb, K., Sindhya, K., Hakanen, J.: Multi-objective optimization in: Decision sciences: Theory and practice (2016)
8. Deb, K., Agrawal, S., Pratap, A., Meyarivan, T.: A fast elitist non-dominated sorting genetic algorithm for multi-objective optimization: NSGA-II. In: Schoenauer, M., et al. (eds.) PPSN 2000. LNCS, vol. 1917, pp. 849–858. Springer, Heidelberg (2000). https://doi.org/10.1007/3-540-45356-3_83
9. Debnath, D., Vanegas, F., Boiteau, S., Gonzalez, F.: An integrated geometric obstacle avoidance and genetic algorithm tsp model for UAV path planning. Drones **8**(7), 302 (2024)
10. Dvorak, J.S., Pampolini, L.F., Jackson, J.J., Seyyedhasani, H., Sama, M.P., Goff, B.: Predicting quality and yield of growing alfalfa from a UAV. Trans. ASABE **64**(1), 63–72 (2021)
11. Fabra, F., Wubben, J., Calafate, C.T., Cano, J.C., Manzoni, P.: Efficient and coordinated vertical takeoff of UAV swarms. In: 2020 IEEE 91st Vehicular Technology Conference (VTC2020-Spring), pp. 1–5. IEEE (2020)
12. Faiçal, B.S., et al.: An adaptive approach for UAV-based pesticide spraying in dynamic environments. Comput. Electron. Agric. **138**, 210–223 (2017)

13. Farid, A.M., Egerton, S., Barca, J.C., Kamal, M.A.S.: Adaptive multi-objective search in a swarm vs swarm context. In: 2018 IEEE International Conference on Systems, Man, and Cybernetics (SMC), pp. 3641–3646. IEEE (2018)
14. Farid, A.M., Mouhoub, M.: Evolutionary mapping with multiple unmanned aerial vehicles. In: 2022 IEEE International Conference on Systems, Man and Cybernetics (SMC), pp. 1–7. IEEE (2022)
15. Farid, A.M., Mouhoub, M.: A multi-objective approach for unmanned aerial vehicle mapping. In: 2023 International Conference on Unmanned Aircraft Systems (ICUAS), pp. 257–264. IEEE (2023)
16. Javaid, S., et al.: Communication and control in collaborative UAVs: recent advances and future trends. IEEE Trans. Intell. Transp. Syst. **24**(6), 5719–5739 (2023)
17. Jin, H., et al.: A survey of energy efficient methods for UAV communication. Veh. Commun. 100594 (2023)
18. King, A.: Technology: the future of agriculture. Nature **544**(7651), S21–S23 (2017)
19. Korani, W., Mouhoub, M.: Discrete mother tree optimization for the traveling salesman problem. In: Yang, H., Pasupa, K., Leung, A.C.-S., Kwok, J.T., Chan, J.H., King, I. (eds.) ICONIP 2020. LNCS, vol. 12533, pp. 25–37. Springer, Cham (2020). https://doi.org/10.1007/978-3-030-63833-7_3
20. Lavers, A.: Guidelines on good practice for aerial application of pesticides. Food and Agriculture Organization of the United Nations (2001)
21. Ma, B., et al.: Deep reinforcement learning of UAV tracking control under wind disturbances environments. IEEE Trans. Instrum. Meas. **72**, 1–13 (2023)
22. Meng, Y., Su, J., Song, J., Chen, W.H., Lan, Y.: Experimental evaluation of UAV spraying for peach trees of different shapes: effects of operational parameters on droplet distribution. Comput. Electron. Agric. **170**, 105282 (2020)
23. Ming, R., Jiang, R., Luo, H., Lai, T., Guo, E., Zhou, Z.: Comparative analysis of different UAV swarm control methods on unmanned farms. Agronomy **13**(10), 2499 (2023)
24. Mouhoub, M., Ahmed, S.: Constrained optimization with partial CP-nets. In: 2018 IEEE International Conference on Systems, Man, and Cybernetics (SMC),. pp. 3361–3366. IEEE (2018)
25. Naous, T., Itani, M., Awad, M., Sharafeddine, S.: Reinforcement learning in the sky: a survey on enabling intelligence in NTN-based communications. IEEE Access (2023)
26. O'Grady, M., Langton, D., O'Hare, G.: Edge computing: a tractable model for smart agriculture? Artif. Intell. Agric. **3**, 42–51 (2019)
27. Radoglou-Grammatikis, P., Sarigiannidis, P., Lagkas, T., Moscholios, I.: A compilation of UAV applications for precision agriculture. Comput. Netw. **172**, 107148 (2020)
28. Rahman, M.F.F., Fan, S., Zhang, Y., Chen, L.: A comparative study on application of unmanned aerial vehicle systems in agriculture. Agriculture **11**(1), 22 (2021)
29. Rebelo, C., Nascimento, J.: Measurement of soil tillage using UAV high-resolution 3d data. Remote Sens. **13**(21), 4336 (2021)
30. Rosselló, L.B., Alkilabi, M., Tuci, E., Bersini, H., Reina, A.: Emergent orchestras: a modular framework for musical robot swarms. In: ALIFE 2024: Proceedings of the 2024 Artificial Life Conference. MIT Press (2024)
31. Sun, J., Meng, Y., Tan, G.: An integer programming approach for the Chinese postman problem with time-dependent travel time. J. Comb. Optim. **29**, 565–588 (2015)
32. Velusamy, P., Rajendran, S., Mahendran, R.K., Naseer, S., Shafiq, M., Choi, J.G.: Unmanned aerial vehicles in precision agriculture: applications and challenges. Energies **15**(1), 217 (2021)
33. Xu, L., Song, B., Cao, M.: A new approach to optimal smooth path planning of mobile robots with continuous-curvature constraint. Syst. Sci. Control Eng. **9**(1), 138–149 (2021)

34. Zhang, Q., Li, H.: MOEA/D: a multiobjective evolutionary algorithm based on decomposition. IEEE Trans. Evol. Comput. **11**(6), 712–731 (2007)
35. Zhang, S., Guo, J., Wang, Z.: Combing k-means clustering and local weighted maximum discriminant projections for weed species recognition. Front. Comput. Sci. **1**, 4 (2019)
36. Zhu, M., Skulstad, R., Zhao, L., Zhang, H., Li, G.: MPC based path planning for collision avoidance under colregs. In: 2022 IEEE International Conference on Systems, Man and Cybernetics (SMC), pp. 1–7. IEEE (2022)

Statistically Consistent Total Least-Squares Estimation of Object Scales

Arne Hasselbring(✉) and Udo Frese

Faculty 3, Mathematics and Computer Science, University of Bremen, Postfach 330 440, 28334 Bremen, Germany
{arha,ufrese}@uni-bremen.de

Abstract. Estimating object poses is a fundamental problem in computer vision in general as well as for robotic manipulation in particular. Most approaches require a known 3D model of the object. One step towards a more general formulation is to estimate the object's width, height and depth with the pose, e. g. consider a generic box, cylinder or plate instead of one with known dimensions.

This paper investigates the last stage of such a pipeline, namely least-squares estimating pose and scales from point correspondences aggregated into a fixed size matrix. Therefore it encapsulates the scaled $SO(3)$ manifold in a so-called $\boxplus$-operator and derives a Gauss-Newton based optimizer with initial guess on that.

We find that the resulting estimator is strongly biased towards small scales. This is due to the structure of the least-squares loss: Noise in recognized object points is multiplied with the to be estimated transformation matrix, violating the additive noise assumption. It has no effect in the prevalent use of this loss for pose estimation but affects the scale.

We propose a solution to this bias based on an approximation of total least-squares that preserves the advantage of a fixed size representation and show that it provides relatively consistent uncertainty estimates.

Keywords: Least-squares estimation · 9D object pose estimation · RGB-D perception

1 Introduction

Object pose estimation is an important perception skill in a variety of applications, such as household robots. In particular, for tasks such as grasping, robot applications require a metrical 6D pose (translation + rotation), not just a 2D bounding box in an image. 6D object pose estimation is a much researched problem, with progress measured by the BOP challenge [11]. Traditionally, CAD models and large image datasets of the involved objects have been required. This is challenged by the approach of category-level pose estimation: A robot, for instance in a kitchen, may deal with a variety of boxes that share the same cuboid geometry, but have different dimensions. Instead of having separate detectors for each kind of box, we want to handle all boxes using the same detector. Then the 3 scaling degrees of freedom need to be estimated along with the pose, making it a 9D estimation problem. The same can be done for other categories, e. g. cans, plates, mugs, etc.

J. Röning and J. Filipe (Eds.): ROBOVIS 2025, CCIS 2629, pp. 208–227, 2026.
https://doi.org/10.1007/978-3-032-00986-9_15

Most modern 6D pose estimation approaches [19,24] generate point pairs $\mathbf{p}_i^O, \mathbf{p}_i^C$ in object, respectively camera frame and match these to obtain a pose. Usually the $\mathbf{p}_i^C$ come directly from the sensor, the $\mathbf{p}_i^O$ from a recognition process, e. g. by keypoints or a CNN. The last stage of this matching is usually least-squares. There are various cases, but all minimize a loss that's a second order term in the coefficients of the 4×4 transformation matrix $\mathbf{T} \in SE(3)$ representing the pose. This can be directly seen, if the points in camera frame are 3D, e. g. from a depth camera:

$$\hat{\mathbf{T}} = \arg \min_{\mathbf{T} \in SE(3)} \mathcal{L}_{\text{pp}}(\mathbf{T}), \tag{1}$$

$$\mathcal{L}_{\text{pp}}(\mathbf{T}) = \sum_i \|\mathbf{T}\mathbf{p}_i^O - \mathbf{p}_i^C\|_2^2 = \sum_i (\mathbf{T}\mathbf{p}_i^O - \mathbf{p}_i^C)^\top (\mathbf{T}\mathbf{p}_i^O - \mathbf{p}_i^C) \tag{2}$$

In this point cloud matching, $\mathcal{L}_{\text{pp}}$ is actually even linear in the rotation part of $\mathbf{T}$, which is exploited by the well-known Umeyama algorithm [22]. The point matches can also be weighted by a covariance matrix $\mathbf{\Sigma}_i$, making $\mathcal{L}_{\text{ppc}}$ quadratic.

$$\mathcal{L}_{\text{ppc}}(\mathbf{T}) = \sum_i \|\mathbf{T}\mathbf{p}_i^O - \mathbf{p}_i^C\|_{\mathbf{\Sigma}_i^{-1}}^2 = \sum_i \|\mathbf{\Sigma}_i^{-\frac{1}{2}} (\mathbf{T}\mathbf{p}_i^O - \mathbf{p}_i^C)\|_2^2 \tag{3}$$

For perspective matches, the $\mathbf{p}_i^C$ is replaced by image coordinates $\left(\begin{smallmatrix} u_i \\ v_i \end{smallmatrix}\right)$. The resulting function is non-linear in the coefficients of $\mathbf{T}$ due to the division in the perspective projection. However, it can be approximated linearly by multiplying with the denominator, the direct linear method [8, §7.1].

$$\mathcal{L}_{\text{persp}}(\mathbf{T}) = \sum_i \left\| \left(\begin{smallmatrix} -f & 0 & u-u_0 & 0 \\ 0 & -f & v-v_0 & 0 \end{smallmatrix}\right) \mathbf{T}\mathbf{p}_i^O \right\|_2^2 \tag{4}$$

Here, f is the focal length and $\left(\begin{smallmatrix} u_0 \\ v_0 \end{smallmatrix}\right)$ the image center.

Depth measurements d_i corresponding to $\mathbf{p}_i^O$ can also be expressed.

$$\mathcal{L}_{\text{depth}}(\mathbf{T}) = \sum_i \left(\left(\begin{smallmatrix} 0 & 0 & 1 & 0 \end{smallmatrix}\right) \mathbf{T}\mathbf{p}_i^O - d_i \right)^2 \tag{5}$$

This also allows to model an RGB-D camera more precisely with $\mathcal{L}_{\text{persp}} + \mathcal{L}_{\text{depth}}$ instead of matching points with $\mathcal{L}_{\text{pp}}$. All different variants condense the information from the raw measurements into a 13×13 matrix $\mathbf{\Omega}$.

$$\mathcal{L}(\mathbf{T}) = \bar{\mathbf{T}}^\top \mathbf{\Omega} \bar{\mathbf{T}}, \tag{6}$$

where $\bar{\mathbf{T}}$ is a flattened vector of the 12 non-constant coefficients of $\mathbf{T}$ and a constant 1. The latter allows to include the first and zeroth order terms of $\mathcal{L}(\mathbf{T})$ in $\mathbf{\Omega}$ (details in Subsect. 3.2).

This representation has been used to estimate the object's pose [19] along with a covariance matrix. Such an uncertainty measure is useful in robotics applications e. g. to prevent grasping objects with insufficient information and decide for a better viewing angle. Furthermore, it allows fusing the pose with other information [20]. Our initial idea was to extend the framework to estimating the object's pose and three-axes scale (object axes), because $\mathbf{T}$ in (2)–(5) can already scale and only the optimization in (1) needs to be adapted. Section 3 derives how this is done in detail.

However, it turns out that the resulting least-squares estimator has a strong bias towards smaller scales and also inconsistent covariance. This is because noise in $\mathbf{p}_i^O$ is multiplied by $\mathbf{T}$ and thus not additive as least-squares theory assumes. Section 4 analyzes this observation and proposes a solution using total least-squares theory [4]. While in general total least squares is much more computationally expensive, we propose an approximation that is statistically relatively consistent in experiments and needs only slightly more time. In particular, as (6) it condenses an arbitrary number of points into a fixed size representation.

Thus, this paper contributes a novel algorithm to estimate object poses with three-axes scale, including the following subcontributions:

- A formalization of the space of scaling transformations as $\boxplus$-manifold.
- An optimization method based on Gauss-Newton.
- An investigation of a bias caused by noise multiplied by variables and its correction by a total least-squares approximation.

The paper is organized as follows: after an overview of related work in Sect. 2, the Sects. 3 and 4 discuss the least-squares and total least-squares approach to the simple point-to-point loss (2). Section 5 extends to the perspective (4) and depth (5) loss. Finally, Sect. 6 presents experimental results.

2 Related Work

In the category-level pose estimation domain, Wang et al. [24] predict normalized object coordinates ("NOCS maps") by a neural network. They compare regression and classification approaches for the output. In order to estimate the transformation, they align the masked point cloud from a depth camera with the predicted NOCS map using RANSAC and least-squares [22]. A similar method is used in [16]. Our work applies to that approach, as it could replace the point alignment.

Wei et al. [25] split the estimation into a learned object scale predictor and a classic RANSAC PnP algorithm for translation and rotation. Other approaches [6, 12] directly predict the transformation and shape parameters using a neural network. This requires the network to generalize over camera intrinsics, and it is harder to fuse the result with other input modalities.

Regarding uncertainty in pose estimation, Brachmann et al. [3] use random forests to predict noise in pixel coordinate measurements. However, they don't provide uncertainty information about the predicted transformation. Wursthorn et al. [26] use deep ensembles to quantify the uncertainty of pose estimation. This comes at a cost in inference time though, and their uncertainty metric provides less information than a covariance matrix. Richter-Klug and Frese [19] predict pixelwise weights using a CNN and use them for least-squares estimation, which provides a covariance matrix of the estimate. This is methodically closest to our approach is it uses the same $\boxplus$-Gauss-Newton formalism as we do.

The problem of finding an orthonormal matrix that minimizes the squared error between two sets of corresponding points has been discovered across disciplines, e. g. as Wahba's problem [23] or orthogonal Procrustes problem [21]. There are analytic solutions based on the singular value decomposition for certain variants of the problem. For instance, Kabsch's algorithm [13] allows weighting factors per point. Umeyama's algorithm [22] does not explicitly include weighting, but outputs a single isotropic scaling factor. Everson [5] investigates the Procrustes problem including isotropic scaling.

Computing the pose from 3D-2D correspondences is a long researched problem in computer vision [14,15,17,27]. In these works the focus lies on finding a global solution algebraically, e. g. by Gröbner bases. They model noisy data at most as isotropic per point and do not provide a measure of uncertainty.

3 Least-Squares Estimation of Pose and Scale

Starting from an image of an object, there are three steps to determine its transformation matrix ($\mathbf{T} = \mathbf{T}_{C \leftarrow O}$) and its uncertainty $\boldsymbol{\Sigma}$, as depicted in Fig. 1:

1. Identify pixels u_i, v_i in the image that correspond to certain 3D points $\mathbf{p}_i^O$ of the object, either with keypoints (sparse) or by a CNN (dense)
2. Aggregate measurements into a fixed size (13×13) information matrix $\boldsymbol{\Omega}$.
   (a) Aggregate perspective measurements u_i, v_i by (4)
   (b) If available, aggregate depth measurements d_i by (5)
   (c) Alternatively convert u_i, v_i, d_i to 3D-points $\mathbf{p}_i^C$ and aggregrate by (2)
3. Obtain the max-likelihood transformation by minimizing the aggregated loss $\bar{\mathbf{T}}^\top \boldsymbol{\Omega} \bar{\mathbf{T}}$ over the manifold of valid transformations $\mathbf{T}$.
   (a) Find a valid initial guess $\mathbf{T}_0$
   (b) Iterate: Perform a Gauss-Newton iteration using a $\boxplus$-operator to encapsulate the manifold
   (c) Obtain a covariance matrix $\boldsymbol{\Sigma}$ from the converged Gauss-Newton

Such an approach has been used by [19] with a CNN in the first step to estimate poses with uncertainty. For estimating object scales using this method, we need to extend the following steps:

- The optimizer. In our framework, this means describing the transformation space as $\boxplus$-manifold (cf. Subsect. 3.1).
- The initial guess. The previous approach evaluates a fixed set of rotations and recovers the optimal translation as a linear function of the rotation. We still use a fixed set of rotations, but the optimal scale requires the solution of a 4×4 linear equation per rotation (cf. Subsect. 3.3).

Notably, the neural network that predicts 3D points requires no change, except to output normalized coordinates. Constructing the information matrix needs no adaptation either.

In the paper we use homogenous points $\mathbf{p} \in \mathbb{R}^4$ with $\mathbf{p}_4 = 1$ to flag a location vector. Occasionally, we will need only the 3 actual coordinates, denoted as $\mathbf{p}_{\blacksquare}$. Similarly, for a matrix $\mathbf{A} \in \mathbb{R}^{4\times 4}$, $\mathbf{A}_{\blacksquare}$ denotes the left/upper 3×3 part.

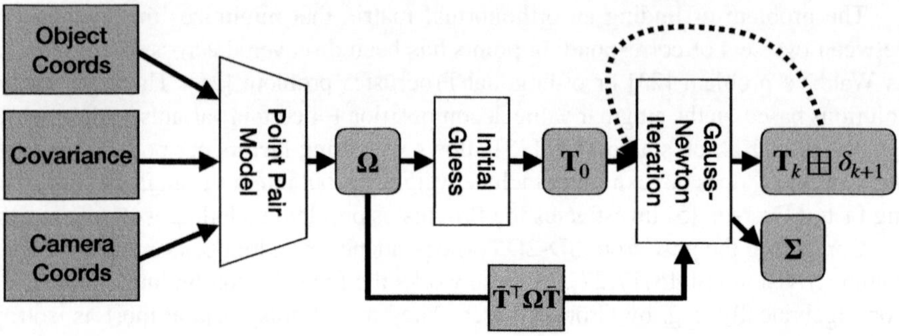

Fig. 1. System overview. The object coordinates, camera coordinates and covariance matrices are supplied externally, e. g. by a neural network from an RGB image and a depth camera. The sensor model condenses the problem to a fixed size matrix $\mathbf{\Omega}$. From this, the initial guess $\mathbf{T}_0$ is calculated. Finally, Gauss-Newton produces a δ_{k+1} that is added via $\boxplus$ to the iterate, and a covariance matrix.

3.1 The Scaled $SO(3)$ Manifold

We want to model 3D transformations from object to camera coordinates that allow positive scaling along the object axes. Ignoring translation for now, these scaling-followed-by-rotation matrices are described by the following state space:

$$\begin{aligned}\mathcal{Q} &= \{\mathbf{R}\,\mathrm{diag}(\mathbf{s}) \mid \mathbf{R} \in SO(3), \mathbf{s} \in \mathbb{R}^3_{>0}\} \\ &= \{\mathbf{Q} \mid \exists \mathbf{s} \in \mathbb{R}^3_{>0} \colon \mathbf{Q}^\top \mathbf{Q} = \mathrm{diag}(\mathbf{s})^2 \wedge \det(\mathbf{Q}) > 0\} \\ &= \{\mathbf{Q} \mid \mathbf{Q}_i^T \mathbf{Q}_j = 0 \,\forall\, i \neq j \wedge \det(\mathbf{Q}) > 0\}. \end{aligned} \tag{7}$$

In order to use an iterative optimizer and the notion of Gaussian distributions on this space, we view it as $\boxplus$-manifold [10]. This method encapsulates the manifold structure in two closed, smooth operators defining a local parameterization (tangent space) of perturbations to a state.

$$\boxplus \colon \mathcal{Q} \times \mathbb{R}^d \to \mathcal{Q} \qquad\qquad \boxminus \colon \mathcal{Q} \times \mathcal{Q} \to \mathbb{R}^d \tag{8}$$

The $\boxplus$-operator takes a a manifold element $\mathbf{Q}$ and adds a vector δ from the d-dimensional tangent space, returning a new manifold element $\mathbf{Q} \boxplus \delta$. The inverse operator $\boxminus$ returns the tangent space vector required to go from one manifold element to another, i. e. $\mathbf{Q}_1 \boxplus (\mathbf{Q}_2 \boxminus \mathbf{Q}_1) = \mathbf{Q}_2$.

In order to define these operators on our "scaled $SO(3)$" manifold, we need two auxiliary functions, σ and ρ, which extract the scaling and rotating components from Q, respectively.

$$\sigma \colon \mathcal{Q} \to \{\mathrm{diag}(\mathbf{s}) \mid \mathbf{s} \in \mathbb{R}^3_{>0}\}, \qquad \mathbf{Q} \mapsto \sqrt{\mathbf{Q}^\top \mathbf{Q}} \tag{9}$$

$$\rho \colon \mathcal{Q} \to SO(3) \qquad \mathbf{Q} \mapsto \mathbf{Q} \cdot \sigma(\mathbf{Q})^{-1} \tag{10}$$

The well-definedness of these functions is proven in [9, Appendix A]. It is straightforward that $\mathbf{Q} = \rho(\mathbf{Q})\sigma(\mathbf{Q})$, but ρ and σ do not commute in general.

Furthermore, we need two functions based on the matrix exponential (with $[\mathbf{x}]_\times$ denoting the cross product matrix), and their corresponding inverses:

$$\exp_\times : \mathbb{R}^3 \to SO(3) \qquad \mathbf{r} \mapsto \exp[\mathbf{r}]_\times \tag{11}$$

$$\exp_\circ : \mathbb{R}^3 \to \{\operatorname{diag}(\mathbf{s}) \mid \mathbf{s} \in \mathbb{R}^3_{>0}\} \qquad \mathbf{s} \mapsto \exp \operatorname{diag} \mathbf{s} \tag{12}$$

$$\log_\times : SO(3) \to \mathbb{R}^3 \qquad \log_\circ : \{\operatorname{diag}(\mathbf{s}) \mid \mathbf{s} \in \mathbb{R}^3_{>0}\} \to \mathbb{R}^3 \tag{13}$$

$\exp_\times$ corresponds to the well-known Rodrigues formula to convert an axis-angle into a rotation matrix, and $\exp_\circ$ maps real numbers to a diagonal positive scaling matrix by exponentiating them element-wise. While the $\circ$-mappings are actually bijective, $\exp_\times$ is only injective within $\|\mathbf{r}\| < \pi$. Furthermore, for the $\circ$-functions, the usual rules still apply, as they work element-wise on the diagonal. On the contrary, $\exp_\times(\mathbf{r}_1)\exp_\times(\mathbf{r}_2) = \exp_\times(\mathbf{r}_1 + \mathbf{r}_2)$ does not hold in general.

Writing $\delta \in \mathbb{R}^6 = (\delta_\times, \delta_\circ)$, the $\boxplus$- and $\boxminus$-operators on $\mathcal{Q}$ are then defined as

$$\boxplus : \mathcal{Q} \times \mathbb{R}^6 \to \mathcal{Q} \qquad (\mathbf{Q}, \delta) \mapsto \exp_\times \delta_\times \mathbf{Q} \exp_\circ \delta_\circ \tag{14}$$

$$\boxminus : \mathcal{Q} \times \mathcal{Q} \to \mathbb{R}^6 \qquad (\mathbf{Q}_2, \mathbf{Q}_1) \mapsto (\log_\times(\rho(\mathbf{Q}_2)\rho(\mathbf{Q}_1)^{-1}), \log_\circ(\sigma(\mathbf{Q}_1)^{-1}\sigma(\mathbf{Q}_2)))^\top$$

This means that $\boxplus$ uses $\delta_\times$ as axis-angle representation of a rotation and $\delta_\circ$ as logarithmic per-axis scale factors. $\boxminus$ recovers the tangent vector that is required to move from one state to another. This behavior is formalized by three axioms that need to hold for $\boxplus$-manifolds, for which the proof is given in [9, Appendix B].

In order to incorporate object translations, we extend our state space to full 4×4 transformation matrices:

$$\mathcal{T} = \left\{ \begin{pmatrix} \mathbf{Q} & \mathbf{t} \\ \mathbf{0} & 1 \end{pmatrix} \middle| \mathbf{Q} \in \mathcal{Q}, \mathbf{t} \in \mathbb{R}^3 \right\} \tag{15}$$

$\mathbb{R}^3$ satisfies the $\boxplus$-axioms with the usual vector addition/subtraction [10]. Thus we define $\boxplus$- and $\boxminus$-operators on $\mathcal{T}$ (with $\mathbb{R}^9$ as tangent space) that act independently on $\mathbf{Q}$ and $\mathbf{t}$, which makes $\mathcal{T}$ a 9-dimensional $\boxplus$-manifold. The optimization itself does not need the $\boxminus$-operator. It is however used in the definitions of an expected value, a covariance matrix and the Mahalanobis distance on $\mathbf{T}$. A normal distribution on a $\boxplus$-manifold is defined by

$$\mathcal{N}(\mu, \boldsymbol{\Sigma}) \sim \mu \boxplus \mathcal{N}(0, \boldsymbol{\Sigma}). \tag{16}$$

This means the uncertainty of a transformation is quantified by a covariance matrix $\boldsymbol{\Sigma} \in \mathbb{R}^{9\times 9}$ on the tangent space at the mean $\mu \in \mathcal{T}$.

3.2 Point Pair Sensor Model

In our context, a sensor model is a function that maps a object-in-camera transformation matrix $\mathbf{T} = \mathbf{T}_{C\leftarrow O} \in \mathcal{T}$ (the variable in the optimization) to a residual. The squared norm of this residual is then the loss to be minimized, e. g. (2)–(5). Our sensor models are linear, thus we want to express them as a matrix-vector product, flattening $\mathbf{T} \in \mathbb{R}^{4\times 4}$ into $\bar{\mathbf{T}} \in \mathbb{R}^{13}$ defined as

$$\bar{\mathbf{T}} = \left(T_{11}\ T_{12}\ T_{13}\ T_{21}\ T_{22}\ T_{23}\ T_{31}\ T_{32}\ T_{33}\ 1\ T_{14}\ T_{24}\ T_{34}\right)^\top. \tag{17}$$

It consists of the rotation part in row major order, a constant 1 and the translation column. Including the 1 in the flattened transformation allows us to use a single Jacobian for affine linear functions. The position of the 1 between rotation/scaling and translation coefficients is motivated by the block decomposition for taking the Schur complement in Eq. (22). Similarly, a homogeneous vector $\mathbf{p} \in \mathbb{R}^4$ can be converted to a matrix $\bar{\mathbf{p}} \in \mathbb{R}^{4\times 13}$ such that $\mathbf{Tp} = \bar{\mathbf{p}}\bar{\mathbf{T}}$, expressing the matrix vector product $\mathbf{Tp}$ as a linear operation on the matrix coefficients.

$$\bar{\mathbf{p}} = \begin{pmatrix} p_1 & p_2 & p_3 & 0 & 0 & 0 & 0 & 0 & 0 & 0 & p_4 & 0 & 0 \\ 0 & 0 & 0 & p_1 & p_2 & p_3 & 0 & 0 & 0 & 0 & 0 & p_4 & 0 \\ 0 & 0 & 0 & 0 & 0 & 0 & p_1 & p_2 & p_3 & 0 & 0 & 0 & p_4 \\ 0 & 0 & 0 & 0 & 0 & 0 & 0 & 0 & 0 & p_4 & 0 & 0 & 0 \end{pmatrix} \tag{18}$$

Using this notation, a sensor model with M measurements is represented by a Jacobian $\mathbf{M} \in \mathbb{R}^{M\times 13}$. In addition, a covariance matrix $\mathbf{\Sigma} \in \mathbb{R}^{M\times M}$ represents noise in the measurements, such that at the true transformation $\mathbf{T}^*$

$$\mathbf{\Sigma}^{-\frac{1}{2}}\mathbf{M}\bar{\mathbf{T}}^* \sim \mathcal{N}(\mathbf{0}, \mathbf{I}_M). \tag{19}$$

The Hessian of the resulting normalized least-squares objective $\mathcal{L}(\mathbf{T}) = \|\mathbf{\Sigma}^{-\frac{1}{2}}\mathbf{M}\bar{\mathbf{T}}\|^2$ (up to a factor of 2) is called the *information matrix* $\mathbf{\Omega} = \mathbf{M}^\top\mathbf{\Sigma}^{-1}\mathbf{M} \in \mathbb{R}^{13\times 13}$. Equation (19) implies that $\bar{\mathbf{T}}^{*\top}\mathbf{\Omega}\bar{\mathbf{T}}^*$ is χ^2-distributed with M degrees of freedom.

The point pair sensor model assumes a set of N points of which the coordinates relative to the camera $\mathbf{p}_i^C \in \mathbb{R}^4$ and relative to the object $\mathbf{p}_i^O \in \mathbb{R}^4$ (with $\mathbf{p}_{i4}^C = \mathbf{p}_{i4}^O = 1$) are known. In a setting where the object scales should be estimated, it makes sense for the object coordinates to be normalized to the range $[0, 1]$, as done in [24]. The Jacobian for a single 3D point measurement is then

$$\mathbf{M}_{\text{pp},i} = \begin{pmatrix} \mathbf{I}_3 & -\mathbf{p}_{i\blacksquare}^C \end{pmatrix} \bar{\mathbf{p}}_i^O. \tag{20}$$

If the point measurements are independent, the $3N \times 3N$ covariance matrix becomes 3×3 block-diagonal and is parameterized by $\mathbf{\Sigma}_i \in \mathbb{R}^{3\times 3}$ per point. Then each point contributes the summand $\mathbf{M}_{\text{pp},i}^\top\mathbf{\Sigma}_i^{-1}\mathbf{M}_{\text{pp},i}$ to $\mathbf{\Omega}$.

3.3 Initial Guess

The iterative Gauss-Newton algorithm needs a starting transformation $\mathbf{T}_0$. Often RANSAC is used before the final least-squares to handle outliers which also provides an initial guess. We take here the view to aggregate all measurements into $\mathbf{\Omega}$ and thus provide an algorithm to obtain an initial guess from $\mathbf{\Omega}$.

We can decompose the optimization into rotation, scale and translation:

$$\min_{\mathbf{T}\in\mathcal{T}} \bar{\mathbf{T}}^\top\mathbf{\Omega}\bar{\mathbf{T}} = \min_{\mathbf{R}\in SO(3)} \min_{\mathbf{s}\in\mathbb{R}^3_{>0}} \min_{\mathbf{t}\in\mathbb{R}^3} \bar{\mathbf{T}}^\top\mathbf{\Omega}\bar{\mathbf{T}}, \quad \text{with } \mathbf{T} = \begin{pmatrix} \mathbf{Q} & \mathbf{t} \\ \mathbf{0} & 1 \end{pmatrix}, \mathbf{Q} = \mathbf{R}\,\text{diag}(\mathbf{s}) \tag{21}$$

We minimize for $\mathbf{t}$ by Schur complement, decomposing $\bar{\mathbf{T}} = \binom{\bar{\mathbf{Q}}}{\mathbf{t}}$ into the 9 rotation coefficients with the fixed 1 as $\bar{\mathbf{Q}}$, and the 3 translation coefficients $\mathbf{t}$:

$$= \min_{\mathbf{R}\in SO(3)} \min_{\mathbf{s}\in\mathbb{R}^3_{>0}} \bar{\mathbf{Q}}^\top (\boldsymbol{\Omega}_Q - \boldsymbol{\Omega}_{Qt}\boldsymbol{\Omega}_t^{-1}\boldsymbol{\Omega}_{Qt}^\top)\bar{\mathbf{Q}}, \quad \text{with } \boldsymbol{\Omega} = \begin{pmatrix} \boldsymbol{\Omega}_Q & \boldsymbol{\Omega}_{Qt} \\ \boldsymbol{\Omega}_{Qt}^\top & \boldsymbol{\Omega}_t \end{pmatrix} \tag{22}$$

For a given rotation $\mathbf{R}$, $\mathbf{Q}$ is linear in the scale $\mathbf{s}$. Hence the flattened $\bar{\mathbf{Q}}$ can be expressed as a matrix vector product with $\mathbf{s}$:

$$\bar{\mathbf{Q}} = \breve{\mathbf{R}}\begin{pmatrix}\mathbf{s}\\1\end{pmatrix}, \quad \breve{\mathbf{R}} = \begin{pmatrix}\operatorname{diag} \mathbf{R}_{i\bullet} & \}\text{i=1..3} \ \mathbf{0}_{9\times 1} \\ \mathbf{0}_{1\times 3} & 1\end{pmatrix} \tag{23}$$

$$\min_{\mathbf{R}\in SO(3)} \min_{\mathbf{s}\in\mathbb{R}^3_{>0}} (\mathbf{s}^\top\ 1)\, \breve{\mathbf{R}}^\top (\boldsymbol{\Omega}_Q - \boldsymbol{\Omega}_{Qt}\boldsymbol{\Omega}_t^{-1}\boldsymbol{\Omega}_{Qt}^\top)\breve{\mathbf{R}}\begin{pmatrix}\mathbf{s}\\1\end{pmatrix}. \tag{24}$$

The inner optimization problem is quadratic in $\mathbf{s}$ and can thus be solved analytically as a 4×4 linear system. If the optimal $\mathbf{s}$ for some $\mathbf{R}$ isn't positive, it's simply discarded. Thus for a given rotation, we calculate the optimal scale $\mathbf{s}$ and subsequently the optimal translation $\mathbf{t}$ as $-\boldsymbol{\Omega}_t^{-1}\boldsymbol{\Omega}_{Qt}^\top\bar{\mathbf{Q}}$. The rotational space can be efficiently sampled by a grid, by selecting each of the 60 vertices of a football (truncated icosahedron) as the x-axis and rotating around it in 22.5° steps. The initial guess is made by calculating the loss for each of the 960 grid rotations (with the induced optimal scale and translation) and choosing the minimum.

3.4 Gauss-Newton on the Manifold

The initial guess is refined by the Gauss-Newton algorithm on the previously defined $\boxplus$-manifold, following the principles from [10]. In each iteration the current value $\mathbf{T}_k$ is changed by some δ in the tangential space using $\boxplus$. This δ is determined optimally in a linearized way:

$$\mathbf{T}_{k+1} \approx \mathbf{T}_k \boxplus \operatorname{lin} \arg\min_{\delta\in\mathbb{R}^9} \overline{(\mathbf{T}_k \boxplus \delta)}^\top \boldsymbol{\Omega}\overline{(\mathbf{T}_k \boxplus \delta)} \tag{25}$$

The linearization of the $\boxplus$-operator is represented by the Jacobian $\mathbf{J}_{\boxplus,\delta}(\mathbf{T}) \in \mathbb{R}^{13\times 10}$, which satisfies locally for $\delta \in \mathbb{R}^9 \approx 0$ that $\overline{\mathbf{T} \boxplus \delta} \approx \mathbf{J}_{\boxplus,\delta}(\mathbf{T})\left(\delta^\top\ 1\right)^\top$. It is given in [9, Appendix C].

The resulting unconstrained quadratic optimization problem Eq. (27) can be solved by Cholesky decomposition to obtain the Gauss-Newton step, which is then applied to the iterate via the real nonlinear $\boxplus$-operator in Eq. (29). The matrix $\mathbf{K}$ regularizes the linearized least-squares problem, such that empirically step size 1 can be chosen. After N iterations, the final estimate $\hat{\mathbf{T}}$ is available, including a covariance $\hat{\boldsymbol{\Sigma}}$. This approximately parameterizes the distribution of the true transformation $\mathbf{T}^*$, i. e. $\mathbf{T}^* \sim \mathcal{N}(\hat{\mathbf{T}}, \hat{\boldsymbol{\Sigma}})$.

$$\mathbf{J}_k = \mathbf{J}_{\boxplus,\delta}(\mathbf{T}_k) \tag{26}$$

$$\delta_{k+1} = \arg\min_{\delta\in\mathbb{R}^9} \left(\delta^\top\ 1\right)(\mathbf{J}_k^\top\boldsymbol{\Omega}\mathbf{J}_k + \mathbf{K})\begin{pmatrix}\delta\\1\end{pmatrix} \tag{27}$$

$$
\begin{aligned}
&= -\mathbf{H}_k^{-1}\mathbf{g}_k, \quad \text{with} \begin{pmatrix} \mathbf{H}_k & \mathbf{g}_k \\ \mathbf{g}_k^T & c_k \end{pmatrix} = \mathbf{J}_k^\top \boldsymbol{\Omega} \mathbf{J}_k + \mathbf{K} && (28)\\
\mathbf{T}_{k+1} &= \mathbf{T}_k \boxplus \delta_{k+1} && (29)\\
\hat{\mathbf{T}} &= \mathbf{T}_N \qquad \hat{\Sigma} = \mathbf{H}_N^{-1}, \quad \text{with } \mathbf{K} = 0 && (30)
\end{aligned}
$$

4 Inconsistency and Total Least Squares Correction

By now, we have a complete algorithm to obtain a 9D transformation from point pair measurements. Point measurements are aggregated into the fixed size matrix $\boldsymbol{\Omega}$, from which an initial guess is made, which is refined by Gauss-Newton to yield an estimate with covariance. However, running it on sample data (cf. Subsect. 6.1, experiment *PP2*) reveals that there is a problem. There is a bias towards smaller object size of 10%. This bias is not reflected in the estimated covariance matrix, such that the results are inconsistent by a factor of 6.

The reason is that the noisy object coordinates $\mathbf{p}_i^O$ are multiplied by the optimization variable $\mathbf{T}$ in (2). This is not allowed in standard least-squares problems, where the noise must be confined to the "right-hand side of the equation", i. e. additive as noise in $\mathbf{p}_i^C$. In our case, the optimizer can scale the noise in the object coordinates down to reduce the error. This creates a bias towards smaller scales. This problem does not appear when a 6D pose is fitted, since the orthonormal rotation matrix preserves the noise level. In fact, it has been shown that the solution to the unitarily-constrained total least squares problem is the same as the standard orthogonal Procrustes solution [1].

This leads us to the insight that for estimating scales consistently, we do need to model the problem as total least squares [7] which allows a noisy data matrix. We follow the approach from [4] and [18, §15.3] to normalize the squared residual by its variance *at the current parameters*, instead of at the true parameters.

4.1 Loss Function

In standard least squares the normalization with the variance is a constant precomputed weighting factor for the minimization and included in the matrix $\boldsymbol{\Omega}$ in (6). By constrast the current parameters $\bar{\mathbf{T}}$ change during optimization, so normalization at the current parameters makes the loss more complex. The direct interpretation of this paradigm results in a loss function with a sum of fractions, one per scalar measurement j. We use the index j for scalar measurements, while i indexes logical measurements (e. g. a 3D point pair is one logical measurement that contributes 3 scalar measurements).

$$
\mathcal{L}_{\text{tls}}(\mathbf{T}) = \sum_{j=1}^{M} \frac{\left(\mathbf{M}_j \bar{\mathbf{T}}\right)^2}{V(\mathbf{M}_j \bar{\mathbf{T}})} \tag{31}
$$

For a scalar measurement j, where the Jacobian $\mathbf{M}_j$ is just a row vector, the denominator $V(\mathbf{M}_j\bar{\mathbf{T}})$ is the quadratic form $\bar{\mathbf{T}}^\top \operatorname{Cov}(\mathbf{M}_j)\bar{\mathbf{T}}$. $\operatorname{Cov}(\mathbf{M}_j)$ depends on the specific sensor model and the noise in the quantities affecting $\mathbf{M}_j$ (e. g. $\mathbf{p}^O$ and $\mathbf{p}^C$), but again can be precomputed as it does not change during optimization. The dependency on $\bar{\mathbf{T}}$ during optimization is purely quadratic.

Therefore, the previous parameterization of the optimization problem by $\boldsymbol{\Omega}$ must be split into a set of matrices for the numerators and denominators, which we call $\boldsymbol{\Omega}_j^U$ and $\boldsymbol{\Omega}_j^L$, respectively.

$$\boldsymbol{\Omega}_j^U = \mathbf{M}_j^\top \mathbf{M}_j \qquad \boldsymbol{\Omega}_j^L = \mathrm{Cov}(\mathbf{M}_j) \tag{32}$$

$$\mathcal{L}_{\text{tls}}(\mathbf{T}) = \sum_{j=1}^{M} \frac{\bar{\mathbf{T}}^\top \boldsymbol{\Omega}_j^U \bar{\mathbf{T}}}{\bar{\mathbf{T}}^\top \boldsymbol{\Omega}_j^L \bar{\mathbf{T}}} \tag{33}$$

If there is noise only in the right hand side, $\boldsymbol{\Omega}_j^L$ is only non-zero at the diagonal entry corresponding to the fixed 1 of $\bar{\mathbf{T}}$ and hence the denominator constant. There are three problems with this formula:

1. Each measurement contributes a summand, so the problem cannot be represented by a constant number of parameters.
2. The measurements are assumed to be independent which they aren't, e. g. some random variables are shared or correlated within a logical measurement (e. g. the $x/y/z$ measurements of one point).
3. This function does not have the quadratic form that Gauss-Newton expects.

For the first problem, we require that the denominators (i. e. variances of individual measurements) are not too different (i. e. within the same order of magnitude). Then, $\sum_{j=1}^{M} \frac{x_j}{y_j} \approx M \frac{\sum x_j}{\sum y_j}$ is a valid approximation and we set

$$\boldsymbol{\Omega}^U = \sum_{j=1}^{M} \boldsymbol{\Omega}_j^U \qquad \boldsymbol{\Omega}^L = \frac{1}{M} \sum_{j=1}^{M} \boldsymbol{\Omega}_j^L \tag{34}$$

$$\tilde{\mathcal{L}}_{\text{tls}}(\mathbf{T}) = \frac{\bar{\mathbf{T}}^\top \boldsymbol{\Omega}^U \bar{\mathbf{T}}}{\bar{\mathbf{T}}^\top \boldsymbol{\Omega}^L \bar{\mathbf{T}}} \tag{35}$$

This is a rather strong approximation. But it is also very beneficial, because it again combines all measurements into a fixed size representation $(\boldsymbol{\Omega}^U, \boldsymbol{\Omega}^L)$.

The second problem is partially addressed by keeping the weight matrix $\boldsymbol{\Sigma}^{-\frac{1}{2}}$ in (19) corresponding to noise in the right-hand side (e. g. $\mathbf{p}_i^C$). In textbook total least squares such a weight appears in the denominator, but being scalar that can not handle correlation in $x/y/z$ components. Furthermore, this approach improves the sum-of-fractions approximation in (35) as it makes the constant part of $\boldsymbol{\Omega}_j^L$ one and hence equal for all j.

4.2 Optimization

As in normal Gauss-Newton, we replace $\bar{\mathbf{T}}$ by $\mathbf{J}_k \left(\begin{smallmatrix}\delta \\ 1\end{smallmatrix}\right)$ and regularize the numerator, so the modified Gauss-Newton step becomes

$$\delta_{k+1}^{\text{tls}} = \arg\min_{\delta \in \mathbb{R}^9} \frac{(\delta^\top \; 1)\,(\mathbf{J}_k^\top \boldsymbol{\Omega}^U \mathbf{J}_k + \mathbf{K}) \begin{pmatrix}\delta \\ 1\end{pmatrix}}{(\delta^\top \; 1)\, \mathbf{J}_k^\top \boldsymbol{\Omega}^L \mathbf{J}_k \begin{pmatrix}\delta \\ 1\end{pmatrix}}. \tag{36}$$

In Gauss-Newton, the linearized least squares problem is quadratic and can be solved exactly. This would be complicated here. It's also not necessary since (36) is only an approximation itself. So we opted for using the full gradient at $\delta = 0$ of the fraction, but only the scaled nominator's Hessian, making it a preconditioner.

$$\tilde{\delta}^{\mathrm{tls}}_{k+1} = -\left(\frac{\mathbf{H}^U_k}{c^L_k}\right)^{-1}\left(\frac{\mathbf{g}^U_k}{c^L_k} - \frac{c^U_k}{{c^L_k}^2}\mathbf{g}^L_k\right) \tag{37}$$

$$\text{with } \begin{pmatrix} \mathbf{H}^U_k & \mathbf{g}^U_k \\ \mathbf{g}^{U\top}_k & c^U_k \end{pmatrix} = \mathbf{J}^\top_k \boldsymbol{\Omega}^U \mathbf{J}_k + \mathbf{K}, \quad \begin{pmatrix} \mathbf{H}^L_k & \mathbf{g}^L_k \\ \mathbf{g}^{L\top}_k & c^L_k \end{pmatrix} = \mathbf{J}^\top_k \boldsymbol{\Omega}^L \mathbf{J}_k \tag{38}$$

Note that the Hessian only affects the steps not the final result [18, §15.5]. We don't reduce the fraction $\frac{\mathbf{H}^U_k}{c_L}$ here to highlight the similarity to the multi-sensor case in Subsect. 5.3. The initial guess is not adapted and uses only $\boldsymbol{\Omega}^U$, since the scale bias is small enough to be refined by Gauss-Newton. Furthermore, the initial guess is not involved in the final covariance matrix.

4.3 Covariance Matrix

It is proven in [4] that for sufficiently high signal-to-noise ratios the posterior covariance matrix of the *unconstrained* TLS-problem (33) is given by

$$\hat{\boldsymbol{\Sigma}} = \left(\sum_{j=1}^{M} \frac{\boldsymbol{\Omega}^U_j}{\hat{\mathbf{T}}^\top \boldsymbol{\Omega}^L_j \hat{\mathbf{T}}}\right)^{-1}. \tag{39}$$

In our case, the approximations from Subsect. 4.1 are also employed here. Apart from that, the optimization is constrained, i. e. the $\boxplus$-Jacobian needs to be considered as in Subsect. 3.4. The result is the matrix factor in front of the gradient in (37). This also justifies using that factor instead of the full fraction's Hessian in the optimization.

$$\hat{\boldsymbol{\Sigma}} = \left(\frac{\mathbf{H}^U_N}{c^L_N}\right)^{-1}, \quad \text{with } \mathbf{K} = 0 \tag{40}$$

4.4 Application to the Point Pair Sensor Model

In the sensor model from Subsect. 3.2, the measurement uncertainty was represented by a single covariance matrix that normalizes the residual to unit variance. For the total least squares approach, we need to attribute the uncertainty to the object and camera coordinates. Both are assumed to be normal distributed around their true values (*), and the points are assumed independent.

$$\mathbf{p}^O_i \sim \mathcal{N}(\mathbf{p}^{O*}_i, \boldsymbol{\Sigma}^O_i) \qquad \mathbf{p}^C_i \sim \mathcal{N}(\mathbf{p}^{C*}_i, \boldsymbol{\Sigma}^C_i) \tag{41}$$

For the fourth homogeneous component of $\mathbf{p}^O_i, \mathbf{p}^C_i$ model zero noise. Then, with the right-hand side decorrelation/normalization in the numerator as explained above, we get the information matrix

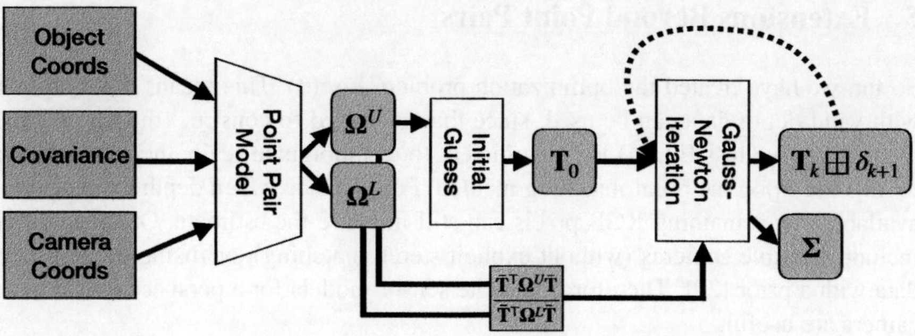

Fig. 2. The point pair model produces two matrices that represent a quadratic fraction. Only the numerator is used in the initial guess, but Gauss-Newton approximates optimization of the entire fraction.

$$\mathbf{\Omega}^U_{\text{pp}} = \sum_{i=1}^{N} \mathbf{M}_{\text{pp},i}^\top \mathbf{\Sigma}_{i\blacksquare}^{C\ -1} \mathbf{M}_{\text{pp},i}. \tag{42}$$

The corresponding denominator $\mathbf{\Omega}^L$ is difficult to derive from $\text{Cov}(\mathbf{M}_{\text{pp},j})$ as the flattening from the $\bar{\ }$-operator hinders algebraic manipulation. So, we derive it from the original measurement model (3) and then convert it into $\mathbf{\Omega}^L$ according to the flattening of $\mathbf{T}$ as $\bar{\mathbf{T}}$.

$$\bar{\mathbf{T}}^\top \mathbf{\Omega}^L \bar{\mathbf{T}} = \frac{1}{M} \sum_{j=1}^{M} V((\mathbf{\Sigma}^{C^{-\frac{1}{2}}} \mathbf{M}_{\text{pp}})_j \bar{\mathbf{T}}) \tag{43}$$

$$= \frac{1}{3N} \sum_{i=1}^{N} \operatorname{tr} \operatorname{Cov} \left(\mathbf{\Sigma}_i^{C^{-\frac{1}{2}}} (\mathbf{T}\mathbf{p}_i^O - \mathbf{p}_i^C) \right) \tag{44}$$

$$= \frac{1}{3N} \sum_{i=1}^{N} \operatorname{tr} \left(\mathbf{\Sigma}_i^{C^{-\frac{1}{2}}} \left(\mathbf{T}\mathbf{\Sigma}_i^O \mathbf{T}^\top + \mathbf{\Sigma}_i^C \right) \mathbf{\Sigma}_i^{C^{-\frac{1}{2}\top}} \right) \tag{45}$$

$$= 1 + \frac{1}{3N} \sum_{i=1}^{N} \operatorname{tr} \left(\mathbf{\Sigma}_i^{C^{-\frac{1}{2}}} \mathbf{T}\mathbf{\Sigma}_i^O \mathbf{T}^\top \mathbf{\Sigma}_i^{C^{-\frac{1}{2}\top}} \right) \tag{46}$$

This expression is clearly quadratic in the entries of $\mathbf{T}$ and hence can be expressed by a suitable $\mathbf{\Omega}^L$. Lemma 1 [9, Appendix D] gives the concrete formula using the Kronecker product. Our modified system is shown in Fig. 2.

$$\mathbf{\Omega}^L_{\text{pp}} = \begin{pmatrix} \frac{1}{3N} \sum_{i=1}^{N} \mathbf{\Sigma}_{i\blacksquare}^{C\ -1} \otimes \mathbf{\Sigma}_{i\blacksquare}^{O} & \mathbf{0}_{9\times 1} & \mathbf{0}_{9\times 3} \\ \mathbf{0}_{1\times 9} & 1 & \mathbf{0}_{1\times 3} \\ \mathbf{0}_{3\times 9} & \mathbf{0}_{3\times 1} & \mathbf{0}_{3\times 3} \end{pmatrix}. \tag{47}$$

5 Extensions Beyond Point Pairs

So far, we have treated the optimization problem Eq. (3). This means that only pixels with valid depth data can be used, since that is needed to construct the $\mathbf{p}_i^C$. Although the perspective loss Eq. (4) is not sufficient to disambiguate scale, there are still ways to improve upon the point matching method. For instance, when depth data is partially available, the remaining RGB pixels can still improve the estimate. Other possibilites include multiple cameras (without explicit stereo matching), or fusing the perspective data with a prior [20]. Therefore, separate sensor models for a perspective and a depth camera are useful.

The steps to obtain an information matrix from RGB and depth data are described in detail in [19]. However, the normalization by a variable variance is new, hence the sensor models are restated here.

5.1 Perspective Sensor Model

In the perspective camera model, each object pixel generates two scalar measurements. The Jacobian corresponding to Eq. (4) is

$$\mathbf{M}_{\text{persp},i} = \mathbf{P}_i \bar{\mathbf{p}}_i^O, \quad \text{with } \mathbf{P}_i = \begin{pmatrix} -f & 0 & u_i - u_0 & 0 \\ 0 & -f & v_i - v_0 & 0 \end{pmatrix} \tag{48}$$

where f, $\binom{u_0}{v_0}$ are focal length and optical center of the camera, and $\binom{u_i}{v_i}$ are the pixel coordinates where $\mathbf{p}_i^O$ was observed. From this, obtaining $\boldsymbol{\Omega}_{\text{persp}}^U$ is straightforward by Eqs. (32) and (34). As above, $\mathbf{p}_i^O$ is assumed to be normal distributed around its true value with covariance $\boldsymbol{\Sigma}_i^O$.

The denominator is obtained with the same strategy as in Subsect. 4.4, where $\mathbf{P}_i$ takes the role that $\boldsymbol{\Sigma}_i^{C^{-\frac{1}{2}}}$ had before.

$$\bar{\mathbf{T}}^\top \boldsymbol{\Omega}_{\text{persp}}^L \bar{\mathbf{T}} = \frac{1}{M} \sum_{j=1}^{M} V(\mathbf{M}_{\text{persp},j} \bar{\mathbf{T}}) = \frac{1}{2N} \sum_{i=1}^{N} \operatorname{tr} \operatorname{Cov} \left(\mathbf{P}_i \mathbf{T} \mathbf{p}_i^O \right) \tag{49}$$

$$= \frac{1}{2N} \sum_{i=1}^{N} \operatorname{tr} \left(\mathbf{P}_i \mathbf{T} \boldsymbol{\Sigma}_i^O \mathbf{T}^\top \mathbf{P}_i^\top \right) \tag{50}$$

Again with [9, Lemma 1] the denominator is

$$\boldsymbol{\Omega}_{\text{persp}}^L = \begin{pmatrix} \frac{1}{2N} \sum_{i=1}^{N} (\mathbf{P}_i^\top \mathbf{P}_i)_{\blacksquare} \otimes \boldsymbol{\Sigma}_{i\blacksquare}^O & \mathbf{0}_{9\times 1} & \mathbf{0}_{9\times 3} \\ \mathbf{0}_{1\times 9} & 0 & \mathbf{0}_{1\times 3} \\ \mathbf{0}_{3\times 9} & \mathbf{0}_{3\times 1} & \mathbf{0}_{3\times 3} \end{pmatrix}. \tag{51}$$

The fact that $\boldsymbol{\Omega}_{\text{persp},10,10}^L$ is 0 corresponds to the scale invariance of the perspective residual.

5.2 Depth Sensor Model

For the depth sensor model, each pixel is a single measurement, i. e. $N = M$. Depth $d_i \sim \mathcal{N}(d_i^*, (\sigma_i^d)^2)$ is measured at the pixel where $\mathbf{p}_i^O$ is recognized. The Jacobian corresponding to Eq. (5) is

$$\mathbf{M}_{\text{depth},i} = \mathbf{D}_i \bar{\mathbf{p}}_i^O, \quad \text{with } \mathbf{D}_i = \begin{pmatrix} 0 \; 0 \; 1 \; -d_i \end{pmatrix}. \tag{52}$$

$\mathbf{\Omega}_{\text{depth}}^U$ is calculated from the Jacobian and the right-hand side variance $(\sigma_i^d)^2$. As in the point pair model, the weighting factor $\frac{1}{\sigma_i^d}$ is included in the nominator to make all denominators have 1 as constant part and improve the sum-of-fractions approximation. The derivation of $\mathbf{\Omega}_{\text{depth}}^L$ is analogous using [9, Lemma 1].

$$\bar{\mathbf{T}}^\top \mathbf{\Omega}_{\text{depth}}^L \bar{\mathbf{T}} = \frac{1}{M} \sum_{j=1}^{M} V\left(\frac{1}{\sigma_j^d} \mathbf{M}_{\text{depth},j} \bar{\mathbf{T}}\right) \tag{53}$$

$$= \frac{1}{N} \sum_{i=1}^{N} \operatorname{tr} \operatorname{Cov}\left(\frac{1}{\sigma_i^d} \left(\mathbf{Z}\mathbf{T}\mathbf{p}_i^O - d_i\right)\right), \text{with } \mathbf{Z} = \begin{pmatrix} 0 \; 0 \; 1 \; 0 \end{pmatrix} \tag{54}$$

$$= \frac{1}{N} \sum_{i=1}^{N} \operatorname{tr}\left(\frac{1}{\sigma_i^d} \left(\mathbf{Z}\mathbf{T}\mathbf{\Sigma}_i^O \mathbf{T}^\top \mathbf{Z}^\top + {\sigma_i^d}^2\right) \frac{1}{\sigma_i^d}\right) \tag{55}$$

$$= 1 + \frac{1}{N} \sum_{i=1}^{N} \operatorname{tr}\left(\left(\frac{1}{\sigma_i^d}\mathbf{Z}\right)\mathbf{T}\mathbf{\Sigma}_i^O \mathbf{T}^\top \left(\frac{1}{\sigma_i^d}\mathbf{Z}\right)^\top\right) \tag{56}$$

$$\mathbf{\Omega}_{\text{depth}}^L = \begin{pmatrix} \sum_{i=1}^{N} \left({\sigma_i^d}^{-2} \mathbf{Z}^\top \mathbf{Z}\right)_{\blacksquare} \otimes \mathbf{\Sigma}_{i\blacksquare}^O & \mathbf{0}_{9\times1} & \mathbf{0}_{9\times3} \\ \mathbf{0}_{1\times9} & 1 & \mathbf{0}_{1\times3} \\ \mathbf{0}_{3\times9} & \mathbf{0}_{3\times1} & \mathbf{0}_{3\times3} \end{pmatrix}. \tag{57}$$

5.3 Combining Sensor Models

The residuals in the perspective camera model all have a factor of the pixel's depth, which the depth residuals do not have. This potentially violates the assumption of variances in the same order of magnitude that underlies Eq. (34). Therefore, each sensor's contribution to the loss is normalized separately.

$$\mathcal{L}_{\text{persp+depth}}(\mathbf{T}) = \frac{\bar{\mathbf{T}}^\top \mathbf{\Omega}_{\text{persp}}^U \bar{\mathbf{T}}}{\bar{\mathbf{T}}^\top \mathbf{\Omega}_{\text{persp}}^L \bar{\mathbf{T}}} + \frac{\bar{\mathbf{T}}^\top \mathbf{\Omega}_{\text{depth}}^U \bar{\mathbf{T}}}{\bar{\mathbf{T}}^\top \mathbf{\Omega}_{\text{depth}}^L \bar{\mathbf{T}}} \tag{58}$$

Although this doubles the number of parameters involved in the optimization process, it is still a small constant instead of growing with the number of measurements. Similarly, if multiple cameras or other sensors were used, each would be normalized separately. This affects the modified Gauss-Newton step Eq. (37), where the Hessians and gradients from all S sensors have to be added.

$$\tilde{\delta}_{k+1}^{\text{tls}} = -\left(\sum_{l=1}^{S} \frac{\mathbf{H}_{l,k}^U}{c_{l,k}^L}\right)^{-1} \left(\sum_{l=1}^{S} \frac{\mathbf{g}_{l,k}^U}{c_{l,k}^L} - \frac{c_{l,k}^U}{{c_{l,k}^L}^2} \mathbf{g}_{l,k}^L\right) \tag{59}$$

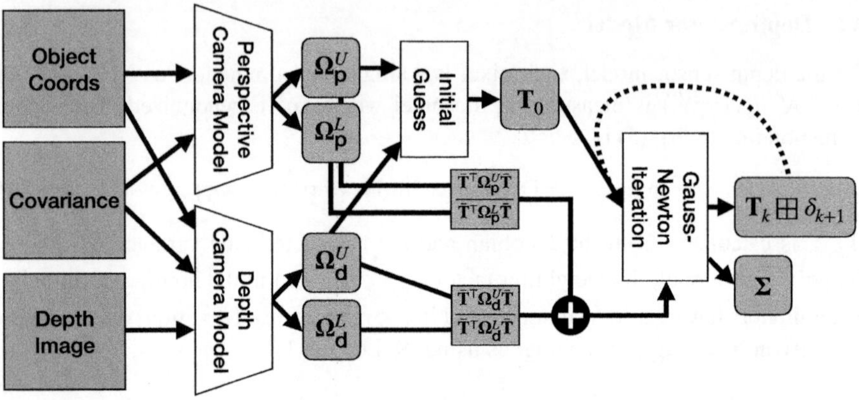

Fig. 3. Both sensor models output matrices representing a quadratic fraction. The initial guess uses both nominators. Gauss-Newton optimizes the sum of these fractions.

The overall relation of the individual parts can be seen in Fig. 3.

For the initial guess, the information from multiple sensors has to be aggregated as well. As stated in Subsect. 4.2, the initial guess does not handle the denominator matrix. Therefore, $\mathbf{\Omega}^U_{\text{persp}}$ and $\mathbf{\Omega}^U_{\text{depth}}$ can not simply be added. At least the factor of each pixel's depth in the residual of the perspective camera model should be compensated. A good guess for this factor is the mean of depth measurements $\bar{d}$, so that the initial guess is made from $\mathbf{\Omega}^U_{\text{persp}} + \bar{d}^2\mathbf{\Omega}^U_{\text{depth}}$.

6 Experiments and Results

We evaluate our approach with simulated data. This way, we can focus on the statistical properties of our approach and have control over noise in the data.

Since our algorithm outputs the parameters of a distribution, we want to show that the true pose is consistent with this distribution. A measure for this is the squared Mahalanobis distance, which should be χ^2-distributed with as many degrees of freedom as the tangent space's dimensionality.

$$\chi^2 = (\mathbf{T}^* \boxminus \hat{\mathbf{T}})^\top \hat{\mathbf{\Sigma}}^{-1} (\mathbf{T}^* \boxminus \hat{\mathbf{T}}) \tag{60}$$

In particular its expected value should be 6 for pose and 9 for pose and scale.

6.1 Point Pair Model

Each experiment is a series of 1000 trials in which certain quantities are randomized, i. e. at least the point measurements. For each trial, a set of $N = 1000$ true 3D object points $\mathbf{p}_i^{O*}$ is generated, all coordinates uniformly sampled from $[0, 1]$. The corresponding true camera points $\mathbf{p}_i^{C*}$ are obtained by $\mathbf{T}^*\mathbf{p}_i^{O*}$. The object or camera points, or both, are corrupted by additive Gaussian noise to form the measurements. Finally, a

Table 1. Overview of the experiments. Common parameters are the number of points $N = 1000$, the true 3D object point distribution and the number of trials (1000).

Name	Noise	True Transformation	Algorithm
PP1	$\sigma^C = 0.1\,\mathrm{m}$	$\mathbf{T}^* = \mathbf{I}$	LS
PP2	$\sigma^O = 0.1$	$\mathbf{T}^* = \mathbf{I}$	LS
PP3	$\sigma^O = 0.1$	$\mathbf{T}^* = \mathbf{I}$	TLS
PP4	$\sigma^O \sim U([0.05, 0.1])$ rotated $\sigma^C \sim U([0.01\,\mathrm{m}, 0.1\,\mathrm{m}])$ rotated	$\mathbf{R}^* = \mathbf{I}, \mathbf{t}^* = (0\,\mathrm{m}, 0\,\mathrm{m}, 1\,\mathrm{m})$ $\mathbf{s}^* = (0.04\,\mathrm{m}, 0.08\,\mathrm{m}, 0.12\,\mathrm{m})$	TLS
PP5	$\sigma^O \sim U([0.05, 0.1])$ rotated $\sigma^C \sim U([0.01\,\mathrm{m}, 0.1\,\mathrm{m}])$ rotated	$\mathbf{R}^* \sim U(SO(3))$ $\mathbf{t}^* \sim U([-1\,\mathrm{m}, 1\,\mathrm{m}]^3)$ $\mathbf{s}^* \sim U([0.02\,\mathrm{m}, 0.3\,\mathrm{m}]^3)$	TLS
PD1	$\sigma^O \sim U([0.05, 0.1])$ rotated $\sigma^d = 0.01\,\mathrm{m}$	$\mathbf{R}^* = \mathbf{I}, \mathbf{t}^* = (0\,\mathrm{m}, 0\,\mathrm{m}, 1\,\mathrm{m})$ $\mathbf{s}^* = (0.04\,\mathrm{m}, 0.08\,\mathrm{m}, 0.12\,\mathrm{m})$	TLS
PD2	$\sigma^O \sim U([0.05, 0.1])$ rotated $\sigma^d = 0.01\,\mathrm{m}$	$\mathbf{R}^* \sim U(SO(3))$ $\mathbf{t}^* \sim U([-0.2\,\mathrm{m}, 0.2\,\mathrm{m}]^2 \times [0.2\,\mathrm{m}, 2\,\mathrm{m}])$ $\mathbf{s}^* \sim U([0.02\,\mathrm{m}, 0.3\,\mathrm{m}]^3)$	TLS

Table 2. Overview of the results. The $\overline{\chi^2}$ metric would ideally be 9. The scale ratio is the average ratio of predicted and true scales over all axes. The bias in *PP2* is noticable.

Name	PP1	PP2	PP3	PP4	PP5	PD1	PD2
$\overline{\chi^2}$	9.1003	332.36	10.272	11.189	13.842	9.3517	9.4690
Scale Ratio	1.0005	0.8930	0.9998	1.0022	1.0026	0.9997	1.0001

transformation and its covariance is computed using the algorithm from Sect. 3 (LS) or Sect. 4 (TLS). The parameters of all experiments are summarized in Table 1.

In order to demonstrate the relevance of total least squares, we start with a simple experiment: The true object transformation $\mathbf{T}^*$ is set to the identity matrix. We start with isotropic noise, identical for all points (i. e. $\mathbf{\Sigma}^{O/C} = \sigma^2\mathbf{I}_3, \sigma = 0.1$). When the noise is in the camera points only, we are in the classic least-squares case (*PP1*). Therefore, the LS estimator yields consistent results: Over 1000 trials, the average squared Mahalanobis distance is close to the expected 9 (cf. Table 2) and its cumulative distribution matches a χ^2 distribution with 9 degrees of freedom (cf. Fig. 4).

However, with noise in the object points, the classic least-squares approach fails (*PP2*). Although the least-squares problem is properly scaled at the true parameters (the averaged $\bar{\mathbf{T}}^{*\top}\mathbf{\Omega}\bar{\mathbf{T}}^*$ matches the expectation of 3000 measurements), the averaged squared Mahalanobis distance is much higher than the expected 9 degrees of freedom (cf. Table 2). Looking at the average value of the estimated scales ($\rho(\mathbf{T}_\blacksquare)$), we find that they are systematically lower than their true values. This is the effect explained in Sect. 4, that by making the object smaller, the noise's contribution to the residual is

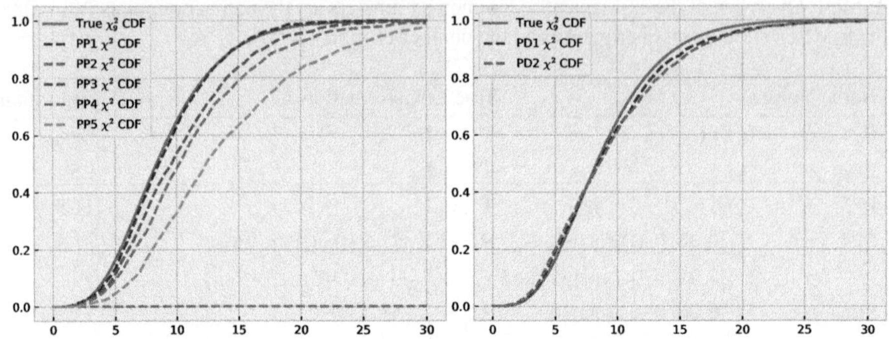

Fig. 4. Cumulative distributions of the Mahalanobis distance from the experiments (left: point pair, right: perspective and depth camera). The curve of *PP1* closely matches the true χ^2 distribution with 9 degrees of freedom. *PP2* (visible at the bottom) is shifted far off to the right due to inconsistency. *PP3*, *PP4*, and *PP5* are a bit off to the right (i. e. the estimation tends to be overconfident), as the involved approximations take increasing effect at those settings.

reduced. The other components in the mean of estimated transformations (calculated by fixed-point iteration over the $\boxplus$-manifold [10, §3.5]) are unbiased.

With similarly generated data, the TLS approach from Sect. 4 yields relatively consistent results (cf. *PP3* in Table 2 and Fig. 4).

We can move to more complex settings (*PP4*). We set the true object transformation to a scale of $(0.04\,\mathrm{m}, 0.08\,\mathrm{m}, 0.12\,\mathrm{m})$ and 1 m ahead of the camera, and corrupt both object and camera points by noise. The noise is drawn for each point independently from a 3D covariance matrix with random rotation and standard deviations drawn uniformly from $[0.05, 0.1]$ for the object points and $[0.01\,\mathrm{m}, 0.1\,\mathrm{m}]$ for the camera points. In this setting, we still get an acceptable average Mahalanobis distance of ≈ 11.

As final validation, we randomize the ground truth transformation (*PP5*). The rotation is chosen uniformly over $SO(3)$ [2], translation is uniformly from $[-1\,\mathrm{m}, 1\,\mathrm{m}]$ and scales from the $[0.02\,\mathrm{m}, 0.3\,\mathrm{m}]$, independently per axis. This is roughly the range of household objects. At this point, the approximations start to show (cf. Table 2). The difference in axes scale affects the variances of the $x/y/z$ components and makes the approximation Eq. (35) worse. Still, the results are far better than even the simple example without total least squares.

In summary, as long as the scales of the axes of the object are not orders of magnitude apart and the noise level is relatively low, the transformation can be estimated sufficiently consistent.

6.2 Perspective and Depth Camera Model

We now evaluate transformation estimation using the perspective and depth camera model from Sect. 5. The process is similar, except how the true object coordinates are obtained. For each trial, a 32×32 depth image is generated by sampling uniformly within an object diameter of the object's true z-translation, i. e. the true object is a random point cloud. This depth image is then transformed into camera points using a pixel coordinate grid and a camera matrix. The focal length is chosen depending on the object diameter and distance to the camera, such that the resulting object coordinates are approximately normalized. Both the depth image and the object points are then independently corrupted by noise. Experiment *PD1* is similar to *PP4* with a fixed object transformation (cf. Table 1). For the random object transformations in *PD2*, the true translation is roughly sampled from the cameras view frustrum. The results can be seen in Fig. 4 and Table 2 and are both unbiased and consistent.

6.3 Limitations

The normal distribution requirements on $\mathbf{p}^O, \Sigma^O, d, \sigma^{d^2}$ are not exactly fulfilled by input data available from real sensors (e. g. the prediction of a CNN from RGB data and a depth sensor). Yet, single pixel outliers are uncommon, since a CNN rather fails by misidentifying the entire visible part of the object. In that case, any estimation approach must clearly fail.

Other CNN failure modes have been examined in [19]: The predicted per-pixel uncertainties will usually be overconfident since they were trained on the same data as the $\mathbf{p}_i^O$ itself, which have lower uncertainty than the $\mathbf{p}_i^O$ at evaluation time. This can be corrected by normalizing $\hat{\Sigma}$ by the observed χ^2 error [18, §15.1]. In addition, the predicted $\mathbf{p}_i^O$ are correlated, e. g. the predictions on a texture-less surface are implicitly interpolated from features at the boundaries and thus do not add independent information. That is, although the covariance for individual pixels may be correct, the fusion of those measurements is not as certain as the number of measurements suggests. The CNN can however learn another correction factor by a loss on $\hat{\mathbf{T}}, \hat{\Sigma}$ (the least-squares estimation is differentiable) [19].

7 Conclusion and Future Work

Many object pose estimation algorithms match a set of point pairs, either 3D-3D or 3D-2D, with least-squares. We showed how this process can be extended to also estimate object-axes scales, by optimizing over the scaled $SO(3)$ manifold using a $\boxplus$-operator that encapsulates the manifold.

However, a problem comes up that's hidden in the original pose formulation already, but does not have an effect there: There is noise in both sides of the match, one of them is multiplied with the scale. Ignoring this creates a bias towards smaller scales, because that also scales the noise down. This bias is not reflected by the uncertainty estimate rendering it inconsistent.

The paper discusses a solution for this problem using total least squares by normalizing every measurement with the variance at the current parameters. Normally, this approach would not allow to combine all measurements into a fixed size representation. However, we propose an approximation to achieve this, which in the experiments proved relatively consistent.

In future work, our fusion stage will be combined with a neural network to predict object coordinates and uncertainties to construct a complete 9D pose estimation system. Further lines of research go for fusion with a prior, other sensors or fusion over time, where a system might remember the object's scale, even if the pose has changed.

Acknowledgements. The research reported in this paper has been supported by the German Research Foundation DFG, as a part of Collaborative Research Center (Sonderforschungsbereich) 1320 Project-ID 329551904 EASE - Everyday Activity Science and Engineering, University of Bremen (http://www.ease-crc.org/). The research was conducted in subproject R02 Multi-cue perception supported by background knowledge.

Disclosure of Interests. The authors have no competing interests to declare that are relevant to the content of this article.

References

1. Arun, K.S.: A unitarily constrained total least squares problem in signal processing. SIAM J. Matrix Anal. Appl. **13**(3), 729–745 (1992)
2. Arvo, J.: Fast random rotation matrices. In: Kirk, D. (ed.) Graphics Gems III, pp. 117–120. Academic Press (1991)
3. Brachmann, E., Michel, F., Krull, A., Yang, M.Y., Gumhold, S., Rother, C.: Uncertainty-driven 6D pose estimation of objects and scenes from a single RGB image. In: IEEE/CVF CVPR, pp. 3364–3372 (2016)
4. Crassidis, J.L., Cheng, Y.: Error-covariance analysis of the total least squares problem. AIAA J. Guidance, Control Dyn. **37**(4), 1053–1063 (2014)
5. Everson, R.: Orthogonal, but not orthonormal. City University of New York (Mar, Procrustes problems. Technical report (1997)
6. Fu, Y., Wang, X.: Category-level 6D object pose estimation in the wild: a semi-supervised learning approach and a new dataset. In: 36th NeurIPS (2022)
7. Golub, G.H., Van Loan, C.F.: An analysis of the total least squares problem. SIAM J. Numer. Anal. **17**(6), 883–893 (1980)
8. Hartley, R., Zisserman, A.: Multiple View Geometry in Computer Vision. Cambridge University Press, Cambridge (2003)
9. Hasselbring, A., Frese, U.: Statistically consistent total least-squares estimation of object scales (2024). https://www.informatik.uni-bremen.de/agebv2/downloads/published/hasselbring_robovis_25.pdf. with appendices
10. Hertzberg, C., Wagner, R., Frese, U., Schröder, L.: Integrating generic sensor fusion algorithms with sound state representations through encapsulation of manifolds. Inf. Fusion **14**(1), 57–77 (2013)
11. Hodaň, T., et al.: BOP challenge 2023 on detection, segmentation and pose estimation of seen and unseen rigid objects. In: IEEE/CVF CVPR Workshop CV4MR (2024)
12. Irshad, M.Z., Kollar, T., Laskey, M., Stone, K., Kira, Z.: CenterSnap: single-shot multi-object 3D shape reconstruction and categorical 6D pose and size estimation. In: IEEE ICRA (2022)
13. Kabsch, W.: A solution for the best rotation to relate two sets of vectors. Acta Crystallogr. **A32**, 922–923 (1976)
14. Kneip, L., Furgale, P.: OpenGV: a unified and generalized approach to real-time calibrated geometric vision. In: IEEE ICRA, pp. 1–8 (2014)
15. Kneip, L., Furgale, P., Siegwart, R.: Using multi-camera systems in robotics: efficient solutions to the NPnP problem. In: IEEE ICRA, pp. 3770–3776 (2013)
16. Lee, T., Lee, B.U., Kim, M., Kweon, I.S.: Category-level metric scale object shape and pose estimation. IEEE RA-L **6**(4), 8575–8582 (2021)
17. Lepetit, V., Moreno-Noguer, F., Fua, P.: EPnP: an accurate O(n) solution to the PnP problem. IJCV **81**(2), 155–166 (2009)

18. Press, W.H., Teukolsky, S.A., Vetterling, W.T., Flannery, B.P.: Numerical Recipes, 3rd edn. Cambridge University Press, Cambridge (2007)
19. Richter-Klug, J., Frese, U.: Towards meaningful uncertainty information for CNN based 6D pose estimates. In: Proceedings of the 12th International Conference on Computer Vision Systems, pp. 408–422 (2019)
20. Richter-Klug, J., Mania, P., Kazhoyan, G., Beetz, M., Frese, U.: Improving object pose estimation by fusion with a multimodal prior - utilizing uncertainty-based CNN pipelines for robotics. IEEE RA-L **7**(2), 2282–2288 (2022)
21. Schönemann, P.H.: A generalized solution of the orthogonal Procrustes problem. Psychometrika **31**(1), 1–10 (1966)
22. Umeyama, S.: Least-squares estimation of transformation parameters between two point patterns. IEEE PAMI **13**(4), 376–380 (1991)
23. Wahba, G.: A least squares estimate of satellite attitude. SIAM Rev. **7**(3), 409 (1965)
24. Wang, H., Sridhar, S., Huang, J., Valentin, J., Song, S., Guibas, L.J.: Normalized object coordinate space for category-level 6D object pose and size estimation. In: IEEE/CVF CVPR, pp. 2637–2646 (2019)
25. Wei, J., Song, X., Liu, W., Kneip, L., Li, H., Ji, P.: RGB-based category-level object pose estimation via decoupled metric scale recovery. In: IEEE ICRA, pp. 2036–2042 (2024)
26. Wursthorn, K., Hillemann, M., Ulrich, M.: Uncertainty quantification with deep ensembles for 6D object pose estimation. In: ISPRS Annals of the Photogrammetry, Remote Sensing and Spatial Information Sciences, vol. X-2-2024 (2024)
27. Zheng, Y., Kuang, Y., Sugimoto, S., Åström, K., Okutomi, M.: Revisiting the PnP problem: a fast, general and optimal solution. In: IEEE ICCV, pp. 2344–2351 (2013)

Silent Speech Interface Based on Surface Electromyography Using Arduino and Ensemble Learning

William Kyle Deveza(✉), Joseph Bryan Ibarra, and Marloun Sejera

Mapúa University, Manila, Philippines
{wkadeveza,jbgibarra,mpsejera}@mymail.mapua.edu.ph, {wkadeveza,jbgibarra,mpsejera}@mapua.edu.ph

Abstract. A silent speech interface (SSI) allows people to interact with machines. It solves issues regarding the use of machines or devices in noisy environments or use by people incapable of producing audible speech. In this study, an SSI was made by classifying spectrogram images of the surface electromyography signals on the corner of the mouths of seven participants. The signals were digitized by an Arduino board. The Arduino board was connected to a PC via Bluetooth Low Energy. The signals were filtered and amplified as part of preprocessing. Then, short-time Fourier transformed was applied to change their domains to time and frequency, from which the spectrogram images were created. Afterward, the images were preprocessed using ResNetv2. The classification was done by four ensembles of four deep learning, base models, ResNet50V2, VGG16, CNN-LSTM, and MLP. The accuracy scores of the base models were 80.00%, 70.00%, 81.67%, and 71.67%. The soft-voting ensemble, neural network stacked ensemble, linear SVC stacked ensemble, and SVC stacked ensemble achieved accuracy scores of 90.00%, 81.67%, 91.67%, and 93.33%. The results indicated that the proposed silent speech interface was viable and could be improved through certain recommended actions.

Keywords: Surface electromyography · Ensemble learning · Short-time fourier Transform

1 Introduction

Human-machine interaction (HMI) is increasingly becoming more intuitive and convenient for users. One method of interaction with machines is by voice. Audible speech commands can be given to personal computers or smartphones to instruct the device to perform a task. However, these pose a privacy risk to the user and are susceptible to environmental noise. Moreover, they require users to produce intelligible speech, but people may be incapable due to medical conditions or loud environmental noise [1]. A silent speech interface (SSI) addresses these issues. SSI can be constructed by processing signals captured from muscle movements related to speech.

J. Röning and J. Filipe (Eds.): ROBOVIS 2025, CCIS 2629, pp. 228–249, 2026.
https://doi.org/10.1007/978-3-032-00986-9_16

Reference [1] offered a wearable device for SSI without distinguishable movements. The device of the study captured neuromuscular signals to rebuild the speech of the user from a convolutional neural network, capable of communicating with devices and other people. Then, the signals were used in a natural language interface with bone-conduction feedback. Thus, a bi-directional interface between the user and the computer was achieved. Data was collected from three participants and silent speech. Among the recommendations of [1] were a more generalized model for silent speech recognition and the inclusion of a wider vocabulary. In another study by Chandrashekhar, an SSI was made for the benefit of patients with speech disorders. Surface electromyographic (sEMG) signals were recorded and classified as speech by a machine learning (ML) model and a Support Vector Machine model. The study concluded that the SVM model attained the highest accuracy after comparing the F1-Scores of eight models. Chandrashekhar notes that his study was limited to the comparison of pattern recognition (PR) and ML models that were trained with a small dataset of English vowels and one consonant. This study also collected data from one participant and the submental triangle [2]. Abdullah and Chemmangat sought to create a computationally efficient SSI with fewer electrodes for the comfort of the user. To achieve their objective, a channel reduction technique and a Decision Tree model were used. The vocabulary developed by Abdullah and Chemmangat included fifty words. Furthermore, the extraction and use of only the time-domain features of the signals led to a faster model performance and complexity reduction. The study reduced the number of electrodes to four and used data from the EMG UKA Trial Corpus, which incorporated recordings of silent, whispered, and audible speech [3].

Research in SSI could improve in (1) sensing technique complexity that inhibits user comfort during use; (2) selection of participants and speech spoken in different ways; and (3) comparing performances of deep learning (DL) models in classifying sEMG signals as speech. The lack of a system with reduced complexity and an improved sensing technique that can accurately classify speech from sEMG signals using an ensemble of DL models was identified as the research problem of this study.

The research aim of this study was to create a system that could classify silent speech from surface electromyographic signals using an ensemble made of deep learning models – specifically, to make an algorithm for signal acquisition, processing, and classification of surface electromyography signals with an F1-Score of at least 90%.

The contributions of the study included:

- The introduction of a silent speech interface that used a minimal number of electrodes and an optimized algorithm for a silent speech interface with a personal computer even in a noisy environment.
- A hardware prototype that demonstrated the feasibility of a portable wireless peripheral device, which could be further refined.
- Comparisons of the performances of four DL models, vital for guiding future research.
- Discussing four algorithms of ensemble learning. Three of which hit the F1-Score objective while two performed better than the best base models of the ensemble.

2 Review of Related Literature

2.1 Silent Speech Interface

SSIs can be made with different kinds of sensors for capturing visual information or myoelectrical signals. With myoelectrical signals from human bodies, SSIs can perform speech recognition. They provide a private interface between the user and the machine. Furthermore, they are inclusive and provide interfacing for persons with speech disorders [3, 4].

Current SSIs are challenged to improve sensing techniques and robustness against inter-session, intra-subject, and inter-subject variabilities. Inter-session variability is the changes in the session such as repositioning the electrodes. Weather and other external factors also contribute to the inter-session variability. On the other hand, intra-subject variability is the variation in speaking and inter-subject variability arises from the differences in the anatomy of subjects [5]. Reference [6] addressed inter-session variability by placing the electrodes at the same locations.

In this study, a silent speech interface was made that could classify silent or mimed speech by the movement of muscles. The interface utilized an sEMG sensor mapped on the face and a speech classification algorithm incorporating deep learning. To address inter-session variability, the positions of the electrodes always followed their initial positions, targeting the same muscle groups. Furthermore, diversifying the samples for the dataset addressed inter-subject variability.

2.2 Data Collection

In [1], data were collected from three persons including one female. A total of 31 h of silent speech was recorded. However, [1] recommended the inclusion of larger data and a wider vocabulary of words. The study by Chandrashekhar included 1020 recordings of five vowels, taken from one participant. Furthermore, it recommended the inclusion of more words in the dataset for training the machine-learning models [2]. Study [3] used 50 words from the EMG UKA Trial Corpus to form its dataset. While the previous studies recorded only silent speech, the corpus from EMG UKA included audible and whispered speech.

Reference [7] incorporated ten digits spoken in English and Chinese. The data were sampled from twelve healthy volunteers that consisted of seven males and five females. In a different study by Kapur [8], three multiple sclerosis (MS) patients were sampled to make a dataset consisting of 15 different sentences, each repeated ten times.

The study made a dataset with three English phrases, recorded from different participants that were selected by purposive sampling. The age, sex, height, weight, and body mass index (BMI) of the subjects were recorded.

2.3 Signal Acquisition and Processing

Kapur, Kapur, and Maes created a composite sEMG signal from seven electrodes and applied a representation transformation to it. The envelopes of the signals were characterized by a mel-frequency cepstral coefficient. A periodogram from the frames of the envelopes is modified using a discrete cosine transform (DCT) before being fed to a convolutional neural network [1].

In a study by Chandrashekhar, sEMG signals were acquired by a Myoware sensor on the submental triangle with a sampling rate of 2000 Hz. The signals were applied to a short-time Fourier Transform (STFT) algorithm to create spectrograms of the signals. The spectrograms of the signals are then used for input to the classifier model [2].

Abdullah and Chemmangat initially used 6 electrodes to acquire the necessary sEMG signal. The sensors were strategically placed to recognize words. The time-domain features of the signal were extracted [3].

Signals were sampled at a frequency of 2048 Hz in [7] and filtered by a fourth-order bandpass Butterworth filter. The signals were further cleaned by a notch filter, removing harmonics and interferences from the power line. Originally, the system in [7] used 120 channels. After optimizing the channels, the number was reduced to ten.

Eight sEMG sensors were placed on MS patients for signal capturing [8]. The signals were filtered using a Butterworth filter to remove power line noise and harmonics. Heartbeat artifacts were removed using a Ricker wavelet.

According to [9], other than crosstalk, sEMG signals are affected by other kinds of noise. There are four categories of noise. These are inherent instability of the signal, motion artifact, inherent noise in electronics equipment, and ambient noise. Furthermore, the same reference adds that the raw EMG signal itself cannot be used. Hence, signal processing needs to be performed on the raw signal.

The study used a minimum number of sEMG electrodes placed on the muscles for articulating speech. The sEMG signals from muscle activity were sensed by the electrodes. The electrodes were connected to a commercial sEMG sensor that was powered by two DC batteries. This setup did not have any power line noise. A microprocessor board received the signals from the sensors and sent the signals to a PC for further processing. The algorithm for signal processing involved filtering unwanted signals and amplifying the wanted signals. Then, the envelopes were retrieved, and spectrograms were generated from them. The conversion of the envelopes into the time-frequency domain were done by STFT.

2.4 Application of Deep Learning in Silent Speech Interface

Recent advancements in sEMG and deep learning paved the way to improve direct speech synthesis [5]. Novel ML models have been developed for managing particular processes like combining data from different subjects [4].

Both studies by Kapur used a convolutional neural network (CNN) trained on a GPU from NVIDIA, the GeForce Titan X [1, 8]. In his first study [1], the CNN model was trained with an 80/20 random splitting of its collected data. The word accuracy (WAcc) was 92.01%. The CNN model in [8] was trained using an Adam optimizer and evaluated using stratified cross-validation with a train-validation-test split of 60–20-20. The accuracy of the model was tested on 3 patients and was recorded to be 79%, 87%, and 77%.

A previous study also incorporated the comparison of certain supervised ML models, including select DL models. Chandrashekhar used the first version of the Myoware Muscle Sensor to retrieve sEMG signals. He analyzed PR, ML, and CNN models using their performances in F1 scores, accuracy, and confusion matrices. He concluded that the SVM model had the highest accuracy of 80.10% and an F1 score of 0.81 [2]. However, the signal processing was limited to the on-board capabilities of the muscle sensor and the spectrogram function of MATLAB prior to speech classification.

A supervised decision-tree algorithm in [3] was made. It was trained using features of the sEMG signals in the time domain. The overall system WAcc was 95.17%. Reference [10] recognized mimed or silently spoken speech using sEMG data. It used an attention bidirectional long short-term memory (LSTM) architecture for speech recognition. It also needed six channels. The signals from the six channels underwent STFT and were fed through a CNN to extract their features in the time-frequency domain. The classification system had reached an accuracy of 97%. Another study created and compared CNN, bi-directional LSTM, and multilayer perceptron (MLP) models. The bi-directional LSTM returned the highest accuracy [11]. MLP is a deep neural network wherein all threshold logic units are fully connected. In contrast, in CNN, neurons are not fully connected to the preceding layer or input. RNNs are generally used on sequential data [12].

Deep transfer learning (DTL) significantly reduces the cost of training a model. There are four common approaches to DTL. The first is finetuning a pre-trained model on new data. Examples of a pre-trained model are VGG and ResNet which had been trained on ImageNet. The second and third approaches involve freezing either convolutional layers or selected layers. The fourth approach involves transferring features using adversarial methods. Pre-trained models can be applied to work with images in different fields such as medical imaging [13].

For fine-tuning the performance of algorithms involving DL, ensemble learning may be employed. Ensemble learning combines the predictions of numerous base models to achieve better performance. Base models may be combined using majority voting or weighted voting. The predictions of the base models may also be combined to train a separate algorithm, the meta learner, in stacking. Ensemble learning has seen applications in classification and has the potential to improve on deep learning techniques [14]. However, even with the clear benefits of using ensemble learning, there is a dearth of research on its application in silent speech interfaces. In one previous research work, a voting ensemble ResNet model for classification of the NATO alphabet was made with an accuracy of 86% [15].

A comparative analysis of supervised deep learning models fed with processed signals was included in this study. The architectures of interest included ResNet50V2, VGG16, CNN-LSTM, and MLP. The ResNet50V2 and VGG16 layers were loaded using their available weights on ImageNet. These four models are referred to as base models in this paper hereafter. The CNN models based on ResNet50V2 and VGG16 are also referred to in this paper as ResNet50V2 and VGG16 even though they had been added with hidden layers for simplicity. LSTM would be paired with convolutional layers. The models were trained using a GPU on Linux with a balanced dataset and train-validation-test split. The meta learners were trained on the predictions of the four mentioned models. The performances of the DL models and ensemble learning approaches in F1-Score and confusion matrices were compared.

3 Methods

3.1 Conceptual Framework

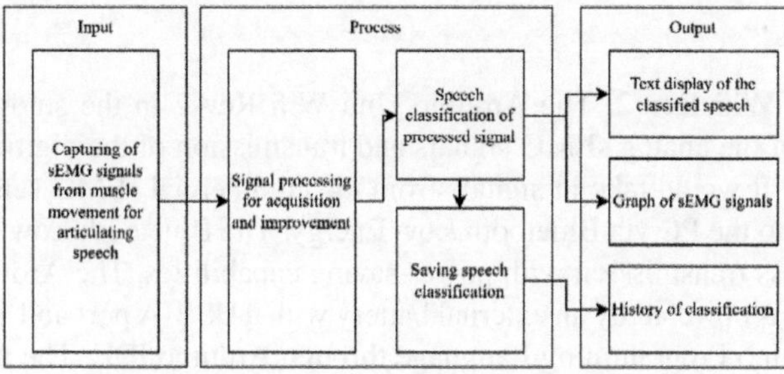

Fig. 1. Conceptual framework used in the study.

Figure 1 illustrates the conceptual framework of the system by showing the inputs, processes, and outputs. At the input side of the system are the captured analog sEMG signals. Two electrodes of the system were placed across the muscles responsible for articulating speech. The potential differences were measured across the electrodes. Another electrode was connected to another part of the body far away from the other pair. This acted as a reference. The surface myoelectric signals were transduced into electrical signals. These electrical signals, or sEMG signals, were subsequently sent to the commercial sEMG sensor.

The signals from the electrodes were retrieved by the commercial sEMG sensor. The sensor was equipped with a differential input amplifier that produced the difference signal between the two electrodes. The output was the envelope of the difference signal. The sensor would provide initial amplification to the signal with a multiplier of 4,140 V/V.

The envelope signal was transmitted to the Arduino Uno Wifi Rev 2 board. The microcontroller board had an analog-to-digital converter that would convert the envelope signal into a digital signal, sampled at a rate of 10,000 Hz. The resolution of the ADC had a range from 0 to 1023. The digital signal was transmitted via Bluetooth Low Energy to the receiving PC on Windows 10.

The digital signal itself is unsuitable for speech classification. Hence, the software program would further filter the digital signal and perform digital amplification. A low-pass filter was applied to remove unwanted signals from neighboring muscle groups. The spectrogram of the envelope of the signal was calculated using Librosa. The spectrogram was preprocessed and fed into four DL speech classification models.

With the spectrogram, the four DL models would begin classification. The classification was any of the three English phrases. The output of the DL models was the probabilities of each class. The probabilities were stacked to form the features of the classification. These probabilities were used to train the meta learner. The meta-learner was the final classifier. The classification would be saved throughout the user session.

At the output of the system, the classification would be displayed on the GUI on the screen of the PC. The user could view the current and previous speech classifications on the GUI. The unprocessed envelope of the digital signals of the current speech classification was also displayed on a separate page of the GUI. Once the user started the termination of the GUI, the software program would delete the stored information after creating a CSV file of the history.

3.2 Materials

Arduino Uno Wifi Rev 2. The Arduino Uno Wifi Rev 2 in the study was used for the reception of the analog sEMG signals and transmission of the digitized sEMG signals to the PC. It would take in signals from the commercial sEMG sensor and would transmit those to the PC via Bluetooth Low Energy. The Bluetooth Low Energy feature allowed wireless transmission with power-saving capabilities. The Arduino microcontroller board was powered by an external battery with a USB-A port and would be coded using the Arduino Programming Language through Arduino IDE. The microcontroller board would accept inputs from its analog pin and transmit the data to the PC. The program was made to run indefinitely until it was interrupted by disconnecting the battery or shutting down the GUI.

Commercial sEMG Sensor. The commercial sEMG sensor was responsible for the initial signal processing of the analog sEMG signals by amplifying and filtering them. In the study, there was one sensor, and it was powered by two 9-V DC batteries. The ground pin and the output signal pin of the sensor board were connected to the Arduino Uno Wifi Rev 2 board on the printed circuit board. A TRS connector was included on the board for the electrodes and cables. The sensor is pictured in Fig. 2.

Fig. 2. Commercial sEMG sensor.

Electrodes and Cables. The electrodes were coated with Polymer Ag/AgCl. They are of adhesive, wet, single-use type. The three electrodes were strategically placed and one acted as the reference electrode. The remaining two would capture the movements of the muscle groups. The sensor cables connected the electrodes to the commercial sEMG sensor.

Other Materials. The hardware of the system also consisted of two 9-V DC batteries, a battery box, a push button, and two switches. The batteries were enclosed in a battery box. The cable of the Arduino Uno Wifi Rev 2 comes out of the box for connecting to a DC battery. The switches would connect or disconnect the two 9-V DC batteries to the commercial sEMG sensor.

3.3 Figure Setup

Fig. 3. Front (left photo) and back (right photo) of the housing.

Figure 3 shows the housing of the hardware in two perspectives. In the top image, A is the electrode snap connectors and cables. B is the USB-A cable for powering on the Arduino board. C is a strap. Finally, D is the push button for transmission. In the bottom image, there are two switches. These are used for connecting and disconnecting the two 9-VDC batteries.

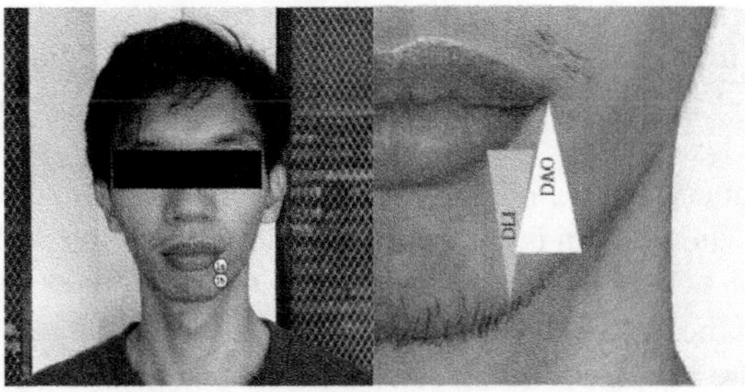

Fig. 4. Electrode placement (left) and muscle groups (right).

The placement of the pair of electrodes would be based on the configuration from [16] as depicted on the left image of Fig. 4. The movement of DAO and DLI was sensed by the sEMG electrodes. These muscles are depicted in the right image of Fig. 4. A reference electrode was placed on the left shoulder. A bipolar configuration at the targeted sites would improve the signal-to-noise ratio (SNR) of the analog sEMG signals by enhancing the common-mode rejection ratio (CMRR) of the onboard differential amplifier of the sEMG sensor [6].

3.4 I/O Wiring

Figure 5 illustrates the connections of the hardware components of the system. Starting from the top-left corner, the electrodes and cables are depicted to connect through the

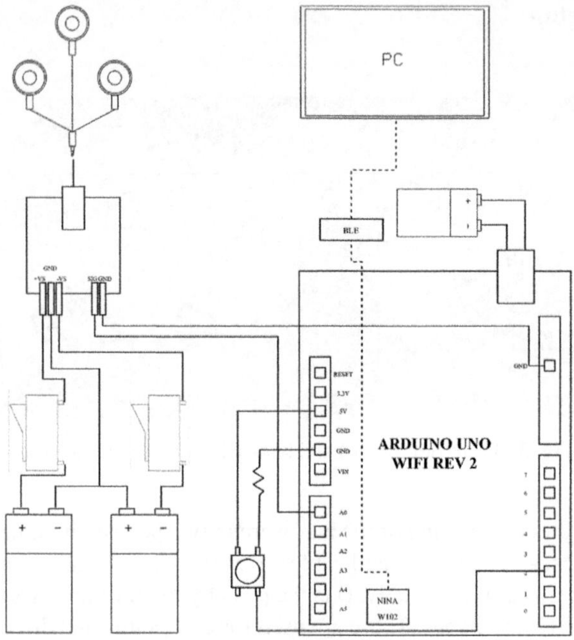

Fig. 5. I/O wiring.

TRS connector to the sEMG sensor. The sEMG sensor has five pins. From the left, these are +VS, GND, −VS, SIG, and GND. +VS and −VS are connected to their respective rocker switches. These rocker switches are connected to 9-VDC batteries. The negative terminal of one battery and the positive terminal of the other are connected at the GND pin of the sensor. The SIG pin is connected to the A0 pin of the Arduino Uno Wifi Rev 2 board. The second GND pin is connected to the GND pin of the Arduino board.

To the right of the two 9-V batteries, there is a push button with four pins. The pins on the same side are normally disconnected until the button is pushed. The top-left pin is connected to the +5 pin of the Arduino board. Meanwhile, the top-right pin is connected to a resistor, which is connected to GND. The bottom right pin is connected to Digital Pin 2 of the board. When the button is pressed, the Digital Pin 2 should read a high voltage.

The Arduino Uno Wifi Rev 2 board was powered by a separate battery, connected by USB-A. The NINA W102 chip enables WiFi and BLE communications. Using BLE, the board can connect to the PC on Windows 10.

For configuring the Arduino board for BLE communications, the ArduinoBLE library was used. The board was designated as a peripheral device, while the PC was the central device. The UUIDs of the peripheral (peripheralServiceUuid), state of the push button (dataTransFlagCharUuid), and envelope data (MSensorA0CharUUID) were declared. A BLE service (SemgService) was declared; additionally, the envelope data and push button state were set to transmit as bytes. These characteristics were also set to notify – the central device was made to continuously receive information while the push button was pressed.

3.5 Data Collection

Data was collected from seven participants, five males and two females. The average age of the participants was 30 years. The average BMI was 20.73. The participants were asked to silently speak the English phrases, "fire under control", "increase pressure", and "hose", with seldom audible and whispered speech. The phrases were chosen with the intention of a sample use case of the SSI in firefighting. A total of 600 recordings were saved. These were split to train, validation, and test data by 0.8-0.1-0.1 split. To extend the train data, augmentation was performed.

3.6 Signal Preprocessing

A summary of preprocessing is illustrated in Fig. 6. After capturing the sEMG signals, they were processed on-board by the sEMG sensor, Arduino microcontroller board, and PC.

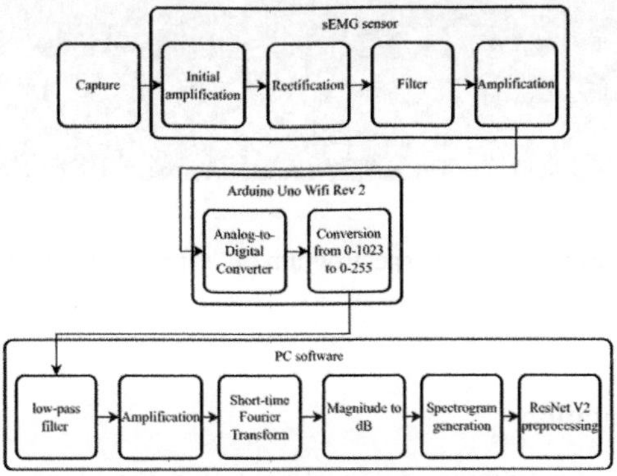

Fig. 6. Preprocessing.

The sEMG sensor provided initial amplification of 4,140 V/V. The sEMG signals were also rectified and filtered to generate the envelope. The envelope signals were then amplified and sent to the Arduino microcontroller board. The Arduino Uno Wifi Rev 2 sampled the envelope signals at a rate of 10,000 Hz. The samples were coded from 0–1023, being further converted to 0–255 for byte transmission to the PC.

The software of the study provided further filtering by use of a 4th-order low-pass filter from SciPy. The low-pass filter was accessed from the "butter" method of SciPy.Signal and was configured with a sampling frequency of 10,000 Hz and a cut-off frequency of 500 Hz. The filtered data were amplified by Python. The amplified data were transformed into the time-frequency domain using short-time Fourier transform (STFT), interfaced from the Librosa library. Amplified data shorter than the 256-long window of the STFT transform were padded with zeros. The STFT was configured with a window length of 200, a hop length of 100, and conversion of the input data into float64. The configuration allowed a compromise between the temporal and frequency resolutions. The STFT magnitudes were retrieved and converted into dB, with the maximum magnitude of the amplified data as the reference value. For uniformity, the x-axis of the spectrogram stood for time, and the y-axis was set up as logarithmic. Also, no plot labels or axes were included. The spectrograms were saved locally on the PC. A sample spectrogram is given in Fig. 7. The colormap used was 'magma', where the lowest value was represented by black and the higher value by the opposite. With the axes and labels removed, the spectrogram was preprocessed using ResNet V2. The preprocessing function of ResNet V2 returned pixel values scaled between −1 and 1 for each sample. Through a scale between −1 and 1, the negative and positive values of the spectrogram were retained.

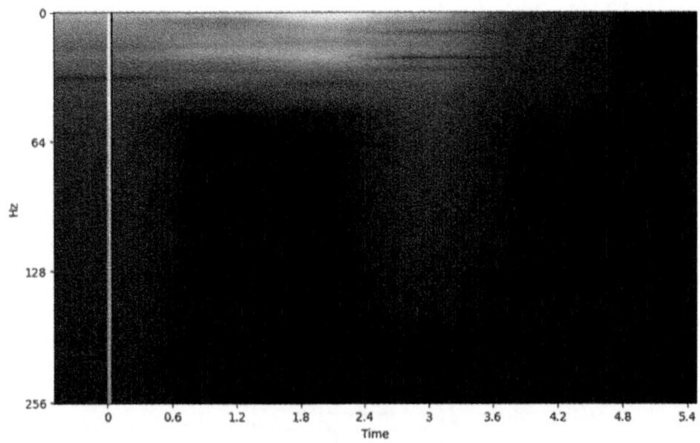

Fig. 7. Sample spectrogram of "Fire under control".

3.7 Data Augmentation

To increase the data for training, data augmentation was done on the acquired sEMG signals. Several techniques were used, including time shifting, time warping, magnitude warping, and adding Gaussian noise. Time shifting the signals simulated the delay in silently speaking. Both time warping and magnitude warping simulated the muscle movement variations for speaking. Gaussian noise simulated the addition of possible noise.

The augmentation had been done before transforming the signals into the time-frequency domain. No augmentation had been done on the spectrogram images because there were no possible realistic variations in the images. Popular techniques such as image shifting and rotation were not used with spectrograms.

3.8 Deep Learning Base Models

Tensorflow and Keras were used to develop the four deep learning base models, ResNet50V2, VGG16, CNN-LSTM, and MLP. For CNN-LSTM, ResNet50V2 was used as a base model for the convolutional layers via deep transfer learning. Most of the layers of the ResNet50V2 were frozen. Some layers from the top were retrained, while the top-most layer was removed for the manual addition of layers. The accuracy, precision, recall, F1-Scores, and confusion matrix were imported from Scikit-Learn. Matplotlib was used to visualize and save the confusion matrices.

Before training, the dataset was shuffled. Image data generator of Keras loaded the images and split them into train, validation, and test datasets, following a 0.8-0.1-0.1 split. The images were preprocessed using ResNetV2. The sizes of the spectrogram images were uniform at 224 × 224 for all models. The train data in each mini-batch were shuffled by the data generator while the validation and test data were not. The train data was also augmented to increase its size.

All models used the Nadam optimizer. To improve regularization and avoid overfitting, all models had normalization and dropout layers. During the training of the models, callbacks from Keras were implemented. EarlyStopping was used to stop the training after signs of overfitting, and ReduceLROnPlateau was utilized to reduce the learning rate by a magnitude of 10 for better validation performances. The former monitored validation accuracy and the latter monitored validation loss. The two had patience values of 3 and 1 respectively.

For manual hyperparameter tuning, the script for building the models iterated over possible values of the dropout rate and batch size. The final values are discussed under the respective section of each model. Due to limited hardware, only certain hyperparameters and possible values were used in tuning and the performances of each generated model were not saved.

Convolutional Neural Network Model Based on ResNet50V2. The CNN model had an input layer, accepting 224 × 224 spectrogram images with 3 channels.

The output of the ResNet50V2 base model was passed through a functional layer and a global average pooling 2D layer. Succeeding the pooling layer was a dense layer with 256 units and an activation layer with a function of ReLu. A batch normalization layer was added before a dropout layer. The final output was a dense layer with a number of units equivalent to the number of classes, 3, and an activation layer with the function Softmax for multiple classifications.

The CNN model was trained using a starting learning rate of 1e−3, dropout rate of 0.5, batch size of 16, and a starting number of epochs of 10. Beta1 and beta2 of the Nadam optimizer were 0.9 and 0.999 respectively. 39 layers from the top of the ResNet50V2 model were retrained, freezing the remaining 64 layers.

Convolutional Neural Network Model Based on VGG16. The top of the VGG16 model was not included, and two layers from the top were retrained.

The output of the VGG16 layers was pooled by the global average pooling 2D layer. A hidden layer followed the pooling layer with 128 units and ReLu activation. A batch normalization layer with a dropout layer followed the hidden layer. The output layer was another dense layer with a number of units equal to the number of classes and ReLu activation.

CNN Long Short-Term Memory Model. The CNN-LSTM had an input layer with a shape of 224 × 224. It was reshaped to include the timestep variable. The timestep was one, representing one spectrogram image.

The ResNet50V2 base model was wrapped in a TimeDistributed layer. The output of the base model was also passed through a TimeDistributed global average pooling 2D layer. Afterward, there was an LSTM layer with 256 units, not returning sequences. It had an activation layer with the ReLu function.

Layer normalization was employed after the LSTM layer. A dense layer with 128 units, activation with function ReLu, and another layer normalization follows. A dropout layer was added after the last normalization. A dense layer serves as the output, with a number of units of three and Softmax activation.

The CNN-LSTM model was fitted using a starting 1e-3 learning rate, 0.5 dropout rate, 16 batch size, and 10 epochs. The optimal values for beta1 and beta2 of the Nadam optimizer were found to be 0.2 and 0.999. The number of trainable layers from the top was the same as the CNN model at 39. The remaining 93 layers were frozen.

Multilayer Perceptron Model. The input layer of the MLP model also accepted a shape size of 224 $\times$ 224 with 3 channels for RGB. It was followed by a flatten layer.

The MLP model had four dense layers with units of 256, 256, 128, and 64. Their activation function is ReLU. Each dense layer was followed by a batch normalization layer. A dropout layer followed the final batch normalization layer.

The output layer of the MLP model was a dense layer. The starting learning rate, dropout rate, batch size, and number of epochs used for fitting the MLP model were 1e$-$3, 0.5, 8, and 10 respectively. For the Nadam optimizer, beta1 and beta2 were 0.9 and 0.999 respectively. The other value considered for the dropout rate was 0.7.

The saved deep learning models and meta learner were loaded using Keras by the software for the classification of speech. When the DL models were loaded, they were also wrapped to be compatible with Scikit-Learn.

3.9 Ensemble Learning

Ensemble learning was employed to increase the performance in the accuracy of silent speech classification. The four DL base models were combined to create four different algorithms. The first algorithm used a soft-voting ensemble. The other three algorithms were stacked ensembles using different meta learners.

Soft Voting Ensemble. The voting ensemble from the four DL models used soft voting. The probabilities from the classification results of the validation set using the four DL models were multiplied by their respective weights. The weights were calculated by the contribution of the F1-Score of one model to the total F1-Scores of the four models. The weighted probabilities are then summed to find the final set of probabilities.

Stacking Ensemble. The stacking ensemble was done by creating a meta learner. To train the meta learner, the probability results of the classification of the validation set using the four DL models were used. The probabilities were stacked column-wise, representing the features of one classification. These probabilities were scaled using StandardScaler of Scikit-Learn. The StandardScaler class and meta learner classes were connected using make_pipeline.

Three algorithms were used as the meta learner. These were MLP, linear Support Vector Classification (SVC), and SVC, accessed from Scikit-Learn. GridSearchCV was used to find the optimal hyperparameters. No data augmentation was done on the validation set to prevent data leakage using GridSearchCV. Hereafter, neural network (NN) is used to refer to the MLP meta learner to avoid confusion with the MLP base model.

The NN meta learner was instantiated as an MLPClassifier from Scikit-Learn. Its learning rate is adaptive. It was initialized with automatic mini batching, early stopping, shuffling, and a 42 random state. It has three hidden layers with units 256, 128, and 64. The activation function of the hidden layers was ReLu. The strength of the regularization, alpha, was 0.01, and the solver was Adam.

The class LinearSVC was used to create a linear SVC meta learner. The 'l2' penalty was used along with a squared hinge loss. The weights were balanced, the random state was 42, and the dual parameter was set to be automatic. Fitting the intercept was done with a scale of 0.001. The maximum number of iterations was 100e3, and C was 0.01.

The last meta learner, SVC, was initialized with balanced class weights and a 42 random state. The value of C, coef0, and polynomial degree were 0.01, 0.1, and 1 or (linear) respectively. The kernel of the SVC is polynomial. A shrinking heuristic was used. The value of gamma was set to automatic.

The meta learners were fitted using the whole probability results of the classification by the base models. They were evaluated using the test dataset.

4 Results

Table 1 shows the best scores returned from manual tuning of the hyperparameters of the ResNet50V2, VGG16, CNN-LSTM, and MLP models. The validation accuracy of each model was equal to their corresponding micro-averaged F1-Score due to the nature of the speech classification. Furthermore, because of the balanced dataset, the macro-averaged F1-Scores were also equal to the weighted averages.

Table 1. F1-Scores of DL base models on the validation set.

Metrics		ResNet50V2	VGG16	CNN-LSTM	MLP
Validation	Loss	0.9026	0.7527	1.0566	0.7131
	Accuracy (%)	80.00	70.00	81.67	71.67
Macro average (%)	Precision	79.97	70.00	81.67	71.81
	Recall	80.00	70.00	81.67	71.67
	F1-Score	79.95	67.41	81.67	71.28
Weighted average (%)	Precision	79.97	70.00	81.67	71.81
	Recall	80.00	70.00	81.67	71.67
	F1-Score	79.95	67.41	81.67	71.28

The MLP model posted the lowest validation loss at 0.7131, but the CNN-LSTM model built from transfer learning of ResNet50V2 scored the highest validation accuracy. Moreover, the F1-Scores of the CNN-LSTM model using the different weighting techniques were consistently higher than those of ResNet50V2, VGG16, and MLP. The ResNet50V2 model scored second while the MLP model scored third in F1-Score. The VGG16 model got the lowest F1-Score in the three averaging techniques.

The confusion matrices of the ResNet50V2, VGG16, CNN-LSTM, and MLP models are depicted in Fig. 8. The true labels are represented on the y-axis, while the predicted labes are represented on the x-axis. The classification reports are shown in Table 2.

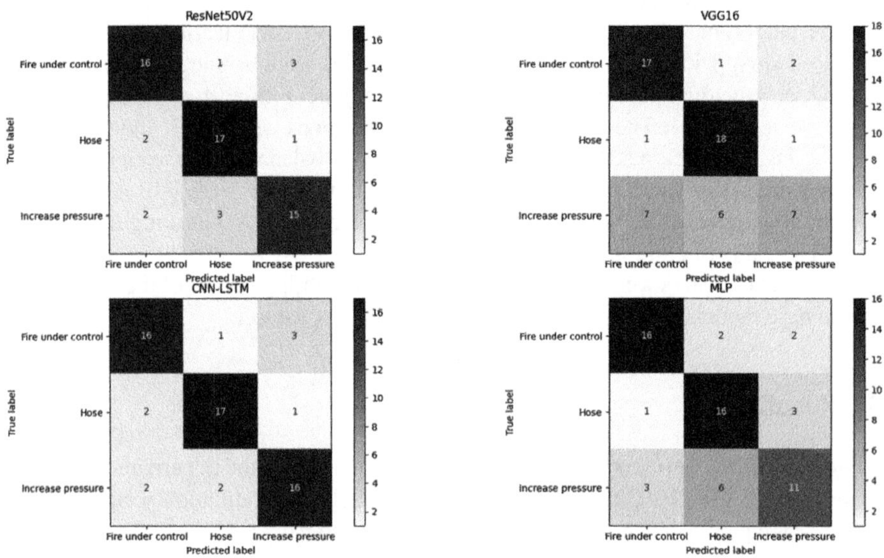

Fig. 8. Confusion matrices of the base models.

Across the four models, "hose" consistently had the greatest number of true classifications, while "increase pressure" had the least as seen in the confusion matrixes. For the ResNet50V2 model "fire under control" was misclassified as "hose" once and "increase pressure" thrice. "Increase pressure" was misclassified as "fire under control" five times. Compared to the CNN-LSTM model, the Resnet50V2 model tied it for the highest accuracy in classifying "fire under control" and "hose". It also tied with the MLP model for the highest F1-Score for "fire under control". In two of the classifications, "fire under control" and "hose", the F1-Scores were at least 80% at 80% and 83%, while "increase pressure" got 77%. The number for the recall of "increase pressure" suggests that the ResNet50V2 would tend to misclassify "increase pressure" as either of the other two to produce false negatives.

The VGG16 model had the greatest number of correct classifications of "fire under control" and "hose", but it had the highest misclassifications of "increase pressure". Because of the disproportionate number of false positive results of "fire under control", its precision was only 68% while its recall was 85%. Similarly, "hose" also had a high number of false positives that led to a 72% precision. The F1-Scores of "fire under control" and "hose" were 76% and 80% respectively. The VGG16 model had a low F1-Score on classifying "increase pressure" due to the high number of false negatives.

Table 2. F1-Scores in decimal of the DL base models per classification.

Phrase	Metric	ResNet50V2	VGG16	CNN-LSTM	MLP
Fire under control	Precision	0.80	0.68	0.80	0.80
	Recall	0.80	0.85	0.80	0.80
	F1-Score	0.80	0.76	0.80	0.80
Hose	Precision	0.81	0.72	0.85	0.67
	Recall	0.85	0.90	0.85	0.80
	F1-Score	0.83	0.80	0.85	0.73
Increase pressure	Precision	0.79	0.70	0.80	0.69
	Recall	0.75	0.35	0.80	0.55
	F1-Score	0.77	0.47	0.80	0.61

From the confusion matrix of the CNN-LSTM model, the scores of the model in precision, recall, and F1-Score on "fire under control" and "increase pressure" were 80%. On the other hand, "increase pressure" had scores of 85%.

The MLP model had the second worst performance in classifying "increase pressure" with only 11 right classifications. "Fire under control" and "hose" each had 16 right classifications. Only "fire under control" reached 80% on the F1-Score metric.

The variances in the marks in precision, recall, and F1-Score on each phrase of the DL base models suggested room for improvement in the F1-Score. For example, the lower number of false negatives and recall of the VGG16 model were better than that of the other three models. Conversely, the VGG16 model could improve its performance in classifying "increase pressure".

The F1-Score of the voting ensemble along with the performances of the other ensemble algorithms is shown in Table 3. Of the four meta-learner algorithms, the NN posted the lowest results. Possibly, this was because of overfitting on the training data of stacked probabilities. Next, the soft-voting ensemble got a 90% F1-Score. The linear SVC and SVC meta learners got 91.67% and 93.33% respectively. The CNN-LSTM model – the base model with best performance – was also evaluated using the same test set. It got a 90.00% F1-Score. Table 4 contains the scores of all base models. The differences in the scores of the base models may had been caused by the random splitting of the initial data.

The confusion matrices in Fig. 9 and the classification reports as Table 5 of the three meta learners were generated using Scikit-Learn. While the 81.67% F1-Score of the NN meta learner on Table 4 suggested that it did not improve on the best-performing base model (CNN-LSTM on the validation set), the individual scores in precision and recall were different. For "fire under control", the precision suggested that no false positives – or misclassifications of the other two as this phrase – occurred. However, it had a great number of false negatives that resulted in a 60% recall. The number of false negatives during the classification of "hose" and "increase pressure" was lower for a recall value of 95% and 90%.

Table 3. F1-Scores of ensemble algorithms.

Metrics		Soft voting	Stacking – NN	Stacking – Linear SVC	Stacking - SVC	CNN-LSTM (base)
	Accuracy (%)	80.00	81.67	91.67	93.33	90.00
Macro average (%)	Precision	–	84.87	91.65	93.33	90.45
	Recall	–	81.67	91.67	93.33	90.00
	F1-Score	–	81.12	91.62	93.33	90.07
Weighted average (%)	Precision	–	84.84	91.65	93.33	90.45
	Recall	–	81.67	91.67	93.33	90.00
	F1-Score	–	81.12	91.62	93.33	90.07

Table 4. F1-Scores of the DL base models on the test set.

Model or algorithm	Accuracy (%)
ResNet50V2	83.33
VGG16	73.33
CNN-LSTM	90.00
MLP	80.00

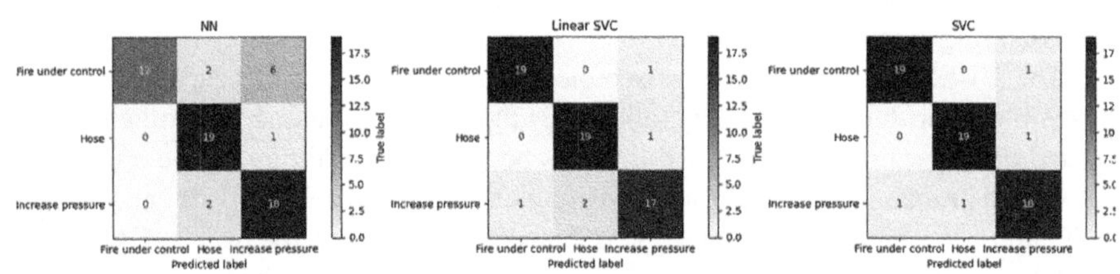

Fig. 9. Confusion matrices of the stacking ensembles.

The linear SVC meta learner returned better performance than the base models with a total F1-Score of 91.67% in Table 4. Precision, recall, and F1-Score of "fire under control" were consistent at 95%. The 90% precision of "hose" and 85% recall of "increase pressure" suggest a level of confusion among the two.

Like the linear SVC meta learner, the SVC meta learner performed better than the CNN-LSTM base model. It showed more consistent results than the linear SVC meta learner. The 90% precision and recall of "increase pressure", combined with the consistent 95% scores of the other two phrases, suggests that the phrase was the source of confusion.

Table 5. F1-Scores in decimal of stacking ensembles per classification.

Phrase	Metric	NN	Linear SVC	SVC
Fire under control	Precision	1.00	0.95	0.95
	Recall	0.60	0.95	0.95
	F1-Score	0.75	0.95	0.95
Hose	Precision	0.83	0.90	0.95
	Recall	0.95	0.95	0.95
	F1-Score	0.88	0.93	0.95
Increase pressure	Precision	0.72	0.89	0.90
	Recall	0.90	0.85	0.90
	F1-Score	0.80	0.87	0.90

Among the base models, the CNN-LSTM base model posted the highest F1-Score, followed by the ResNet50V2, MLP, and VGG16 models. Three ensemble algorithms posted higher results than the performance of the CNN-LSTM base model on the validation set. These were the soft-voting ensemble, stacking ensemble with a linear SVC meta learner, and stacking ensemble with an SVC meta learner. The latter posted the highest performance, while the both SVC meta learners improved on the performance of the CNN-LSTM base model on the test set.

5 Conclusion

A silent speech interface was made using an sEMG sensor, Arduino Uno Wifi Rev 2 board, and deep learning models. Complexity in the sensing technique was avoided by using only two electrodes to measure the sEMG signal on the DAO and DLI muscle groups. Seven participants were recorded speaking silent, whispered, and audible speech. Furthermore, the performances of three models, CNN, CNN-LSTM, and MLP, were compared with one another.

The software program reliably performed the preprocessing procedures while the preprocessing algorithm and DL base models, ResNet50V2, VGG16, CNN-LSTM, and MLP, returned F1-scores of 80%, 70%, 81.67%, and 71.67%, respectively. The variances in the performance of each base model implied that the ensemble algorithms could have improved performances. The F1-Scores of the base models were used to calculate the individual weights for the soft-voting ensemble algorithm.

Four ensemble algorithms were made to improve the performances of the four base models. The first ensemble used soft voting while the rest of the three used a meta learner. These meta learners were a neural network or MLP, linear SVC, and SVC. The soft-voting ensemble achieved a 90% F1-Score. The stacking ensemble algorithms with a NN, linear SVC, and SVC meta learner returned F1-Scores of 81.67%, 91.67%, and 93.33%. The soft-voting ensemble, linear-SVC ensemble, and SVC ensemble were able to achieve the target F1-Score of at least 90%, while the latter two performed better than the base models on the same test set.

6 Additional Work

To further discuss and compare the possible performance differences among the four ensemble learning algorithms as recommended, additional testing was done. However, due to time and paper limitations, this added section is kept short.

The initial test set was combined with the initial validation set for generating the new training set for the ensembles. The performances of the DL base models on the combined dataset are presented on Fig. 10 and Table 6.

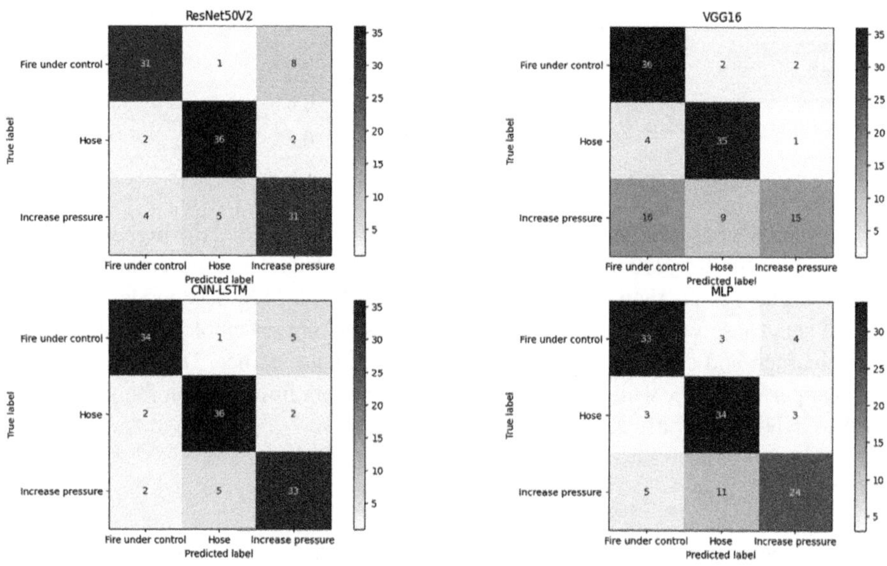

Fig. 10. Confusion matrices of the DL base models using the combined dataset.

Table 6. F1-Scores of DL base models per classification on the combined dataset.

Phrase	Metric	ResNet50V2	VGG16	CNN-LSTM	MLP
Fire under control	Precision	0.84	0.64	0.89	0.67
	Recall	0.78	0.90	0.85	0.90
	F1-Score	0.81	0.75	0.87	0.77
Hose	Precision	0.86	0.76	0.86	0.60
	Recall	0.90	0.88	0.90	0.88
	F1-Score	0.88	0.81	0.88	0.71
Increase pressure	Precision	0.76	0.83	0.83	0.60
	Recall	0.78	0.38	0.83	0.15
	F1-Score	0.77	0.52	0.83	0.24

Following the same methods, the ensemble algorithms were tested on 57 new data. The F1-Scores of the DL base models and ensemble algorithms are shown in Table 7. Moreover, Fig. 11 and Table 8 detail the performances of the stacking ensembles. The numbers are lower than before; yet, this may be because of the discussed variabilities and lack of optimization of the models and algorithms. Of note, the stacking ensemble with a neural network meta learner outperformed the other models and algorithms. In contrast, the other stacking ensembles underperformed, suggesting poorer generalization.

Table 7. F1-Scores of the ensemble algorithms on additional testing.

Model or algorithm	Accuracy (%)
ResNet50V2	77.19
VGG16	71.93
CNN-LSTM	66.67
MLP	63.16
Soft-voting	68.42
Stacking – NN	78.95
Stacking – Linear SVC	66.67
Stacking - SVC	75.44

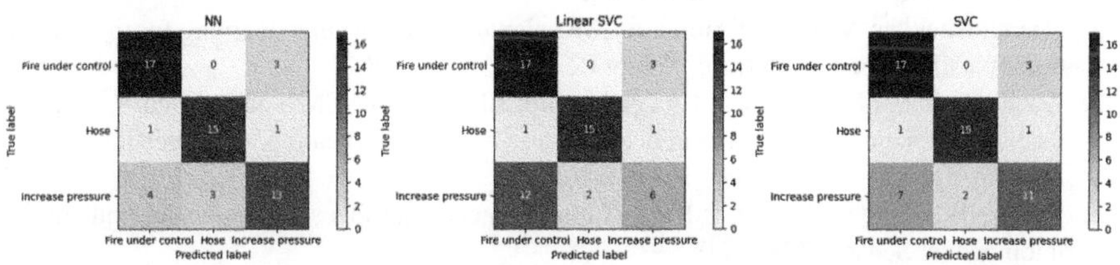

Fig. 11. Confusion matrices of the stacking ensembles on additional testing.

Table 8. F1-Scores of stacking ensembles per classification on additional testing.

Phrase	Metric	NN	Linear SVC	SVC
Fire under control	Precision	0.77	0.57	0.68
	Recall	0.85	0.85	0.85
	F1-Score	0.81	0.68	0.76
Hose	Precision	0.83	0.88	0.88
	Recall	0.88	0.88	0.88
	F1-Score	0.86	0.88	0.88

(*continued*)

Table 8. (*continued*)

Phrase	Metric	NN	Linear SVC	SVC
Increase pressure	Precision	0.76	0.60	0.73
	Recall	0.65	0.30	0.55
	F1-Score	0.70	0.40	0.63

Changing the units of the convolutional layers of the NN meta learner yielded better results. From the original sequence of 256, 128, and 64 units to a new sequence of 256, 256, and 64 units, the algorithm attained an accuracy of 80.70%.

For future work, the additional work done suggested that more data is needed to improve the generalization of the algorithms especially against variabilities. Furthermore, with new data, optimizing the base models and ensemble algorithms is also necessary. Lastly, future research can also include a more exhaustive comparison of the trained architectures and algorithms.

References

1. Kapur, A., Kapur, S., Maes, P.: AlterEgo: a personalized wearable silent speech interface. In: International Conference on Intelligent User Interfaces, Proceedings IUI, pp. 43–53. Association for Computing Machinery (2018)
2. Chandrashekhar, V.: Classification of EMG signals using machine learning for the construction of a silent speech interface. Young Res. **5**, 266–283 (2021)
3. Abdullah, A., Chemmangat, K.: A computationally efficient sEMG based silent speech interface using channel reduction and decision tree based classification. In: Procedia Computer Science, pp. 120–129. Elsevier B.V. (2020)
4. Denby, B., Csapó, T.G., Wand, M.: Future speech interfaces with sensors and machine intelligence. Sensors **23** (2023)
5. Gonzalez-Lopez, J.A., Gomez-Alanis, A., Martín Doñas, J.M., Pérez-Córdoba, J.L., Gomez, A.M.: Silent speech interfaces for speech restoration: a review. IEEE Access **8**, 177995–178021 (2020)
6. Maier-Hein, L., Metze, F., Schultz, T., Waibel, A.: Session independent non-audible speech recognition using surface electromyography. In: 2005 IEEE Workshop on Automatic Speech Recognition and Understanding, pp. 331–336. IEEE (2005)
7. Zhu, M., et al.: Towards optimizing electrode configurations for silent speech recognition based on high-density surface electromyography. J. Neural Eng. **18** (2021). https://doi.org/10.1088/1741-2552/abca14
8. Kapur, A., Sarawgi, U., Wadkins, E., Wu, M., Hollenstein, N., Maes, P.: Non-invasive silent speech recognition in multiple sclerosis with dysphonia. In: Machine Learning for Health Workshop, pp. 25–38. PMLR (2020)
9. Reaz, M.B.I., Hussain, M.S., Mohd-Yasin, F.: Techniques of EMG signal analysis: detection, processing, classification and applications. Biol Proced Online **8**, 11–35 (2006)
10. Ye, H., et al.: Attention bidirectional LSTM networks based mime speech recognition using sEMG data. In: Conference Proceedings - IEEE International Conference on Systems, Man and Cybernetics, pp. 3162–3167. Institute of Electrical and Electronics Engineers Inc. (2020)

11. Wang, Y., et al.: Silent speech decoding using spectrogram features based on neuromuscular activities. Brain Sci. **10**, 1–14 (2020). https://doi.org/10.3390/brainsci10070442
12. Géron, A.: Hands-On Machine Learning with Scikit-Learn, Keras, and TensorFlow. O'Reilly Media, Inc. (2022)
13. Iman, M., Arabnia, H.R., Rasheed, K.: A review of deep transfer learning and recent advancements. Technol. (Basel) **11** (2023)
14. Mienye, I.D., Sun, Y.: A survey of ensemble learning: concepts, algorithms, applications, and prospects. IEEE Access **10**, 99129–99149 (2022)
15. Lai, W., Yang, Q., Mao, Y., Sun, E., Ye, J.: Knowledge distilled ensemble model for sEMG-based silent speech interface (2023)
16. Stepp, C.E., Heaton, J.T., Rolland, R.G., Hillman, R.E.: Neck and face surface electromyography for prosthetic voice control after total laryngectomy. IEEE Trans. Neural Syst. Rehabil. Eng. **17**, 146–155 (2009). https://doi.org/10.1109/TNSRE.2009.2017805

PENet: A Joint Panoptic Edge Detection Network

Yang Zhou(✉) and Giuseppe Loianno

New York University, Brooklyn, NY 11201, USA
{yangzhou,loiannog}@nyu.edu

Abstract. In recent years, compact and efficient scene understanding representations have gained popularity in increasing situational awareness and autonomy of robotic systems. In this work, we illustrate the concept of a panoptic edge segmentation and propose PENet, a novel detection network called that combines semantic edge detection and instance-level perception into a compact panoptic edge representation. This is obtained through a joint network by multi-task learning that concurrently predicts semantic edges, instance centers and offset flow map without bounding box predictions exploiting the cross-task correlations among the tasks. The proposed approach allows extending semantic edge detection to panoptic edge detection which encapsulates both category-aware and instance-aware segmentation. We validate the proposed panoptic edge segmentation method and demonstrate its effectiveness on the real-world Cityscapes dataset.

Keywords: Panoptic edge detection · Semantic segmentation · Edge detection · Scene understanding

1 Introduction

Semantic scene understanding [7] is an important task in different areas such as autonomous driving, search and rescue, and robot navigation. A compact environmental representation with geometric and semantic information can raise robots' situational awareness and assist them execute complex autonomous tasks. Camera sensors are widely used in the robotics field for semantic scene understanding due to their low cost, ability to obtain semantic information from the appearance and textures of the scene, and compatibility with Size, Weight, and Power (SWaP) constraints of small-scale robots.

The recent trend of deep learning has produced different semantic representations in computer vision and robotics. Researchers' interests span from object detection [19], semantic segmentation [18], panoptic segmentation [17] and scene understanding [22]. Semantic edge which was first proposed in CASENet [24] classifies each edge pixel with corresponding semantic categories. It offers a unique representation that jointly combines geometric and semantic information. Other works including [1,25] and [11] improve the accuracy of semantic edge detection by proposing different alignment mechanisms and feature fusion strategies. Our previous work FENet [26] proposes the

J. Röning and J. Filipe (Eds.): ROBOVIS 2025, CCIS 2629, pp. 250–264, 2026.
https://doi.org/10.1007/978-3-032-00986-9_17

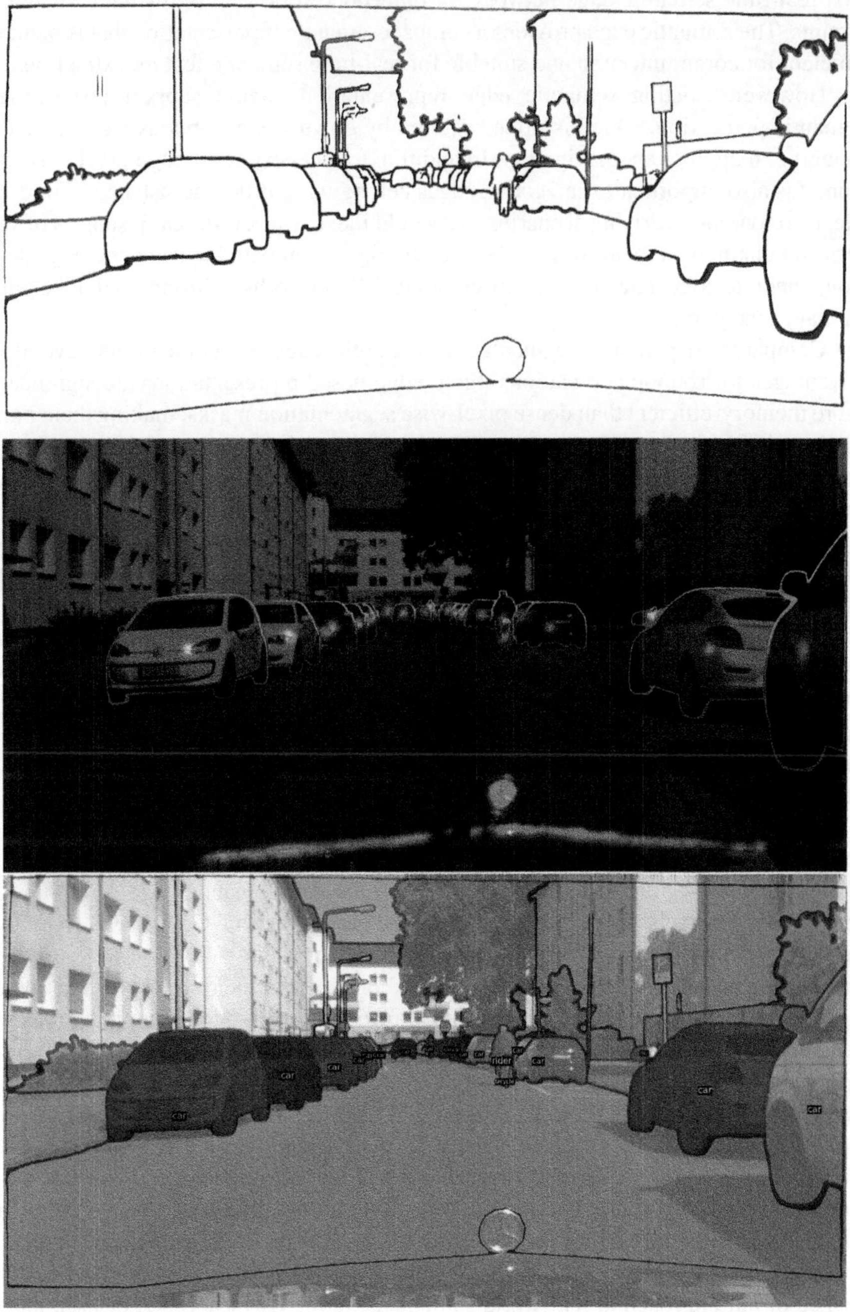

Fig. 1. Combining the semantic edge detection (top) and Instance center and offset regression (center), our proposed PENet (bottom) can obtain panoptic edges that differentiate different categories and instances of edges. We fill the closed instance edge contours for visualization purpose.

first real-time semantic edge network for embedded robotic systems with SWaP constraints. The semantic edge provides a compact semantic representation that is memory-efficient for communication and suitable for real-time semantic feature extraction.

However, existing semantic edge representation cannot support instance-level semantic perception, which is often required by downstream robotics tasks, including planning, mapping, and navigation. In addition to category-level edge pixel classification, it is also important to categorize edges belonging to different instances. For example, in autonomous driving scenarios, we would like to track different instances of vehicles and distinguish them from each other. In Fig. 1, compared to semantic edge detection, panoptic edge detection can differentiate different vehicle instances that belong to the same category.

Compared to panoptic segmentation, panoptic edge detection offers several key advantages for robotic applications. First, edge-based representations are significantly more memory-efficient than dense pixel-wise segmentation masks, making them particularly suitable for resource-constrained robots and real-time communication. Second, edges inherently capture the geometric structure and boundaries of objects, which is crucial for tasks like obstacle avoidance, manipulation, and precise navigation. Finally, by combining semantic and instance information in a compact edge representation, panoptic edges provide all the essential scene understanding information while maintaining computational efficiency.

To address this issue, in this work, we propose a novel approach that combines instance information with semantic edge representation. In [12], the authors propose the first panoptic edge detection method. They combine the information from object detection and semantic edge detection branches respectively. Both branches share the same feature encoder. By fusing the information of the output from both tasks, the final panoptic edge detection result is obtained.

Compared to [11], our approach reformulates the semantic edge definition from multi-label per pixel to single-label per pixel, in order to address the issue of inter-class instance edge. We formulate the panoptic upon the new semantic edge definition. Our method does not rely on bounding-box based object detection. Conversely, we employ one sub-network to predict the semantic edges, and an additional sub-network to predict the edge category, the center, and edge pixels' offset from their corresponding centers. Finally, we employ a clustering technique to fuse the center and offset predictions with semantic edge detection to predict the final panoptic edge detection result. Our proposed approach shares a joint encoder for all sub-networks producing a feature embedding that is memory friendly and efficient.

This paper presents several contributions. First, we provide a formulation of panoptic edge since this is not straightforward as for other types of segmentation tasks. Second, we propose a novel panoptic edge detection multi-task learning design that jointly predicts semantic edges, instance centers, and offset without bounding box predictions exploiting the cross-task correlations. Finally, we demonstrate and validate the performance of our approach in real-world settings using the Cityscapes [5] dataset, and we open source our implementation.

2 Related Works

Panoptic Segmentation. This segmentation task can generate a scene representation that contains the segmentation mask of "stuff" (non-instance such as sky and road) and "thing" (such as cars and humans which we need to identify different instances), therefore, unifying semantic segmentation and instance segmentation. Panoptic Segmentation also separates objects' instances with different instance ID [17]. UPSNet [23] proposes a unified panoptic segmentation network which combines a semantic segmentation head with a Mask R-CNN [9] style instance segmentation head and introduces a parameter-free panoptic head to predict the panoptic label. Panoptic FPN [16] also uses a semantic segmentation branch and a Mask R-CNN instance segmentation branch, but it uses a shared Feature Pyramid Network network as the backbone. FPSNet [8] solves the same problem as a dense pixel-wise classification problem, which predicts a class label or an instance ID for each pixel, which runs faster than the above methods. Panoptic-DeepLab [3] uses a class-agnostic instance segmentation branch that includes a simple instance center regression, which improves the accuracy of panoptic segmentation with a simple and fast design.

Our work is inspired by the design choice of Panoptic-DeepLab. However, rather than separating the prediction of the instance edges and semantic edges, we obtain the instance edges by combining the prediction of semantic edges, the center prediction of instances, and center regression of the instances. Finally, we fuse the semantic edges with the instance edges to produce the panoptic edges.

Semantic Edge Detection. This type of segmentation is different compared to semantic segmentation. Semantic segmentation predicts the category of the pixel inside the target, while semantic edge only focuses on the boundary of the target and predicts the multi-label categories of the boundary pixels. CASENet [24] is the first approach to propose the semantic edge detection method. It predicts edge pixels and classifies the category of each edge pixel. Notably, each edge pixel can belong to multiple categories. Later, SEAL [25] and STEAL [1] improve the quality of the semantic edge detection by aligning edges using latent variable optimization and reasoning the annotation noise. DFF [11] adaptively adjusts the weights of feature maps from different levels according to the high-level feature map, which further boosts up the accuracy of semantic edge detection. More recently, in order to deploy real-time semantic edge detection on edge computing devices, our FENet work [26] proposes the first real-time semantic edge detection method which can run on an embedded robotic platform at more than 30 Hz.

This work extends semantic edge detection to panoptic edge detection by introducing center regression and head regression. We adopt a fusion strategy to fuse the object center, object offset, and semantic labels to produce the panoptic edges. In this area, the closest related work PEN [12] cannot directly regress the instance edge pixel and employs the bounding-box of the object detection to solve this task. The approach simply combines object detection with semantic edge detection to coarsely produce panoptic edges without properly exploiting cross-task correlations.

3 Methodology

3.1 Panoptic Edge Formulation

CASENet [24] formulates category-aware semantic edge such that each semantic edge pixel can map to multiple labels. However, if we want to extend the formulation of semantic edge to panoptic edge segmentation, we need to ensure that each pixel on the two sides of two overlapping instances with different semantic category labels should only reflect a single category label, so that the instance labels of these edges do not have ambiguity. This is reflected in our network design and shown in Sect. 3.5. Specifically, we first reformulate the semantic edge by adding a constraint in the network design such that each semantic edge pixel only maps to a single category label. We split semantic edge pixels to two sets: "thing" edge pixels and "stuff" edge pixels similar to the definition of Panoptic Segmentation [17] based on their semantic categories. To be noticed, we use the concept of "thing" edge and instance edge interchangeably. "thing" edge pixels of the same category can have different instances (e.g., contours of cars), whereas "stuff" edge pixels do not have different instances (e.g., contours of the sky).

Therefore, we map each semantic edge pixel p_i to a single semantic category label ($S_i \in 1, \cdots K$) and a single instance ID ($ID_i \in \mathbb{N}_0$): $f : p_i \rightarrow S_i$, $g : p_i \rightarrow ID_i$, $S_i \in 1 \cdots K$ where: 1) K is the total number of semantic categories; 2) $\forall g(p_i) < D$, where $D \in \mathbb{N}$ is set to be a large enough integer and larger than the largest instance ID among all semantic category label; 3) $\|\{g(p_i)\}\| = \|\{p_i\}\|$, $\forall p_i$ s.t. $f(p_i) = S$ which means all instance IDs of edge pixels that belong to the same category have unique instance ID among their own set. We define the panoptic edge label for each "stuff" pixel and "thing" pixel as $S_i * D + ID_i$. Each panoptic edge label is unique among all edge segments. Since "stuff" edges do not have different instances, without loss of generality, we can map all "stuff" edge pixels of same category S to any given instance ID where S is a "stuff" category.

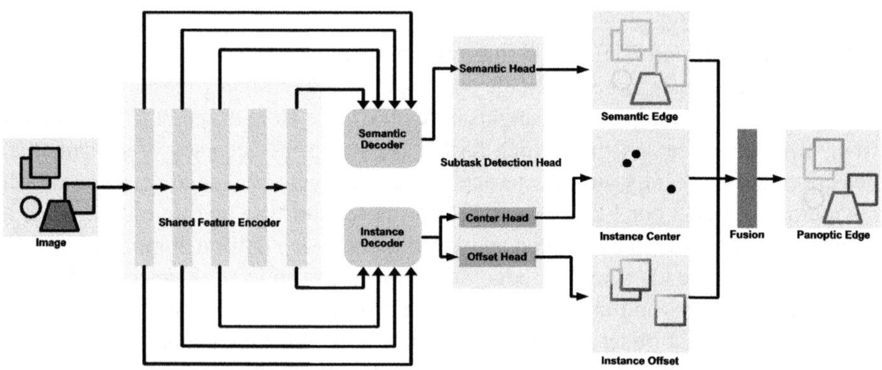

Fig. 2. The Semantic and Instance Decoder aggregate the input features from shared encoder to decode features for subtask heads, including the semantic head which outputs semantic edges, the center head which outputs instance center regression and the offset head which outputs instance offset regression. Finally, a Fusion module fuses them to obtain the Panoptic Edge. To be noted, each pixels are assigned with unique semantic label and instance label.

3.2 Panoptic Edge Detection Model Overview

We predict the panoptic edge by predicting the instance ID and semantic label of each pixel. We call these two tasks instance edge prediction and semantic edge prediction. We illustrate the proposed model architecture in Fig. 2.

We use a shared feature encoder for two sub-networks of semantic edge prediction and instance edge prediction. Assume the input image has dimension $3 \times H \times W$. The sub-network of semantic edge prediction outputs a probability map with dimension of $(K + 1) \times H \times W$, where K is the number of semantic labels. This probability map predicts the probabilities of K labels and the non-edge labels for each pixel. The instance edge sub-network outputs the instance center regression and instance offset regression. The instance center regression outputs the geometric center of each instance edge with the dimension of $1 \times H \times W$. The instance offset regression outputs the offset vector maps with dimensions of $2 \times H \times W$ from the current edge pixels to their instance center. Given instance centers and corresponding instance offsets, we can compute the instance IDs for edge pixels.

In the following sections, we detail our proposed framework. We introduce the shared feature encoder in Sect. 3.3. We show the design of semantic decoder and instance decoder in Sect. 3.4. We also show the panoptic edge fusion strategy in Sect. 3.6. Finally, we show the loss function to train our proposed network in Sect. 3.7.

3.3 Shared Feature Encoder

The shared feature encoder (see Fig. 2) module uses a backbone network to produce multi-level feature maps for all three subtasks: the semantic edge detection, the instance center regression and the instance offset regression. The Shared Feature Encoder outputs feature maps from different levels to the decoders. Low-level feature maps provide geometric details of the edges, whereas high-level feature maps provide semantic clues for category classification.

We use ResNet [10] as the backbone network with a replacement of the first block as three 3×3 convolution layers which first layer has stride 2 followed by a 3×3 max-pooling with stride 2. Thus, the spatial resolution of the feature maps after the first block is $\frac{H}{4} \times \frac{W}{4}$.

3.4 Semantic Decoder and Instance Decoder

The semantic decoder and instance decoder take inputs from the different levels of Shared Feature Encoder, fuse the information across each level, and output the decoded features for their subtasks. The output of the semantic decoder will be used by semantic head to produce the semantic edge map. The output of the instance decoder will be utilized by center head and offset head to generate instance center map and instance offset map respectively. Both decoders share the same meta-architecture illustrated in Fig. 3.

The features of last encoder block pass into a Astrous Spatial Pyramid Pooling (ASPP) module [2]. The features of the three additional encoder blocks pass into a Projection module. The Projection module projects the features to desired projection channel sizes. We experiment with two different Projection modules. The basic one is a 1×1 convolution layer that projects the input feature channels to smaller values. We call

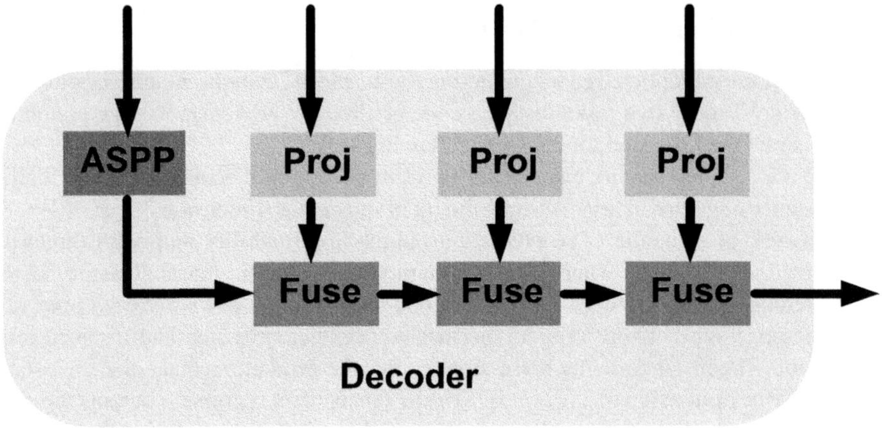

Fig. 3. The Decoder Module fuses features from different levels of encoder using ASPP, Projection and Fuse module.

the basic Projection module Proj-A. The advanced one, called Proj-B, is a self-attention module powered by Criss-Cross Attention (CC) [14]. The CC module applies axis-wise attention for each element in the feature maps. Then it adds the input feature maps as the residual term to obtain the self-attention output of the feature map. Applying Criss-Cross Attention recursively two times can aggregate the information of all pixels to each pixel. Compared to non-local attention, which requires an attention map with the same spatial resolution as the input feature map, Criss-Cross Attention is memory efficient and computation-efficient. This advanced module first projects the features to projection channel sizes using the convolution layer. Subsequently, it applies the Criss-Cross Attention recursively two times. Finally, it applies another convolution layer.

The fuse module shown in Fig. 4 upsamples the low-resolution features and concatenates them with the projected features with high-resolution. The Fuse module then uses a depthwise separable convolution with a 5×5 convolution layer and a 1×1 convolution layer to fuse the features.

3.5 Subtask Detection Head

The subtask detection heads including semantic head, center head and offset head predict the subtask output using aggregated features from the semantic decoders and instance decoders. The format of these subtasks are illustrated in Fig. 2. We use square to demonstrate the same-category "thing" edges, and others are "stuff" edges. All subtask detection heads consist of three convolution layers with kernel size 3×3. The semantic head decodes the feature into the $(K+1) \times H \times W$ semantic label map, which predicts the probability of the semantic edge category. The center head decodes the feature into $1 \times H \times W$ gaussian heat map, which predicts the possible center locations of "thing" edges. The offset head decodes the feature into a $2 \times H \times W$ feature map, which represents the instance center offset vector from semantic edge pixel to its instance center of "thing" edges.

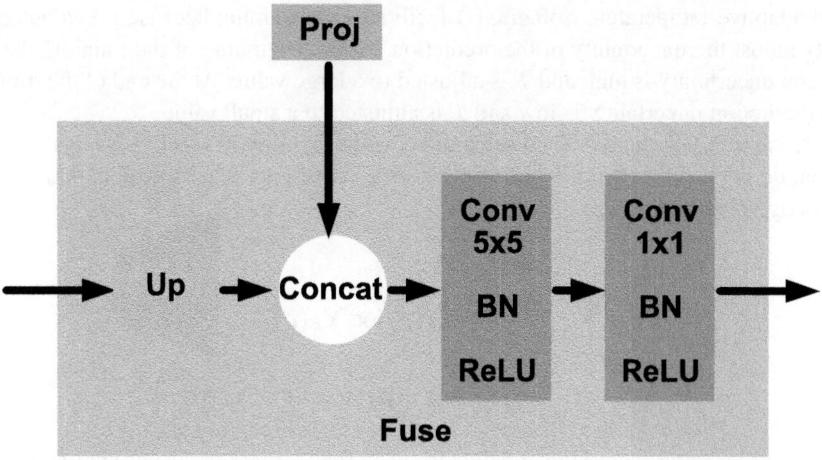

Fig. 4. The Fuse module combines low-level and high-level features by upsampling and convolutions.

3.6 Panoptic Edge Fusion Module

The heuristics-based panoptic edge fusion module fuses the semantic edges, the instance centers and the instance offsets to produce the panoptic edge label. We first do a clustering step for the predicted instance center since the predicted heatmap of the instance center contains noises. Given semantic labels of edge pixels, We determine the instance center of an instance edge pixel that has a corresponding semantic edge label according to 1) The distance between the instance center and the pixel; 2) The instance offset vector from the pixel to the instance center. We generate a vector according to the direction of the normalized offset vector and the magnitude of the distance from the pixel to the predicted instance center. Then, we identify the nearest predicted instance center to the endpoint of the vector. This ensures that each instance edge is associated with a distinct instance ID. Finally, we merge the semantic edge prediction and instance edge prediction to obtain the panoptic edge prediction.

3.7 Loss Function

Our problem is a multi-task learning problem. Therefore, the loss is composed of three parts, one for each subtasks. For semantic edge detection, inspired by CASENet [24] and DUpsampling [20], we combine $\mathrm{Softmax}(\cdot)$ with temperature T and reweighted cross entropy loss to obtain the semantic edge prediction loss L_s. We first apply an adaptive-temperature on the multi-label prediction, then we re-weight loss of edge and non-edge pixels using the percentage ratio of them. Compared to conventional $\mathrm{Softmax}(\cdot)$, the adaptive-temperature $\mathrm{Softmax}(\cdot)$ scales down the input by an adaptive trainable temperature T

$$\mathrm{AdaSoftMax}(x) = \mathrm{Softmax}(x/T). \tag{1}$$

The adaptive-temperature $\mathrm{Softmax}(\cdot)$ facilitates the training because it can automatically adjust the uncertainty of the prediction. At the beginning of the training, the prediction uncertainty is high and T is adjusted to a large value. At the end of the training, the prediction uncertainty is low and T is adjusted to a small value.

Assume $\mathbf{Y}_k$ is the predicted semantic edge probability of label k, $\overline{\mathbf{Y}}_k$ is the binary semantic edge groundtruth label of class k, $\mathbf{p}$ represents pixel location, and γ is the non-edge pixel percentage

$$\begin{aligned}\hat{\mathbf{Y}} &= \mathrm{AdaSoftMax}(\mathbf{Y}),\\ \mathcal{L}_s &= \sum_k \sum_{\mathbf{p}} \Big\{ -\gamma \overline{\mathbf{Y}}_k(\mathbf{p}) \log \hat{\mathbf{Y}}_k(\mathbf{p}) \\ &\quad -(1-\gamma)\left(1-\overline{\mathbf{Y}}_k(\mathbf{p})\right) \log\left(1-\hat{\mathbf{Y}}_k(\mathbf{p})\right) \Big\}.\end{aligned} \tag{2}$$

For instance center regression and the instance offset regression, we use the L_2 norm as the loss function for the instance center regression task as L_c where c_i is the predicted center and $\overline{c}_i$ is the groundtruth center, and we use the L_1 norm as the loss function for the offset regression task as L_o where o_i is the predicted offset and $\overline{o}_i$ is the groundtruth offset

$$L_c = \sum \|c_i - \overline{c}_i\|_2, \quad L_o = \sum \|o_i - \overline{o}_i\|_1. \tag{3}$$

The final loss function is

$$L = \alpha_s L_s + \alpha_c L_c + \alpha_o L_o. \tag{4}$$

4 Experiments

4.1 Groundtruth Generation

We evaluated our method on the Cityscapes [5] dataset, which contains original panoptic segmentation groundtruth annotations. The splits of training, validation and testing samples are 2975, 500, and 1525. The dataset contains 8 "thing" classes and 11 "stuff" classes. We convert the original panoptic segmentation mask annotation to panoptic edge annotation by applying erosion and exclusive OR (XOR) operator $\oplus$ from the panoptic segmentation label. Assuming the original panoptic segmentation label is $\mathbf{P}$, we can obtain panoptic edge label $\mathbf{PE}$ as follows where r is the width of the edges. In this work, we try to tackle thin edge setting $r = 2$.

$$\mathbf{PE} = \mathrm{erosion}(\mathbf{P}, r) \oplus \mathbf{P}. \tag{5}$$

4.2 Implementation Details

We implement our pipeline based on Detectron2 [21]. We use Adam [15] optimizer with the base learning rate as 0.001. We train our model with 90000 iterations based on ResNet$-18/50$ model [10].

4.3 Evaluation Protocol

We evaluate our method using protocols similar to panoptic segmentation. [17] proposes a Panoptic Quality (PQ) to evaluates panoptic segmentation, and [4] proposes Boundary PQ that uses $\min\{\text{BoundaryIoU}, \text{MaskIoU}\}$ instead of pure MaskIoU used in previous work to address the boundary prediction accuracy of panoptic segmentation. In this work, we employ the Boundary PQ metric, but only use Boundary IoU in the computation instead of $\min\{\text{BoundaryIoU}, \text{MaskIoU}\}$ since we do not have any mask prediction task.

We define the panoptic edge PQ metric as follows. The IoU_{edge} is the intersection over union of edge prediction and edge groundtruth. The PQ metric can be computed separately for "stuff" edges and "thing" edges, the final PQ is the average of the PQ metric of all edge segments

$$\text{IoU} = \frac{\text{Edge}_{\text{pred}} \cap \text{Edge}_{\text{gt}}}{\text{Edge}_{\text{pred}} \cup \text{Edge}_{\text{gt}}}, \tag{6}$$

$$\text{PQ} = \underbrace{\frac{\sum_{(p,g)\in TP} \text{IoU}_{\text{edge}}(p,g)}{|TP|}}_{\text{semantic edge quality (SQ)}} \times \underbrace{\frac{|TP|}{|TP| + \frac{1}{2}|FP| + \frac{1}{2}|FN|}}_{\text{recognition quality (RQ)}}. \tag{7}$$

In panoptic segmentation tasks, the IoU threshold of True Positives (TP), False Positives (FP), False Negatives (FN) is 50%. Since the alignment between edges are more difficult than masks, we set the threshold as 10%. Otherwise, predictions would be hard to match the ground truth which leads to extremely low RQ metric. We also evaluate the computation (FLOPS), model parameter size to validate the inference efficiency and memory footprint, in order to design an efficient and memory-friendly robotic perception model.

4.4 Quantitative Result

In this section, we show the quantitative result of our approach. Since we propose a new panoptic edge definition and an evaluation metric, and the most related work [13] uses a different definition (multi-label edges) and metric (bounding-box based RQ metric), we cannot directly compare with this method. Therefore, we will focus on ablation study for different design choices.

In Table 1, we show 6 PENet variants from the aspect of reweighted loss, encoder model, projection channels and project module. We experiment the effect of adopting reweighted loss in Eq. 2, the size of the encoder between ResNet-50 and ResNet-18, whether pretraining only on ImageNet (I) or ImageNet(I) and Semantic Edge Detection (SE) tasks, the size of the projection channels in Sect. 3.4, and project module mentioned in Sect. 3.4 through abltation studies.

In Table 2, we show the ablation analysis of the different modules. By comparing variants PENet-A and PENet-B, we show that adopting the reweighted loss rather than the average loss of edge pixels and non-edge pixels is effective. In addition, by comparing variants PENet-B and PENet-C, we show that the output channels of the Projection

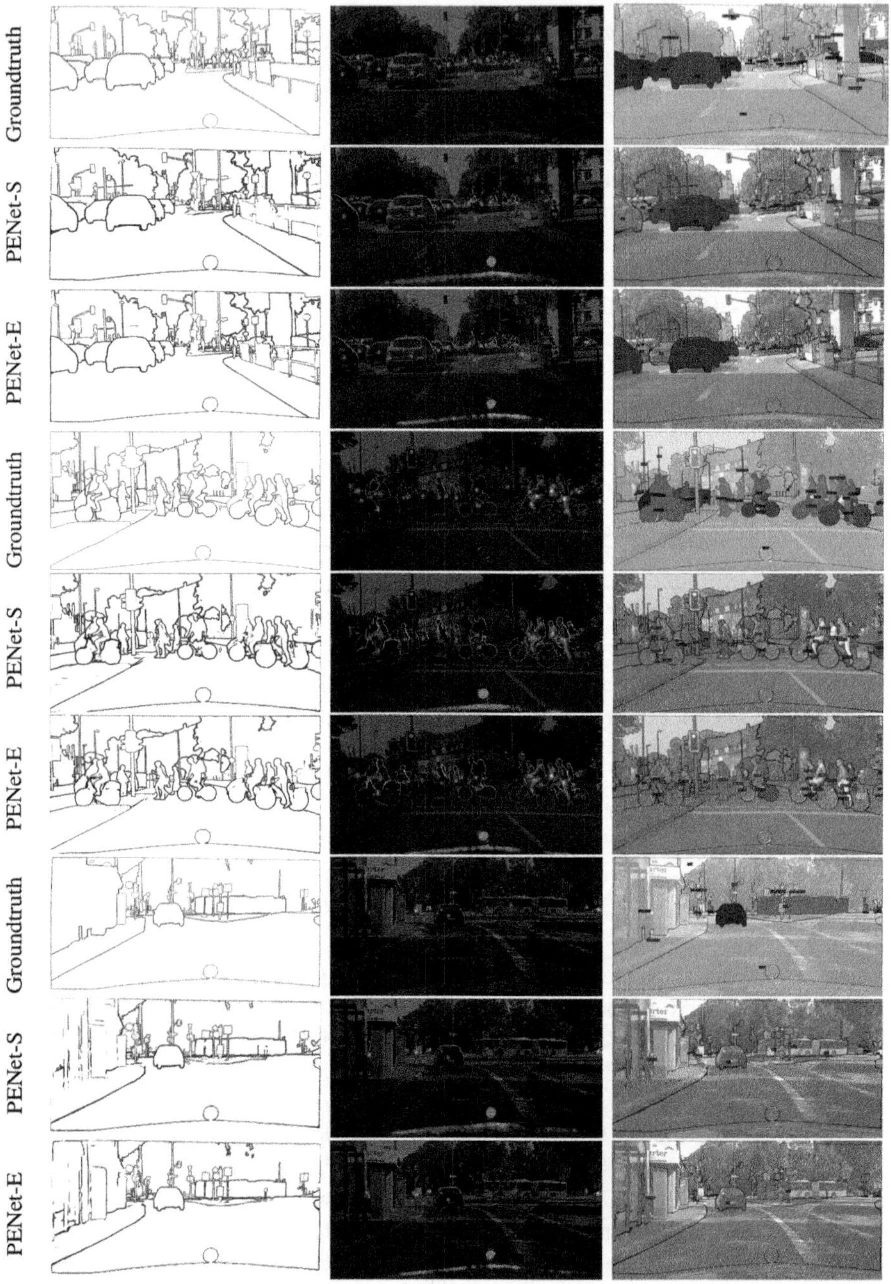

Fig. 5. Qualitative Result. Columns from left to right: semantic edge, instance center heatmap with instance offset flow map, panoptic edge. We show that both PENet-S and PENet-E are robust to small objects and cluttered environments. Both qualitative results are close to the groundtruths. PENet-S performs slightly worse than PENet in the detailed areas.

Table 1. Design space of PENet variants.

Model	Reweighted Loss	Encoder	Pretrain	Projection Channels	Projection Module
PENet-A		ResNet-50	I	$[16, 32, 64]$	A
PENet-B	✓	ResNet-50	I	$[16, 32, 64]$	A
PENet-C	✓	ResNet-50	I	$[1, 1, 1]$	A
PENet-D	✓	ResNet-50	I	$[16, 32, 64]$	B
PENet-E	✓	ResNet-50	I + SE	$[16, 32, 64]$	B
PENet-S	✓	ResNet-18	-	$[1, 1, 1]$	A

Table 2. Results for different settings of Reweighted loss, ResNet Depth, Pretrain method, Projection Channels and Projection Module Type. The **bold** value shows the best result and the underline value shows the second-best result.

Model	PQ ↑	SQ ↑	RQ ↑	FLOPS(T)↓	Params Size(MiB) ↓
PENet-A	17.659	27.172	61.282	0.433	30.376
PENet-B	20.557	27.714	72.689	0.433	30.376
PENet-C	20.617	27.385	**74.131**	0.425	30.243
PENet-D	20.889	28.007	73.341	0.420	30.272
PENet-E	**21.047**	**28.396**	72.322	0.420	30.272
PENet-S	18.887	26.447	69.277	**0.286**	**20.700**

Table 3. Detailed PQ evaluation of "thing" and "stuff" edges. The **bold** value shows the best result and the underline value shows the second-best result.

Model	PQ_{th}	SQ_{th}	RQ_{th}	PQ_{st}	SQ_{st}	RQ_{st}
PENet-A	**17.33**	26.40	**73.47**	19.47	30.13	59.10
PENet-B	16.74	26.65	70.61	24.85	30.91	80.62
PENet-C	16.95	26.26	72.84	24.82	30.59	**81.69**
PENet-D	17.25	**26.91**	72.06	25.12	31.25	80.82
PENet-E	16.33	26.87	68.17	**25.96**	**31.95**	81.54
PENet-S	14.51	25.40	64.41	23.39	29.52	78.67

Module do not affect the performance by a large margin, so we can use smaller projection channels to decrease memory usage (M: [16,32,64], S: [1,1,1]). We show by comparing PENet-B and PENet-D that Proj-B Module which utilizes criss-cross attention mechanism improves the performance against Proj-A Module and also decreases the required FLOPS computation. The variants PENet-A/B/C/D/E use ImageNet [6]-pretrained backbone model weights. The difference between PENet-D and PENet-E is that the semantic edge detection branch of the PENet-E model is pretrained for a semantic detection task before the joint training. We can see that the PENet-E model outperforms all other models and becomes the best model of our approach. Additionally, we propose a variant PENet-S with ResNet-18 backbone that consumes 34% less computation and 31.85% memory size while maintaining competitive performance against other variants.

In Table 3, we show detailed PQ evaluation results across "thing" and "stuff" edges. Most models perform better on "stuff" edges compared to "thing" edges, as "stuff" edges are simpler to detect without requiring instance-level discrimination. The Recognition Quality (RQ) metrics show higher values for "stuff" edges, reaching up to 81.69% (PENet-C) compared to 73.47% (PENet-A) for "thing" edges. While PENet-E achieves the best overall performance, it shows a trade-off between "stuff" edge detection (PQ_{st}: 25.96%) and "thing" edge detection (PQ_{th}: 16.33%). In contrast, PENet-A demonstrates better performance on "thing" edges (PQ_{th}: 17.33%) but lower performance on "stuff" edges (PQ_{st}: 19.47%). The lightweight PENet-S shows competitive performance on "stuff" edges while maintaining reasonable accuracy on "thing" edges, suggesting its potential for resource-constrained applications.

4.5 Qualitative Result

In this section, we show the qualitative result of different samples on our best model PENet-E and small mobile-friendly model PENet-S. Our method has been proven to be robust against different small instance objects, environment-cluttered conditions and overlapping cases. In Fig. 5, we show semantic edge, instance center heatmap with offset flow map, and the final panoptic edge. We overlay the image on the last two columns for easier recognition of edge alignments. We fill in the complete edge contours to visualize the completeness of the panoptic edge prediction. We observe that small model PENet-S tends to predict opened instance contours compared to PENet-E. Both models works well on instance center and offset prediction tasks. The bottleneck of the final panoptic edge detection is the performance of semantic edge detection, especially for edges in the cluttered area. From some small area, we do not expect the performance to be perfect since some categories and instances of the edges cannot even be recognized by human.

5 Conclusion

In this work, we proposed PENet, a novel learning-based panoptic edge detection approach. We formulate a novel panoptic edge definition and evaluation metric and we design the approach as a multi-task joint network to exploit the cross-correlation information flow across the tasks. Our method is accurate and memory-friendly, and we evaluate our method on the real-world Cityscapes dataset and demonstrate its effectiveness. Future works will investigate how the proposed method can be effectively applied and be useful to multiple downstream robotic tasks to improve the situation awareness and safety of robotic operations.

Acknowledgments. This work was supported in part through the NYU IT HPC resources, services, and staff expertise.

Supplementary Material.

Codes: https://t.ly/U3sDD

Video: https://www.youtube.com/watch?v=_5F5WhbWUD4

References

1. Acuna, D., Kar, A., Fidler, S.: Devil is in the edges: learning semantic boundaries from noisy annotations. In: Proceedings of the IEEE/CVF Conference on Computer Vision and Pattern Recognition, pp. 11075–11083 (2019)
2. Chen, L.C., Papandreou, G., Schroff, F., Adam, H.: Rethinking atrous convolution for semantic image segmentation. ArXiv **abs/1706.05587** (2017)
3. Cheng, B., et al.: Panoptic-deeplab: a simple, strong, and fast baseline for bottom-up panoptic segmentation. In: Proceedings of the IEEE/CVF Conference on Computer Vision and Pattern Recognition, pp. 12475–12485 (2020)
4. Cheng, B., Girshick, R., Dollár, P., Berg, A.C., Kirillov, A.: Boundary iou: improving object-centric image segmentation evaluation. In: Proceedings of the IEEE/CVF Conference on Computer Vision and Pattern Recognition, pp. 15334–15342 (2021)
5. Cordts, M., et al.: The cityscapes dataset for semantic urban scene understanding. In: Proceedings of the IEEE Conference on Computer Vision and Pattern Recognition, pp. 3213–3223 (2016)
6. Deng, J., Dong, W., Socher, R., Li, L.J., Li, K., Fei-Fei, L.: Imagenet: a large-scale hierarchical image database. In: IEEE Conference on Computer Vision and Pattern Recognition, pp. 248–255 (2009). https://doi.org/10.1109/CVPR.2009.5206848
7. Garg, S., et al.: Semantics for robotic mapping, perception and interaction: a survey. Found. Trends® Robot. **8**(1–2), 1–224 (2020)
8. de Geus, D., Meletis, P., Dubbelman, G.: Fast panoptic segmentation network. IEEE Robot. Autom. Lett. **5**(2), 1742–1749 (2020)
9. He, K., Gkioxari, G., Dollár, P., Girshick, R.: Mask R-CNN. In: Proceedings of the IEEE International Conference on Computer Vision, pp. 2961–2969 (2017)
10. He, K., Zhang, X., Ren, S., Sun, J.: Deep residual learning for image recognition. In: Proceedings of the IEEE Conference on Computer Vision and Pattern Recognition, pp. 770–778 (2016)
11. Hu, Y., Chen, Y., Li, X., Feng, J.: Dynamic feature fusion for semantic edge detection. In: Proceedings of the Twenty-Eighth International Joint Conference on Artificial Intelligence, IJCAI-19, pp. 782–788 (2019)
12. Hu, Y., Zou, Y., Feng, J.: Panoptic edge detection. arXiv preprint arXiv:1906.00590 (2019)
13. Hu, Y., Zou, Y., Feng, J.: Panoptic edge detection. arXiv preprint arXiv:1906 (2019)
14. Huang, Z., Wang, X., Huang, L., Huang, C., Wei, Y., Liu, W.: CCNet: criss-cross attention for semantic segmentation. In: Proceedings of the IEEE/CVF International Conference on Computer Vision, pp. 603–612 (2019)
15. Kingma, D.P., Ba, J.: Adam: a method for stochastic optimization. In: 3rd International Conference on Learning Representations (ICLR) (2015)
16. Kirillov, A., Girshick, R., He, K., Dollár, P.: Panoptic feature pyramid networks. In: Proceedings of the IEEE/CVF Conference on Computer Vision and Pattern Recognition, pp. 6399–6408 (2019)
17. Kirillov, A., He, K., Girshick, R., Rother, C., Dollár, P.: Panoptic segmentation. In: Proceedings of the IEEE/CVF Conference on Computer Vision and Pattern Recognition, pp. 9404–9413 (2019)

18. Long, J., Shelhamer, E., Darrell, T.: Fully convolutional networks for semantic segmentation. In: Proceedings of the IEEE Conference on Computer Vision and Pattern Recognition, pp. 3431–3440 (2015)
19. Ren, S., He, K., Girshick, R., Sun, J.: Faster R-CNN: towards real-time object detection with region proposal networks. Adv. Neural. Inf. Process. Syst. **28**, 91–99 (2015)
20. Tian, Z., He, T., Shen, C., Yan, Y.: Decoders matter for semantic segmentation: data-dependent decoding enables flexible feature aggregation. In: Proceedings of the IEEE/CVF Conference on Computer Vision and Pattern Recognition, pp. 3126–3135 (2019)
21. Wu, Y., Kirillov, A., Massa, F., Lo, W.Y., Girshick, R.: Detectron2 (2019). https://github.com/facebookresearch/detectron2
22. Xiao, T., Liu, Y., Zhou, B., Jiang, Y., Sun, J.: Unified perceptual parsing for scene understanding. In: Proceedings of the European Conference on Computer Vision (ECCV), pp. 418–434 (2018)
23. Xiong, Y., et al.: Upsnet: a unified panoptic segmentation network. In: Proceedings of the IEEE/CVF Conference on Computer Vision and Pattern Recognition, pp. 8818–8826 (2019)
24. Yu, Z., Feng, C., Liu, M.Y., Ramalingam, S.: CASENet: deep category-aware semantic edge detection. In: The IEEE Conference on Computer Vision and Pattern Recognition (CVPR), pp. 5964–5973 (2017)
25. Yu, Z., et al.: Simultaneous edge alignment and learning. In: Proceedings of the European Conference on Computer Vision (ECCV), pp. 388–404 (2018)
26. Zhou, Y., Ge, R., McGrath, G., Loianno, G.: Fenet: fast real-time semantic edge detection network. In: IEEE International Symposium on Safety, Security, and Rescue Robotics (SSRR), pp. 246–251. IEEE (2020)

Norm-Based Stability Conditions for Neutral Systems with Discrete Delays

Ozlem Faydasicok[1(✉)] and Sabri Arik[2]

[1] Department of Mathematics, Faculty of Science, Istanbul University, Istanbul, Turkey
kozlem@istanbul.edu.tr
[2] Department of Computer Engineering, Faculty of Engineering, Istanbul University-Cerrahpasa, Istanbul, Turkey
ariks@istanbul.edu.tr

Abstract. This research article deals with stability problems for neutral systems possessing discrete time delay terms in state variables and discrete neutral delay terms in time derivative of state variables. By analysing some suitable Lyapunov functional candidates, we derive a set of new norm-based conditions that determine global stability of neutral systems involving discrete delay terms. The proposed norm-based global asymptotic stability conditions impose some constraints on the norms of the constant system matrices independently of the delay parameters. We will give a numerical example of neutral systems to demonstrate the feasibility of proposed stability criteria. Since deriving sufficient stability criteria for linear neutral systems including discrete delay terms in the system equations is a difficult task to achieve, the stability conditions proposed in this research article can be considered as beneficial contributions to the topic of stability of neutral systems.

Keywords: Stability analysis · Neutral systems · Discrete delays terms · Lyapunov theorems · Matrix theory

1 Introduction

In the last years, a remarkable number of research papers have extensively studied the stability of neutral-type systems, which involve time delay parameters in states and neutral delay parameters in time derivative of the states. Such neutral systems are sometimes used for modelling of various classes of physical processes such as partial element equivalent circuit models, different flexible systems and as well as population ecology (e.g. see [1–16]). From the application poibt of view, stability is one of the most critical issues in analysing dynamics of neutral systems. In general, stability analysis of neutral systems is conducted by employing proper Lyapunov functionals. The determination of the stability conditions via Lyapunov approach totally depends on the mathematical models of theese neutral systems. Specially, the introduction of the forms of delay parameters into the differential equations representing neutral systems has a significant impact on determining the desired stability conditions. In the literature, the stability issues of neutral systems admitting discrete delays has been given much attention and,

J. Röning and J. Filipe (Eds.): ROBOVIS 2025, CCIS 2629, pp. 265–274, 2026.
https://doi.org/10.1007/978-3-032-00986-9_18

by using different different methods and techhiques combined with the Lyapunov stability theorems, many researcher papers have peresented different criteria for stability of neutral systems [7–17]. In our article, we derive some new norm-based conditions which determine global asymptotic stability of the model of examined neutral systems including discrete delay terms by defining some suitable Lyapunov functionals. We also give a numerical example to indicate the applicability of determined stability criteria.

Notations: Let $x = (x_1, x_2, ..., x_n)^T$ and $A = (a_{ij})_{n\times n}$. A is said to be positive definite, if it has all positive eigenvalues. A positive definite matrix A is denoted by $A > 0$. $\lambda_m(A)$ denotes the minimum eigenvalue of A. The following norms are also noted:

$$||x||_2 = \sqrt{\sum_{i=1}^{n} x_i^2}, \quad ||A||_2 = [\lambda_M(A^T A)]^{1/2}$$

where $\lambda_M(A)$ is the maximum eigenvalue of $A^T A$.

2 Neutral Systems with Discrete Delays

The basic goal in this section is to determine the stability conditions for neutral systems including discrete delays, which is expressed by a set of state equations possessing the form:

$$\dot{x}_i(t) = \sum_{j=1}^{n} a_{ij}x_j(t) + \sum_{j=1}^{n} b_{ij}x_j(t-\tau_j) + \sum_{j=1}^{n} c_{ij}\dot{x}_j(t-\zeta_j), \quad i = 1, \cdots, n. \quad (1)$$

In system (1), $x_i(t)$ represents the ith state variable, the constants a_{ij}, b_{ij} and c_{ij} are the system parameters. τ_j and ζ_j are delay parameters. Let $\varpi = max\{\tau, \zeta\}$ where $\tau = max\{\tau_j\}$ and $\zeta = max\{\zeta_j\}$, $\forall j$. Then, accompanying neutral system (1) are initial conditions of the system $x_i(t) = \vartheta_i(t)$ and $\dot{x}_i(t) = \varrho_i(t)$ in $C([-\varpi, 0], R)$ with the set $C([-\varpi, 0], R)$ involving the continuous functions that range from $[-\varpi, 0]$ to R.

The constant parameters a_{ij}, b_{ij} and c_{ij} of system (1) will be respectively represented by $A = (a_{ij})$, $B = (b_{ij})$ and $C = (c_{ij})$. The delays τ_j and ζ_j will be respectively called time delays and neutral delays.

Note that system decribed in (1) can be directly put in a vector-matrix equation stated by

$$\dot{x}(t) = Ax(t) + Bx(t-\tau) + C\dot{x}(t-\zeta) \quad (2)$$

In system (2), $x(t) = (x_1(t), x_2(t), \cdots, x_n(t))^T$ denotes state vector, $x(t-\tau) = (x_1(t-\tau_1), x_2(t-\tau_2), \cdots, x_n(t-\tau_n))^T$ denotes state vector involving time delays and $\dot{x}(t-\zeta) = (\dot{x}_1(t-\zeta_1), \dot{x}_2(t-\zeta_2), \cdots, \dot{x}_n(t-\zeta_n))^T$ is a vector involving time derivatives of states together with neutral delays.

In a past few decades, many researchers have focused on determination of sufficient stability conditions for neutral system (2), (see. [7]–[29]). The authors of the papers [7]–[29] have basically employed the Lyapunov stability theorems combining with various techniques and methods, and have determined alternative sets of sufficient stability conditions associated with system (2). The stability conditions obtained in the past literature have mainly stated in different forms of linear matrix inequalities (LMIs). In this context, the validation of stability conditions in the LMI forms essentially require to solve some high order matrix inequalities. Therefore, the stability conditions, which are determined to be in the LMI forms, may not be easy to verify. Considering this fact, we will propose some novel delay-independent stability conditions for system given in (1), which are stated in terms of norms of constant system matrices. One of main advantages of these conditions is that they can be easliy verified by simply checking some algebraic norm inequalities.

3 Stability Analysis

The key objective of the current section will be proposing some new and improved criteria which guarantee global asymptotic stability of continuous-time neutral system represented by (1). We proceed with the following stability conditions for system (1):

Theorem 1. *For system (1), let*

$$\alpha = \lambda_m(-A - A^T) - ||A^T(A - A^T)||_2 - ||A^T B||_2 - ||A^T C||_2 - ||B||_2 - ||C||_2 - \frac{1}{2}||B^T(A - A^T)||_2 - \frac{1}{2}||C^T(A - A^T)||_2,$$

$$\beta = ||A^T B||_2 + ||B||_2 + \frac{1}{2}||B^T(A - A^T)||_2 + 2||B||_2^2 + 2||B^T C||_2$$

$$\gamma = ||A^T C||_2 + 2||B^T C||_2 + ||C||_2 + 2||C||_2^2 + \frac{1}{2}||C^T(A - A^T)||_2$$

Then, neutral system (1) is globally asymptotically stable if $-A - A^T > 0$, $\alpha - \beta > 0$ *and* $\gamma < 2$.

Proof. We employ a proper Lyapunov functional given by $V(t) = V_1(t) + V_2(t)$ in which functionals $V_1(t)$ and $V_2(t)$ are respectively stated by

$$V_1(t) = x^T(t)x(t) - \frac{1}{2}x^T(t)(A^T + A)x(t) \tag{3}$$

and

$$V_2(t) = \sum_{i=1}^{n}\Big(\int_{t-\tau_i}^{t} \beta x_i^2(\rho)d\rho + \int_{t-\zeta_i}^{t} \gamma \dot{x}_i^2(\varphi)d\varphi\Big) \tag{4}$$

The condition $-A - A^T > 0$ ensures that $V_1(t)$ defined by (3) is positive definite. When examining time derivative of $V_1(t)$ expressed by (4) associated with trajectories of neutral system (1), we get that

$$\dot{V}_1(t) = 2\dot{x}^T(t)x(t) - \dot{x}^T(t)(A^T + A)x(t) \tag{5}$$

Adding the zero term

$$2\dot{x}^T(t)\dot{x}(t) - 2\dot{x}^T(t)\dot{x}(t) = 0$$

to the right hand side of (5) leads to

$$\dot{V}_1(t) = 2\dot{x}^T(t)x(t) - \dot{x}^T(t)(A^T + A)x(t) + 2\dot{x}^T(t)\dot{x}(t) - 2\dot{x}^T(t)\dot{x}(t) \tag{6}$$

(6) is equivalent to

$$\begin{aligned}
\dot{V}_1(t) &= 2\dot{x}^T(t)x(t) - \dot{x}^T(t)(A^T + A)x(t) + 2\dot{x}^T(t)\dot{x}(t) - 2\dot{x}^T(t)\dot{x}(t) \\
&= 2\dot{x}^T(t)\Big(x(t) - \frac{1}{2}(A^T + A)x(t) + \dot{x}(t)\Big) - 2\dot{x}^T(t)\dot{x}(t) \\
&= 2\Big(Ax(t) + Bx(t-\tau) + C\dot{x}(t-\zeta)\Big)^T \times \\
&\quad \Big(x(t) + \frac{1}{2}(A - A^T)x(t) + Bx(t-\tau) + C\dot{x}(t-\zeta)\Big) \\
&\quad -2\dot{x}^T(t)\dot{x}(t) \\
&= -2x^T(t)(-A^T)x(t) + x^T(t)A^T(A - A^T)x(t) + 2x^T(t)A^TBx(t-\tau) \\
&\quad +2x^T(t)A^TC\dot{x}(t-\zeta) + 2x^T(t-\tau)B^Tx(t) + x^T(t-\tau)B^T(A - A^T)x(t) \\
&\quad +2x^T(t-\tau)B^TBx(t-\tau) + 2x^T(t-\tau)B^TC\dot{x}(t-\zeta) \\
&\quad +2\dot{x}^T(t-\zeta)C^Tx(t) + \dot{x}^T(t-\zeta)C^T(A - A^T)x(t) \\
&\quad +2\dot{x}^T(t-\zeta)C^TBx(t-\tau) + 2\dot{x}^T(t-\zeta)C^TC\dot{x}(t-\zeta) - 2\dot{x}^T(t)\dot{x}(t)
\end{aligned} \tag{7}$$

Exploiting a few basic properties of matrix and vector norms, we derive from equation (7) that

$$\begin{aligned}
\dot{V}_1(t) \le &- x^T(t)(-A - A^T)x(t) + ||A^T(A - A^T)||_2||x(t)||_2^2 - 2\dot{x}^T(t)\dot{x}(t) \\
&+ 2||A^TB||_2||x(t)||_2||x(t-\tau)||_2 + 2||A^TC||_2||x(t)||_2||\dot{x}(t-\zeta)||_2 \\
&+ 2||B^T||_2||x(t)||_2||x(t-\tau)||_2 + ||B^T(A - A^T)||_2||x(t)||_2||x(t-\tau)||_2 \\
&+ 2||B||_2^2||x(t-\tau)||_2^2 + 2||B^TC||_2||x(t-\tau)||_2||\dot{x}(t-\zeta)||_2 \\
&+ 2||C||_2||x(t)||_2||\dot{x}(t-\zeta)||_2 + ||C^T(A - A^T)||_2||x(t)||_2||\dot{x}(t-\zeta)||_2 \\
&+ 2||C^TB||_2||x(t-\tau)||_2||\dot{x}(t-\zeta)||_2 + 2||C||_2^2||\dot{x}(t-\zeta)||_2^2
\end{aligned} \tag{8}$$

From (8), we directly obtain:

$$\begin{aligned}\dot{V}_1(t) \le & -\lambda_m(-A-A^T)||x(t)||_2^2 + ||A^T(A-A^T)||_2||x(t)||_2^2 - 2||\dot{x}(t)||_2^2 \\ & + ||A^TB||_2(||x(t)||_2^2 + ||x(t-\tau)||_2^2) + ||A^TC||_2(||x(t)||_2^2 + ||\dot{x}(t-\zeta)||_2^2) \\ & + ||B||_2(||x(t)||_2^2 + ||x(t-\tau)||_2^2) \\ & + \frac{1}{2}||B^T(A-A^T)||_2(||x(t)||_2^2 + ||x(t-\tau)||_2^2) \\ & + 2||B||_2^2||x(t-\tau)||_2^2 + ||B^TC||_2(||x(t-\tau)||_2^2 + ||\dot{x}(t-\zeta)||_2^2) \\ & + ||C||_2(||x(t)||_2^2 + ||\dot{x}(t-\zeta)||_2^2) \\ & + \frac{1}{2}||C^T(A-A^T)||_2(||x(t)||_2^2 + ||\dot{x}(t-\zeta)||_2^2) \\ & + ||C^TB||_2(||x(t-\tau)||_2^2 + ||\dot{x}(t-\zeta)||_2^2) + 2||C||_2^2||\dot{x}(t-\zeta)||_2^2\end{aligned} \tag{9}$$

(9) leads to

$$\begin{aligned}\dot{V}_1(t) \le & \Big(-\lambda_m(-A-A^T) + ||A^T(A-A^T)||_2 + ||A^TB||_2 + ||A^TC||_2 + ||B||_2 \\ & + ||C||_2 + \frac{1}{2}||B^T(A-A^T)||_2 + \frac{1}{2}||C^T(A-A^T)||_2\Big)||x(t)||_2^2 \\ & + \Big(||A^TB||_2 + ||B||_2 + \frac{1}{2}||B^T(A-A^T)||_2 + 2||B||_2^2 + 2||B^TC||_2\Big)||x(t-\tau)||_2^2 \\ & + \Big(||A^TC||_2 + 2||B^TC||_2 + ||C||_2 + 2||C||_2^2 \\ & + \frac{1}{2}||C^T(A-A^T)||_2\Big)||\dot{x}(t-\zeta)||_2^2 - 2||\dot{x}(t)||_2^2 \\ = & -\alpha||x(t)||_2^2 + \beta||x(t-\tau)||_2^2 + \gamma||\dot{x}(t-\zeta)||_2^2 - 2||\dot{x}(t)||_2^2\end{aligned} \tag{10}$$

When examining time derivative of $V_2(t)$ stated by (4) associated with trajectories of neutral system (1), we get that

$$\begin{aligned}\dot{V}_2(t) &= \sum_{i=1}^{n}\Big(\beta x_i^2(t) - \beta x_i^2(t-\tau_i) + \gamma\dot{x}_i^2(t) - \gamma\dot{x}_i^2(t-\zeta_i)\Big) \\ &= \beta||x(t)||_2^2 - \beta||x(t-\tau)||_2^2 + \gamma||\dot{x}(t)||_2^2 - \gamma||\dot{x}(t-\zeta)||_2^2\end{aligned} \tag{11}$$

If we combine (11) with (10), then we will obtain

$$\begin{aligned}\dot{V}(t) = \dot{V}_1(t) + \dot{V}_2(t) &\le -\alpha||x(t)||_2^2 + \beta||x(t)||_2^2 + \gamma||\dot{x}(t)||_2^2 - 2||\dot{x}(t)||_2^2 \\ &= -(\alpha-\beta)||x(t)||_2^2 - (2-\gamma)||\dot{x}(t)||_2^2\end{aligned} \tag{12}$$

In (12), if we choose $\alpha - \beta > 0$ and $\gamma < 2$, then $\dot{V}(t) < 0$ for all $x(t) \neq 0$ or $\dot{x}(t) \neq 0$. When $x(t) = \dot{x}(t) = 0$, we have $\dot{V}_1(t) = 0$. Thus, from (11), $\dot{V}(t)$ turns into the following

$$\dot{V}(t) = -\beta||x(t-\tau)||_2^2 - \gamma||\dot{x}(t-\zeta)||_2^2 \tag{13}$$

One can simply conclude from (13) that $\dot{V}(t)$ will be absolutely negative definite if $||x(t-\tau)||_2 \neq 0$ or $||\dot{x}(t-\zeta)||_2 \neq 0$. Finally, if $x(t) = \dot{x}(t) = x(t-\tau) = \dot{x}(t-\zeta) = 0$, then we can directly observe from (6) and (11) that $\dot{V}(t) = 0$. It can be noted from this analysis that $\dot{V}(t) = 0$ only at the equilibrium point, proving that $\dot{V}(t) < 0$ other than the origin. Hence, system given by (1) is asymptotically stable. Our next step is to prove $V(t)$ is radially unbounded, meaning the property that $V(t) \rightarrow \infty$ in the case of $||x(t)|| \rightarrow \infty$. To this end, we need to show that $V_1(t)$ given by (4) is radially unbounded as $V_2(t) \geq 0$. Since $-A - A^T > 0$, from (3), we can directly derive the condition for $V(t)$:

$$V(t) \geq ||x(t)||_2^2 \tag{14}$$

Therefore, from (14), we can directly observe that $V(t) \rightarrow \infty$ as $||x(t)|| \rightarrow \infty$. Thus, this condition proves global asymptotic stability of neutral system (1).

In what follows, it is procceded with an alternative stability result:

Theorem 2. *For system (1), let*

$$\hat{\alpha} = \lambda_m(-A - A^T) - ||A^T(A - A^T)||_2 - (\xi_1 + \xi_2)||A||_2^2 - \xi_3 - \xi_4$$
$$-\frac{1}{2}||B^T(A - A^T)||_2 - \frac{1}{2}||C^T(A - A^T)||_2,$$

$$\hat{\beta} = (\frac{1}{\xi_1} + \frac{1}{\xi_3} + 2\xi_5 + 2)||B||_2^2 + \frac{1}{2}||B^T(A - A^T)||_2$$

and

$$\hat{\gamma} = (\frac{1}{\xi_2} + \frac{1}{\xi_4} + \frac{2}{\xi_5} + 2)||C||_2^2 + \frac{1}{2}||C^T(A - A^T)||_2$$

where ξ_1, ξ_2, ξ_3, ξ_4 and ξ_5 are some positive constants. Then, neutral system (1) is globally asymptotically stable if $-A - A^T > 0$, $\hat{\alpha} - \hat{\beta} > 0$ and $\hat{\gamma} < 2$.

Proof. Employ a suitable Lyapunov functional given by $W(t) = V_1(t) + V_3(t)$ in which $V_1(t)$ is the previously defined Lyapunov functional in (3) and $V_3(t)$ is formed as given below:

$$V_3(t) = \sum_{i=1}^{n} \left(\hat{\beta} \int_{t-\tau_i}^{t} x_i^2(\rho) d\rho + \hat{\gamma} \int_{t-\zeta_i}^{t} \dot{x}_i^2(\varphi) d\varphi \right) \tag{15}$$

When examining the time derivative of $V_3(t)$ expressed by (15) associated with trajectories of neutral system (1), we get that

$$\begin{aligned}\dot{V}_3(t) &= \sum_{i=1}^{n} \left(\hat{\beta} x_i^2(t) - \hat{\beta} x_i^2(t-\tau_i) + \hat{\gamma} \dot{x}_i^2(t) - \hat{\gamma} \dot{x}_i^2(t-\zeta_i) \right) \\ &= \hat{\beta}||x(t)||_2^2 - \hat{\beta}||x(t-\tau)||_2^2 + \hat{\gamma}||\dot{x}(t)||_2^2 - \hat{\gamma}||\dot{x}(t-\zeta)||_2^2\end{aligned} \tag{16}$$

We now note some key inequalities:

$$\begin{aligned}2x^T(t)A^TBx(t-\tau) \leq& \xi_1 x^T(t)A^TAx(t) + \frac{1}{\xi_1}x^T(t-\tau)B^TBx(t-\tau)\\ \leq& \xi_1||A||_2^2||x(t)||_2^2 + \frac{1}{\xi_1}||B||_2^2||x(t-\tau)||_2^2\end{aligned} \tag{17}$$

$$\begin{aligned}2x^T(t)A^TC\dot{x}(t-\zeta) \leq& \xi_2 x^T(t)A^TAx(t) + \frac{1}{\xi_2}\dot{x}^T(t-\zeta)C^TC\dot{x}(t-\zeta)\\ \leq& \xi_2||A||_2^2||x(t)||_2^2 + \frac{1}{\xi_2}||C||_2^2||\dot{x}(t-\zeta)||_2^2,\end{aligned} \tag{18}$$

$$\begin{aligned}2x^T(t-\tau)B^Tx(t) \leq& \xi_3 x^T(t)x(t) + \frac{1}{\xi_3}x^T(t-\tau)B^TBx(t-\tau)\\ \leq& \xi_3 x(t)||_2^2 + \frac{1}{\xi_3}||B||_2^2||x(t-\tau)||_2^2,\end{aligned} \tag{19}$$

$$\begin{aligned}2\dot{x}^T(t-\zeta)C^Tx(t) \leq& \xi_4 x^T(t)x(t) + \frac{1}{\xi_4}\dot{x}^T(t-\zeta)C^TC\dot{x}(t-\zeta)\\ \leq& \xi_4||x(t)||_2^2 + \frac{1}{\xi_4}||C||_2^2||\dot{x}(t-\zeta)||_2^2,\end{aligned} \tag{20}$$

and

$$\begin{aligned}&2x^T(t-\tau)B^TC\dot{x}(t-\zeta) = 2\dot{x}^T(t-\zeta)C^TBx(t-\tau)\\ &\leq \xi_5 x^T(t-\tau)B^TBx(t-\tau) + \frac{1}{\xi_5}\dot{x}^T(t-\zeta)C^TC\dot{x}(t-\zeta)\\ &\leq \xi_5||B||_2^2||x(t-\tau)||_2^2 + \frac{1}{\xi_5}||C||_2^2||\dot{x}(t-\zeta)||_2^2\end{aligned} \tag{21}$$

Using (17)–(21) in (7) results in

$$\begin{aligned}\dot{V}_1(t) \leq& -\lambda_m(-A-A^T)||x(t)||_2^2 + ||A^T(A-A^T)||_2||x(t)||_2^2 + \xi_1||A||_2^2||x(t)||_2^2\\ &+ \frac{1}{\xi_1}||B||_2^2||x(t-\tau)||_2^2 + \xi_2||A||_2^2||x(t)||_2^2 + \frac{1}{\xi_2}||C||_2^2||\dot{x}(t-\zeta)||_2^2\\ &+ \xi_3 x(t)||_2^2 + \frac{1}{\xi_3}||B||_2^2||x(t-\tau)||_2^2\\ &+ \frac{1}{2}||B^T(A-A^T)||_2(||x(t)||_2^2 + ||x(t-\tau)||_2^2)\\ &+ 2||B||_2^2||x(t-\tau)||_2^2 + \xi_4||x(t)||_2^2 + \frac{1}{\xi_4}||C||_2^2||\dot{x}(t-\zeta)||_2^2\\ &+ \frac{1}{2}||C^T(A-A^T)||_2(||x(t)||_2^2 + ||\dot{x}(t-\zeta)||_2^2)2\xi_5||B||_2^2||x(t-\tau)||_2^2\\ &+ + \frac{2}{\xi_5}||C||_2^2||\dot{x}(t-\zeta)||_2^2 + 2||C||_2^2||\dot{x}(t-\zeta)||_2^2 - 2||\dot{x}(t)||_2^2\end{aligned}$$

which can be directly written as

$$\begin{aligned}\dot{V}_1(t) \leq &- \Big(\lambda_m(-A - A^T) - ||A^T(A - A^T)||_2 - (\xi_1 + \xi_2)||A||_2^2 - \xi_3 - \xi_4 \\ &- \frac{1}{2}||B^T(A - A^T)||_2 - \frac{1}{2}||C^T(A - A^T)||_2\Big)||x(t)||_2^2 - 2||\dot{x}(t)||_2^2 \\ &+ \Big((\frac{1}{\xi_1} + \frac{1}{\xi_3} + 2\xi_5 + 2)||B||_2^2 + \frac{1}{2}||B^T(A - A^T)||_2\Big)||x(t - \tau)||_2^2 \\ &+ \Big((\frac{1}{\xi_2} + \frac{1}{\xi_4} + \frac{2}{\xi_5} + 2)||C||_2^2 + \frac{1}{2}||C^T(A - A^T)||_2\Big)||\dot{x}(t - \zeta)||_2^2\end{aligned}$$

$$= - \hat{\alpha}||x(t)||_2^2 + \hat{\beta}||x(t - \tau)||_2^2 + \hat{\gamma}||\dot{x}(t - \zeta)||_2^2 2||\dot{x}(t)||_2^2 \tag{22}$$

If we combine (22) with (16), then we will get that

$$\begin{aligned}\dot{W}(t) = \dot{V}_1(t) + \dot{V}_3(t) &\leq (-\hat{\alpha} + \hat{\beta})||x(t)||_2^2 + \hat{\gamma}||\dot{x}(t)||_2^2 - 2||\dot{x}(t)||_2^2 \\ &= -(\hat{\alpha} - \hat{\beta})||x(t)||_2^2 - (2 - \hat{\gamma})||\dot{x}(t)||_2^2\end{aligned} \tag{23}$$

In (16), if we choose $\hat{\alpha} - \hat{\beta} > 0$ and $\hat{\gamma} < 2$, then $\dot{W}(t)$ will obviously be negative definite for all $x(t) \neq 0$ or $\dot{x}(t) \neq 0$. When $x(t) = \dot{x}(t) = 0$, we will have $\dot{V}_1(t) = 0$. Then, from (16), $\dot{W}(t)$ can be shown to staisfy

$$\dot{W}(t) = -\beta||x(t - \tau)||_2^2 - \gamma||\dot{x}(t - \zeta)||_2^2 \tag{24}$$

One can simply conclude from (24) that $\dot{W}(t)$ will be absolutely negative definite if $||x(t - \tau)||_2 \neq 0$ or $||\dot{x}(t - \zeta)||_2 \neq 0$. Finally, if $x(t) = \dot{x}(t) = x(t - \tau) = \dot{x}(t - \zeta) = 0$, then we can directly observe from (6) and (11) that $\dot{W}(t) = 0$. It can be noted from this analysis that $\dot{V}(t) = 0$ only at equilibrium point, proving that $\dot{W}(t) < 0$ other than the origin. Hence, system given by (1) is asymptotically stable. One may note the fact that the rest of the proof of this theorem is almost same as that of Thorem 1.

It may be of great interest to note that, in the case of A being a symmetric matrix, some simple and compact stability conditions associated with sytem (1) can be easily obtained from the resuts of Theroems 1 and 2.

Theorem 3. *In system (1), let $A = A^T$ and define*

$$\begin{aligned}\tilde{\alpha} &= 2\lambda_m(-A) - ||AB||_2 - ||AC||_2 - ||B||_2 - ||C||_2, \\ \tilde{\beta} &= ||AB||_2 + ||B||_2 + 2||B||_2^2 + 2||B^TC||_2, \\ \tilde{\gamma} &= ||AC||_2 + 2||B^TC||_2 + ||C||_2 + 2||C||_2^2.\end{aligned}$$

Then, (1) is globally asymptotically stable if $-A > 0$, $\tilde{\alpha} - \tilde{\beta} > 0$ and $\tilde{\gamma} < 2$.

Theorem 4. *In system (1), let $A = A^T$ and define*

$$\bar{\alpha} = 2\lambda_m(-A) - (\bar{\xi}_1 + \bar{\xi}_2)||A||_2^2 - \bar{\xi}_3 - \bar{\xi}_4,$$
$$\bar{\beta} = (\frac{1}{\bar{\xi}_1} + \frac{1}{\bar{\xi}_3} + 2\bar{\xi}_5 + 2)||B||_2^2,$$
$$\bar{\gamma} = (\frac{1}{\bar{\xi}_2} + \frac{1}{\bar{\xi}_4} + \frac{2}{\bar{\xi}_5} + 2)||C||_2^2.$$

Then, neutral system (1) is globally asymptotically stable if $-A > 0$, $\bar{\alpha} - \bar{\beta} > 0$ and $\bar{\gamma} < 2$ where $\bar{\xi}_1$, $\bar{\xi}_2$, $\bar{\xi}_3$, $\bar{\xi}_4$ and $\bar{\xi}_5$ are some positive constants.

We now give an example to indicate the applicability of our conditions:

Example: Choose the system matrices of neutral system (1) as follows

$$A = \begin{bmatrix} -4a & a & a & a \\ a & -4a & a & a \\ a & a & -4a & a \\ a & a & a & -4a \end{bmatrix}, B = \begin{bmatrix} b & b & b & b \\ b & -b & b & -b \\ b & b & -b & -b \\ -b & b & b & -b \end{bmatrix}, C = \begin{bmatrix} c & c & c & -c \\ c & -c & c & c \\ c & c & -c & c \\ c & -c & -c & -c \end{bmatrix}$$

In this numerical example, a, b and c are chosen to be positive constant elements. For A, B and C, it can be calculated that $\lambda_m(-A) = a$, $||A||_2 = 5a$, $||B||_2 = 2b$, $||C||_2 = 2c$, $||AB||_2 = 10ab$, $||AC||_2 = 10ac$ and $||B^TC||_2 = 4bc$. Note that $-A$ staisfies the condition of being a positive definite matrix. Now, applying the results of Theorem 3 in the case of this example, we get that $\tilde{\alpha} - \tilde{\beta} = 2a - 20ab - 4b - 8b^2 - 10ac - 8bc - 2c > 0$ and $\tilde{\gamma} = 10ac + 8bc + 2c + 8c^2 < 2$. Let $a = 1$ and $b = c = \frac{1}{20}$. Then, we obtain $\tilde{\alpha} - \tilde{\beta} = 0.16 > 0$ and $\tilde{\gamma} = 0.64 < 2$. Thus, Threom 3 establishes stability of a neutral system, whose parameters are particularized in the example, under the conditions: $a = 1$, $b = \frac{1}{20}$ and $c = \frac{1}{20}$.

In Theorem 4, first let $\bar{\xi}_1 = \bar{\xi}_2 = \bar{\xi}_3 = \bar{\xi}_4 = \frac{1}{32}$ and $\bar{\xi}_5 = 1$, and then choose $a = 1$, $b = \frac{3}{20}$ and $c = \frac{3}{10}$. In this case, we calculate $\bar{\alpha} - \bar{\beta} = 2a - \frac{25}{16}a^2 - \frac{1}{16} - (4 + \frac{1}{16})4b^2 = 0.375 - 0.365 = 0.01 > 0$ and $\bar{\gamma} = 4.0625||C||_2^2 = 16.25c^2 = 1.4625 < 2$. Thus, Threom 4 establishes the stability of the neutral system given in this example under the conditions that $a = 1$, $b = \frac{3}{20}$ and $c = \frac{3}{10}$.

4 Conclusions

This paper has focused on stability problems for neutral systems involving some discrete time delay parameters in state variables and some discrete neutral delay parameters in time derivative of state variables of considered system. By employing some proper Lyapunov functional candidates, some applicable and alternative sufficient algebraic stability conditions have been determined for the class of linear neutral systems possessing discrete delay terms. The proposed results have proved global asymptotic stability of such neutral-type systems by imposing easily verifiable algebraic conditions on constant system parameters independently of the delay parameters. We have examined a numerical example to indicate some basic advantages of our obtained conditions. Since, the determination of desired stability criteria for the model of a linear neutral system having discrete delay terms in the system equations is a difficult problem to deal with, because of complexity of mathematical models of this class of systems, the simple stability criteria proposed in this research article might be interpreted as important and valuable contributions to stability analyzes of neutral systems.

References

1. Yue, D., Han, Q.L.: A delay-dependent stability criterion of neutral systems and its application to a partial element equivalent circuit model. IEEE Trans. Circuits Syst. II Express Briefs **51**(2), 685–689 (2004)
2. Fu, X., Pang, X., Huang, Y.: Robust H-infinity filtering for neutral systems with multi-delay and application in the flexible system. Cybern. Inf. Technol. **18**(4), 120–130 (2018)
3. Bellen, A., Guglielmi, N., Ruehli, A.E.: Methods for linear systems of circuit delay differential equations of neutral type. IEEE Trans. Circ. Syst. I: Fund. Theory Appl. **51**(1), 212–215 (1999)
4. Ngoc, P.H.A., Trinh, H.: Stability analysis of nonlinear neutral functional differential equations. SIAM J. Control. Optim. **55**(6), 3947–3968 (2017)
5. Ngoc, P.H.A., Trinh, H.: Novel criteria for exponential stability of linear neutral time-varying differential systems. IEEE Trans. Autom. Control **61**(6), 1590–1594 (2016)
6. Hale, J.K., Lunel, S.M.V.: Introduction to Functional Differential Equations. Springer-Verlag, New York, USA (1993)
7. He, Y., Wang, Q.G., Lin, C., Wu, M.: Augmented Lyapunov functional and delay-dependent stability criteria for neutral systems. Int. J. Robust Nonlinear Control **15**(18), 923–933 (2005)
8. Ivanescu, D., Niculescu, S.I., Dugard, L., Dion, J.M., Verriest, E.I.: On delay-dependent stability for linear neutral systems. Automatica **39**(2), 255–261 (2003)
9. Balasubramaniam, P., Krishnasamy, R., Rakkiyappan, R.: Delay-dependent stability of neutral systems with time-varying delays using delay-decomposition approach. Appl. Math. Model. **36**(5), 2253–2261 (2012)
10. Lun, R., Wu, H., Bai, J.: New delay-dependent robust stability criteria for uncertain neutral systems with mixed delays. J. Franklin Inst. **351**(3), 1386–1399 (2014)
11. Chen, Y., Xue, A., Lu, R., Zhou, S.: On robustly exponential stability of uncertain neutral systems with time-varying delays and nonlinear perturbations. Nonlinear Anal. Theory Methods Appl. **68**(8), 2464–2470 (2008)
12. Han, Q.L.: Improved stability criteria and controller design for linear neutral systems. Automatica **45**(8), 1948–1952 (2009)
13. Gao, J., Su, H., Ji, X., Chu, J.: Stability analysis for a class of neutral systems with mixed delays and sector-bounded nonlinearity. Nonlinear Anal. Real World Appl. **9**(5), 2350–2360 (2008)
14. Qian, W., Liu, J., Sun, Y., Fei, S.: A less conservative robust stability criteria for uncertain neutral systems with mixed delays. Math. Comput. Simul. **80**(5), 1007–1017 (2010)
15. Li, H., Zhong, S., Li, H.: Some new simple stability criteria of linear neutral systems with a single delay. J. Comput. Appl. Math. **200**(1), 441–447 (2007)
16. Altun, Y.: Improved results on the stability analysis of linear neutral systems with delay decay approach. Math. Methods Appl. Sci. **43**(3), 1467–1483 (2020)
17. Wang, T., Li, T., Zhang, G., Fei, S.: Further triple integral approach to mixed-delay-dependent stability of time-delay neutral systems. ISA Trans. **70**, 116–124 (2017)

Evaluating Pose Awareness and 3D Consistency in Semantic Matching

Paolo Sebeto[1(✉)], Jean-Baptiste Weibel[1,2], Christian Hartl-Nesic[1], and Markus Vincze[1]

[1] Automation and Control Institute, TU Wien, Gußhausstraße 27–29, 1040 Wien, Austria
{sebeto,weibel,hartl,vincze}@acin.tuwien.ac.at

[2] Institute of Forest Engineering, Department of Forest and Soil Science, University of Natural Resources and Life Sciences Vienna, Peter-Jordan-Straße 82/III, 1190 Wien, Austria

Abstract. Semantic matching is increasingly adopted in robotics as a flexible approach for generalizing point transfer across different manipulation tasks, creating a need for suitable benchmark datasets and a reassessment of existing evaluation metrics. Point correspondences used for manipulation require not only pixel-level precision but also accuracy in 3D space. Current methods and evaluation metrics suffer from a bias toward the pixel position relative to the image at the expense of accurate 3D localization. Objects' orientation differences between source and target images severely affect matching results. In this paper, we introduce a novel evaluation procedure for assessing pose-aware and 3D-consistent semantic matching, supported by a synthetic dataset, **SemanticHouseCat3D**, that includes rich annotations of household objects. Our evaluation features a new orientation-based assessment that bins point matching metrics according to changes in object orientation and precisely measures the 3D accuracy of estimated image points after their re-projection. Using SemanticHouseCat3D, we conduct an exhaustive evaluation of state-of-the-art methods and investigate the influence of full-image context on performance compared to techniques like object cropping and segmentation. Our results indicate that while foundation models are reliable and adaptable across different domains, there is a critical need for improving semantic matching methods in terms of pose awareness and feature localization. The dataset is available at https://sites.google.com/view/semantichousecat3d/.

Keywords: Semantic correspondence · Benchmark dataset · Keypoint matching

1 Introduction

Semantic Matching is concerned with establishing pixel-level correspondences between two images containing different instances of the same object or same

J. Röning and J. Filipe (Eds.): ROBOVIS 2025, CCIS 2629, pp. 275–293, 2026.
https://doi.org/10.1007/978-3-032-00986-9_19

category. This task has been applied to various image editing applications, such as attributes transfer [20], appearance transfer [33], color transfer [14,22] or dense visual alignment [27]. At the same time, there is growing interest in its application to robotics, including affordance region transfer [11,17], object manipulation [16,32], and category-level object pose estimation [10]. Existing semantic matching techniques exhibit a bias toward the pixel location of points within the image, rather than understanding their true position on the object in 3D space. This leads to significant errors when objects undergo changes in orientation between source and target images. A recent work [37] introduced a pose-awareness evaluation where four coarse poses (i.e., front, back, left, right) are predicted based on deep features' similarity. However, this provides only a general understanding of the evaluated methods' sensitivity to pose variations, without quantifying the specific orientation or translation differences between object instances. Additionally, existing methods neglect 3D consistency, by which we refer to the accuracy with which a matched point, when re-projected from the image to its 3D location, aligns with its ground truth counterpart in 3D space. Without ensuring 3D consistency, correspondences may not only misalign keypoints in the image but also fail to preserve their true spatial relationships in the real world. Figure 1 illustrates these issues using a recent state-of-the-art method for points transfer on a mobile manipulator. In robotics, such errors can have substantial consequences, as precise spatial awareness is crucial for tasks requiring interaction with objects. Pose awareness, defined as a method's ability to accurately recognize the spatial configuration of points in 3D space irrespective of how the object appears in 2D images, along with 3D consistency, constitutes key challenges in semantic matching that require more attention, especially in applications involving precise spatial interactions.

A deeper evaluation of pose awareness and 3D consistency is currently limited by the lack of object pose annotations in existing semantic matching benchmark datasets, except for the azimuth label available in SPair-71k [25]. Moreover, existing benchmarks may not be appropriate for current robotics applications of semantic matching, which are centered around manipulation of everyday household objects. They often focus on object categories such as animals or vehicles. A stronger focus on smaller, daily-use items would help to better assess a method's real-world applicability.

To address the aforementioned challenges and the lack of datasets and evaluation metrics specifically targeting pose awareness and 3D consistency, we developed SemanticHouseCat3D, a synthetic dataset of household objects tailored for semantic matching. By utilizing synthetic data and leveraging accurate and consistently oriented 3D meshes from the HouseCat6D [18] dataset, we enable precise 3D consistency measurements and establish a one-to-one correspondence between every pixel in an image frame and its corresponding 3D position. This precision is crucial for accurately assessing how well estimated image points align with their true 3D counterparts, a capability that is typically unavailable in general-purpose semantic matching scenarios where pre-aligned meshes are not provided.

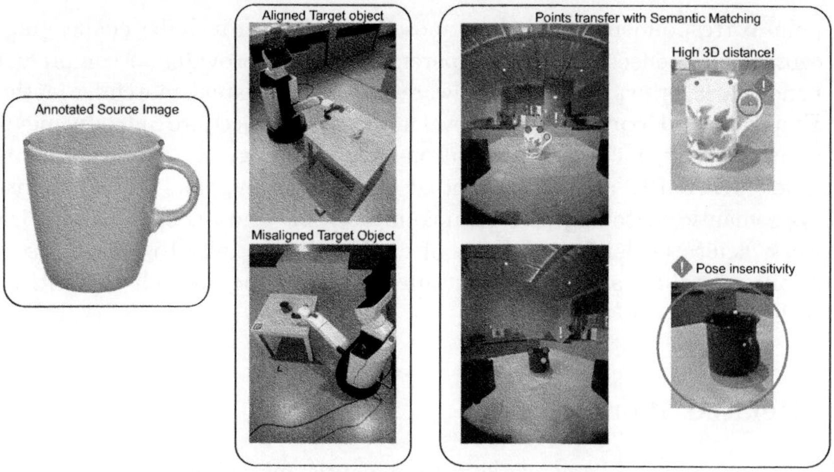

Fig. 1. Examples of point transfer from an annotated image using the SD+DINO [38] semantic matching algorithm with the hand camera of a Toyota HSR robot. These examples highlight challenges in 3D consistency and pose awareness: in the top image, the inferred point is close in pixel space but has a high 3D error, falling outside the object. In the bottom image, the method shows insensitivity to pose variation, maintaining a bias toward the point structure in the source image.

SemanticHouseCat3D consists of image pairs annotated with semantic keypoint correspondences and precise object poses. Keypoint annotations were initially generated using the Normalized Object Coordinate Space (NOCS) representation, leveraging the pre-aligned 3D meshes, and manually refined to ensure accuracy in a number of more challenging scenes. The dataset includes a total of 1,659 rendered frames across six categories, with 250 annotated image pairs per category, totaling 1,500 image pairs overall. Scenes were constructed using publicly available assets and rendered using BlenderProc [5]. Additionally, the dataset encompasses two challenging object categories—metallic cutlery and transparent glasses—with reflective and transparent surfaces.

Thanks to SemanticHouseCat3D, we provide an exhaustive evaluation of recent state-of-the-art semantic matching methods with respect to pose awareness and 3D consistency. We assess performance across various view angle variations and evaluate techniques aimed at focusing semantic matching methods on objects, such as cropping and segmentation, to determine their impact on matching accuracy. The synthetic nature of the dataset allows us to generate corresponding point clouds for each frame, enabling the evaluation of distance errors not only in pixel space but also in 3D space, offering a more physically meaningful metric for robotic tasks.

In summary, our contributions are:

- **SemanticHouseCat3D:** A new synthetic dataset specifically designed for semantic matching of household objects, featuring rich annotations for key-

point correspondences and object poses. The dataset includes challenging categories with reflective and transparent materials, providing a comprehensive benchmark for evaluating pose-aware and 3D consistent matching methods.
- **Evaluation Procedure:** A novel evaluation procedure introducing pose-aware metrics, including orientation-based binning, 3D Average End Point Error (3D AEPE) and 3D Percentage of Correct Keypoints (PCK), for assessing semantic matching performance in both 2D and 3D spaces. This framework facilitates detailed analysis of methods' sensitivity to object pose variations and their ability to maintain 3D consistency, which are critical for real-world robotic applications.

2 Related Works

We categorize the related works into semantic matching techniques, applied semantic matching for robotics, and existing benchmark datasets.

2.1 Semantic Matching

Semantic matching algorithms have progressively refined point matching processes, including feature extraction, cost aggregation, and displacement computation, using both supervised and unsupervised methods. Key developments include NCNet [28], which introduced 4D convolutions for cost volume refinement later expanded in [23] with non-isotropic 4D kernels and [24], with convolutional Hough matching. SFNet [21] with a refinement of high-level features using kernel soft argmax for optical flow and leveraging foreground masks for supervision. Transformer-based approaches for cost aggregation [3,4], and hybrid feature aggregation and cost aggregation combining self- and cross-attention [15], have further enhanced performance.

More recently, visual foundation models, such as DINO [2] and Stable Diffusion [29], which are pre-trained on large datasets using self-supervised or generative tasks, have surpassed traditional methods by learning more powerful descriptors for semantic matching. The fusion of features from multiple foundation models [38] has set a new benchmark, particularly in zero-shot settings. Additionally, improving the geometrical accuracy of keypoints through a feature post-processing head, combined with pre-training on "geometrically-aware" datasets [37], now represents the state-of-the-art in strongly supervised semantic matching.

Our work aims to challenge these methods in terms of pose awareness and geometrical accuracy, two key factors for successful robotic applications.

2.2 Applied Semantic Matching

A key work exploring point matching for robotic applications is Dense Object Nets (DON) [8]. DON uses object masks and 3D scene reconstructions to learn dense object descriptors through a self-supervised pixel-wise contrastive loss.

While DON achieves category generalization as a secondary outcome, being primarily trained for dense object correspondences for specific objects, the more recent DODUO [16] builds on semantically-aware flow to train a flow estimation model in an unsupervised manner, achieving generalizable dense correspondences.

The field of object pose estimation has greatly benefited from semantically aware point matching. Notably, Goodwin et al. [10] was one of the first to demonstrate the use of pre-trained DINO descriptors in a zero-shot manner for category-level object pose estimation, a concept later adopted in other works such as ZS6D [1] for single-object instances.

Other applications of semantic features include AffCorrs [11], where annotated affordance regions are used to segment corresponding parts in a target scene, Robo-ABC [17], which transfers affordance contact points from a pre-collected memory, and Click to Grasp [32], where a user-selected interaction region on a source image is used to optimize a grasp pose for a semantically corresponding area in a target image.

All these methods involve the interaction of semantic deep features with a 3D environment and often highlight limited pose awareness. This limitation motivates us to develop a new benchmark, allowing semantic matching pipelines to clearly evaluate their effectiveness when interacting with objects in varying poses.

2.3 Datasets for Semantic Matching

Over the years, several datasets have been developed to evaluate the accuracy and robustness of semantic matching methods in diverse scenarios. PF-PASCAL and PF-WILLOW [12] are among the most widely used datasets. PF-PASCAL focuses on object correspondences in real-world scenes across 20 object categories, while PF-WILLOW provides simpler object instances with keypoint annotations in more controlled settings. SPair-71k [25] is a more comprehensive dataset that addresses the limitations of earlier datasets by introducing greater variability in object scale, viewpoint, and occlusion. With over 70,000 image pairs and fine-grained semantic keypoint annotations, SPair-71k is regarded as one of the most challenging benchmarks.

Other notable datasets include TSS [31], which has manually annotated dense flow fields for 400 semantically related image pairs; Caltech-101 [6], which contains 1,515 image pairs from 101 categories with segmentation annotations; and CUB [34], which provides image pairs of birds annotated with semantic keypoints.

The most recent dataset, AP-10k [37], derived from animal pose estimation, contains 261k training, 17k validation, and 36k testing image pairs across 23 families and 54 species of animals. It was designed to improve semantic matching methods, particularly for geometry-ambiguous matching cases.

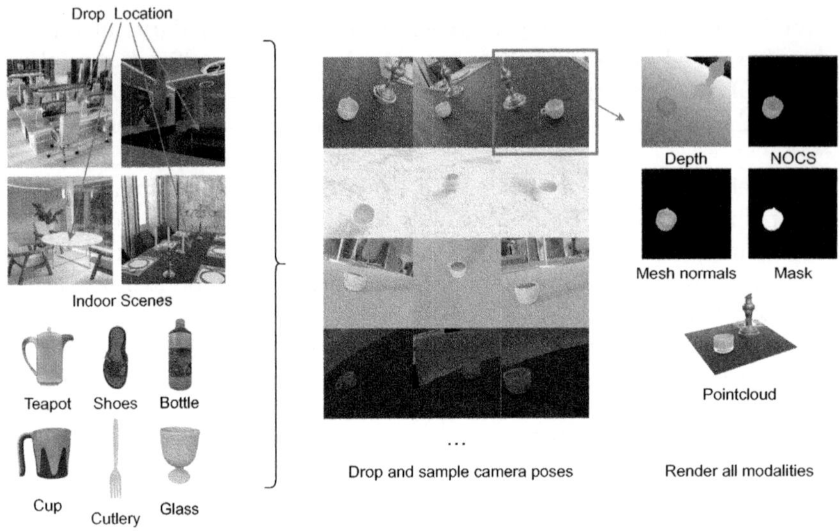

Fig. 2. Rendering pipeline of the SemanticHouseCat3D dataset.

3 The SemanticHouseCat3D Dataset

To promote research on semantic matching with a focus on robotics applications, we developed the SemanticHouseCat3D dataset, which features household rendered scenes containing objects spanning six categories from the HouseCat6D dataset [18], along with freely available assets. Each rendering includes an RGB image, a depth image, an instance mask, a point cloud, a NOCS [35] map, a mesh normals map and 6D object pose annotations. These frames are used to annotate image pairs within each category with semantic point correspondences, which serve as ground truth for benchmarking existing methods.

The availability of 6D pose annotations for the objects enables us to precisely measure how sensitive a semantic matching method is to variations in orientation between objects in the source and target images.

3.1 Rendering Pipeline

To create the SemanticHouseCat3D dataset, we employed a structured rendering pipeline using objects from six categories of the HouseCat6D dataset [18] illustrated in Fig. 2. These categories include high-quality meshes of common household items, with photometrically challenging objects such as glasses and cutlery. The entire rendering process was performed using the BlenderProc [5] procedural rendering pipeline.

The first step in our pipeline involves preparing indoor scenes—typical room environments—that include at least one planar surface, such as a table, where the objects are placed at chosen points.

Next, we iterate through all objects in each category and place them in the designated spot within each room. For each object, we sample a number of camera poses from a spherical shell region around the object. The camera positions are randomly offset in the XY plane, with offsets sampled from the range $[-0.1, 0.1]m$. The shell has an inner sphere radius of $0.4m$ and an outer sphere radius of $0.7m$, with a minimum elevation angle of 5 deg. The in-plane rotation of the camera is uniformly sampled from the range $[-30, 30]$ deg.

For each of the sampled camera poses, a corresponding frame is rendered, generating several outputs: an RGB image, a depth map, an instance mask, a NOCS map, and a mesh normals map, along with a point cloud. Additionally, the 6D object pose of the item in each frame is annotated and stored in a database.

3.2 Handling Symmetries

In the process of generating keypoint correspondences for semantic matching, it is crucial to account for object symmetries, as they prevent establishing unique correspondences. For instance, a point on the rim of a cylindrical glass cannot be uniquely identified due to the object's rotational symmetry around its central axis. We use meshes that are meaningfully and consistently oriented within each category around their respective axes and planes of symmetry. This consistent alignment allows for accurate detection and adjustment of symmetries during the generation of keypoint correspondences. We consider cylindrical and planar symmetries, present in the glass and bottle categories, respectively.

We classify the symmetry of an object using a heuristic based on the eigenvalues derived from a Principal Component Analysis (PCA) of the object's 3D shape.

Since our dataset contains only two types of symmetries, we focus on identifying whether an object has cylindrical symmetry. An object is classified as cylindrical, particularly an elongated cylinder, if the first (largest) eigenvalue is greater than the second, and the third eigenvalue is at least 90% of the second. This pattern reflects a tall, elongated shape along one axis (height), with similar dimensions along the other two axes (forming the base), typical of cylindrical objects. If the object does not meet these criteria, it is classified as having planar symmetry.

These adjustments provide consistency in the generation of keypoint correspondences and provide accurate annotations for objects with symmetries, which would otherwise make the annotation process geometrically ambiguous.

Orientation Adjustment. Once the symmetry type is determined, we adjust the object's orientation to align appropriately with the camera's viewpoint when generating the Normalized Object Coordinate Space (NOCS) and mesh normals maps used in the automatic annotation process.

- Cylindrical Symmetry: For objects with cylindrical symmetry, we rotate the object around its vertical (z) axis by an angle equal to the difference between

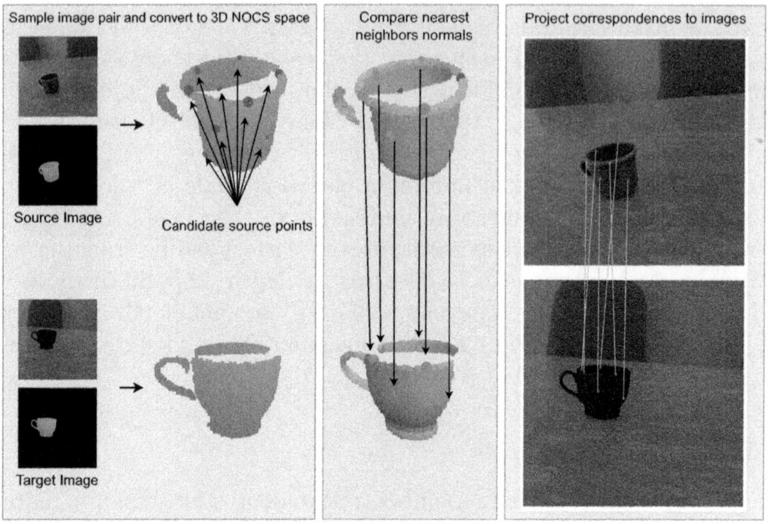

Fig. 3. Automatic keypoints annotation steps.

the object's forward vector (local x-axis) and the viewing vector (from the camera to the object's center), projected onto the horizontal (xy) plane. This alignment minimizes the angular difference between the object's orientation and the camera's viewpoint, ensuring consistent mapping of corresponding points despite the rotational symmetry.

- Planar Symmetry: For objects with planar symmetry, we check the alignment of the object's forward vector and the viewing vector in the xy-plane. If the dot product of their normalized projections is negative (i.e., they point in opposite directions), we rotate the object by 180°C around the z-axis. This adjustment ensures that the object's front face is consistently oriented relative to the camera, resolving ambiguity due to planar symmetry.

3.3 Keypoints Annotation Procedure

A key aspect of evaluating semantic matching methods is the accurate annotation of semantically similar keypoints across different object instances; however, a formal and precise definition of such keypoints has not been explicitly provided in previous literature. In this work, we introduce a clear definition to guide our annotation process and ensure consistency across the dataset (Fig. 3).

We define **semantically similar keypoints** as:

Image points on different objects within the same category that correspond to the same object part and maintain a consistent relative geometric placement from the viewer's perspective, after accounting for symmetries.

Given the synthetic nature of our dataset, we can annotate ground-truth semantic correspondences by leveraging the rendered NOCS and mesh normals maps. NOCS (Normalized Object Coordinate Space) maps are RGB images where each point on the object is color-coded to correspond uniquely to its 3D position within a unit cube $\{x, y, z\} \in [0, 1]$. This normalization is achieved by uniformly scaling a 3D model such that its tight bounding box has a unit diagonal, and centering the model within the NOCS space.

The mesh normals map encodes each point's surface normal in the object's original space as an RGB value. Both RGB mappings require that all 3D models within a category are consistently aligned.

Our annotation process begins by randomly sampling an image pair within the same category, ensuring that the two images depict different objects and have not been previously selected. From the source image, we sample a set of keypoints by applying the Farthest Point Sampling (FPS) algorithm [13] to select n points from the NOCS map. This sampling ensures a spatially diverse selection of points from the object's surface.

For each sampled keypoint in the source image, we search for a corresponding point in the target image by identifying its nearest neighbor in NOCS space from the target image's NOCS map under a threshold t_{NOCS}.

This choice is motivated by the assumption that different objects within one category possess a distribution of surface points that once scaled and rotated to have a consistent orientation enable the alignment of several of their parts that rather differ in texture or high frequency details. This criteria has been exploited in other works such as [7].

At this stage, once the proximity in NOCS space has been established, we validate the correspondences based on the alignment of their corresponding surface normals. Given an angle threshold t_{norm}, let $\mathbf{A}$ and $\mathbf{B}$ be a pair of selected points and $\mathbf{n}_A$ and $\mathbf{n}_B$ the corresponding surface normal vectors retrieved from the rendered RGB mapping we want the pair to satisfy

$$\angle(\mathbf{n}_A, \mathbf{n}_B) < t_{norm} \tag{1}$$

Such a constraint is needed for object categories with concavities. In those types of objects, two points on the outer and inner surface could be close within the established distance threshold if the object is thin enough but the corresponding surface normals will have opposite directions.

The keypoint correspondence is retained only if the pair satisfies these criteria. We continue this process for each of the sampled keypoints in the source image, and if at least one valid correspondence is found, the image pair is retained for annotation. If no valid correspondences are identified, the image pair is discarded, and a new pair is sampled.

This process is repeated until a predefined number of valid image pairs has been annotated, ensuring a sufficient number of candidate ground-truth correspondences for each category.

The automatic annotation step is followed by a final step of manual refinement. This will account for those point pairs that were matched correctly given the established criteria but are not "semantically" correct because of slight variations of source and target objects' shapes. Additionally, certain categories can have parts placed in varying positions which the NOCS and normals criteria can not account for and need manual annotation (e.g. a teapot having a side handle rather than a back handle). For the final distribution of image pairs and point pairs across different angles and for each category see Table 1.

Table 1. Distribution of annotated point pairs (PP) and image pairs (IP) per category and across orientation difference angle bins.

		Orientation Differences Bins (deg)											
		0–30		30–60		60–90		90–120		120–150		150–180	
Category	Total PP	IP	PP	IP	PP	IP	PP	IP	PP	IP	PP	IP	PP
bottle	957	57	297	89	399	62	171	31	64	8	22	3	4
cup	964	40	197	108	428	59	205	29	93	9	26	5	15
cutlery	1659	30	222	78	526	62	415	30	177	22	140	28	179
glass	969	117	457	116	453	16	55	1	4	0	0	0	0
shoe	1023	37	165	112	490	54	226	28	83	17	52	2	7
teapot	932	48	210	101	377	64	224	26	84	7	24	4	13
Total	6504	329	1548	604	2673	317	1296	145	505	63	264	42	218

4 Benchmark Evaluations on SemanticHouseCat3D

In this section we present the evaluations of baseline state-of-the-art methods on SemanticHouseCat3D with their results summarized in Table 3-5 and Fig. 4–5.

4.1 Evaluation Procedure

Each evaluated method computes deep feature maps. For each method, we follow a standardized procedure: we compute the feature map for both source and target images, resulting in a tensor with a number of channels specific to each model and a spatial resolution lower than that of the original images. Input images are pre-processed to a specific resolution unique to each method. After computing the feature maps, we upsample them to the original image resolution using bilinear interpolation, obtaining one feature vector per pixel. We then compute the cosine similarity between the upsampled feature maps and retrieve the correspondences of the annotated query points using the argmax operation. Table 2 reports the shape of feature maps computed using each of the baseline methods before interpolating them.

Table 2. Shapes of feature maps computed with each of the baseline methods before the upsampling step.

Method	Feature Map Shape (Channels × Height × Width)
DINOv1 [2,38]	384 × 55 × 55
DINOv2 [26,38]	768 × 60 × 60
DIFT [30]	1280 × 48 × 48
SD+DINO [38]	1536 × 60 × 60
GeoAware [37]	768 × 60 × 60

All methods have been evaluated using their publicly available versions. For DINOv1 [2] and DINOv2 [26], we use feature computation parameters provided by [38]. For GeoAware [37], we evaluate the strongly supervised model pre-trained on AP-10K without adaptive flip.

We introduce two novel evaluation metrics made possible by our dataset: a binned Percentage of Correct Keypoints (PCK) based on orientation differences between the objects in source and target images, with bins of 30°, a 3D Average Endpoint Error (3D AEPE) and a 3D PCK which considers correct keypoints based on metric distances rather than pixel-space distances.

For all evaluations, each method is evaluated with three input types: the full original image, a tightly cropped image containing only the bounding box around the object of interest, and a masked image that retains only the object of interest. This approach reflects common practices in robotics, where smaller input images (e.g., cropped) or focused input (e.g., masked) are used to enhance attention on the object or reduce computational load.

Considering the distribution of annotated samples in the dataset (see Table 1), we exclude the bin spanning 150° to 180° due to an insufficient sample size in this range, which would render the computed metrics statistically unreliable.

4.2 Evaluation Metrics

The **Percentage of Correct Keypoints (PCK)** measures the percentage of inferred keypoints with a distance from the groundtruth under the $\alpha_{bbox} \cdot \max(H_{bbox}, W_{bbox})$ threshold in an image pair and averaged over all the image pairs in a dataset. The values H_{bbox} and W_{bbox} are the height and width of the tight bounding box surrounding the object of interest.

The **3D Average End Point Error (3D AEPE)** measures the averaged Euclidean distance in meters between the 3D location of the back-projected inferred matching point retrieved from the corresponding point cloud and the 3D location of the groundtruth point obtained in the same manner.

The **3D** PCK_τ measures the percentage of keypoints which after being lifted to a 3D point have a distance from the groundtruth under the τ threshold. We designate $\tau = 2cm$ deeming it a representative threshold for feasible manipulation of the objects included in the dataset.

4.3 Discussion

Standard PCK Evaluations. Table 3 and Table 4 present the standard PCK evaluations of baseline methods on our dataset.

Table 3. PCK@α_{bbox} [%], α_{bbox} = $\{0.05, 0.10, 0.15\}$ evaluation of baseline methods on SemanticHouseCat3D. **Bold** and underlined values indicate respectively the best and second best result achieved for each metric across the different models and input modalities.

Method	Input	PCK@0.05$_{bbox}$	PCK@0.10$_{bbox}$	PCK@0.15$_{bbox}$
DINOv1 [2,38]	Full Image	11.4	28.8	43.1
	Crop	16.1	33.6	47.8
	Segmented Image	15.4	33.5	47.1
DINOv2 [26,38]	Full Image	20.5	42.1	57.2
	Crop	21.9	42.1	56.5
	Segmented Image	20.4	41.9	56.2
DIFT [30]	Full Image	24.2	45.3	58.1
	Crop	<u>24.5</u>	42.7	56.3
	Segmented Image	**24.8**	46.0	58.7
SD+DINO [38]	Full Image	24.2	**46.9**	**61.2**
	Crop	23.1	43.7	57.5
	Segmented Image	24.1	<u>46.4</u>	<u>60.1</u>
GeoAware [37]	Full Image	20.2	39.9	53.4
	Crop	18.3	36.1	48.8
	Segmented Image	19.6	38.4	51.8

The general trend shows that stable diffusion-based DIFT [30] and the feature aggregation method SD+DINO [38] achieve the best performances. DINOv1 features benefit significantly from both cropping and segmenting the image, consistently improving matching performance in these conditions. DIFT also shows performance gains with segmentation; notably, for the "cutlery" category, DIFT improves by 9.5%, likely due to segmentation helping the method localize thin objects more accurately and reduce artifacts from reflective materials. GeoAware, while achieving state-of-the-art performance on the SPair-71k [25] dataset with a strongly supervised model, performs poorly when tested in a different domain. The "bottle" category is the only one in which its performance remains competitive, likely because it was included in SPair-71k, the dataset on which it was trained.

Table 4. Per class PCK@0.10 [%] evaluation of baseline methods on SemanticHouseCat3D. **Bold** and underlined values indicate respectively the best and second best result achieved for each category across the different models and input modalities.

Method	Input	Bottle	Cup	Cutlery	Glass	Shoe	Teapot	All
DINOv1 [2,38]	Full Image	25.0	18.0	38.6	34.7	27.9	28.9	28.8
	Crop	26.4	22.7	43.3	45.0	28.7	35.4	33.6
	Segmented Image	26.6	21.7	46.7	43.4	31.5	31.2	33.5
DINOv2 [26,38]	Full Image	31.5	25.0	<u>60.7</u>	52.9	36.4	46.2	42.1
	Crop	29.2	25.1	59.6	54.3	37.0	47.5	42.1
	Segmented Image	30.9	25.5	57.6	53.8	36.5	46.9	41.9
DIFT [30]	Full Image	34.2	27.0	48.8	**75.0**	**38.4**	48.2	45.3
	Crop	32.2	25.7	48.4	72.5	32.6	44.8	42.7
	Segmented Image	<u>36.6</u>	25.2	57.5	<u>73.6</u>	<u>37.4</u>	45.9	46.0
SD+DINO [38]	Full Image	**36.9**	28.1	**61.0**	72.8	32.9	**49.6**	**46.9**
	Crop	35.5	<u>26.9</u>	57.4	62.0	34.4	45.9	43.7
	Segmented Image	36.2	**29.9**	58.6	69.3	35.8	<u>48.5</u>	46.4
GeoAware [37]	Full Image	36.3	24.9	45.3	65.4	29.3	38.3	39.9
	Crop	32.7	21.8	43.2	58.0	25.6	35.6	36.1
	Segmented Image	34.6	24.3	42.3	63.9	27.5	37.9	38.4

Pose Aware PCK Evaluations. The binned PCK evaluation results are presented in Fig. 4 and Fig. 5.

The most noticeable trend is the decline in matching performance as the orientation angle difference between source and target images increases—a behavior previously noted but quantified here for the first time. Diffusion-based features from DIFT exhibit the best matching performance when objects are well-aligned, with a sharp decline as the angle increases. Conversely, DINOv2 features are more robust to orientation changes, performing well across all α values in the PCK evaluation. The use of either a masked or cropped input is particularly beneficial for lower thresholds, as evidenced by the performance of both DIFT and DINOv2 in the $\alpha = 0.05$ plot.

Similar trends appear in the per-category plots in Fig. 5. For example, DINOv2 shows robustness to angle changes in the "bottle" category, with an almost linear performance curve. However, both DINOv1 and DINOv2 exhibit a significant drop in performance for lower bins compared to other methods. By inspecting the image pairs in this bin and analyzing inferred correspondences, we observe that both models are more sensitive to texture cues such as logos, labels, or barcodes. Thus, even when bottles are aligned in the images, points near logos or text may be matched with other points on different logos or text areas, even if they are arranged differently on each object. These correspondences are wrong according to the definition given in Subsect. 3.3.

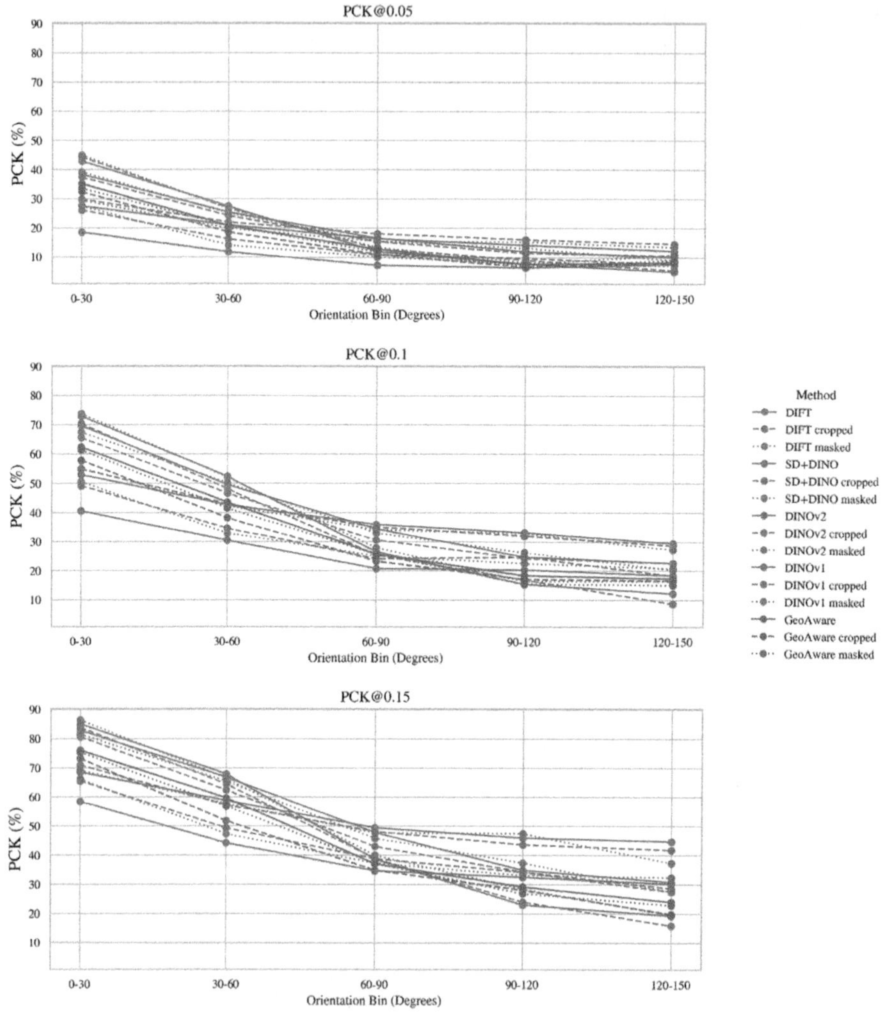

Fig. 4. PCK@0.10 [%] evaluation of baseline methods across orientation angle difference bins on SemanticHouseCat3D across all classes.

Both DINO models also seem more sensitive to transparent materials like glass compared to reflective materials like cutlery, where they show better performance.

Although SD+DINO, which aggregates DINO and diffusion features, performs best on average, it does not capture the best characteristics of each model in terms of PCK.

3D Consistency Evaluations. Table 5 presents the results of the 3D AEPE evaluations alongside the 3D PCK_{2cm}.

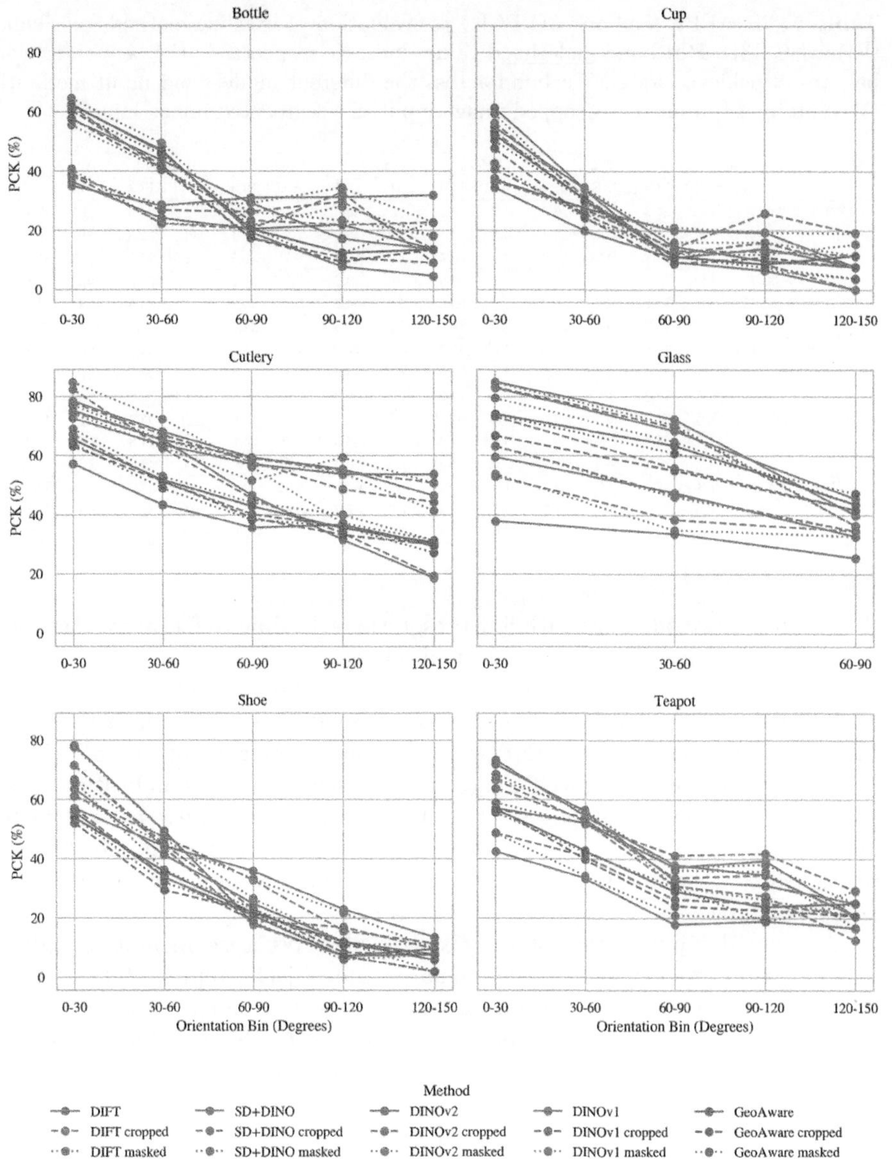

Fig. 5. Per class PCK@0.10 [%] evaluation of baseline methods across orientation angle difference bins on SemanticHouseCat3D.

An interesting observation from Table 5 is the contrasting impact of input modalities on matching accuracy and precision. Using cropped images consistently yields lower AEPE scores, indicating more precise localization of matching points. For instance, SD+DINO with cropped input achieves the best overall performance with an AEPE of 4.4 cm. Cropping enhances spatial precision as

Table 5. 3D AEPE [cm] and 3D PCK_{2cm} evaluation of baseline methods on SemanticHouseCat3D. **Bold** and underlined values indicate respectively the best and second best result achieved for each column across the different models and input modalities (F - Full image input, C - Cropped image input, S - segmented image input).

Method	Input	Bottle		Cup		Cutlery		Glass		Shoe		Teapot		All	
		AEPE	PCK_{2cm}	AEPE	PCK_{2cm}	AEPE	PCK_{2cm}	AEPE	PCK_{2cm}	AEPE	PCK_{2cm}	AEPE	PCK_{2cm}	AEPE	PCK_{2cm}
DINOv1 [2,38]	F	12.6	27.3	10.1	26.6	4.7	38.2	11.2	30.5	10.7	17.0	19.8	22.9	11.5	27.1
	C	6.8	29.6	4.0	33.9	4.5	45.8	5.2	45.3	7.5	20.1	8.0	32.3	6.0	34.5
	S	10.0	27.2	11.5	27.8	4.3	46.4	13.4	42.4	8.7	20.5	11.9	25.9	10.0	31.7
DINOv2 [26,38]	F	14.6	30.3	10.5	35.0	3.1	58.9	10.3	50.8	7.6	26.2	15.6	37.6	10.3	39.8
	C	5.6	34.1	4.6	**40.5**	2.7	63.6	4.4	54.7	**5.9**	**29.3**	6.3	46.5	4.9	44.8
	S	9.9	30.9	9.2	33.3	2.9	56.8	7.5	49.5	7.1	27.7	8.6	41.3	7.5	39.9
DIFT [30]	F	10.7	36.8	7.9	34.6	16.2	47.7	5.1	**73.1**	10.0	28.0	11.7	42.1	10.2	43.7
	C	**4.7**	36.6	**3.3**	39.0	4.4	52.3	**2.6**	73.0	6.1	25.8	6.1	43.0	4.5	44.9
	S	8.0	38.2	12.3	30.8	3.7	54.9	7.4	68.9	8.0	26.0	12.1	39.6	8.6	43.1
SD+DINO [38]	F	5.2	**39.6**	6.8	40.0	**2.6**	**63.8**	4.5	70.8	6.7	25.6	4.9	**47.8**	5.1	**47.9**
	C	**4.7**	37.8	3.5	38.7	3.0	61.0	5.1	63.5	**5.9**	25.6	**4.4**	44.8	**4.4**	45.2
	S	8.9	37.2	6.3	38.1	3.0	58.3	7.6	66.0	7.0	27.0	7.1	44.6	6.7	45.2
GeoAware [37]	F	7.3	37.4	14.8	32.5	18.4	45.7	10.7	63.5	21.2	19.4	22.1	35.9	15.7	39.1
	C	10.0	34.6	6.8	31.0	4.6	45.4	7.6	57.2	9.0	18.2	10.0	32.6	8.0	36.5
	S	11.7	35.4	7.3	31.8	5.6	41.4	7.3	60.8	11.8	17.9	9.3	34.2	8.8	36.9

the different methods work with fixed resolutions, leading to feature vectors that represent a smaller region of the original image.

However, when examining the 3D PCK_{2cm} values, cropping does not necessarily increase the number of correct correspondences across all methods and categories. A case such as DIFT with the 'glass' category or the SD+DINO method overall achieve higher PCK_{2cm} values with full images, indicating better matching accuracy. This suggests that the background context present in full images provides a richer semantic environment, enabling methods to leverage relationships between the object and its surroundings for more accurate keypoint matching.

Segmented input images show mixed results. While segmentation reduces background interference, it doesn't enlarge the object's representation in the image, so the feature map resolution for the object remains similar to that in full images. Consequently, segmentation improves AEPE over full images but doesn't match the effectiveness of cropped inputs in terms of precision, nor does it consistently enhance matching accuracy.

This contrast highlights a trade-off between precision and accuracy based on the input modality. Cropping focuses solely on the object, improving spatial precision but potentially losing contextual cues that aid in accurate matching. Conversely, full images retain the background context, enhancing matching accuracy but possibly at the expense of spatial precision due to the object occupying a smaller portion of the image and feature maps.

5 Conclusions

In this paper, we introduced **SemanticHouseCat3D**, a synthetic dataset aimed at advancing semantic matching with a focus on pose awareness in household objects. Built from high-quality 3D models, our dataset fills critical gaps by providing challenging scenarios with significant orientation changes, reflective and transparent materials, and categories relevant to robotic manipulation.

Our evaluation of state-of-the-art methods, including zero-shot and strongly supervised approaches, highlighted limitations in handling pose variations and achieving 3D accuracy. The evaluation, featuring angle-difference binning and 3D AEPE metrics, showed that while DINOv2 is robust to pose changes, diffusion-based methods like DIFT perform best when objects are aligned. All methods, however, still struggle with orientation variations, underscoring the need for inherently pose-aware techniques.

Our observations point to a contrasting impact of input modalities on matching accuracy and precision. Cropping input images yields lower 3D AEPE, a sign of more precise localization of matching point on the object thanks to the removal of distractions and farther regions depicted in the image. This improvement in precision does not consistently translate to higher matching accuracy. A method like SD+DINO based on feature aggregation from two other foundation models greatly benefits from the context present in full images which provides valuable semantic information that aids in correctly matching keypoints.

Looking ahead, integrating advanced feature upsampling techniques could further improve 3D localization capabilities. Recent methods like FeatUp [9] have shown promise in preserving semantic information during upsampling and restore lost spatial information in deep features. Advances in monocular depth estimation, such as Marigold [19] and DepthAnything [36], open possibilities for upsampling processes informed by scene structure, potentially enhancing pixel- and meter-level alignment. Such improvements could make semantic matching methods more viable for robotics applications that demand high precision in 3D object recognition and manipulation.

Acknowledgment. The authors gratefully acknowledge the financial support of Festo AG & Co. KG.

Disclosure of Interests. The authors declare that they have no conflict of interest.

References

1. Ausserlechner, P., Haberger, D., Thalhammer, S., Weibel, J.B., Vincze, M.: ZS6D: zero-shot 6d object pose estimation using vision transformers. In: 2024 IEEE International Conference on Robotics and Automation (ICRA), pp. 463–469. IEEE (2024)
2. Caron, M., et al.: Emerging properties in self-supervised vision transformers. In: Proceedings of the IEEE/CVF International Conference on Computer Vision, pp. 9650–9660 (2021)
3. Cho, S., Hong, S., Jeon, S., Lee, Y., Sohn, K., Kim, S.: CATs: cost aggregation transformers for visual correspondence. Adv. Neural. Inf. Process. Syst. **34**, 9011–9023 (2021)
4. Cho, S., Hong, S., Kim, S.: CATs++: boosting cost aggregation with convolutions and transformers. IEEE Transactions on Pattern Analysis and Machine Intelligence (2022)

5. Denninger, M., et al.: BlenderProc: reducing the reality gap with photorealistic rendering. In: 16th Robotics: Science and Systems, RSS 2020, Workshops (2020)
6. Fei-Fei, L., Fergus, R., Perona, P.: Learning generative visual models from few training examples: an incremental Bayesian approach tested on 101 object categories. In: 2004 Conference on Computer Vision and Pattern Recognition Workshop, pp. 178–178 (2004). https://doi.org/10.1109/CVPR.2004.383
7. Feng, Q., Atanasov, N.: Fully convolutional geometric features for category-level object alignment. In: 2020 IEEE/RSJ International Conference on Intelligent Robots and Systems (IROS), pp. 8492–8498. IEEE (2020)
8. Florence, P.R., Manuelli, L., Tedrake, R.: Dense object nets: Learning dense visual object descriptors by and for robotic manipulation. arXiv preprint arXiv:1806.08756 (2018)
9. Fu, S., Hamilton, M., Brandt, L.E., Feldmann, A., Zhang, Z., Freeman, W.T.: FeatUp: A model-agnostic framework for features at any resolution (2024)
10. Goodwin, W., Vaze, S., Havoutis, I., Posner, I.: Zero-shot category-level object pose estimation. In: European Conference on Computer Vision, pp. 516–532. Springer (2022)
11. Hadjivelichkov, D., Zwane, S., Agapito, L., Deisenroth, M.P., Kanoulas, D.: One-shot transfer of affordance regions? Affcorrs! In: Conference on Robot Learning, pp. 550–560. PMLR (2023)
12. Ham, B., Cho, M., Schmid, C., Ponce, J.: Proposal flow: semantic correspondences from object proposals. IEEE Trans. Pattern Anal. Mach. Intell. **40**, 1711–1725 (2017). https://api.semanticscholar.org/CorpusID:6050505
13. Han, M., et al.: QuickFPS: architecture and algorithm co-design for farthest point sampling in large-scale point clouds. IEEE Trans. Comput. Aided Des. Integr. Circuits Syst. **42**(11), 4011–4024 (2023). https://doi.org/10.1109/TCAD.2023.3274922
14. He, M., Liao, J., Chen, D., Yuan, L., Sander, P.V.: Progressive color transfer with dense semantic correspondences. ACM Trans. Graph. (TOG) **38**(2), 1–18 (2019)
15. Hong, S., Cho, S., Kim, S., Lin, S.: Unifying feature and cost aggregation with transformers for semantic and visual correspondence. In: The Twelfth International Conference on Learning Representations (2024). https://openreview.net/forum?id=fQHb1uZzl7
16. Jiang, Z., Jiang, H., Zhu, Y.: Doduo: learning dense visual correspondence from unsupervised semantic-aware flow. In: 2024 IEEE International Conference on Robotics and Automation (ICRA), pp. 12420–12427. IEEE (2024)
17. Ju, Y., Hu, K., Zhang, G., Zhang, G., Jiang, M., Xu, H.: Robo-ABC: Affordance generalization beyond categories via semantic correspondence for robot manipulation. arXiv preprint arXiv:2401.07487 (2024)
18. Jung, H., et al.: HouseCat6D-a large-scale multi-modal category level 6d object perception dataset with household objects in realistic scenarios. In: Proceedings of the IEEE/CVF Conference on Computer Vision and Pattern Recognition, pp. 22498–22508 (2024)
19. Ke, B., Obukhov, A., Huang, S., Metzger, N., Daudt, R.C., Schindler, K.: Repurposing diffusion-based image generators for monocular depth estimation. In: Proceedings of the IEEE/CVF Conference on Computer Vision and Pattern Recognition, pp. 9492–9502 (2024)
20. Kim, S., Min, D., Jeong, S., Kim, S., Jeon, S., Sohn, K.: Semantic attribute matching networks. In: Proceedings of the IEEE/CVF Conference on Computer Vision and Pattern Recognition, pp. 12339–12348 (2019)

21. Lee, J., Kim, D., Ponce, J., Ham, B.: SFNet: learning object-aware semantic correspondence. In: Proceedings of the IEEE/CVF Conference on Computer Vision and Pattern Recognition (CVPR) (2019)
22. Lee, J., Kim, E., Lee, Y., Kim, D., Chang, J., Choo, J.: Reference-based sketch image colorization using augmented-self reference and dense semantic correspondence. In: Proceedings of the IEEE/CVF Conference on Computer Vision and Pattern Recognition, pp. 5801–5810 (2020)
23. Li, S., Han, K., Costain, T.W., Howard-Jenkins, H., Prisacariu, V.: Correspondence networks with adaptive neighbourhood consensus. In: Proceedings of the IEEE/CVF Conference on Computer Vision and Pattern Recognition (CVPR) (2020)
24. Min, J., Cho, M.: Convolutional hough matching networks. In: Proceedings of the IEEE/CVF Conference on Computer Vision and Pattern Recognition (CVPR), pp. 2940–2950 (June 2021)
25. Min, J., Lee, J., Ponce, J., Cho, M.: SPair-71k: A large-scale benchmark for semantic correspondence. arXiv preprint arXiv:1908.10543 (2019)
26. Oquab, M., et al.: DINOv2: learning robust visual features without supervision. Trans. Mach. Learn. Res. (2023)
27. Peebles, W., Zhu, J.Y., Zhang, R., Torralba, A., Efros, A.A., Shechtman, E.: Gan-supervised dense visual alignment. In: Proceedings of the IEEE/CVF Conference on Computer Vision and Pattern Recognition, pp. 13470–13481 (2022)
28. Rocco, I., Cimpoi, M., Arandjelović, R., Torii, A., Pajdla, T., Sivic, J.: Neighbourhood consensus networks. Adv. Neural Inf. Process. Syst. **31** (2018)
29. Rombach, R., Blattmann, A., Lorenz, D., Esser, P., Ommer, B.: High-resolution image synthesis with latent diffusion models. In: Proceedings of the IEEE/CVF Conference on Computer Vision and Pattern Recognition, pp. 10684–10695 (2022)
30. Tang, L., Jia, M., Wang, Q., Phoo, C.P., Hariharan, B.: Emergent correspondence from image diffusion. Adv. Neural. Inf. Process. Syst. **36**, 1363–1389 (2023)
31. Taniai, T., Sinha, S.N., Sato, Y.: Joint recovery of dense correspondence and cosegmentation in two images. In: Proceedings of the IEEE Conference on Computer Vision and Pattern Recognition, pp. 4246–4255 (2016)
32. Tsagkas, N., Rome, J., Ramamoorthy, S., Mac Aodha, O., Lu, C.X.: Click to grasp: Zero-shot precise manipulation via visual diffusion descriptors. arXiv preprint arXiv:2403.14526 (2024)
33. Tumanyan, N., Bar-Tal, O., Bagon, S., Dekel, T.: Splicing ViT features for semantic appearance transfer. In: Proceedings of the IEEE/CVF Conference on Computer Vision and Pattern Recognition (CVPR), pp. 10748–10757 (2022)
34. Wah, C., Branson, S., Welinder, P., Perona, P., Belongie, S.: The Caltech-UCSD birds-200-2011 dataset (2011)
35. Wang, H., Sridhar, S., Huang, J., Valentin, J., Song, S., Guibas, L.J.: Normalized object coordinate space for category-level 6D object pose and size estimation. In: Proceedings of the IEEE/CVF Conference on Computer Vision and Pattern Recognition (CVPR) (2019)
36. Yang, L., et al.: Depth anything v2. arXiv preprint arXiv:2406.09414 (2024)
37. Zhang, J., et al.: Telling left from right: identifying geometry-aware semantic correspondence. In: Proceedings of the IEEE/CVF Conference on Computer Vision and Pattern Recognition, pp. 3076–3085 (2024)
38. Zhang, J., et al.: A tale of two features: stable diffusion complements DINO for zero-shot semantic correspondence. Adv. Neural Inf. Process. Syst. **36** (2024)

Detection, Characterization, and Localization of Oranges and Their Stems Using RGB-D Camera and Image Processing

Alaeddin Bani Milhim(✉), Colton Cunningham, and The Leo Nguyen

California State University, Fresno, Fresno, CA 93740, USA
abanimilhim@mail.fresnostate.edu

Abstract. This paper presents an advanced image processing technique for detection, characterization, and localization of orange fruits and their stems, using an RGB-D camera, addressing a critical challenge in agricultural automation. Additionally, this work investigates the performance of RGB-D camera for orange fruit and its stem characterizations, alongside with the Super-Resolution Convolutional Neural Network (SRCNN) techniques to enhance image quality for improved detection accuracy. The proposed method captures the images of orange fruits, converts them into HSV color space, isolates the orange fruit using binary masking, identifies the largest visible fruit, detects its stem, characterizes both the fruits and their stems, and precisely localizes both the fruit and stem features using pinhole camera modeling. The effectiveness of the super-resolution approach was evaluated by comparing the results of a higher resolution camera, RGB-D camera, and RGB-D camera with super-resolution enhancement. The super resolution approach was concluded to significantly improve stem detection and localization, with the proposed image processing method achieving localization results within a maximum absolute error of 4.5° and 1.7% deviation from measured values. These findings demonstrate promising potential for achieving high-accuracy localization of orange fruit and stems, facilitating precise gripping and cutting action in automated harvesting systems.

Keywords: Image processing · Super-resolution convolutional neural network · Orange fruit detection · Stem characterization · Automated harvesting

1 Introduction

Image processing plays a crucial role in advancing automated fruit harvesting, enabling precise identification and localization of produce, which are essential for maintaining high yield and quality. Traditional manual harvesting, while widely practiced, is labor-intensive and time-consuming, with inconsistencies due to human error and variations in picking techniques [1]. Another established method, mechanical harvesting, such as tree shaking, involves collecting a fruit/nut from a tree with no perception of the fruit/nut. While this approach addresses labor shortages and reduces the lengthy hours required for manual harvesting, it cannot adapt its technique based on the produce's

J. Röning and J. Filipe (Eds.): ROBOVIS 2025, CCIS 2629, pp. 294–311, 2026.
https://doi.org/10.1007/978-3-032-00986-9_20

condition, potentially affecting overall quality. Automated harvesting systems leverage image processing techniques, often enhanced by Artificial Intelligence (AI), to accurately detect and assess fruit ripeness and position, providing a consistent, efficient, and scalable alternative to manual methods. This approach not only improves harvest accuracy but also addresses labor challenges, ensuring reliable and high-quality outcomes [2, 3].

Numerous research efforts have been reported on developing image processing techniques and improvement for citrus fruit recognition [4–14]. Hannan et al. [4] discussed a five-stage image processing method for detecting orange fruits. The results of different segmentation scenarios indicated that over 90% of the visually recognized fruits were detected in the 110 images tested, with a false detection rate of 4%. McCarthy et al. [5] discussed different broad sensing methods including monocular vision, stereo vision, multi-spectral imaging, and range sensing. This paper proposes that combining these methods and sensors can yield accurate results in outdoor environments, which have different lighting conditions compared to indoor environments. Y. Changhui [6] addressed the challenge of fruit recognition in scenarios involving overlapped fruit by developing a convex hull-based method to localize and reconstruct overlapped citrus fruits, enhancing harvesting robot accuracy. Leveraging the spherical shape and hue-based imaging, this method determines central picking points and radii with an average positioning error of 6.51% and a reconstruction error of 8.84%, meeting citrus harvesting requirements. Jimenez et al. [7, 8] proposed a preliminary method employing a laser-based machine vision system for the automatic identification of fruits. The proposed technique achieved a detection rate of approximately 80–90% for citrus harvesting. The primary challenge in this study was fine-tuning the algorithm to achieve a low false detection rate while meeting the sensor requirements. Thendral et al. [9] employed edge-based and color-based segmentation techniques to detect citrus fruits. While edge-based segmentation was unsuccessful, color-based segmentation achieved an accuracy of 85% for fruit recognition. However, the study did not address the localization of the detected fruits. Liu et al. [10] proposed a recognition algorithm for citrus fruits based on RealSense technology, which utilizes depth-point cloud data at a close-shot range of 160 mm, achieving an accuracy of 79.17% on average. Dorj et al. [11] addressed the challenges of removing "clutter objects" from fruit images, where clutter objects can include background features such as leaves, branches, sky, and soil. However, the proposed processing method falls short in tracking or detecting all elements within the image.

Ukwuoma et al. [12] proposed a deep learning-based system for fruit categorization and identification using the Fruits-360 dataset. Their experiment included Convolutional Neural Networks (CNNs) and You Only Look Once (YOLO) techniques for feature extraction, demonstrating a loss and accuracy model based on ResNet-50. Ultimately, they achieved a categorization accuracy of 99% using advanced algorithms. Jiang et al. [13] argued that accurate fruit detection, classification, and localization requires images with sufficient resolution. Optical zoom methods can improve image quality of faraway objects but can be expensive due to the need for adjustable focal length, while digital zoom can enlarge images without enhancing resolution, often causing blur and artifacts [14]. Instead, Jiang *et al.* [13] explored machine learning-based super-resolution, achieving significant improvements in image quality. Although the reported results highlight super-resolution methods potential in image resolution enhancement, this research primarily focused on plant structures rather than fruit detection.

To effectively harvest citrus, precise detection and characterization of the stem are essential, allowing the end-effector to accurately determine the optimal cutting point. Current methods primarily focus on the detection and characterization of the citrus fruit itself, often overlooking the critical role of stem identification. This work addresses this gap by introducing a technique for detecting and characterizing both the citrus fruit and its stem using a single RGB-D camera, paving the way for automated citrus tree harvesting. The technique is also adaptable to other areas, including packaging and manufacturing. While RGB-D cameras provide valuable depth information, they are limited by lower resolution and lack of zoom capabilities, which can pose challenges for detailed imaging.

This paper is organized as follows. Section 2 describes the experimental setup and methodology for processing images of oranges and their stems. Section 3 details the orange image processing procedure, while Sect. 4 covers the stem detection and characterization. Orange fruit and its stem localization is addressed in Sect. 5. Section 6 presents results and discussions. Finally, conclusions are drawn in Sect. 7.

2 Methodology and Experimental Setup

2.1 Methodology Structure

The goal of this study is to develop an approach for detecting both orange fruits and their stems using a single RGB-D camera. Intel RealSense depth camera (i.e. D457) was selected for its capability to capture depth information through stereo vision techniques while simultaneously providing color images in the RGB color space [15, 16]. However, one limitation of this camera is its relatively low image resolution of 1280×720 pixels. The Intel RealSense depth camera was chosen for its crucial depth information capabilities essential for automated fruit harvesting, despite having a lower resolution compared to other available RGB cameras. High-resolution imaging is crucial for accurately detecting and localizing the features of the orange fruit and its stem. To determine whether the lower resolution of the Intel RealSense depth camera significantly affects fruit detection and localization, this study evaluates the effectiveness of current camera technology and image enhancement techniques in accurately recognizing orange fruits and their stems. To assess these methods, three different image-capturing approaches were implemented: capturing images with a high-resolution camera (e.g. mobile-phone camera), capturing images with an Intel RealSense depth camera, and capturing images with an Intel RealSense camera followed by image enhancement algorithms. This comparative analysis aims to evaluate the effectiveness of the super-resolution enhancement in accurately characterizing both the orange and its stem. The technical specifications of the two cameras used in this study are outlined in Table 1. The images in this experiment were processed using the MATLAB Image Processing Toolbox and computed using MATLAB version R2023b on an Asus ROG G15 laptop, equipped with an NIVIDIA GeForce RTX 3060 graphics processing unit.

Table 1. Technical specifications of the cameras used in this study.

Specification	Intel RealSense D457 Camera	12 MP Mobile-phone Camera
RGB Field of view	90° × 65°	120°
RGB Resolution	1280 × 720	4032 × 3024
RGB Frame rate	30 fps	N/A
Depth Field of View	87° × 58°	N/A
Depth Resolution	1280 × 720	N/A
Depth Range	52 cm–20 m	N/A

2.2 Test Apparatus

One of the main challenges in fruit detection approaches is the impact of poor lighting conditions [17]. Harsh lighting can degrade the quality of captured images, resulting in inaccurate detection, localization, orientation, and characterization of orange fruits. To mitigate this issue, data collection for this experiment was conducted in a controlled environment, where lighting and other factors were carefully managed. This controlled setting allows for the optimization of the detection algorithms without the confounding effects of variable lighting conditions. Once optimal performance is achieved in the lab setting, the experiment will be extended to real-world conditions.

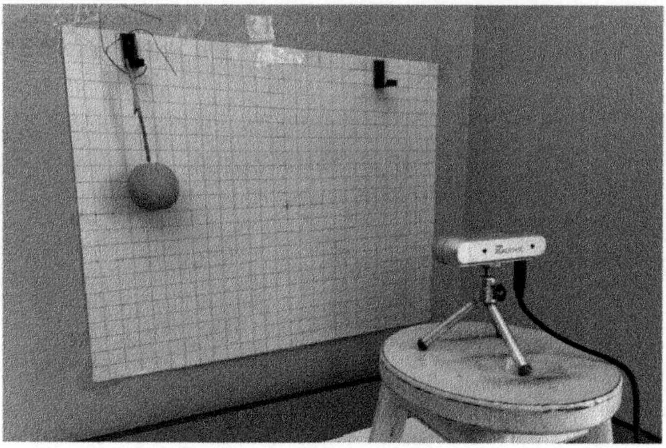

Fig. 1. Photo of the testing apparatus used to collect the data.

The testing apparatus used in this work consists of a camera mounted on a stage, with artificial oranges and stems placed in front of a white grid background, as illustrated in Fig. 1. The dimensions of the artificial oranges and stems used in this work are comparable to that of real orange fruits, ensuring that the experimental conditions closely mimic real-world scenarios. The white grid background behind the orange was used to evaluate the accuracy of the detection algorithm. The performance of the detection algorithm was evaluated based on six characteristics: percent difference in orange orientation, stem orientation, orange centroid location, orange width, orange height, and the stem base location. To assess the relative error between the measured values and the detected values from the camera and the proposed methodology, two performance metrics were implemented: absolute difference (ε_X) and percentage difference ($\varepsilon_X\%$), as shown below:

$$\varepsilon_X = |X_{calculated} - X_{measured}| \tag{1}$$

$$\varepsilon_X\% = \frac{X_{calculated} - X_{measured}}{X_{measured}} \times 100\% \tag{2}$$

where $X_{calculated}$ refers to the quantity produced from the detection algorithm, and $X_{measured}$ refers to the manually obtained measurements using the white grid background and software measuring tools (i.e. Adobe Acrobat). Absolute difference was chosen as the error metric for angles due to the values of the measured angle being small, which would consequently produce a high percent difference. Figure 2 illustrates the process of obtaining known measured values for comparison with the detected values produced by the detection algorithm methodology present in this paper.

In this study, the orientation, position, and features of the orange fruits and their stems were detected under various stem angles and lighting conditions. The five stem orientations tested were –30º, –15º, 0º, 15º, 30º, with two levels of illumination: mid-level and high-level. After obtaining the orange and its stem feature results, the percent difference between the camera-detected feature values and the known measured values was calculated to assess accuracy. These error results were then averaged across the five stem orientations for each feature to evaluate the system's overall performance.

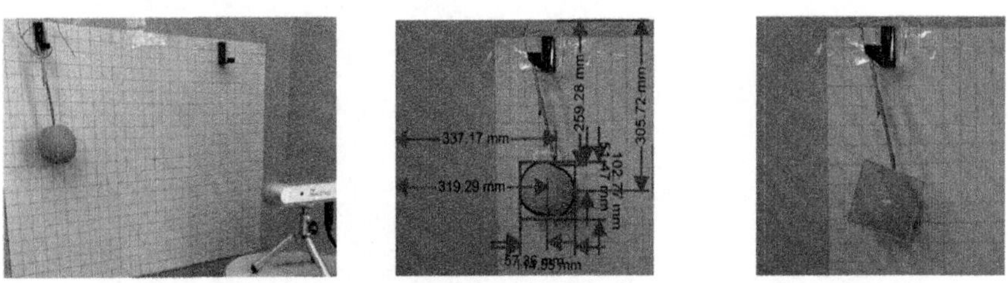

(a) (b) (c)

Fig. 2. Illustration of the methodology for comparing measured values with calculated values. (a) Capture image. (b) Manually Measure Image Localization features using Adobe Acrobat electronic measuring tool. (c) Compare known localization results to detection methodologies detected results.

2.3 Orange Detection and Characterization

Super-resolution is a computer vision algorithm that enhances the quality of low-resolution images by generating missing details through training images. Among the most used super-resolution algorithms are the Super-Resolution Convoluted Neural Network (SRCNN), Enhanced Super Resolution Convoluted Neural Network (ESPCN), and Super-Resolution Generative Adversarial Network (SRGAN). Super resolution demonstrated more consistent and higher recognition performance compared to bilinear and cubic spline interpolation [18]. Due to its promising results and cost-effective capability to enhance low-quality images, SRCNN was selected as the image resolution enhancement technique for this study. MATLAB's comprehensive SRCNN toolbox further supported its selection for this application.

Table 2. List of parameters chosen to build the CNN model.

Parameter	Parameter Value
Network Depth	10
Number of filters	32
Patch Size	256 × 256
Learning Rate	0.0001
Batch Size	1
Epochs	181
Training Data size	1302

Once the orange images were captured by the camera, the images were enhanced using the SRCNN technique. The data used to train the CNN model in this study was obtained from a orange dataset created for image classification [19]. This data set contained 434 high-resolution images of orange fruits under uniform lighting of four orange varieties: Murcott, Ponkan, Tangerine, and Tankan. The 434 images were then augmented by randomly rotating the images, to produce a grand total of 1302 training images. The parameters used to train the CNN model are outlined in Table 2.

Super-Resolution Performance Metrics. There are two main categories of metrics available to assess the image performance of a CNN model: full-reference quality metrics and no-reference quality metrics [20, 21]. Full-reference quality metrics require a pristine reference image for comparison to the super-resolved image, quantifying the image enhancement provided by the super-resolution algorithm. In contrast, no-reference quality metrics do not require a reference image. Instead, they rely on machine learning models trained on databases of pristine images to evaluate the quality improvement of the super-resolution model [22].

The advantage to full-reference quality metrics is their ability to capture subtle differences between images, often aligning more closely with human perception of quality. However, the main drawback is they require a pristine reference image for comparison, which may not be feasible in real-time applications. Conversely, the advantage to no-reference quality metrics is their ability to evaluate the quality of an image without a reference image, which makes them suitable for real time applications. However, their results are generally less accurate than full-reference metrics, which can cause discrepancies with human perception of image quality.

In this work, both full-reference and no-reference quality metrics were employed to evaluate the super-resolution model's ability to recover lost information. The no-reference quality metric selected for this analysis is the Natural Image Quality Evaluator (NIQE). NIQE is calculated by extracting statistical features from the image, which are then compared to a pre-trained model of natural scene statics, resulting in a score that quantifies the deviation from natural image quality. A lower NIQE score indicates better image quality, while a higher score suggests more distortion or unnatural artifacts in the image.

(a) (b) (c) (d)

Fig. 3. Illustrating of the calculation process for full-reference quality metrics. (a) Capture image. (b) Blur the image. (c) Super-resolve the blurred image. (d) Compare (b) and (c) to obtain the metrics.

The other metric used to assess the super-resolution model's ability to recover lost information is the full-reference image metrics. To assess the effectiveness of this technique, a pristine reference image is required as a ground truth for comparing images before and after enhancement. In this study, a pristine reference image was first captured with the Intel RealSense camera, while a blurred version of this original image represents the pre-enhanced image. The super-resolved blurred image, created by applying the super-resolution technique, represents the post-enhancement image. The blurry version was generated by resizing the pristine image, effectively reducing its resolution. The process for obtaining the full-reference quality metrics is described in Fig. 3.

The full-reference quality metrics chosen for this work include Mean Square Error (MSE), Peak-Signal-To-Noise ratio (PSNR), and Structural Similarity Index Metric (SSIM). Higher PSNR and SSIM values, along with a lower MSE value indicate better image quality. The formulas for the MSE, PSNR, and SSIM are outlined in the following equations [21].

$$MSE = \frac{1}{mn}\sum_{i=0}^{m-1}\sum_{j=0}^{n-1}[f(i,j) - g(i,j]^2 \tag{3}$$

$$PSNR = 10 * log_{10}(\frac{255^2}{MSE}) \tag{4}$$

$$SSIM = \frac{(2\mu_x\mu_y + C_1)(2\sigma_{xy} + C_2)}{(\mu_x^2 + \mu_y^2 + C_1)(\sigma_x^2 + \sigma_y^2 + C_2)} \tag{5}$$

where f and g represent the two images, each with a width of m pixels and a height of n pixels, x and y represent the pixels in a 7×7 window from images f and g, respectively.

μ_x and μ_y are the average pixel values within the 7×7 window, σ_{xy} is the covariance of the pixel values in the window, and C_1 and C_2 are constants introduced to stabilize the division with weak denominators.

3 Orange Fruit Image Processing Steps

3.1 Filter Orange Image

After capturing the image and applying super-resolution, a bilateral filtering process was applied to the super-resolved image. Bilateral filtering is a noise reduction technique that preserves edges while smoothing the image. This method was implemented to remove any noise, or artifacts introduced by the super-resolution model before further preprocessing. Figure 4 (a-c) illustrates the filtering process.

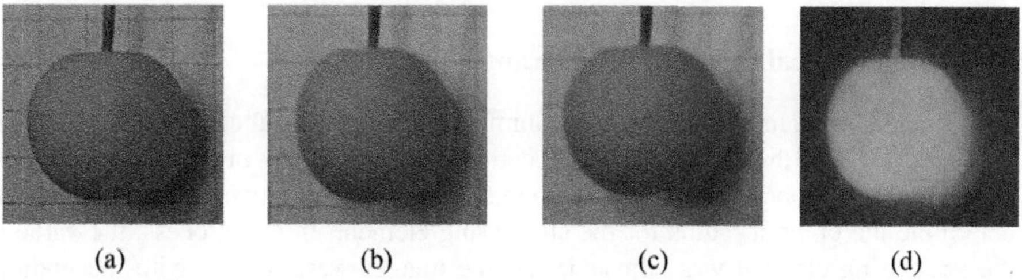

Fig. 4. Image preprocessing illustration showcasing (a) original image, (b) super resolving original image, (c) bilateral filtering super resolved image, and (d) converting filtered image to HSV color space.

3.2 Preprocess Orange Image

The preprocessing stage converts RGB images into HSV color space to more effectively manage variations in lighting and color intensity, as shown in Fig. 4.d. The Hue (H) represents the color type, measured in degrees on a 0° to 360° color wheel and determined by the dominant RGB component, while Saturation (S) indicates the color's intensity or purity and Value (V) component, representing the brightness of the color, is defined as the maximum of the normalized RGB values. The following equations transform an RGB color into its corresponding HSV values:

$$H = \begin{cases} (G - B)/(max - \min), & if \ \max = R \\ 2 + (B - R)/(max - \min), & if \ \max = G \\ 4 + (R - G)/(max - \min), & if \ \max = B \end{cases} \tag{6}$$

$$H = H + 360, ifH < 0 \tag{7}$$

$$S = \begin{cases} (max - \min)/max, & if \ V \neq 0 \\ S = 0, & if \ V = 0 \end{cases} \tag{8}$$

$$V = max \tag{9}$$

where *max* is the maximum color value among the RGB color channels, and *min* is the minimum color value among the RGB color channels.

3.3 Segmentation

To locate the pixels that represented orange fruits, a binary mask was created based upon a predetermined threshold for hue, saturation, and value. The threshold represents a range of color values that an orange fruit can range from. The mask will then assign all pixels in that image with an HSV color value within the threshold range a 1 value, and all pixels that contain HSV values outside of the threshold with a 0 value. This binary mask was then used to extract only the pixels in the image that belonged to the orange fruit.

3.4 Morphological Operations for Orange Image

To further enhance image quality and minimize noise, median filtering techniques were employed to refine the binary mask for locating the oranges. This process helped smooth out the mask contours and reduced noise in the image. An iterative process was used to determine the optimal radius for the structuring element. In this process, the value of the structuring element was adjusted, and the images were filtered with the updated structuring element. After multiple trials, the structuring element that produced the highest accuracy was selected for this work.

In this context, efficiency is defined by the accuracy in detecting complete orange shapes within the image, rather than merely identifying orange-colored regions. For example, in Fig. 5, although 14 orange regions were initially detected, only 2 of these corresponded to oranges that were suitable for harvesting. A higher efficiency would result in the detected regions more closely matching the actual count of 2 usable oranges. Through an analysis of 5 different images and 10 disk sizes, a disk with radius of 8 was determined to be the optimal setting, offering the best balance between noise reduction and detail preservation.

3.5 Extract Orange Features

Following segmentation, MATLAB's contour detection algorithms were employed to determine the boundaries of each orange. Once the contours of the oranges were identified, key features such as area, centroid, and perimeter were extracted using MATLAB function. Specific attention was given to the orange with the largest area within the captured image, as larger fruits are typically more representative and easier to analyze in isolation, providing clearer data for testing and application development (See Figs. 6.a and 6.b). A contour was then drawn around the largest orange to accurately delineate its boundary, which is essential for further analysis. Subsequently, a bounding box was constructed around the same orange, defining a rectangular outline to simplify orientation estimation and spatial analysis (see Fig. 6.c).

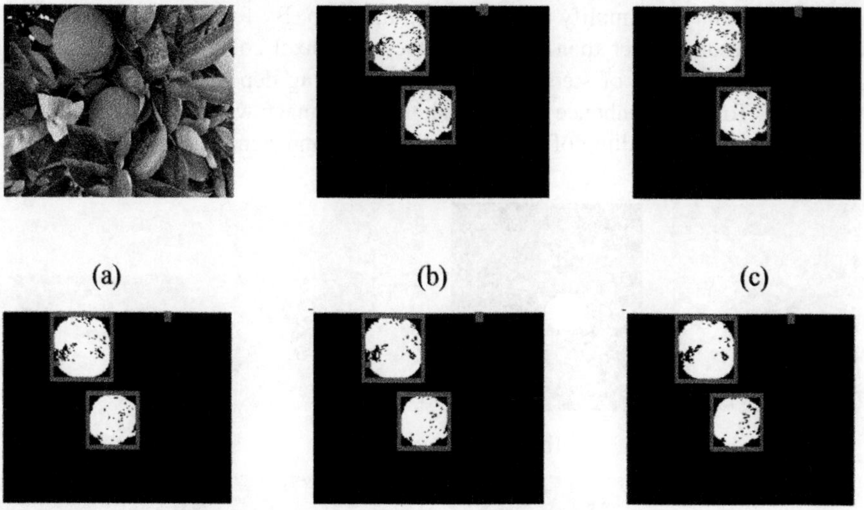

Fig. 5. Filtered orange images with different structuring element sizes, r represents the disk radius: (a) original image. (b) filtered with $r = 2$, (c) filtered with $r = 4$, (d) filtered with $r = 6$, (e) filtered with $r = 8$, and (f) filtered with $r = 9$.

4 Stem Detection and Characterization

4.1 Locate Stem Region

Once the largest orange was detected, the next task was to identify and analyze its stem. To achieve this, a bounding box was positioned above the orange's centroid, adjusted to a predetermined ideal depth and width based on prior testing. This strategic placement was designed to exclusively capture the area where the stem was most likely to be located (See Fig. 6.c).

4.2 Super-Resolve and Filter Stem Region

The cropped stem region was then super-resolved to improve its image quality. The purpose of improving the image quality of the stem region was to achieve more accurate position and orientation measurements of the stem. Once the stem region had been super-resolved, it was filtered using bilateral filtering to reduce any noise that might have been introduced from the super resolution algorithm while still preserving the edges of the image (See Fig. 6.d).

4.3 Preprocess Stem Image

Initially, the stem was attempted to be identified using the HSV color space; however, this approach proved ineffective due to the wide color variation of orange stems, which frequently fell outside the predefined HSV detection ranges. To overcome this challenge, another method was developed that involved capturing images of the oranges against a white background to simplify distinguishing the stem. By focusing on identifying the white background rather than relying on the stem pixel color, this approach offered a more reliable means of stem identification, reducing dependence on color-specific thresholds. To further enhance the method, the stem image was converted to grayscale, allowing for better handling of variations in lighting and stem color.

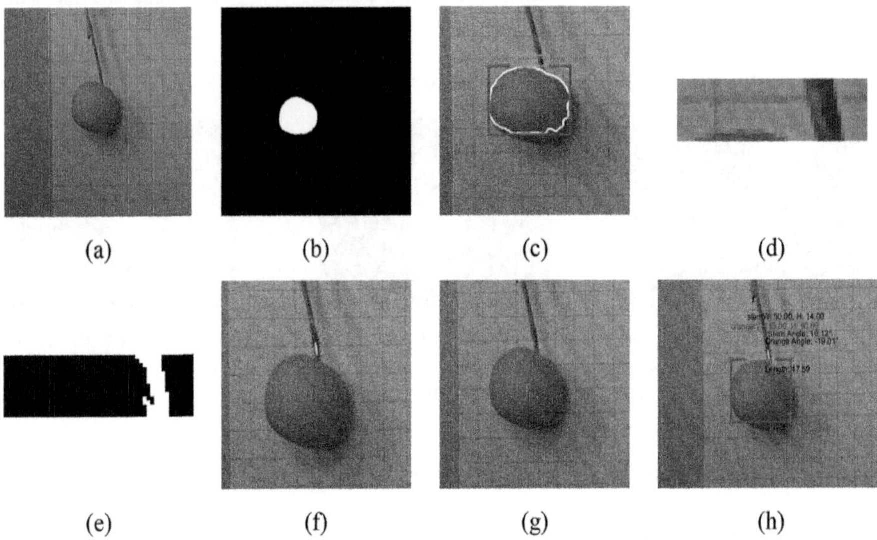

Fig. 6. Illustrating the image capturing, detection, and characterization process. (a) Capture image. (b) Apply a binary mask. (c) Create contour, orange bounding box, and stem search box. (d) Super-resolve stem image. (e) Apply a binary mask to stem image. (f) Calculate stem orientation and coordinates. (g) Calculate the orange orientation. (h) Calculate all other characteristics.

4.4 Locate and Characterize the Stem

To locate the stem within the cropped stem location region, a white binary mask was created to isolate the background. The binary was created by setting a threshold of pixel values that correspond to the backgrounds under varying lighting settings. This binary mask was then applied to remove all non-stem pixels, effectively isolating the stem in the cropped image for further analysis as shown in Figs. 6.d-e.

After isolating the stem, the x and y positions of the stem at the base of the orange was calculated as well as the stem's orientation. With the base location of the stem identified, a line was drawn from the orange's centroid to this base, allowing for the orange's orientation to be calculated, as illustrated in Figs. 6.e-h.

5 Orange Fruit Localization

After calculating the positions of the orange and stem in pixel units, the depths of their centroids were measured using the stereo vision capabilities of the Intel RealSense camera. This depth information enabled the conversion of pixel coordinates into real-world dimensions using the pinhole camera model equations. The pinhole camera model establishes a trigonometric relationship between an object's 3D dimensions and its 2D projection onto the camera's sensor through a pinhole, enabling accurate spatial calculations, as shown in Fig. 7 [22].

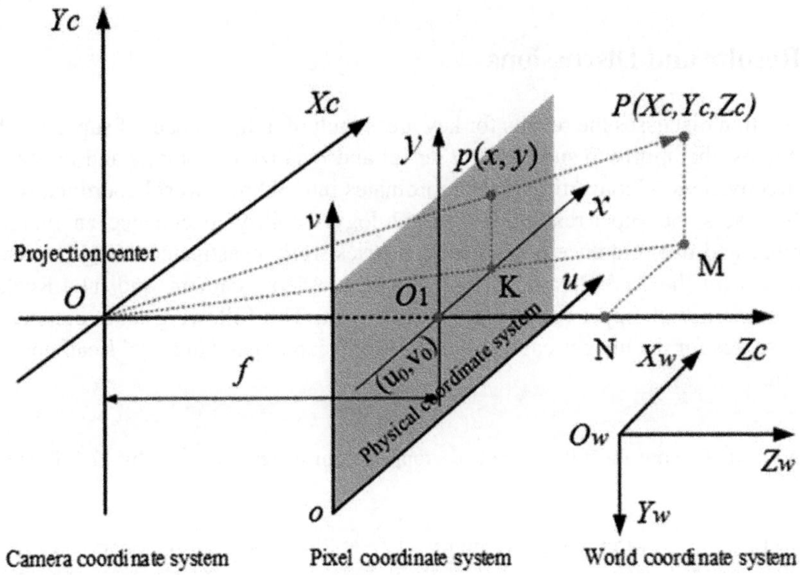

Fig. 7. Trigonometric relationship between 2D projection coordinate system to 3D real world coordinate system using Pinhole Camera Modeling [22].

If the object's depth is known, the 2D pixel coordinates can be converted into 3D real-world coordinates using the following equations [22]:

$$x = f_x \frac{X_c}{Z_c} \tag{10}$$

$$y = f_y \frac{Y_C}{Z_c} \tag{11}$$

where x and y represent the pixel coordinate in the 2D image. f_x and f_y denote the camera's focal length in the x and y directions, respectively. X_c, Y_C, and Z_c correspond to the object's 3D real-work coordinates.

In image processing, pixel coordinates are measured relative to the top-left corner, where the (0,0) point represents the top-left corner of the image. However, in a 3D world coordinate system, it is more conventional to position the origin (0,0) at the center of the image. To align the 2D image coordinate with this 3D convention, the pinhole camera model was adjusted accordingly. The following modified equations (Eq. 10 and 11) were implemented to convert the 2D pixel coordinate to 3D real-world units, with the origin centered at the middle of the image.

$$X_c = \frac{Z_c}{f_x}(x - \mu_0) \tag{12}$$

$$Y_c = \frac{Z_c}{f_y}(y - v_0) \tag{13}$$

where μ_0 is the camera's principal point in the x direction and v_0 is the camera's principal point in the Y direction.

6 Results and Discussions

This section discusses the results for key areas including the impact of super-resolution techniques, the ability to successfully detect and localize the orange and its stem, and the effectiveness of converting pixel coordinates into 3D real-world coordinates.

To assess the super-resolution methodology's ability to enhance an image, no-reference and full-reference performance metrics were investigated. NIQE scores were calculated for the 12 MP camera, Intel RealSense depth camera, and Intel RealSense depth camera with super-resolution enhancement. The following table compares the NIQE scores for the images captured using 12MP camera and the Intel RealSense depth camera.

Table 3. NIQE score for full orange and cropped stem images captured by 12 MP and D457 cameras.

Image Type	12 MP Camera NIQE		D457 Camera NIQE	
	Orange Image	Cropped Stem Image	Orange Image	Cropped Stem Image
Original Image	3.1	6.9	4.4	18.9
Bilateral Filtered Image	3.9	8.6	4.6	18.9
Super-resolved Image	N/A	N/A	5.0	6.4

Table 3 indicates that the 12 MP camera captured the highest-quality original images for both the full orange and the cropped stem scenes, achieving NIQE values of 3.1 and 6.9, respectively. This outcome was expected, given the significantly higher resolution of the 12 MP camera compared to the D457 camera. It can be noted that applying Bilateral Filtering to the full orange and stem images led to a reduction in image quality for the 12 MP camera, whereas the D457 images were less impacted by the filtering process. Applying super-resolution to the D457 camera's cropped stem image significantly improved image quality, reducing the NIQE from 18.9 to 6.4. However, super-resolving the full orange image from the same camera slightly degraded its quality, as the NIQE score increased from 4.4 to 5.0. This increase suggests that the super-resolution techniques were less effective for the full orange image, likely because the original image already had sufficient resolution and did not benefit from additional enhancement.

As mentioned earlier, the blurred version of the original image represents the pre-enhancement image (i.e. blurry image). Localization features were then detected from both the blurry image and the super-resolved blurry image. These detected values were compared to those from the original pristine image, serving as the ground truth. The results were averaged across multiple trials, resolutions, stem orientations, and lighting conditions. Five trials were conducted at stem orientations of 30°, 15°, 0°, –15°, –30°. Additionally, two distinct lighting scenarios were applied. Finally, input image resolution was tested at full, half, and one-fifth resolution. Tables 4 and 5 present the full-reference quality metrics used to evaluate the super-resolution model on the full image and the cropped stem image captured by Intel RealSense camera, respectively.

Table 4. Full-reference quality metrics for the full image produced by Intel RealSense camera.

	MSE Value	MSE % diff from noisy	PSNR Value	PSNR % diff from noisy	SSIM Value	SSIM % diff from noisy
Blurry Image	637.80	N/A	20.08	N/A	0.44	N/A
Bilateral Filtered Image	200.80	68.50	25.15	25.20	0.70	60.10
Super-resolved Image	145.90	77.10	26.56	32.20	0.80	82.20

Table 5. Full-reference quality metrics for the cropped stem image produced by Intel RealSense camera.

	MSE Value	MSE % diff from noisy	PSNR Value	PSNR % diff from noisy	SSIM Value	SSIM % diff from noisy
Blurry Image	643.76	N/A	20.04	N/A	0.55	N/A
Bilateral Filtered Image	200.11	68.90	25.18	25.60	0.78	43.30
Super-resolved Image	290.76	54.80	23.92	19.30	0.84	53.00

A lower MSE, along with higher PSNR and SSIM, correlates to better image quality. Based on the collected data, the super-resolution technique outperformed bilateral filtering by achieving a lower MSE for the full orange image whereas bilateral filtering produced lower MSE value in the stem image. As shown in Table 4 for the full image, the super-resolution method also produced a higher PSNR score of 26.56, compared to the bilateral filtering PSNR score of 25.15. However, for the cropped stem image, bilateral filtering yielded a better PSNR score of 25.18, while the super-resolution achieved a lower PSNR score of 23.92 (see Table 5). Additionally, the super-resolution model delivered a higher SSIM than bilateral filtering for both the full orange image and cropped stem image. Given its lower MSE and higher PSNR and SSIM for the full orange image, it was concluded that super-resolution is a superior enhancement technique compared to bilateral filtering for the full image of the orange. Furthermore, for the cropped stem image, super-resolution demonstrated better performance in reducing noise (reflected by the lower MSE) and preserving structural information (evidenced by the higher SSIM). However, the lower PSNR for the cropped stem image suggests that the super-resolution technique may be introducing artifacts, which negatively affect the PSNR. Despite this, super-resolution was still found to be more effective overall in terms of noise reduction and structure preservation in the stem region.

It is worth noting that the images studied are blurred rather than lacking in detail, suggesting that a bilateral filter may outperform super-resolution in terms of edge preservation. However, in real-world scenarios, images are most likely to lack detail, making super-resolution techniques more effective for enhancing image quality in such cases.

In addition to the full-reference and no-reference performance metrics, the feature measurement accuracy rate was investigated as outlined in Table 6.

Table 6. Feature measurement accuracy rate for a blurry image and super-resolved blurry image.

	Blurry Images	Super-resolved Images
Orange Orientation AVG Error (ε_X)	4.3°	3.9°
Stem Orientation AVG Error (ε_X)	4.1°	3.0°
Orange Centroid x AVG Error (ε_X%)	0.2%	0.3%
Orange Centroid Y AVG Error (ε_X%))	0.4%	0.7%
Orange Width AVG Error (ε_X%))	1.4%	2.1%
Orange Height AVG Error (ε_X%))	1.8%	3.9%
Stem Base x AVG Error (ε_X%))	0.4%	0.5%
Stem Base y AVG Error (ε_X%))	0.8%	0.8%

The results in Table 6 indicate that the super-resolution technique enhanced the accuracy of the extracted orientation values for both the orange and its stem. Specifically, the average error in the stem orientation improved from 4.1° to 3.0°, while the error in the orange orientation decreased from 4.3° to 3.9°, which aligns with the image quality metrics in Tables 4 and 5. While super-resolution enhanced the detection accuracy of orange and stem orientation, it is worthy to note that it did not significantly impact the accuracy of other measurements, as those values remained comparable.

The second set of results investigates the model's effectiveness in accurately detecting and localizing both the orange and its stem, showcasing its potential for precise agricultural applications. Following the procedure outlined in the Methodology section, the average results were obtained as shown in Table 7.

Table 7 shows that the accuracy rates for the 12 MP camera and the D457 camera used in this study are comparable. This result corroborates Liu's decision in selecting a RealSense depth camera and the Intel RealSense depth camera's effectiveness with orange localization [10].

Table 7. Feature measurement accuracy rate for the 12 MP camera and the D457 camera.

	12 MP Camera	D457 Camera
Orange Orientation (ε_X)	4.3°	4.2 °
Stem Orientation (ε_X)	3.8 °	4.5 °
Orange centroid x location (ε_X %)	0.3%	0.2%
Orange Centroid Y (ε_X %)	0.7%	0.4%
Orange width (ε_X %)	1.1%	0.9%
Orange Height (ε_X %)	4.9%	1.7%
Stem base x location (ε_X %)	0.7%	0.3%
stem base y location (ε_X %)	1.0%	0.7%

Lastly, to evaluate the accuracy of converting pixel coordinates to 3D coordinates using the pinhole camera model, six test were conducted. These tests measured both the detected *x* and *y* coordinates of the orange centroids and their corresponding measured x and y coordinates (See Table 8).

Table 8. Detected and measured orange centroid locations using the pinhole camera model.

Test Trial	ε_x	ε_y
1	0.1 in	0.3 in
2	0.1 in	0.1 in
3	0.4 in	0.1 in
4	0.2 in	0.1 in
5	0.1 in	0.1 in
6	0.0 in	0.1 in

The results from the pinhole camera models closely matched the known measured values, with an average difference of 0.15 inches in the *x* centroid location and 0.13 inches in the *y* centroid location, including the notable deviation in trail # 3. This deviation may have been caused by manual measurement errors, likely due the challenge of precisely locating the exact centroid of the orange in Adobe Acrobat.

7 Conclusions and Future Work

A key challenge in orange automation is accurately detecting and localizing both oranges and their stems under varying lighting conditions. This paper presents an advanced image detection method using a single RGB-D camera. Additionally, it evaluates SRCNN's effectiveness in improving detection accuracy for low-resolution images. The evaluation approaches compare the performance metrics across three image-capturing methods: a high-resolution mobile-phone camera, Intel RealSense depth camera, and Intel RealSense depth camera with super-resolution enhancement.

Based on these NIQE results, it can be concluded that the 12 MP camera produces the highest quality original images, and the super-resolution technique is most effective when applied to the cropped stem region, rather than the entire image that contains both the orange and the stem. Furthermore, super-resolution enhancement technique was found to be more effective overall in terms of noise reduction and structure preservation in the stem region. For the cropped stem region, super-resolution effectively reduced noise (with lower MSE) and preserved structural information (higher SSIM). However, super-resolution resulted in a lower PSNR compared to bilateral filtering, likely due to introduced artifacts by the super-resolution process. The detection methodology produced orientation and dimensional results within 10° and 5% of known values. Using pinhole camera model for 3D localization yielded a maximum error of 0.4 inches from the actual value.

A key challenge with the proposed methodology lies in stem identification, as the detection model currently relies on a white background, a condition not representative of orange fruits growing on a tree. Future work should focus on enhancing this methodology to enable reliable stem detection against more natural, non-white background, aligning with real-world conditions.

Acknowledgments. The work was partially supported by the Economic Development Administration (EDA) Project Grant 077907908, Fresno-Merced Future of Food Innovation (F3) Coalition.

References

1. Kuta, L., Li, Z., Stopa, R., Komarnicki, P., Slupska, M.: The influence of manual harvesting on the quality of picked apples and the Picker's muscle load. Comput. Electron. Agric. **175**, 105511 (2020). ISSN 0168–1699. https://doi.org/10.1016/j.compag.2020.105511
2. Jimenez, A., Ceres, R., Pons, J.: A survey of computer vison methods for locating fruit on trees. Trans. ASABE **43**, 1911–1920 (2000). https://doi.org/10.13031/2013.3096
3. Fu, L., Gao, F., Wu, J., Li, R., Karkee, M., Zhang, Q.: Application of consumer RGB-D cameras for fruit detection and localization in field: a critical review. Comput. Electron. Agric. **177**, 105687 (2020). https://doi.org/10.1016/j.compag.2020.105687
4. Hannan, M.W., Burks, T.F., Bulanon, D.M.: A machine vision algorithm combining adaptive segmentation and shape analysis for orange fruit detection. Agric. Eng. Int.: CIGR J. **XI** (2009)
5. McCarthy, C.L., Hancock, N.H., Raine, S.R.: Applied machine vision of plants: a review with implications for field deployment in automated farming operations. Intell. Serv. Robot. **3**, 209–217 (2010). https://doi.org/10.1007/s11370-010-0075-2
6. Changhui, Y., Youcheng, H., Lin, H., Sa, L., Yanping, L.: Overlapped fruit recognition for citrus harvesting robot in natural scenes. In: 2017 2nd International Conference on Robotics and Automation Engineering (ICRAE), Shanghai, China, pp. 398–402, 2017. https://doi.org/10.1109/ICRAE.2017.8291418

7. Jimenez, A.R., Ceres, R., Pons, J.L.: A machine vision system using a laser radar applied to robotic fruit harvesting. In: Proceedings of the IEEE Workshop on Computer Vision Beyond the Visible Spectrum: Methods and Applications (CVBVS'99), Hilton Head, SC, pp. 110–119, 1999
8. Jimenez, A.R., Ceres, R., Pons, J.L.: A vision system based on a laser range-finder applied to robotic fruit harvesting. Mach. Vis. Appl. **11**, 321–329 (2000)
9. Thendral, R., Suhasini, A., Senthil, N.: A comparative analysis of edge and color based segmentation for orange fruit recognition. In: 2014 International Conference on Communication and Signal Processing, Melmaruvathur, India, 2014, pp. 463–466, 2014. https://doi.org/10.1109/ICCSP.2014.6949884
10. Liu, J., Yuan, Y., Zhou, Y., Zhu, X., Syed, T.N.: Experiments and analysis of close-shot identification of on-branch citrus fruit with realSense. Sensors (5), 1510 (2018). https://doi.org/10.3390/s18051510
11. Dorj, U.O., Lee, M., Yun, S.S.: An yield estimation in citrus orchards via fruit detection and counting using image processing. Comput. Electron. Agric. **140**, 103–112 (2017). https://doi.org/10.1016/j.compag.2017.05.019
12. Ukwuoma, C.C., Zhiguang, Q., Bin Heyat, M.B., Liaqat, A., Almaspoor, Z., Monday, H.N.: Recent advancements in fruit detection and classification using deep learning techniques. Math. Probl. Eng. Article ID 9210947, 29 (2022). https://doi.org/10.1155/2022/9210947
13. Jiang, Z., Das Choudhury, S., Roychowdhury, A., Sarkar, S.: High-throughput plant phenotyping using deep learning. Front. Plant Sci. **14**, 1292483 (2023). https://pmc.ncbi.nlm.nih.gov/articles/PMC11204869/
14. Wang, X., et al.: A review of image super-resolution approaches based on deep learning and applications in remote sensing. Remote Sensing **14**(21), 5423 (2022). https://doi.org/10.3390/rs14215423
15. Intel Realsense, 2024. https://www.intelRealSense.com/depth-camera-d457/
16. Tadic, V., et al.: Perspectives of RealSense and ZED depth sensors for robotic vision applications. Machines **10**(3), 183 (2022). https://doi.org/10.3390/machines10030183
17. Sun, B., Liu, K., Feng, L., Peng, H., Yang, Z.: The surface defects detection of citrus on trees based on a support vector machine. Agronomy **13**, 43 (2023). https://doi.org/10.3390/agronomy13010043
18. Lin, F., Fookes, C., Chandran, V., Sridharan, S.: Super-Resolved Faces for Improved Face Recognition from Surveillance Video. Advances in Biometrics **4642**, 1 (2007). https://doi.org/10.1007/978-3-540-74549-5_1
19. Huang, M.L., Chen, Y.A.: Citrus dataset for image classification. Data Brief **51**, 109628 (2023). https://doi.org/10.1016/j.dib.2023.109628
20. Yamamoto, K., Togami, T., Yamaguchi, N.: Super-resolution of plant disease images for the acceleration of image-based phenotyping and vigor diagnosis in agriculture. Sensors **17**, 2557 (2017). https://doi.org/10.3390/s17112557
21. Ma, C., Yang, C.Y., Yang, X., Yang, M.H.: Learning a no-reference quality metric for single-image super-resolution. Comput. Vis. Image Underst. **158**, 1–16 (2017). https://doi.org/10.1016/j.cviu.2016.12.009
22. Yang, C.H., et al.: Integrated detection of citrus fruits and branches using a convolutional neural network. Comput. Electron. Agric.. Electron. Agric. **174**, 105469 (2020). https://doi.org/10.1016/j.compag.2020.105469

Scene-Aware Prediction of Diverse Human Movement Goals

Qiaoyue Yang[1(✉)], Amadeus Weber[1], Magnus Jung[2], Ayoub Al-Hamadi[2], and Sven Wachsmuth[1]

[1] COSY@Home-Lab, Faculty of Technology, Bielefeld University, 33619 Bielefeld, Germany
{qyang,amweber,swachsmuth}@techfak.uni-bielefeld.de

[2] Institute for Information Technology and Communications (IIKT), Otto von Guericke University Magdeburg, 39106 Magdeburg, Germany
{magnus.jung,ayoub.al-hamadi}@ovgu.de

Abstract. Anticipation of human behaviours facilitates autonomous systems in proactive planning. Human behaviour could be stochastic due to varying goals. Human goals typically guide their own movement and could therefore help to predict the human trajectory and human motion in the long-term. To infer the human movement intentions, the environmental context plays a significant role, in addition to the social cues expressed by the individual. Previous works on human goals prediction either require semantic knowledge of the scene, or only tackle interactions with objects. In this paper, we propose a novel multi-goal prediction method using the generative model to address the stochasticity of human movement. It leverages the current RGB scene and the human pose to predict diverse potential future goals of human movement based on the Conditional Variational Autoencoder (CVAE). Our results demonstrate that our approach is capable of generating multiple movement goals in the scene via samplings in latent space of the CVAE and exhibits generalization capability across scenarios in GTA-IM dataset and PROX dataset. Code is publicly available at https://github.com/Q-Y-Yang/DiverseGoalsPrediction.git.

Keywords: Human intentions · Human goals prediction · Probablistic motion prediction · Variational autoencoder

1 Introduction

Human behaviour is inherently stochastic, for example, a person could suddenly change his or her mind while being engaged in an activity. But this is often driven by goals. To understand human movement intentions, human trajectory prediction resolves 2D waypoints along the path and human motion/pose prediction tackles 3D full body motion. In order to cover uncertainties in the future, probabilistic forecasting attracts more attention than deterministic methods [30, 31].

J. Röning and J. Filipe (Eds.): ROBOVIS 2025, CCIS 2629, pp. 312–327, 2026.
https://doi.org/10.1007/978-3-032-00986-9_21

Long-term human trajectory can be planned conditioned on the future movement destinations [1,3,5,26], and these waypoints also contribute to the accuracy of long-term human motion predictions [2,4]. The intention of a person is often implicitly hidden in the mind because people do not always express them verbally. But it is usually associated with the surrounding environment, for example, the desire to interact with a specific object such as a table, chair, cup, coffee machine, fridge, etc. [6], or to navigate in the environment such as passing through a doorway and walking up the stairs.

In human robot cooperation, it is imperative for robots to possess visual perception capabilities towards humans as partners, rather than merely detecting humans as common obstacles. For instance, these applies to environments where humans and robots coexist, such as public areas like museums and shops where robots provide services to customers [7], and home scenarios where robots perform as a helper to healthcare [7] and housework. In robot navigation, a multilayer costmap [32] is usually deployed to guide the global and local planning. Among them, a social navigation layer [33] provides the possibility to adjust the costs for navigating around humans. Predicting potential goals of human partners benefits the robot's behavioral planning in a proactive and safe way, for instance, avoiding impeding the potential movement areas of human counterparts in advance [6]. Besides, in autonomous driving, self-driving cars should also be capable of anticipating pedestrians' potential movement destinations, in order to react in advance to avoid accidents.

Possible human goals in the scenario could help overcome the difficulty of long-term forecasting of human trajectories and human motions by serving as priors. These future goals could also directly benefit proactive autonomous systems. In this work, we propose a method based on Conditional Variational Autoencoders (CVAE) that forecasts scene-aware future goals of the human movement from only a single frame of the current scene and the human pose. Figure 1 demonstrates scene-compliant predictions of the human movement goals. The contributions of this paper can be summarized as:

(1) An end-to-end method for predicting scene-compliant targets of long-term human motion, based on the current RGB scene image and the human pose.
(2) Addressing stochastic nature of human behaviour by anticipating multiple possible targets, without the need for multiple goal positions as labels.

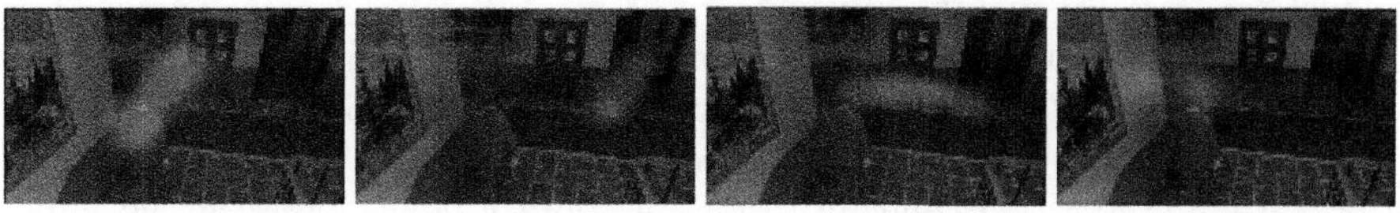

(a) (b) (c) (d)

Fig. 1. Predictions of possible movement areas in the future. (a) The subject walks straight to the door. (b) The subject turns right towards the doors. (c) The subject turns right into the corridor. (d) The subject turns left into the corridor.

2 Related Work

Goal-directed Forecasting. Previous works leverage goal prediction to address long-term human trajectory and motion prediction problems [1–5,26,28,29]. [28, 29] forecast deterministic human motion along a set of contact points in the scene point cloud, but they do not take into account multiple potential human intentions. [2] predict human motion goals based on a sequence of heatmaps of past human joints and a scene image to benefit long term 3D motion prediction. However, a set of joint heatmaps during a past time slot might not fit in a single scene frame because the scene may have changed over time. Additionally, generating a sequence of heatmaps of human joints is not computational efficient during inference on the real robot, because the time required increases linearly with the number of heatmaps. In the real application, the requirement for a fixed length of history reduces flexibility, i.e. the prediction system can only work if such a length of history is available. [27] also utilizes a series of observed 2D human poses and images to forecast 3D human poses. However, it only predicts a fixed future path and poses, neglecting the inherent stochasticity of human behaviors.

In outdoor scenarios from bird view, a semantic map is often required to incorporate scene information and derive movement goals. For instance, Y-net [3] uses a semantic segmentation map of the scene and the past trajectory to forecast goals and waypoints based on U-Net architectures. The SNS-LSTM model [5] takes the observed trajectory, a navigation map and a semantic map as inputs to extract future positions by LSTM (long short-term memory). GoalGAN [8] also firstly predicts goals via a convolutional neural network (CNN) from an RGB scene and dynamic features of the pedestrian. PECNet [1] proposes an endpoint variational autoencoder (VAE) to predict final goals of all pedestrians based on history trajectories and ground truth endpoints, but the ground truth endpoints are not available during inference. [26] divides the boundary of the scene into grids as potential destinations. However, other areas of the scene are neglected and dividing into grids could corrupt the scene information by introducing artifacts.

In home scenarios, the layout of the environment could be changed more frequently, compared to public environments such as streets, museums, and train stations. For instance, tables and chairs at home can be easily moved. If the forecasting relies on a pre-established model of the environment, then the home model has to be frequently adjusted.

In addition, some approaches concentrate on human object interactions. The probabilistic transition model [6] predicts the human's navigation goal in accordance with past human poses and object interactions. [4] propose a GoalNet that estimates positions and directions of contact points between the human and the interactive object with known object geometry. Nevertheless, they can only handle targets related to interactive objects, and do not cover other aspects of an entire scene.

Variational Autoencoders (VAEs). VAE as one of the generative models has achieved promising performances in various applications such as image reconstruction, image generation, representation learning, semi-supervised learning, anomaly detection, and data augmentation [21]. An Autoencoder (AE) learns a compressed representation of the input data via an encoder network and reconstructs the input from that compressed latent space through a decoder network [23]. VAE [10] further extends the compressed space to a probabilistic distribution such as a Gaussian distribution and generates new samples from that distribution. The Conditional Variational Autoencoder (CVAE) [22] was originally proposed to generate new handwritten digits from the MNIST dataset by conditioning on 10 classes of digits. It further proved great performances in face image manipulation conditioned on a set of face attributes such as gender, expression, hair colour, age, and eyewear etc. [24].

3 Proposed Method

3.1 Problem Formulation

The problem we address in this work is to predict human movement goals G in the future time T from the perspective of the current time 0. To cover the stochastic nature of human behaviour, multiple goals G_T^F should be resolved, given the human H_0 and the scene S_0 at zero time, as in Eq. 1. The future time horizon is defined by a criterion that the future position at time T is already present in the scene at time 0.

$$(S_0, H_0) \rightarrow G_T^F. \tag{1}$$

3.2 Proposed Approach

Our approach forecasts interactive goals by learning features of goal areas, such as walking along a corridor, going towards a chair, instead of relying on a past trajectory as previous methods did. Given a past trajectory, it is possible to calculate the speed and direction of movement, and therefore estimate the future position. However, this only works if a fixed-length history is available and if the person does not change their mind during this time period. Instead, our approach predicts potential interaction goals in the scene at every moment by sampling in a 200-dimensional latent space.

Figure 2 illustrates the overall pipeline of our approach. The model $\mathcal{F}$ takes a scene image S_0 and a heatmap of human joints $H_{J,0}$ at current time 0 as inputs, to anticipate multiple goals G_T^F with corresponding confidence scores C_T^F at frame T in the future,

$$\left(G_T^F, C_T^F\right) = \mathcal{F}\left(S_0, H_{J,0}\right), \tag{2}$$

where F refers to the number of forecasts, and T is defined to 2 s in our case.

Concretely, the encoder $\mathcal{F}_{encode}$ learns a latent vector z from the inputs, and the decoder $\mathcal{F}_{decode}$ predicts goal heatmaps $\hat{H}_{G,T}$ at frame T from the samplings of the latent vector z with the condition of the joint heatmap $H_{J,0}$,

$$z \sim \mathcal{N}(0, \mathbf{I}) = \mathcal{F}_{encode}(S_0, H_{J,0}), \tag{3}$$

$$\hat{H}_{G,T} = \mathcal{F}_{decode}(H_{J,0}, z). \tag{4}$$

The assumption of the Gaussian distribution for the approximated posterior $q_{encode}(\mathbf{z} \mid (S_0, H_{J,0}))$ makes gradient decent more efficient [21]. The distribution of the latent variable $p(\mathbf{z})$ is also assumed to be a high-dimensional mixture of Gaussians with zero mean and unit variance $\mathcal{N}(0, \mathbf{I})$ [20]. The dimension of our latent vector $\mathbf{z}$ is set to 200, since higher dimensions have stronger capability to represent complex features of scenes [12,13]. Lighter areas of the output $\hat{H}_{G,T}$ indicate higher probabilities of being goal areas.

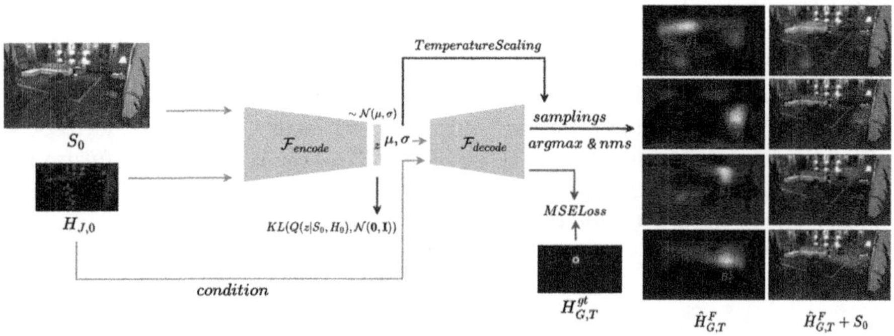

Fig. 2. Method. The encoder takes a scene image and a heatmap of human joints as input. The encoded latent vector z and the heatmap of human joints as condition are fed to the decoder. In the training stage, the MSE loss between the ground truth goal heatmap and the decoder output, and the KL divergence between the posterior of z and the Gaussian distribution are computed to optimise the weights of the CVAE (blue arrows only exist during training). During inference, temperature scaling is used to generate multiple samples as diverse goal areas (purple arrows only work during inference). The results $\hat{H}^F_{G,T}$ show the predicted destination in the sofa, the chair, the desk and the way to another room respectively (from top to bottom).

3.3 Training and Loss Function

We use the torso position at time T as the ground truth goal position at time 0 and generate the corresponding ground truth goal heatmap $H^{gt}_{G,T}$, so that manual labelling is not necessary. In particular, our method does not require labelling of multiple goals within the scene, despite the capability to predict various goals.

The model is trained with a loss function L consisting of a KL-divergence L_{KL} between the variational posterior $q_{encode}(\mathbf{z} \mid (S_0, H_{J,0}))$ of encoder and a normal distribution $\mathcal{N}(\mu, \sigma\mathbf{I})$, and Mean Squared Error (MSE) L_{MSE} between the predicted goal heatmap $\hat{H}_{G,T}$ and the ground truth goal heatmap $H^{gt}_{G,T}$,

$$L = L_{KL} + L_{MSE}, \tag{5}$$

$$L_{KL} = KL[q_{encode}(\mathbf{z} \mid (S_0, H_{J,0}))||\mathcal{N}(\mu, \sigma\mathbf{I})], \tag{6}$$

$$L_{MSE} = MSE(\hat{H}_{G,T}, H^{gt}_{G,T}). \tag{7}$$

Unlike other goal prediction methods [2,8], a L_2 loss that measures distance between the predicted goal position and the ground truth goal position is not chosen in our approach. Our ground truth is not just a coordinate of the target position, but a heatmap generated by a Gaussian distribution centred on the target coordinate. The size of the generated goal area is determined by the criterion that the features of the target area are covered. A too large area of the ground truth goal results in greater inaccuracy of goal positions and a too small area lacks features. The purpose of using MSE loss between the predicted and ground truth heatmaps is to implicitly learn features of goal areas from the scene, which benefits the generalization of predictions. Comparably, [8] uses a cross entropy loss for the probability that a predicted grid cell corresponds to the ground-truth goal. However, the grid segmentation of the scene could corrupt spatial information, for instance, a door may be divided into two or more grid cells.

3.4 Inference via Generation

We generate more than one prediction $\hat{H}^{(f)}_{G,T}$ via temperature scaling (changing the variance σ of the latent vector z) [15] to address the stochasticity of human behaviour during inference, even though the ground truth goal is only fixed during training. Equation 8 describes the reparametrization trick [10] of VAE with temperature scaling:

$$z = \mu + \sigma \cdot \varepsilon \cdot \tau, \tag{8}$$

where $\varepsilon \sim N(0, 1)$ works as white noise, τ refers to the temperature that controls diversity of generation. A higher scaling τ leads to more variety to cover potential possibilities for future goals. It turns to deterministic prediction when $\tau \to 1$, which can be applied to scenes such as stair climbing where there are not many behavioural options.

In the post-processing stage, bounding boxes of possible goal areas B^N_T are extracted by selecting N $argmax$ of each generated goal heatmap $\hat{H}^{(f)}_{G,T}$ (Eq. 9). These raw bounding boxes B^N_T are then merged by performing non-maximal suppression (NMS) [11] to propose M bounding boxes predictions B^M_T with corresponding confidence scores C^M_T (Eq. 10). The purpose of this is to take into account local maxima rather than solely extracting one $argmax$, as the output heatmap often displays multiple local maxima. Finally, each predicted goal $G_T^{(m)}$ is extracted by *argmax* operation from every proposed bounding box $B_T^{(m)}$ (Eq. 11). The goals G_T^M can be ranked by their corresponding confidence scores C_T^M, and the goal with the highest confidence score can be selected as a final prediction. In particular, the size of the bounding boxes is determined by the size of the ground truth target area, the former being slightly larger than the latter to ensure that the bounding boxes are able to detect the region of interest.

$$B_T^N = argmax(\hat{H}_{G,T}^{(f)}), \tag{9}$$

$$B_T^M, C_T^M = NMS(B_T^N), \tag{10}$$

$$G_T^M = argmax(B_T^M), \tag{11}$$

where N denotes the number of raw bounding boxes, and M denotes the number of proposed bounding boxes with the corresponding confidence scores.

4 Experiments

4.1 Experimental Setups

Datasets. GTA Indoor Motion dataset (GTA-IM) [2] is a synthetic dataset that contains various human behaviors such as going upstairs and downstairs, walking towards another room, going to sit on a chair or sofa, lying on a bed, going to drink in the kitchen, etc. It also includes 10 different scenes, multiple subjects, and provides 21 human joints positions in the camera coordinate and in the world coordinate. Notably, the camera in the GTA game engine moves along with the subject so that it keeps capturing the human, which is similar with cameras on mobile robots rather than fixed cameras in the space. PROX (Proximal Relationships with Object eXclusion) [25] is a real-world dataset that records human movements in and interactions with the world. It includes 12 scenarios such as bedrooms, living rooms, offices, and sitting booths [25]. 10 of these were used for training, and the remaining two scenarios were used to test the model's ability to generalise across scenes. Compared to the synthetic GTA-IM dataset [2], the scenes of PROX data are more compact and disordered. For instance, more pieces of furniture are placed in the room, facing in different directions.

Evaluation Metric. Final Displacement Error (FDE) [16] measures average Euclidean distance between predicted and ground truth goals (endpoints). This metric is frequently deployed in trajectory prediction to assess the accuracy of destination forecasts, so it is also highly applicable to our research. FDE_{avg}, as in Eq. 12, computes the average error across multiple goal predictions for each test data, and then averages these errors over the entire test set. FDE_{min}, as in Eq. 13, selects the prediction with the smallest error for each test data and then averages these minimal errors across all test data. The assessment is performed in 2D image space in pixels.

$$FDE_{avg} = \frac{1}{S}\frac{1}{F}\sum_{s=1}^{S}\sum_{f=1}^{F}\min_{m}\|G_T^{gt} - G_T^{(s,f,m)}\|_2, \quad (12)$$

$$FDE_{min} = \frac{1}{S}\sum_{s=1}^{S}\min_{f}\min_{m}\|G_T^{gt} - G_T^{(s,f,m)}\|_2, \quad (13)$$

where S refers to the set of test data and F refers to the number of probabilistic forecasts for the test data. G_T^{gt} and G_T represent the ground truth goal coordinate and the predicted goal coordinate respectively. m denotes the local maxima that yields the minimal error of every forecast f. For deterministic goal prediction, F equals to 1, and $F = 3, 5, 10$ are evaluated for probabilistic prediction.

Baseline. Given the limited research on probabilistic destination forecasting in indoor scenarios, we compare our Goal CVAE with the GoalNet [2] in GTA-IM dataset and PROX dataset. GoalNet [2] was reproduced since it is not open-sourced, and we retrained and evaluated under the same conditions as our method. Since the baseline does not provide the information how to generate probabilistic forecasts in their paper, we deployed our Inference via Generation as explained in Sect. 3.4 on the baseline model. A 1-second history was used by the GoalNet [2] to predict destinations 2 s ahead.

Implementation Details. Our work is implemented in PyTorch [19], trained with the ADAM optimizer [18]. 2 Epochs were trained with a batch size of 64 on NVIDIA GeForce GTX 1060. Learning rate is 10^{-4}. In order to avoid overfitting and ensure the diversity of our predictions, the frames per second (FPS) of training data was reduced to 5, so that there are fewer duplicate inputs.

4.2 Results

Qualitative Analysis

Deterministic Predictions. Our CVAE also shows promising results for deterministic target prediction without temperature scaling. Figure 3 (a) and (b) present single forecasts in scenes where only one fixed behaviour can be performed. The prediction errors of these two scenes are 5 and 2 pixels respectively. Figure 4 shows goal heatmaps of deterministic predictions and the corresponding scenes in the real world. One subject is going to the table and the other continues to lie on the bed.

(a) (b)

Fig. 3. Deterministic Predictions in GTA-IM. Within the bounding boxes of the predicted goal areas, the red dots represent the predicted goal positions and the green dots represent the ground truth goal positions. (a) Climbing stair. (b) Standing still. (Color figure online)

Fig. 4. Deterministic Predictions in PROX. The left column displays the predicted goal heatmaps, from which the goal areas are extracted. The right column presents the corresponding scenes with the predicted goals.

Probabilistic Predictions. When the temperature $\tau > 1$, the model turns to generative prediction. As shown in Fig. 5, there is a trend towards more diversity as τ increases, with more forecasts being delivered. Figure 6 presents various predictions with increasing temperature τ in the real world. A larger τ covers more possibilities of potential goals within the scene.

Fig. 5. Probabilistic Predictions in GTA-IM. From left to right by column, the temperature $\tau = 1, 200, 500$. $\tau = 1$ means deterministic prediction.

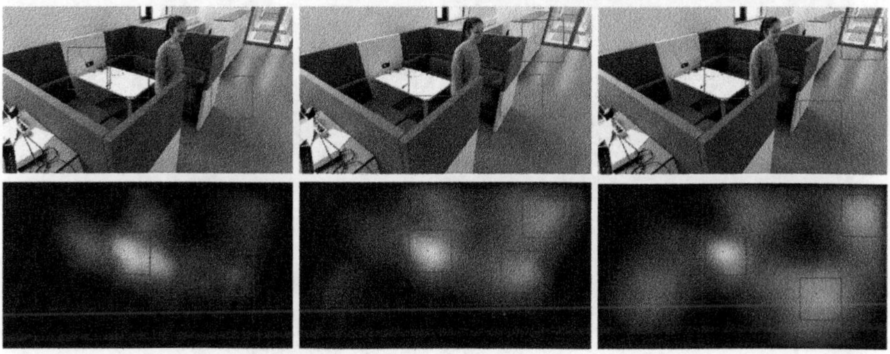

Fig. 6. Probabilistic Predictions in PROX. From top to bottom by row, the temperature $\tau = 100, 200, 300$. The subject would turn left and walk through the open space to the door, or back to the table behind.

Generalization across Scenarios. Although our model is trained on real movement sequences of subjects without diverse manual labels, it shows generalization to behavioural options that never happened and to scenes unseen during training. Figure 7 (a) anticipates the sofa as one of the potential target areas, even though the subjects never go to this sofa in our training data. Figure 7 (b) is a bedroom not encompassed within our training dataset, but our model still delivers highly plausible forecasts. In this moment, the subject could either go to the bed or sit on the chair positioned behind. Two scenes of PROX dataset that are not seen during training, as shown in Fig. 8, also yield promising predictions. In particular, the bedroom depicted at the bottom right of Fig. 8 has a relatively compact layout.

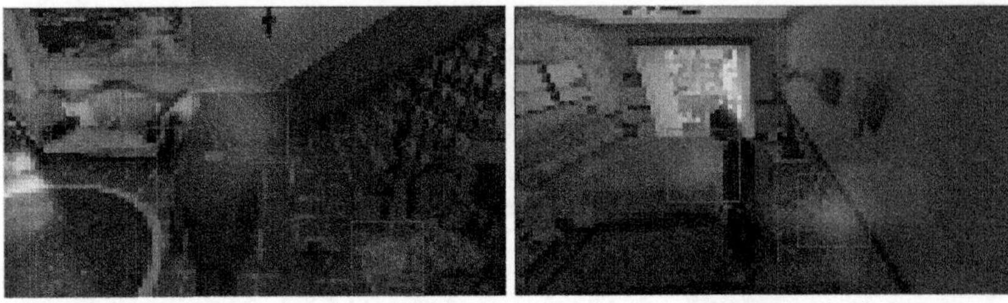

(a) (b)

Fig. 7. Generalization across Scenarios in GTA-IM. (a) Generalisation to interactive objects. (b) Generalisation to unseen scenes.

Fig. 8. Generalization across Scenarios in PROX. Predictions in scenarios not seen during training. (Top) The subject walks through the open space. (Bottom) The subject sits on the chair, or may go to the bed.

Table 1. The final displacement errors (FDEs) in pixel of our model compared to the baseline [2] in GTA-IM dataset and PROX dataset. The lower, the better. We set the temperature τ to 100 in the evaluation of probabilistic predictions.

	GTA-IM				PROX			
Method	$F=1$	$F=3$	$F=5$	$F=10$	$F=1$	$F=3$	$F=5$	$F=10$
GoalNet (min)	22.5	23.4	22.7	17.1	24.4	27.0	24.9	21.5
Ours (min)	**10.9**	**7.9**	**6.8**	**5.2**	**10.38**	**7.0**	**6.2**	**5.4**
GoalNet (avg)	–	38.2	37.9	38.3	–	40.1	39.9	39.5
Ours (avg)	–	**13.1**	**13.3**	**12.9**	–	**10.1**	**10.1**	**10.0**

Quantitative Analysis. Average final displacement errors ($FDEs_{avg}$) and minimal final displacement errors ($FDEs_{min}$) are analyzed as defined in Eq. 12 and 13. Table 1 lists the FDEs of deterministic prediction ($F = 1$) and probabilistic prediction with varying numbers of samples ($F = 3, 5, 10$) for our method and the baseline in GTA-IM and PROX dataset respectively. Overall, our minimal and average errors in both probabilistic and deterministic forecasting are significantly lower than the baseline in both benchmarking datasets. Our $FDEs_{min}$ continue to decrease as the number of forecasts increases, indicating that more accurate predictions are generated. Our $FDEs_{avg}$ remain nearly constant even with the increasing number of forecasts, showing that the generation quality is stable, as the temperature parameter τ remains constant during this evaluation.

Moreover, in order to enable real-time deployment of our model on edge devices for robotic applications, the Average Inference Time (AIT) was also measured. Our average inference time of 43.8 ms guarantees real-time capability for applications, and is also around 11% faster than the baseline, as listed in Table 2.

Table 2. Average Inference Time (AIT) in millisecond of our model and the baseline [2].

Method	GoalNet	Ours
Average Inference Time (AIT)	49.4	**43.8**

Ablation Study. We conducted ablation studies to test the effects of the components in our method, as listed in Table 3. First, the dimension of the latent space was investigated. With a smaller dimension of latent space, the performance of deterministic and probabilistic predictions is worse, indicating that 30 dimensions are not sufficient to represent features.

Table 3. Ablation Studies. ✗ denotes the impossibility of generating predictions. $F = 3$ in the evaluation of probabilistic prediction.

Method	Deterministic Prediction		Probabilistic Prediction	
	FDE_{min} (GTA)	FDE_{min} (PROX)	FDE_{min} (GTA)	FDE_{min} (PROX)
Ours (Z = 30)	15.6	14.9	12.9	12.3
Ours (condition on history trajectory)	18.3	15.5	✗	✗
Ours (condition on torso heatmap)	13.3	12.4	✗	✗
w/o condition	✗	✗	✗	✗
w/o multi-maxima	20.4	21.3	17.7	19.1
Our full model	10.9	10.3	7.9	7.0

Second, we tested different conditions of the CVAE. Our model, whether conditioned on the human history trajectory, a torso heatmap, or left unconditioned, is not capable of probabilistic prediction, because it cannot generate multiple maxima. In particular, when conditioning on a set of human trajectory points, it is easy to overfit to positions close to the last trajectory point in the history, indicating that the scene context does not contribute to the prediction. Its deterministic forecasting is also less accurate. Conditioning on a torso heatmap means $H_{J,0}$ only contains one Gaussian around the torso position without other joints to represent the human position. It performs slightly worse than our proposed model in deterministic prediction, while it also has no capability for probabilistic prediction because it can only generate a single maximum. Additionally, we removed the condition in our training and inference, which makes our model a VAE. The input modality becomes a scene image without explicit information of the human. It is found out that no scene structure is learned and no target can be predicted. This proves the necessity of human information, as our model is not designed to detect humans within the scene image and intuitively the current location is required to derive the future destination.

Third, extracting only one maximum from the predicted heatmap has larger errors than extracting multiple maxima, which demonstrate the positive effect of multi-maxima that takes local maxima into account.

The temperature parameter τ introduces variation into sampling process of the latent space [14]. The setting of this parameter is a trade-off between anticipating a single but possibly more precise destination and generating more flexible predictions according to the scene. Table 4 investigates the influence of τ in probabilistic forecasting. As the τ rises, the average FDE continues to increase. Because a higher temperature scaling factor yields more bad samples due to more variation. The averaged minimum FDE is relatively stable up to $\tau = 300$, which demonstrates the stable capability to generate good samples.

Table 4. Ablation study on the parameter τ for inference via generation. $F = 3$.

Parameters	$\tau = 50$	$\tau = 80$	$\tau = 200$	$\tau = 300$	$\tau = 500$
FDE_{avg}	11.9	12.1	15.1	16.1	19.8
FDE_{min}	7.6	8.6	8.6	8.5	9.9

Limitations and Future Work. Our evaluations show that our multi-goal prediction provides more accurate samples than just predicting one deterministic goal. But so far the generation by random sampling is not fully controlled to only sample in the real data distribution of the latent space. Currently, we are mostly able to distinguish good samples from bad ones, as the bad samples usually have a lower variance of values or lower maximal values, indicating low confidence in the prediction. The efficient generation of effective samples is still a challenging problem [34] and is planned to be explored in the future.

In the robotic applications, apart from selecting a final prediction with the highest confidence score among the M forecasts, the historical trajectory of the human can also be used to guide the selection of an optimal prediction. This is because a future position can be estimated based on the current position and velocity. Therefore, the final prediction could be chosen by selecting a forecast that minimizes the distance to the simple estimate of the future position. The prediction accuracy using confidence scores or using historical trajectory could be compared in the future.

5 Conclusion

In summary, our work presents a scene-aware method for anticipating diverse human movement goals. Firstly, we trained the CVAE model to deliver pixel-wise outputs, and then in post-processing extracted target areas represented by bounding boxes and predicted the coordinates of the human movement goal. Secondly, in the inference stage, diverse goals are obtained by sampling in the latent space via temperature scaling. Besides, our model shows the generalization capability across interactive objects in the scene and unknown scenarios, since it has been trained to implicitly understand the features of scenes within the target area. The evaluation shows that our method significantly outperforms the baseline. In the future, the integration of this method into a collaborative robot environment is planned, for instance, our predicted goal heatmap could be transferred to the social cost layer for robot navigation.

Acknowledgments. This work was funded by Deutsche Forschungsgemeinschaft (DFG, German Research Foundation) under grant number 502483052.

Disclosure of Interests. The authors have no competing interests to declare that are relevant to the content of this article.

References

1. Mangalam, K., et al.: It is not the journey but the destination: endpoint conditioned trajectory prediction. Computer Vision – ECCV, pp. 759–776 (2020)
2. Cao, Z., Gao, H., Mangalam, K., Cai, Q., Vo, M., Malik, J.: Long-term human motion prediction with scene context. In: Computer Vision – ECCV: 16th European Conference, Glasgow, UK, August 23–28, Proceedings, Part I, pp. 387–404 (2020)
3. Mangalam, K., An, Y., Girase, H., Malik, J.: From goals, waypoints & paths to long term human trajectory forecasting. In: IEEE/CVF International Conference On Computer Vision (ICCV), pp. 15213–15222 (2021)
4. Hassan, M., et al.: Stochastic scene-aware motion prediction. In: Proceedings of International Conference On Computer Vision (ICCV), pp. 11354–11364 (2021)
5. Lisotto, M., Coscia, P., Ballan, L.: Social and scene-aware trajectory prediction in crowded spaces. In: 2019 IEEE/CVF International Conference On Computer Vision Workshops, ICCV Workshops, Seoul, Korea (South), October 27-28, pp. 2567–2574 (2019)
6. Bruckschen, L., Dengler, N., Bennewitz, M.: Human motion prediction based on object interactions. In: European Conference on Mobile Robots (ECMR), pp. 1–6 (2019)

7. Bartneck, C., Belpaeme, T., Eyssel, F., Kanda, T., Keijsers, M., Šabanović, S.: Human-robot interaction : an introduction. (Cambridge University Press) (2020)
8. Dendorfer, P., Ošep, A., Leal-Taixé, L.: Goal-GAN: multimodal trajectory prediction based on goal position estimation. In: Computer Vision – ACCV, pp. 405–420 (2020)
9. Sohn, K., Lee, H., Yan, X.: Learning structured output representation using deep conditional generative models. In: Advances In Neural Information Processing Systems. vol. 28 (2015)
10. Kingma, D., Welling, M.: Auto-encoding variational bayes. In: 2nd International Conference On Learning Representations, ICLR, Banff, AB, Canada, April 14-16, Conference Track Proceedings (2014)
11. Neubeck, A., Van Gool, L.: Efficient non-maximum suppression. In: Proceedings Of The 18th International Conference on Pattern Recognition, Vol. 03, pp. 850–855 (2006)
12. White, T.: Sampling Generative Networks (2016). https://arxiv.org/abs/1609.04468
13. Foster, D.: Generative Deep Learning: Teaching Machines to Paint, Write, Compose, and Play (O'Reilly Media, Inc.,) (2020)
14. Foster, D.: Generative Deep Learning: Teaching Machines to Paint, Write, Compose, and Play (O'Reilly Media) (2019)
15. Mehta, S., Kirkland, A., Lameris, H., Beskow, J., Székely, É., Henter, G.: OverFlow: putting flows on top of neural transducers for better TTS. In: Proceedings of Interspeech, pp. 4279–4283 (2023)
16. Alahi, A., Goel, K., Ramanathan, V., Robicquet, A., Fei-Fei, L., Savarese, S.: Social LSTM: human trajectory prediction in crowded spaces. In: Proceedings of the IEEE Conference on Computer Vision and Pattern Recognition (CVPR) (2016)
17. Ionescu, C., Papava, D., Olaru, V., Sminchisescu, C.: Human3.6M: large scale datasets and predictive methods for 3D human sensing in natural environments. In: IEEE Transactions on Pattern Analysis and Machine Intelligence, vol. 36, pp. 1325–1339 (2014)
18. Kingma, D., Ba, J.: Adam: a method for stochastic optimization. In: International Conference on Learning Representations (ICLR) (2015)
19. Paszke, A., et al.: PyTorch: an imperative style, high-performance deep learning library. In: Proceedings of the 33rd International Conference on Neural Information Processing Systems (2019)
20. Chan, S.: Tutorial on Diffusion Models for Imaging and Vision (2024) https://arxiv.org/abs/2403.18103
21. Sanchez, D.: Variational autoencoders - theory and applications: exploring variational autoencoder models and their applications in generative modeling, representation learning, and beyond. Adv. Deep Learn. Tech. **4**, 18–32 (2024)
22. Kingma, D., Rezende, D., Mohamed, S., Welling, M.: Semi-Supervised Learning with Deep Generative Models (2014)
23. Wei, R., Garcia, C., El-Sayed, A., Peterson, V., Mahmood, A.: Variations in variational autoencoders - a comparative evaluation. IEEE Access **8**, 153651–153670 (2020)
24. Yan, X., Yang, J., Sohn, K., Lee, H.: Attribute2Image: conditional image generation from visual attributes. In: Computer Vision – ECCV, pp. 776–791 (2016)
25. Hassan, M., Choutas, V., Tzionas, D., Black, M.: Resolving 3D human pose ambiguities with 3D scene constraints. In: International Conference on Computer Vision, pp. 2282–2292 (2019)

26. Tran, H., Le, V., Tran, T.: Goal-driven long-term trajectory prediction. In: 2021 IEEE Winter Conference on Applications of Computer Vision (WACV), pp. 796–805 (2020)
27. Mohamed, A., Chen, H., Wang, Z., Claudel, C.: Skeleton-graph: long-term 3D motion prediction from 2D observations using deep spatio-temporal graph CNNs. CoRR abs/2109.10257 (2021)
28. Scofano, L., Sampieri, A., Schiele, E., Matteis, E., Leal-Taixé, L., Galasso, F.: Staged contact-aware global human motion forecasting. In: BMVC, pp. 589–594 (2023)
29. Mao, W., Liu, M., Hartley, R., Salzmann, M.: Contact-aware Human Motion Forecasting (2022)
30. Lyu, K., Chen, H., Liu, Z., Zhang, B., Wang, R.: 3D human motion prediction: a survey. Neurocomputing **489**, 345–365 (2022)
31. Marchellus, M., Park, I.: Deep learning for 3D human motion prediction: state-of-the-art and future trends. IEEE Access **10**, 35919–35931 (2022)
32. Marder-Eppstein, E., Berger, E., Foote, T., Gerkey, B., Konolige, K.: The office marathon: robust navigation in an indoor office environment. In: IEEE International Conference on Robotics and Automation, pp. 300–307 (2010)
33. Lu, D., Hershberger, D., Smart, W.: Layered costmaps for context-sensitive navigation. In: IEEE/RSJ International Conference on Intelligent Robots and Systems, pp. 709–715 (2014)
34. Yuan, Y., Kitani, K.: DLow: diversifying latent flows for diverse human motion prediction. In: Proceedings of the European Conference on Computer Vision (ECCV) (2020)

Explainable Detection of Logical and Structural Anomalies Based on Multimodal Large Language Models

Noeko Fujii(✉) and Tetsuya Sakai

Graduate School of Fundamental Science and Engineering, Waseda University, Tokyo 169-8555, Japan
noeko.fujii@akane.waseda.jp, tetsuya@waseda.jp

Abstract. Large Language Models are rapidly evolving in the field of Natural Language Processing as well as Vision and Language. In particular, GPT-4o integrates images and text, and is capable of effective Visual Question Answering. However, GPT-4o is limited in its ability to accurately detect the quantity (count or volume), position, and size of objects in a given image, which hinders its practical application to industrial Anomaly Detection (AD).

In order to improve the accuracy and interpretability of AD, this study proposes a new pipeline that utilizes GPT-4o to improve both logical and structural AD accuracies and to output natural language explanations of the detected anomalies. Our system first performs a first-pass logical AD by leveraging the results of the MM-Grounding-DINO object detection model and the SAM2 object segmentation model. It then constructs a multimodal prompt in order to make GPT-4o perform AD with accompanied by natural language explanations of the nature of the anomalies. Experimental results with the MVTec LOCO AD dataset show that our system outperforms existing models in a logical AD task, although it performs less well in a structural AD task. Moreover, to the best of our knowledge, our system is the first to achieve explainable AD that can handle both structural and logical anomalies.

Keyword: Anomaly detection · Large language models · Logical anomalies · Structural anomalies

1 Introduction

With the rapid progress of Large Language Models (LLMs), the field of visual language modelling (VLM) is going through significant development. In particular, OpenAI's GPT-4V [4] and its extension GPT-4o [5] have attracted considerable attention for their high performance in extracting complex visual features and generating natural language descriptions. GPT-4o effectively integrates image and textual features and is able to generate natural language explanations, which can be used in a wide range of applications including Visual Question Answering (VQA), where it has substantially outperformed traditional VLMs.

J. Röning and J. Filipe (Eds.): ROBOVIS 2025, CCIS 2629, pp. 328–347, 2026.
https://doi.org/10.1007/978-3-032-00986-9_22

Meanwhile, in the field of industrial Anomaly Detection (AD), recent studies have demonstrated that models that combine LLMs and visual processing can achieve high generalisation abilities. With the growing demand for automation of quality control and inspection processes in manufacturing, datasets such as MVTec LOCO AD [2] (See Fig. 1) have been developed to target not only *structural anomalies* (i.e., physical problems with the objects in the image) but also *logical anomalies* such as product placement and quantity anomalies in a given image.

Given the above developments, VQA-oriented research using GPT-4V in visual AD has gained momentum. Performance improvements have been reported through various prompts [1], such as those containing quantitative analysis results of anomaly localisation [3], task description, class context, normality rules and reference images. However, VQA-oriented approaches to logical AD using GPT-4o have not yet been fully explored. More specifically, there are significant technical challenges with GPT-4o at present. The most prominent problem is its limited ability to recognise the quantity (count or volume), position, and size of objects. For example, when there are multiple identical objects as shown in Fig. 2, GPT-4o often cannot count the number of objects accurately. This hinders its practical applications in industry, for example, for automatic visual AD in a product line.

In light of the above considerations, we propose a pipeline approach that achieves highly accurate explainable AD. First, we employ the MM-Grounding-DINO object detection model [7] to detect the quantity, position, and size of objects in an image; second, we utilise the Segment Anything Model 2 (SAM2) [8] to obtain an accurately segmented image of each object. Third, we perform a first-pass logical AD, and then utilize the result to design a one-shot multimodal prompt for GPT-4o in order to make it return structural and logical AD results with a natural language explanation that describes what is wrong with the input image.

Our main contributions are as follows.

- We propose a new pipeline architecture for explainable AD that can handle both structural and logical AD tasks. To the best of our knowledge, our system is the first to achieve explainable AD that can handle both structural and logical anomalies. Since the natural language explanations of the detected anomalies are more informative than plain AD results, we expect them to be of high utility for practical AD applications.
- We use the widely used MVTec LOCO AD dataset [2] to demonstrate the effectiveness of our system in a one-shot setting, i.e., when the prompt includes exactly one normal image (i.e., an image without any anomalies) as a positive example along with the input image. In a logical AD task, our system outperforms existing models, owing to our pipeline approach that incorporates a first-pass Logical Anomaly Detector. While our system performs less well in a structural AD task, it shows high accuracy when handling relatively large objects such as breakfast boxes and bottles.

The remainder of this paper is structured as follows. Section 2 discusses related work. Section 3 proposes our pipeline approach to explainable logical and structural AD. Section 4 describes our experiment settings, and Sect. 5 reports on the results. Section 6 provides discussions, and Sect. 7 concludes this paper.

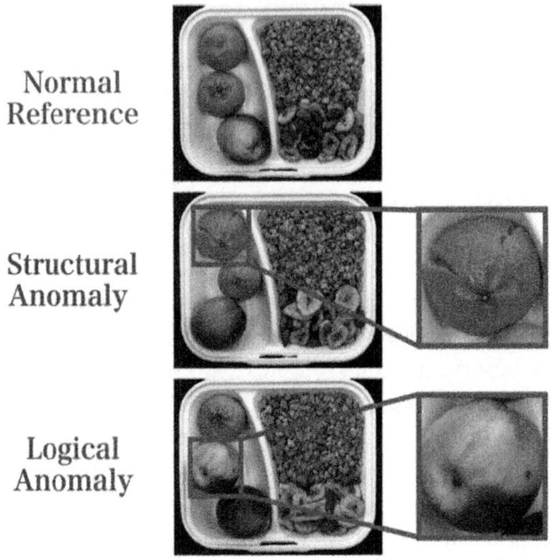

Fig. 1. Examples of structural and logical anomalies from the *breakfast box* category of the MVTec LOCO AD data set [2]. Structural anomalies are physical problems with the objects themselves, such as scratches, dirt, damage or foreign objects, while logical anomalies refer to the fact that the individual components themselves are normal, but they collectively deviate from the placement or quantity constraints.

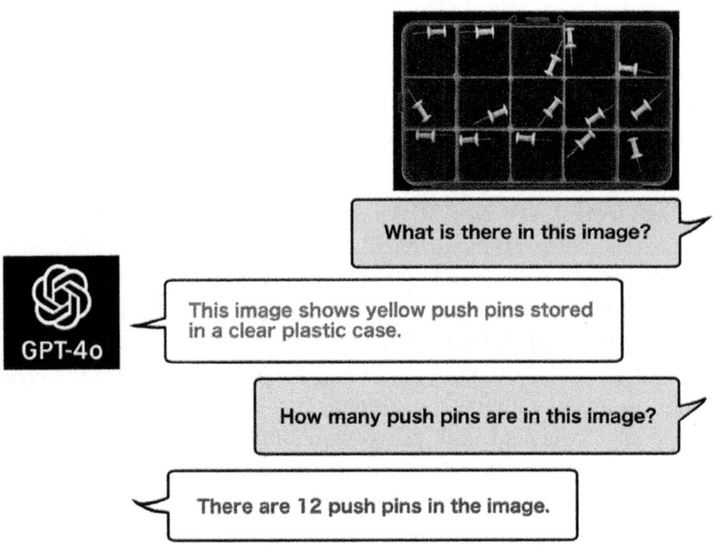

Fig. 2. Example of object detection results with straight GPT-4o (MVTec LOCO AD dataset [2]) GPT-4o often cannot count the number of objects in the input image correctly.

2 Related Work

2.1 Structural and Logical Anomalies

Structural anomalies refer to physical damage or imperfections in the object itself, such as scratches, stains, cracks or breaks, which are visually visible. Logical anomalies, on the other hand, refer to semantic inconsistencies to expected rules or behaviour. Unlike physical structural anomalies such as dents, scratches and stains, these are anomalies caused by violations of rules such as the arrangement, quantity or order of individual objects, even if the objects themselves are normal.

The release of the MVTec LOCO AD dataset [2] was an important milestone in the study of the logical AD task. This dataset contains images with structural and logical anomalies as well as normal images, and provides a comprehensive collection of patterns of logical anomalies that actually occur in manufacturing. One of the existing industrial AD methods, GCAD [2], features a dual structure combining local and global network branches. Local branches reconstruct low-level features to identify structural anomalies and detect local structural changes. Global branches, on the other hand, utilise the global context to detect anomalies in long-range dependencies between elements. This dual structure makes it possible to detect both structural and logical anomalies. The global network branch approach of GCAD has since been adopted by EfficientAD [10] and GLCF [11]; these systems focus on logical AD.

CSAD [12] achieved SOTA performances in logical and structural AD by integrating an unsupervised component segmentation method with a Patch Histogram module and a Local-Global Student-Teacher module; the segmentation method automatically generates training labels by utilising multiple foundation models including SAM [9] and Grounding DINO [6].

However, these methods only output anomaly scores and cannot provide an explanation of the nature of the detected AD. Hence, we discuss *explainable* AD in the next section.

2.2 Visual Anomaly Detection Using Large Language Models

Methods for visual AD can be broadly classified into full-shot unsupervised learning and zero-shot/few-shots approaches. While full-shot unsupervised learning [13–15] shows high accuracy, it requires a large amount of reference data. Hence, zero-shot and few-shot visual AD has attracted much attention in recent years [16–18]. In particular, an approach that utilises the multimodal pre-learning model CLIP [17] has shown excellent results in AD with limited data. Furthermore, the rapid development of Large Visual Language Models has opened up new possibilities. For example, AnomalyGPT [19] utilises GPT-based VLMs and outperforms previous methods in AD with small samples. Of particular note is the study of leveraging GPT-4V the form of Visual Question Answering (VQA): performance improvements have been reported through various prompt designs that feature quantitative analysis in anomaly localisation [3], task description, class context, normality rules and reference images [1]. These GPT-based studies achieve explainable AD by designing appropriate prompts.

In spite of the above recent developments, the potential of the VQA approach for logical AD using GPT-4o has not yet been fully explored. Therefore, in the present study, we extend the prompt design of Xu et al. [1] and investigate the effectiveness of GPT-4o in detecting visual anomalies in a one-shot setting, with a particular focus on quantity, position, and size anomalies. To the best of our knowledge, our system is the first to achieve explainable AD that can handle both structural and logical anomalies.

3 Methods

This section describes our proposed method, which combines existing generic foundation models to form a pipeline customised for explainable AD.

3.1 Overview

In order to build a pipeline customised for AD, we make use of three foundation models: the MM-Grounding-DINO object detection model [7], the SAM2 segmentation model [8], and the GPT-4o visual language model [5]. Figure 3 shows the overview of our pipeline; it consists of the following three steps.

Object Detection. (Sect. 3.2) An input image I and an object tag set T are fed to MM-Grounding-DINO and the quantity and bounding box information of each object are obtained (Fig. 3 left). The output is denoted by T^*.

Segmentation Generation. (Sect. 3.3) The input image I and the above output T^* are fed to SAM2 and, for each object o, the segmented image Io is obtained (Fig. 3 middle).

Anomaly Detection. First (Sect. 3.4), for each object o in the image, the quantity and bounding box information from T^* and Io are processed by our Logical Anomaly Detector, and the detection result is obtained as a short natural language text; we denote the set of texts obtained for the entire image by D. Second (Sect. 3.5), a prompt P is designed based on D in order to let GPT-4o perform explainable AD. The input image I and the prompt P are then fed to GPT-4o, which outputs either a binary AD result B (i.e., whether an anomaly exists or not) or an anomaly score S in the [0,1] range, and a textual explanation E of the anomaly.

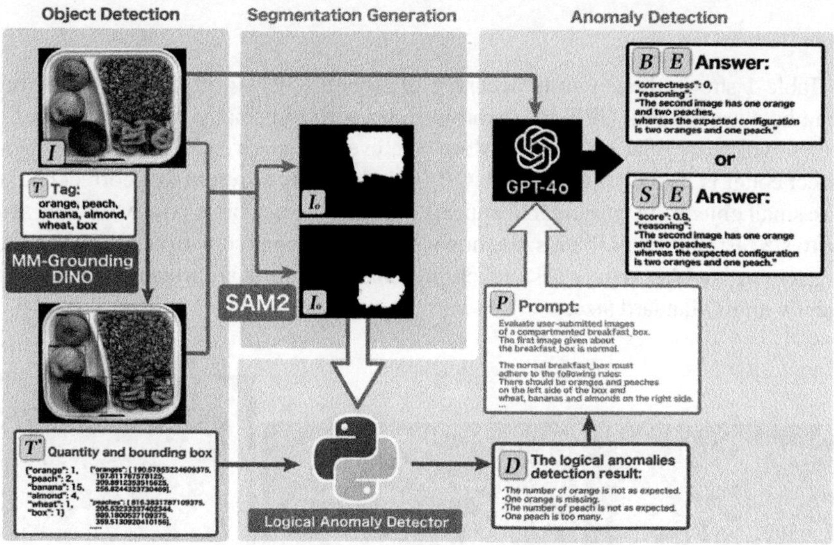

Fig. 3. Overview of the proposed framework.

3.2 Object Detection with MM-Grounding-DINO

First, we demonstrate the limited accuracy of "straight" GPT-4o with regard to counting the number of objects and detecting their size, as this is what motivated us to propose our pipeline architecture. We selected four different object types (pushpins, oranges, washers, long screws) from the MVTec LOCO AD dataset [2] (See Fig. 4: details will be given in Sect. 4.1), randomly sampled $n = 50$ images for each object type, and asked GPT-4o to count the number of objects in the image using the following two different prompt templates.

Prompt 1: "How many [object type] are in the image?"
Prompt 2: "There are [correct number of objects] with [object type] in the image. How many [object type] are in the image?"

Note that Prompt 2 is absurd for humans—the correct answer is deliberately included in the prompt.

Table 1. Counting accuracy of straight GPT-4o.

object name	Prompt 1	Prompt 2
pushpins ($n = 50$)	0.000	0.780
oranges ($n = 50$)	0.960	1.000
washers ($n = 50$)	0.480	1.000
long screws ($n = 50$)	0.025	0.650

Table 1 shows the counting accuracy of straight GPT-4o in this pilot experiment. It can be observed that GPT-4o performs very poorly especially for pushpins and long screws, which are relatively small. Moreover, even when given Prompt 2 (in which the correct count is actually mentioned), GPT-4o often fails to return this correct count for these small objects. In particular, it appears that GPT-4o performs poorly for long screws due to size estimation problems: as shown in Fig. 4, images sometimes contain not only long screws but also short ones, which prevents GPT-4o from properly associating an object with its standard size.

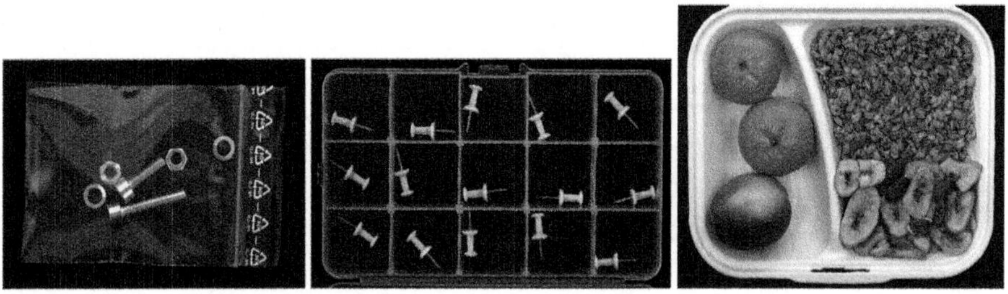

Fig. 4. Images from the MVTec LOCO AD dataset [2] containing four different object types.

To solve the above problem in object detection, Step 1 of our pipeline framework employs MM-Grounding-DINO [7], an open-source model that extends Grounding-DINO [6]. The original Grounding-DINO model is known for its high performance in tasks such as Open Vocabulary Detection, Phrase Grounding, and Referring Expression Comprehension; the new MM-Grounding-DINO model utilises the MMDetection toolbox of OpenMMLab project, and has been pre-trained and fine-tuned with further datasets. As MM-Grounding-DINO accommodates open-set object detection, it can be fine-tuned for specialised tasks; in our case, we leverage it to detect object quantity (count or volume), position, and size. More specifically, we fine-tuned MM-Grounding-DINO using an instance segmentation dataset that we created from the training set of the MVTec LOCO AD dataset [2]. The segmentation dataset contains images from five categories (*breakfast box, juice bottle, pushpins, screw bag, splicing connectors*), and each category is associated with a set of tags, as shown in Table 2. The segmentation dataset includes 132 *pushpins* images, 132 *screw bag* images, 396 *juice bottle* images, and 396 *splicing connectors* images. (We left out images from the breakfast box category as the images in this category contain only large food items such as oranges.) Our fine-tuned model takes as input an image from one of the categories and a corresponding set of tags, identifies the objects in the image, and obtains the quantity and bounding box (i.e., position and size) of each object.

Table 2. Category tags of objects that are input to MM-Grounding-DINO.

Category	Tag
breakfast box	orange, peach, box, wheat, banana, almond
juice bottle	bottle, juice content, fruit, label, text
pushpins	box, pushpin, partition
screw bag	screw, washer, nut, plastic bag
splicing connectors	connector, clamp, red cable, yellow cable, blue cable

3.3 Segmentation Generation with SAM2

The Segment Anything Model 2 (SAM2), released by Meta on 29 July 2024, is a generic model for segmentation on arbitrary objects, capable of extracting object boundaries with high accuracy. SAM2 is based on a wealth of annotation data and has the ability to recognise object shapes and boundaries in more detail than conventional segmentation models. In particular, they provide consistent accuracy for objects of different shapes and sizes and are capable of segmenting fine-grained features.

In Step 2 of our pipeline, the object detection results obtained from MM-Grounding-DINO are used to generate a segmentation image for each object using SAM2. More specifically, the bounding box information of each object detected by MM-Grounding-DINO is input to SAM2 to create a segmentation mask for each object. The resulting segmentation image enables the exact shape and size of the object to be captured.

3.4 Logical Anomaly Detector

The first part of our AD component (See Fig. 3) performs the first-pass logical AD using our own AD model. The model sets threshold values for various objects based on normal images in our training data; these thresholds represent the normal ranges of the quantity (count or volume), position, and size of objects. Input objects deviating from these thresholds are detected as abnormal. When a logical anomaly in terms of quantity, position, or size is detected, this module also outputs a natural language explanation such as "The number of bananas and almonds is wrong." and "One short screw is missing." These explanations are later used by GPT-4o, in the final part of our AD component (to be described in Sect. 3.5).

3.5 One-Shot Multimodal Prompt-Based AD Using GPT-4o

The second part of our AD component (See Fig. 3) involves multimodal prompt engineering in order to make GPT-4o perform explainable AD. Our multimodal prompt consists of one normal image as a positive example, one test image (i.e., target of AD), plus four textual instruction components: task instruction, class context, structural and logical rules, Logical Anomaly Detection results with additional instructions. We adopted the first two of these from Xu et al. [1]; the rest are our own designs and are indicated with an * below, where we describe the components using Fig. 5.

Task Instruction

The task instruction component is shown in red in Fig. 5. The first half is in Part (a) of the prompt, which explains the task to GPT-4o. In our experiments, the ${CLASS_NAME} variable is either 'breakfast box', 'juice bottle', 'pushpins', 'screw bag', or 'splicing connectors'. The second half of task instruction is in Part (c) of the prompt, where the output expected from GPT-4o is specified. We make GPT-4o perform both structural and logical AD and outputs either a binary AD result B ((0: normal, 1: abnormal) or an anomaly score S in the [0−1] range. In either case, a natural language explanation E is also output. The explanation describes the nature of the anomaly if there is any; otherwise, it argues why the input image can be considered normal.

We initially tried making GPT-4o output B and S at the same time using a single prompt, but this approach made GPT-4o always return either 0.0 or 1.0 for S. Hence we devised separate prompts for obtaining B with E and for obtaining S with E. Figure 5(c) shows how we make GPT-4o return S with E.

Class Context

This component, shown in blue in Fig. 5 (a), describes what are the expected quantity, shape, colour, etc. for each object in a normal image.

Structural and Logical Rules*

This component, shown in green in Fig. 5 (a), defines the normality criteria for structural and logical AD in words. Here is another example from the breakfast box category: 'There should be oranges and peaches on the left side of the box and wheat, bananas and almonds on the right side.'

Logical Anomaly Detector Results with Additional Instructions*

This component, shown in purple in Fig. 5 (b), passes on the first-pass results from the Logical Anomaly Detector to GPT-4o. The first part of this component contains the detected objects and the quantity, position and size information. In addition, if logical anomalies have been detected, the corresponding natural language explanations are passed on to GPT-4o. On the other hand, if no anomalies were found, we instruct GPT-4o as follows: 'Please prioritise the following condition: **The number of the objects is normal in the second image. Ignore the number anomalies.**' This is to prevent GPT-4o from returning false alarms even though the Logical Anomaly Detector judged the input image to be normal. In Fig. 5, this section is shown in purple.

Part (a) : task instruction (first half), class context, structural and logical rules

Evaluate user-submitted images of a compartmented ${CLASS_NAME}.
The first image given about the ${CLASS_NAME} is normal. The objects in the first image:

{"pushpins": 15, "box": 1}

The normal ${CLASS_NAME} must adhere to the following rules:
There are no big stains, cracks, or foreign objects on the plastic box or pushpins.

Please determine whether the second image given about the ${CLASS_NAME} contains anomalies or defects.
If yes, give a specific reason.
Also, to evaluate the possibility of abnormality, calculate an abnormality score in the range 0 to 1.
The higher the score, the higher the possibility of abnormality.
Output the abnormality score as a numerical value to indicate the degree of possibility of abnormality.
It may have defects such as broken parts, and contaminations.

Part (b): Logical Anomaly Detector results, additional instruction

The objects in the second image:
{"pushpins": 15, "box": 1}

[If no logical anomaly is detected]
>>>>>>>>>>>>>>
Please prioritize the following condition:
The number of the objects is normal in the second image. Ignore the number anomalies.
The number anomalies: Missing screws or washers, or nuts; Too many screws or washers, or nuts; Extra screws or washers, or nuts;
>>>>>>>>>>>>>>

[If logical anomaly is detected]
The second image contains the following anomalies. Please explain in detail in your reason:
The number of pushpins is not as expected.
There is a missing push pin in row 1, column 4.

Part (c): task instruction (second half)

Your answer should contain 2 parts:
"reasoning": a string, that describes what you think about the given image;
"score": an abnormality score in the range 0 to 1;
Output example: {"explanation": a string, "score": a float, an abnormality score in the range 0 to 1;} Your response must be a valid JSON string starting with { and should contain nothing else because we will directly execute it in Python. No indent or ¥n in json structure formatting is needed. No ``` or ```json is needed.

Fig. 5. An example prompt for explainable AD output.

4 Experimental Settings

This section reports on our experiments for evaluating the effectiveness of our Logical Anomaly Detector component as well as our final explainable AD results.

4.1 The MVTec LOCO AD Dataset

Our experiments use the widely used MVTec LOCO AD dataset, which contains images of five product categories (*breakfast box*, *juice bottle*, *pushpins*, *screw bag*, *splicing connectors*), each with images with logical anomalies, structural anomalies, and those without anomalies (i.e., normal images). The dataset consists of 1,778 normal images for training, 305 normal images for validation, and 1,568 images for testing; the test set contains 575 normal images, 561 images with logical anomalies, and 432 images with structural anomalies. Table 3 shows the breakdown of images included in the test data. We use the entire test data (n = 1,568) to test our system.

Table 3. Statistics of the images in the test data of MVTec LOCO AD.

Category	Normal	Logically anomalous	Structurally anomalous	Total
breakfast box	102	83	90	275
juice bottle	94	142	94	330
pushpins	138	91	81	310
screw bag	122	137	82	341
splicing connectors	119	108	85	312
Total	575	561	432	1568

The query images in the juice bottle and splicing connectors categories are associated with three normal images while those in the other categories are associated with only one. For the two categories mentioned above, one normal image was automatically selected from the three and used as the normal image part of the aforementioned prompt for GPT-4o. Thus, our prompts are one-shot for all five product categories.

MVTec LOCO AD contains five types of logical anomalies as described below.

Count Anomaly. The number of an object is different from what is considered normal. Instances where an object that should be present is missing in the image also belong to this anomaly type.

Quantity Anomaly. The volume of an object is different from (i.e., either more or less than) the expected amount.

Size Anomaly. The size of an object is different from (i.e., larger or smaller than) what is considered normal.

Position Anomaly. An object that should be present is in an inappropriate position within the image. For example, a fruit may be in the wrong partition within the *breakfast box*, or a label on a *juice bottle* may be misaligned from its standard position.

Matching Anomaly. This occurs when multiple objects are paired in a manner that is outside the norm. For example, a label on a bottle may not match the content of the bottle; the colour of a cable may not match that of an accompanying connector.

Table 4 shows the number of instances for each combination of product category and logical anomaly type.

Table 4. Number of test images for each combination of product category and logical anomaly type. Note that the Total cell for *breakfast box* says 89 instead of 83 (See Table 3): there are duplicate counts due to 6 images that contain multiple logical anomaly types.

Category	Count anomaly	Quantity anomaly	Size anomaly	Position anomaly	Matching anomaly	Total
breakfast box	66	20	0	3	N/A	89
juice bottle	53	36	0	31	22	142
pushpins	80	0	0	11	N/A	91
screw bag	72	0	65	0	N/A	137
splicing connectors	50	0	21	25	12	108
Total	321	56	86	70	34	567

4.2 Evaluation Measures

Following previous work, we use Accuracy (ACC) and Area Under the Receiver Operating Characteristic Curve (AUROC) [20] as our primary evaluation measures. For each product category, we conduct five trials and report the average effectiveness score over the trials for all evaluation measures.

5 Results

5.1 Evaluating the Logical Anomaly Detector

First, we evaluate the Logical Anomaly Detector component of our system (Fig. 3 left to middle), which gives us our first-pass logical AD results. As we have described in Sect. 3, the input to our Logical Anomaly Detector are T^* (which contains the quantity and bounding box information for each object in the query image) and the Io (segmented image) for each object.

Table 5 shows the accuracy results of our Logical Anomaly Detector for each anomaly type. As quantity anomalies and size anomalies are the same from the viewpoint of our system that relies on the object segmentation images obtained from SAM2, the two anomaly types are merged in this table. There are two cells that say "Detected by GPT-4o": this means that our system bypasses the Logical Anomaly Detector and let GPT-4o detect the anomalies directly, because these combinations of product category and anomaly type involve only large objects, which the straight GPT-4o can handle with sufficient accuracy. Also, cells marked with an 'N/A' means that there are no anomalies in that product category (See Table 4).

Table 5. Accuracy of our Logical Anomaly Detector per anomaly type. (n = #normal + #logically anomalous).

Category	Count anomaly	Quantity & Size anomaly	Position anomaly	Matching anomaly
breakfast box ($n = 102 + 83 = 185$)	0.994	0.967	Detected by GPT-4o	N/A
juice bottle ($n = 94 + 142 = 236$)	1.000	1.000	1.000	Detected by GPT-4o
pushpins ($n = 138 + 91 = 229$)	1.000	0.978	1.000	N/A
screw bag ($n = 122 + 137 = 259$)	0.995	1.000	1.000	N/A
splicing connectors ($n = 119 + 108 = 227$)	0.994	1.000	1.000	1.000

It can be observed that our Logical Anomaly Detector is highly accurate. In particular, it achieves 100% accuracy for all four product categories in position AD, thanks to the accuracy of the bounding boxes obtained by MM-Grounding-DINO.

5.2 Evaluating the Final AD Effectiveness in a 3-Class Setting (Normal vs. Logical Anomalies vs. Structural Anomalies)

In this experiment, we evaluated the effectiveness of the final AD results output by GPT-4o in a 3-class setting, where the test data contained normal images, images with logical anomalies, and those with structural anomalies.

Table 6 compares our results with existing models in terms of Average AUROC as this is the measure widely reported in previous work. From the table, it can be observed that our system performs comparably with SOTAs. In particular, for the breakfast box category, our system outperforms all other models, including CSAD (95.7% vs 92.7% in Average AUROC). While our system underperforms CSAD in terms of the overall Average AUROC, the difference is very small (93.1% vs 95.3%).

From this 3-class experiment, however, it is not clear whether our system suffers more with logical anomalies or with structural anomalies. Hence, Sects. 5.3 and 5.4 examine two 2-class settings separately: normal vs. logical anomalies, and normal vs. structural anomalies.

Table 6. Comparison of our final AD results with other models under the 3-class setting in terms of Average AUROC.

Category	EfficientAD [10]	PSAD [22]	ComAD [23]	CSAD [12]	**Ours**
breakfast box	86.9	92.4	86.3	92.7	**95.7**
juice bottle	**99.0**	98.6	96.6	95.2	96.3
pushpins	96.9	94.9	93.4	**98.6**	93.5
screw bag	73.7	**97.5**	80.2	96.5	94.1
splicing connectors	**97.0**	90.6	94.1	93.5	86.0
average	90.7	94.8	90.1	**95.3**	93.1

5.3 Evaluating the Final AD Effectiveness in 2-Class Settings (Normal vs. Logical Anomalies)

First, we focus on logical AD. Table 7 compares the final AD results under a 2-class setting (normal vs. logical anomaly images) with other models in terms of Average ACC, copied from previous work; Table 8 does the same in terms of Average AUROC. The scores of the existing systems were copied from previous work. Our main findings are as follows.

- In terms of Average ACC (Table 7), our system and LogiCode are the overall winners, tied with an Average ACC of 0.989. While LogiCode performs best for the breakfast box and juice bottle categories, our system performs best for the other categories, which contain smaller objects.
- In terms of Average AUROC (Table 8), our system is the overall winner. While PSAD performs best for the breakfast box, juice bottle, and pushpins categories, it can be observed that it underperforms our system substantially for the splicing connectors category.

Table 7. Comparison of our final AD results with other models under a 2-class setting (normal vs. logically anomalous) in terms of Average ACC.

Category	EfficientAD-S	EfficientAD-M	LogiCode [24]	**Ours**
breakfast box	0.935	0.862	**0.992**	0.978
juice bottle	0.952	0.875	**0.989**	0.987
pushpins	0.839	0.814	0.990	**0.991**
screw bag	0.950	0.878	0.981	**0.992**
splicing connectors	0.885	0.768	0.989	**0.996**
average	0.912	0.839	**0.989**	**0.989**

Table 8. Comparison of our final AD results with other models under a 2-class setting (normal vs. logically anomalous) in terms of Average AUROC.

Category	EfficientAD[10]	PSAD [22]	ComAD [23]	CSAD[12]	**Ours**
breakfast box	85.5	**100.0**	91.1	94.4	98.7
juice bottle	98.4	**99.1**	95.0	94.9	97.9
pushpins	97.7	**100.0**	95.7	99.5	99.9
screw bag	56.7	99.3	71.9	**99.9**	99.4
splicing connectors	95.5	91.9	93.3	94.8	**99.1**
average	86.8	98.1	89.4	96.7	**99.0**

5.4 Evaluating the Final AD Effectiveness in 2-Class Settings (Normal vs. Structural Anomalies)

Next, we focus on structural AD. Table 9 compares the final AD results under a 2-class setting with other models in terms of Average AUROC. The following observations can be made.

- Our system substantially underperforms EfficientAD (87.3% vs. 94.7%). This is largely due to our poor performance for the *splicing connectors* category (72.9%). That is, while our system performs well in *logical* AD for *splicing connectors* (See Tables 10), it performs poorly in *structural* AD.
- Our system outperforms the others for the *breakfast box* category. This is because this category involves large objects such as fruits, and GPT-4o is generally capable of handling large objects.

From the above two 2-class experiments, it is clear that our system performs well in logical AD, but that there is room for improvement in structural AD. That is, while the first-pass Logical Anomaly Detector is highly useful for logical AD in the final step, it is less so for structural AD in the final step.

Table 9. Comparison of our final AD results with other models under a 2-class setting (normal vs. structurally anomalous) in terms of Average AUROC.

Category	EfficientAD [10]	PSAD [22]	ComAD [23]	CSAD [12]	**Ours**
breakfast box	88.4	84.9	81.6	91.1	**92.7**
juice bottle	**99.7**	98.2	98.2	95.6	94.8
pushpins	96.1	89.8	91.1	**97.8**	87.1
screw bag	90.7	**95.7**	88.5	93.2	88.8
splicing connectors	**98.5**	89.3	94.9	92.2	72.9
average	**94.7**	91.6	90.9	94.0	87.3

5.5 Effect of Asking for an Explanation

Table 10 shows, in a 3-class setting (normal vs. logically anomalous vs. structurally anomalous), the effect of making GPT-4o provide an explanation on the AD accuracy. The ACC score in the 'Without explanation' was obtained by deleting the request to provide an explanation from the input prompt. It can be observed that making GPT-4o provide an explanation improves the overall accuracy, although this has a negative effect on the *pushpins* category and no effect on the *splicing connectors* category. The results suggest that formulating explainable AD prompts is beneficial at least for images that involve large objects, e.g., fruits in breakfast boxes and bottles.

Table 10. Effect of making GPT-4o output an explanation for the AD result in terms of ACC (n = #normal + #logically anomalous + #structurally anomalous).

Category	With explanation	Without explanation
breakfast box ($n = 102 + 83 + 90 = 275$)	**0.931**	0.905
juice bottle ($n = 94 + 142 + 94 = 330$)	**0.952**	0.952
pushpins ($n = 138 + 91 + 81 = 310$)	0.884	**0.890**
screw bag ($n = 122 + 137 + 82 = 341$)	**0.962**	0.848
splicing connectors ($n = 119 + 108 + 85 = 312$)	**0.862**	0.846
average	**0.918**	0.888

5.6 Examples of Our Explainable AD Results

Figure 6 shows two examples of correct explanations output by our system for the pushpins category. The left half of this figure shows parts of our prompts for GPT-4o, and the right half shows the output of GPT-4o in our system. In the top image, GPT-4o returns a perfect explanation for logical anomalies: 'The bottom image contains only 12 pushpins instead of the expected 15. There are missing pushpins in row 1, column 4; row 2, column 4; and row 3, column 4.' In the bottom example, GPT-4o's response correctly explains not only a count anomaly (i.e., type of logical anomaly) but also a structural anomaly: 'The second image contains 16 pushpins instead of the expected 15, and there is a red pushpin among the yellow ones, indicating a foreign object.' (The latter image is categorised as structurally anomalous in the dataset.) Note that in both cases, GPT-4o paraphrases the output of our Logical Anomaly Detector when explaining logical anomalies. Explaining the nature of detected anomalies in this way is probably very informative and useful in practical applications.

On the other hand, Fig. 7 shows two examples of incorrect explanations output by our system for the pushpins category. The top image is free from anomalies, but because the explanation returned by the Logical Anomaly Detector claims that 'The pushpin may be the wrong size or damaged,' GPT-4o concludes that there is a structural anomaly: 'The second image shows a pushpin with a bent pin, which is a defect.' On the other hand, the bottom image contains a structural anomaly, but because the first-pass Logical Anomaly Detector finds nothing wrong with the image, GPT-4o agrees with it.

Thus, while our final explainable AD results can be accurate and useful when the Logical Anomaly Detector passes on good results to GPT-4o, if this first-pass AD fails, GPT-4o cannot do any better. Moreover, there is room for improvement in our system especially for structural AD of small objects such as pushpins.

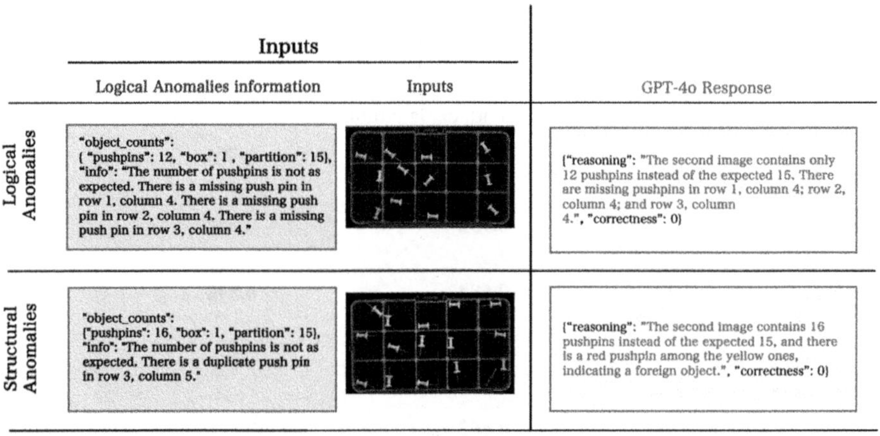

Fig. 6. Examples of correct explanations from the pushpins category (MVTec LOCO AD dataset [2]).

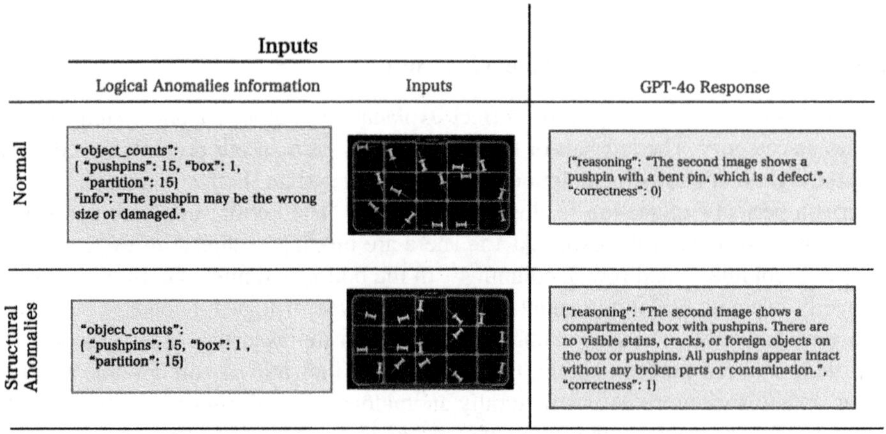

Fig. 7. Examples of incorrect explanations from the pushpins category (MVTec LOCO AD dataset [2]).

6 Limitations of Our Approach

We have demonstrated that our pipeline approach that incorporates a Logical Anomaly Detector prior to prompt construction for GPT-4o is effective for explainable AD. However, while our system handles large objects such as bottles effectively, its effectiveness is limited in structural AD of small objects such as pushpins and cables. This may be a fundamental problem with Visual Language Models, as they tend to capture the entire image rather than minute details, perhaps similarly to humans. While our system took a one-shot approach (i.e., providing only one normal image in the prompt), alternative approaches that rely on more training data (with high-definition images) are probably required for handling these cases.

Another limitation of the present study is our reliance on the MVTec LOCO AD dataset, which only covers five categories. Datasets with a wider variety of real products will be required in order to demonstrate the robustness and practicality of our system.

7 Conclusions

We proposed a pipeline architecture for explainable AD, for handling logical and structural anomalies in product images. Our system comprises an object detection step using MM-Grounding-DINO, a segmentation generation step using SAM2, and an AD step in which a first-pass logical AD is performed and then a one-shot multimodal prompt is constructed for GPT-4o to return AD results with natural language explanations. Our main findings are as follows.

- In a 3-class AD setting where normal, logically anomalous, and structurally anomalous images are used as input, our system performs similarly to the CSAD (93.1% vs. 95.3% in terms of Average AUROC). In particular, our system performs best in the breakfast box category (Table 6).
- In a 2-class AD setting where normal and logically anomalous images are used as input, our system achieves the SOTA performance. For example, our system achieves 99.0% in terms of Average AUROC, by performing exceptionally well (99.1%) for the splicing connectors category (Table 8).
- In a 2-class AD setting where normal and structurally anomalous images are used as input, our system performs less well (87.3% in terms of Average AUROC), due to its low performance for the splicing connectors category (72.9%). This is probably because our first-pass Logical Anomaly Detector is less useful for structural AD than for logical AD in the final step.
- Our system can output informative natural language explanations of the nature of the detected anomalies. However, there is room for improvement in terms of AD accuracy, especially in structural AD for small objects such as pushpins.

As future work, we would like to conduct a quantitative evaluation of the quality and utility of the natural language explanations that our system provides. Moreover, as our current system handles small objects less well than large objects such as bottles in structural AD, we would like to consider performing AD optimised for each object type and then consolidating the results for the entire input image.

References

1. Xu, X., Cao, Y., Chen, Y., Shen, W., Huang, X.: Customizing visual-language foundation models for multi-modal anomaly detection and reasoning. arXiv preprint arXiv:2403.11083 (2024)
2. Bergmann, P., Batzner, K., Fauser, M., Sattlegger, D., Steger, C.: Beyond dents and scratches: logical constraints in unsupervised anomaly detection and localisation. Int. J. Comput. Vis. **130**(4), 947–969 (2022)
3. Zhang, J., et al.: GPT-4V-AD: exploring the grounding potential of VQA-oriented GPT-4V for zero-shot anomaly detection. arXiv preprint arXiv:2311.02612 (2023)
4. OpenAI. gpt-4v(ision) system card, 2023. Accessed 20 Oct 2024
5. OpenAI. gpt-4o system card, 2024. Accessed 20 Oct 2024
6. Liu, S., et al.: Grounding DINO: marrying DINO with grounded pre-training for open-set object detection. arXiv preprint arXiv:2303.05499 (2023)
7. Zhao, X., et al.: An open and comprehensive pipeline for unified object grounding and detection. arXiv preprint arXiv:2401.02361 (2024)
8. Ravi, N., et al.: Sam 2: segment anything in images and videos. arXiv preprint arXiv:2408.00714 (2024)
9. Kirillov, A., et al.: Segment anything. In. Proceedings of the IEEE/CVF International Conference on Computer Vision, pp. 4015–4026 (2023)
10. Batzner, K., Heckler, L., König, R.: EfficientAD: accurate visual anomaly detection at millisecond-level latencies (2024)
11. Yao, H., Yu, W., Luo, W., Qiang, Z., Luo, D., Zhang, X.: Learning global-local correspondence with semantic bottleneck for logical anomaly detection. IEEE Trans. Circuits and Syst. Video Technol. (2023)
12. Hsieh, Y.-H., Lai, S.-H.: CSAD: unsupervised component segmentation for logical anomaly detection. arXiv preprint arXiv:2408.15628 (2024)
13. Hu, T., et al.: AnomalyDiffusion: few-shot anomaly image generation with diffusion model. In. AAAI (2024)
14. Rudolph, M., Wandt, B., Rosenhahn, B.: Same same but different: semi-supervised defect detection with normalising flows. In: Proceedings of the IEEE/ CVF Winter Conference on Applications of Computer Vision, pp. 1907–1916 (2021)
15. He, H., et al.: A diffusion-based framework for multi-class anomaly detection. In: AAAI (2024)
16. Liu, Z., Zhou, Y., Xu, Y., Wang, Z.: SimpleNet: a simple network for image anomaly detection and localisation. In: Proceedings of the IEEE/CVF Conference on Computer Vision and Pattern Recognition, pp. 20402–20411 (2023)
17. Radford, A., et al.: Learning transferable visual models from natural language supervision. In: International Conference on Machine Learning, pp. 8748–8763. PMLR (2021)
18. Cao, Y., et al.: Segment any anomaly without training via hybrid prompt regularization. arXiv preprint arXiv :2305.10724 (2023)
19. Gu, Z., Zhu, B., Zhu, G., Chen, Y., Tang, M., Wang, J.: AnomalyGPT: detecting industrial anomalies using large vision-language models. arXiv preprint arXiv:2308.15366 (2023)
20. McClish, D.K.: Analysing a portion of the ROC curve. Med. Decis. Mak. **9**, 190–195 (1989)
21. Bradley, A.P.: The use of the area under the ROC curve in the evaluation of machine learning algorithms. Pattern Recogn. **30**, 1145–1159 (1997)
22. Kim, S., et al.: Few-shot part segmentation reveals compositional logic for industrial anomaly detection. In: Proceedings of the AAAI Conference on Artificial Intelligence, vol. 38, pp. 8591–8599 (2024)

23. Liu, T., et al.: Component-aware anomaly detection framework for adjustable and logical industrial visual inspection. Adv. Eng. Inform. **58**, 102161 (2023)
24. Zhang, Y., Cao, Y., Xu, X., Shen, W.: LogiCode: an LLM-driven framework for logical anomaly detection. arXiv preprint arXiv:2406.04687 (2024)

Learn Where I Can Walk: Auto-labeling of Walked Areas Using Monocular Camera Trajectory

Helmut Engelhardt(✉), Matthias Kalenberg, Jörg Franke, and Sina Martin

Institute for Factory Automation and Production Systems, Friedrich-Alexander Universität Erlangen-Nürnberg (FAU), Egerlandstraße 7, 91058 Erlangen, Germany
{helmut.engelhardt,matthias.kalenberg,joerg.franke, sina.martin}@faps.fau.de

Abstract. This paper presents Learn Where I Can Walk (LWICW), a novel auto-labeling approach for segmenting walked areas using a trajectory estimated from multiple sequential monocular camera images, aimed at training supervised segmentation models for the navigation of visually impaired people. The proposed method uses images sourced from Mapillary, which is a collaborative platform to share street-level images. The approach involves extracting the walked path of the camera operator through the camera poses, the filtering of occluded walking path poses using Depth Anything V2, and the application of Segment Anything Model 2 (SAM 2) for segmentation. The LWICW auto-labels are validated against a manually labeled dataset from Mapillary and compared to the state-of-the-art zero-shot segmentation model Grounded SAM 2. The LWICW method achieves an overall mean Intersection over Union (mIoU) of 93.9% and a mean F_1 score (mF_1) of 96.6%, which represents a performance improvement of +1.6% points on mIoU and +1.0% points on mF_1 compared to the Grounded SAM 2 approach.

Keywords: Self-supervised visual learning · Auto-labeling · People navigation · Person navigation system · Walkable area detection

1 Introduction

Identifying walkable areas is essential for the safe navigation of visually impaired people or other person navigation system [12]. However, this task is challenging due to the limited availability of publicly available and suitable datasets. Most available datasets are focused on autonomous driving and are of limited use for the navigation of visually impaired people, as they are recorded from the perspective of a car [8–10,36]. This restricts the dataset's scope to roads and areas accessible by cars, excluding various surfaces accessible to pedestrians. Therefore, more general datasets are needed to train models for the navigation of visually impaired people. In addition, the creation of new datasets is a time-consuming and expensive process, as they are mostly labeled by human annotators. This creates a demand for auto-labeling approaches that eliminate

J. Röning and J. Filipe (Eds.): ROBOVIS 2025, CCIS 2629, pp. 348–363, 2026.
https://doi.org/10.1007/978-3-032-00986-9_23

the need for human-labeled data. For a global source of pedestrian-level images, we utilize Mapillary, although the proposed approach can be applied to any camera sequence that captures the perspective of a pedestrian walking on a path. Mapillary is a collaborative platform founded in 2014 that allows users to capture, share, and use street-level images from around the world, currently containing more than two billion recorded images worldwide [1]. Users can contribute by uploading photos along with additional location data taken with smartphones or cameras while driving, cycling, or walking. The inclusion of pedestrian-captured images makes Mapillary a valuable source of worldwide pedestrian-level data for the navigation of visually impaired people. To address the challenges described above, this paper proposes an auto-labeling approach to detect walkable areas using only multiple sequential images from pedestrian-level recordings. The proposed approach utilizes the path taken by the camera operator to segment the corresponding traversed areas, effectively identifying walkable regions.

The contributions of this paper include:

- A novel auto-labeling method for labeling walked areas using only multiple sequential monocular camera images.
- Masking occluded paths using Depth Anything V2, eliminating the need for additional depth sensor data.
- Segmentation of walked areas from the pedestrian path using SAM 2.
- Validation with a self-labeled dataset from Mapillary.

2 Related Work

Robust detection of walkable areas is essential for advanced assistance systems designed to aid the navigation of visually impaired people. However, research has primarily focused on detection drivable areas for autonomous driving. Furthermore, available datasets from the pedestrian perspective are limited or lack annotations for semantic segmentation. This scarcity makes supervised learning approaches challenging to implement. To overcome this shortage of labeled data, auto-labeling approaches have been proposed.

2.1 Manually Labeled Datasets for Supervised Approaches

Previous work on pedestrian path segmentation relies on extensive labeled datasets [28,31]. Several datasets have been annotated for supervised learning in autonomous navigation but are mainly focused on driving scenes (Table 1). Additionally, the datasets for sidewalk scenes lack semantic segmentation annotations, making them unsuitable for supervised learning of walkable area segmentation.

2.2 Auto-labeling Approaches

Auto-labeling approaches have been proposed to improve the adaptability of models to new environments and to eliminate the need for human supervision. By analyzing the flatness of the environment with a 3D sensor, it is possible to create area labels

Table 1. Comparison of datasets with semantic annotations and depth data availability across various scenes.

Datasets	Total images	Semantic annotation		Depths		Scenes
		images	classes	num	type	
ApolloScape [10]	147K	147K	25	51K	LiDAR	Driving
BDD100K [36]	100K	10K	19	–	–	Driving
Cityscapes [8]	25K	25K	30	25K	Stereo	Driving
KITTI [9]	15K	400	12	400[a]	LiDAR	Driving
Mapillary Vistas [21]	25K	25K	29	–	–	Street[b]
SOID [3]	50K	–	–	–	–	Sidewalk
SideGuide [22]	492K	–	–	180K	Stereo	Sidewalk

[a] KITTI Stereo 2015 Benchmark.

[b] Includes both driving and pedestrian environments.

automatically. All flat and continuous areas are then marked as drivable or walkable. Common sensors for this purpose include stereo cameras [7,20,29,33] and 3D-LiDAR [6,18,30]. Stereo cameras have also been explored to mark walkable areas for visually impaired people [11,14]. However, these methods have limitations in distinguishing between areas of similar height, such as sidewalks and roads. Other auto-labeling approaches for self-supervised drivable area detection commonly utilize the vehicle trajectory to learn which areas are drivable [4,5,16,20,25–27,32,34,37]. In robotics, the force-torque signal [34] or acoustic features of the ground [37] have been used to automatically classify the ground and use this information to auto-label different areas in the image.

2.3 Zero-Shot Semantic Segmentation

Zero-shot semantic segmentation aims to classify and segment novel classes without explicit training on labeled examples for those classes. Recent advancements in zero-shot learning and open-set segmentation have enabled models to classify unseen classes using high-level semantic information, often extracted from word embeddings or visual-language models. For instance, models like LSeg [15] leverage a language-guided approach by using text embeddings to perform zero-shot segmentation, allowing for flexible identification of classes like "sidewalk", "path" or "road" based solely on textual descriptions.

Grounded SAM [24] is also notable in this context and has shown remarkable results on zero-shot segmentation on the Segmentation in the Wild (SGinW) benchmark. Grounded SAM combines the Segment Anything Model (SAM) [13,23] with zero-shot object detection through Grounding DINO [17], enabling the segmentation of walkable surfaces by interpreting text prompts such as "sidewalk." or "path.". Specifically, Grounding DINO proposes bounding boxes based on the given text prompts, and SAM refines the segmentation within these bounding boxes. This zero-shot segmentation capability is particularly useful for auto-labeling and knowledge distillation into supervised models.

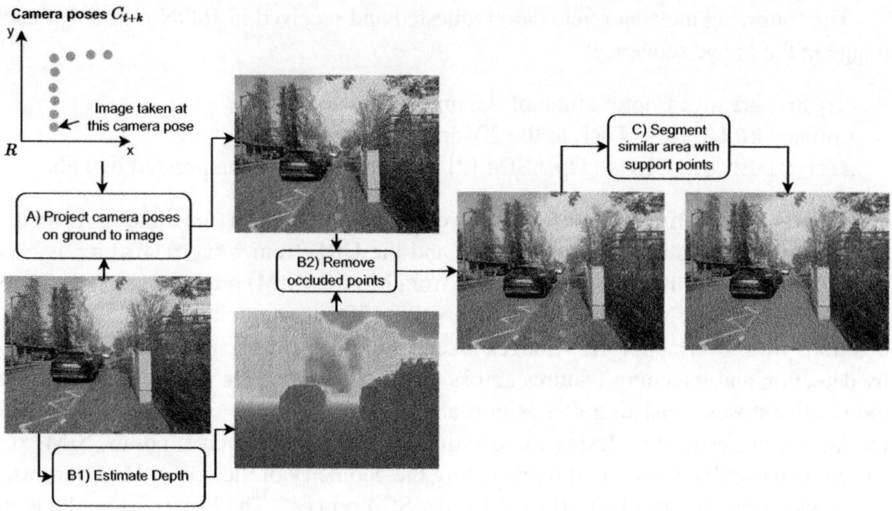

Fig. 1. Overview of the proposed auto-labeling process. In the first step A) the walked trajectory of the camera operator is projected based on the camera poses subtracted by the height above the ground into the image (Sect. 3.2). In step B1) the depth is estimated from the input image and used in B2) to filter out projected points occluded by obstacles (Sect. 3.3). As last step C) the remaining points are used as prompt for segmentation (Sect. 3.4).

3 Method

In the following section, the LWICW method for auto-labeling walked areas using only multiple sequential camera images is presented. The approach is based on the following steps and depicted in Fig. 1:

1. Image Sequence Download (Sect. 3.1)
2. Extraction of Camera Operator's Path Using Camera Positions (Sect. 3.2 and Fig. 1A)
3. Filtering of Occluded Path Positions (Sect. 3.3 and Fig. 1B)
4. Segmentation of Walked Area (Sect. 3.4 and Fig. 1C)

The following sections present each step in detail. The experimental results for the proposed method are described in Sect. 4.

3.1 Image Sequence Download

Mapillary provides a web API that allows users to download images and their metadata. The API offers endpoints for accessing image sequences, metadata, and other related data. To retrieve a complete image sequence, the API endpoint (https://graph.mapillary.com/images) for requesting images is used with the `sequence_ids` filter parameter. Image sequence IDs representing images from a pedestrian's perspective are identified manually using the Mapillary Web User Interface.

The following metadata fields are requested and received in JSON format for each image in the image sequence:

- `captured_at`: Capture time of the image.
- `thumb_2048_url`: URL to the 2048px wide image.
- `sfm_cluster`: URL to OpenSfM [2] data in JSON and compressed by zlib.

The URLs from `thumb_2048_url` are used to download the images from the sequence in a resolution of 2048 × 1536, and the URL from `sfm_cluster` is used to download the results from the Structure from Motion (SfM) process run on the Mapillary server. The SfM process generates sparse 3D structures and estimates camera positions from overlapping 2D images taken from different perspectives. This is done by detecting and matching features across the images. Once the features are matched, the relative poses consisting of position and orientation of the cameras that captured the images are estimated. Using these estimated poses and matched points, SfM constructs a sparse 3D point cloud representing the geometry of the scene. Mapillary uses the open-source library OpenSfM [2] for the SfM process. The library is available on GitHub[1] and can therefore also be applied to custom-recorded image sequences. The `sfm_data` from the OpenSfM pipeline contains the following data:

- cameras: The camera type name along with its estimated intrinsic camera parameters and distortion coefficients.
- reference_lla: Latitude and longitude of the reference coordinate system origin R.
- shots: The camera pose transformation $\mathbf{T}_{C_{t+k}}^{R}$ estimated by the reconstruction process at image $t+k$ from the camera coordinate system C_{t+k} to the reference coordinate system R.
- points: Reconstructed 3D points of the scene with its 3D position vector $\boldsymbol{t}_{point,i}$ in the reference coordinate system R.

Further information on the file format can be found here: https://opensfm.org/docs/dataset.html#reconstruction-file-format.

3.2 Extraction of Camera Operator's Path Using Camera Positions

To project the future trajectory taken by the camera operator, the estimated homogeneous transformations, $\mathbf{T}_{C_{t+k}}^{R}$, from the OpenSfM data are utilized. Here, t represents the current frame, and $t+k$ represents the frame after k frames. These transformations are stored from the camera coordinate system C to the reference coordinate system R. Therefore, each transformation is first inverted to obtain the camera pose C_{t+k} in the reference coordinate system R (Fig. 2):

$$\mathbf{T}_{R}^{C_{t+k}} = {\mathbf{T}_{C_{t+k}}^{R}}^{-1} \tag{1}$$

To calculate the position of the camera operator on the ground from its camera pose, the height above the ground h for the camera is needed. For the estimation of the height, the reconstructed 3D points estimated by the OpenSfM method are used. For each camera

[1] https://github.com/mapillary/OpenSfM.

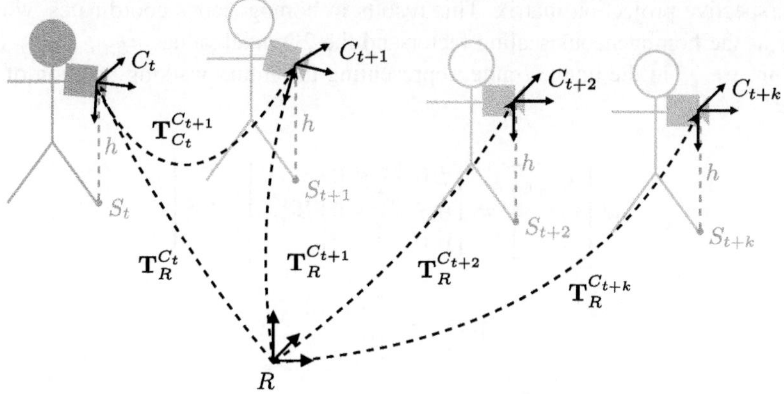

Fig. 2. Camera extrinsic for the auto-labeling process. The camera operator's walked trajectory **S** can be estimated through the poses of the camera C. In this example the camera operator is moving toward the right with C_{t+k} indicating future poses of the camera after k frames. The point S represents the pose on the ground directly beneath the camera C, at a distance h. The camera poses are reconstructed using the OpenSfM pipeline, with each pose stored relative to a reference coordinate system labeled R. The transformation between the reference coordinate system R and the camera coordinate system C is denoted as $\mathbf{T}_R^{C_{t+k}}$.

pose $\mathbf{T}_R^{C_{t+k}}$ the close 3D points are searched, with a search space limited to a range from 0.5 m to 2 m below the camera position and within a radius of 0.3 m in x- and y-direction in reference coordinate system to increase the likelihood to find a ground-level 3D point. It is assumed that the camera is at least 0.5 m and at most 2 m above the ground. The height above ground h_{t+k} for the camera position k is then calculated by subtracting the z-value of each found 3D point $z_{point_{k,l}}$ from the z-value of the camera pose $z_{C_{t+k}}$ and calculating the median of these results:

$$h_{t+k,l} = z_{C_{t+k}} - z_{point_{k,l}} \tag{2}$$

$$h_{t+k} = \text{median}(h_{t+k,1}, h_{t+k,2}, \dots, h_{t+k,l}) \tag{3}$$

This step is repeated for every camera position k of the image sequence. As the reconstructed 3D point cloud is sparse, not every camera position has a 3D point matching the filter criteria. Therefore, the median value of all remaining calculated heights h_{t+k} is used as the height above ground for all camera positions:

$$h = \text{median}(h_t, h_{t+1}, \dots, h_{t+k}) \tag{4}$$

With the estimated height above ground h, the corresponding ground poses S_{t+k} can now be calculated:

$$S_{t+k} = C_{t+k} - h \tag{5}$$

As the next step, the ground positions S_{t+k} are projected onto the current image frame by transforming the ground positions to the camera coordinate system and applying the perspective projection matrix. This results in homogeneous coordinates, where w serves as the homogeneous scaling factor and the 2D pixel values $u_{S_{t+k}}, v_{S_{t+k}}$ define the point $\mathbf{p}_{S_{t+k}}$ in the image frame, representing the future walking position of the k frame:

$$w \begin{bmatrix} u_{S_{t+k}} \\ v_{S_{t+k}} \\ 1 \end{bmatrix} = \begin{bmatrix} f & 0 & \frac{w_{\text{image}}}{2} & 0 \\ 0 & f & \frac{h_{\text{image}}}{2} & 0 \\ 0 & 0 & 1 & 0 \end{bmatrix} \mathbf{T}_R^{C_t} \begin{bmatrix} x_{S_{t+k}} \\ y_{S_{t+k}} \\ z_{S_{t+k}} \\ 1 \end{bmatrix} \tag{6}$$

$$\mathbf{p}_{S_{t+k}} = \begin{bmatrix} u_{S_{t+k}} \\ v_{S_{t+k}} \end{bmatrix} \tag{7}$$

3.3 Filtering of Occluded Path Positions

Parts of the future path may be occluded and should not be used for segmentation and must be filtered out. Since the Mapillary data does not contain depth sensor data and the 3D point cloud from SfM is too sparse, the Depth Anything V2 model for Metric Depth Estimation [35] is used as an alternative to estimate depth and mask occluded positions along the camera operator's ground path. The detailed parameters of the used model can be found in Table 2. The model was trained on the Virtual KITTI 2 Dataset to predict metric depth values in outdoor environments for each pixel of a given 2D color image. However, our experiments indicate that the estimated depth values deviate from the calculated depth to the camera operator path poses, which are based on the camera poses produced by the OpenSfM reconstruction. To correct for this deviation, the values of the estimated depth image $\mathbf{D}_{\text{estimated}}$ are scaled based on the calculated distances to the first two subsequent camera operator's ground positions, $z_{S_{t+1}}^{C_t}$ and $z_{S_{t+2}}^{C_t}$, relative to the current image frame C_t.

$$\begin{bmatrix} x_{S_{t+k}}^{C_t} \\ y_{S_{t+k}}^{C_t} \\ z_{S_{t+k}}^{C_t} \end{bmatrix} = \mathbf{T}_R^{C_t} \cdot S_{t+k} \tag{8}$$

The corresponding depth values in the estimated depth image for these two subsequent camera operator's ground positions are obtained at the calculated 2D image pixel coordinates $(u_{S_{t+1}}, v_{S_{t+1}})$ and $(u_{S_{t+2}}, v_{S_{t+2}})$, as described in Sect. 3.2.

$$\mathbf{D}_{\text{scaled}} = \mathbf{D}_{\text{estimated}} \cdot \frac{1}{2} \sum_{i=1}^{2} \frac{z_{S_{t+i}}^{C_t}}{\mathbf{D}_{\text{estimated}}(u_{S_{t+i}}, v_{S_{t+i}})} \tag{9}$$

The scaled depth image $\mathbf{D}_{\text{scaled}}$ is then used to filter out occluded camera operator positions. This is done by removing ground positions where the known z-distance from the camera to the camera operator ground point $z_{S_{t+k}}^{C_t}$ exceeds the estimated depth value by a factor of α. This discrepancy indicates that the line of sight is likely occluded by an object, as the estimated depth is closer than the actual distance to the camera operator ground point S_{t+k}. Here $\alpha = 1.2$ is used to give room for a small error margin. The filtered camera operator path point set $\mathbf{S}_{\text{filtered}}$ is thus defined as:

$$\mathbf{S}_{\text{filtered}} = \left\{ \mathbf{p}_{S_{t+k}} \in \mathbf{S} \;\middle|\; z_{S_{t+k}}^{C_t} \leq \alpha \cdot \mathbf{D}_{\text{scaled}}(\mathbf{p}_{S_{t+k}}) \right\} \tag{10}$$

where $\mathbf{S} = \{\mathbf{p}_{S_{t+k}} \mid k = 1, 2, \ldots, N\}$ is the original 2D pixel coordinate set along the camera operator's path. Each $\mathbf{p}_{S_{t+k}} = (u_{S_{t+k}}, v_{S_{t+k}})$ represents a 2D pixel coordinate and $\mathbf{D}_{\text{scaled}}(\mathbf{p}_i)$ is the estimated scaled depth at point $\mathbf{p}_i$.

Table 2. Parameters of the used Depth Anything V2 model for depth estimation from 2D color images.

Model	Depth Anything V2 Large (335 M params)
Training Dataset	Virtual KITTI v2
Max. estimated depth	80 m
Image input resolution	512 × 384

3.4 Segmentation of Walked Area

For the segmentation of the walked area, the Segment Anything Model 2 (SAM 2) [23] (Table 3) is used along with the filtered projected 2D points $\mathbf{S}_{\text{filtered}}$ of the camera operator's path. Three different approaches have been evaluated:

1. Use of all filtered points as a prompt for the segmentation task of the model.
2. Rasterization of the filtered points before prompting the segmentation task of the model.
3. Repetition of the segmentation process for each point that is not within the previous segmentation mask.

The initial approach results in sparse masks due to the fact that SAM 2 is trained to use only a few points for segmentation. The use of too many points resulted in reduced and sparse segmentation quality.

The second approach aims to reduce the number of points provided to SAM 2 for segmentation. To achieve this, the image is divided into a grid with 12 rows and 16 columns. Additionally, the $z_{S_{t+k}}^{C_t}$ value is segmented into 3 m sections in order to better separate points that are further away and therefore closer together. Only the first point from the camera operator's path within each grid cell and section is then used for segmentation.

The third approach also targets reducing the number of points. Here, the segmentation process is repeated in the case of outlying points. First, a segmentation mask is created using only the first point. Then, all subsequent points that fall within the generated segmentation mask are skipped. If a point is outside the mask, the segmentation is repeated with this additional point included.

The third approach produced the best segmentation results, as only the necessary points were selected, ensuring that no potentially significant points were skipped. This approach is also used evaluating the LWICL method against manually labeled as described in Sect. 4. An example for the different segmentation results for each method are shown in Fig. 3

Table 3. Model parameters of the used Segment Anything Model 2 for the segmentation of the walked area.

Model	Hiera Large (224.4 M params)
Image input resolution	2048 × 1536

(a) (b) (c)

Fig. 3. Segmentation results for proposed point selection approaches for prompting SAM 2. Filtered out points (yellow); selected points for SAM 2 segmentation (turquoise); remaining positions (red/blue). (a) All filtered points S_{filtered} used. (b) 12×16 grid and 3 m distance-based section rasterization of points. (c) Incremental selection, starting with the first point and repeating for outliers of the segmentation mask. (Color figure online)

4 Experimental Results

In this section, the experimental results of the proposed method for auto-labeling walked areas using camera trajectory data are presented. The performance of the method is evaluated on a manually labeled dataset from Mapillary, which includes various scenarios such as sidewalks, paved footpaths, and low structured environments (Fig. 4). The results are compared with the state-of-the-art zero-shot segmentation model, Grounded SAM 2. Both quantitative and qualitative results are reported to demonstrate the effectiveness and robustness of the LWICW approach.

4.1 Manually-Labeled Mapillary Dataset

To validate the presented approach, 263 images from five different sequences obtained from Mapillary, capturing scenes from a pedestrian's perspective, were manually labeled with ground truth data for the walked areas. Sequences from three different scenarios have been selected and labeled:

- Sidewalk
- Paved Footpath
- Low Structured Environment

Example images from these scenarios, along with their labeled ground truth masks, are shown in Fig. 4.

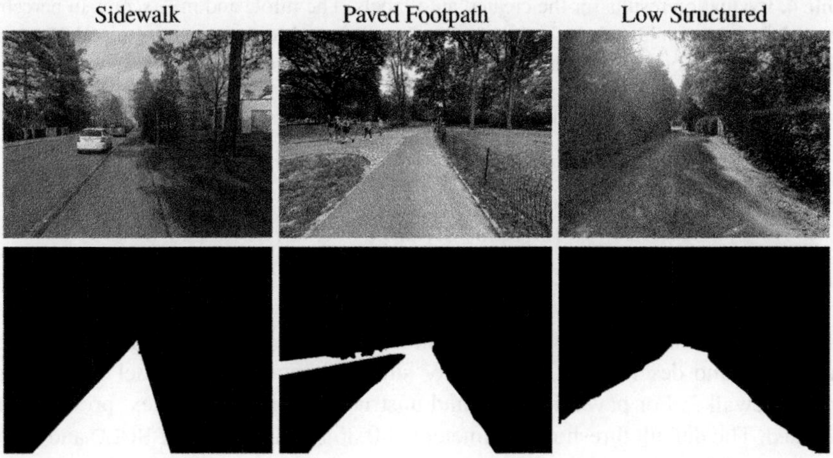

Fig. 4. Examples of manually labeled images along with their labeled ground truth from different scenarios.

4.2 Quantitative Results

For the measurement of the quantitative performance of the presented approach, the mean Intersection over Union (mIoU) metric

$$\mathrm{mIoU} = \frac{1}{N}\sum_{k=1}^{N}\frac{\mathrm{TP}_k}{\mathrm{TP}_k + \mathrm{FP}_k + \mathrm{FN}_k} \tag{11}$$

and the mean F_1 (mF_1) score

$$\mathrm{mF}_1 = \frac{1}{N}\sum_{k=1}^{N}\frac{2\mathrm{TP}_k}{2\mathrm{TP}_k + \mathrm{FP}_k + \mathrm{FN}_k} \tag{12}$$

are calculated. Where True Positives (TP) is the number of pixels correctly segmented as walkable area, False Positives (FP) is the number of pixels incorrectly segmented as walkable area and False Negatives (FN) is the number of pixels incorrectly segmented as not walkable area. The index k corresponds to each ground truth image and N is the total number of images. The results are presented in the next Sect. 4.

The mIoU measures the overlap between the predicted segmentation mask and the ground truth mask. It provides a direct sense of how well the predicted mask aligns with the actual segmentation mask, with a higher IoU indicating better segmentation accuracy.

The mF_1 score also measures how well the predicted segmentation mask matches the ground truth mask by balancing precision and recall. This balance can make it more sensitive to small or thin structures compared to mIoU. Also, a higher score indicates better segmentation accuracy.

The measurements are compared to the state-of-the-art zero-shot segmentation model, Grounded SAM 2 [24]. The Grounding DINO SwinT OGC model is used for

Table 4. Evaluation results for the created auto-labels. The mIoU and mF_1 scores in percent are reported for each evaluated method and scenario compared to the ground truth. Higher values indicate better performance, with the best result in each column marked in bold.

	All		Sidewalk		Paved Footpath		Low Structured	
	mIoU	mF_1	mIoU	mF_1	mIoU	mF_1	mIoU	mF_1
Grounded SAM 2	92.3	95.6	92.0	95.5	94.4	96.9	**95.7**	**97.8**
LWICW (Ours)	**93.9**	**96.6**	**93.7**	**96.5**	**95.8**	**97.7**	93.6	96.6

box proposals component, while the segmentation model SAM 2 is the same model as used in 3.4 and described in Table 3. For sidewalk images, the model was prompted with "sidewalk.". For paved footpath and unstructured images, the text prompt "path." was used. The default threshold parameters of 0.35 for `BOX_THRESHOLD` and 0.25 for `TEXT_THRESHOLD` were applied.

Table 4 presents the evaluation results for the created auto-labels with the proposed LWICW method and Grounded SAM 2 on the different scenarios. The table reports the mIoU and mF_1 scores for all scenarios combined, as well as for each individual scenario Sidewalk, Paved Footpath, and Low Structured Environment. Higher values indicate better segmentation accuracy, with the best results in each column highlighted in bold.

Overall, the proposed LWICW method outperforms the state-of-the-art zero-shot Grounded SAM 2 by +1.6 pp on mIoU and +1.0 pp on mF_1. This suggests that LWICW is more accurate in labeling walked areas across various environments.

In the sidewalk and paved footpath scenarios, LWICW outperforms Grounded SAM 2, achieving higher mIoU and mF_1 scores in both cases. For sidewalks, LWICW scores achieved a +1.7 pp (mIoU) and +1.0 pp (mF_1) improvement. In the paved footpath scenario, LWICW could improve +1.4 pp (mIoU) and +0.8 pp (mF_1), compared to Grounded SAM 2. These results indicate that LWICW's segmentation approach better handles structured environments, potentially due to its more effective handling of boundaries.

In the unstructured environment scenario, Grounded SAM 2 outperforms LWICW, with an mIoU of 95.7% and mF_1 of 97.8%, compared to LWICW's 93.6% and 96.6%. This may be attributed to the enhanced capacity of Grounded SAM 2 to address inhomogeneous areas, where boundaries are less clearly defined.

4.3 Qualitative Results

To evaluate the qualitative performance of the proposed approach, the segmentation results produced by the LWICW method are compared with those generated by Grounded SAM 2. Figure 5 presents examples from three different labeled scenarios: sidewalk, paved footpath, and unstructured environments. For each scenario, the input image, the walked area segmentation by Grounded SAM 2, and the walked area segmentation by LWICW are shown. In general, LWICW produced more precise segmentation masks, especially for environments with similar structured paths.

Fig. 5. Auto-labeling segmentation examples across different scenarios, compared with Grounded SAM 2. The first proposed segmentation mask of Grounded SAM 2 is shown in purple, and the second proposed mask is shown in red. (Color figure online)

- Sidewalk Scenario: LWICW produced more consistent boundaries along sidewalks and curb, especially not segmenting the gutter line and elevated curb as walked area, while Grounded SAM 2 struggles on images where the bounding box of the sidewalk also captures the street.
- Paved Footpath Scenario: Both methods effectively captured paved footpaths, while Grounded SAM 2 sometimes also capture the gutter line as walkable area.
- Low Structured Scenario: Grounded SAM 2 outperformed LWICW here by correctly expanding walkable areas over inhomogeneous areas.

In Fig. 6 the limitation cases encountered during the evaluation are shown:

- Figure 6a: The current method only uses the poses of the recorded images without interpolating the trajectory between the poses. Therefore, when turning, the future poses of the trajectory may not fall within the region of the previous trajectory, leading to segmentation failure.

(a) (b) (c) (d)

Fig. 6. Limitations of the proposed auto-labeling segmentation method. Filtered out points (yellow); selected points for SAM 2 segmentation (red/turquoise); remaining positions (red/blue). (a) Previous area is not segmented when turning, as no trajectory points fall within it. (b) Walkable manholes are excluded incorrectly. (c) Second point used for depth scaling intersects with a person. (d) Incorrectly estimated camera position results in mid-air points. (Color figure online)

- Figure 6b: Surfaces that varied too much, such as manholes, were sometimes excluded from the segmentation.
- Figure 6c: Depth estimation was inaccurate when the first two points used for the value scaling of depth image intersected with moving objects, such as pedestrians.
- Figure 6d: Incorrect camera positions estimated by OpenSfM caused projected points to appear mid-air, leading to segmentation failure.

Despite these challenges, the LWICW method showed robustness across a range of conditions, highlighting its potential to auto-label walkable areas for training supervised segmentation networks for real-world navigation scenarios of visual impaired people.

5 Conclusion

The proposed method for automatically labeling walked areas in images has been validated using a manually-labeled dataset from Mapillary. The results demonstrate that the method can label walked areas with slightly better accuracy compared to the state-of-the-art zero-shot segmentation. The method is able to label walked areas without the need for human supervision. Notably, LWICW outperforms in structured environments, particularly in effectively handling boundaries and producing precise segmentation masks for walkable areas. In contrast, Grounded SAM 2 faces challenges in environments where bounding boxes extend too far or overlap similar surfaces, such as streets.

Future work could involve exploring alternative visual odometry algorithms to address mismatches in camera positions from OpenSfM. In addition, fusing this approach with Grounded SAM 2 could leverage the strengths of both methods. Depth prediction might also be improved, potentially eliminating the need for corrective scaling, by fine-tuning the depth estimation model through self-supervised learning on the specific image sequence beforehand [19].

Acknowledgments. This publication has emanated from research supported by the Federal Ministry of Education and Research (BMBF) under founding code 16SV9081.

Disclosure of Interests. The authors have no competing interests to declare that are relevant to the content of this article.

References

1. Mapillary. https://www.mapillary.com/. Accessed 10 Jan 2025
2. OpenSfM. https://opensfm.org/. Accessed 10 Jan 2025
3. Ahmed, F., Yeasin, M.: Optimization and evaluation of deep architectures for ambient awareness on a sidewalk. In: 2017 International Joint Conference on Neural Networks (IJCNN), pp. 2692–2697. IEEE (2017)
4. Alamikkotervo, E., Ojala, R., Seppänen, A., Tammi, K.: TADAP: trajectory-aided drivable area auto-labeling with Pretrained self-supervised features in winter driving conditions. IEEE Trans. Intell. Veh. 1–10 (2024). https://doi.org/10.1109/TIV.2024.3397853
5. Barnes, D., Maddern, W., Posner, I.: Find Your Own Way: Weakly-Supervised Segmentation of Path Proposals for Urban Autonomy (2017)
6. Chen, E., Ho, C., Maulimov, M., Wang, C., Scherer, S.: Learning-on-the-Drive: Self-supervised Adaptation of Visual Offroad Traversability Models (2023)
7. Cho, J., Kim, Y., Jung, H., Oh, C., Youn, J., Sohn, K.: Multi-task self-supervised visual representation learning for monocular road segmentation. In: 2018 IEEE International Conference on Multimedia and Expo (ICME), pp. 1–6. IEEE, San Diego, CA (2018). https://doi.org/10.1109/ICME.2018.8486472
8. Cordts, M., et al.: The cityscapes dataset. In: CVPR Workshop on the Future of Datasets in Vision. vol. 2, p. 1 (2015)
9. Geiger, A., Lenz, P., Stiller, C., Urtasun, R.: Vision meets robotics: the KITTI dataset. Int. J. Robot. Res. (IJRR) **32**(11), 1231–1237 (2013)
10. Huang, X., et al.: The ApolloScape dataset for autonomous driving. In: Proceedings of the IEEE Conference on Computer Vision and Pattern Recognition Workshops, pp. 954–960 (2018)
11. Imai, K., Kitahara, I., Kameda, Y.: Detecting walkable plane areas by using RGB-D camera and accelerometer for visually impaired people. In: 2017 3DTV Conference: The True Vision - Capture, Transmission and Display of 3D Video (3DTV-CON), pp. 1–4 (2017). https://doi.org/10.1109/3DTV.2017.8280422
12. Kalenberg, M., Hofmann, C., Martin, S., Franke, J.: Human Comfort Factors in People Navigation: Literature Review, Taxonomy and Framework. In: Filipe, J., Röning, J. (eds.) Robotics, Computer Vision and Intelligent Systems, pp. 225–243. Springer Nature Switzerland, Cham (2024)
13. Kirillov, A., et al.: Segment Anything. arXiv:2304.02643 (2023)
14. Lee, Y.H., Medioni, G.: RGB-D camera based wearable navigation system for the visually impaired. Comput. Vis. Image Underst. **149**, 3–20 (2016). https://doi.org/10.1016/j.cviu.2016.03.019
15. Li, B., Weinberger, K.Q., Belongie, S.J., Koltun, V., Ranftl, R.: Language-driven Semantic Segmentation. CoRR abs/2201.03546 (2022). https://arxiv.org/abs/2201.03546
16. Lieb, D., Lookingbill, A., Thrun, S.: Adaptive road following using self-supervised learning and reverse optical flow. In: Robotics: Science and Systems I. Robotics: Science and Systems Foundation (2005). https://doi.org/10.15607/RSS.2005.I.036
17. Liu, S., et al.: Grounding DINO: Marrying DINO with Grounded Pre-training for Open-Set Object Detection. arXiv preprint arXiv:2303.05499 (2023)
18. Liu, Z., Yu, S., Zheng, N.: A co-point mapping-based approach to drivable area detection for self-driving cars. Engineering **4**(4), 479–490 (2018). https://doi.org/10.1016/j.eng.2018.07.010

19. Lyu, X., et al.: HR-Depth: High Resolution Self-Supervised Monocular Depth Estimation. ArXiv abs/2012.07356 (2020). https://doi.org/10.1609/aaai.v35i3.16329
20. Mayr, J., Unger, C., Tombari, F.: Self-supervised learning of the drivable area for autonomous vehicles. In: 2018 IEEE/RSJ International Conference on Intelligent Robots and Systems (IROS), pp. 362–369. IEEE, Madrid (2018). https://doi.org/10.1109/IROS.2018.8594480
21. Neuhold, G., Ollmann, T., Rota Bulo, S., Kontschieder, P.: The mapillary vistas dataset for semantic understanding of street scenes. In: Proceedings of the IEEE International Conference on Computer Vision, pp. 4990–4999 (2017)
22. Park, K., et al.: SideGuide: a large-scale sidewalk dataset for guiding impaired people. In: 2020 IEEE/RSJ International Conference on Intelligent Robots and Systems (IROS), pp. 10022–10029. IEEE, Las Vegas, NV, USA (2020). https://doi.org/10.1109/IROS45743.2020.9340734
23. Ravi, N., et al.: SAM 2: Segment Anything in Images and Videos (2024). https://arxiv.org/abs/2408.00714
24. Ren, T., et al.: Grounded SAM: Assembling Open-World Models for Diverse Visual Tasks (2024)
25. Schmid, R., et al.: Self-supervised traversability prediction by learning to reconstruct safe terrain. In: 2022 IEEE/RSJ International Conference on Intelligent Robots and Systems (IROS), pp. 12419–12425. IEEE, Kyoto, Japan (2022). https://doi.org/10.1109/IROS47612.2022.9981368
26. Seo, J., Kim, T., Kwak, K., Min, J., Shim, I.: ScaTE: a scalable framework for self- supervised traversability estimation in unstructured environments. IEEE Robot. Autom. Lett. **8**(2), 888–895 (2023). https://doi.org/10.1109/LRA.2023.3234768
27. Seo, J., Sim, S., Shim, I.: Learning off-road terrain traversability with self-supervisions only. IEEE Robot. Autom. Lett. **8**(8), 4617–4624 (2023). https://doi.org/10.1109/LRA.2023.3284356
28. Sessner, J., Schmid, M., Lauer-Schmalz, M., Franke, J.: Path segmentation with artificial neural networks in low structured environments for the navigation of visually impaired people. In: 2020 8th IEEE RAS/EMBS International Conference for Biomedical Robotics and Biomechatronics (BioRob), pp. 1242–1247. IEEE, New York City, NY, USA (2020). https://doi.org/10.1109/BioRob49111.2020.9224324
29. Shinzato, P.Y., Gomes, D., Wolf, D.F.: Road estimation with sparse 3D points from stereo data. In: 17th International IEEE Conference on Intelligent Transportation Systems (ITSC), pp. 1688–1693. IEEE, Qingdao, China (2014). https://doi.org/10.1109/ITSC.2014.6957936
30. Shinzato, P.Y., Wolf, D.F., Stiller, C.: Road terrain detection: avoiding common obstacle detection assumptions using sensor fusion. In: 2014 IEEE Intelligent Vehicles Symposium Proceedings, pp. 687–692. IEEE, MI, USA (2014). https://doi.org/10.1109/IVS.2014.6856454
31. Sun, C., Su, J., Shi, Z., Guan, Y.: P-Minder: a CNN based sidewalk segmentation approach for phubber safety applications. In: 2019 IEEE International Conference on Image Processing (ICIP), pp. 4160–4164. IEEE, Taipei, Taiwan (2019). https://doi.org/10.1109/ICIP.2019.8803417
32. Tang, L., Ding, X., Yin, H., Wang, Y., Xiong, R.: From one to many: unsupervised traversable area segmentation in off-road environment. In: 2017 IEEE International Conference on Robotics and Biomimetics (ROBIO), pp. 787–792. IEEE, Macau (2017). https://doi.org/10.1109/ROBIO.2017.8324513
33. Wang, H., Sun, Y., Liu, M.: Self-supervised drivable area and road anomaly segmentation using RGB-D data for robotic wheelchairs. IEEE Robot. Autom. Lett. **4**(4), 4386–4393 (2019). https://doi.org/10.1109/LRA.2019.2932874

34. Wellhausen, L., Dosovitskiy, A., Ranftl, R., Walas, K., Cadena, C., Hutter, M.: Where should i walk? Predicting terrain properties from images via self-supervised learning. IEEE Robot. Autom. Lett. **4**(2), 1509–1516 (2019). https://doi.org/10.1109/LRA.2019.2895390
35. Yang, L., et al.: Depth Anything V2. arXiv:2406.09414 (2024)
36. Yu, F., et al.: BDD100K: a diverse driving dataset for heterogeneous multitask learning. In: The IEEE Conference on Computer Vision and Pattern Recognition (CVPR) (2020)
37. Zurn, J., Burgard, W., Valada, A.: Self-supervised visual terrain classification from unsupervised acoustic feature learning. IEEE Trans. Rob. **37**(2), 466–481 (2021). https://doi.org/10.1109/TRO.2020.3031214

Material Classification Using Visio-Tactile Sensor for Haptic Feedback Generation

Md Golam Rabby Shuvo(✉), Sonya Coleman, Dermot Kerr, and Justin Quinn

School of Computing Engineering, and Intelligent Systems, Ulster University, Londonderry, UK
m.shuvo@ulster.ac.uk

Abstract. The flexibility, versatility and enhanced perception of visio-tactile sensors could be beneficial for advanced robotic systems and other applications requiring precise haptic feedback. In this paper, we present a comprehensive framework that combines material classification and haptic feedback through the use of GelSight sensors. The study includes the creation of a diverse material dataset, consisting of 13 material classes of 42 distinct indoor and outdoor items, each item with multiple video samples captured over different regions and pressing conditions by human-held GelSight mini sensors. We introduce a method for detecting pressing events from recorded video samples and extracting key frames that capture important material features. We employ both traditional and deep learning-based feature extraction techniques to model material characteristics. These features are then used to classify materials with high accuracy through supervised learning methods using different image resolutions. For the traditional approach, Histogram of Oriented Gradients (HOG) feature descriptor combined with SVM gives 95.41% accuracy using the new image dataset. After fine-tuning five pre-trained models for transfer learning on our dataset, Dense-Net121 (96.42%), InceptionV3 (96.32%), and VGG16 (95.77%) models show promising results, and the ensemble of these 3 fine-tuned models provides highest accuracy of 97.63%. The results demonstrate the feasibility of using GelSight-based material classification for haptic feedback, with potential implications for virtual reality, robotic manipulation, and human-computer interaction applications.

Keywords: Material classification · Haptic feedback · Visio-tactile sensor · Feature extraction · Machine learning · Deep learning

1 Introduction

Haptic describes the sense of touch as well as the perception and object manipulation that follow from any type of touch-based interaction. The primary objective of haptic technology is to simulate touch sensation. It refers to systems that permit users to interact with digital or physical environments by utilizing the sense of touch. This technology simulates the sense of touch through applying forces, vibrations, or motions to the user [30]. Haptic feedback is the main element of haptic technologies, where devices return physical feedback to the user when they interact with a virtual object or a physical machine. For instance, when a user uses a smartphone and feels a slight vibration while

J. Röning and J. Filipe (Eds.): ROBOVIS 2025, CCIS 2629, pp. 364–382, 2026.
https://doi.org/10.1007/978-3-032-00986-9_24

pressing a button on the screen, that's haptic feedback. In a more advanced setting, haptic devices can simulate textures, resistance, or even the weight of virtual objects, enhancing the realism of virtual experiences [6].

For the haptic feedback, material classification plays an important task in helping automation grow in different fields, especially in robotics and manufacturing. Precise recognition of materials is vital for robots to interact with various objects in dynamic surroundings, aiding activities like manufacturing inspection, handling and sorting [18]. The latest advances in vision-based touch sensing introduce clear opportunities for improved material classification. Unlike using visual or touch systems on their own, vision-based touch sensors, like the GelSight Mini, capture detailed surface texture data that greatly improves how materials are recognized [38]. Mixing touch data with visual signals allows a robotic setup to "feel" and "see" the texture, creating a strong combination for differentiating materials.

GelSight technology first came about for studying touch-sensing in complicated tasks like robot gripping. This technology offers detailed texture information, which helps in grouping materials that have similar visual appearances [20]. However, using this detailed tactile data proves complex for data handling and requires strong classification methods to interpret sophisticated higher dimensional information correctly. Telling apart materials with tiny texture differences - like metal, plastic or ceramic - needs techniques that grab both large and small features. This challenge shows the necessity for advanced feature extraction methods. Solving this issue needs a broad strategy that visits both traditional and deep learning methods to keep computing efficient and precise.

This research aims to contribute to the tactile sensing and material classification within robotics and computer vision, by building a diverse material dataset with the GelSight Mini. This sensor records a variety of data that humans have gathered from different indoor and outdoor items in various conditions. The dataset has materials often used in manufacturing, linking the research to real-world applications such as checking quality and automating processes. We explore traditional feature extraction methods, such as Histogram of Oriented Gradients (HOG) [8], Local Binary Patterns (LBP) [27], Scale-Invariant Feature Transform (SIFT) [26], along with traditional classifiers and deep learning methods, for supervised machine learning. The study explores how these techniques perform in this application area. It also fine-tunes the pre-trained models like ResNet50 [12], InceptionV3 [31], VGG16 [29], Dense-Net121 [14], EffiencientNetB2 [32] to improve feature quality, thus improving classification success with small amounts of data. Our main goal involves improving classification accuracy and connecting these findings with touch feedback for haptic interactions. By studying vision based tactile sensors, this work opens pathways for reliable material classification, fixing important gaps in research and increasing the practical use of touch sensors in smart manufacturing.

The paper is organized as follows. In Sect. 2 related works and motivation for the work are discussed. In Sect. 3 materials, dataset, and methods are described in detail, including feature extraction, classification, and transfer learning models. In Sect. 4, the experimental results of classifications are displayed to demonstrate the efficiency and connection towards haptic feedback. In Sect. 5, the study and future directions are summarized.

2 Related Work

Tactile sensing technology has expanded quickly because robotics and human-computer interaction need systems that could mimic human touch sensitivity. These sensors give important information about texture, hardness and structural traits of objects, allowing machines to understand physical interactions very accurately [7]. Traditional tactile sensors, like piezoelectric [19] and capacitive [21] ones, have had some success in measuring forces or noticing surface details [24, 28]. However, they frequently miss the fine details needed for precise material recognition. Recent visio-tactile sensors, which mix sight and touch sensing—offer higher sensitivity and spatial resolution, making these useful for robots that require delicate object handling [36]. Unlike traditional sensors, these sensors show spatial mapping of applying force across surfaces when they touch, helping robots grasp and move things more easily.

GelSight is a special type of sensor that combines sight and touch. It captures detailed surface topography upon touch, translating touch into visual data, with the help of a high-resolution camera under a soft and deformable gel [17, 39]. This system helps to identify material surfaces because it notices small deformations, which signify textures, and other material properties [20]. GelSight's soft gel layer bends around surfaces, making it good at picking up small details that other tactile sensors miss, such as tiny textures and sharp edges [10]. Current research highlights that GelSight works well in recognizing materials and objects. Yuan et al. [38] showed that GelSight could classify different textures accurately on diverse materials by representing touch information as images that machine learning algorithms can interpret.

Recently, datasets collected by GelSight have become popular. Yang et al. [34] provided the "Touch and Go" dataset, where humans gathered GelSight data in many different indoor and outdoor places. They collected detailed information for self-supervised learning across 13,900 touches and 3,971 different objects. This dataset stands out because of its variety and method of using personal viewpoints for data collection and offers a benchmarking for cross-modal tasks, unlike datasets from labs like "VisGel" [22] or "The Feeling of Success" [4] which mostly collected data in lab environments using robots. These earlier datasets usually focused on repetitive tasks for object recognition, whereas our GelSight dataset is designed for classifying materials among objects, highlighting both indoor and outdoor material differences, and distinct haptic properties with less objects.

Material classification commonly depends on feature extraction from images using methods like the Histogram of Oriented Gradients (HOG), Scale-Invariant Feature Transform (SIFT), and Local Binary Patterns (LBP), which emphasize texture and shape characteristics [8, 25]. HOG has been heavily used in visual tasks and works well even when light changes, and thus is appropriate to use with tactile images captured by GelSight. Research by Liang et al. [23] determined that HOG works well for object recognition when used with Support Vector Machines (SVM), achieving good accuracy over significant textures. In [15], Support Vector Machine (SVM) and Random Forest (RF) classifiers provide high classification rate in texture recognition upon haptic perception using a bionic tactile sensor. Among many traditional classifiers, SVM and RF are widely used in detection, recognition, and classification relating materials.

Deep learning models have advanced material classification by using large datasets and high-resolution images. Earlier studies on estimating materials with GelSight effectively utilized convolutional neural networks that were initially trained using natural image data [36, 40]. Convolutional Neural Networks (CNNs) find detailed, multi-layer features, so they match complex material characteristics. Transfer learning with models like ResNet50, InceptionV3, DenseNet121, EfficientNetB2, VGG16, uses existing knowledge from big image datasets, giving better results in tasks like tactile-based classification [1, 3]. Fine-tuning pre-trained models has proven beneficial for the image classification tasks [33], thus making them appropriate for use with GelSight data, as the sensor's unique touch images need very detailed feature extraction to spot small changes and textures that show material differences [20, 38]. Ensemble methods join predictions from many models, which have emerged as a robust approach for improving classification performance [9]. Studies using ensemble transfer learning show better accuracy and strength in recognition and detection tasks [2, 5].

The use of GelSight sensors is growing in robotic tasks for haptic feedback as new designs extend the limits of touch understanding. In virtual reality, GelSight helps identify materials and creates real touch feelings [11], while in robotic work, GelSight's touch feedback helps with accurate and careful control [10]. Studies show GelSight helps with holding objects steady and guessing how hard materials are, it uses haptic information about texture and softness, so robots adjust their hold and manage things correctly [4, 37]. GelSight mixes sight and touch information connecting haptic feedback to improve object recognition in challenging situations [35]. These studies show that GelSight sensors are useful for robot handling and quick material identification, which fits with haptic feedback in our research.

3 Materials and Methods

3.1 GelSight Mini

We have used a GelSight Mini tactile sensor for our research from GelSight Inc. [16]. The GelSight Mini is a touch sensor using an 8MP camera and RGB lights. It is small, around 1.5 cm wide. It collects clear data by recording how 4.25 mm soft gel changes shape when it touches a surface. Many colorful lights illuminated on the gel, which contains markers within it. The black dots (illustrated in Fig. 1.(c)) are markers which bend with the gel, giving information about the surface of the object. The gel matches the shape of the object and GelSight captures many images, allowing for detailed 2D and 3D study, important for figuring out what the materials are.

GelSight generally captures a video where direction, depth and tilt might be determined by studying each video's frame. It takes pictures at 25 frames each second in an 18.6×14.3 mm area. It works well with robots and vision tasks using ROS/ROS2 and PyTouch. Figure 1 illustrates a GelSight Mini sensor taking a sample of Rockery Stone.

(a) (b) (c)

Fig. 1. (a) Picture of GelSight Mini, (b) Recording sample of Rockery Stone using GelSight Mini, and (c) An image sample of Rockery Stone.

3.2 Dataset Creation

Material Selection. The dataset includes 13 types of material to cover different tactile properties needed for strong material classification. Each type includes 3–4 representative items to keep variety within each group. For example, in the Plastic class, items like a water bottle, plastic bag and food container show differences in feeling and stiffness. In the Metal class, items go from hard and heavy things (cast iron, stainless steel) to softer ones (aluminum foil, drink can), enabling the GelSight sensor to check both hard and soft surfaces. Figure 2 visualizes selected 42 items in 13 material classes, demonstrating the variety and touch challenges each class brings. This material selection aims to mimic real textures and shapes that a touch-vision system might find, creating a dataset that fits many different situations.

Recording Video Samples. Video examples were collected for each chosen item. There are 3–4 recordings per item, capturing various surface details and touch experiences. Each video lasts around 11–12 s, showing different angles, pressures and lighting. In the process, the GelSight sensor was moved across each item's surface, using slide, lift and press actions to collect unique spots and detailed textures. This method resulted in different video frames showing various regions and angles to capture small changes in surface patterns. Although the GelSight naturally reveals force data through the elastomeric gel deformation [38], exact force measurements were not needed for the proposed visuo-tactile classification task.

Frame Selection and Labelling. Selecting frames from video samples is an important step in creating the dataset, pertaining to those that give useful touch and visual information, while avoiding repeated information. We developed Algorithm 1 to select frames with strong touch contact and distinct texture details. Our video samples were already sorted by each material class subfolder in the dataset folder, the whole dataset folder fed into the algorithm with other inputs.

First, it compares each frame to a reference image when the sensor was untouched, skipping frames with little contact using a similarity threshold of 0.5. For frames with clear interaction, it measures the mean absolute difference between consecutive frames to detect significant pressing events, using a threshold value of 2 to find frames where meaningful surface deformation occurred. Then, it crops each chosen frame to the marker region of [300:2100, 400:2750] pixels for consistency and focus on touch interaction.

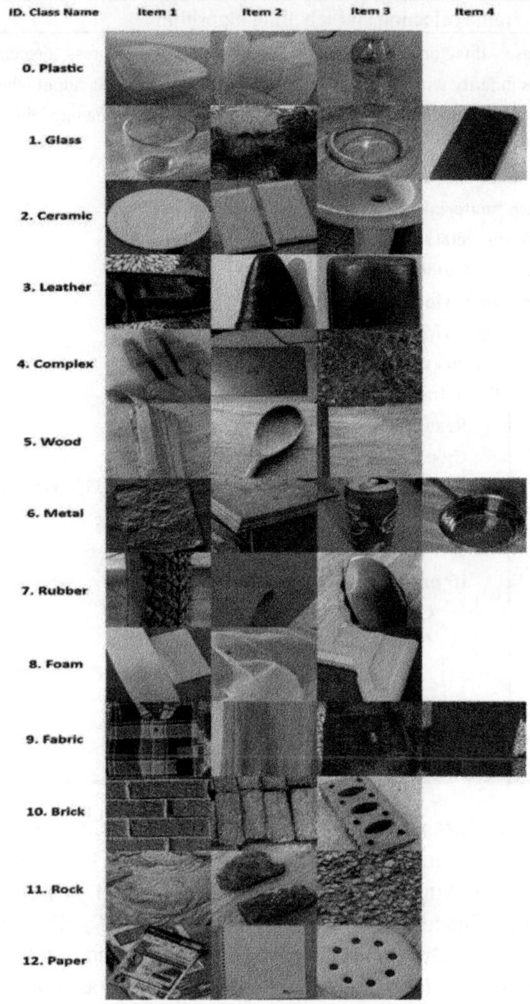

Fig. 2. Overview of 13 material classes and 42 selected items.

This algorithm generates a dataset full of touch features, cutting out repeated images and keeping varied, high-quality samples with important material properties.

Final Image Dataset. The final set of data contains 796 images for each of the 13 material classes, totaling 10,348 images. Each image has a size of 2350 $\times$ 1800 pixels. This selected set of images balances the number of samples in each group, providing enough data to train, validation and test models that classify materials.

Algorithm 1: Frame selection and labelling algorithm.

Input: Dataset directory with videos, reference image, press detection threshold (**thres old_value**), similarity with reference (**similarity_threshold**), and output label file.

Output: Selected, cropped frames saved as images with corresponding labels written to label file.

```
Load 'reference_gray' ← grayscale(reference_image)
Open 'label_file' for writing
For each 'material_class' in material class dataset folder:
    Assign 'class_index' to 'material_class'
    Create 'frames' folder if it doesn't exist
    For each 'video' in 'material_class':
        Open video capture 'cap'
        Set 'prev_frame' ← None
        While frames are available in 'video':
            Read 'frame' and convert to 'gray_frame'
            Crop region [300:2100, 400:2750]                     #cropping markers region
            Calculate mean absolute difference (MAD) with 'reference_gray'
            If MAD < 'similarity_threshold': continue            #skipping not -touched frame
            If 'prev_frame' is not None:
                Calculate MAD with 'prev_frame'
                If MAD > 'threshold_value':                      #detecting significant press
                    Save 'frame' and write 'class_index' to 'label_file'
            Set 'prev_frame' ← 'gray_frame'
        Release 'cap'
Close 'label_file'
```

Contrary to Other Datasets. Table 1 shows how our dataset and earlier GelSight datasets are different in source, setting and touch variety. Our collection has 42 objects and 10,348 touches, making it one of the largest gathered by humans. Other datasets like 'The Feeling of Success' [4] and 'VisGel' [22] were gathered by robots in controlled tabletop settings. Our dataset covers both indoor and outdoor areas, capturing a wider range of real-world textures. 'Touch and Go' [34] has more objects (3,971) and touches (13,900) in indoor settings, but our dataset offers a mix of quantity and different environments. Our dataset balances the number of samples with differences in settings, capturing natural surface details in various places. This flexibility is very useful for visuo-tactile projects that require real-life data.

Table 1. Real-world GelSight datasets, a simple comparison with past datasets.

Dataset	Items	Touches	Environment	Source
The Feeling of Success [4]	106	9300	Table-top	Robot
VisGel [22]	195	12000	Table-top	Robot
Touch and Go [34]	3971	13900	Indoor	Human
Material Dataset (Ours)	42	10348	Indoor and Outdoor	Human

3.3 Traditional Feature Extraction and Classification

This research utilized different traditional image processing and machine learning methods to find and sort material details from GelSight sensor information. We specifically applied Histogram of Oriented Gradients (HOG), Local Binary Patterns (LBP) and Scale-Invariant Feature Transform (SIFT) to obtain features. These feature descriptions were tested with two guided classifiers: Support Vector Machine (SVM) and Random Forest (RF).

Histogram of Oriented Gradients (HOG). HOG studied gradient orientations in small areas, determining edge and texture details that are important for finding material patterns. The gradient of each pixel is measured in the x-axis and y-axis, then sorted into orientation bins, creating a histogram that shows local edge directions and stays strong against light changes [8]. This technique, often used for identifying objects, is described by the following key steps for our implementation.

- Calculate Gradients: For each pixel, the gradient G_x and G_y along the x and y axes are calculated as in Eq. 1 and Eq. 2.

$$G_x = f(x+1, y) - f(x-1, y) \tag{1}$$

$$G_y = f(x, y+1) - f(x, y-1) \tag{2}$$

- Calculation of gradient magnitude (Eq. 3) and gradient orientation (Eq. 4).

$$magnitude = \sqrt{G_x^2 + G_y^2} \tag{3}$$

$$orientation = arctan(\frac{G_y}{G_x}) \tag{4}$$

- Histogram Binning: Gradients are then converted into orientation bins, inside regions of 16x16 pixels. These binned values are adjusted to L2 normalization in bigger blocks to maintain stability against light variations.

Local Binary Patterns (LBP). LBP secures surrounding texture by recording brightness differences between nearby pixels. For one pixel, the brightness of each nearby pixel is checked against the middle pixel, creating a pattern of 0s and 1s that shows nearby texture details [27]. This pattern stays unchanged with simple light adjustments, so it is very effective for capturing detailed textures. The value of LBP is calculated as in Eq. 5, where $s(x) = 1$ if $x \geq 0$ and $s(x) = 0$ if $x < 0$.

$$LBP(x, y) = \sum_{p=0}^{p-1} s\big(I_p - I(x, y)\big) \times 2^p \tag{5}$$

Scale-Invariant Feature Transform (SIFT). SIFT discovers unique key points that do not change with size, rotation or light [26]. The image is shown at many sizes by slowly smoothing it with a Gaussian filter, and key points are determined by measuring local extremes in Difference of Gaussian (DoG) representation:

$$D(x, y, \sigma) = L(x, y, k\sigma) - L(x, y, \sigma) \tag{6}$$

where k is a constant value and $L(x, y, \sigma)$ refers to the image softened at level σ. This method identifies unique spots within every material's surface.

Support Vector Machine (SVM). SVM, a supervised learning algorithm, locates an optimal hyperplane to divide classes in the feature space [13]. Initially made for two-class classification, SVM might adapt for multiple classes using methods like one-vs-one or one-vs-rest. In the one-vs-one method, each pair of classes gets its own SVM model, while in one-vs-rest, one model trains per class against all other classes. For a specific decision function when there are only two choices,

$$f(x) = w^T x + b \tag{7}$$

SVM improves the gap between classes with the condition of $y_i\left(w^T x_i + b\right)$ for every training example (x_i, y_i). Multiclass classification happens by merging outcomes from the two-class classifiers. This enables a SVM to manage different material types well in the proposed classification task.

Random Forest (RF). RF is an ensemble learning technique using many decision trees, each trained with different parts of the data [15]. Every tree chooses its category and the main decision comes from the choice that most trees agree on, giving the model better stability and reducing overfitting. The RF classifier works well for data with many features, like texture details, because it deals with complex interactions between these features. Also, because it uses randomness and takes averages from many trees, it stays strong against noise, giving dependable results when classifying materials where small texture changes are important.

3.4 Ensemble Transfer Learning

To improve how well the material classification task works with GelSight sensor data, we examined an ensemble transfer learning approach. After looking at traditional feature extraction and classification methods, we decided to try deep learning techniques by using pre-trained models, which help with strong feature extraction. The five pre-trained models used in this research were ResNet50, InceptionV3, VGG16, DenseNet121 and EfficientNetB2. These models were chosen because they work really well in different image classification tasks, pre-trained on the same dataset that includes our material classes, and can adjust to various types of data through transfer learning.

1. **ResNet50** is a deep residual network with 50 layers, first trained on the ImageNet dataset [12]. This network uses skip connections, which help solve the dissipating gradient issue in deep networks. It accepts an input size of 224 × 224 pixels and contains 25.6 million parameters. ResNet50's depth and skip links allow it to capture high-level features well and avoid overfitting. In TensorFlow, ResNet50 includes 50 layers with around 177 trainable layers when split into TensorFlow's parameter collections.
2. **InceptionV3** is a deep structured neural network trained with the ImageNet dataset, known for using different filter sizes together [31]. This design helps the model recognize features at many levels. It is good at classifying images with different

detail levels. InceptionV3 has 48 layers and about 23.8 million parameters. It accepts images sized 299 × 299 pixels as inputs, bigger than some models, thus it perceives finer details. TensorFlow's InceptionV3 model includes 313 layers that can be trained. This is because of its intricate design with different filter sizes and pathways.

3. **VGG16** is a convolutional neural network with a simple design, it contains 16 layers and has trained on the ImageNet dataset [29]. VGG16 is renowned for using small 3x3 filters. It has a deep structure, which allows it to recognize detailed parts of images. The model includes 138 million parameters. It takes input images of size 224 × 224 pixels. Although it needs more computation because of many parameters, its design fits tasks with high-resolution images, such as the GelSight dataset, where capturing detail matters a lot. VGG16 involves 23 trainable layers in TensorFlow.
4. **DenseNet121** is a newer design famous for its dense connection style. Each part links to all other parts in a tightly connected way. Trained on the ImageNet dataset, DenseNet121 holds 121 layers and about 8 million parameters [14]. It needs an input size of 224 × 224 pixels. The denser connections let features be used again efficiently and give it fewer parameters than other deep models. TensorFlow's DenseNet121 has approximately 428 adjustable layers when divided into parameter groups.
5. **EfficientNetB2** belongs to the EfficientNet group, shaped to refine effectiveness by balancing depth, width and resolution of the network. Trained with ImageNet, EfficientNetB2 includes 18 layers and approximately 8 million parameters [32]. Input sizes at 260 × 260 pixels, offering a strong balance of computational efficiency and precision. EfficientNetB2 in TensorFlow includes 342 trainable layers because of its scaling setup, which manages depth, width and resolution effectively.

We trained all the pre-trained models on the top layers with our GelSight material dataset. The last fully connected layers changed to fit the number of material classes utilised. Slowly unfreezing the last 10–40 layers and training them with a smaller learning rate helped, which protected the existing pre-trained weights. The number of layers chosen varied based on the structure of the model. This method allowed better comprehension of the GelSight images by fine-tuning the pre-trained models to the specific characteristics of the material while keeping their image recognition skill to generalize from ImageNet.

To raise classification accuracy and reliability, the ensemble averaging approach was checked on different combinations of the pre-trained models. The ensemble method focuses on taking the average of class probabilities given by different models. For each test sample, the models like InceptionV3, DenseNet121 and VGG16 provided class probabilities through the test generator. These probabilities were averaged from all models to get the final ensemble predictions. This allowed the strengths of each single model to add to the final classification choice. This learning helps in reducing overfitting and increasing performance by easing the bias of single models. The average predictions from the best-performing fine-tuned models were put together to create the final outcome, ending in a more dependable and correct classification of the material classes.

4 Experimental Results

The experiments for materials classification using the GelSight sensor images include two main approaches. Our tests aimed to check how well both methods worked using our custom GelSight dataset with 10,348 images representing 13 classes of material, each having a very high-resolution of 2350 × 1800 pixels. The dataset was divided into training (60%), validation (20%) and testing (20%) sets, representing each class evenly in every set.

The experiments using the traditional approaches employed Python 3.12 with Scikit-Learn library for feature extraction and classification. For deep learning experiments, TensorFlow, Keras and OpenCV libraries were utilized. Model training operated on a NVIDIA GeForce RTX 4070 Ti allowing efficient training and adjustment of transfer learning models on the high-resolution dataset.

4.1 Traditional Feature Extraction and Classification

At first, experiments were conducted using a dataset of small images (size 254 × 254) to lessen computing effort while keeping important details and later moved to higher image sizes of 655 × 500 to maintain the aspect ratio. Feature descriptors methods employed were Histogram of Oriented Gradients (HOG), Local Binary Patterns (LBP) and Scale-Invariant Feature Transform (SIFT). Every feature group was combined with the Support Vector Machine (SVM) and the Random Forest (RF) and the classification accuracy calculated.

Initial Experiments Using 254 × 254 Images. HOG regularly exceeded the performance of other feature descriptors using both the SVM and RF classifiers. HOG + SVM obtained the highest accuracy among the traditional methods, as shown in Table 2. Although LBP works quickly to describe texture, it did not perform well, showing an accuracy of only 12.22% (LBP + SVM) using this dataset. This result signals that it was not successful in extracting the unique features from the touch images.

Table 2. Traditional classification results on 254 × 254.

Feature Extraction	Classification	Accuracy
HOG	SVM	**92.19%**
HOG	RF	75.66%
LBP	SVM	12.22%
LBP	RF	72.12%
SIFT	SVM	66.81%
SIFT	RF	70.28%

Experiments Using 655 × 500 Images. We maintained the GelSight sensor's original image shape and utilised HOG, LBP and SIFT. HOG + SVM obtained a high accuracy of 94.92%, see Table 3. Next, we used Grid Search cross-validation with 4-folds for hyperparameter tuning on HOG + SVM. This process optimized the parameters (C = 100, gamma = 0.001, kernel = 'rbf') and improved accuracy to 95.12%. Figure 3 and Table 4 illustrate the confusion matrix and classification report on the test set for this model.

Table 3. Traditional classification results on 655 × 500.

Feature Extraction	Classification	Accuracy
HOG	SVM	**94.92%**
HOG	RF	79.06%
LBP	SVM	11.59%
LBP	RF	77.29%
SIFT	SVM	68.51%
SIFT	RF	69.16%

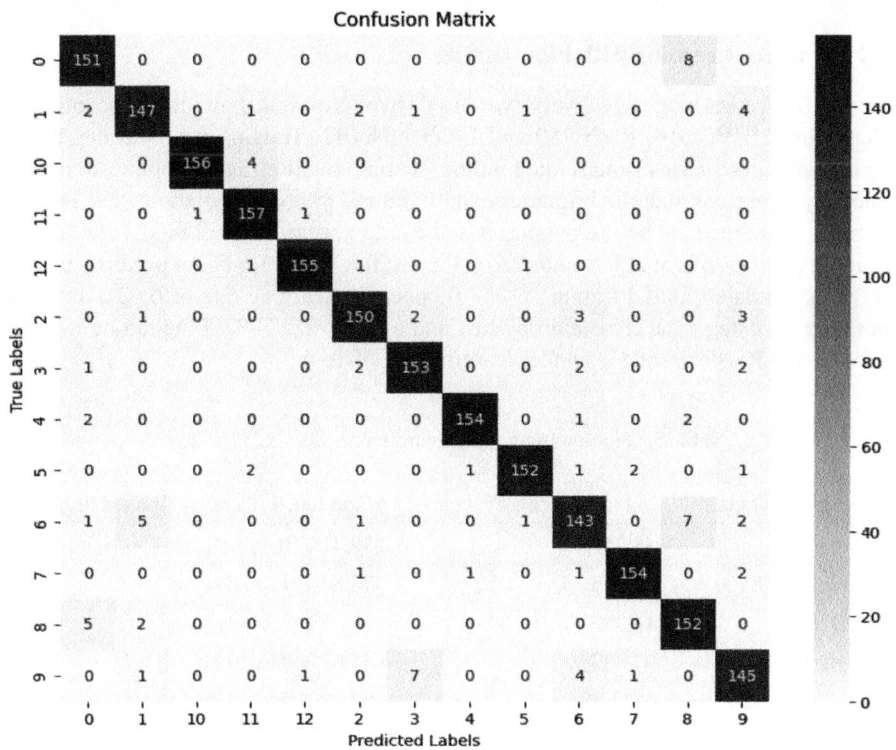

Fig. 3. Confusion matrix for HOG and SVM with best hyperparameters.

Table 4. Classification report for HOG and SVM with best hyperparameters.

Class	Precision	Recall	F1-Score	Support
0	0.93	0.95	0.94	159
1	0.94	0.92	0.93	159
10	0.99	0.97	0.98	160
11	0.95	0.99	0.97	159
12	0.99	0.97	0.98	159
2	0.96	0.94	0.95	159
3	0.94	0.96	0.95	160
4	0.99	0.97	0.98	159
5	0.98	0.96	0.97	159
6	0.92	0.89	0.91	160
7	0.98	0.97	0.97	159
8	0.90	0.96	0.93	159
9	0.91	0.91	0.91	159
Accuracy			**0.95**	2070
Macro avg	0.95	0.95	0.95	2070

4.2 Transfer Learning with Fine-Tuning

To use deep learning effectively, we used five pre-trained models: InceptionV3, DenseNet121, VGG16, ResNet50 and EfficientNetB2. Training data was augmented by applying geometric changes like flipping, scaling, rotation, and cropping, along with intensity adaptions such as brightness and contrast, to create variations and increase samples within the set before passing into the data generator. Each model started with training on the top layer, then adjusted on the last few layers for better performance and this was validated. Initial training used 10 epochs, a learning rate of 0.001, an Adam optimizer, a categorical cross entropy loss and a batch size of 32. Fine-tuning involved another 10–50 epochs and a smaller learning rate of 1e-4.

Table 5. Fine-tuning transfer learning results on 254 × 254.

Pre-trained Models	Initial Training Accuracy	Fine-tuned Accuracy (trained layers)
InceptionV3	55.94%	**79.41%** (last 30 layers)
DenseNet121	67.72%	78.80% (last 30 layers)
VGG16	44.30%	72.45% (last 4 layers)
ResNet50	07.30%	31.61% (last 30 layers)
EfficientNetB2	08.00%	07.96% (last 20 layers)

254 × 254 Image Dataset. Models were fine-tuned to 10 epochs. DenseNet121 and InceptionV3 models reached good accuracy after fine-tuning using images of size 254 × 254, achieving 78.80% and 79.41% respectively, see Table 5. VGG16 also improved with fine-tuning. However, ResNet50 and EfficientNetB2 often showed poor results, probably because of overfitting or because they did not extract features well from this dataset.

655 × 500 Image Dataset. Models were fine-tuned to 50 epochs. Evaluating the pre-trained models using 655 × 500 images resulted in significant improvements in precision, especially for DenseNet121 (96.42%) and InceptionV3 (96.32%) after careful adjustments as shown in Table 6. Fine-tuning on larger images enabled the models to notice smaller texture elements. Figure 4 illustrates the accuracy and loss curves for the fine-tuned InceptionV3, DenseNet121, and VGG16 models respectively.

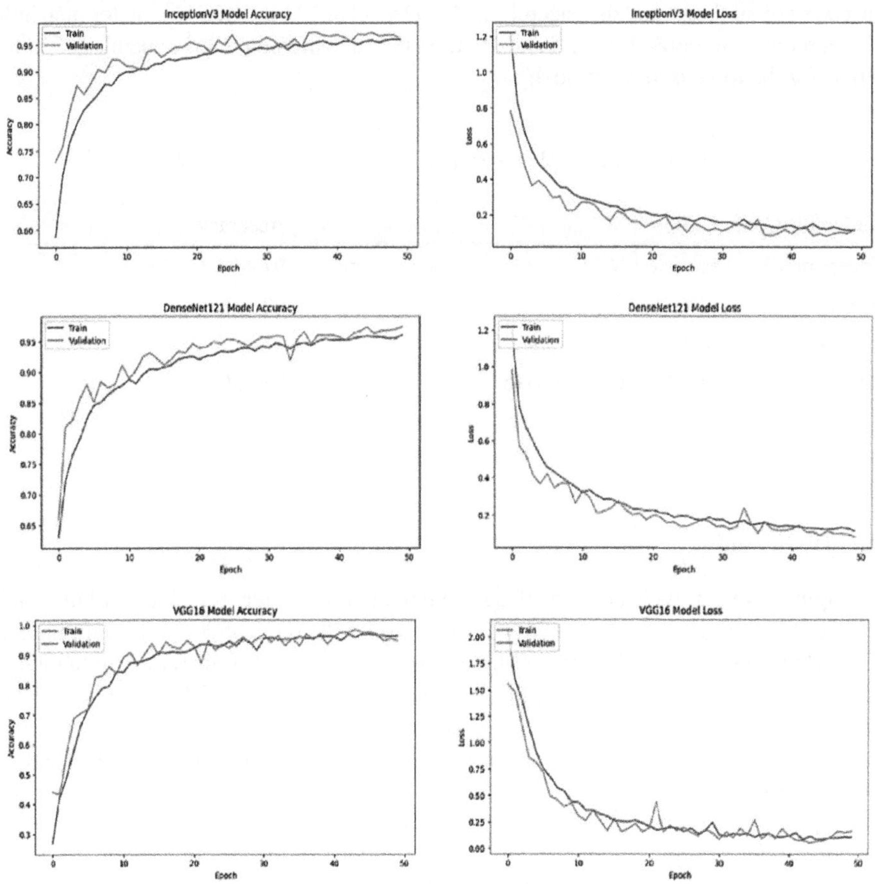

Fig. 4. Accuracy vs loss curves for 3 fine-tuned models to 50 epochs.

Ensemble with Average Predictions. After checking each model on its own, we tried ensemble techniques to refine classification results more, using the test data. The leading three models, InceptionV3, DenseNet121 and VGG16, were tested in various combinations to form an ensemble. The final result for each combination is found by taking

Table 6. Fine-tuning transfer learning results on 655 × 500.

Pre-trained Models	Initial Training Accuracy	Fine-tuned Accuracy (trained layers)
InceptionV3	59.13%	96.32% (from 259 layers)
DenseNet121	65.49%	**96.42%** (from 380 layers)
VGG16	35.12%	95.77% (from 10 layers)

the average from the set of predictions given by the chosen models. Table 7 displays ensemble transfer learning results. The best accuracy (97.63%) was achieved using an ensemble of all three models (InceptionV3 + DenseNet121 + VGG16), better than individual model outcomes. Figure 5 and Table 8 show a confusion matrix and classification report for the top ensemble model.

Table 7. Ensemble transfer learning results on 655 × 500.

Ensemble Configuration	Accuracy
InceptionV3 + DenseNet121	97.43%
DenseNet121 + VGG16	97.10%
VGG16 + InceptinV3	97.44%
InceptionV3 + DenseNet121 + VGG16	**97.63%**

4.3 Discussion

GelSight sensors provide clear touch data, enabling us to capture tiny details of materials for accurate sorting. All experiments work well with the 655 × 500 image dataset. Traditional methods like HOG with SVM work well, but ensemble transfer learning models performed best. Fine-tuning InceptionV3, DenseNet121 and VGG16 models achieves high correctness with high-resolution images. This precision is crucial for accurately completing robotic tasks in busy environments, where fast and accurate material sorting requires them to adjust their actions quickly. In manufacturing, a robot with touch sensing can make decisions about how it grips items based on the material, improving safety and work quality.

By turning touch data into touch responses, we help robots adapt to different materials, like gently holding delicate objects or securely grasping rough ones, making robotic systems more flexible and reactive. Our results indicate that adding touch sensing and machine learning brings robots closer to human-like feeling and better handling. GelSight sensing helps not only in classifying materials but also shows a path to robots that interact more precisely and naturally with real-time touch feedback.

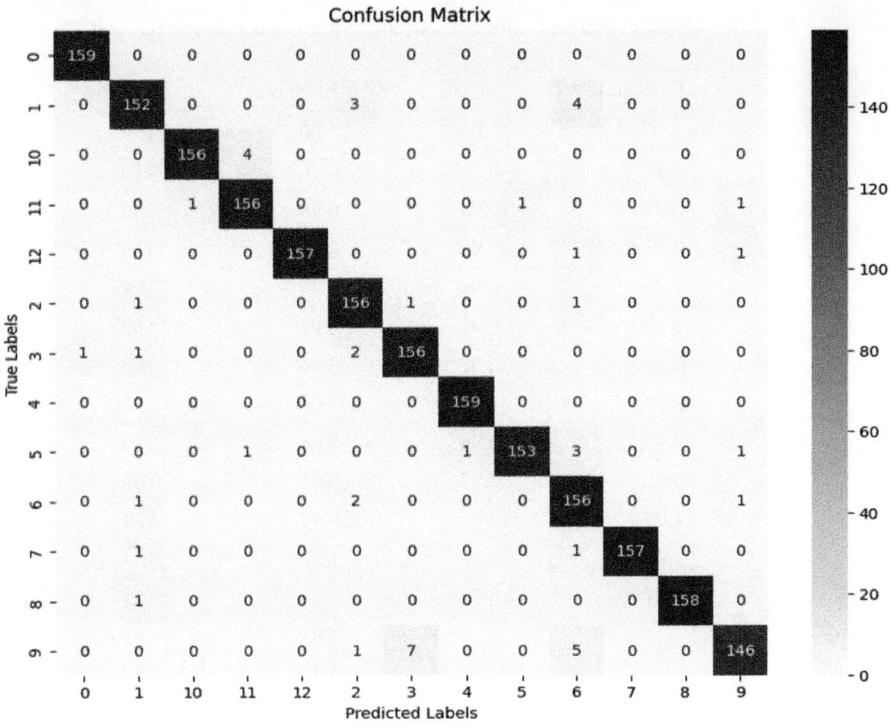

Fig. 5. Confusion matrix for best ensemble transfer learning on test set.

5 Conclusion

This study shows how GelSight-based material identification could enable robotic touch systems for flexible and effective handling of different materials. We developed and classified a large collection of detailed touch images. We investigated how well basic feature descriptors work with traditional classifiers, following ensemble transfer learning methods. Ensemble models usually achieve good classification accuracy. These models fit situations needing accurate feedback quickly in complicated surroundings.

Future work will expand this study by looking at real-time model usage to permit quick touch feedback and material changes in robot systems. Improving models for quicker conclusions, maybe using simpler designs or model pruning, becomes important to match the needs of real-time uses. Also, examining the combination of different sensors, like combined GelSight data with heat or sound sensing, could provide a fuller understanding of material features, enhancing classification precision and touch response skills.

Adding more types of materials, different environmental settings and various textures to the dataset probably strengthens the model. Automation of the frame selection process reduces manual work and helps in growing the dataset. Bringing these classification models into robot systems with touch feedback possibly allows for special handling methods for each material. This change means that robots act in a safer and more accurate

Table 8. Classification report for best ensemble transfer learning on test set.

Class	Precision	Recall	F1-Score	Support
0	0.99	1.00	1.00	159
1	0.97	0.96	0.96	159
2	0.99	0.97	0.98	160
3	0.97	0.98	0.97	159
4	1.00	0.99	0.99	159
5	0.95	0.98	0.97	159
6	0.95	0.97	0.96	160
7	0.99	1.00	1.00	159
8	0.99	0.96	0.98	159
9	0.91	0.97	0.94	160
10	1.00	0.99	0.99	159
11	1.00	0.99	1.00	159
12	0.97	0.92	0.94	159
Accuracy			**0.98**	2070
Macro avg	0.98	0.98	0.98	2070

way with different materials. These improvements drive manufacturing robots, especially for tasks requiring quick, human-like touch responses.

Acknowledgments. This research is funded by Innovate UK under the Smart Manufacturing Data Hub project (contract no. 10017032) – www.smdh.uk.

References

1. Aral, R.A., Keskin, Ş.R., Kaya, M., Hacıömeroğlu, M.: Classification of TrashNet dataset based on deep learning models. In: 2018 IEEE International Conference on Big Data (Big Data), pp. 2058–2062 (2018). https://doi.org/10.1109/BigData.2018.8622212
2. Bian, P., Li, W., Jin, Y., Zhi, R.: Ensemble feature learning for material recognition with convolutional neural networks. J. Image Video Process. **2018**, 64 (2018). https://doi.org/10.1186/s13640-018-0300-z
3. Bircanoğlu, C., Atay, M., Beşer, F., Genç, Ö., Kızrak, M.A.: RecycleNet: intelligent waste sorting using deep neural networks. In: 2018 Innovations in Intelligent Systems and Applications (INISTA), pp. 1–7 (2018). https://doi.org/10.1109/INISTA.2018.8466276
4. Calandra, R., Owens, A., Upadhyaya, M., Yuan, W.Z., Lin, J., Adelson, E.H., et al.: The feeling of success: does touch sensing help predict grasp outcomes? In: Conference on Robotic learning (CoRL), pp. 314–323 (2017). https://doi.org/10.48550/arXiv.1710.05512
5. Casado-Garcia, A., Heras, J.: Ensemble methods for object detection. In: ECAI 2020. IOS Press, pp. 2688–2695 (2020). https://doi.org/10.3233/FAIA200407

6. Culbertson, H., Schorr, S.B., Okamura, A.M.: Haptics: the present and future of artificial touch sensation. Annu. Rev. Control Robot. Auton. Syst. **1**, 385–409 (2018). https://doi.org/10.1146/annurev-control-060117-105043
7. Dahiya, R.S., Metta, G., Valle, M., Sandini, G.: Tactile sensing—from humans to humanoids. IEEE Trans. Rob. **26**(1), 1–20 (2010). https://doi.org/10.1109/TRO.2009.2033627
8. Dalal, N., Triggs, B.: Histograms of oriented gradients for human detection. In: 2005 IEEE Computer Society Conference on Computer Vision and Pattern Recognition (CVPR'05), pp. 886–893 (2005). https://doi.org/10.1109/CVPR.2005.177
9. Dietterich, T.G.: Ensemble methods in machine learning. In: Multiple Classifier Systems. MCS 2000. LNCS, vol. 1857, pp. 1–15. Springer, Berlin, Heidelberg (2000). https://doi.org/10.1007/3-540-45014-9_1
10. Dong, S., Yuan, W., Adelson, E.H.: Improved GelSight tactile sensor for measuring geometry and slip. In: 2017 IEEE/RSJ International Conference on Intelligent Robots and Systems (IROS), pp. 137–144 (2017). https://doi.org/10.1109/IROS.2017.8202149
11. Gomes, D.F., Paoletti, P., Luo, S.: Generation of GelSight tactile images for Sim2Real learning. IEEE Robot. Autom. Lett. **6**(2), 4177–4184 (2021). https://doi.org/10.1109/LRA.2021.3063925
12. He, K., Zhang, X., Ren, S., Sun, J.: Deep residual learning for image recognition. In: 2016 IEEE Conference on Computer Vision and Pattern Recognition (CVPR), pp. 770–778 (2016). https://doi.org/10.1109/CVPR.2016.90
13. Hearst, M.A., Dumais, S.T., Osuna, E., Platt, J., Scholkopf, B.: Support vector machines. IEEE Intell. Syst. Appl. **13**(4), 18–28 (1998). https://doi.org/10.1109/5254.708428
14. Huang, G., Liu, Z., Van Der Maaten, L., Weinberger, K.Q.: Densely connected convolutional networks. In: 2017 IEEE Conference on Computer Vision and Pattern Recognition (CVPR), pp. 2261–2269 (2017). https://doi.org/10.1109/CVPR.2017.243
15. Huang, S., Wu, H.: Texture recognition based on perception data from a bionic tactile sensor. Sensors **21**(15), 5224 (2021). https://doi.org/10.3390/s21155224
16. Inc., G.: GelSight Mini: A portable high-resolution tactile sensor. GelSight Inc. https://www.gelsight.com/gelsightmini/. Accessed 07 Nov 2024
17. Johnson, M.K., Adelson, E.H.: Retrographic sensing for the measurement of surface texture and shape. In: 2009 IEEE Conference on Computer Vision and Pattern Recognition, pp. 1070–1077 (2009). https://doi.org/10.1109/CVPR.2009.5206534
18. Kerr, E., McGinnity, T.M., Coleman, S.: Material recognition using tactile sensing. Expert Syst. Appl. **94**, 94–111 (2018). https://doi.org/10.1016/j.eswa.2017.10.045
19. Kolesar, E.S., Dyson, C.S.: Object imaging with a piezoelectric robotic tactile sensor. J. Microelectromechanical Syst. **4**(2), 87–96 (1995). https://doi.org/10.1109/84.388117
20. Li, R., Adelson, E.H.: Sensing and recognizing surface textures using a GelSight sensor. In: 2013 IEEE Conference on Computer Vision and Pattern Recognition, pp. 1241–1247 (2013). https://doi.org/10.1109/CVPR.2013.164
21. Li, T., Luo, H., Qin, L., Wang, X., Xiong, Z., Ding, H., et al.: Flexible capacitive tactile sensor based on micropatterned dielectric layer. Small **12**(36), 5042–5048 (2016). https://doi.org/10.1002/smll.201600760
22. Li, Y., Zhu, J.-Y., Tedrake, R., Torralba, A.: Connecting touch and vision via cross-modal prediction. In: 2019 IEEE/CVF Conference on Computer Vision and Pattern Recognition (CVPR), pp. 10601–10610 (2019). https://doi.org/10.1109/CVPR.2019.01086
23. Liang, C.-W., Juang, C.-F.: Moving object classification using local shape and HOG features in wavelet-transformed space with hierarchical SVM classifiers. Appl. Soft Comput. **28**, 483–497 (2015). https://doi.org/10.1016/j.asoc.2014.09.051
24. Liu, W., Yu, P., Gu, C., Cheng, X., Fu, X.: Fingertip piezoelectric tactile sensor array for roughness encoding under varying scanning velocity. IEEE Sens. J. **17**(21), 6867–6879 (2017). https://doi.org/10.1109/JSEN.2017.2721740

25. Lorenzo-Navarro, J., Castrillón, M., Ramón, E., Freire, D.: Evaluation of LBP and HOG descriptors for clothing attribute description. In: Distante, C., Battiato, S., Cavallaro, A. (eds.) Video Analytics for Audience Measurement. VAAM 2014. LNCS, vol. 8811, pp. 53–65. Springer, Cham (2014). https://doi.org/10.1007/978-3-319-12811-5_4
26. Lowe, D.G.: Distinctive image features from scale-invariant keypoints. Int. J. Comput. Vision **60**, 91–110 (2004). https://doi.org/10.1023/B:VISI.0000029664.99615.94
27. Ojala, T., Pietikainen, M., Maenpaa, T.: Multiresolution gray-scale and rotation invariant texture classification with local binary patterns. IEEE Trans. Pattern Anal. Mach. Intell. **24**(7), 971–987 (2002). https://doi.org/10.1109/TPAMI.2002.1017623
28. Qiu, J., Guo, X., Chu, R., Wang, S., Zeng, W., Qu, L., et al.: Rapid-response, low detection limit, and high-sensitivity capacitive flexible tactile sensor based on three-dimensional porous dielectric layer for wearable electronic skin. ACS Appl. Mater. Interfaces **11**(43), 40716–40725 (2019). https://doi.org/10.1021/acsami.9b16511
29. Simonyan, K., Zisserman, A.: Very Deep Convolutional Networks for Large-Scale Image Recognition. arXiv preprint arXiv:1409.1556 (2014). http://arxiv.org/abs/1409.1556
30. Sun, Z., Zhu, M., Shan, X., Lee, C.: Augmented tactile-perception and haptic-feedback rings as human-machine interfaces aiming for immersive interactions. Nat. Commun. **13**, 5224 (2022). https://doi.org/10.1038/s41467-022-32745-8
31. Szegedy, C., Vanhoucke, V., Ioffe, S., Shlens, J., Wojna, Z.: Rethinking the inception architecture for computer vision. In: 2016 IEEE Conference on Computer Vision and Pattern Recognition (CVPR), pp. 2818–2826 (2016). https://doi.org/10.1109/CVPR.2016.308
32. Tan, M., Le, Q.V.: EfficientNet: Rethinking Model Scaling for Convolutional Neural Networks (2019). arXiv preprint arXiv:1905.11946. http://arxiv.org/abs/1905.11946
33. Too, E.C., Yujian, L., Njuki, S., Yingchun, L.: A comparative study of fine-tuning deep learning models for plant disease identification. Comput. Electron. Agric. **161**, 272–279 (2019). https://doi.org/10.1016/j.compag.2018.03.032
34. Yang, F., Ma, C., Zhang, J., Zhu, J., Yuan, W., Owens, A.: Touch and go: learning from human-collected vision and touch (2022). arXiv preprint arXiv:2211.12498. https://arxiv.org/abs/2211.12498
35. Yuan, W., Mo, Y., Wang, S., Adelson. E.H.: Active clothing material perception using tactile sensing and deep learning. In: 2018 IEEE International Conference on Robotics and Automation (ICRA), pp. 4842–4849 (2018). https://doi.org/10.1109/ICRA.2018.8461164
36. Yuan, W., Wang, S., Dong, S., Adelson, E.H.: Connecting look and feel: associating the visual and tactile properties of physical materials. In: 2017 IEEE Conference on Computer Vision and Pattern Recognition (CVPR), pp. 4494–4502 (2017). https://doi.org/10.1109/CVPR.2017.478
37. Yuan, W., Srinivasan, M.A., Adelson, E.H.: Estimating object hardness with a GelSight touch sensor. In: 2016 IEEE/RSJ International Conference on Intelligent Robots and Systems (IROS), pp. 208–215 (2016). https://doi.org/10.1109/IROS.2016.7759057
38. Yuan, W., Dong, S., Adelson, E.H.: GelSight: high-resolution robot tactile sensors for estimating geometry and force. Sensors **17**(12), 2762 (2017). https://doi.org/10.3390/s17122762
39. Yuan, W., Li, R., Srinivasan, M.A., Adelson, E.H.: Measurement of shear and slip with a GelSight tactile sensor. In: 2015 IEEE International Conference on Robotics and Automation (ICRA), pp. 304–311 (2015). https://doi.org/10.1109/ICRA.2015.7139016
40. Yuan, W., Zhu, C., Owens, A., Srinivasan, M.A., Adelson, E.H.: Shape-independent hardness estimation using deep learning and a gelsight tactile sensor. In: 2017 IEEE International Conference on Robotics and Automation (ICRA), pp. 951–958 (2017). https://doi.org/10.1109/ICRA.2017.7989116

Pipeline Inspection a Case Study for Human Cognition Inspired Condition Management System

Hariom Dhungana(✉)

Western Norway University of Applied Sciences, Inndalsveien 28, 5063 Bergen, Norway
hdhu@hvl.no

Abstract. Subsea pipelines are critical in transporting production in the modern oil and gas industry. However, over time, factors like corrosion or deformations can cause degradation, potentially leading to significant economic and environmental harm if not promptly addressed. As a result, regular inspection of subsea pipelines is essential to prevent catastrophic events. A human cognition-inspired condition management framework has been proposed in an ongoing project. The system is designed to leverage various data sources and integrate them with analytical models and knowledge-based systems to assist in equipment diagnosis and recommend optimized operation and maintenance strategies. Multisensory integration is the process by which the brain combines information from different sensory modalities to form a coherent perception of the environment. We sought an integrated dataset containing various observations, such as equipment, environmental, and operational data, to demonstrate the experimental verification of the multi-sensor integration mechanism and the different stages of condition monitoring stages of the framework. For a comprehensive and optimal case study, we selected the Subpipe inspection dataset, showcasing pipeline localization, fault detection, and fault diagnostic tests performed on the dataset.

Keywords: Subsea pipelines · Condition management · Data analysis · Image processing

1 Introduction

The integrity of pipelines is critical for the safe and efficient transport of oil, gas, and other fluids, and undetected corrosion can lead to serious failures, environmental hazards, and financial losses. Subsea pipelines are vital to oil and gas infrastructure, transporting resources from offshore extraction sites to the mainland. Offshore production accounted for significant volume, and as near-shore reservoirs deplete, the industry is moving into deeper and harsher environments [1]. However, subsea pipelines face risks from corrosion, deformation, and extreme weather, with failures potentially causing severe economic and environmental damage despite relatively low failure rates. Timely fault detection is crucial to prevent catastrophic outcomes [2]. Routine inspections using a lightweight autonomous underwater vehicle (LAUV) collect data through various sensors, including images and video footage, inertial measurement units (IMUs), echo

J. Röning and J. Filipe (Eds.): ROBOVIS 2025, CCIS 2629, pp. 383–396, 2026.
https://doi.org/10.1007/978-3-032-00986-9_25

sounders, and other pipe-tracking instruments, with onboard coordinators providing annotations subject to quality control [3].

With the growing importance of automated monitoring systems, advancements in maintenance engineering have significantly improved the efficiency and accuracy of visual inspection processes. Human cognition-inspired condition monitoring aims to develop systems capable of simulating human intelligence, allowing frameworks to perform tasks that involve learning, reasoning, perception, and decision-making [4]. Figure 1 illustrates a schematic representation of the decision-making framework designed for maintenance planning, drawing inspiration from the functioning of the human brain. The framework emulates cognitive processes, such as perception, analysis, and decision-making, to optimize and streamline maintenance strategies. Despite achieving human-like accuracy on various tasks, AI systems, particularly those using deep neural networks, lack human-level intelligence and depend on large datasets to learn distribution patterns [5,6]. Human intelligence encompasses accurate task performance and complex cognitive abilities—such as learning from limited data, adapting

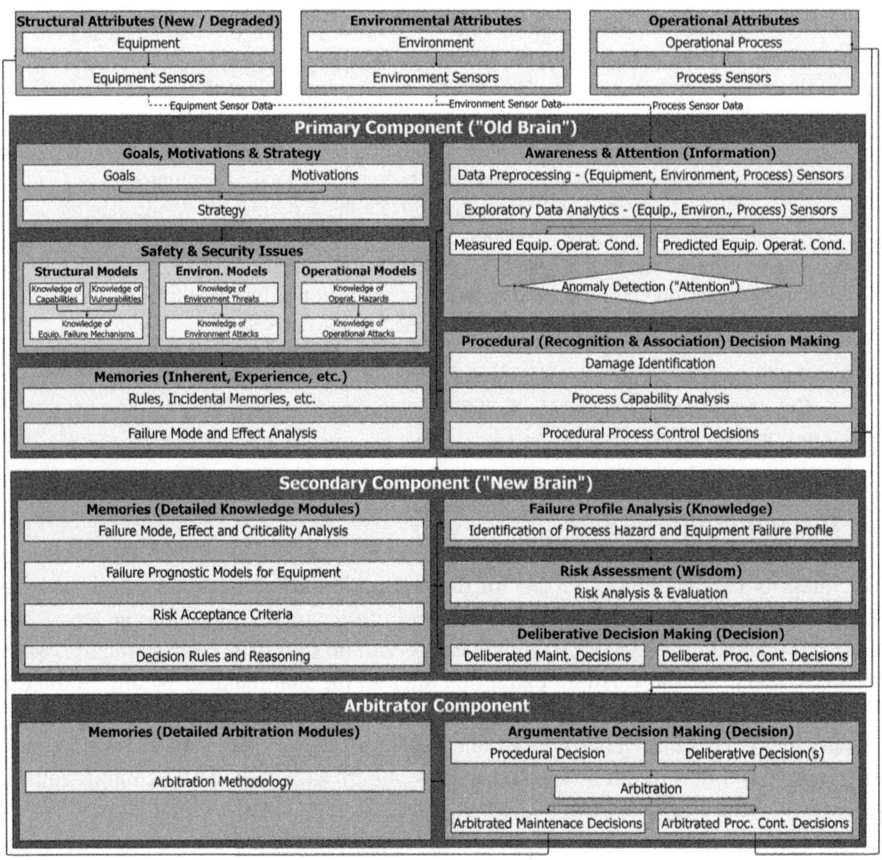

Fig. 1. Human cognition-inspired condition monitoring framework for industrial processes [4].

to new situations, and making ethical judgments—making an understanding of these processes crucial for developing truly human-like AI [7].

The typical stages of condition monitoring include four sub-modules: fault detection, fault identification, fault quantification, and fault prognostics [8]. Once a fault is detected, it is necessary to identify the fault type, including which parts or locations of the equipment or infrastructure indicate degradation during the condition monitoring process [9]. Fault identification is crucial for effective decision-making in condition management, demanding both high accuracy and clear interpretability [10]. In evaluating the framework, we seek multi-sensor inspection datasets encompassing various parameters, enabling the extraction of diverse information and facilitating cross-verification among the data. In that context, we found SubPipe: A submarine pipeline inspection dataset; the detailed information about the experimental platform can be found in [3].

Figure 2 illustrates the showcasing of the multi-sensor integration approach for multiple condition monitoring tasks. RGB images facilitate pipe localization, clamp size estimation, and corrosion analysis, such as determining length and width. Sonar images are employed to detect clamps and identify corrosion and other faults. Inertial navigation system (INS) data supports pipe localization and cross-verification of measurements. Additional sensors, such as forward-looking echo sounders, temperature gauges, altimeters, pressure sensors, and depth meters, contribute to a comprehensive understanding of the monitored pipeline environment.

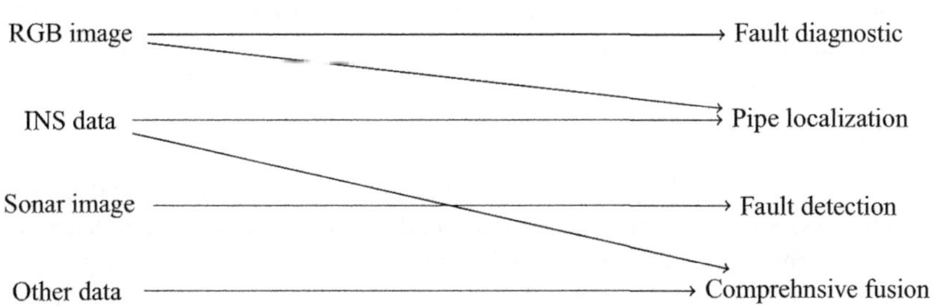

Fig. 2. An overview of information extraction across various condition monitoring stages using multi-sensor inspection datasets. Pipe localization can be achieved using RGB images and INS data. Corrosion and clamp dimensions can be estimated through RGB images, while corrosion pits can be detected using side-scan sonar (SSS) images. Additionally, specific measurements can be cross-verified by integrating data from different sensors to enhance reliability and accuracy.

1.1 Comprehensive Sensing

Comprehensive sensing or multisensory integration, whatever the terms used, refers to the integration and use of multiple types of sensors and data modalities to achieve a holistic understanding of a system. Similarly, humans rely on various sense organs for perception rather than depending solely on a single observation mode [11]. For example, when vision is impaired due to low light or obstructions, they instinctively turn to their sense of balance, touch, or auditory cues to navigate their surroundings. Similarly, the combination of visual and inertial sensors provides a more comprehensive understanding of motion and the environment, effectively compensating for the limitations of individual sensors. As highlighted in [12], this integration enhances robustness against challenges such as poor texture, motion blur, and occlusions. In monocular systems, such multi-sensor fusion also enables scale observability, akin to how humans estimate size and distance by blending visual cues with motion feedback.

1.2 Pipeline Localization or Navigation

Humans rely on color and shape cues from their surroundings to navigate and orient themselves, leveraging both visual processing and cognitive mapping abilities. When we encounter familiar colors or shapes, our brain quickly associates them with past experiences, aiding in recognition and location identification. Human navigation, Visual Odometry (VO), and Visual Simultaneous Localization and Mapping (V-SLAM) share fundamental principles in perceiving and mapping the environment while estimating movement. Hence, we intend to solve the pipeline localization problem via visual signal processing. V-SLAM uses cameras to capture images, extract features, and recognize landmarks, creating a detailed map of the environment. As humans update their mental map while moving and use it to avoid obstacles or find paths, V-SLAM continuously updates its map while simultaneously estimating the camera's position. Both processes integrate visual information with motion cues to achieve localization and mapping, ensuring effective navigation in complex, unfamiliar settings. In essence, VO is a subset of the broader V-SLAM framework, which only builds a precise motion path by reconstructing camera poses.

1.3 Fault Detection

Humans detect anomalies by observing changes in their surroundings and identifying key landmarks. Similarly, fault (like corrosion, deformation, erosion, and leaks) detection is a fundamental challenge in pipeline inspection. From a visual inspection perspective, object detection techniques have become pivotal in advancing fault detection and classification. Traditional inspection methods often rely on manual evaluations or basic imaging, which can be time-consuming and prone to human error. By leveraging state-of-the-art object detection algorithms, such as those based on deep learning frameworks, we intend to detect fault areas with high precision and speed.

1.4 Fault Diagnosis

Fault diagnostics focuses on identifying fault types and evaluating their severity. For corrosion detection, this includes determining the type of corrosion and measuring its dimensions (length, width, and depth). Image segmentation, which divides images into meaningful regions, isolates areas of interest, such as corroded patches on pipeline surfaces. By segmenting images from subsea inspections, corrosion dimensions can be precisely measured. Advanced segmentation methods enhance accuracy by clearly defining corrosion boundaries, supporting automated analysis, efficient maintenance planning, and practical risk assessment for pipeline integrity.

Based on these four activities, the subsequent subsections outline the related works, data description, evaluation metrics, and preliminary results. Section 6 discusses the dataset's limitations, focusing on factors such as the number of features, coverage, and annotation quality. It highlights gaps in data representation, potential biases, and challenges in capturing real-world variations, which may affect inspection reliability. Finally, Sect. 7 concludes the paper and offers an outlook on possible extensions.

2 Related Works

This section presents the stages of condition monitoring in terms of comprehensive sensing, localization, fault detection, and fault diagnosis. Comprehensive sensing is achieved through data fusion; pipeline localization is carried out using V-SLAM and VO, fault detection is performed through object detection, and fault diagnosis is accomplished using image segmentation techniques.

2.1 Data Fusion

Relying on a single data source for decision-making can lead to errors due to the limitations of the sensing mechanism or environmental factors. Data fusion improves the reliability of measurements by combining information from multiple sources, helping to cross-verify results. This process allows for more accurate anomaly detection and the removal of outliers, leading to more robust and trustworthy outputs. For example, the robustness to poor texture, motion blur, and occlusions was enhanced through the combination of visual and inertial sensors, which also enable scale observability in monocular systems [12].

2.2 V-SLAM and Visual Odometry

VO is a fundamental component of a complete SLAM system, providing incremental motion estimation of a camera, as described in [13]. However, additional processes such as loop closure detection and global optimization are necessary for a full SLAM implementation to ensure a metrically consistent map [14]. These algorithms reduce uncertainty by repeatedly measuring static features from varying viewpoints. In [15], fractional V-SLAM-based VO was applied to estimate UAV positions using monocular cameras, leveraging feature matching across consecutive frames to infer motion and relative positions.

The Lucas-Kanade method estimates optical flow by solving a local weighted least-squares problem, assuming constant motion, brightness constancy, and spatial smoothness. It processes consecutive frames by calculating spatial and temporal gradients, solving for displacement vectors, and integrating these vectors to generate a trajectory [16]. It is computationally efficient and ideal for small-displacement tracking. The method solves for optical flow under the assumption of constant motion in a local neighborhood based on brightness constancy.

$$I(x, y, t) = I(x + u, y + v, t + 1), \tag{1}$$

where $I(x, y, t)$ represents the image intensity at position (x, y) and time t, and (u, v) denotes the displacement vector. Expanding using the Taylor series and neglecting higher-order terms, the equation simplifies to:

aaaaaaaaaa

$$I_x u + I_y v + I_t = 0, \tag{2}$$

where I_x, I_y are the spatial intensity gradients, I_t is the temporal gradient, and u, v are the optical flow components. For a local window W, the optical flow is determined by solving the linear system:

$$\mathbf{A}\mathbf{d} = \mathbf{b}, \tag{3}$$

where $\mathbf{A} = I_x I_y \vdots\vdots I_x I_y, \quad \mathbf{b} = -I_t \vdots - I_t, \quad \mathbf{d} = uv$. The solution is obtained using the weighted least-squares approach:

$$\mathbf{d} = (\mathbf{A}^T\mathbf{A})^{-1}\mathbf{A}^T\mathbf{b}. \tag{4}$$

The estimated optical flow vectors $\mathbf{d} = [u, v]^T$ are then integrated over time to compute the trajectory. Given an initial position $\mathbf{p}_0$, the position at time t is updated iteratively as:

$$\mathbf{p}(t) = \mathbf{p}(t-1) + \mathbf{d}(t). \tag{5}$$

2.3 Object Detection

Over the past two decades, object detection has significantly advanced, shaping the landscape of computer vision research. Key aspects, such as historical milestones, datasets, evaluation metrics, system components, and state-of-the-art methods, are comprehensively reviewed in [17]. Object detection involves localizing objects in images and identifying their categories, traditionally using a three-stage process: region selection, feature extraction, and classification [18]. The introduction of YOLO in 2015 revolutionized the field with a unified, end-to-end approach, treating detection as regression and outperforming earlier, multi-stage methods [19].

2.4 Image Segmentation

Image segmentation is vital in visual understanding systems, particularly for fault diagnosis. It involves assigning semantic labels to pixels (semantic segmentation) or isolating individual objects (instance segmentation) [20]. Advanced techniques like U-Net and Mask R-CNN excel at delineating corrosion boundaries, enabling automated analyses for improved maintenance planning and risk assessment. The Segment Anything (SA) project, introducing the SAM model and the SA-1B dataset with over 1 billion masks, achieves zero-shot generalization with performance rivaling supervised models, advancing segmentation in computer vision research [21].

3 Data Description

SubPipe is a dataset recorded during a survey mission by OceanScan-MST1 near a 1 km underwater pipeline in Porto, Portugal. The dataset includes measurements from onboard sensors and the robot's estimated state. Detailed information about the experimental data collection platform and data description can be found in [3]. Figure 3 illustrates the experimental setup for Subpipe data collection, which consists of two downward-looking RGB cameras and a Klein 3500 sss scanner. Additional sensors capture forward-looking echo sounder data, temperature, altitude, pressure, and depth. SubPipe features five video sequences (7âĂŞ9 min each), with the high-resolution camera recorded at 240 Hz and the low-resolution at 4 Hz. SSS images were annotated in COCO format for object detection and resized to 640 × 640 pixels for algorithm compatibility. The dataset includes ground truth annotations for object detection, image segmentation, and visual-inertial localization. RGB images are semantically segmented, while SSS images are annotated for object detection tasks, enhancing the dataset's utility across multiple research domains. The brief summary of data category according to the human cognition-inspired framework is given in Table 1

Table 1. Datasets description based on framework cluster.

	Sensors	Data attributes
Equipment sensing	RGB cameras (Cam0, Cam1)	Image size 2704 × 1520, 1936 × 1216
	SSS cameras (HF, LF)	Image size 5000 × 500, 2500 × 500
Environment sensing	Temperature sensor	°C
	Pressure sensor	(hpa)
Operation sensing	INS (Position and Orientation)	m, m/s/s
	DVL (Velocity)	m/s
	Depth	m
	Altitude	m

4 Evaluation Metric

This section presents the evaluation metrics for localization, fault detection, and fault diagnostics according to the paper's structure.

Pipeline Navigation. A localization problem typically involves determining the position and orientation of a system, such as a sensor within a given environment. In the context of visual inspection tasks, localization algorithms produce an estimated trajectory that represents the path taken by the LAUV during its inspection. This trajectory is critical for mapping, navigation, and identifying areas of interest in the inspected environment. Absolute Trajectory Error (ATE) and Relative Pose Error (RPE) are utilized in this work as key localization metrics, following the approach outlined in [22].

The ATE measures the global consistency by comparing the absolute distances between the estimated trajectory $\mathbf{P}_{1:n}$ and the ground truth trajectory $\mathbf{Q}_{1:n}$. Since both trajectories may be defined in arbitrary coordinate frames, they must first be aligned. This alignment is achieved using Horn's method, which computes the rigid-body transformation $\mathbf{S}$ that minimizes the least-squares error between the two trajectories.

The RPE is an evaluation metric used to measure the local accuracy of a trajectory over a fixed time interval Δ. This metric is particularly valuable for assessing the performance of visual odometry systems, as it quantifies the drift in the estimated trajectory.

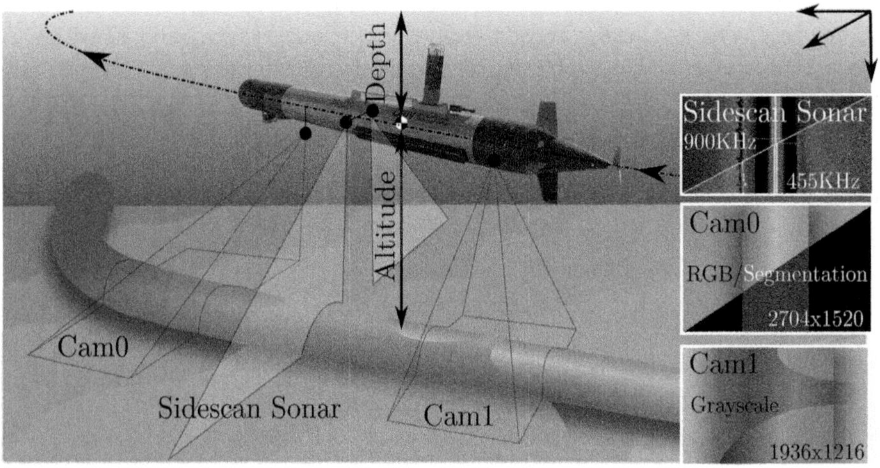

Fig. 3. Pipeline inspection mission using OceanScan's LAUV Adapted from [3]. The dataset includes data from a monochrome and an RGB camera (with pipe segmentation annotations for the RGB), side-scan sonar images with pipeline bounding box annotations for object detection, as well as temperature, altitude, depth measurements, and the robot's pose, velocity, and acceleration.

Clamp Detection. In object detection evaluation for image analysis, precision, recall, and F1 score are fundamental metrics to measure the performance of a model. Precision quantifies the accuracy of the detections by calculating the proportion of correctly predicted objects (True Positives) out of all predicted objects, helping identify false positives. Recall, on the other hand, measures the ability of the model to detect all relevant objects by computing the ratio of correctly detected objects to the total ground truth objects, emphasizing false negatives. The F1 score, the harmonic mean of precision and recall, provides a balanced measure of accuracy, especially when there is a trade-off between precision and recall. These metrics collectively assess the reliability and completeness of object detection models, making them crucial in evaluating corrosion or clamp detection performance.

Pipe and Clamp Segmentation. In image segmentation, two widely used evaluation metrics are the Intersection over Union (IoU), also known as the Jaccard Index, and the

Dice Coefficient (F1 Score for Segmentation). The IoU measures the overlap between the predicted segmentation (P) and the ground truth (G) by calculating the ratio of their intersection to their union. It ranges from 0 to 1, with higher values indicating better segmentation. The Dice Coefficient, closely related to the F1 Score, computes the similarity between P and G. It also ranges from 0 to 1 and is especially useful in imbalanced class distributions. Together, these metrics provide a robust assessment of segmentation accuracy, with IoU focusing on spatial overlap and Dice emphasizing similarity.

5 Preliminary Results

This section aims to demonstrate how observed data from various sensors can be utilized to perform critical condition monitoring tasks. Specifically, pipeline localization and clamp size estimation are achieved using RGB images, and object detection is achieved using SSSLF images. These results showcase how sensor data supports precise localization and structural assessments in subsea pipeline inspection for maintenance decision-making.

Figure 4 shows the trajectory of the LAUV from Chunk 2 based on data from the INS sensor. The trajectory spans a length of 463.4 m and was collected around 9 min. For the first 400 m, the LAUV moves smoothly, but beyond this point, its orientation exhibits some irregularities, showing random variations in its movement. The LAUV's control mechanism uses actuators like rudders to adjust its movement, and changes in direction lead to sudden shifts in forces such as thrust or speed. The shift after 14,000 samples seems like the vehicle deviated momentarily from its orientation, resulting in fluctuations, especially during sharp turns.

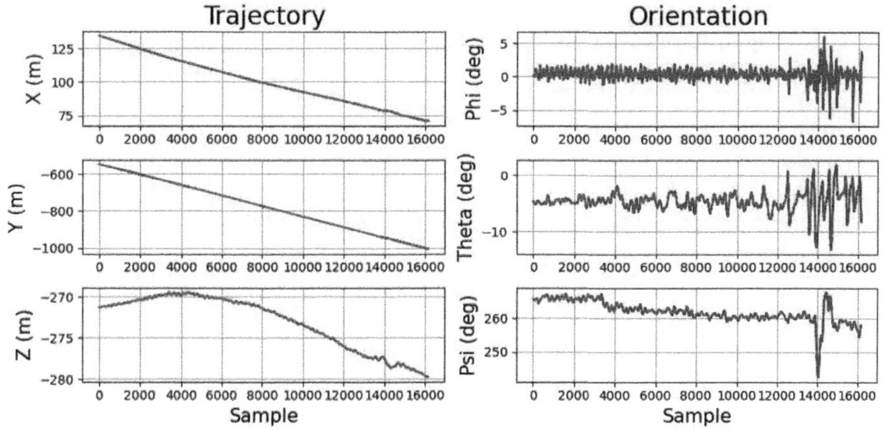

Fig. 4. Trajectory obtained from INS observation.

Figure 5 shows the LAUV trajectory from both the INS sensor and Camera0 images. The left graph illustrates vision-based localization using the first 100 images from Chunk2 data of Cam0, where optical flow with the Lucas-Kanade method is applied to track feature points between consecutive images, estimate the essential matrix, and recover the camera pose (rotation and translation) to build the visual odometry trajectory. The right graph displays the same 100 observations from the INS position. The trajectory obtained from optical flow differs significantly from the trajectory derived from the INS data. This discrepancy highlights the limitations of basic VO techniques and suggests the need for more advanced visual odometry methods that can better integrate sensor fusion, handle more complex motion, and improve accuracy in dynamic environments. The pipe localization metrics, including ATE and RPE, for the first 100 images across all five chunks of the dataset are listed in Table 2.

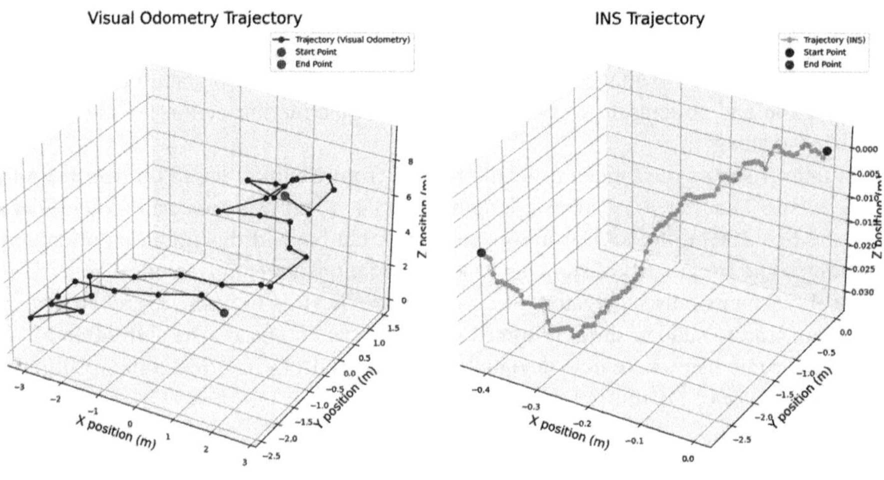

Fig. 5. Trajectory obtained from camera inspection and INS observation.

Sonar cameras utilize sound waves to detect objects and obstacles in their surroundings, making them ideal for low-visibility environments. In object detection, sonar cameras capture reflected sound waves to identify objects' shapes, distances, and sizes. For the experimental verification of object detection, we used SSSLF images. The object detection labels were created by pairing .pbm images from the Image folder with their corresponding .txt files from the YOLO annotation Label folder, assigning class 0 if a label exists and class 1 otherwise. The dataset was then split into training and testing sets with an 80–20 ratio. A convolutional neural network (CNN)-based binary image classification model was implemented for object detection, comprising convolutional, max-pooling, and dense layers, with a sigmoid activation function for the final output. The model was trained on the training set and evaluated on the test set using precision and recall metrics. Figure 6 shows the detected object with rectangular YOLO annotations from the Chunk 2 data of the 693573947.93.pbm image. The object detection metrics, including precision and recall, for 20% of each chunk are provided in Table 2.

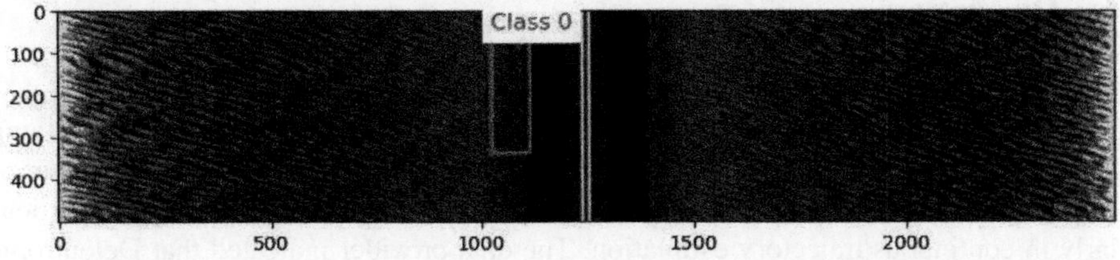

Fig. 6. Clamp annotation from the SSSLF image used for object detection.

We used the DeepLabV3 model from PyTorch's torchvision models for the experimental verification of image segmentation. segmentation module to perform semantic segmentation on an input image. It loads a pre-trained DeepLabV3 model, fine-tuned on the COCO dataset, ensuring robust generalization. The code applies necessary transformations to the input image, including resizing, normalizing, and converting it into a tensor. After performing segmentation using the model, the predicted mask is compared with the ground truth mask. Figure. 7 shows Image segmentation results, including the original image, predicted segmentation, and ground truth, which are visualized side by side. The predicted segmentation mask fails to segment the pipeline and clamp accurately due to challenges in object visibility. The image segmentation metrics, including IoU and Dice Coefficient, to evaluate the segmentation performance by comparing the predicted and ground truth binary masks for the first 100 images across chunk2 of the dataset are listed in Table 2.

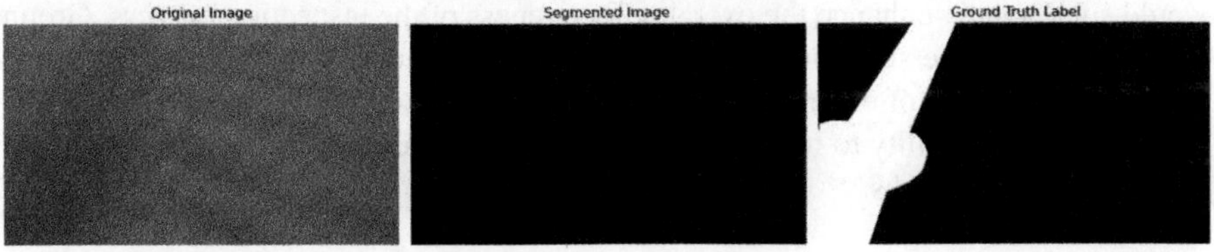

Fig. 7. Visualization of the original image, predicted segmentation mask, and ground truth mask displayed side by side for comparison.

Table 2. Initial results for navigation, object detection and image segmentation.

	Navigation		Object detection		Image segmentation	
Data	ATE	RPE	Precision	Recall	IoU	Dice Coefficient
Chunk0	7.53	0.78	0.98	1.0	X	X
Chunk1	7.96	0.69	0.94	1.0	X	X
Chunk2	5.58	0.30	0.4	0.69	0.8	0.75
Chunk3	4.25	0.99	0.79	1.0	X	X
Chunk4	0.45	0.01	0.94	0.98	X	X

6 Discussion

In pipeline navigation using camera images, the performance of both VO and V-SLAM technologies depends heavily on feature matching, which is essential for determining the camera's movement and creating accurate 3D maps. However, when the number of feature matches is insufficient, these systems encounter significant challenges, particularly in continuous trajectory estimation. The data provider indicated that Delentropy, derived from entropy, is the lowest among other subsea datasets. Since Delentropy (a measure of disorder or randomness) is low in the subsurface pipeline inspection dataset, the available data may be inadequate for accurately interpreting the structure and condition of the pipeline. This highlights the need for advanced visual navigation modules to guide inspection tools through complex pipeline systems precisely. Geometry-based V-SLAM algorithms and traditional VO approaches rely heavily on identifying and tracking distinct features in an environment. These methods often fail in low-textured areas where discernible features are sparse or repetitive, resulting in track loss, poor feature matching, or degraded motion estimation accuracy.

Since the dataset also includes INS data, combining the INS for trajectory estimation with the visual information from the camera can enhance overall navigation and localization performance, enabling accurate path mapping even in GPS-denied environments. This fusion would enable more robust and reliable pipeline inspections, similar to human navigation, especially when individual sense observation may be prone to errors.

Furthermore, an advanced segmentation module is crucial to improving the identification and localization of key pipeline features and faults, ensuring more reliable fault diagnostics and precise pipeline localization during inspections. These advancements would significantly enhance the overall effectiveness of the inspection process. Ground truth data for image segmentation is limited to only Chunk 2 out of the five chunks, restricting the scope of extensive experiments across the dataset. As a result, this limitation hinders the ability to fully evaluate segmentation performance and generalize the results across all chunks.

7 Conclusion

To experimentally verify the different stages of condition monitoring—such as comprehensive sensing, pipeline localization, fault detection, and fault diagnostics—within the human cognition-inspired condition management framework, we utilized an integrated dataset containing diverse observations, including equipment, environmental, and operational data. For each stage, we provided an example implementation and a brief discussion of related works and the corresponding evaluation metrics. This demonstrates that the dataset applies to various stages of condition monitoring. In future work, we aim to focus on precise and highly accurate information extraction to enable effective decision-making.

Acknowledgments. The authors thank Maneesh Singh, Knut Øvsthus, and Anne-Lena Kampen for their valuable discussions.

References

1. Ho, M., El-Borgi, S., Patil, D., Song, G.: Inspection and monitoring systems subsea pipelines: a review paper. Struct. Health Monit. **19**, 606–645 (2020)
2. Hasan, S., Sweet, L., Hults, J., Valbuena, G., Singh, B.: Corrosion risk-based subsea pipeline design. Int. J. Press. Vessels Pip. **159**, 1–14 (2018)
3. Álvarez-Tuñón, O., Marnet, L.R., Antal, L., Aubard, M., Costa, M., Brodskiy, Y.: SubPipe: a submarine pipeline inspection dataset for segmentation and visual-inertial localization. In: OCEANS 2024-Singapore. IEEE (2024)
4. Singh, M., Øvsthus, K., Kampen, A.-L., Dhungana, H.: Development of a human cognition inspired condition management system for equipment. Int. J. Syst. Assur. Eng. Manag. **1**, 1–10 (2024)
5. Cambria, E., Mao, R., Chen, M., Wang, Z., Ho, S.B., Murugesan, S.: Seven pillars for the future of artificial intelligence. IEEE Intell. Syst. **38**, 62–69 (2023)
6. Dhungana, H.: A machine learning approach for wind turbine power forecasting for maintenance planning. Energy Inform. **8**, 1–25 (2025)
7. Mao, R., Liu, Q., Li, X., Cambria, E., Hussain, A.: Guest editorial: cognitive analysis for humans and AI. Cogn. Comput. **16**, 3316–3318 (2024)
8. Dhungana, H.: Rule-based decision making in biologically inspired condition management system. Int. Conf. Agents Artif. Intell. **2**, 1245–1254 (2024)
9. Dhungana, P., Singh, R.K., Dhungana, H.: Machine learning model for fault detection in safety critical system. In: International Conference on Applications in Electronics Pervading Industry, Environment and Society, pp. 499–507, Springer, Cham (2024)
10. Dhungana, H.: Case based decision making in biologically inspired condition management system. In: 7th International Conference on Inventive Computation Technologies, ICICT 2024, pp. 335–339 (2024)
11. Feldman, J.: The simplicity principle in perception and cognition. Wiley Interdisciplinary Reviews: Cognitive Science, vol. 7, pp. 330–340 (2016)
12. Campos, C., Elvira, R., Rodriguez, J.J., Montiel, J.M., Tardos, J.D.: ORB-SLAM3: an accurate open-source library for visual, visual-inertial, and multimap SLAM. IEEE Trans. Robot. **37**, 1874–1890 (2021)
13. Scaramuzza, D., Fraundorfer, F.: Tutorial: visual odometry. IEEE Robot. Autom. Mag. **18**, 80–92 (2011)
14. Aitken, J.M., et al.: Simultaneous localization and mapping for inspection robots in water and sewer pipe networks: a review. IEEE Access **9**, 140173–140198 (2021)
15. Dhungana, H., Bellotti, F., Berta, R., De Gloria, A.: Position Estimation of Small UAV from Monocular Camera by Using Matched Features, vol. 177 LNNS (2021)
16. Lucas, B.D., Kanade, T.: An iterative image registration technique with an application to stereo vision. In: IJCAI'81: 7th International Joint Conference on Artificial Intelligence, vol. 2, pp. 674–679 (1981)
17. Zou, Z., Chen, K., Shi, Z., Guo, Y., Ye, J.: Object detection in 20 years: a survey. Proc. IEEE **111**, 257–276 (2023)
18. Zhao, Z.Q., Zheng, P., Xu, S.T., Wu, X.: Object detection with deep learning: a review. IEEE Trans. Neural Netw. Learn. Syst. **30**, 3212–3232 (2019)
19. Redmon, J., Divvala, S., Girshick, R., Farhadi, A.: You only look once: unified, real-time object detection. In: Proceedings of the IEEE Computer Society Conference on Computer Vision and Pattern Recognition, vol. 2016-December, pp. 779–788 (2015)
20. Minaee, S., Boykov, Y., Porikli, F., Plaza, A., Kehtarnavaz, N., Terzopoulos, D.: Image segmentation using deep learning: a survey. IEEE Trans. Pattern Anal. Mach. Intell. **44**, 3523–3542 (2022)

21. Kirillov, A., et al.: Segment anything. In: Proceedings of the IEEE International Conference on Computer Vision, pp. 3992–4003 (2023)
22. Sturm, J., Engelhard, N., Endres, F., Burgard, W., Cremers, D.: A benchmark for the evaluation of RGB-D SLAM systems. In: IEEE International Conference on Intelligent Robots and Systems, pp. 573–580 (2012)

Active Closure: Symbolic Active Contour for Spatial Automated Reasoning

J. I. Olszewska(✉)

School of Computing and Engineering, University of the West of Scotland, Paisley, U.K.
joanna.olszewska@ieee.org

Abstract. Reducing the gap between quantitative visual data and qualitative spatial information such as qualitative spatial relations (QSR) is crucial for many intelligent and autonomous systems (AS) requiring the automated analysis of complex, visual scenes containing multiple objects of interest. Hence, our paper proposes to directly relate symbolic spatial knowledge to computer-vision concepts, in particular, to a new active-contour-based, symbolic concept. Indeed, active contours are deformable curves that evolve under forces computed from geometric and photometric properties of visual objects in order to delineate these target objects' shapes. The active contours could not only be applied to generate the quantitative visual data related to the extracted objects of interest, but the computation of these active contours' centroids could also be used to define centers of reference which are necessary for the determination of our spatial directional relations and projective relations among the objects of interest. In particular, this paper introduces the use of active contours to intrinsically define objects-of-interest's closure which is useful for our spatial topological relations, leading to the symbolic active closure concept. This presented symbolic AI approach for qualitative spatial reasoning based on active contours has been successfully validated on geographical-related imagery, while being reliable, explainable, and sustainable.

Keywords: Intelligent Systems · Robotic Systems · Autonomous Systems · Scene Analysis and Understanding · Visual-Based Navigation · Geospatial Artificial Intelligence (GeoAI) · Knowledge-Based Systems · Cognitive Systems · Knowledge Representation and Reasoning · Computer Vision · Explainable Artificial Intelligence (XAI) · Sustainable Artificial Intelligence

1 Introduction

Nowadays, a growing number of autonomous systems (AS) are used to help with the United Nations (UN) sustainable goals [22], such as building *sustainable cities and communities* by improving smart cities [4,68], caring about *life on land* by developing smart agriculture [42,58], preserving *life below water* by managing oceans [14], assessing marine life pollution [48], or contributing to the *climate action* by aiding in weather forecasting, studying climate changes [2,34] as well as assisting in natural disaster management and rescue missions [25] - with many of these AS relying on Geographical Information Systems (GIS) [11,24,36,59] and contributing to the field of Geographical Artificial Intelligence (GeoAI) [74].

J. Röning and J. Filipe (Eds.): ROBOVIS 2025, CCIS 2629, pp. 397–413, 2026.
https://doi.org/10.1007/978-3-032-00986-9_26

In particular, spatial reasoning is of a prime importance for AS used in GeoAI-based applications [19,33,45] and beyond [54].

Spatial reasoning involves both high-level qualitative symbolic concepts and low-level quantitative feature representations [72]. While quantitative representations rely on metric measurements within spatio-visual imagery [32], qualitative spatial relations [17] project the perceived scene into an abstract representation and allow the action of reasoning on semantically meaningful concepts.

In order to define prototypes for representing spatial scenes from real-world images, to acquire knowledge about them as well as to understand and to interpret them, performing qualitative spatial reasoning (QSR) represents a major advantage compared to other approaches such as those describing visual information with simple linguistic forms, e.g. consisting of sparse words [3,9], or those limited to sole quantitative visual data [41,69].

For this purpose, knowledge representations involving qualitative spatial relations to describe spatial structures have been developed. In particular, spatial reasoning relies on relations which have been mostly defined as binary ones [64], such as the topological spatial relations like the RCC-8 model [60] or the directional spatial relations, using the cardinal spatial model [37] and its enhancement [28], or the clock model [55]. Moreover, [73] uses binary spatial relations at the symbolic level for its bimodal spatial reasoning framework.

To reason on spatial relations among a greater number of objects (at least three), ternary spatial relations such as ternary projective relations have been developed. Hence, a fuzzy definition of the ternary spatial relation 'between' has been proposed in [8], and improved for the case of spatially extended objects in [15], but it is limited in terms of accuracy. In [16], the 5-intersection model is introduced, but it has a restricted applicability. On the other hand, [49] has formalized semantic concepts such as 'above' as ternary spatial relations by applying the clock representation.

Besides, spatial relations have been recently studied in conjunction with Large Language Models (LLM) like ChatGPT [70] or Vision Language Models (VLM) [12], but these approaches need better explainability [62] and are not yet sustainable, while they present better performance when associated with approaches such as symbolic QSR or ontologies [35].

Since the new-generation of AS [66] is required to be reliable [5,6] and transparent [27,71], one also needs to take care when integrating computer vision (CV) methods into AS [52], since not all CV approaches are equally explainable [43] and therefore verifiable [20,63].

Hence, in AS applications that involve finding objects-of-interest's border, computer vision methods helping in automatically detecting contours are sought for. Among the segmentation methods available in the literature [65,74], which detect edges of foreground and background objects alike, the active contour approach provides a meaningful and coherent delineation of objects of interests [10]. The active contour analytical model has been established in 1980s [31] and then improved in the following years and decades by introducing e.g., level sets [56,75], active shapes with template matching [7]; by adding region-based criteria [47], or by setting the multi-feature vector flow [29] mathematical framework which allows to embed any type of features to compute active contours [51]. Deep Learning (DL) based active contour models such as DeepContour have also been introduced [67]. These methods usually require greedy power resources as well as a huge amount of image data and of very high resolution to be trained and tested on. However, such resources and/or amount of data are not always available for the specific applications they have to be used for [46], while their modelling relies on not-yet explainable concepts [23,39].

On the other hand, more recently, the *snake-in-tree* model of the active contours [53] has been demonstrated to be both efficient and intrinsically explainable so this modelling approach has been adopted in this work.

Thence, in this paper, we focus on the conceptualization of advanced qualitative spatial relations directly in terms of computer vision theory. For this purpose, we integrate our active contour model into the qualitative spatial relations, and we propose a new active-contour-based closure concept which we called *active closure*. Its symbolic representation is fully explainable [74] and can be seamlessly integrated within a larger AI system or AS [44]. Further advantages of our approach are that it does not drain huge CPU resources [30,40] and it does not require high-resolution images [46] or data training [13], so it avoids dataset biases [68] and provides a sustainable as well as a multi-scale solution for GeoAI-based systems [38].

This approach moves forward qualitative spatial reasoning, as it fully maintains the advantages of the symbolic reasoning, while being totally connected to real-world metrics and visual data.

Therefore, in order to create a fully automatic system for qualitative spatial reasoning based on visual information and to bridge the semantic gap, visual data (i.e. input images) are first processed by means of active contours [29]. Indeed, active contours are an image-processing method for segmenting objects of interest considering both their geometric and photometric properties. This approach efficiently extracts objects of interest's shape and automatically defines their boundaries in the image plane. Qualitative spatial reasoning could be then performed on the new spatial relations which are themselves formalized in terms of the active contour model.

Thus, our active-contour-based spatial relations define a new set of semantic concepts allowing the study of complex spatio-visual imagery through the acquisition of knowledge and the automatic reasoning on them to solve the related spatial problems.

Besides, it is worth noting that this work is focused on the AI-based analysis of 2D spatial images, with our presented approach having the capability to be extended to adequate 3D models such as [50] by applying our 2D approach in the different views.

The contribution of this paper is the modelling of spatial relations using the symbolic active-contour-based approach for the automatic analysis of visual data. This involves the definition of the new active closure concept and the symbolic representation of topological, directional, and projective spatial relations in terms of this active closure notion. Moreover, this has led to the development of a whole AI system which is both explainable and sustainable and which combines quantitative image processing consisting in segmenting visual objects of interest together with semantic image interpretation through qualitative spatial reasoning.

The paper is structured as follows. In Sect. 2, we present our approach called 'active closure' which is based on the active contour definition to directly model spatial relations, namely, topological, directional, and projective ones. All these relations have been integrated in an explainable and sustainable framework for automatic image analysis and scene understanding, and the resulting system has been successfully tested in context of Geospatial artificial intelligence (GeoAI) applications as reported in Sect. 3. Conclusions are drawn up in Sect. 4.

2 Active-Contour-Based QSR

We first introduce the active contour model which defines the visual object's shape and centroid based on quantitative data (Sect. 2.1) and then we propose the active closure concept. Next, we present its use for qualitative spatial reasoning. In particular, we integrate this active contour model into the definitions of topological (Sect. 2.2), directional (Sect. 2.3), and projective (Sect. 2.4) relations among objects of interest.

2.1 Active Contour Model

Active contours are a powerful approach to segment objects of interest in images [21]. The active contour model (Fig. 1) is an initial contour that deforms towards the boundaries of the object of interest, guided by forces derived from energy functions which govern the evolution of the deformation and guarantee that it stops at the boundaries of the object of interest [51]. This approach is particularly useful for automated object's shape detection and boundaries delineation.

In this work, we concentrate on the multi-feature vector flow (MFVF) active contours [29] which have been proven to be very efficient in real-world, complex scenes, and which allow precise foreground segmentation, without any kind of assumption about the object appearance, i.e. without the need of training process. Indeed, given an image $I(x,y)$, the multi-feature active contour is a parametric planar deformable curve $C(s) = [C_x(s), C_y(s)]$, with $0 \leq s \leq 1$, which evolves from an initial position to object boundaries. In this framework, the convergence of the curve is guided by internal and external forces, which are involved in a gradient descent process. The internal forces constrain the active contour shape, in the way to ensure regularity and smoothness of the curvature. The MFVF external force regroups all the selected features in one bidirectional force which computation is based on the MFVF field $\Xi(x,y) = [\xi_u(x,y), \xi_v(x,y)]$, enabling the active contour to reach its final accurate position even in complex situations.

Formally, the deformable curve $C(s,t)$ is modeled itself by a B-spline paradigm in order to be computationally efficient, and must satisfy the following dynamic equations,

$$C_{xt}(s,t) = \alpha\, C_x''(s,t) - \beta\, C_x''''(s,t) + \xi_u(x,y) \tag{1}$$

$$C_{yt}(s,t) = \alpha\, C_y''(s,t) - \beta\, C_y''''(s,t) + \xi_v(x,y), \tag{2}$$

where C_x'', C_y'', C_x'''', C_y'''', respectively, are the second and fourth-order derivatives with respect to the parameter s of the curve, α is the curvature elasticity coefficient, and β is the curvature rigidity coefficient.

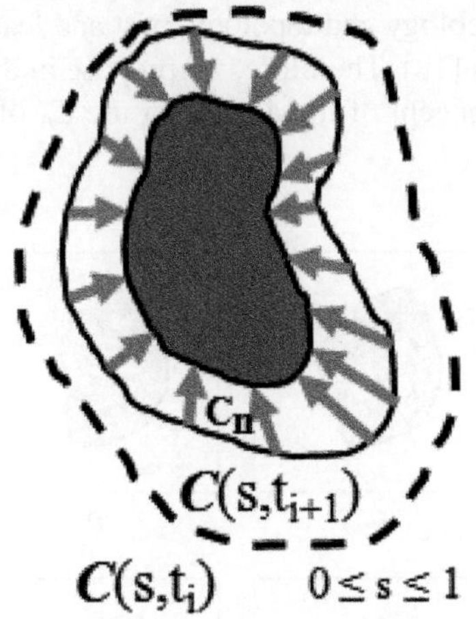

Fig. 1. Evolution process of the parametric active contour.

The active contour found by solving Eqs. (1)–(2) could be, in practice, roughly initialized from a distance of the target, since the MFVF force offers a large capture range. This obtained fast, multi-feature active contour owns high-deformation capabilities that are well suited for segmenting non-rigid objects whose shapes change markedly over space and/or time.

To relate the image-processing method of above-mentioned active contours with qualitative spatial reasoning, we introduce the definition of the *active closure* or the closure C_n of an object of interest n in terms of active contours, as follows:

$$C_n \equiv_{def} \{(x,y) \in I(x,y) \mid (x,y) \in \mathcal{C}_n(s)\}, \tag{3}$$

where (x,y) represent a pixel in the given image $I(x,y)$, and $\mathcal{C}_n(s)$ is the active contour corresponding to the *nth* object of interest in the image I as per Eqs. (1)-(2).

On the other hand, the position of the object n could be defined in the $I(x,y)$ image space by computing its contour centroid $O_n^{centroid}$ as follows:

$$O_n^{centroid} = (O_n^x, O_n^y) = \frac{1}{L_n} \int_0^{L_n} \mathcal{C}_n(s)\, ds, \tag{4}$$

where L_n is the length of the corresponding active contour $\mathcal{C}_n(s)$.

2.2 Active-Contour-Based Topological Relations

Qualitative spatial reasoning relies on binary relations among two spatial objects A and B such as topological relations which are usually formalized using Region Connection Calculus (RCC-8) [26,61].

Indeed, RCC-8 [60] is a well-known mereotopological theory which extends the mereology, or theory of the part, with topological relations. It is usually based on the connected relation $CO(A,B)$ between two spatial regions or entities A and B. Many strategies to integrate mereology and topology exist and lead to different definitions of mereotopological relations [18]. Therefore, we propose in this work to redefine RCC-8 properties based on the concept of the active closure C_n of the objects of interest we introduced in Sect. 2.1.

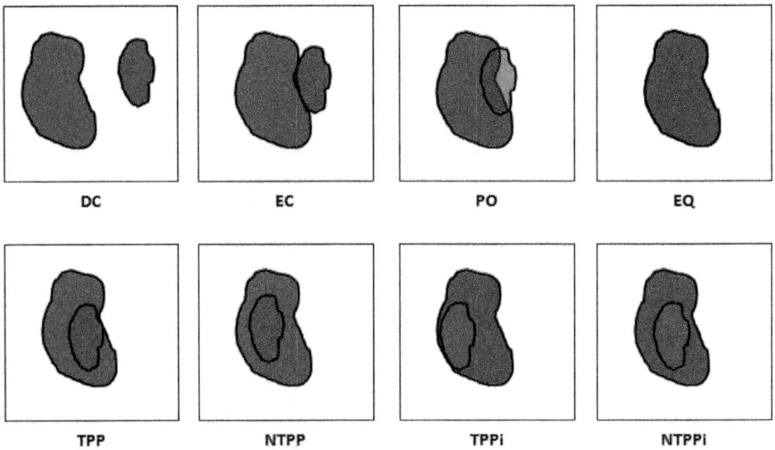

Fig. 2. Topological spatial relations modelled using Region Connection Calculus (RCC-8).

As two regions are connected if and only if their topological closures share a common point and as we set the correspondence between the closure C_n and the active contour $\boldsymbol{C}_n(s)$ in Eq. (3), the connection can be modeled in terms of the active contours as a result of the following definition:

$$CO(A,B) \equiv_{def} C_A \cap B \neq \emptyset. \tag{5}$$

RCC-8 is based on eight jointly exhaustive and pairwise disjoint (JPED) relations, namely, disconnected (*DC*), externally connected (*EC*), partially overlapping (*PO*), equal (*EQ*), tangential proper part (*TPP*), non-tangential proper part (*NTPP*), tangential proper part inverse (*TPPi*), non-tangential proper part inverse (*NTPPi*), all presented in Fig. 2. These relations imply to define at first some fundamental notions such as the overlap $OV(A,B)$:

$$OV(A,B) \equiv_{def} A \cap B \neq \emptyset; \tag{6}$$

the parthood $PT(A,B)$ could be modeled such as:

$$PT(A,B) \equiv_{def} A \subseteq B \wedge A \neq \emptyset, \tag{7}$$

with inclusion defined as:

$$A \subseteq B \equiv_{def} \forall (x,y)((x,y) \in A \rightarrow (x,y) \in B), \tag{8}$$

while the proper parthood $PP(A,B)$ concept is defined as follows:

$$PP(A,B) \equiv_{def} PT(A,B) \wedge A \neq B, \tag{9}$$

i.e.

$$PP(A,B) \equiv_{def} PT(A,B) \wedge \neg PT(B,A). \tag{10}$$

Thence, we can remodel the RCC-8 relations in terms of active contours considering Eq. (3) and Eqs. (5)-(10).

In first order logic, the RCC-8 relations in terms of active contours are thus as follows:

$$DC(A,B) \equiv_{def} C_A \cap B = \emptyset, \tag{11}$$

$$EC(A,B) \equiv_{def} C_A \cap B \neq \emptyset \wedge A \cap B = \emptyset, \tag{12}$$

$$\begin{aligned} PO(A,B) \equiv_{def} & A \cap B \neq \emptyset \\ & \wedge \neg PT(A,B) \wedge \neg PT(B,A), \end{aligned} \tag{13}$$

$$EQ(A,B) \equiv_{def} PT(A,B) \wedge PT(B,A), \tag{14}$$

$$TPP(A,B) \equiv_{def} PP(A,B) \wedge C_A - B \neq \emptyset, \tag{15}$$

$$NTPP(A,B) \equiv_{def} PP(A,B) \wedge C_A - B = \emptyset, \tag{16}$$

$$TPPi(A,B) \equiv_{def} TPP(B,A), \tag{17}$$

$$NTPPi(A,B) \equiv_{def} NTPP(B,A). \tag{18}$$

The proposed model of RCC-8 relations in terms of active contours (Eqs. (11–18)) is part of a wider, coherent set of active-contour-based spatial relations we established in this paper in order to perform reliable, qualitative spatial reasoning about complex, real-world objects as presented in Section 3. The other active-contour-based spatial relations deal with directional and projective concepts and are presented in Sects. 2.3–2.4, respectively.

2.3 Active-Contour-Based Directional Relations

Spatial directional relations have been modeled by a variety of approaches such as cardinal relations or traditional 'left' and 'right' concepts [37]. These formalisms own the advantage to have a linguistic meaning, but often lead to the uncertainty on the directional relative positions between objects in complex scenes. Other spatial relations deal with a varying granularity to describe the space such as OPRA or STAR [18], but thus loose their semantic interpretation.

In this work, we propose to use the clock representation [55] which is both semantically meaningful and spatially discriminant, and leads to JPED relations. Indeed, the image plane is divided in twelve parts around any object of interest of the scene similarly to a clock face as illustrated in Fig. 3, and each portion of the space is then corresponding to an hour.

Thence, we formalize spatial directional relations using the clock representation and the active closure defined in Eq. (3).

For this purpose, we consider O_{REF}, O_{REL}, which are the centroids defined in Eq. (4), based on the active contours of objects A and B, respectively. We could thus define

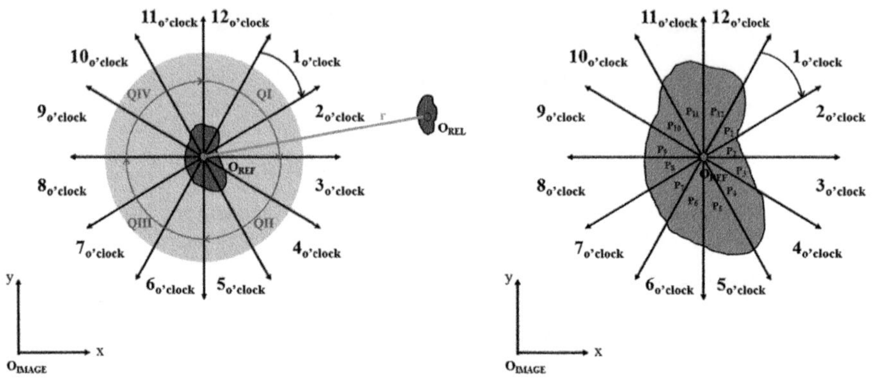

Fig. 3. Directional spatial relations using clock representation.

the *Angle* concept as the relative angle between the line $O_{REF} - O_{REL}$ and the axis X of the analyzed image plane.

As an example of the clock formalism based on active contours, we define the relation *isAt2oclock* between the objects A and B, in first order logic, as follows:

$$\begin{aligned} isAt2oclock(A,B) \equiv_{def} & Angle(O_{REF}, O_{REL}) \\ & \in Angle2clock(O_{REF}, O_{REL}), \end{aligned} \tag{19}$$

with

$$\begin{aligned} & Angle2clock(O_{REF}, O_{REL}) \equiv_{def} \\ & \quad \exists O_{REF}, O_{REL}(Angle(O_{REF}, O_{REL}) \leq \tfrac{\pi}{6} \\ & \quad \cap Angle(O_{REF}, O_{REL}) > 0). \end{aligned} \tag{20}$$

Hence, we have linked symbolic spatial relations such as directional relations (Eqs. 20) to active contours through the centroid notion defined in Eq. (4) in order to allow qualitative spatial reasoning directly on quantitative visual data. The use of the active contour model for projective spatial relations through the centroid definition is detailed in Sect. 2.4.

2.4 Active-Contour-Based Projective Relations

Projective relations involve semantic concepts such as 'above', 'before', 'between', etc., and they could be implemented as binary [8, 15, 76] or ternary models [16]. We focus on ternary projective relations which avoid common pitfalls of such relations usually considered as binary, as demonstrated in [49]. In particular, we consider the most common projective relations, namely, *above* (*ab*), *below* (*bl*), *before* (*bf*), *after* (*af*), and *between* (*bt*) we formalized as ternary ones with the clock model for sake of efficiency [49] and coherence with the spatial relations introduced in previous sections.

Hence, we propose in this work to redefine these five ternary projective relations in terms of active contours through the centroid notion defined in Eq. (4). It is worth noting that the definitions are valid for both convex and concave objects and that the center of each related clock is set to the centroid of the corresponding object, computed by Eq. (4), as shown in Fig. 4.

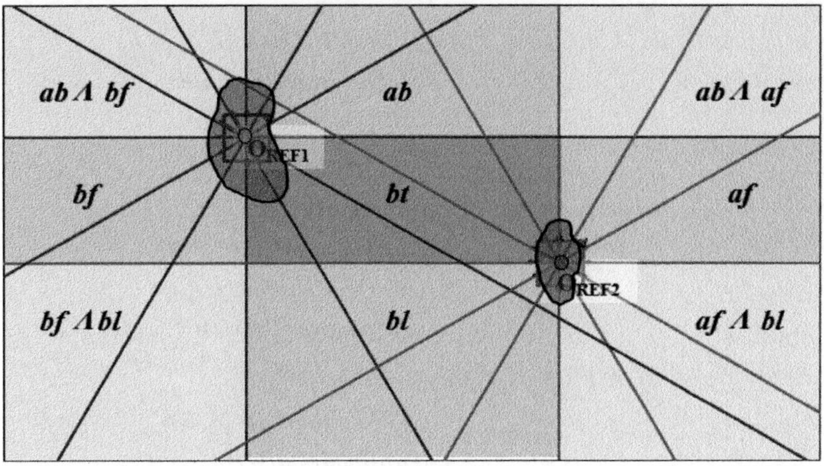

Fig. 4. Projective ternary spatial relations (*above* (*ab*), *below* (*bl*), $before$ (bf), $after$ (af), and *between* (*bt*)) using the clock representation.

For this purpose, we use the *quadrant Q* concept as introduced in [49] and illustrated in Fig. 3(a), where we consider *A* the object of reference with the corresponding centroid O_{REF} and *B* the target object with the related centroid O_{REL}. Thus, taking into account the Eq. 4, we define $isInQuadrantIOf$ in first order logic as follows:

$$\begin{aligned} &isInQuadrantIOf(A,B) \equiv_{def} \\ &\quad Angle(O_{REF},O_{REL}) \\ &\quad \in (Angle12clock(O_{REF},O_{REL}) \\ &\qquad \cup Angle1clock(O_{REF},O_{REL}) \\ &\qquad \cup Angle2clock(O_{REF},O_{REL})), \end{aligned} \tag{21}$$

where the concepts based on active contours' centroids such as $Angle(O_{REF},O_{REL})$ and $Angle2clock(O_{REF},O_{REL})$ have been defined in Eq. (20), respectively, and where $Angle12clock(O_{REF},O_{REL})$ and $Angle1clock(O_{REF},O_{REL})$ are defined in a similar way as in Eq. (20). We can note that any object of interest is located in at least one of the four quadrants, i.e. *QI*, *QII*, *QIII* or *QIV*.

Thence, considering the Eqs. (4), (21) and (20) and using first-order logic, we propose the respective definitions of the projective relations *above* (*ab*), *below* (*bl*), *before* (*bf*), *after* (*af*), and *between* (*bt*), as follows:

$$\begin{aligned} ab(A,B,C) \equiv_{def} &(isInQuadrantIVOf(A,B) \\ &\cup isInQuadrantIOf(A,B)) \\ &\cap (isInQuadrantIVOf(A,C) \\ &\cup isInQuadrantIOf(A,C)), \end{aligned} \tag{22}$$

$$
\begin{aligned}
bl(A,B,C) \equiv_{def} (&isInQuadrantIIIOf(A,B)\\
&\cup isInQuadrantIIOf(A,B))\\
&\cap (isInQuadrantIIIOf(A,C)\\
&\cup isInQuadrantIIOf(A,C)),
\end{aligned} \tag{23}
$$

$$
\begin{aligned}
bf(A,B,C) \equiv_{def} (&isInQuadrantIVOf(A,B)\\
&\cup isInQuadrantIIIOf(A,B))\\
&\cap (isInQuadrantIVOf(A,C)\\
&\cup isInQuadrantIIIOf(A,C),
\end{aligned} \tag{24}
$$

$$
\begin{aligned}
af(A,B,C) \equiv_{def} (&isInQuadrantIOf(A,B)\\
&\cup isInQuadrantIIOf(A,B))\\
&\cap (isInQuadrantIOf(A,C)\\
&\cup isInQuadrantIIOf(A,C)).,
\end{aligned} \tag{25}
$$

$$
\begin{aligned}
bt(A,B,C) \equiv_{def} (&isInQuadrantIIOf(A,B)\\
&\cup isInQuadrantIVOf(A,C)),
\end{aligned} \tag{26}
$$

where all these ternary projective spatial relations are illustrated in Fig. 4.

It is worthwhile to mention that all the Eqs. (22)-(26) follow the notation $rl(A,B,C)$, where rl is the ternary relation (i.e. ab, bl, bf, af, or bt) among three objects of interest A, B, and C and means "A is in the relation rl with B and C". In this case, the first object A is considered as the target object, whereas the two other objects B and C are the reference objects with the centroids O_{REF1} and O_{REF2}, respectively. The order of the reference objects B and C is not usually interchangeable in these relations, since it affects the orientation of the ternary relation, which is in this case from the reference object B to the reference object C.

3 Experiments and Results

In order to validate our relations and to prove their usefulness for spatio-visual automated analysis in context of Geographical Artificial Intelligence (GeoAI), we have carried out experiments with the spatial relations presented in Sect. 2 implemented into an imagery-based autonomous system.

To run the experiments, we have used a GIS database consists of 400 images with various geographical content such as maps, graphics (e.g. Fig. 5), and real-world pictures, including aerial and satellite photographs from the University of South California (USC) Viterbi SIPI standard dataset (e.g. Fig. 8), with a 512×512 image resolution. Further 100 higher-resolution images have also been taken from open-data standard datasets such as OpenStreetMap [57] (e.g. Fig. 6) and Sentinel maps[1] (e.g. Fig. 7).

[1] https://www.sentinelmap.eu.

Indeed, geographical images present many challenges such as complex scenes, objects of interest with both concavities and convexities, varying illumination, different camera view points, as well as varying (from low-level to high-level) image resolutions.

The first experiment consists in automatically computing the topological relations defined in Sect. 2.2 on the dataset and comparing the results with the ground truth ones obtained by applying the standard RCC-8 relations ([60]) on the same dataset by three independent persons. To illustrate this experiment, the computations for Fig. 5 generate the following list of found topological relations: `DC(B,G)`, `DC(B,R)`, `DC(G,Y)`, `DC(R,Y)`, `EC(B,Y)`, `EC(G,R)`. We can observe that this list is in accordance to the listed humans' observations. In this experiment, the accuracy performance achieved by our topological relations is 99.8%.

The second experiment is related to our directional relations modeled in Sect. 2.3. For this purpose, a series of queries is carried out about the directional relations between objects of interest for all the GIS-database images. As an example, in the Fig. 5, the relation *isAt3oclock* is found for the reference object R and the target object B, the relation *isAt4oclock* is found for the reference object R and the target object Y, and the relation *isAt5oclock* is found for the reference object R and the target object G. Hence, our system provides each time a single, correct answer. Compared to standard relations such as $left$ defined for GIS systems ([1]), which generate three answers for such relations, our definitions provide more discriminant directional relations, which are semantically meaningful. When tested for the entire GIS dataset and considering that the $precision\ of\ answers = \#correct\ answers / \#queries$, the average precision of our system in regards to ground truth values is of 99.9%.

(a)

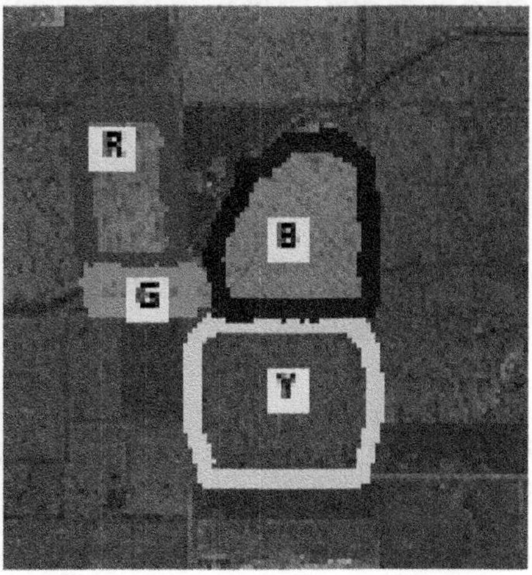

(b)

Fig. 5. Sample results of the experiments on the GIS dataset. The sample image (a) presents an aerial view of fields defining thus multiple objects of interest. It is worth mentioning that, in this example, the computation of topological and directional relations has involved four objects of interest (b).

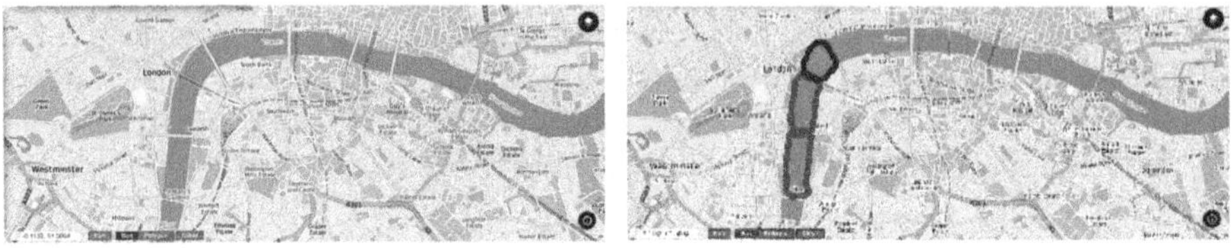

(a) (b)

Fig. 6. Sample results of the experiments on the GIS dataset. The image (a) presents an aerial view of the London sections of the river Thames defining thus multiple objects of interest. In this example, the computation of topological and directional relations has involved three objects of interest (b).

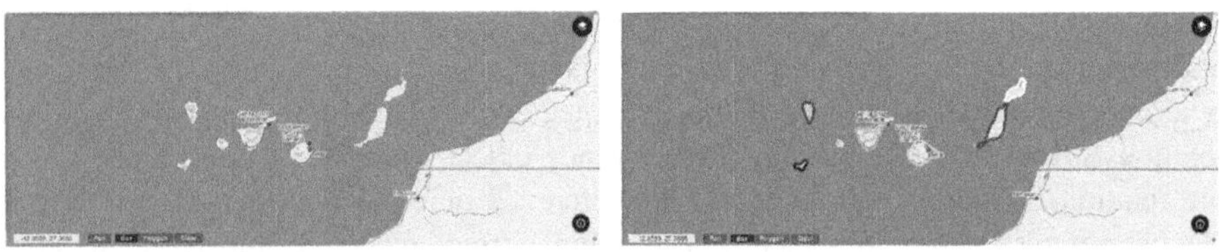

(a) (b)

Fig. 7. Sample results of the experiments on the GIS dataset. The image (a) presents an aerial view of the Canary Islands defining thus multiple objects of interest. In this example, the computation of topological and directional relations has involved seven objects of interest (b).

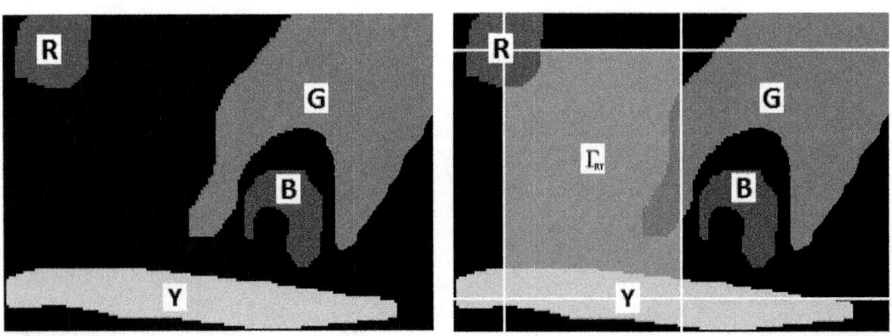

(a) (b)

Fig. 8. Sample results of the experiments on the GIS dataset. The sample image (a) presents objects of interest with both concavities and convexities. To test the degree of satisfaction of the ternary relation *between* for the image, the pink area called Γ_{RY} is automatically defined as illustrated in (b), and then, the objects crossing or lying in this area are automatically detected and considered to be *between* the objects R and Y. Best viewed in color. (Color figure online)

In the third experiment, we have quantitatively assessed the performance of our formalism of the projective relations described in Sect. 2.4 on the GIS dataset. For this purpose, we consider that the area between two reference objects B and C is equal to

Table 1. Satisfaction degree of the ternary relation *between* for all the objects of interest present in Fig. 8(a), from ◇ [8], from □ [15], and our.

O_{REL}	O_{REF1}	O_{REF2}	◇	□	**our**
B	G	R	0.41	0.02	0.00
B	G	Y	0.77	0.95	0.86
B	R	Y	0.52	0.22	0.00
G	R	Y	0.12	0.10	0.06
R	B	G	0.27	0.00	0.00

Γ_{BC}, and that the degree of satisfaction of the relation $rl(A,B,C)$ by the target object A is defined as follows:

$$s(A) = \frac{|area(A) \cap \Gamma_{BC}|}{|area(A)|}. \tag{27}$$

In particular, the results of the assessment applying (27) to the relation *between* defined in (26) as well as the comparisons with the works of [8, 15] are reported in Table 1 for the synthetic image presented in Fig. 8(a).

We can observe that our definition of the *between* relation provides better results than those obtained using state-of-the-art approaches, i.e. fuzzy mathematical morphology techniques ([8]) and ([15]). Furthermore, our approach leads to consistent values that is not the case for the other methods. Indeed for the $bt(B,G,R)$ and $bt(R,B,G)$ relations, the value of our definition is, in both cases, equal to zero which is conform with the intuition, whereas [8] approach's values are far from zero, while [15] values are once zero, once not.

The consistency and the accuracy of the values computed for all the dataset on the basis of the proposed formalism of the ternary relations as well as their concordance with the human interpretation of the semantics of these spatial relationships demonstrate the validity of the proposed semantic relations.

Hence, the evaluation of the results shows that our active-contour-based formalism of the spatial relations provides a very precise and consistent definition of these spatial concepts, allowing reliable qualitative spatial reasoning, while being both explainable and sustainable.

4 Conclusions

In this paper, qualitative spatial relations have been formalized in first-order logic and involved an innovative symbolic representation of the computer-vision concept of active contours by introducing the new active closure notion, reducing thus the semantic gap, while increasing representation consistency. Furthermore, on one hand, topological relations such as RCC-8 have been remodeled in terms of active contours instead of connection, leading to new mereotopologic relations. On the other hand, the directional relations and projective relations using the clock representation have been redefined based on the active contour's centroid notion. All these new binary and ternary spatial relations provide a powerful knowledge model combining visual descriptors and semantics, in order to describe multiple objects' relative positions and to perform reasoning on them. As demonstrated in the GeoAI context, this conceptualization brings a new insight in the study of explainable automated interpretation and sustainable content analysis of image data by autonomous systems.

References

1. Aksoy, S., Koperski, K., Tusk, C., Marchisio, G., Tilton, J.C.: Learning Bayesian classifiers for scene classification with a visual grammar. IEEE Trans. Geosci. Remote Sens. **43**(3), 581–589 (2005)
2. Amiri, Z., Heidari, A., Jafari Navimipour, N.: Comprehensive survey of artificial intelligence techniques and strategies for climate change mitigation. Energy **308**, 1–26 (2024)
3. Baylock, N., Swain, B., Allen, J.: TESLA: a tool for annotating geospatial language corpora. In: Proceedings of the Conference of the North Amercian Chapter of the Association for Artificial Intelligence (2009)
4. Bayomi, N., Fernandez, J.E.: Eyes in the sky: drones applications in the built environment under climate change challenges. Drones **7**(10), 1–42 (2023)
5. Binder, R.: Software dependability measurement at the age of 36. IEEE Comput. **57**(4), 1–18 (2024). https://arxiv.org/abs/2311.10039
6. Black, R., Davenport, J.H., Olszewska, J.I., Roessler, J., Smith, A.L., Wright, J.: Artificial Intelligence and Software Testing: Building Systems You Can Trust. BCS Press (2022)
7. Blake, A., Isard, M.: Active Contours. Springer (1998)
8. Bloch, I., Colliot, O., Cesar, R.M.: On the ternary spatial relation "between". IEEE Trans. Syst. Man. Cybern. - Part B: Cybern. **36**(2), 312–327 (2006)
9. Cai, G., Lee, K., Lee, I.: Itinerary recommender system with semantic trajectory pattern mining from geo-tagged photos. Expert Syst. Appl. **94**, 32–40 (2018)
10. Cai, P., Cai, Z., Fan, Y., Wu, W.: Image contour detection based on visual pathway information transfer mechanism. Neural Process. Lett. **56**(1), 1–20 (2024)
11. Castro-Santos, L., Lamas-Galdo, M.I., Filgueira-Vizoso, A.: Managing the oceans: site selection of a floating offshore wind farm based on GIS spatial analysis. Mar. Policy **113**, 1–8 (2020)
12. Chen, B., et al.: SpatialVLM: endowing vision-language models with spatial reasoning capabilities. In: Proceedings of the IEEE Conference on Computer Vision and Pattern Recognition (CVPR), pp. 14455–14465 (2024)
13. Chen, C., et al.: Self-supervised place recognition by refining temporal and featural pseudo labels From panoramic data. IEEE Robot. Autom. Lett. 1–8 (2024)
14. Chenier, R., Sagram, M., Omari, K., Jirovec, A.: Earth observation and artificial intelligence for improving safety to navigation in Canada low-impact shipping corridors. ISPRS Int. J. Geo Inf. **9**(6), 1–15 (2020)
15. Cinbis, R.G., Aksoy, S.: Relative position-based spatial relationships using mathematical morphology. In: Proceedings of the IEEE International Conference on Image Processing (ICIP'07), pp. II.97–II.100 (2007)
16. Clementini, E., Skiadopoulos, S., Billen, R., Tarquini, F.: A reasoning system of ternary projective relations. IEEE Trans. Knowl. Data Eng. **22**(2), 161–178 (2010)
17. Cohn, A.G., et al.: Cognitive Vision Systems: Sampling the Spectrum of Approaches, chap. Cognitive vision: Integrating symbolic qualitative representations with computer vision, pp. 211–234. Springer (2005)
18. Cohn, A.G., Renz, J.: Handbook of Knowledge Representation, chap. Elsevier, Qualitative spatial reasoning (2007)

19. Davison, A.: FutureMapping: The computational structure of spatial AI systems. arXiv:1803.11288, pp. 1–19 (2018)
20. Dennis, L., Fisher, M.: Verifiable Autonomous Systems. Cambridge University Press (2023)
21. Ge, Q., Xiao, L., Wang, L.Q., Zhang, Z.R., Wei, Z.H.: A hybrid active contour model with structure feature for image segmentation. In: Proceedings of the IEEE International Conference on Image Processing (ICIP'14), pp. 1242–1246 (2014)
22. Guenat, S., Purnell, P., Davies, Z.G., et al.: Meeting sustainable development goals via robotics and autonomous systems. Nat. Commun. **13**(1), 1–10 (2022)
23. Gunning, D., Stefik, M., Choi, J., Miller, T., Stumpf, S., Yang, G.-Z.: XAI–Explainable artificial intelligence. Sci. Robot. **4**(37), 1–5 (2019)
24. Guven, D.S., Yenigun, K., Isinkaralar, O., et al.: Modeling flood hazard impacts using GIS-based HEC-RAS technique towards climate risk in Sanliurfa, Turkiye. Nat. Hazards 1–19 (2024)
25. Hernandez, D., Cano, J.-C., Silla, F., Calafate, C.T., Cecilia, J.M.: AI-enabled autonomous drones for fast climate change crisis assessment. IEEE Internet Things J. **9**(10), 7286–7297 (2022)
26. Hogenboom, F., Borgman, B., Frasincar, F., Kaymak, U.: Spatial knowledge representation on the Semantic Web. In: Proceedings of the IEEE International Conference on Semantic Computing, pp. 252–259 (2010)
27. Houghtaling, M.A., et al.: Standardizing an ontology for ethically aligned robotic and autonomous systems. IEEE Trans. Syst. Man Cybern. Syst. **54**(3), 1791–1804 (2024)
28. Hudelot, C., Atif, J., Bloch, I.: A spatial relation ontology using mathematical morphology and description logics for spatial reasoning. In: Proceedings of the European Conference on Artificial Intelligence (ECAI'08), pp. 21–25 (2008)
29. J. I. Olszewska et al.: Multi-feature vector flow for active contour tracking. In: Proceedings of the IEEE International Conference on Acoustics, Speech and Signal Processing (ICASSP'08), pp. 721–724 (2008)
30. Jiang, Z.: Deep learning for spatiotemporal Big data: opportunities and challenges. In: Proceedings of the IEEE International Conference on Big Data, pp. 1157–1161 (2023)
31. Kass, M., Witkin, A., Terzopoulos, D.: Snakes: active contour models. Int. J. Comput. Vision **1**(4), 321–331 (1988)
32. Kurup, U., Lebiere, C., Stentz, A., Hebert, M.: Using expectations to drive cognitive behavior. In: Proceedings of the AAAI Conference on Artificial Intelligence, pp. 221–227 (2012)
33. Laurinia, R., Favetta, F.: About external geographic information and knowledge in smart cities. Int. Arch. Photogramm. Remote. Sens. Spat. Inf. Sci. **42**, 51–58 (2017)
34. Leal Filho, W., Wall, T., Rui Mucova, S.A., et al.: Deploying artificial intelligence for climate change adaptation. Technol. Forecast. Soc. Chang. **180**, 1–20 (2022)
35. Li, F., Hogg, D.C., Cohn, A.G.: Advancing spatial reasoning in large language models: an in-depth evaluation and enhancement using the StepGame benchmark. In: Proceedings of the AAAI Conference on Artificial Intelligence (AAAI), pp. 18500–18507 (2024)
36. Li, W., Batty, M., Goodchild, M.F.: Real-time GIS for smart cities. Int. J. Geogr. Inf. Sci. **34**(2), 311–324 (2020)
37. Ligozat, G.: Qualitative Spatial and Temporal Reasoning. John Wiley & Sons (2011)
38. Liu, P. and Filip Biljecki, F.: A review of spatially-explicit GeoAI applications in urban geography. Int. J. Appl. Earth Observ. Geoinf. **112**, 1–12 (2022)
39. Longo, L., Brcic, M., Cabitza, F., et al.: Explainable artificial intelligence (XAI) 2.0: a manifesto of open challenges and interdisciplinary research directions. Inf. Fusion **106**, 1–22 (2024)
40. Lowry, S., et al.: Visual place recognition: a survey. IEEE Trans. Rob. **32**(1), 1–19 (2016)

41. Ma, Z., Nie, F., Yang, Y., Uijilings, J., Sebe, N., Hauptmann, A.: Discriminating joint feature analysis for multimedia data understanding. IEEE Trans. Multimedia **14**(6), 1662–1672 (2012)
42. Mandal, S., Yadav, A., Panme, F.A., Devi, K.M., Shravan Kumar, S.M.: Adaption of smart applications in agriculture to enhance production. Smart Agric. Technol. **7**, 1–11 (2024)
43. Minh, D., Wang, H.X., Li, Y.F., Nguyen, T.N.: Explainable artificial intelligence: a comprehensive review. Artif. Intell. Rev. **112**, 1–66 (2022)
44. Mobasheri, A.: A rule-based spatial reasoning approach for Openstreetmap data quality enrichment: case study of routing and navigation. Sensors **17**(11), 1–19 (2017)
45. Molina, M., Stent, A.: Generating descriptions that summarize geospatial and temporal data. In: Proceedings of the IEEE International Conference on Tools with Artificial Intelligence (ICTAI), pp. 485–492 (2009)
46. Moradi, M., Yan, K., Colwell, D., Samwald, M., Asgari, R.: Model-agnostic explainable artificial intelligence for object detection in image data. Eng. Appl. Artif. Intell. **137**, 1–33 (2024)
47. Mumford, D., Shah, J.: Optimal approximations by piecewise smooth functions and associated variational problems. Commun. Pure Appl. Math. **42**(5), 577–685 (1989)
48. Ning, J., Pang, S., Arifin, Z., et al.: The diversity of artificial intelligence applications in marine pollution: a systematic literature review. J. Mar. Sci. Eng. **12**(7), 1–26 (2024)
49. Olszewska, J.I.: Clock-modeled ternary spatial reltations for visual scene analysis. In: Proceedings of the ACL International Conference on Computational Semantics Workshop (IWCS'13), pp. 20–30 (2013)
50. Olszewska, J.I.: 3D spatial reasoning using the clock model. Res. Dev. Intell. Syst. **32**, 147–154 (2015)
51. Olszewska, J.I.: Active contour based optical character recognition for automated scene understanding. Neurocomputing **161**, 65–71 (2015)
52. Olszewska, J.I.: Designing transparent and autonomous intelligent vision systems. In: Proceedings of the International Conference on Agents and Artificial Intelligence (ICAART), pp. 850–856 (2019)
53. Olszewska, J.I.: Snakes in Trees: an explainable artificial intelligence approach for automatic object detection and recognition. In: Proceedings of the International Conference on Agents and Artificial Intelligence (ICAART), pp. 996–1002 (2022)
54. Olszewska, J.I.: Operational modeling of temporal intervals for intelligent systems. In: Proceedings of the International Conference on Robotics, Computer Vision and Intelligent Systems (ROBOVIS 2024). Communications in Computer and Information Science, vol. 2077. Springer Nature, pp. 334–344 (2024)
55. Olszewska, J.I., McCluskey, T.L.: Ontology-coupled active contours for dynamic video scene understanding. In: Proceedings of the IEEE International Conference on Intelligent Engineering Systems, pp. 369–374 (2011)
56. Osher, S., Sethian, J.A.: Fronts propagating with curvature-dependent speed: algorithms based on Hamilton-Jacobi formulations. J. Comput. Phys. **16**(9), 2361–2368 (1988)
57. Panphattarasap, P., Calway, A.: Automated map reading: image based localisation in 2-D maps using binary semantic descriptors. In: Proceedings of the IEEE International Conference on Intelligent Robots and Systems (IROS), pp. 6341–6348 (2018)
58. Pearson, S., et al.: Robotics and autonomous systems for net zero agriculture. Current Robot. Rep. **3**(2), 57–64 (2022)
59. Raihan, A.: A systematic review of Geographic Information Systems (GIS) in agriculture for evidence-based decision making and sustainability. Global Sustain. Res. **3**(1), 1–24 (2024)
60. Randell, D.A., Cui, Z., Cohn, A.G.: A spatial logic based on regions and connection. In: Proceedings of the International Conference on Knowledge Representation and Reasoning, pp. 165–176 (1992)

61. Randell, D.A., Landini, G., Galton, A.: Discrete mereotopology for spatial reasoning in automated histological image analysis. IEEE Trans. Pattern Anal. Mach. Intell. **35**(3), 568–581 (2013)
62. Rane, N.L., Paramesha, M.: Explainable artificial intelligence (XAI) as a foundation for trustworthy artificial intelligence. Trustworthy Artificial Intelligence in Industry and Society, pp. 1–27 (2024)
63. Redfield, S., Olszewska, J.I., Leahy, K., Murahwi, Z., Araiza-Illan, D., Fisher, M.: Verification of autonomous systems: the road ahead. In: 40th Anniversary of the IEEE International Conference on Robotics and Automation (ICRA) (2024)
64. Renz, J., Nebel, B.: Handbook of Spatial Logics, chap. Springer Verlag, Qualitative spatial reasoning using constraint calculi (2007)
65. Ronneberger, O., Fischer, P., Brox, T.: U-Net: convolutional networks for biomedical image segmentation. In: IEEE Conference on Medical Image Computing and Computer-Assisted Intervention (MICCAI), pp. 234–241 (2015)
66. Schoitsch, E.: Trustworthy smart autonomous systems-of-systems–resilient technology, economy and society. In: 29th Interdisciplinary Information Management Talks (IDMIT) (2021)
67. Shen, W., Wang, X., Wang, Y., Bai, X., Zhang, Z.: DeepContour: a deep convolutional feature learned by positive-sharing loss for contour detection. In: Proceedings of the IEEE Conference on Computer Vision and Pattern Recognition (CVPR), pp. 3982–3991 (2015)
68. Thakker, D., Mishra, B.K., Abdullatif, A., Mazumdar, S., Simpson, S.: Explainable artificial intelligence for developing smart cities solutions. Smart Cities **3**(4), 1353–1382 (2020)
69. Van, T.T., Le, T.M.: Content-based image retrieval based on binary signatures cluster graph. Expert Syst. **35**(1) (2018)
70. Wang, J., et al.: Is a picture worth a thousand words? Delving into spatial reasoning for vision language models. arXiv:2406.14852 pp. 1–11 (2024)
71. Winfield, A.F.T., et al.: IEEE P7001: a proposed standard on transparency. Front. Robot. AI **8**, 1–11 (2021)
72. Wintermute, S., Laird, J.E.: Predicate projcetion in a bimodal spatial reasoning system. In: Proceedings of the AAAI Conference on Artificial Intelligence (2007)
73. Wintermute, S., Laird, J.E.: Bimodal spatial reasoning with continuous motion. In: Proceedings of the AAAI Conference on Artificial Intelligence, pp. 1331–1337 (2008)
74. Xing, J., Sieber, R.: The challenges of integrating explainable artificial intelligence into GeoAI. Trans. GIS **27**(3), 626–645 (2023)
75. Xue, P., Niu, S.: A novel active contour model based on features for image segmentation. Pattern Recogn. **155**, 1–10 (2024)
76. Zhang, K., Wang, X., Zhong, Y.: Research on fundemental theory of spatial directional relation. In: Proceedings of the IEEE International Conference on Cloud Computing and Intelligence Systems, pp. 65–69 (2011)

Synth it Like KITTI: Synthetic Data Generation for Object Detection in Driving Scenarios

Richard Marcus[1(✉)], Christian Vogel[1], Inga Jatzkowski[2], Niklas Knoop[2], and Marc Stamminger[1]

[1] Chair of Visual Computing, Friedrich-Alexander-Universität Erlangen-Nürnberg, Erlangen, Germany
{richard.marcus,christian.chr.vogel,marc.stamminger}@fau.de
[2] e:fs TechHub GmbH, gaimersheim, Germany
{inga.jatzkowski,niklas.knoop}@efs-techhub.com

Abstract. An important factor in advancing autonomous driving systems is simulation. Yet, there is rather small progress for transferability between the virtual and real world. We revisit this problem for 3D object detection on LiDAR point clouds and propose a dataset generation pipeline based on the CARLA simulator. Utilizing domain randomization strategies and careful modeling, we are able to train an object detector on the synthetic data and demonstrate strong generalization capabilities to the KITTI dataset. Furthermore, we compare different virtual sensor variants to gather insights, which sensor attributes can be responsible for the prevalent domain gap. Finally, fine-tuning with a small portion of real data almost matches the baseline and with the full training set slightly surpasses it.

Keywords: LiDAR · Object Detection · Simulation

1 Introduction

Autonomous Driving has gained a lot of traction in recent years, but practical applications remain limited. One of the reasons for this is that machine learning systems are held back by the uncertainty of their predictions and the cost of generating real-world training data. For both issues, synthetic data poses a solution, as simulating test drives is more affordable and scalable. It is also possible to provoke rare scenarios or critical situations that otherwise would endanger humans.

However, driving simulations still lack in realism, resulting in a *domain gap* between synthetic and real-world data. This is difficult to overcome as modeling the real world requires good physical-based sensors as well as detailed environments and materials. Conversely, this may only be true to some extent for the special case of 3D object detection in LiDAR point clouds. The respective sensors are operating with a rather low resolution and light computations are simpler in comparison to photorealistic rendering, which suggests that it is possible to succeed with points sampled from the basic geometry.

Yet, approaches in that direction have not reached convincing results. In particular, training a neural network for object detection on synthetic data has not proven to

J. Röning and J. Filipe (Eds.): ROBOVIS 2025, CCIS 2629, pp. 414–432, 2026.
https://doi.org/10.1007/978-3-032-00986-9_27

be practical for real-world application to the best of our knowledge. Only using synthetic data causes detections to be magnitudes worse, and real-data fine-tuning shows no improvements beyond the non-synthetic baseline. Moreover, existing synthetic datasets and simulations often do not provide the necessary data or the correct format to evaluate 3D object detection on point clouds on common benchmarks. We improve this with a customized CARLA [8] simulation, resulting in a robust and diverse synthetic dataset (cf. 1).

Fig. 1. Typical samples from our synthetic dataset. We mimic the KITTI configuration and use multiple maps for data generation.

1.1 Contribution

Our contribution in this has three aspects: First, we implement the LiDAR sensor and model surface interactions so that the resulting point clouds closely resemble those generated by the real device. For this, we add a heuristic LiDAR intensity model and adjust the sensor parameters.

Second, we leverage domain randomization and adaption concepts. Instead of exactly modeling the real world, we evaluate randomizing certain aspects like the environment, the traffic, the movement of the vehicle and the sensor responses for better generalization. Notably, we confirm that adapting bounding box labeling biases are a crucial factor for achieving high detection precision on real data.

Third, we define a pipeline for generating synthetic object detection datasets, including a modular setup for ease of use and modification, effectively lowering the entry barrier for further research. The simulation scripts and processed synthetic datasets are available at https://github.com/richardmarcus/synth-it-like-kitti.

2 Related Work

To build a competitive system for this, it is necessary to look at both real world datasets and existing simulation approaches for object detection and domain adaption.

2.1 Datasets

The traditional way to perform object detection tasks for autonomous driving is using real sensor data from test drives. The respective algorithms are based on visual sensors like LiDAR, radar, or camera images. Neural networks have emerged as the standard solution in recent research but require ground truth labels for training. There are semi-automatic approaches [1], but considerable human effort is still necessary for large-scale datasets.

For our approach, the primary focus was 3D object detection, which commonly relies on LiDAR point clouds. The KITTI dataset [13] offers an established benchmark for comparing the performance of object detection systems. As such, it is the perfect candidate to evaluate how well objects can be detected when training on synthetic data. The test vehicle for the KITTI dataset is equipped with a stereo camera setup and a Velodyne LiDAR sensor [31].

Another popular dataset is Waymo [27], which especially stands out for the number and diversity of captured scenarios. It uses a rather complex sensor setup with five cameras and LiDAR sensors. There are further datasets with 3D object labels like Argoverse2 [33], nuScenes [5] or [17], but in general it is not trivial to compare results and have compatible formats between these. Our work mainly takes KITTI as an example of how well a synthetic dataset can mimic a real one.

2.2 Object Detection

Given these labeled datasets, the task of object detection also includes predicting the dimensions and rotation of the vehicle, even when there are only partial observations of the respective objects.

Approaches. To isolate the impacts of the point clouds, we limited our experiments to architectures that use only LiDAR point clouds as input. Aside from the distance, these sensors also measure *intensity* values based on the strength of the reflected signal. We call the phenomenon that some rays do not return a signal as *raydrop*. Due to material properties some high frequency details can become visible, in particular retro-reflective surfaces as can be found on number plates. This offers additional features for accurately detecting cars in point clouds.

Voxel-based methods such as SECOND [34] or Voxel-R-CNN [6] have proven to robustly extract features from point clouds for object detection and thus may lead to good generalization between point clouds generated by different sensors. Furthermore, we are mostly interested in the relative change of detection quality when incorporating synthetic data and less in the behavior of different detection architectures, so we base all experiments on Voxel-R-CNN. We use the implementation provided by OpenPCDet [28], a framework that supports different object detection models and datasets. This complements the modular nature of our pipeline and allows us to use additional models and datasets for future experiments.

Domain Adaptation. Domain adaption regarding object detection in driving scenarios is covered quite well. On the one hand, there is work that directly examines the domain shift between synthetic and real datasets [14,30], where we rather focus on the aspect of data collection, i.e., how typical road scenes are structured or the composition of datasets. This is more in line with methods that show good performance for optimizing the domain gap and robustness between different real datasets [32,35,36]. However, our goal is to be able to directly generate data that can be used for generalization purposes, independent of the network architecture, so that we can gather more insight on what actually impedes the object detections. One such issue has already been identified by the works mentioned above, namely the difference in vehicle dimensions between different datasets. We will revisit this topic in Sect. 3.3. Finally, the core idea behind our randomization concepts are closely related to the findings of Tobin et al.: "With enough variability in the simulator, the real world may appear to the model as just another variation". [29].

2.3 Simulation

For synthetic data generation, the open source driving simulator CARLA [8] has seen widespread adoption for training neural networks on car perception tasks. CARLA is built on the Unreal Engine [11]. Features include its scalable architecture with one server and multiple clients controlling different parts of the simulation, a flexible Python API for writing custom clients, and a basic sensor suite for autonomous driving applications. Other tools like NVIDIA DriveSim [20] are not easily accessible or, in the case of AirSim [26], do not offer as much support for driving simulation integrations.

There are several approaches regarding object detection in synthetic environments [2,7,21,24,25], but direct use is often difficult as 3D data often is not available and there are no benchmarks on real data.

While we make use of some concepts of these approaches, we base our code on a simple standalone implementation for generating data in the KITTI format from CARLA [19]. Overall, the specific combination of 3D bounding boxes and evaluation on real datasets was often not the main focus, which our work is supposed to address.

Synthetic 3D Object Detection on Real Data. There are also some approaches that have already gathered insights for using synthetically trained networks on real data [15], e.g., that fine-tuning results in significantly better performance on the target domain compared to training on both datasets simultaneously [10]. Other works like CADET [3] (based on AVOD [16]) use the same KITTI benchmarks we target, so we can compare our results. The same is true for IntensitySim [18], which uses data from VKITTI2 [4, 12], a synthetic remodeling of KITTI instead of CARLA. It consists of selected sequences, summing up to about 2k frames. In addition to sampling point clouds from the depth maps, it also utilizes a GAN trained on real data to simulate raydrop. Our approach will employ further methods to increase the realism of the synthetic data.

3 Synthetic Data Generation for Object Detection

We use the CARLA simulator and define a pipeline to gather a robust training dataset, which is evaluated in 4. Our build is based on version 0.9.15, which is the latest CARLA release that uses Unreal Engine 4.

3.1 Simulation Pipeline

Our simulation pipeline consists of three stages: data generation, data processing, and object detection. This modular approach allows more flexibility for different experiments and for future use by the research community. See Fig. 2 for the resulting pipeline.

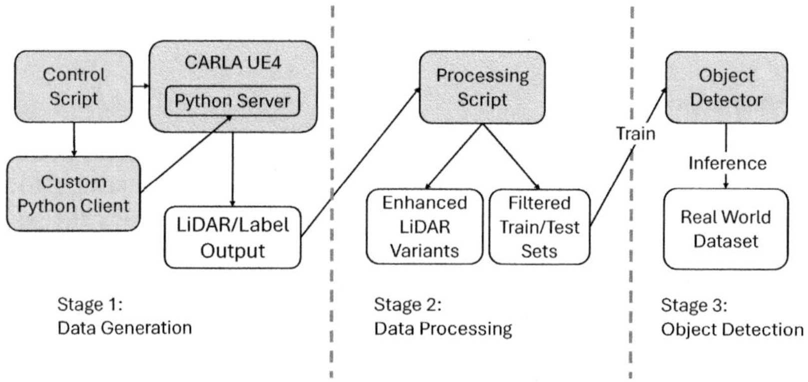

Fig. 2. Modular Sim2Real Pipeline: The simulation generates an intermediate output. A processing script enhances the realism of the data and prepares it for object detection.

Stage 1: Data Generation. The first stage largely consists of the CARLA simulator, which is controlled by a custom python client script that interacts with the CARLA server. The CARLA server can run in an off-screen mode, which simplifies remote and simultaneous data generation.

Our main addition in this stage is a monitor script that handles errors from both, the CARLA server and the custom python client since CARLA exhibits stability issues [9] regarding frequent restarts of the main simulation.

The simulator generates the relevant data directly in a KITTI compatible format, so additional modules could be added that, for example, directly test certain perception tasks in the loop. For this work, we only generate the dataset for offline use.

Stage 2: Data Processing. The resulting dataset includes denser data than necessary for the final dataset, i.e., the point clouds are downsampled or some of the bounding boxes filtered out. Furthermore, we record data that helps to process the generated data to produce more LiDAR variants. Providing processing scripts as well as the final data enables future research usage and experiment variants even without setting up the CARLA environment.

Stage 3: Object Detection. The processed data is then used for training an object detector, where we compare different sensor configurations to observe the generalization behavior. The core concept behind this is that we train on synthetic data but employ the trained network for unseen, real-world data.

3.2 Realistic World Modeling

We will now move onto our approaches to increase the realism of the synthetic data. For better overview, there will be no explicit division of the aforementioned stages, instead our findings will be grouped into world, label and sensor modeling.

Variation in Vehicle Behavior. The simulation in CARLA is populated by a number of traffic participants that are controlled by CARLA's internal traffic manager. By default, these traffic participants move quite uniformly and show little variation in behavior. To make the behavior of these vehicles more realistic, a number of behavior variations were applied. Vehicles can exceed the speed limit by up to $30\,\mathrm{km\,h^{-1}}$. They can vary the distance they keep to the leading vehicle between 20 cm and 3 m and can have an offset from the center line of the lane of up to 20 cm in either direction.

Vehicles can perform lane changes to the left or right randomly and may also decide to make a U-turn in the middle of the road, disregarding traffic rules. A side effect of this behavior variation is the occasional occurrence of collisions between vehicles that can produce traffic jams in the simulation. In addition to the traffic participants, several vehicles are spawned parking on the shoulder along the road. These vehicles can be triggered to start driving off at any point in the simulation. Although potential resulting traffic deadlocks make the data collection less efficient, we can cover a higher variety of scenarios that way, which can potentially increase the robustness of the object detection when training on that data.

Environment Randomization. A different important factor is the environment captured during test drives, which is usually quite diverse in real scenarios. Aside from the road users, structures like trash bins, bushes, boxes, or tables appear frequently in the real world. CARLA covers this by offering a selection of *props* that are used in the default maps, but can also be placed randomly. With the maps itself, CARLA models different sceneries, we use the default maps Town01 to Town07 as well as Town10HD and Town15, which add more urban environments, see Fig. 3. Overall, we randomize the number of driving vehicles, parking vehicles and props, as well as the type of road users and maps.

3.3 Realistic Bounding Boxes

A known issue in Carla is that bounding boxes retrieved from the simulation can have an incorrect size depending on the blueprint, which is addressed in GitHub issue [23]. While it also should be possible to retrieve the actual volume from the vehicle model, the issue provides a script that reconstructs more consistent bounding box sizes from multiple simulated LiDAR measurements of each vehicle. As this avoids any source build adaptations, we use the resulting JSON file to replace the dimensions and center point of the vehicle bounding boxes returned by CARLA during synthetic data generation.

Special care also has to be taken for vehicles that are baked into the default CARLA maps. These are not registered as actors for the traffic simulation and thus are not provided with bounding boxes. Still, our simulator can handle these, as long as they are either defined in the *parking layer* or can be identified by their name.

A more conceptual issue are the actual sizes of cars and the partial visibility in LiDAR scans. The former has already been identified as cause for lacking generalization between datasets captured in regions where the average car dimensions differ, but there also can be a difference in how tight the annotated bounding boxes are in respect to the vehicle. While we can measure the size discrepancy between the ground truth bounding box and the extents of the points inside it, there is no direct way to decide whether larger values arise simply from larger vehicles or the labeling bias. Yet, this also means that by trying to emulate this effect, we can cover both effects to a certain degree depending on the amount of shrinking we apply.

Fig. 3. Bird-eye-view perspective screenshots of the nine CARLA maps, from which the synthetic dataset was created. Notably, Town10 (bottom left) and Town15 (top right) increase the proportion of urban environments.

We implement this by reducing the dimensions of the CARLA bounding boxes by $a + b \times d$ meters, where d is the delta between the bounding box and the extents of the points inside and the absolute reduction a and the factor b are empirically chosen. For our experiment, we chose a conservative instantiation and start with an initial upwards shift to largely prevent ground points to be inside the boxes. The most crucial dimension is the length, as cars can vary greatly in length and there are many cases where the front or back points towards the ego-vehicle. We chose $a = 0.2\,\mathrm{m}$ and $b = 0.25$. We use a similar variation of $a = 0.05\,\mathrm{m}$ and $b = 0.25$ for the width. Even though in theory this could reduce the overall dimensions by half, in practice, either a sufficient number of rays hit vehicles from at least one side or the car is filtered out because of low visibility anyway. Last, we allow only slight variation of $a = 0.05\,\mathrm{m}$ and $b = 0.05$ for the height, as this is rather simple to estimate from the recorded data. An example of the shrunk boxes can be seen in 4.

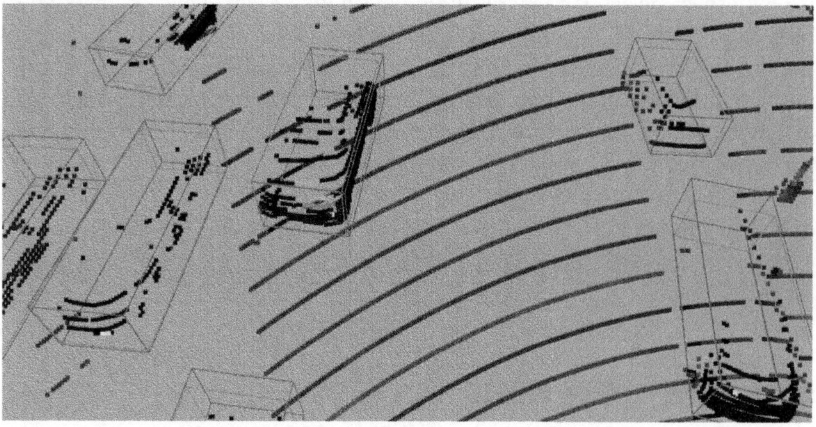

Fig. 4. Original bounding boxes in purple, shrunk ones in green. (Color figure online)

3.4 Realistic Sensor Modeling

Sensor Setup. We adapt the sensor configuration of the KITTI dataset and use two stereo camera setups, grayscale and RGB, as well as a LiDAR sensor. Skeletons for further cameras like depth or semantic segmentation are also already configurable via CARLA.

While usually not modeled realistically in simulations, ground height variations and steering motions have a big impact on the resulting point cloud as small deviations in pitch, yaw, and roll cause the sensor to see objects in very different locations relative to the world.

We model this by randomizing the sensor rotation during data collection. The randomization of the vehicle behavior and the inclusion of parking processes has already introduced a great variety of different rotations, but the object positions have appeared very centered. Adding this additional step effectively brings the data distribution very close to the real-world dataset (cf. Figure 5). Notably, both cannot easily be implemented as a post process, as translating and rotating vehicle points does not take into account that the sensor sees different parts of the objects depending on their relative transformation.

LiDAR Implementation. The CARLA simulator comes with a basic ray cast LiDAR implementation. This implementation uses a line trace from the Unreal Engine and returns the first blocking hit of that trace regardless of the material that was hit. In reality, a LiDAR is usually able to penetrate glass-like materials at least to a certain degree. In order to replicate this behavior within CARLA, we added a modified version of the original ray cast LiDAR. This modified LiDAR uses the original line trace of the basic LiDAR.

In order to enable a LiDAR sensor to penetrate vehicle windows in CARLA, the collision meshes for moving object had to be adapted. By default, CARLA uses low resolution collision meshes for dynamic vehicles for LiDAR and radar sensors. These collision meshes consist of a low resolution mesh with a single custom material for the entire vehicle. Thus, a line trace would hit the collision mesh with its custom material but not the underlying structure. Only the custom material is returned, but not the true material of the vehicle under the collision mesh. This has the effect that for the modified LiDAR no secondary line trace is triggered when hitting a window of a moving vehicle with the initial line trace as the material returned is not glass. In order to circumvent this issue and get the correct materials for moving vehicles, new collision meshes for all vehicle blueprints were generated that preserve the vehicle's materials.

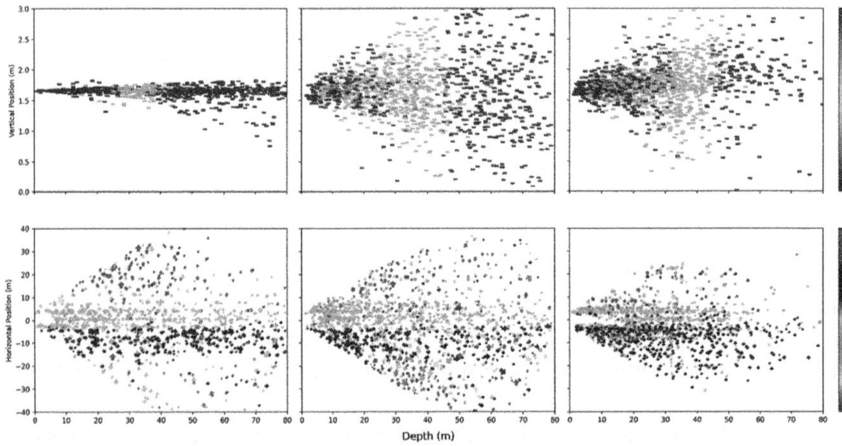

Fig. 5. Bounding box distribution plots: top row shows side view, bottom row BEV; left is synthetic data before sensor randomization, middle after and right KITTI data.

The Unreal Engine provides methods to obtain the underlying material of a hit point from a line trace. In order to achieve this, returning the face index of the hit point must be activated in the trace parameters of the line trace. Returning the physical material of the hit point can also be activated in the trace parameters but is unimportant for CARLA as the physical material is not set for most if not all components. The hit result returned by the line trace then allows retrieving a pointer to the underlying component that was hit. With the face index of the hit point, a pointer to the material of the component for that specific face index of the triangle mesh can be retrieved. This material pointer can then be used to get the material's name. As a last step, we use a lookup table to categorize materials into broader categories by name, so e.g., 'Glass' and 'Window' are categorized as glass materials but 'GlassContainer' , the waste container for glass, is not. With this, we avoid dependency on the actual transparency attribute.

If the blocking hit of the original was a glass-like material, it shoots a secondary multi-hit line trace from the first hit point ignoring blocking hits along the trace. From this secondary line trace, we return the first hit that does not hit a glass-like material. The modified LiDAR returns two hits, the first and the last hit. If the first hit was a solid material, both hits are the same. Otherwise, the first hit is the one that hit the glass, the second hit is the one that hit a solid material after passing though the glass.

Basic LiDAR Variants. To analyze the importance of sensor specifics in the simulation, our simulation supports LiDAR configurations beyond the basic KITTI setup, which essentially means that different sampling strategies will be employed. Also, sensors use a higher angular resolution compared to the KITTI dataset in order to simulate different frequency operation later on.

- **First Hit.** This is basically the default behavior of the CARLA LiDAR, which can be compared to a real sensor that always reports the first reflection but, in contrast to reality, always receives a return signal when geometry is hit, i.e., not in the sky. We disable other CARLA settings like atmospheric intensity values or randomly dropping and shifting points.
- **Strongest Hit.** This variant adds transparency effects but nothing further.
- **Original Boxes.** This configuration is the same as Strongest Hit, but uses the original corrected CARLA bounding boxes instead of the ones that model the human labeling bias, it is labeled with a "*" in the tables below.
- **Sampled Depth.** A different approach is a pseudo-LiDAR generated from a depth camera that uses the same position as the LiDAR sensor. The camera uses a resolution of 2048 by 512 and an FOV of 120 degrees. From that we sample points depending on azimuth, elevation of the points and angular resolution and FOV of Strongest Hit. Notably, the default behavior in CARLA is to not include transparent objects in the depth.

LiDAR Intensity Model. The first variant is a sensor modeling that is closer to the actual Velodyne sensor, which uses two optical centers for detecting returning laser rays. The upper one has a narrower FOV and the lower one a wider FOV, resulting in more points sampled in the farther regions of a LiDAR scan, cf. Figure 6. This is simply configured as two separate sensors in CARLA, whose output is merged to a single point cloud.

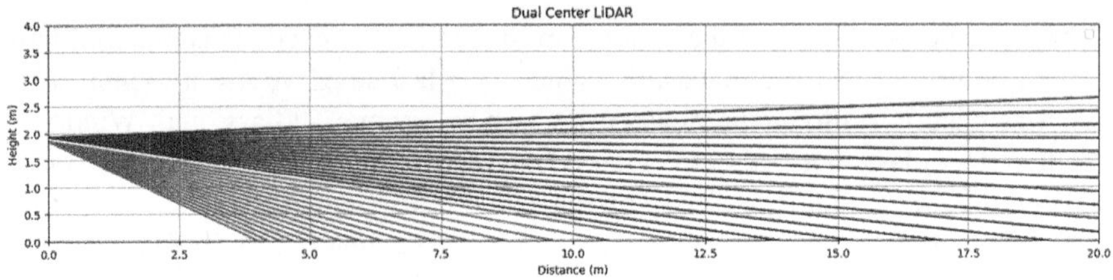

Fig. 6. Dual sensor model: the Velodyne sensor internally consists of two separate entities with different optical center and FOV (picture only shows 32 lines instead of 64 for better illustration.

In addition to the two hit points, the modified LiDAR also returns the surface normal in each hit point. This allows us to model the intensity of the synthetic points a posteriori, as it depends on the incident angle and the surface properties. The latter is modeled by combining a statistical surface model and the projection of the camera image onto the point cloud. To be precise, we use the grayscale value G for the base brightness B for each point with image coordinates x and y and randomize the contribution with two factors $r1 \in [0.25, 0.5]$ and $r2 \in [0.2, 0.3]$:

$$B(x, y) = r1 \times G(x, y) + r2 \tag{1}$$

The LiDAR sensor simultaneously is the camera and the light source and in contrast to a model like Phong [22] that uses a separate specular reflection, we combine diffuse and specular components by randomizing the intensity falloff at the angle between the Normal $\boldsymbol{N}$ and the light source $\boldsymbol{L}$ via the parameter $n \in [0, 8]$. Intensity is then defined as:

$$I = B \times (\boldsymbol{N} \cdot \boldsymbol{L})^n \tag{2}$$

Overall, this model results in lower intensity values for highly reflective materials, but this is equalized by the randomization of the base color. As statistically there are more vehicles with lower intensity values, there is no reason for specific further normalization. To increase the realism of this model, we introduce several approximations inspired by real-world data. We add per-vehicle brightness and reflectivity, global distance falloff and try to model the noise attributes of the Velodyne sensor. Finally, we extract potential retro-reflective surfaces via brightness peaks in the projected camera images and map these toward higher intensity values.

Like this, the model always produces positive intensity values. To simulate raydrop, where the sensor does not receive a return signal from a light ray, we subtract a small epsilon, so that some values close to 0 become negative. This results in some points with intensity values of 0, which is also true for real point clouds in the KITTI dataset. Only when the intensity values become negative, raydrop removes the respective points.

Finally, we empirically determine randomization values that mimic the intensity behavior of the Velodyne sensor and reach an average intensity of about 0.3, resulting in results comparable to KITTI, see Fig. 7

(a) CARLA intensity

(b) KITTI intensity

Fig. 7. Comparing synthetic and real intensity.

Overall, this allows us to generate more realistic point clouds, we define four settings:

- **Dual Velodyne.** Aside from the sensor configuration with two optical centers and FOVs (cf. Fig 6, there is no further modification. It is the base for the following variants.
- **Noise.** Adds Gaussian noise with $\mu = 0$ and $\sigma = 0.1$
- **Intensity.** Here, the intensity values predicted by our heuristic model are directly used as input for the object detector. All other variants use 0 for compatibility as proposed by OpenPCDet [28].
- **Raydrop.** This variant is also based on the modeled intensity, but simply filters out points with intensity lower than 0 without forwarding this information to the neural network.

(a) First Hit **(b)** Second Hit **(c)** Depth **(d)** Dual Sensor

(e) Gaussian Noise **(f)** Intensity **(g)** Raydrop **(h)** KITTI

Fig. 8. Point clouds resulting from different sensor configurations. Bottom right is a reference picture from a real KITTI point cloud. The other pictures show the same frame from the synthetic CARLA dataset.

4 Object Detection Training and Evaluation

With the defined methods and LiDAR variants, we move on to generating the actual dataset and performing the evaluation. We will first test on synthetic, then on real data, and finally examine the effects of pre-training on the simulated data and fine-tuning with samples from the KITTI train set.

4.1 Data Collection

To generate the synthetic dataset for object detection, we configure our simulation to spawn the ego-vehicle randomly at one of the map's predefined spawn points and collect up to 100 frames before reloading, recording only every 100th frame to further decrease redundancy in the dataset.

A single simulation run is real-time-capable depending on hardware, the number of actors, parallel sensors and data written. This results in between 10 and 120 FPS, which fits well for typical sensors that produce data at 10 Hz. While there is potential for replacing the CARLA ray cast with a faster implementation, our focus is offline data generation. We roughly obtain 1000 frames per hour, taking into account waiting periods, where the car is stationary or no other actors in perception range, and loading times between map change or simulation restart. This is a reasonable time for data generation, but can be reduced substantially when only using the necessary sensors and driving longer sequences without reloading. Similar to KITTI, we generate 15k frames and use roughly half of them for training and the rest for validation.

For evaluation, we use the eight variants described in Sects. 3.4 and 3.4. *Strongest** and *Strongest* have identical point clouds, but the former uses the original, bigger 3D bounding boxes, while all others have differences in point cloud structure (cf. Figure 8).

We use the metrics of the official KITTI benchmark. The quality of detections is measured with average precision using the PASCAL criteria with 40 recall positions and a 70 percent overlap for the 3D bounding boxes. Depending on the occlusion and truncation level and the size of the object in the camera images, the labels are categorized as *Easy*, *Moderate* or *Hard* or are excluded completely (look back to Fig. 5 for the distribution of these).

Aside from the 3D boxes, other benchmarks also include the Bird's Eye View (BEV), 2D Bounding Box or Average Orientation Similarity (AOS). We do so as well, as it allows for insights regarding the size accuracy of the predictions, but mainly focus on the 3D results otherwise. If not stated otherwise, the object detector is Voxel-R-CNN.

4.2 Object Detection on Synthetic Data

First, we evaluate on the CARLA validation set, see Tab. 1. We notice that the original big labels perform better. This is expected as these are consistent, meaning that there is no size variance that depends on the visibility of the object. In turn, this should have worse results when evaluating on real data, which we will look at in the next experiments. Among the variants with shrunk bounding boxes, the one that uses the simulated intensity values shows the best precision, especially for samples in the Hard category.

Here, it confirms that it can provide important cues to identify vehicles correctly. Also, the dual sensor variant helps for these cases as it samples more points in the distance.

Table 1. Training on CARLA train set and testing on CARLA validation set.

	3D			BEV			2D			AOS		
	Easy	Mod.	Hard	Easy	Mod.	Hard	Easy	Mod.	Hard	Easy	Mod.	Hard
Strongest*	97.25	93.18	86.77	97.31	94.4	89.33	97.21	94.29	89.23	92.31	89.34	84.3
Strongest	94.87	89.53	85.3	94.89	89.63	86.98	94.8	88.24	84.19	89.31	83.27	79.25
First Hit	94.76	86.89	81.58	94.86	89.47	81.94	94.81	86.86	81.62	89.69	82.11	76.92
Depth	94.8	89.35	84.1	94.83	89.49	86.73	94.78	89.25	84.07	89.4	84.2	79.14
Dual	94.72	89.61	87.04	94.78	89.64	89.5	94.64	89.43	86.75	89.69	84.62	81.87
Noise	94.84	89.48	86.96	94.88	90.02	89.46	94.82	89.3	86.65	89.3	84.28	81.58
Intensity	**94.91**	**89.88**	**87.82**	94.96	90.41	89.89	94.84	89.62	87.06	89.41	84.5	81.83
Raydrop	94.75	89.44	86.91	94.83	90.96	88.91	94.25	88.81	86.18	89.06	83.88	81.17

Next is using real data for training and evaluating on the simulated data (results in Table. 2). We immediately see the precision deterioration when using the bigger bounding boxes as ground truth. The impact on the less size sensitive metrics like AOS is considerably smaller, which means that the detections are still reasonable.

For the variants with the smaller bounding boxes, this is less severe but still prevalent. It is difficult to exactly estimate the extent of the different aspects of the remaining domain shift. As we only have tackled the labeling bias and not the actual size differences between the real and synthetic dataset, there might be further potential to improve the results.

Comparing the different variants among each other, the dual sensor modeling and the simulated intensity now show clear benefits. This confirms that the window holes are a strong indicator for detecting vehicles. Especially for the moderate and hard category, the real-data-trained model has problems to detect vehicles from the depth sampled point clouds. Here, the resolution distribution of the depth map causes more sparsity in the relevant regions, even though the overall number of points is comparable.

Table 2. Training on KITTI and validation on CARLA.

	3D			BEV			2D			AOS		
	Easy	Mod	Hard	Easy	Mod	Hard	Easy	Mod	Hard	Easy	Mod	Hard
Strongest*	57.44	43.92	38.15	88.41	76.33	67.23	93.68	84.34	78.50	87.83	77.35	71.34
Strongest	87.05	68.34	63.04	95.59	88.97	83.53	95.67	86.38	81.31	89.65	79.17	73.96
First Hit	85.81	62.67	55.65	94.12	82.85	73.58	94.46	80.56	73.1	88.45	74.07	66.84
Depth	90.17	65.18	58.07	95.06	86.01	78.49	95.72	80.8	75.33	89.35	73.66	68.02
Dual	89.95	**76.06**	69.31	95.54	89.91	84.75	96.14	89.97	86.84	89.91	82.49	78.80
Noise	89.59	74.21	68.94	95.52	89.83	84.73	96.3	89.94	86.66	90.15	82.55	78.80
Intensity	**91.17**	75.36	**70.19**	96.42	90.86	85.89	96.92	88.51	83.53	90.86	81.36	76.25
Raydrop	89.5	74.04	68.61	95.21	89.6	84.44	96.01	89.78	86.43	89.5	82.12	78.2

4.3 Object Detection on Real Data

The second part of the evaluation is performed on the KITTI evaluation set. We move to the main application of our approach: the transfer from synthetically trained systems to real scenarios. In some areas, we see similar results: problems with the bigger bounding boxes in the synthetic data and advantages for the dual sensor modeling. However, there are also distinct differences. First, training on the depth sampled point clouds works quite well. The reason for this is that the neural network still learns to detect vehicles with fewer points from the depth data. There are only problems, when the training data is denser than the testing data. Second, the simulated intensity values degrade the performance on real point clouds, even though it showed the most benefits before. This implies that the neural network learns some pattern from the simulated intensity that does not translate to real data.

Table 3. Training on synthetic datasets and testing on KITTI evaluation set. Comparison with training on real train set (bottom row) and related work.

	3D			BEV			2D			AOS		
	Easy	Mod	Hard	Easy	Mod	Hard	Easy	Mod	Hard	Easy	Mod	Hard
DepthSim	63.78	50.5	48.70	75.32	62.43	62.07	79.24	66.59	66.84	78.58	65.05	65.05
IntensitySim	63.22	51.74	50.27	80.33	70.77	69.74	83.83	72.78	71.95	82.10	70.54	69.42
CADET	35.85	29.4	24.99	57.32	49.63	43.25	-	-	-	-	-	-
Strongest*	44.77	37.27	34.02	75.51	65.21	61.48	90.28	80.8	78.55	90.15	80.4	78.06
Strongest	74.5	62.77	59.89	86.16	77.36	77.07	90.05	80.72	79.36	89.98	80.41	78.97
First Hit	65.21	53.95	52.29	82.34	71.47	71.64	86.24	74.95	75.09	86.04	74.51	74.53
Depth	76.0	61.77	59.66	87.06	77.59	77.5	90.11	78.72	78.57	90.06	78.5	78.26
Dual	**76.89**	**64.29**	**61.52**	86.13	77.63	77.32	90.12	81.24	80.04	90.07	80.98	79.7
Noise	75.79	64.22	60.49	85.2	77.78	77.42	89.78	81.11	79.02	89.74	80.8	78.65
Intensity	66.5	55.53	53.8	81.68	73.48	72.06	88.99	78.91	78.14	88.87	78.37	77.5
Raydrop	74.34	62.77	60.79	84.14	77.47	77.14	88.91	81.02	79.86	88.88	80.81	79.57
KITTI	91.94	82.9	80.45	95.36	91.19	88.94	98.46	94.65	92.34	98.43	94.52	92.14

Looking at related work, one interesting approach we can use for comparison is IntensitySim [18], where training is performed on point clouds sampled from VKITTI2. We call their base variant *DepthSim* in Tab. 3. Since VKITTI and the 3D object labels are very close to the original KITTI dataset, it shows satisfactory detection precision without special processing. IntensitySim also adds raydrop but does not use the intensity values for training, which slightly improves results. We observe even stronger generalization for our variant without vehicle windows, but adding intensity based raydrop on top of that shows no further improvement. Overall, our CARLA based variants significantly outperform IntensitySim, validating that sensor modeling and randomization are important for generalization.

The second competitor is CADET [3], where we can draw similar conclusions. It is based on CARLA but adds no further modifications during data generation. Our most comparable setting is the one with the original bounding boxes, which lacks behind in precision for evaluation on the real dataset. But, considering that with AVOD it uses an older architecture, and the LiDAR simulation in CADET does not implement transparency effects, the results are quite close. It is not clear how much AVOD would gain from the window modeling, as in contrast to Voxel-R-CNN it also uses camera images as direct input. Nonetheless, this suggests, that the sensor modeling itself has a stronger impact than the randomization strategies (Table. 5) .

Table 4. Few Shot Setting: Fine-tuning with 30 Epochs and about 400 frames from KITTI train set, testing on KITTI evaluation set.

	3D			BEV			2D			AOS		
Strongest*	91.51	81.52	79.0	94.69	88.43	87.77	97.99	92.06	91.51	97.91	91.8	91.07
Strongest	91.98	81.39	78.76	95.43	88.47	87.14	98.63	92.38	91.1	98.55	92.05	90.65
First Hit	91.41	80.11	78.0	94.94	88.11	86.21	98.23	91.7	90.45	98.13	91.38	90.0
Depth	91.56	80.45	78.08	94.87	88.56	87.09	97.46	91.96	90.51	97.4	91.68	90.12
Dual	**91.96**	**81.64**	**79.32**	95.57	88.74	87.96	98.65	91.96	91.53	98.57	91.65	91.09
Noise	91.47	80.15	78.51	94.99	88.39	87.47	98.24	92.08	91.2	98.19	91.8	90.79
Intensity	90.95	80.09	78.63	94.8	88.4	87.87	97.48	92.25	91.46	97.41	91.96	91.04
Raydrop	91.53	80.51	78.4	93.81	88.0	87.13	97.86	91.67	91.24	97.79	91.37	78.20
KITTI	91.94	82.9	80.45	95.36	91.19	88.94	98.46	94.65	92.34	98.43	94.52	92.14

Table 5. Fine-tuning with 30 Epochs on full KITTI train set, testing on KITTI evaluation set.

	3D			BEV			2D			AOS		
	Easy	Mod	Hard	Easy	Mod	Hard	Easy	Mod	Hard	Easy	Mod	Hard
Strongest*	92.66	83.32	81.91	95.61	90.98	89.19	98.65	94.54	93.04	98.62	94.39	92.82
Strongest	91.98	82.61	80.89	95.55	90.73	88.62	98.70	94.28	92.06	98.67	94.09	91.80
First Hit	92.22	82.65	81.19	95.56	90.35	88.66	98.55	93.87	92.09	98.52	93.73	91.89
Depth	92.25	82.82	81.04	95.67	90.63	88.63	98.79	94.15	92.38	98.76	93.97	92.14
Dual	**92.56**	82.84	81.25	95.47	90.46	88.60	98.46	93.98	92.05	98.43	93.82	91.81
Noise	92.30	82.82	81.29	95.74	90.06	88.65	98.76	94.00	92.12	98.73	93.86	91.90
Intensity	91.92	82.58	81.09	95.06	90.65	88.52	98.38	94.39	92.80	98.34	94.22	92.57
Raydrop	92.17	**83.15**	**81.73**	95.59	90.94	88.70	98.67	94.48	92.54	98.63	94.32	92.29
KITTI	91.94	82.9	80.45	95.36	91.19	88.94	98.46	94.65	92.34	98.43	94.52	92.14

Another approach is combining real and synthetic data for training. Adding fine-tuning with only 400 frames of real data, see Tab. 4, can quickly almost close the domain gap. While the overall ranking between our sensor variants mostly remains the same, they do converge to a degree where there is very little difference and even the bigger bounding boxes make no difference anymore.

Finally, using the synthetic data more in a pretraining setting and training with the full KITTI set afterwards can increase the detection precision beyond the real-data baseline. While there is only a small advantage, it is especially noteworthy that the underperforming raydrop variant and the big bounding boxes yield the best results. This indicates that the more consistent bounding boxes offer a better initialization, and further variance in the vehicle point clouds leads to improved robustness.

4.4 Limitations

Although they are not effective for every tested setting, all sensor variants except the minor point jittering showed contributions to the generalization capabilities between real and synthetic data. This is expected for Voxel-R-CNN, as the simulated measurement error in real LiDAR data is mostly ignored through the voxelization. Other networks might very well behave differently for our modeled sensor effects.

Further limitations for determining the strength of the impact on the detection performance arise for the randomization approach. Especially for the environment, it is not trivial to have two comparable datasets with different degrees of randomization because there is non-deterministic behavior in the simulation.

Another concern is the 3D object detection benchmarking itself. The score strongly depends on the difficulty categories and filtered object labels as well as the size of the bounding boxes. This makes it difficult to have a single synthetic dataset that generalizes well to arbitrary real-world data and could impede the effectiveness of randomization beyond the distribution of the target data.

Still, analyzing KITTI, our synthetic data proved to be effective for use on real data.

5 Conclusion

In summary, we have narrowed the gap between synthetic and real-world datasets. In particular, for direct synthetic to real evaluation and vice versa, our data modeling shows a significant improvement compared to previous work, enabling effective synthetic pretraining for the KITTI dataset. Finally, our modular approach can serve for future experiments and is suited for adaption to arbitrary real-world data configurations.

Acknowledgements. Richard Marcus was supported by the Bayerische Forschungsstiftung (Bavarian Research Foundation) AZ-1423-20. The authors gratefully acknowledge the scientific support and HPC resources provided by the Erlangen National High Performance Computing Center (NHR@FAU) of the Friedrich-Alexander-Universität Erlangen-Nürnberg (FAU) under the NHR project b204dc. NHR funding is provided by federal and Bavarian state authorities. NHR@FAU hardware is partially funded by the German Research Foundation (DFG) âĂŞ 440719683.

References

1. autonomousvision: KITTI-360 annotation tool. https://github.com/autonomousvision/kitti360LabelTool
2. Bavirisetti, D.P., Brobak, E., Espen, P., Kiss, G., Lindseth, F.: Simulated RGB and LiDAR image based training of object detection models in the context of autonomous driving (1). https://www.ntnu.no/ojs/index.php/nikt/article/view/5665
3. Brekke, Å., Vatsendvik, F., Lindseth, F.: Multimodal 3D object detection from simulated pretraining. https://doi.org/10.48550/arXiv.1905.07754. http://arxiv.org/abs/1905.07754
4. Cabon, Y., Murray, N., Humenberger, M.: Virtual KITTI 2. https://doi.org/10.48550/arXiv.2001.10773. http://arxiv.org/abs/2001.10773
5. Caesar, H., et al.: nuScenes: A multimodal dataset for autonomous driving. https://doi.org/10.48550/arXiv.1903.11027. http://arxiv.org/abs/1903.11027
6. Deng, J., Shi, S., Li, P., Zhou, W., Zhang, Y., Li, H.: Voxel r-CNN: Towards high performance voxel-based 3d object detection. https://doi.org/10.48550/arXiv.2012.15712. http://arxiv.org/abs/2012.15712
7. Deschaud, J.E., Duque, D., Richa, J.P., Velasco-Forero, S., Marcotegui, B., Goulette, F.: Paris-CARLA-3D: a real and synthetic outdoor point cloud dataset for challenging tasks in 3D mapping **13**(22), p. 4713. https://doi.org/10.3390/rs13224713. https://www.mdpi.com/2072-4292/13/22/4713, number: 22 Publisher: Multidisciplinary Digital Publishing Institute
8. Dosovitskiy, A., Ros, G., Codevilla, F., Lopez, A., Koltun, V.: CARLA: An open urban driving simulato. https://doi.org/10.48550/arXiv.1711.03938. http://arxiv.org/abs/1711.03938
9. dotchen: CARLA issue regarding stability. https://github.com/carla-simulator/carla/issues/2789
10. Dworak, D., Ciepiela, F., Derbisz, J., Izzat, I., Komorkiewicz, M., Wójcik, M.: Performance of LiDAR object detection deep learning architectures based on artificially generated point cloud data from CARLA simulator, pp. 600–60. https://doi.org/10.1109/MMAR.2019.8864642. https://ieeexplore.ieee.org/document/8864642
11. Epic Games: unreal engine. https://www.unrealengine.com
12. Gaidon, A., Wang, Q., Cabon, Y., Vig, E.: Virtual worlds as proxy for multi-object tracking analysis. https://doi.org/10.48550/arXiv.1605.06457. http://arxiv.org/abs/1605.06457
13. Geiger, A., Lenz, P., Urtasun, R.: Are we ready for autonomous driving? The KITTI vision benchmark suite. In: 2012 IEEE Conference on Computer Vision and Pattern Recognition, pp. 3354–336https://doi.org/10.1109/CVPR.2012.6248074. ISSN: 1063–6919
14. Huch, S., Scalerandi, L., Rivera, E., Lienkamp, M.: Quantifying the LiDAR sim-to-real domain shift: a detailed investigation using object detectors and analyzing point clouds at target-leve.https://doi.org/10.48550/arXiv.2303.01899. http://arxiv.org/abs/2303.01899
15. Iglesias, A., García, M., Aranjuelo, N., Arganda-Carreras, I., Nieto, M.: Analysis of point cloud domain gap effects for 3D object detection evaluation, pp. 278–285. SCITEPRESS - Science and Technology Publication. https://doi.org/10.5220/0012357200003660. https://www.scitepress.org/DigitalLibrary/Link.aspx?doi=10.5220/0012357200003660
16. Ku, J., Mozifian, M., Lee, J., Harakeh, A., Waslander, S.: Joint 3D proposal generation and object detection from view aggregation. https://doi.org/10.48550/arXiv.1712.02294. http://arxiv.org/abs/1712.02294
17. Mao, J., et al.: One million scenes for autonomous driving: ONCE database. https://doi.org/10.48550/arXiv.2106.11037. http://arxiv.org/abs/2106.11037
18. Marcus, R., Gabel, F., Knoop, N., Stamminger, M.: GAN-based LiDAR intensity simulation. vol. 1875, pp. 419–43. https://doi.org/10.1007/978-3-031-39059-3_28. http://arxiv.org/abs/2311.15415
19. Nozarian, F.: fnozarian/CARLA-KITTI. https://github.com/fnozarian/CARLA-KITTI

20. NVIDIA: DRIVE sim. https://developer.nvidia.com/drive/simulation
21. Patel, M., Jung, R.: Simulation-based performance evaluation of 3D object detection methods with deep learning for a LiDAR point cloud dataset in a SOTIF-related use case, pp. 415–426. SCITEPRESS - Science and Technology Publicatio. https://doi.org/10.5220/0012707300003702. https://www.scitepress.org/DigitalLibrary/Link.aspx?doi=10.5220/0012707300003702
22. Phong, B.T.: Illumination for computer generated pictures **18**(6), 311–31. https://doi.org/10.1145/360825.360839. https://dl.acm.org/doi/10.1145/360825.360839
23. Promitzer, P.: CARLA GitHub bounding box workaround. https://github.com/carla-simulator/carla/issues/7007
24. Sanchez, J., Soum-Fontez, L., Deschaud, J.E., Goulette, F.: ParisLuco 3D: a high-quality target dataset for domain generalization of LiDAR perception. https://doi.org/10.48550/arXiv.2310.16542. http://arxiv.org/abs/2310.16542
25. Sekkat, A.R., Mohan, R., Sawade, O., Matthes, E., Valada, A.: AmodalSynthDrive: a synthetic amodal perception dataset for autonomous driving. https://doi.org/10.48550/arXiv.2309.06547. http://arxiv.org/abs/2309.06547
26. Shah, S., Dey, D., Lovett, C., Kapoor, A.: AirSim: High-fidelity visual and physical simulation for autonomous vehicle. https://doi.org/10.48550/arXiv.1705.05065. http://arxiv.org/abs/1705.05065
27. Sun, P., et al.: Scalability in perception for autonomous driving: waymo open dataset, pp. 2446–2454. https://openaccess.thecvf.com/content_CVPR_2020/html/Sun_Scalability_in_Perception_for_Autonomous_Driving_Waymo_Open_Dataset_CVPR_2020_paper.html
28. Team, O.D.: OpenPCDet: An open-source toolbox for 3D object detection from point clouds. https://github.com/open-mmlab/OpenPCDet
29. Tobin, J., Fong, R., Ray, A., Schneider, J., Zaremba, W., Abbeel, P.: Domain randomization for transferring deep neural networks from simulation to the real world. http://arxiv.org/abs/1703.06907
30. Triess, L.T., Rist, C.B., Peter, D., Zöllner, J.M.: A realism metric for generated LiDAR point cloud. https://doi.org/10.48550/arXiv.2208.14958. http://arxiv.org/abs/2208.14958
31. Velodyne: Velodyne HDL-64e data sheet. https://hypertech.co.il/wp-content/uploads/2015/12/HDL-64E-Data-Sheet.pdf
32. Wang, Y., et al.: Train in Germany, test in the USA: Making 3D object detectors generalize. https://doi.org/10.48550/arXiv.2005.08139. http://arxiv.org/abs/2005.08139
33. Wilson, B., et al.: Argoverse 2: Next generation datasets for self-driving perception and forecasting. https://doi.org/10.48550/arXiv.2301.00493. http://arxiv.org/abs/2301.00493
34. Yan, Y., Mao, Y., Li, B.: SECOND: Sparsely embedded convolutional detection **18**(10), 333. https://doi.org/10.3390/s18103337. https://www.mdpi.com/1424-8220/18/10/3337, number: 10 Publisher: Multidisciplinary Digital Publishing Institute
35. Yang, J., Shi, S., Wang, Z., Li, H., Qi, X.: ST3d++: Denoised self-training for unsupervised domain adaptation on 3d object detection.https://doi.org/10.48550/arXiv.2108.06682. http://arxiv.org/abs/2108.06682
36. Zhang, B., Yuan, J., Shi, B., Chen, T., Li, Y., Qiao, Y.: Uni 3D: a unified baseline for multi-dataset 3D object detection. https://doi.org/10.48550/arXiv.2303.06880. http://arxiv.org/abs/2303.06880

NAUTICAL: Navigation Aid Using U-Net and *Theta** with Integrated Collision Avoidance and Landmarking

Yashwardhan Deshmukh, Martin J.-D. Otis(✉), and Salick Diagne

LAR.i Laboratory, Applied Sciences Department, Université du Québec à Chicoutimi, Saguenay, QC G7H 2B1, Canada
martin_otis@uqac.ca
https://lari.uqac.ca/

Abstract. Technologies related to decision support systems in intelligent vessels have reached a high level of maturity in recent years. Meanwhile, autonomous and unmanned vessels have been extensively studied in conjunction with autonomous vehicles using path planning, trajectory generation, location, and logistic optimization. Numerous technologies have been developed for the planning of path and obstacle avoidance strategies in the sea and rivers, but the challenge remains when it comes to avoiding marine mammals, especially under the constraint of optimal trajectory to reduce energy consumption and time. This paper proposes a planner based on both neural network-driven and deterministic approaches. An Attention U-Net is used for semantic segmentation of terrestrial and aquatic areas, followed by the implementation of an artificial potential field to represent the map. Skeletonization and weighted dilation are then carried out to generate an optimal cost map for *Theta** path planning. The proposed Navigation Aid System includes parameters related to the minimum distance from the shore, a maximization of cetacean distance under the constraint of minimizing the total distance traveled by the vessel. The pilot has the option to add waypoints and force the algorithm to reach these locations using a minimal traveled distance. The results show an optimal vessel path for the segmented map, given the constraints.

Keywords: Path planning · Semantic segmentation · Vessel navigation · Path optimization

1 Introduction

The protection of cetaceans coupled with economic development and the increased use of maritime transport routes cause legal problems and problems of social acceptability, which this research project aims to minimize. New industrial projects will use seaways, river or intracoastal waterways to transport their products. As a result, it is expected that a significant increase in shipping is expected to increase noise disturbance (period, duration, and amplitude) from ships, as well as the potential for collisions with cetaceans. Three major problems arise from this: (1) increased frequency and period of noise that

J. Röning and J. Filipe (Eds.): ROBOVIS 2025, CCIS 2629, pp. 433–453, 2026.
https://doi.org/10.1007/978-3-032-00986-9_28

affect Beluga socialization [16], in particular communication between mother and calf through contact calls; (2) reduced ability of females to locate food, resulting in a lack of energy to complete gestation or to raise calves; and (3) possible proximity (or overly risky collision) between ships and certain cetaceans, including right whales [42]. The research project presented in this article aims to solve this problem and make possible the operationalization of sustainable and intelligent logistics on maritime transportation routes. To demonstrate the possibility of combining an increase in maritime traffic with the recovery of beluga and cetacean populations in the Fjords, the research project aims to carry out a proof of concept, firstly, by proposing a simulator as a piloting aid system. The logistics chain instrumentation (through a digital corridor) will allow the location of cetaceans and the availability of their positions through a real-time display on a maritime map dedicated to pilots and ports as suggested in [43]. An optimal trajectory to follow, taking into account a set of constraints (energy, shore distance, cetacean distance, etc.), will be proposed by this new type of navigation decision support system. Therefore, the contribution of this paper is a system that enables optimization of the traveled distance under the constraints of optimal distance under minimal travel, collision avoidance, and maximal distance of cetaceans. There is a cost when changing the heading direction with a rudder: this reduces the velocity of the vessel with the potential to reduce controllability under the constraints of underwater current and wind for inland navigation. Path-planning algorithms such as A*, D*, and Theta* have some issues with steering while maximizing a constraint such as the distance between the cetacean and the vessel while minimizing traveled distance. This paper compares different strategies to find a solution for inland navigation under the constraints of minimizing the traveled distance and maximizing the cetacean-vessel distance while limiting the variation of the heading (the ability to turn is limited). This application leads to an under-optimal traveled distance in order to improve the navigation constraints. Some technologies are compared inside according to performance and the advantages or disadvantages of each technology. This will make it possible to steer ships towards less risky areas to avoid too close proximity to cetaceans.

In order to explain the main contribution, the related works in Sect. 2 present three aspects to optimize path planning, including collision avoidance, travel, and energy minimization. Since the contribution is to reduce the impact of the vessel on inland navigation, a segmentation adapted to navigation is combined with an artificial potential field. The Methodology in Sect. 3 explains how this combination allows the definition of safety zones and then minimizes the path length according to $Theta^*$, Skeletonized $Theta^*$ and A^* algorithms (simple and safe repulsive). A comparison between these algorithms is set forth to select the appropriate one, not only for reducing the length of the path or the processing time but also to limit the variation in the heading angle. The results in Sect. 4 present different study cases with the presence of cetaceans and some waypoints selected by the pilot. Finally, a result demonstrates the impact of reducing velocity near the cetacean with and without proximity avoidance (cetacean-vessel maximum distance) while using the optimal path. These results are presented based on three study cases in the Saguenay-du-Fjord.

2 Related Works

Path planning and collision avoidance are crucial aspects of air and sea navigation. Both fields require sophisticated approaches to ensure safe and efficient travel. In this related works, this section explores path planning from aerial images in Sect. 2.1, collision avoidance for ships in Sect. 2.2, as well as distance minimization and energy optimization in Sect. 2.3. These three key areas play an important role in the development of advanced navigation systems and autonomous vehicles, and a thorough understanding of them is essential to foster ongoing innovation in these constantly evolving sectors.

2.1 Path Planning from Aerial Images

Path planning algorithms are used to determine the optimal trajectory for a robot, such as an Unmanned Aerial Vehicle (UAV) or Unmanned Surface Vessel (USV) while avoiding obstacles and respecting certain constraints linked to the needs of the users and their environment. Although the basic concepts of path planning are applicable to UAVs and USVs, the implementation details may differ due to the unique characteristics of each type of vehicle and its operational environment. In the never-ending quest to improve these path-planning technologies, research has explored various innovative approaches and their specific applications. In [4], the authors study the use of a hybrid algorithm for path planning in unmanned surface vehicles. This innovative approach combines global and local methods, implementing A^* for global planning, while the dynamic window algorithm [74] allows dynamic obstacles to be avoided, demonstrating effective adaptation in complex environments. Continuing this innovative line, Ji, Xianyou et al. [23] propose an optimization algorithm that merges the optimized A^* with the dynamic window approach. This fusion proves particularly beneficial, improving both global and local path planning for autonomous robots evolving on complex and bumpy roads. On the other hand, Erke, Shang et al. [10] present a significant advance with a new algorithm dedicated to path planning for autonomous ground vehicles. This algorithm introduces an evaluation standard, uses a human-generated directive, improves obstacle avoidance, and incorporates a variable-step A^* algorithm to reduce computation time. In contrast, [68] marks a major development with the introduction of Neural A^*, a data-driven search method. This novel approach uses a convolutional encoder to form a fully trainable neural planner, outperforming data-driven planners in terms of optimally and efficiency. Other notable advances include [32], where an autonomous navigation approach for UAVs combines map-based path planning with vision-based obstacle detection. The use of optical flow [19] for collision avoidance demonstrates the feasibility of this method for autonomous navigation. Moving towards multi-layer approaches, Lin, Huei-Yung et al. [6] proposes a path planning algorithm based on reinforcement learning for UAVs. This multi-layer Q-learning approach collects global and local information, planning a collision-free path, while using the B-spline curve to smooth the path. Conversely, in [64], a major challenge is addressed with an algorithm aimed at solving the difficult convergence of reinforcement learning algorithms in three-dimensional path planning. For electric UAV path planning, [2] proposes an algorithm based on the improved optimization of the A^* ant colony. This algorithm considers the accuracy of UAV control and aims to minimize energy consumption, showing a significant reduction compared to the manual patrol of a UAV on an aerial transmission line for image capture. Similarly, [75] presents a path-planning method for unmanned vehicles, combining satellite imagery with the Voronoi field algorithm. This approach improves the A^* evaluation by using an obstacle hazard function related to the boundary of the navigation area, thus reducing the number of redundant nodes in the planned path. In parallel, [12] addresses the autonomous optimal routes for mobile logistics applications using a heuristic algorithm. By converting various environments into binary grids, this algorithm optimizes paths in various contexts, offering path planning for autonomous vehicles based on methods such as particle swarm optimization (PSO) and the bat search algorithm. For scenarios involving multiple UAVs without GPS and communication, [66] presents a feature fusion algorithm. The feature fusion proximal policy optimization (FF-PPO) algorithm uses deep reinforcement learning (DRL) to fuse image information taken by the UAVs. This enables cooperative planning without communication but with an object detection algorithm using the image recognition box to determine whether the UAVs have reached the target. In [3], a path planning method for UAVs uses an opposition-based learning artificial bee colony algorithm. The opposition-based learning artificial bee colony (OABC) algorithm uses an information entropy model to evaluate the information obtained, reducing the number of images required while maintaining 3D reconstruction efficiency. Exploring specific areas, [34] presents a new improved back-and-forth (IBF) algorithm for full coverage path planning with UAVs. Using a modified rectilinear steering mode and auxiliary approaches, it outperforms other methods in complex environments with forbidden zones. These various approaches make a significant contribution to the ongoing evolution of autonomous path-planning technologies. Path planning for autonomous vehicles, whether in the air or on the ocean, is a dynamic area of research where a variety of approaches and algorithms are emerging to meet specific challenges. Traditional methods such as A^* and its variants like $Theta^*$ [52] or S-$Theta^*$ [35,36] and map-based path planning are complemented by innovative approaches, including those based on reinforcement learning, the use of vision data, and the fusion of heuristic methods and optimization algorithms. The contributions also explore the adaptations required for complex environments, such as taking account of dynamic obstacles and energy constraints.

2.2 Collision Avoidance for Vessel

In the field of collision avoidance for Unmanned Surface Vehicles (USVs), several innovative approaches exploit several algorithms and combinations of algorithms. The study in [46] proposes a path planning method for USVs based on the A^* algorithm. This method incorporates a safety distance adapted to dynamic obstacles and ocean currents, demonstrating its effectiveness in congested environments and in simulations in terms of path length and computation time. The authors in [31] introduce improvements to the A^* algorithm for global path planning in automatic ship navigation. These improvements include the establishment of a safety distance, path optimization, and the use of the minimum course alteration algorithm (MCA) to avoid collisions with ships or moving obstacles, in line with COLREGs. These adjustments are proving effective, particularly in complex simulations. Similarly, [14] presents an approach that considers the requirements of the Convention on Rules of the Road (COLREGs), optimizing collision avoidance using an improved dynamic window approach (IDWA) exploiting a deep neural network (Deep Q-network). These results show remarkable effectiveness in complying with maritime regulations and avoiding obstacles. In contrast, [69] subdivides the task into initial motion planning using A^* and B-spline, followed by re-planning with a nonlinear model predictive control (NMPC) that integrates static and COLREG-based obstacle avoidance functions. The proposed event-triggered motion planning and motion re-planning (EMPMR) scheme is compared with an existing scheme, demonstrating superior performance in terms of obstacle avoidance and computation. Other approaches suggest the use of other collision avoidance algorithms such as Dynamic Window or Velocity Obstacles (VO) to manage dynamic environments. Concerning the dynamic window approach, first in [26], the authors present the Collision Avoidance Dynamic Window Approach (CADWA), a dynamic collision avoidance control method for multi-agent systems during formation change. CADWA combines a set of neighbors to detect potential collisions with an objective function focused on collision risk reduction. The aim is to avoid local minima, thereby improving the effectiveness of collision avoidance. Simulation results show that this method allows two agents to complete the formation change without collision. Then, still using an improved version of DWA, paper [70] presents the Utility DWA (UDWA) algorithm for USV navigation. UDWA incorporates considerations for COLREGs and environmental conditions such as wind, optimizing the distance to obstructing vessels to improve the safety and efficiency of USV navigation in windy and rough conditions. Also, in a distributed context, paper [73] presents a distributed algorithm for collision avoidance of USVs with other normal and abnormal USVs, using the Dynamic Enhanced Window (DWA) approach. This algorithm integrates risk detection, responsibility division, and improved distance evaluation with predicted paths, and introduces a rule evaluation function according to international regulations (COLREGS), allowing safe actions in the presence of abnormal USVs. Finally, with a view to complying with international rules, the article [25] proposes a safety algorithm for USVs that complies with COLREGs. This algorithm uses predictions based on the Distance Closest Point of Approach (DCPA) and Time Closest Point of Approach (TCPA), integrating an improved dynamic window approach (CCDWA) to enable USVs to avoid opposing vessels while complying with COLREGs. In the same theme, other algorithms are also combined with the DWA approach. Specifically, in [13,63], DWA is combined with improved Ant Colony Optimisation (ACO), Particle Swarm Optimisation (PSO), and fuzzy control, respectively. In [63], the method incorporates improved heuristic information and a hazard index for dynamic obstacle avoidance in a dynamic environment, showing improved global path-finding capability and local obstacle avoidance. In [13], the method aims to improve the efficiency of finding optimal paths for obstacle avoidance. Here, experimental validation demonstrates that the PSO approach combined with DWA (PSO-CCDWA) reduces navigation time by significant percentages in different encounter scenarios compared to the classical DWA algorithm (CCDWA). Similarly, fuzzy control combined with DWA (FUZZY-CCDWA) reduces the distance traveled in different encounter scenarios. For methods based on Velocity Obstacles, the algorithm presented in [54] uses it to solve the collision avoidance problem for USVs in multiple encounters with an improved version, while integrating COLREGs. This system includes a collision detector and a path replanning algorithm, demonstrating its effectiveness in simulations to allow USVs to avoid multiple dynamic targets while complying with maritime regulations. The authors in [29] also use an improved version of the algorithm that incorporates a collision risk assessment and allows risk-based avoidance decision-making. In a similar approach, paper [40] proposes an autonomous obstacle avoidance algorithm for USVs in multi-vessel encounters. This model integrates a collision detector based on speed obstacles and a path re-planning algorithm using swarm search, enabling USVs to safely avoid several dynamic targets in accordance with maritime rules. Another important contribution is made by paper [55], which proposes a local path planning algorithm for USVs, avoiding static obstacles and moving vessels while respecting COLREGs. It also uses the improved dynamic window approach, incorporates environmental influence to improve collision avoidance, and combines the notion of speed obstacle with COLREGs, demonstrating its effectiveness in COLREG-compliant collision avoidance. To improve the agility and efficiency of the collision avoidance method, the authors in [51] use the collision shielded model predictive control (CS-MPC) algorithm, combining the velocity obstacle method and the predictive model method in complex environments with multiple obstacles. Similarly, a collision avoidance method based on the velocity obstacle is used by the authors in [71] with an improved multi-objective particle swarm optimization. This algorithm demonstrates an ability to avoid dynamic obstacles in accordance with maritime rules and a high adaptability to changing marine environments. Finally, the Proactive Velocity Obstacle (PVO) method presented in [57] is integrated with the Line of Sight (LOS) algorithm as part of Set Based Guidance (SBG). This approach aims to improve collision avoidance decision-making for USVs, ensuring compliance with international regulations (COLREGs) and collision-free navigation in multi-vessel scenarios. On the other hand, and more recently, other techniques integrating AI are used for collision avoidance of USVs, those are based on DRL (Deep Reinforcement Learning). For example, in [60] the authors develop a method based on DRL using visual recognition and a grid representation of the ship encounter situation. The specific neural network, after being trained and evaluated, demonstrates its effectiveness in collision avoidance simulations. At the same time, to simplify the control law, the authors in [27] introduce Smooth Convergence DRL (SCDRL) with an improved deep Q network. Similarly, in [11] an improved algorithm combining a deep Q neural network with integrated features is used to optimize the collision avoidance of USVs. Experiments in a Unity virtual environment confirm optimal performance in terms of collision avoidance. Deep learning can also be exploited using neural networks as in [30,62]. In [30] Convolutional Neural Networks (CNN) and Long- and Short-Term Memory Neural Networks (LSTM) are combined to extract influential features and historical correlations. In addition, a heuristic algorithm based on an improved electromagnetism mechanism is integrated for an optimal real-time strategy. In contrast, the authors in [62] propose a DRL using proximal policy optimization (PPO). This approach uses mathematical models for the USV, generates dynamic obstacles and defines a reward mechanism. High-dimensional state features are constructed, and a deep convolutional neural network (CNN) is designed to handle multi-factor and multi-scalar fusion. Simulations demonstrate efficient decision-making for fast and safe avoidance of dynamic obstacles. To improve specific points of these DRL techniques, other combinations are used. In [20], to reduce the complexity of the model and improve the safety of the obstacle avoidance route, the authors introduce a model-based predictive control (MPC) algorithm assisted by DRL. Simulations demonstrate successful and stable obstacle avoidance. To improve convergence in unstructured environments using a random walk, paper [24] proposes the Twin Delayed Deep Deterministic Policy Gradient (TD3) algorithm. Simulations illustrate efficient obstacle avoidance by the USV without the need for offline path generation. Moreover, in order to reduce redundant information, the method presented in [56] uses two Quaternion Ship Domain (QSD)-based navigation states: the goal-directed state and the collision avoidance state. Separate state spaces are designed for dynamic and static obstacles. The results show that the USV can reach the target point without collision, illustrating the effectiveness of the algorithm for autonomous collision avoidance decision-making. To generate flexible collision avoidance paths while complying with navigation rules, a method using a quantitative collision risk assessment based on the vessel domain and the nearest point of approach (CPA), coupled with a DRL is presented in [5]. Compared with the A^* algorithm, the method demonstrates a better ability to avoid collisions, especially in complex and unexpected scenarios. Furthermore, the study presented in [65] proposes an intelligent hybrid algorithm based on deep reinforcement learning for autonomous navigation and collision avoidance of unmanned surface vehicles (USVs). The model integrates a navigation and collision avoidance framework based on maritime practice, including modeling of ship-to-ship encounters, risk assessment, and consideration of static and dynamic obstacles. The algorithm, which improves on DDPG's sampling mechanics, is proving its effectiveness in collision avoidance simulations in complex environments.

2.3 Travelled Distance and Energy Minimization

In this section, we recall some algorithms designed to optimize both the distance covered by the USV and the energy consumed. These algorithms represent a revolutionary advance in autonomous navigation. These innovative approaches combine state-of-the-art techniques, integrating path planning and collision avoidance, with a particular focus on achieving the dual objectives of efficient path planning and minimizing energy consumption. These algorithms represent a significant advance in the quest for more sustainable and energy-efficient autonomous surface vehicle (ASV) operations. Among these algorithms are those based on the enhancement of A^* as presented in [31,44]. The authors in [31] propose an improvement in A^* that includes setting a safe distance and optimizing the path, as well as using the minimum course alteration algorithm (MCA) to avoid collisions according to COLREGs. Similarly, [44] describes a new maritime path planning algorithm that integrates the A^* algorithm with a collision avoidance algorithm evaluating the Collision Risk Index (CRI). This combination enables the ship to search for COLREG-compliant safe routes. Simulations show an economical and safe optimal route compared to traditional route planning. In this context, other works such as those presented in [1,28], and [67] propose the use of genetic algorithms to optimize the energy consumption of ships while complying with the rules of collision avoidance at sea. In particular, the non-dominated genetic sorting algorithm II (NSGA-II) used in [67] optimizes path planning, significantly reducing the cost of the search effort while maintaining a probability of success similar to conventional methods. In a different context, a double deep Q-learning network (D2QN) is used in [47] to minimize energy consumption and data loss. In [61], the velocity obstacle (VO) method with Modified Quantum Particle Swarm Optimization (MQPSO) is used. In [7], the authors propose a global path planning method that combines PPO (Proximal Policy Optimization Algorithms) and DWA algorithms. It uses two PPO reward modes for global planning and then optimizes the local path with the DWA algorithm based on the inflection point of the global optimal path. Finally, paper [76] proposes an improvement of the D^* Lite algorithm for route planning and avoidance of collisions of unmanned surface vehicles (USV) in unknown environments. By expanding the adjacent search area and setting a safe distance, the algorithm solves the problem of limited maneuverability of USVs. The approach optimizes the path by comparing the estimated distance with the actual distance between waypoints, using a minimum binary heap to significantly reduce search time. Simulations show a significant reduction in planning time and tests on a real USV demonstrate its ability to plan optimized paths while avoiding obstacles in complex environments.

To demonstrate the originality of the approach suggested in this study, Table 1 provides a comparison with the work presented above, particularly those that involve navigation on inland waterways with obstacle avoidance.

3 Methodology

From satellite images, Sect. 3.1 explains the parametric augmentation pipeline used to improve the dataset. Then, the implementation of the dataset preprocessing step is presented. In Sect. 3.2, the training process of a semantic segmentation model is presented to segment terrain types. The segmented images are converted to an artificial potential field as described in Sect. 3.3. Finally, image processing techniques are applied, and then in Sect. 3.4 the implementation of deterministic path-planning algorithms is designed and compared to a neural network path-planning algorithm.

3.1 Satellite Imagery Dataset Creation

First, a manual acquisition of about 60 unlabeled aerial satellite images with varying dimensions was selected, each covering a land area ranging from 500 meters to 5 kilometers, sourced from Google Earth. To create corresponding ground-truth masks, a manual segmentation is executed for each pixel into three labels: water, land, and obstacle.

The dataset then undergoes a parametric augmentation pipeline consisting of random cropping, horizontal and vertical flipping, rotation, brightness, and contrast, and one of Contrast Limited Adaptive Histogram Equalization (CLAHE) [77], Grid Distortion, or Optical Distortion, forming a final dataset of 855 satellite images and their ground truth masks, available on Borealis, an Open Data server (Canadian Dataverse Repository) [38]. The source code is available on OSF [9].

Table 1. Suggested approach compared to recent studies.

Reference	Algorithm	Result	Limits	In-land waterway	COLREG
Sugges-ted ap-proach	APF, U-Net, Skelet-onized-Θ^*	Better optimization of the distance traveled and reduction of proximity to obstacles (islands and coasts) with Skeletonized-Theta*, safer trajectories with added constraints, reduced noise level to 120 dB with reduced speed, improved flexibility and efficiency of trajectory planning with the addition of waypoints.	Could integrate Bathymetric Chart and drone images, should integrate more than one vessel and make an analysis of CO_2 emission and energy consumption.	X	
[69]	A^*	Safer and more time-efficient in real-time than the conventional A* approach, adding a safety distance reduces computation time with an optimal path.	Simulations based on binary maps and satellite images, modeling obstacles as ellipses and using Kalman filters, ocean currents simplified as constant vectors.	X	
[26]	A^*, MCA	Effective autonomous navigation without collisions with coasts, reefs, and other ships, under external disturbances.	Dynamic obstacles limited to other boats only, non-complex environment.	X	X
[73]	A^* CADWA DQN	Effective obstacle avoidance with multiple ships, speed.	Lack of comparative analysis, empirical validation, and discussion on computational complexity and scalability.	X	X

3.2 Semantic Segmentation

Manually obtained image data can have inconsistencies between dimensions across samples and must be preprocessed accordingly to perform segmentation. As a solution, the images and their masks were cropped to the closest size divisible by 256 and then divided all of them into patches of $256 \times 256 \times 3$. The dataset is partitioned by dedicating 30% exclusively to testing and the remaining is used to train 9 segmentation models as shown in Fig. 1, varying in backbone architectures and objective functions. Five backbone architectures are implemented, including VGG-16 [45], ResNet101 [17], DenseNet121, DenseNet169, and DenseNet201 [21]. As a general choice for classification problems, categorical cross-entropy is initially used as an objective function described in (1). To overcome the imbalance between the pixel size of water and land in certain samples of the dataset, a robust custom objective function is implemented consisting of a combination of Dice loss [48] and Focal loss [33] as described in (2). Interestingly, models trained with the custom objective function not only produced more visually accurate segmentation maps, but also experimentally outperformed models

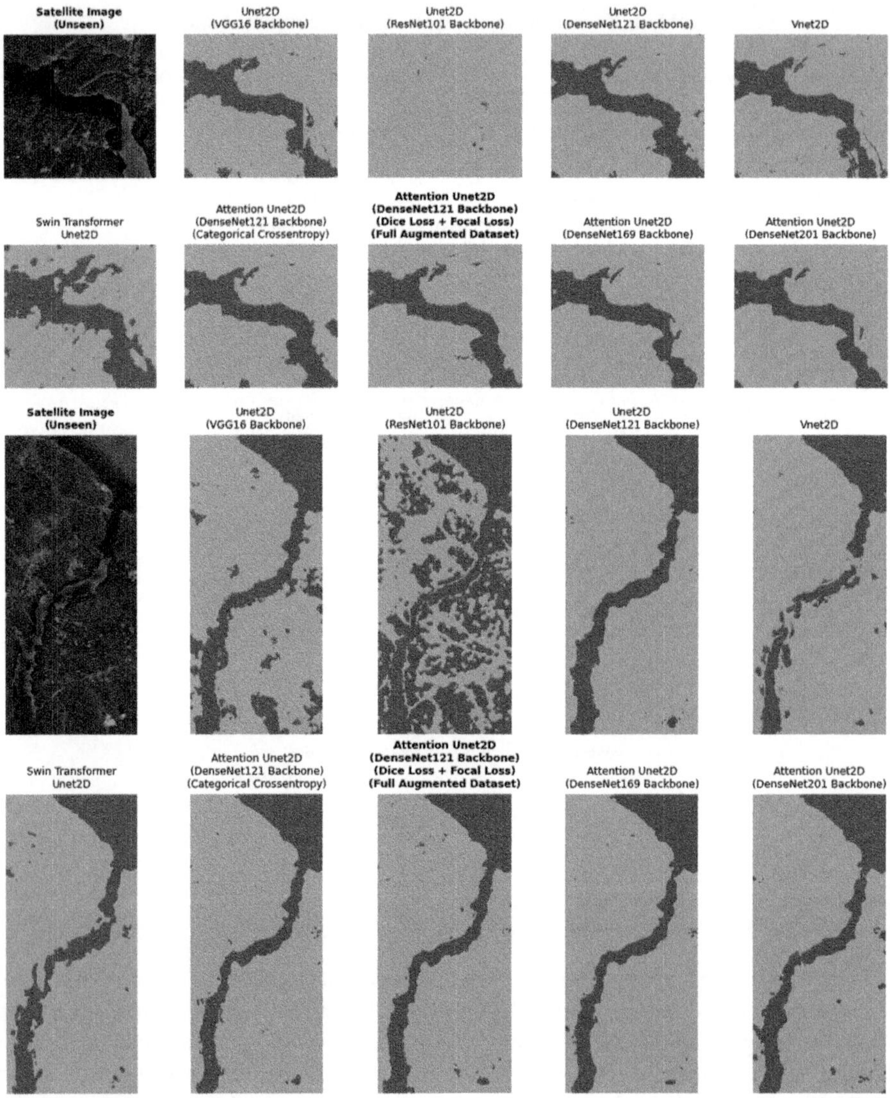

Fig. 1. The semantic segmentation process using nine models applied over two Google Earth satellite images.

with categorical cross entropy as their objective function.

$$L = 1 - (1 + \beta^2) \frac{precision \cdot recall}{\beta^2 \cdot precision + recall} \tag{1}$$

$$L(gt, pr) = -gt \cdot \alpha \cdot (1 - pr)^\gamma \cdot \log(pr) \tag{2}$$

After making predictions on the subdivided image patches, manually stitching them back can cause edge artifacts. This is because the receptive field of the neural network has less information at the edges compared to the center of the patches, causing discontinuities between patches. The open source library [53] uses a 2D windowing function that gradually fades from the center to the edges of the patches, avoiding the edge artifacts without changing the original dimension of the image, and the result is more accurate, as shown in Fig. 2.

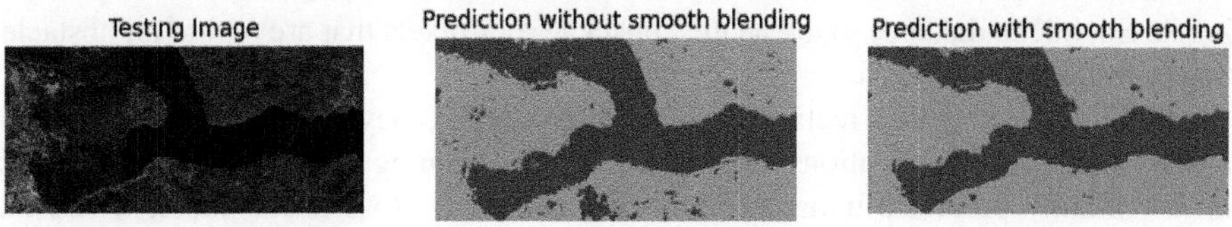

Fig. 2. The impact of the smooth blending algorithm application for the segmentation over one Google Earth satellite image.

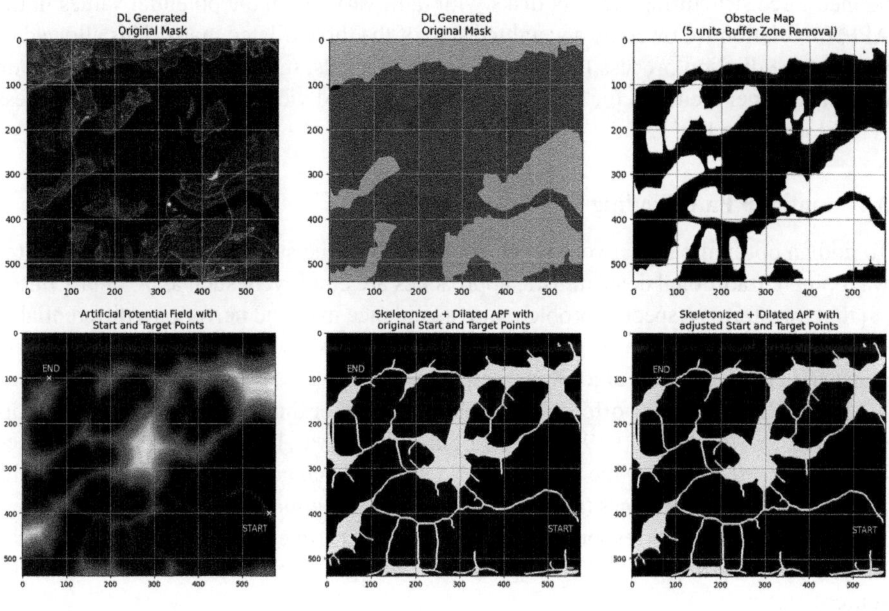

Fig. 3. Process to generate skeletonized and dilated Artificial Potential Field using a 5-unit buffer safety zone.

3.3 Artificial Potential Field

Getting a spatial representation of the environment can be crucial for path-finding algorithms. For this, first, the mask generated by the segmentation model is transformed to sRGB color space through element normalization and a gamma correction of $1/2.2$. The Euclidean distance between the pixels representing individual classes and each pixel in the sRGB mask is computed based on which a pixel is classified as a binary value depending on the class. Obstacles are islands and therefore can be treated as land. The mask is then negated and a distance transform [37] is applied to it such that each pixel is labeled with its distance to the nearest obstacle. A buffer zone normalized to 0.5 percent of the smaller dimension between the height and width of the image is applied to the distance transform to output an obstacle map, which is a binary representation of the environment. An artificial potential field (APF) can be established using a distance transform that provides each pixel of the obstacle map with a potential value representing its Euclidean distance to the nearest obstacle. For pixels that are part of an obstacle, this potential value is zero.

While APFs may be effective for obstacle avoidance, they might seem only suboptimal for real-world applications such as vessel path planning. The algorithms discussed in 3.4 initially predicted unnatural paths that were too close to the shore, where the water is generally shallower. Hence, to parameterize the artificial 3D depth of the water bodies in 2D images, skeletonization [72] is implemented on the APF, followed by an adaptive weighted dilation. Essentially, skeletonization provided a logical mask of the potential field with a high likelihood of having deeper water. To refine the mask, we defined three structuring element disks with radii varying on the potential values in the APF, for dilation followed by a weighted sum of the three dilated maps. This allowed us to adapt the dilation process to different potential levels, making the resulting skeleton map have larger elements for larger potential values and vice versa. The overall process is represented in Fig. 3.

3.4 Optimal Path Finding

To find an optimal path between given coordinates of the start and end target points (or waypoints), traditional deterministic approaches are employed, such as A^* and $Theta^*$ [8] that transforms a specific problem into a guidance map and performs a differentiable A^* on it. The application of three path algorithms is shown in Fig. 4 in two different maps and comparing five algorithm configurations.

In this figure, $Theta^*$ offers a better optimization for the travel distance of 781 units compared to Simple A^* (919 units) and Safe Repulsive A^* (867 units). The distance in the unit corresponds to the sum of the Euclidean distance between each point on the path. A rasterization process (from pixel to latitude, longitude, and altitude coordinates) is needed to find the corresponding value in the meter. An example will be added in the Results section using GeoTIFF image format (using USGS Earth Explorer with ESRI source).

4 Results

The main issue to solve is to avoid cetaceans in complex inland waterways. This section presents the result when applying the algorithms defined in the methodology section using the location of cetacean as a repulsive obstacle (described in Sect. 4.1) and the waypoint as an attractive location (validated in Sect. 4.2) while minimizing the distance traveled. The next two sections describe how these constraints are considered in path optimization. Lastly, Sect. 4.3 describes a simulation of the impact of velocity adaptation on heard noise at the location of the cetacean.

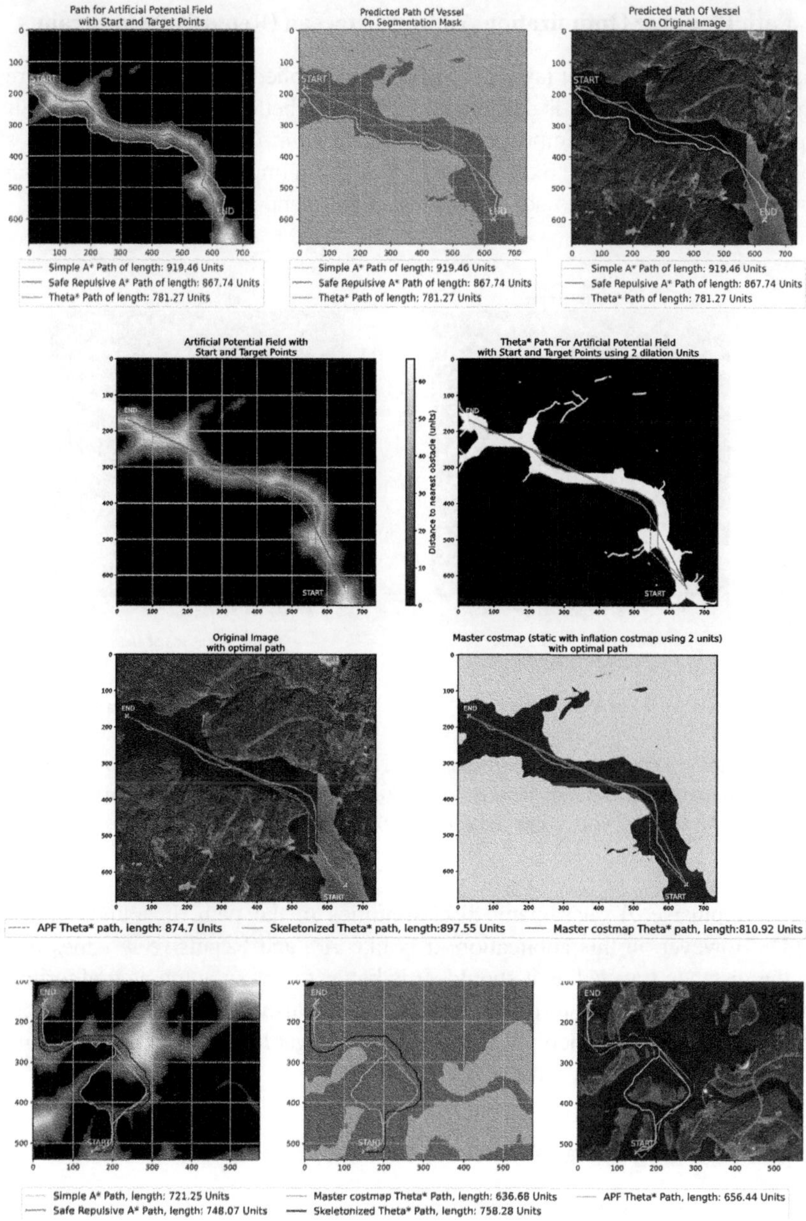

Fig. 4. Evaluation of three path algorithms generation (Simple A^*, Safe Repulsive A^* and $Theta^*$) using master cost map, APF and Skeletonized APF.

4.1 Path Planning Optimization Adding Cetacean (Repulsive) Constraints

Using $Theta^*$ when another layer of constraints is applied generates inadequate results. Therefore, an improvement is designed to help find a better path optimization. Figure 5 compares $Theta^*$ and the improved Skeletonized-$Theta^*$ approach. The result shows a longer travel distance with Skeletonized-$Theta^*$ but improves the entrance to the port and reduces the proximity to obstacles such as the island and the shore.

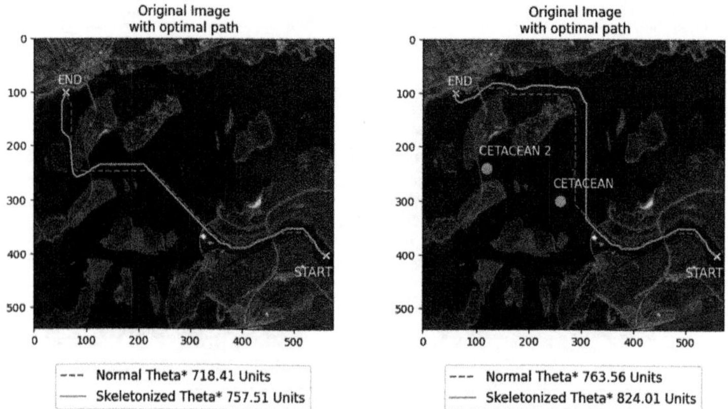

(a) Optimized path without cetacean (b) Optimized path with two cetaceans

Fig. 5. Evaluation of two path algorithms in a complex inland waterway with and without cetacean (repulsive constraints): $Theta^*$ and Skeletonized-$Theta^*$ (Skeletonized and Dilated Artificial Potential Field with 5 units buffer safety zone).

Safe Repulsive A^* has many discontinuities in the path. It sounds better with $Theta^*$. However, in this application, it is like A^*, and Repulsive A^* does not optimize the distance traveled as it should. It is better to get an automated algorithm, but as this system is designed to help the pilot, we can also let the pilot enter some waypoints. The next section then presents the results regarding attractive constraints such as a waypoint given as a constraint from a pilot.

4.2 Path Planning Using Waypoint (Attractive) Constraints

Over a path, it is possible to define a number of waypoints depending on the needs. The autopilot governing law has a threshold distance between both the current vessel location and the waypoint. When this threshold is reached, the next waypoint is selected as the target to be reached. Of course, these waypoints could be added by the pilot, and they define new attractive points to reach by the path-planning algorithm. From Fig. 4, two attractive points are added in the algorithm, therefore generating the results presented in Fig. 6.

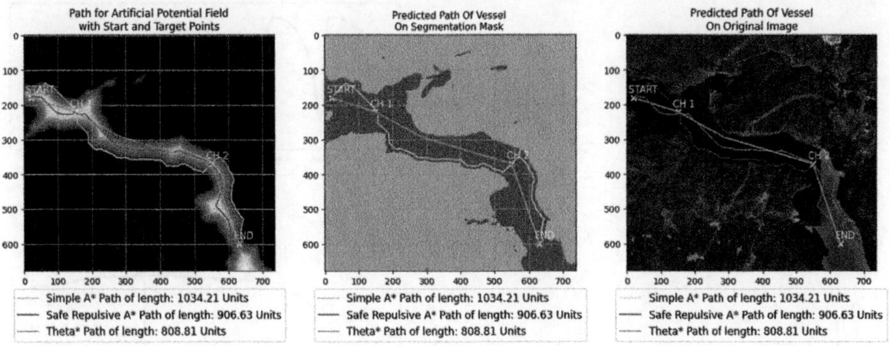

Fig. 6. Evaluation of three path algorithms in a complex inland waterway with waypoint constraints: Simple A^*, Safe Repulsive A^* and $Theta^*$.

4.3 Vessel Control Over the Optimal Path

The Wittekind function [59], integrated in Simulink, is used to estimate the noise of the vessel and an underwater transmission loss [22] allows the estimation of the level of noise heard at the location of the cetacean. The Simulink simulator designed is based on the implementation of the MSS model library [39], specifically adapted to capture the dynamic behavior of the vessels. The integration of the simulator uses a comprehensive set of inputs, including water temperature (3 Celsius), cetacean locations (Fjord of Saguenay, Latitude: 48.258456, Longitude:−69.959307), vessel position and velocity, wind (NORSOK model: direction of 150 degrees, velocity of 15m/s, spectrum over 20 m), underwater current direction (5 degrees) and speed (2 Knots). The simulation uses a cargo length of 175 meters with an initial velocity of 10 Knots. The simulation tracks a set of waypoints using the Integral Line of Sight (ILOS) guidance law such as described in [58] to define the heading setpoint and a PID (Proportional-Integral-Derivative) with a reference feedforward controller that governs the autopilot system. The ILOS guidance law and autopilot are defined in the MSS library. Cetacean detection integrates USV, satellite and UAV imagery with an algorithm described in [41].

$Theta^*$ path of Fig. 6 is used to validate the level of noise heard in a cetacean location with a threshold value of 120 dB which is known to be a higher limit for safety [15]. Then, the simulator tries to reduce the vessel velocity until it reaches the 120dB re 1μPa target to reduce its impact on cetacean, as shown in Fig. 7a. The simulator tries to control the vessel under these constraints in order to reach the waypoints while following the trajectory as described in Fig. 7b. The minimal distance between the vessel and the cetacean is 785 meters and the noise is still near 125dB while the vessel reduces its velocity at 4 knots.

5 Limit of the Study

While the images (satellite and drone) provide a current view of the river (shore constraints while the vessel should be attracted to the center of the river), a Bathymetric

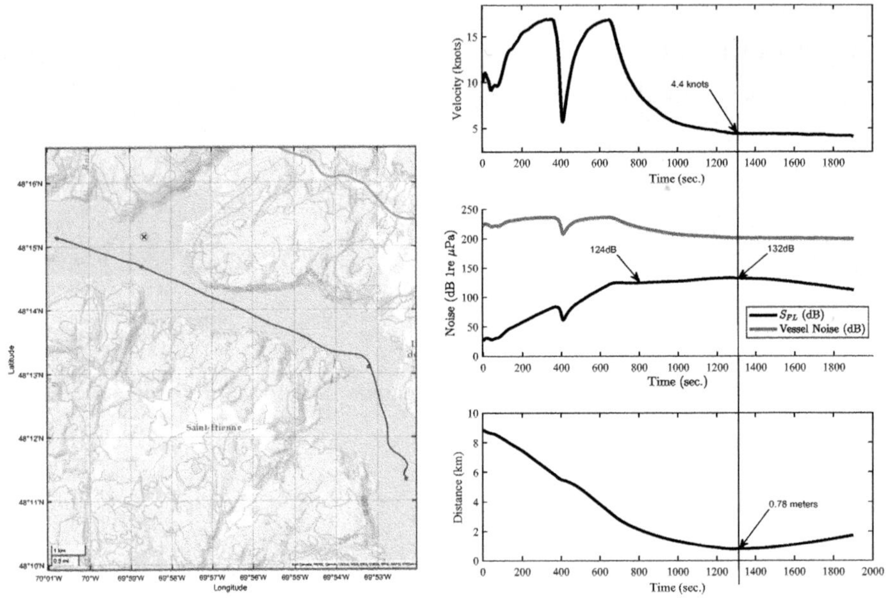

(a) Vessel trajectory simulation ($Theta^*$)

(b) Vessel noise validation

Fig. 7. Vessel trajectory and noise simulation over the path $Theta^*$ with a velocity control in order to limit the noise heard at the cetacean location represented by a blue cross and red circle (USGS Earth Explorer with ESRI source). (Color figure online)

Chart should be added as another layer of constraints in order to be attracted to the deepest underwater level (and push back through the shoals). The current study is limited to satellite images and it should also include drone images in order to find a cetacean location in the front of the vessel (not seen by satellite), but also to locate other kinds of constraints such as small boats without a transponder or Automatic Identification System (AIS) data. In addition, other vessels should be added using the AIS data as repulsive constraints. Finally, this study does not consider bridges and other infrastructures, detected and identified by a drone, LiDAR, or other kinds of embedded camera imagery, which could be added as another kind of repulsive constraint. As an example, the algorithm needs to know the location of the tower foundation and the pile cap and determine the path between these repulsive constraints.

6 Conclusion

The current study uses three layers: obstacle maps (shore and island), repulsive constraints (cetacean) and attractive constraints (waypoints) from satellite images. There is some complexity in generating an accurate mask in order to define the obstacle map, which is the first-layer level for the Artificial Potential Field algorithm. The semantic segmentation step was improved by applying smooth blending on some satellite images, and then a safety zone was added to take into account the uncertainty in the shore segmentation, in particular near small islands or small rivers. The results show that an improved version of $Theta^*$, labeled Skeletonized-$Theta^*$, reaches adequate performance on complexes inland waterways when applied with constraints such as cetacean (repulsive) and manual waypoints entered by the pilot (attractive).

7 Future Works

Although strategies based on collision avoidance decisions exist, as in [49], while considering economic aspects such as damage to ships [50], there is currently no system to estimate optimal ship trajectories (position, speed, acceleration) to control the noise level at the location of cetaceans (noise exposure level as explained by Hirai et al. 2017 [18]). In future work, adding a trajectory to the path planning should increase the autonomy of the ship. Moreover, by adding a model of underwater noise (with a transmission loss model), it should be possible to change the trajectory over the path to limit the noise pollution heard at the cetacean locations. The noise level threshold could be used as repulsive constraints to refine the path. Other layers need to be added, such as the Bathymetric Chart, underwater noise level (with a threshold value of noise heard at the cetacean location), and the usual behaviors of cetaceans over the past years. With an autopilot, this integrated system should be used for a fully autonomous ship with minimal pilot intervention. The research program is therefore aimed at intelligent and transparent logistics, where the use of estimated ship arrival times can help in planning trajectories and scheduling activities.

Acknowledgments. Yashwardhan Deshmukh received financial support from MITACS under the Globalink Research Internship Program (international undergraduate training, 12-week internship) under Application ID 119617.

References

1. Al Maawali, W., Mesbah, M., Al Maashri, A., Saleem, A.: Design of intelligent thruster decision-making system for USVs. Ocean Eng. **285** (2023). https://doi.org/10.1016/j.oceaneng.2023.115431
2. Changxin, Z., et al.: UAV electric patrol path planning based on improved ant colony optimization-a* algorithm. In: IEEE International Conference on Electrical Engineering, Big Data and Algorithms, pp. 1374 – 1380 (2022). https://doi.org/10.1109/EEBDA53927.2022.9744949
3. Chen, H., Liang, Y., Meng, X.: A UAV path planning method for building surface information acquisition utilizing opposition-based learning artificial bee colony algorithm. Remote Sens. **15**(17) (2023). https://doi.org/10.3390/rs15174312
4. Chen, Z., Zhang, Y., Zhang, Y., Nie, Y., Tang, J., Zhu, S.: A hybrid path planning algorithm for unmanned surface vehicles in complex environment with dynamic obstacles. IEEE Access **7**, 126439–126449 (2019). https://doi.org/10.1109/ACCESS.2019.2936689
5. Chun, D.H., Roh, M.I., Lee, H.W., Ha, J., Yu, D.: Deep reinforcement learning-based collision avoidance for an autonomous ship. Ocean Eng. **234** (2021). https://doi.org/10.1016/j.oceaneng.2021.109216

6. Cui, Z., Wang, Y.: UAV path planning based on multi-layer reinforcement learning technique. IEEE Access **9**, 59486–59497 (2021). https://doi.org/10.1109/ACCESS.2021.3073704
7. Dai, J., Chen, D., Yang, S.: Path planning method of unmanned ship based on PPO and DWA. In: SPIE - The International Society for Optical Engineering. vol. 12793 (2023). https://doi.org/10.1117/12.3006648
8. Daniel, K., Nash, A., Koenig, S., Felner, A.: Theta*: any-angle path planning on grids. J. Artif. Intell. Res. **39**, 533–579 (2010). https://doi.org/10.1613/jair.2994
9. Deshmukh, Y., Otis, M.: Source code for inland navigation and vessel optimal path planning. [Source code] OSF (2024). https://doi.org/10.17605/OSF.IO/24ATK
10. Erke, S., Bin, D., Yiming, N., Qi, Z., Liang, X., Dawei, Z.: An improved a-star based path planning algorithm for autonomous land vehicles. Int. J. Adv. Robotic Syst. **17**(5) (2020). https://doi.org/10.1177/1729881420962263
11. Fan, Y., Sun, Z., Wang, G.: A novel intelligent collision avoidance algorithm based on deep reinforcement learning approach for USV. Ocean Eng. **287** (2023). https://doi.org/10.1016/j.oceaneng.2023.115649
12. Fusic, S.J., Sitharthan, R., Masthan, S.S., Hariharan, K.: Autonomous vehicle path planning for smart logistics mobile applications based on modified heuristic algorithm. Measur. Sci. Technol. **34**(3) (2023). https://doi.org/10.1088/1361-6501/aca708
13. Gao, D., Zhou, P., Shi, W., Wang, T., Wang, Y.: A dynamic obstacle avoidance method for unmanned surface vehicle under the international regulations for preventing collisions at sea. J. Marine Sci. Eng. **10**(7) (2022). https://doi.org/10.3390/jmse10070901
14. Guan, W., Wang, K.: Autonomous collision avoidance of unmanned surface vehicles based on improved a-star and dynamic window approach algorithms. IEEE Intell. Transp. Syst. Mag. **15**(3), 36–50 (2023). https://doi.org/10.1109/MITS.2022.3229109
15. Halliday, W.D., Pine, M.K., Insley, S.J.: Underwater noise and arctic marine mammals: review and policy recommendations. Environ. Rev. **28**(4), 438–448 (2020)
16. Halliday, W.D., et al.: Beluga vocalizations decrease in response to vessel traffic in the Mackenzie river estuary. Arctic **72**(4), 337–346 (2019)
17. He, K., Zhang, X., Ren, S., Sun, J.: Deep residual learning for image recognition. In: 2016 IEEE Conference on Computer Vision and Pattern Recognition (CVPR), pp. 770–778 (2015)
18. Hirai, Y., Tsuchiya, T., Shimizu, E.: Estimation of sound exposure level based on relative movement of ship and whale. In: International Congress on Sound and Vibration (2017)
19. Horn, B.K., Schunck, B.G.: Determining optical flow. Artif. Intell. **17**(1–3), 185–203 (1981). https://doi.org/10.1016/0004-3702(81)90024-2
20. Hu, B., Wan, Y., Lei, Y.: Collision avoidance of USV by model predictive control-aided deep reinforcement learning. In: IEEE International Conference on Industrial Technology (2022). https://doi.org/10.1109/ICIT48603.2022.10002769
21. Huang, G., Liu, Z., Weinberger, K.Q.: Densely connected convolutional networks. 2017 IEEE Conference on Computer Vision and Pattern Recognition (CVPR), pp. 2261–2269 (2016)
22. Jalkanen, J.P., et al.: Modelling of ships as a source of underwater noise. Ocean Sci. **14**(6), 1373–1383 (2018)
23. Ji, X., Feng, S., Han, Q., Yin, H., Yu, S.: Improvement and fusion of A* algorithm and dynamic window approach considering complex environmental information. Arab. J. Sci. Eng. **46**(8), 7445–7459 (2021). https://doi.org/10.1007/s13369-021-05445-6
24. Jiang, D., Yuan, M., Xiong, J., Xiao, J., Duan, Y.: Obstacle avoidance USV in multi-static obstacle environments based on a deep reinforcement learning approach. Measur. Control (United Kingdom) (2023). https://doi.org/10.1177/00202940231195937
25. Kim, H.G., Yun, S.J., Choi, Y.H., Ryu, J.K., Suh, J.H.: Collision avoidance algorithm based on colregs for unmanned surface vehicle. J. Mar. Sci. Eng. **9**(8) (2021). https://doi.org/10.3390/jmse9080863

26. Li, L., Sheng, W.: Collision avoidance dynamic window approach in multi-agent system. In: Chinese Automation Congress, pp. 2307–2311 (2020). https://doi.org/10.1109/CAC51589.2020.9327673
27. Li, L., Wu, D., Huang, Y., Yuan, Z.M.: A path planning strategy unified with a colregs collision avoidance function based on deep reinforcement learning and artificial potential field. Appl. Ocean Res. **113** (2021). https://doi.org/10.1016/j.apor.2021.102759
28. Li, Y., Zuo, Y., Shan, Q., Li, T.: Path planning of ship collision avoidance for minimized energy consumption. In: Chinese Control and Decision Conference, p. 177–182 (2021). https://doi.org/10.1109/CCDC52312.2021.9601496
29. Li, Y., Zhang, H.: Collision avoidance decision method for unmanned surface vehicle based on an improved velocity obstacle algorithm. J. Marine Sci. Eng. **10**(8) (2022). https://doi.org/10.3390/jmse10081047
30. Li, Y., Zheng, J.: Deep learning structure for collision avoidance planning of unmanned surface vessel. Proc. Inst. Mech. Eng. Part M: J. Eng. Marit. Environ. **235**(2), 511–520 (2021). https://doi.org/10.1177/1475090220970102
31. Liang, C., Zhang, X., Watanabe, Y., Deng, Y.: Autonomous collision avoidance of unmanned surface vehicles based on improved a star and minimum course alteration algorithms. Appl. Ocean Res. **113** (2021). https://doi.org/10.1016/j.apor.2021.102755
32. Lin, H.Y., Peng, X.Z.: Autonomous quadrotor navigation with vision based obstacle avoidance and path planning. IEEE Access **9**, 102450–102459 (2021). https://doi.org/10.1109/ACCESS.2021.3097945
33. Lin, T.Y., Goyal, P., Girshick, R.B., He, K., Dollár, P.: Focal loss for dense object detection. 2017 IEEE International Conference on Computer Vision (ICCV), pp. 2999–3007 (2017)
34. Mu, X., Gao, W., Li, X., Li, G.: Coverage path planning for UAV based on improved back-and-forth mode. IEEE Access **11**, 114840–114854 (2023). https://doi.org/10.1109/ACCESS.2023.3325483
35. Muñoz, P., R-Moreno, M.D.: S-theta: low steering path-planning algorithm. In: Bramer, M., Petridis, M. (eds.) Research and Development in Intelligent Systems XXIX, pp. 109–121. Springer London, London (2012)
36. Muñoz, P., R-Moreno, M.D., Castaño, B.: 3Dana: a path planning algorithm for surface robotics. Eng. Appl. Artif. Intell. **60**, 175–192 (2017). https://doi.org/10.1016/j.engappai.2017.02.010, https://www.sciencedirect.com/science/article/pii/S0952197617300337
37. Oliphant, T.E., et al.: SciPy: Open source scientific tools for Python (2001). https://www.scipy.org/. [Online; accessed <today’s date>]
38. Otis, M., Deshmukh, Y.: Images for inland navigation and vessel optimal path planning. [dataset] Borealis (2024). https://doi.org/10.5683/SP3/KZNEOU
39. Perez, T., Smogelif, o., Fossenf, T., Sorensen, A.: An overview of the marine systems simulator (MSS): a Simulink toolbox for marine control systems. Model. Ident. Control **27**(4), 259–275 (2006)
40. Ren, J., Zhang, J., Cui, Y.: Autonomous obstacle avoidance algorithm for unmanned surface vehicles based on an improved velocity obstacle method. ISPRS Int. J. Geo-Inf. **10**(9) (2021). https://doi.org/10.3390/ijgi10090618
41. Salah, I.B., Otis, M., Rahem, R., Ardhaoui, M.: Objects detection on the water surface using satellite imagery, drones and vessel-based imaging applied for logistics. In: International conference on Robotic, Computer Vision and Intelligent Systems (ROBOVIS). Springer CCIS (2025)
42. Schoeman, R.P., Patterson-Abrolat, C., Plön, S.: A global review of vessel collisions with marine animals. Front. Marine Sci. **7** (2020)
43. Scott, J.L., et al.: The whalereport alert system: mitigating threats to whales with citizen science. Biol. Cons. **289**, 110422 (2024)

44. Seo, C., Noh, Y., Abebe, M., Kang, Y.J., Park, S., Kwon, C.: Ship collision avoidance route planning using cri-based a* algorithm. Int. J. Naval Archit. Ocean Eng. **15** (2023). https://doi.org/10.1016/j.ijnaoe.2023.100551
45. Simonyan, K., Zisserman, A.: Very deep convolutional networks for large-scale image recognition. In: International Conference on Learning Representations (2015)
46. Singh, Y., Sharma, S., Sutton, R., Hatton, D., Khan, A.: A constrained a* approach towards optimal path planning for an unmanned surface vehicle in a maritime environment containing dynamic obstacles and ocean currents. Ocean Eng. **169**, 187–201 (2018). https://doi.org/10.1016/j.oceaneng.2018.09.016
47. Su, N., Wang, J.B., Zeng, C., Zhang, H., Lin, M., Li, G.Y.: Unmanned-surface-vehicle-aided maritime data collection using deep reinforcement learning. IEEE Internet Things J. **9**(20), 19773–19786 (2022). https://doi.org/10.1109/JIOT.2022.3168589
48. Sudre, C.H., Li, W., Vercauteren, T., Ourselin, S., Jorge Cardoso, M.: Generalised dice overlap as a deep learning loss function for highly unbalanced segmentations. In: Deep Learning in Medical Image Analysis and Multimodal Learning for Clinical Decision Support, pp. 240–248. Lecture notes in computer science, Springer, Cham (2017)
49. Sèbe, M., Kontovas, C.A., Pendleton, L.: A decision-making framework to reduce the risk of collisions between ships and whales. Marine Policy **109** (2019)
50. Sèbe, M., Kontovas, C.A., Pendleton, L.: Reducing whale-ship collisions by better estimating damages to ships. Sci. Total Environ. **713** (2020)
51. Tao, Y., Du, J.: Agile collision avoidance for unmanned surface vehicles based on collision shielded model prediction control algorithm. J. Navig. **75**(5), 1243–1267 (2022). https://doi.org/10.1017/S0373463322000315
52. Van Dang, C., Ahn, H., Lee, D.S., Lee, S.C.: A path planning method based on theta-star search for non-holonomic robots. In: 2022 Joint 12th International Conference on Soft Computing and Intelligent Systems and 23rd International Symposium on Advanced Intelligent Systems, pp. 1–6 (2022). https://doi.org/10.1109/SCISISIS55246.2022.10002141
53. Vooban: Smoothly-blend-image-patches (2017). https://github.com/Vooban/Smoothly-Blend-Image-Patches
54. Wang, D., Zhang, J., Jin, J., Mao, X.: Local collision avoidance algorithm for a unmanned surface vehicle based on steering maneuver considering colregs. IEEE Access **9**, 49233–49248 (2021). https://doi.org/10.1109/ACCESS.2021.3058288
55. Wang, P., Yao, X., Fei, Q., Meng, J.: Research on local path planning for autonomous collision avoidance of USV. In: Chinese Automation Congress, pp. 5368–5373 (2022). https://doi.org/10.1109/CAC57257.2022.10055154
56. Wang, Z., Chen, P., Mou, J., Chen, L.: Colregs-compliant autonomous collision avoidance method based on deep reinforcement learning for USVs. In: IEEE International Conference on Transportation Information and Safety, pp. 1575–1598 (2023). https://doi.org/10.1109/ICTIS60134.2023.10243729
57. Wenming, W., Jialu, D., Yihan, T.: A dynamic collision avoidance solution scheme of unmanned surface vessels based on proactive velocity obstacle and set-based guidance. Ocean Eng. **248** (2022). https://doi.org/10.1016/j.oceaneng.2022.110794
58. Wiig, M.S., Pettersen, K.Y., Ruud, E.L.M., Krogstad, T.R.: An integral line-of-sight guidance law with a speed-dependent lookahead distance. In: European Control Conference, p. 1269–1276 (2018)
59. Wittekind, D.K.: A simple model for the underwater noise source level of ships. J. Ship Prod. Design **30**(1), 7–14 (2014)
60. Woo, J., Kim, N.: Collision avoidance for an unmanned surface vehicle using deep reinforcement learning. Ocean Eng. **199** (2020). https://doi.org/10.1016/j.oceaneng.2020.107001

61. Xia, G., Han, Z., Zhao, B., Wang, X.: Local path planning for unmanned surface vehicle collision avoidance based on modified quantum particle swarm optimization. Complexity **2020** (2020). https://doi.org/10.1155/2020/3095426
62. Xia, J., Zhu, X., Liu, Z., Luo, Y., Wu, Z., Wu, Q.: Research on collision avoidance algorithm of unmanned surface vehicle based on deep reinforcement learning. IEEE Sens. J. **23**(11), 11262–11273 (2023). https://doi.org/10.1109/JSEN.2022.3222575
63. Xia, Z., Liu, T., Zhang, J., Liu, L.: Dynamic obstacle avoidance method of USV based on secure ACO with hazard index. In: IEEE International Conference on Computer and Communications, pp. 2370–2374 (2022). https://doi.org/10.1109/ICCC56324.2022.10065702
64. Xie, R., Meng, Z., Zhou, Y., Ma, Y., Wu, Z.: Heuristic q-learning based on experience replay for three-dimensional path planning of the unmanned aerial vehicle. Sci. Progress **103**(1) (2020). https://doi.org/10.1177/0036850419879024
65. Xu, X., Lu, Y., Liu, G., Cai, P., Zhang, W.: Colregs-abiding hybrid collision avoidance algorithm based on deep reinforcement learning for USVs. Ocean Eng. **247** (2022). https://doi.org/10.1016/j.oceaneng.2022.110749
66. Xu, Y., Wei, Y., Wang, D., Jiang, K., Deng, H.: Multi-UAV path planning in GPS and communication denial environment. Sensors **23**(6) (2023). https://doi.org/10.3390/s23062997
67. Yang, S., Huang, J., Xiang, X., Li, W.: Optimization of USV area coverage path planning based on confidence ellipsoid;. Xi Tong Gong Cheng Yu Dian Zi Ji Shu/Systems Engineering and Electronics **44**(7), 2263–2269 (2022). https://doi.org/10.12305/j.issn.1001-506X.2022.07.22
68. Yonetani, R., Taniai, T., Barekatain, M., Nishimura, M., Kanezaki, A.: Path planning using neural a* search. In: Machine Learning Research. vol. 139, pp. 12029–12039 (2021)
69. Yuan, S., Liu, Z., Sun, Y., Song, S., Wang, Z., Zheng, L.: EMPMR berthing scheme: a novel event-triggered motion planning and motion replanning scheme for unmanned surface vessels. Ocean Eng. **286** (2023). https://doi.org/10.1016/j.oceaneng.2023.115666
70. Yuan, X., Tong, C., He, G., Wang, H.: Unmanned vessel collision avoidance algorithm by dynamic window approach based on colregs considering the effects of the wind and wave. J. Marine Sci. Eng. **11**(9) (2023). https://doi.org/10.3390/jmse11091831, https://www.scopus.com/inward/record.uri?eid=2-s2.0-85172797778&doi=10.3390%2fjmse11091831&partnerID=40&md5=5960bbd04afb23fbfbc6fcd5f2d4e649 cited by: 3; All Open Access, Gold Open Access
71. Zhang, J., Cui, Y., Li, G., Ren, J.: Dynamic path planning algorithm for unmanned surface vehicle under island-reef environment. IEEE Trans. Aerosp. Electron. Syst. **59**(5), 7252–7268 (2023). https://doi.org/10.1109/TAES.2023.3286823
72. Zhang, T.Y., Suen, C.Y.: A fast parallel algorithm for thinning digital patterns. Commun. ACM **27**, 236–239 (1984)
73. Zhang, W.L., Shan, L., Chang, L., Qi, Z.D., Dai, Y.W.: Distributed collision avoidance algorithm for multiple unmanned surface vessels based on improved DWA. Kongzhi yu Juece/Control and Decision **38**(4), 951–962 (2023). https://doi.org/10.13195/j.kzyjc.2021.1744
74. Zhang, Y., Xiao, Z., Yuan, X., Li, S., Liang, S.: Obstacle avoidance of two-wheeled mobile robot based on DWA algorithm. In: Chinese Automation Congress, pp. 5701–5706 (2019). https://doi.org/10.1109/CAC48633.2019.8996425
75. Zhao, J., Ma, X., Yang, B., Chen, Y., Zhou, Z., Xiao, P.: Global path planning of unmanned vehicle based on fusion of a* algorithm and voronoi field. J. Intell. Connected Veh. **5**(3), 250–259 (2022). https://doi.org/10.1108/JICV-01-2022-0001
76. Zhu, X., Yan, B., Yue, Y.: Path planning and collision avoidance in unknown environments for USVs based on an improved d* lite. Appl. Sci. (Switzerland) **11**(17) (2021). https://doi.org/10.3390/app11177863
77. Zuiderveld, K.J.: Contrast limited adaptive histogram equalization. In: Graphics gems (1994)

Entropy-Guided Self-regulated Learning Without Forgetting for Distribution-Shift Continual Learning with Blurred Task Boundaries

Rui Yang[1(✉)], Matthieu Grard[2], Emmanuel Dellandréa[1], and Liming Chen[1]

[1] Ecole Centrale de Lyon, CNRS, Universite Claude Bernard Lyon 1, INSA Lyon, Université Lumière Lyon2, LIRIS, UMR5205, 69130, Ecully, France
{rui.yang1,emmanuel.dellandrea,liming.chen}@ec-lyon.fr

[2] Siléane, 17 rue Descartes, 42000 Saint-Etienne, France
m.grard@sileane.com

Abstract. Continual Learning (CL) aims to endow machines with the human-like ability to continuously acquire novel knowledge while retaining previously learned experiences. Recent research on CL has focused on Domain-Incremental Learning (DIL) or Class-Incremental Learning (CIL) with well-defined task boundaries. However, for real-life applications, e.g., waste sorting, robotic grasping, etc., the model needs to be constantly updated to fit new data. Additionally, there is usually an overlap between new and old data. Thus, task boundaries may not be well-defined, and a more smooth scenario is needed. In this paper, we propose a more general scenario, namely Distribution-Shift Incremental Learning (DS-IL), which enables soft task boundaries with possible mixtures of data distributions over tasks and thereby subsumes the two previous CL scenarios: DIL and CIL are simply DS-IL. Moreover, given the increasingly greater importance of data privacy in real-life applications and, incidentally, data storage efficiency, we further introduce an entropy-guided self-regulated distillation process **without memory**, which leverages data similarities between tasks with soft-boundaries. Experimented on a variety of datasets, our proposed method outperforms or matches state-of-the-art continual learning methods.

Keywords: Continual learning · Entropy · Blurred task boundaries

1 Introduction

In recent years, intelligent systems have been required to possess Continual Learning (CL) ability, *i.e.*, the capability to learn novel knowledge from a new task while preserving previously learned knowledge and experience. However, current intelligent systems usually suffer from a notorious problem named catastrophic forgetting, *i.e.*, they quickly forget previously learned knowledge when learning new tasks.

After years of research, a variety of continual learning scenarios have been proposed. Depending upon the assumptions made for CL, three different scenarios, namely

J. Röning and J. Filipe (Eds.): ROBOVIS 2025, CCIS 2629, pp. 454–468, 2026.
https://doi.org/10.1007/978-3-032-00986-9_29

Task-Incremental Learning (TIL), Domain-Incremental Learning (DIL), and Class-Incremental Learning (CIL) (see details in Fig. 1, Fig. 3 and Fig. 2), were first proposed in [7,22] to evaluate the performance of different CL methods. TIL assumes that task identity is provided for both training and inference, whereas both DIL and CIL assume that task identity is only available during training and remains *unknown* during testing. By definition, it is assumed that novel data of unknown classes occur in CIL over tasks, while novel data of only known classes can appear in DIL. However, the previous three CL settings, as defined in [7,22], assume that during training, task boundaries between tasks are clear and well-defined. For example, a new task must only have new unknown classes in CIL, while a new task must have new images(variety in illumination, background, texture, *etc.*) of known classes in DIL. However, for real-life applications, *e.g.*, waste sorting, data (garbage) are collected from different regions and on different days. If the model updates every day, the garbage collected on one day can be considered to be one single task. In this case, a new task may or may not have new unknown classes or new images from different domains, *i.e.*, there may be an overlap of classes and images between tasks. Thus, there are no well-defined task boundaries, and neither DIL nor CIL can describe this situation.

In [14], a new scenario named New Instances and Classes (NIC) was proposed for their dataset CORe50 [14], where new instances and new classes can occur in a new task. However, it did not propose a clear method for generating NIC on other datasets. In [29], it proposed the Continuous Task Agnostic scenario, which considers the continuous linear transition of task distribution. However, it only studies the linear transition between two tasks, meaning that application of this scenario is limited. Considering the generality of different scenarios, DIL and CIL have attracted much more attention in the literature. Current research, *e.g.*, [3,17,23,27], mainly considers DIL and CIL to be two sub-questions of continual learning that are studied separately. However, both DIL and CIL involve data distribution shifts (see details in Sect. 3). In this paper, we propose a novel CL perspective, namely Distribution-Shift Incremental Learning (DS-IL). More general and based on data distribution shifts, it can subsume the previous CL sub-scenarios and enables mixtures of data distributions over tasks with blurred boundaries.

A general assumption in CL is that past data cannot be entirely stored for privacy or memory constraint reasons. However, the previously learned model can be used for the next training. For a classification problem, the learning model is generally a discriminative model, so that for a given input, the softmax output is the probability distribution of the class labels. However, the information on data distribution is lost after training, meaning that the previous objective function cannot be easily reconstructed by only using a discriminative model. **Regularization-based methods**, *e.g.*, EWC [9], SI [28], Riemannian Walk [2]. These use a second-order approximation (Fisher information, Hessian matrix, etc.) to replace the previous objective function. These methods work well for Task-Incremental Learning, *i.e.*, when the system is informed of the task ID from which the data derive, and struggle against other more challenging scenarios [22]. **Memory-based methods**, *e.g.*, ER [18], LWF [13], iCaRL [17], make use of the actual data, whereas others, *e.g.*, DGR [20], DeepInv [26], rely upon generated data. They use memory or pseudo-memory to replace the previous dataset and approximate the previous objective function. They are better equipped to overcome forgetting than regularization-based methods but usually need an extra memory buffer and more computation. **Parameter isolation methods**, *e.g.*, PNN [19], EFT [23], RKR [21], dedicate different subsets of the model parameters to different tasks. These methods only work when task boundaries are well-defined.

In order to better adapt to real applications, a method that needs less memory budget, more computation efficiency, and more flexibilityÂăis required. We observe that the task boundary is not always rigid between tasks, and that there is usually an overlap of data distributions between different tasks for many continual learning scenarios. In this case, these overlapping data can help us reconstruct the previous objective function, thus retaining knowledge. The remaining challenge is how to find these data. In this paper, we propose to make use of the previous model's entropy information on the current data to identify data similarity. By using this information, we can adjust distillation loss more precisely, based on the degree of familiarity of the learned model with the current data.

The contributions of this paper can be summarized as follows:

- We propose a novel continual learning scenario, namely Domain-Shift Incremental Learning (DS-IL), which enables mixtures of data distributions over tasks with soft task boundaries and thereby subsumes both DIL and CIL;
- In order to deal with mixtures of data distributions between tasks under DS-IL, we introduce an entropy-guided self-regulated knowledge distillation loss which, without memory, preserves previously acquired knowledge based on the degree of familiarity of the learned model with the current task's data;
- Using PACS and CIFAR-100 datasets, we define two novel experimental benchmarks in order to evaluate continual models *w.r.t.* the DS-IL scenario;
- Using the proposed novel DS-IL benchmarks on PACS and CIFAR-100, we show the effectiveness of the proposed ER-LwF (Entropy-Guided Self-Regulated Learning without Forgetting).

2 Related Work

2.1 Domain-Incremental Learning

[7,22] first introduce the concept of Domain-Incremental Learning(DIL), in which there is no new class, but rather novel instances of classes from previous tasks. The objective of DIL is to learn a unified classifier that can classify all samples encountered so far. The core issue in DIL is how to deal with the shift in input space distribution, *e.g.*, changes in background, texture, pose, *etc.* For example, autonomous driving systems trained with the data collected in good weather conditions may encounter extreme weather conditions. DIL needs to learn from the data in extreme weather conditions while preserving the knowledge learned in good weather conditions. ER [18] shows that random selection of exemplars after training and random sampling of a set of memories during training with the new data can already achieve satisfying performances. Furthermore, RM [1] proposes to use diverse data augmentation techniques. MDR [24] introduces the meta-update combined with rich data augmentation. However, DIL still assumes that well-defined task boundaries are known during training. The proposed DS-IL setting extends DIL by enabling mixtures of data distributions over tasks and thereby enabling soft switching over tasks where task boundaries are not well-defined.

2.2 Class-Incremental Learning

Class-Incremental Learning (CIL) is currently the most studied CL scenario, where new classes occur sequentially. Similar to DIL, memory-based methods achieve the best performance. iCaRL [17] first proposes a solution for CIL. It contains 1) an episodic memory selected by the herding rule; 2) a distillation loss of the feature's output; 3) a *nearest-mean-of-exemplars* classifier using the mean feature of the Episodic Memory to classify. PodNet [3] proposes to distill not only the feature's outputs but also the intermediate layers' outputs. SDC [27] proposes to approximate the drift of the prototype's feature by using the current data. BiC [25] finds that the last fully connected layer has a strong bias towards the new classes and proposes to use a linear model to correct the bias. GEM [15] proposes to use memory to limit the current gradient. In this paper, we propose a new memory-free approach that can also cooperate with memory-based methods.

2.3 Task Agnostic Continual Learning

Task Agnostic Continual Learning [29] is the scenario in which task boundaries are unknown or not well-defined. It mainly creates the linear transition between two successive tasks by adjusting the proportion of the data of the two tasks. However, since the transition in a real application is not just linear between two tasks, it is still limited to a real application.

2.4 Knowledge Distillation

The notion of knowledge distillation was first proposed in [6] for model compression. It uses the output of a large model to replace the original label for given data. This new label can help a small model learn faster. LWF [13] first introduced this notion into CL. It considers the previously learned model as the teacher model and replays the memory and the teacher model's output. As aforementioned, many CL methods make use of knowledge distillation as a basic technique. PodNet [3] distills the intermediate layer output as well. RRR [4] distills the attention map of the memory exemplar. UD [11] distills the previous model's uncertainty on the memory exemplar. In this paper, we propose to calculate distillation loss not from memory but from current data, based on the familiarity of the previous model with the current data using entropy in a self-regulated process. We will discuss this in detail in Sect. 4.

3 Distribution-Shift Incremental Learning (DS-IL)

For simplicity without loss of generality, let us consider only two tasks T_1 and T_2 with their data D_1 for $T_1 : \{x_i^1, y_i^1\}_{i \in 1:n_1}$ drawn from a joint distribution $P_1(x, y)$, and D_2 for $T_2 : \{x_i^2, y_i^2\}_{i \in 1:n_2}$ drawn from a joint distribution $P_2(x, y)$. Let l be the loss function (cross-entropy for classification). Let ϕ be the output of the model, and θ its parameters. Then, we can construct the objectives for T_1 and T_2, respectively:

$$T_1 : L_1 = \sum_{1}^{n_1} l(\phi(y|\theta, x_i^1), y_i^1)) \tag{1}$$

$$T_2 : L_2 = \sum_{1}^{n_2} l(\phi(y|\theta, x_i^2), y_i^2)) \tag{2}$$

Gradient descent, such as Stochastic Gradient Descent (SGD), can be used to update the parameters θ to minimize the objective function. If $P_1(x, y)$ equals $P_2(x, y)$, L_1 approximates L_2. Thus, when training only with D_2, L_1 will not increase, and the model will not forget T_1. However, if $P_1(x, y)$ is very different from $P_2(x, y)$, the gradient direction of L_1 may violate the gradient direction of L_2 when updating the parameters only with the gradients of L_2. Therefore, the objective function L_1 will increase, and the phenomenon of *catastrophic forgetting* will occur.

From a Bayesian perspective, joint distribution $P(x, y)$ can be decomposed as follows:

$$P(x, y) = P(x|y)P(y) = P(y|x)P(x) \tag{3}$$

$P(x)$ and $P(y)$ denote the probability density of the input and output, respectively. $P(x|y)$ denotes the conditional probability of an output given an input. $P(x|y)$ denotes the conditional probability of an input given an output. For continual learning, the shift of these four terms is primarily involved, *e.g.*, $P(x)$ mainly changes in Domain-Incremental Learning (DIL), whereas $P(y)$ mainly changes in Class-Incremental Learning (CIL). We can create different scenarios by adjusting the proportion of these four terms.

From this data distribution shift perspective, it is easy to interpret DIL or CIL as DS-IL and extend them for Smooth-DIL or CIL when task transitions are blurred and data distributions mixed up. Thus, DS-IL is a continual learning scenario in which models are to learn knowledge from the successive shifting of $P(x)$, $P(y)$, $P(x|y)$, and $P(y|x)$ over tasks.

3.1 From CIL to DS-IL

For a classic CIL, each new task only contains a few new classes. Thus, the density probability of the previous classes equals zero, and some new output variables y appear. The CIL setting can be considered to be an extreme case of the DS-IL setting where data labels are only available for the novel classes of the second task T_2. Thus, $P(y)$ changes rapidly. By smoothing the change of $P(y)$, we can increase the similarity between tasks and generate a smoother and more flexible version of CIL, as shown in Fig. 2.

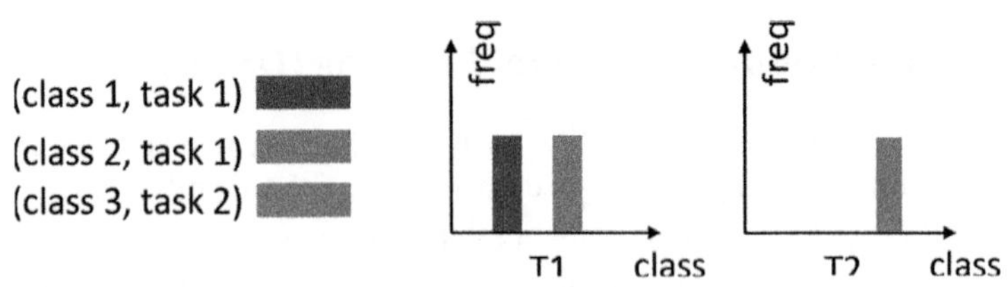

Fig. 1. Illustration of TIL in which the data have both class id and task id. Moreover, task id is provided for both training and testing.

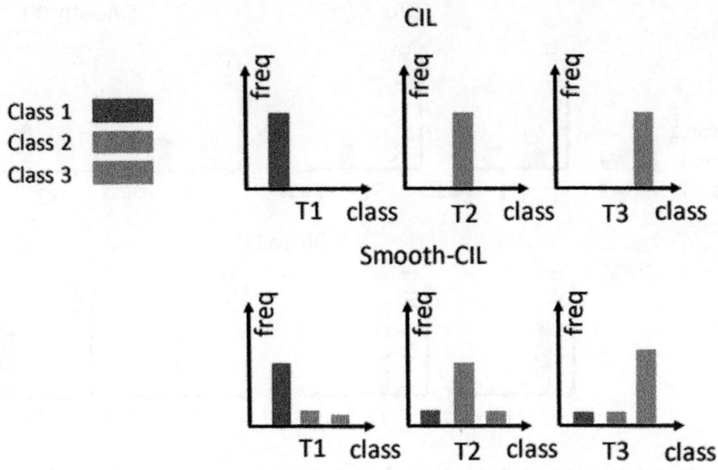

Fig. 2. Illustration of CIL and Smooth-CIL using three tasks with three classes. In the original CIL setting, each task only contains instances of one class. The Smooth-CIL breaks this limit, and each task may have multiple classes. Thus, the shift of $P(y)$ in our scenario is smoother.

3.2 From DIL to DS-IL

The classic DIL defines each domain as a single task with well-defined task boundaries. This means that the domain shift is discontinuous. Thus, we can quickly transform a DIL into a CIL by labeling the data with domain and class labels as shown in Fig. 3, thereby interpreting DIL as DS-IL. However, in many real-life applications, there are no clear and well-defined task boundaries with evident domain labels. Task transitions can be fuzzy, and data distributions of different tasks can overlap and mix up, resulting in a Smooth-DIL as shown in Fig. 3, which is enabled by DS-IL.

4 Entropy-Guided Self-regulated Learning Without Forgetting

To ensure simplicity without loss of generality, we consider the same hypotheses as in Sect. 3. There are only two tasks. From Eq. (1) and Eq. (2), we can derive the joint objective for both task 1 and task 2 as:

$$L_{total} = L_1 + L_2 \tag{4}$$

$$= \sum_{D_1} l(\phi(y|\theta, x_i^1), y_i^1)) + \sum_{D_2} l(\phi(y|\theta, x_i^2), y_i^2)) \tag{5}$$

When training on T_2, if we could store all the data from T_1, then we can construct the objective L_1. However, for CL, we can only use a small part or none of D_1 (dataset for T_1). Thus, the core problem is how to approximate L_1.

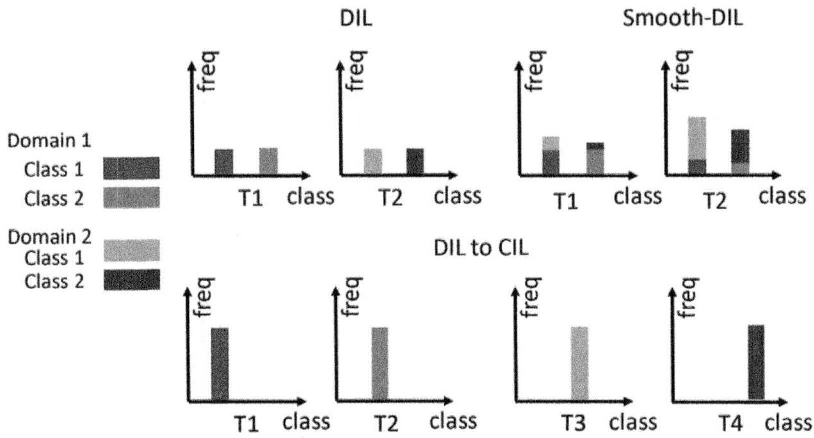

Fig. 3. Assume there are two domains, and each domain contains the same class labels. The classic DIL considers each domain as a single task. In Smooth-DIL, each task can contain two domains, but the distribution of different domains is different for each task. Therefore, from DIL to CIL, we can label data by using both the domain label and the class label. In this figure, there are four different labels, corresponding to four tasks.

4.1 LWF (Learning Without Forgetting)

LWF [13] proposes to use the previous model to generate a soft label and replaces the cross-entropy loss with a distillation loss. In this work, to fit our scenario, we only use the concept of knowledge distillation to represent LWF. θ^* represents the parameters learned from T_1; l_{lwf} corresponds to the distillation loss; M is the memory set which is from D_1 and D_2. Then, the new objective is as follows:

$$\hat{L_{total}} = \hat{L_1} + L_2 \tag{6}$$

$$\hat{L_1} = \sum_M l_{lwf}(\phi(y|\theta, x_i^1), \phi(y|\theta^*, x_i^1))) \tag{7}$$

LWF uses distillation loss to approximate the previous objective function L_1.

4.2 The Proposed ER-LWF Approach

As we discussed in Sect. 3, the distribution shift between tasks is not always rigid and discontinuous. Thus, some current data may possibly be similar to previous data. Here, we use $D_1 \cap D_2$ to represent the set of similar data. It then becomes crucial to find this intersection without access to D_1. We propose to use the output of the previously learned model to verify if the data are similar. Let EI denote the entropy. Then, EI for given data is defined as follows:

$$EI(x, y) = EI(P(y|\theta^*, x)) = EI(softmax(\phi(y|\theta^*, x))) \tag{8}$$

The closer EI is to zero, the more familiar and confident the model is about the input data, and the more corresponding data is valuable for reconstructing the L_1. On the contrary, if EI is large, output distribution is close to discrete uniform distribution. This means that the model hardly classifies the given input data.

Rather than looking for similar data in $D_1 \cap D_2$, we propose to use EI to modulate distillation loss. Given an N-class classifier, the upper-bound of EI over its outputs corresponds to discrete uniform distribution:

$$EI_{upper} = -\sum_{1}^{N}(\frac{1}{N}log(\frac{1}{N})) = log(N) \tag{9}$$

$$0 \leqslant EI(x, y) \leqslant log(N) \tag{10}$$

Thus, we can define our $Entropy - Guided$ weight (EG-weight) for given data as follows:

$$w_{eg}(x, y) = 1 - \frac{EI(x, y)}{log(N)} \tag{11}$$

Then, the previous objective function could be approximated as:

$$\hat{L_1} = \sum_{D_2} w_{eg}(x_i^2, y_i^2) l_{lwf}(\phi(y|\theta, x_i^2), \phi(y|\theta^*, x_i^2))) \tag{12}$$

From Eq. (12), we only use the current data D_2 and our EG-weight to approximate the previous loss function. The benefits of this formulation are threefold:

- Memory is not necessary;
- $w_{eg}(x, y)$ can verify if a model is familiar with data from D_2 or not. If the model is familiar with data, then $w_{eg}(x, y)$ will be close to 1, else it will be close to 0;
- It can be used for online updates.

The corresponding algorithm, ER-LWF, is detailed in Algorithm 1.

5 Experiments

In this section, we first present our experimental protocols under DS-IL in Sect. 5.1 and then introduce the methods we use in Sect. 5.2. Finally, the results are discussed in Sect. 5.3.

5.1 Experimental Protocols

As we discussed in Sect. 3, we can generate a Smooth-CIL and a Smooth-DIL for classic CIL and DIL, respectively. In this section, we continue this idea and conduct experiments on two datasets: PACS and CIFAR-100.

Algorithm 1: ER-LWF for continual learning.

Train(θ, D, n, T)
D: # dataset; θ: # model parameters;
T: # of tasks; N: # of batches
for t = 1:T **do**
  for n = 1:N **do**
    sample data (x_n, y_n) from D_t;
    # CE: Cross-Entropy loss;
    $l_{current} = CE(\phi(y|x_n, \theta), y_n)$;
    if t >1 **then**
      # KD: knowledge distillation loss;
      # θ^*: previous model parameters;
      $l_{lwf} = KD(\phi(y|x_n, \theta), \phi(y|x_n, \theta^*))$
      # $w_{eg}(x_n, y_n)$: EG-weight;
      $l_{ER-LWF} = w_{eg}(x_n, y_n) * l_{lwf}$
    else
      $l_{ER-LWF} = 0$
    end if
    $l_{total} = l_{current} + l_{ER-LWF}$
    $Update(l_{total}, \theta)$
  end for
end for

PACS is an image dataset originally for data generalization [12]. It consists of four domains: photo, art painting, cartoon, and sketch. Each domain contains seven classes. For simplicity, each image is resized to 64×64 for all scenarios, and 20% of each domain is used to construct our test set. We repeated each experiment three times.

First, for DIL, the dataset is divided into four tasks. Each task has one domain. The learning order arbitrarily chosen is: $art - painting \rightarrow cartoon \rightarrow photo \rightarrow sketch$.

We then generate six tasks containing all seven categories for Smooth-DIL. However, the four domains are mixed up with different proportions over the six tasks, and also the domain ratio is randomly generated. To compensate for this randomness, we generate three experiments with varying domain ratios.

In our CIL under the DS-IL perspective, each task contains all the categories. However, there is only one dominant class, and others have few exemplars. PACS has seven classes. Thus, we consider seven tasks, where each task contains only one dominant class.

Similar to Smooth-DIL, Smooth-CIL has six tasks for which the category ratio changes. The category ratio is randomly generated. We generate three experiments with varying proportions of the class.

CIFAR-100 [10] has 20 superclasses, where each superclass contains five classes. Each class comprises 600 images, of which 500 are used for training and 100 for testing. To use the dataset in our experiments, we need to create a notion of the domain in CIFAR-100. For example, there is a superclass *fish* that corresponds to five classes: *aquarium fish*, *flatfish*, *ray*, *shark*, *trout*. Each can be seen as a domain of *fish*. Thus, we use the superclass label as our new class label and the original class label as the domain label. Finally, the original CIFAR-100 is transformed into a dataset containing 20 classes and five domains. For simplicity, we keep the same training set and test set as the original version of CIFAR-100 [10]. We use the original image size that is 32*32*3. Each experiment is repeated three times.

Then, the rest is similar to the PACS dataset. For DIL, each superclass has five domains (subclasses). Thus, we generate five tasks for DIL. Then, we generate eight tasks containing different domain distributions for Smooth-DIL. We created ten tasks for CIL, where each task has two dominant classes. Finally, for Smooth-CIL, we produced eight tasks containing different class label distributions. We provide the details in the material to ensure completeness.

5.2 Training Methods

We use the standard PyTorch [16] implementation of ResNet-18 [5] in both protocols. Because our method does not use memory, we mainly compare our approach to other regularization-based methods (online-EWC, SI, LWF without memory). We also test ER and LWF as the baselines of memory-based methods. FOO-VB [29], which targets the task agnostic CL scenario, is also tested for comparison.

We use **Cumulative** and **Fine-tuning** as the upper bound and lower bound, respectively. **Cumulative** means that all of the data seen so far are available for each training. **Fine-tuning** means that the previous model parameters are used as the initial parameters for the next task. Furthermore, the memory budget is set to 400 for PACS and to 1000 for CIFAR-100.

To ensure a fair comparison, we turn off the data augmentation for all experiments. We rely on the Adam optimizer [8], which is re-initialized for each task. All hyperparameters are selected by a grid search on the validation set. Our network is trained on a single RTX 3070 8GB GPU and an i7-10700 8-core CPU.

5.3 Results

PACS Results. Table 1 and Fig. 4 show the results on the PACS dataset [12]. The results on the Smooth-CIL and Smooth-DIL show that our ER-LWF outperforms all other methods, including even the memory-based ones. In the smooth version, the similarities between different tasks are magnified. Thus, current data are more likely to reconstruct the previous loss function. That is why our method performs well and can even reach the upper bound.

From the DIL column in Table 1, we find that all regularization-based methods fail in this scenario, and that their performance is close to the lower bound (Fine-tuning), including our ER-LWF approach. In contrast, memory-based approaches perform better.

For the results on the PACS CIL, our ER-LWF performs best compared with other regularization-based methods, and its performance is very close to that of LWF with memory. However, there is still a big gap between the upper bound and other methods. This means that only replaying the previous data is not enough, and that the loss function or the gradient requires more constraints.

To conclude, our method does not work on DIL but performs well on the others. Furthermore, it consistently performs better than the LWF without memory.

Table 1. Results on DIL, Smooth-DIL, CIL, and Smooth for the PACS dataset [12]. **Acc** corresponds to Accuracy, while **BF** stands for Backward Transfer defined in [15]. For both of them, the bigger, the better. The budget of memory-based methods is set at 400 images in total. The value here is the percentage and is the average accuracy of the model over all experiments after training on all tasks. We display the best without-memory method in **bold** font. Methods with an asterisk * use memory.

Methods	DIL		Smooth-DIL		CIL		Smooth-CIL	
	Acc(%)↑	BF(%)↑	Acc(%)	BF(%)	Acc(%)	BF(%)	Acc(%)	BF(%)
Cumulative(upper)	54.2 ± 1.3	0.8 ± 0.1	59.5 ± 1.1	6.3 ± 0.3	58.0 ± 1.6	14.7 ± 0.8	58.91 ± 1.4	7.8 ± 0.5
Fine-tuning (lower)	30 ± 3.5	-38.9 ± 4.2	54.2 ± 2.5	4.5 ± 0.5	30.0 ± 2.9	4.7 ± 0.5	50.6 ± 2.6	2.4 ± 0.3
Online-EWC [2]	29.6 ± 2.8	-39.7 ± 4.5	54.8 ± 1.8	$4.6 \pm \pm 0.8$	30.7 ± 2.5	5.4 ± 0.6	50.8 ± 2.5	2.3 ± 0.3
SI [28]	$\mathbf{31.6 \pm 2.5}$	-38.5 ± 4.1	55.8 ± 1.7	$\mathbf{5.6 \pm 0.8}$	30 ± 2.8	4.3 ± 0.6	51.1 ± 2.2	2.7 ± 0.4
FOO-VB [29]	29.6 ± 2.5	$\mathbf{-21.3 \pm 2.7}$	58.5 ± 1.3	5.3 ± 0.6	38.5 ± 2.5	7.5 ± 0.8	55.4 ± 2.5	3.8 ± 0.6
LWF [13]	27.7 ± 3.1	-26.8 ± 2.5	57.4 ± 1.5	5.5 ± 0.7	29.5 ± 2.7	8.2 ± 1.2	55 ± 2.4	5.4 ± 0.5
ER* [18]	44.3 ± 1.8	-12.1 ± 1.5	54.4 ± 1.7	4.1 ± 0.6	37.8 ± 2.3	4.1 ± 0.6	52 ± 1.6	2.8 ± 0.3
LWF(memory)* [13]	47.7 ± 1.7	-7.1 ± 1.1	57.9 ± 1.1	5.9 ± 0.5	39.8 ± 2.2	4.2 ± 0.5	56 ± 1.5	5.3 ± 0.3
ER-LWF (ours)	30.2 ± 2.5	-32.5 ± 3.2	$\mathbf{58.9 \pm 1.3}$	$\mathbf{5.6 \pm 0.5}$	$\mathbf{38.8 \pm 2.5}$	$\mathbf{10.7 \pm 1.0}$	$\mathbf{56.1 \pm 1.8}$	$\mathbf{5.5 \pm 0.4}$

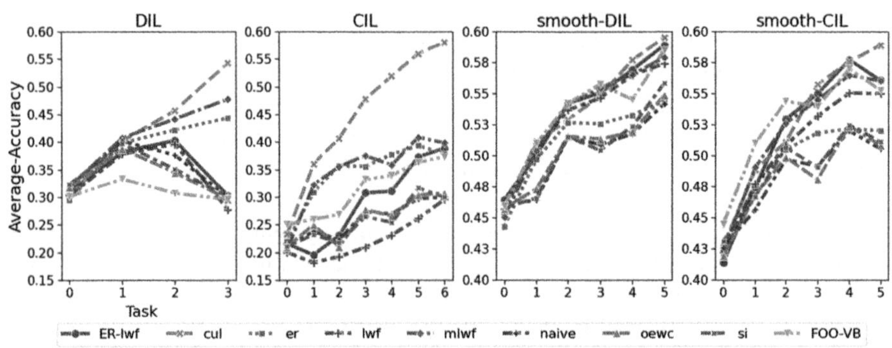

Fig. 4. Results related to the PACS dataset [12]. Testing accuracy (average on three runs) is provided after training on each task for different methods and different scenarios.

CIFAR-100 Results. The results on the CIFAR-100 dataset are presented in Table 2 and Fig. 5. As for Smooth-DIL, CIL, and Smooth-CIL, similar phenomena to the PACS experiments can be observed. Our proposed ER-LWF outperforms all other regularization-based methods, and its performance is even better than memory-based methods for smooth scenarios.

For the DIL setting with CIFAR-100, we do not observe the same result as for PACS. The LWF family's methods all perform well. This can be explained by the way we define the DIL scenario with CIFAR-100. As discussed in Sect. 5.1, CIFAR-100 has 20 superclasses, and each superclass contains five subclasses. In the proposed DIL protocol, each subclass is considered to be a domain, thereby leading to slight differences between tasks. As a result, we can reconstruct the previous objective more efficiently compared with the PACS DIL.

We also find that FOO-VB [29], which initially targets the task agnostic CL scenario (an extremely smooth scenario), is close to our method for the Smooth-DIL and

Smooth-CIL scenarios. However, our method performs much better when data distribution shifts more rapidly, as shown in the DIL and CIL plots of Fig. 5.

Compared to LWF, we designed EG-weight Equation (11) to self-regulate the original LWF loss. This can give more weight to similar data and less weight to unrelated data. Thus, the model can have more plasticity when the current data are different and more stability when the current data are similar. This is confirmed by the results obtained on the CIFAR-100 and PACS, from which we can observe that our method consistently outperforms or matches the performance of LWF without memory.

Table 2. Results on the CIFAR-100 dataset [10]. The budget for memory-based methods is set at 1000. It uses the same setting as Table 1.

Methods	DIL		Smooth-DIL		CIL		Smooth-CIL	
	Acc(%)	BF(%)	Acc(%)	BF(%)	Acc(%)	BF(%)	Acc(%)	BF(%)
Cumulative(upper)	38.8 ± 1.0	−1.4 ± 0.2	41.7 ± 1.2	8.8 ± 0.5	42.9 ± 1.1	14.5 ± 0.7	41.4 ± 1.2	9.2 ± 0.5
Fine-tuning (lower)	28.4 ± 1.5	−26.5 ± 1.2	35.3 ± 1.3	4.7 ± 0.6	15.5 ± 2.9	1.7 ± 0.5	33.1 ± 1.8	3.7 ± 0.5
Online-EWC [2]	30.3 ± 1.6	−30.7 ± 1.5	36.1 ± 1.3	4.6 ± 0.8	15.6 ± 3.1	2.2 ± 0.8	34.4 ± 1.8	4.2 ± 0.4
SI [28]	31.0 ± 1.4	−30.5 ± 1.6	37.7 ± 1.5	6.7 ± 0.8	15.5 ± 2.8	1.4 ± 0.6	33.1 ± 2.3	3.2 ± 0.5
FOO-VB [29]	31.4 ± 1.5	−29.9 ± 1.3	41.4 ± 1.6	7.5 ± 1.1	18.5 ± 2.2	3.4 ± 1.0	40.2 ± 1.5	6.2 ± 0.6
LWF [13]	36.9 ± 1.8	−19.6 ± 1.0	39.8 ± 1.4	5.9 ± 0.7	23.9 ± 2.5	5.9 ± 0.9	38.0 ± 1.6	5.2 ± 0.6
ER* [18]	31.3 ± 1.2	−23.0 ± 1.1	36.2 ± 1.2	4.4 ± 0.5	24.1 ± 1.5	3.4 ± 0.5	36.2 ± 1.5	5.5 ± 0.3
LWF(memory)* [13]	36.7 ± 1.3	−4.8 ± 0.5	39.8 ± 1.2	5.9 ± 0.6	26.0 ± 1.8	7.5 ± 0.6	38.3 ± 1.4	6.9 ± 0.6
ER-LWF (ours)	**37.0 ± 1.5**	**−12.6 ± 0.8**	**41.4 ± 1.2**	**7.9 ± 0.8**	**25.8 ± 2.0**	**8.2 ± 0.6**	**40.3 ± 1.4**	**7.9 ± 0.5**

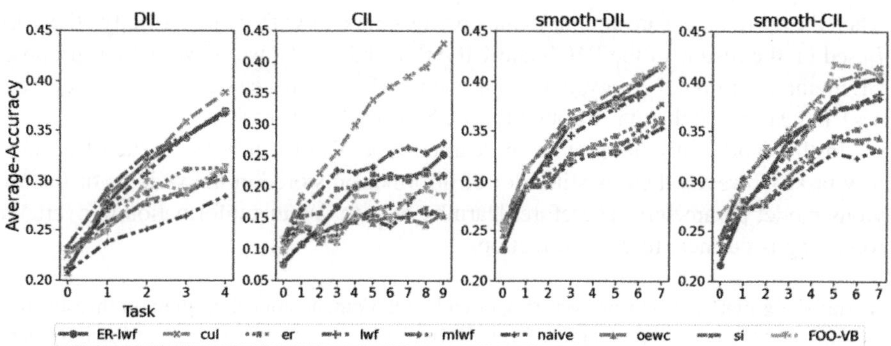

Fig. 5. Results related to the CIFAR-100 dataset [10]. Testing accuracy (average over three runs) is provided after training on each task for different methods and different scenarios.

6 Limitations

In this work, to better fit real-life applications, we make an assumption that task boundaries are blurred, in other words their data distributions overlap or at least have a certain degree of similarity. Smooth-CL setting, *i.e.*, Smooth-DIL and CIL, and regular CL setting, *i.e.* DIL and CIL, correspond to high-level and low-level similarity, respectively. However, if the task boundaries are well-defined with no overlapping of domains, then our method may fail since it makes use of the current data and the previous model output to approximate the previous loss function. If the previous model cannot recognize or provide a meaningful output, the EG-weight Eq. (11) will be close to zero. Then, our method degenerates to **Fine-tuning**. In our experiments, the most difficult CL scenario is the DIL setting on the PACS dataset. Since we assign each domain to a single task in DIL, the similarity between the data of different domains may be very slight when the gap between different domains is too large. In this situation, we cannot find similar data from the current task, meaning that the previous loss function cannot be reconstructed. From the DIL plot of Fig. 4, we can see that model performance degenerates rapidly in the final task. In our experiments, the last task of the DIL corresponds to *sketch*, which is the domain that is most different. We think that this is what accounted for this poor performance.

7 Conclusion

In this paper, we propose a new continual learning paradigm, namely Distribution-Shift Incremental Learning (DS-IL), which, by considering soft task boundaries as encountered in real-world applications, subsumes traditional Domain-Incremental Learning (DIL) and Class-Incremental Learning (CIL) scenarios. Furthermore, we propose ER-LWF, a novel CL method which extends LWF to deal with CL under the DS-IL setting where there are no well-defined task boundaries. It uses the entropy information of the previously learned model's output on the current data to self-regulate the original knowledge distillation loss. This EG-weight can provide the model with more stability when the current data are similar to the previous data, or with more plasticity otherwise. Based on the results of the PACS and CIFAR-100 datasets, we show that our proposed CL method, without memory, consistently outperforms the classic LWF (without memory) and can reach the upper bound for the Smooth-CL scenarios.

In this work, only the previously learned model's output is used when learning a new task. However, there is still a lot of information stored in the weights of the previous model parameters. Therefore, learning how to use this information to overcome forgetting is our next research direction.

Acknowledgments. This work was supported by the French national program of investment of the futur and the regions through the PSPC FAIR Waste project, as well as the French Research Agency, l'Agence Nationale de Recherche (ANR), through the projects Chiron (ANR-20-IADJ-0001-01), Aristotle (ANR-21-FAI1-0009-01), and Astérix (ANR-23-EDIA-0002-001).

References

1. Bang, J., Kim, H., Yoo, Y., Ha, J.W., Choi, J.: Rainbow memory: continual learning with a memory of diverse samples. In: Proceedings of the IEEE/CVF Conference on Computer Vision and Pattern Recognition (CVPR), pp. 8218–8227 (2021)
2. Chaudhry, A., Dokania, P.K., Ajanthan, T., Torr, P.H.S.: Riemannian walk for incremental learning: understanding forgetting and intransigence. In: Ferrari, V., Hebert, M., Sminchisescu, C., Weiss, Y. (eds.) ECCV 2018. LNCS, vol. 11215, pp. 556–572. Springer, Cham (2018). https://doi.org/10.1007/978-3-030-01252-6_33

3. Douillard, A., Cord, M., Ollion, C., Robert, T., Valle, E.: PODNet: pooled outputs distillation for small-tasks incremental learning. In: Proceedings of the IEEE European Conference on Computer Vision (ECCV) (2020)
4. Ebrahimi, S., et al.: Remembering for the right reasons: explanations reduce catastrophic forgetting. In: International Conference on Learning Representations (2021). https://openreview.net/forum?id=tHgJoMfy6nI
5. He, K., Zhang, X., Ren, S., Sun, J.: Deep residual learning for image recognition. In: 2016 IEEE Conference on Computer Vision and Pattern Recognition (CVPR), pp. 770–778 (2016)
6. Hinton, G.E., Vinyals, O., Dean, J.: Distilling the knowledge in a neural network. NIPS abs/1503.02531 (2015)
7. Hsu, Y.C., Liu, Y.C., Ramasamy, A., Kira, Z.: Re-evaluating continual learning scenarios: A categorization and case for strong baselines (2019)
8. Kingma, D.P., Ba, J.: Adam: A method for stochastic optimization. CoRR abs/1412.6980 (2015)
9. Kirkpatrick, J., Pascanu, R., et al.: Overcoming catastrophic forgetting in neural networks. Proc. Natl. Acad. Sci. **114**(13), 3521–3526 (2017)
10. Krizhevsky, A.: Learning multiple layers of features from tiny images. arxiv (2009)
11. Kurmi, V.K., Patro, B.N., Subramanian, V.K., Namboodiri, V.P.: Do not forget to attend to uncertainty while mitigating catastrophic forgetting. WACV (2021)
12. Li, D., Yang, Y., Song, Y., Hospedales, T.M.: Deeper, broader and artier domain generalization. In: 2017 IEEE International Conference on Computer Vision (ICCV), pp. 5543–5551. IEEE Computer Society, Los Alamitos, CA, USA (2017). https://doi.org/10.1109/ICCV.2017.591, https://doi.ieeecomputersociety.org/10.1109/ICCV.2017.591
13. Li, Z., Hoiem, D.: Learning without forgetting. PAMI **40**(12), 2935–2947 (2018). https://doi.org/10.1109/TPAMI.2017.2773081
14. Lomonaco, V., Maltoni, D.: Core50: a new dataset and benchmark for continuous object recognition. CoRR abs/1705.03550 (2017). http://arxiv.org/abs/1705.03550
15. Lopez-Paz, D., Ranzato, M.: Gradient episodic memory for continual learning. In: NIPS (2017)
16. Paszke, A., et al.: PyTorch: an imperative style, high-performance deep learning library. In: Wallach, H., Larochelle, H., Beygelzimer, A., d'Alché-Buc, F., Fox, E., Garnett, R. (eds.) Advances in Neural Information Processing Systems 32, pp. 8024–8035. Curran Associates, Inc. (2019)
17. Rebuffi, S.A., Kolesnikov, A., Sperl, G., Lampert, C.H.: iCaRL: incremental classifier and representation learning. CVPR, pp. 5533–5542 (2017)
18. Rolnick, D., Ahuja, A., Schwarz, J., Lillicrap, T., Wayne, G.: Experience replay for continual learning. In: Wallach, H., Larochelle, H., Beygelzimer, A., d'Alché-Buc, F., Fox, E., Garnett, R. (eds.) Advances in Neural Information Processing Systems. vol. 32. Curran Associates, Inc. (2019). https://proceedings.neurips.cc/paper/2019/file/fa7cdfad1a5aaf8370ebeda47a1ff1c3-Paper.pdf
19. Rusu, A.A., et al.: Progressive neural networks. CoRR abs/1606.04671 (2016). http://arxiv.org/abs/1606.04671
20. Shin, H., Lee, J.K., Kim, J., Kim, J.: Continual learning with deep generative replay. In: NIPS (2017)
21. Singh, P., Mazumder, P., Rai, P., Namboodiri, V.P.: Rectification-based knowledge retention for continual learning. CVPR abs/2103.16597 (2021). https://arxiv.org/abs/2103.16597
22. van de Ven, G.M., Tolias, A.S.: Three scenarios for continual learning. CoRR abs/1904.07734 (2019). http://arxiv.org/abs/1904.07734
23. Verma, V.K., Liang, K.J., Mehta, N., Rai, P., Carin, L.: Efficient feature transformations for discriminative and generative continual learning. CVPR abs/2103.13558 (2021). https://arxiv.org/abs/2103.13558

24. Volpi, R., Larlus, D., Rogez, G.: Continual adaptation of visual representations via domain randomization and meta-learning. In: Proceedings of the IEEE/CVF Conference on Computer Vision and Pattern Recognition (CVPR) (2021)
25. Wu, Y., et al.: Large scale incremental learning. In: Proceedings of the IEEE Conference on Computer Vision and Pattern Recognition, pp. 374–382 (2019)
26. Yin, H., et al.: Dreaming to distill: data-free knowledge transfer via deepinversion. In: The IEEE/CVF Conference on Computer Vision and Pattern Recognition (CVPR) (2020)
27. Yu, L., et al.: Semantic drift compensation for class-incremental learning. In: 2020 IEEE/CVF Conference on Computer Vision and Pattern Recognition (CVPR), pp. 6980–6989 (2020)
28. Zenke, F., Poole, B., Ganguli, S.: Continual learning through synaptic intelligence. In: Precup, D., Teh, Y.W. (eds.) Proceedings of the 34th International Conference on Machine Learning. Proceedings of Machine Learning Research, vol. 70, pp. 3987–3995. PMLR, International Convention Centre, Sydney, Australia (2017). http://proceedings.mlr.press/v70/zenke17a.html
29. Zeno, C., Golan, I., Hoffer, E., Soudry, D.: Task-agnostic continual learning using online variational bayes with fixed-point updates. Neural Comput. **33**(11), 3139–3177 (2021). https://doi.org/10.1162/neco_a_01430

Objects Detection on the Water Surface Using Satellite Imagery, Drones and Vessel-Based Imaging Applied for Logistics

Iheb Ben Salah[1], Martin J.-D. Otis[2](✉), Remy Rahem[3], and Mahassen Ardhaoui[2]

[1] National School of Computer Sciences, Manouba Campus, Manouba, Tunisia
[2] University of Quebec at Chicoutimi, 555 Bd. de l'Université, Chicoutimi, QC G7H 2B1, Canada
martin_otis@uqac.ca
[3] Centre de Géomatique du Québec, Cégep de Chicoutimi, 534 Rue Jacques-Cartier E, Chicoutimi, QC G7H 1Z6, Canada
https://lari.uqac.ca/

Abstract. Automation in the logistic process of vessel transport could be improved using satellite and drone imagery. As an example, finding the location of a point of interest on the surface of the water, such as a human, a buoy, a small ship without AIS or a cetacean, could be used for collision avoidance and search-and-rescue applications. The location could then be used for path planning and logistics. There are a wide variety of objects that can be found on the surface of water. However, there are no studies on the location and differentiation of these objects. This study suggests integrating six datasets from different sources, such as drone and satellite imagery, to validate the concept of mixing different data sources while maintaining adequate detection performance for different objects at the surface of water. Four models (YOLOv8s, YOLOv8m, YOLOv10m and Faster R-CNN:R50-FPN in the Detectron2 framework) were used to validate the feasibility of detecting four different objects (cetacean, small boat, buoy, human, and water (background)) under different conditions. This project will be integrated into an overall system that improves maritime safety and operations.

Keywords: Search and Rescue (SAR) · Maritime safety · Drones · Logistic simulator · Cetacean location · YOLO · Faster R-CNN · Detectron2

1 Introduction

The location of cetaceans is an important factor for navigation safety and social acceptability. Its knowledge could help improve transport logistics and reduce underwater noise pollution for cetaceans [50]. Moreover, human detection in the water is also an important issue after a ship wreck [24]. Between 2015 and 2022, more than 1.8 million people attempted to cross the Mediterranean Sea, with more than 23,000 reported dead or missing [26]. In 2021 alone, 112 ship losses resulted in 654 deaths and 1,044 missing persons, according to the International Maritime Organization (IMO) [37].

J. Röning and J. Filipe (Eds.): ROBOVIS 2025, CCIS 2629, pp. 469–487, 2026.
https://doi.org/10.1007/978-3-032-00986-9_30

Therefore, object detection at the surface of the water is a challenge as the image could come from many sources (satellite [19], drone or aerial imagery [3], vessel/USV-based imagery [30,33]). The characteristics of the water, such as light reflection and absorption, the intensity of light and other meteorological conditions (humidity, wind), combined with the waves, the swell and the foam on the water's surface reduce the detection capacity of objects [53]. The other issues are the size of the object, the geometry and the color at the surface of water. As an example, human and cetacean can appear partially on the surface of water. In this study, two main research applications are considered: maritime transport logistics and search and rescue (SAR). This research focuses specifically on the development and evaluation of a coordinated system using satellite imagery, UAVs, USVs, and advanced object detection models for maritime SAR operations. The study aims to improve the accuracy and speed of the detection of individuals in distress and the location of cetaceans at sea by integrating these technologies into simulated environments and validating their performance using real-world data. The scope of the research covers the following:

1. **Technological Integration:** The study investigates how satellite imagery, UAVs, USVs, and object detection models can be combined to improve the efficiency of SAR operations and cetacean detection.
2. **Simulation and Validation:** High-fidelity simulations are used to test and refine the proposed system, in conjunction with validation through real-time data.
3. **Object Detection Models:** The research explores different models, such as YOLO, and Faster R-CNN (R50-FPN, in the Detectron2 framework), evaluating their suitability for SAR missions and identification of cetaceans in maritime environments.

This project evaluates recent classification algorithms to detect a set of objects (human, cetacean, buoy, island, shore, small ship without AIS) at the surface of water. Despite advances in search and rescue (SAR) technology, there remains a significant gap in the ability to effectively detect and locate individuals in distress or locate cetaceans in vast and challenging marine environments. This raises critical research questions: How can existing satellite imagery, UAV and USV technologies be optimized to improve real-time detection accuracy? What are the most effective object detection models for such environments, and how can they be implemented in a multi-robots system? Therefore, the primary objective of this research is to develop and evaluate a system that combines images from satellites, UAV and USV, and advanced object detection algorithms to improve the identification of objects in the water.

In addition, this study examines the limitations of current SAR operations, focusing on improving detection accuracy and improving response times in maritime emergencies. The study hypotheses are grounded in the assumption that integrating UAVs, USVs, and object detection models will improve rescue efficiency and results. The originality of this study lies in its approach, combining high-fidelity simulations with real-time data to train and evaluate object detection models in SAR operations. In the next Sect. 2, the models used in different applications are presented. Unlike previous studies that focus on satellites, UAVs, or USVs independently, this research explores the coordinated use of all sources, forming a multi-robots system to address real-world challenges in maritime environments. The contribution of this work is two-fold: advancing the field of autonomous vessel logistic in SAR missions and vessel collision avoidance and providing a scalable solution for future operations. The methodology is then presented in Sect. 3. The main findings, presented in the results Sect. 4, are particularly relevant for government agencies, nongovernmental organizations (NGOs), and maritime rescue teams involved in emergency response planning and logistic of maritime transport. Finally, the study presents its limits in Sect. 5 with a final conclusion developed in Sect. 6.

2 Related Works

In recent years, significant progress has been made in developing technologies to improve search and rescue (SAR) operations, particularly in maritime settings. These advances primarily focus on enhancing the speed, accuracy and scope of SAR missions using unmanned aerial vehicles (UAVs), unmanned surface vessels (USVs), and robust object detection models. In addition, satellite imagery is currently used to find and detect cetaceans [19]. Object detection on the surface of water is used in many applications, such as person-overboard scenarios [24] or sea rescue operations [48], hazardous objects near the shore for collision avoidance [31], detection of whales or cetaceans for their protection [10], marine traffic management and security monitoring [35], and also garbage detection [9]. Given the growing number of maritime emergencies, research has increasingly explored how these technologies can work together to provide an efficient response in large and complex environments. First, the related works presents the automatic detection systems in Sect. 2.1, then some examples of the integration of a multisensor system in Sect. 2.2. The integration of these detection systems is then discussed in the Simulation Environments Sect. 2.3 with a special case using multirobots and swarm 2.4.

2.1 Automatic Detection Systems

A critical area of research within SAR is the use of automated detection systems. Studies by Gonçalves and Damas (2022) [18] and Wen et al. (2019) [54] highlight the application of YOLO-based object detection models to identify rescue targets at sea. Gonçalves and Damas (2022) [18] developed a UAV-mounted detection system using YOLOv4-tiny, achieving satisfactory results with a precision of 68% and a recall of 55%. Wen et al. (2019) [54] used a similar YOLOv3 framework, focusing on real-time detection of individuals who have fallen into water, with promising precision in controlled test scenarios. These works underscore the potential of using UAV-based detection models for SAR but also point out challenges like the need for larger, more diverse datasets to improve accuracy in real-world conditions. Then, an improvement is suggested using multi-sensor integration presented in the next Sect. 2.2.

2.2 Multi-sensor Integration for Enhanced Detection

SAR operations often occur in unpredictable environments, where visual conditions can vary significantly considering meteorological conditions and water conditions. To address these challenges, Burke et al. (2019) [7] conducted a pilot study using UAVs equipped with RGB and thermal cameras that demonstrated improved detection accuracy under difficult-to-see conditions. Multi-sensors setups such as these are crucial for ensuring reliable detection in low visibility and nighttime conditions, including snow conditions [14], allowing higher accuracy in SAR applications. The findings of this study [35] emphasize the importance of integrating multiple types of sensors to enhance the efficiency of maritime traffic management and security monitoring.

2.3 Simulation Environments and Custom Datasets for Model Training

Training object detection models in SAR requires datasets that accurately reflect the complexities of maritime environments. Poudel et al. (2023) [46] used a high-fidelity marine simulation environment to evaluate the YOLOv7 models, achieving an impressive detection accuracy of 97.8% with a model re-trained in the SeaDronesSee dataset. Furthermore, Varga et al. (2022) [51] introduced the SeaDronesSee dataset specifically for maritime SAR, providing a benchmark for detecting humans in open water. The work on simulation environments and custom datasets highlights the need for realistic data to improve SAR object detection models, as maritime conditions introduce unique challenges that standard datasets do not typically capture.

2.4 Coordinated Multi-robots System for SAR

Studies by Messmer et al. (2024) [40] explore the coordinated use of UAVs and ground stations for SAR. By leveraging Grad-CAM++ and YOLOv7 models, this research presents a framework for multi-robots system that reduces bandwidth limitations and improves decision-making for SAR operators. Multi-robots coordination not only extends the reach of SAR missions, but also provides more efficient coverage and redundancy in search operations, particularly in large and complex maritime environments.

Although previous research has addressed individual aspects of maritime search and rescue (SAR) technologies, such as UAV-based object detection, multisensor setups, and custom datasets tailored to SAR environments, this study aims to contribute by integrating these components into a coordinated multi-robots system. Specifically, it explores the combined use of UAVs and USVs to expand search coverage, improve detection accuracy, and support operational efficiency. By incorporating high-fidelity simulations alongside real-world data, the study addresses some of the limitations identified in an earlier study, including the need for more diverse datasets and better integration of autonomous systems. This approach seeks to enhance the applicability of object detection models such as YOLO and Faster R-CNN in dynamic maritime settings, providing a foundation for more reliable and adaptable SAR solutions, cetacean monitoring, and small ship (without AIS) tracking (Table 1).

Most studies consider detection (whale/non-whale [19], human/non-human [48]) without combining different objects in a variety of data sources (aerial, vessel on-board camera, satellite). While YOLO is widely used, other models, such as Detectron are less evaluated. Therefore, our study suggests integrating multiple datasets from different sources to evaluate different versions of the YOLO (one-stage object detection) and faster R-CNN: R50-FPN model (two-stage object detection).

Table 1. Comparison of Object Detection Models.

Reference	Simulation	Real-Time	Object Detection Model	Dataset	Single Robot	Multi-robots	Application
Goncalves et al. (2022) [18]	✓	✓	YOLOv4-Tiny	Not Custom (COCO) [34]	✓		SAR
Burke et al. (2019) [7]		✓	Simple Automated System	Custom	✓		SAR
Wen et al. (2019) [54]		✓	YOLOv3	Custom	✓		SAR
Poudel et al. (2023) [46]	✓	✓	YOLOv7 (SDS and COCO)	Custom	✓		SAR
Varga et al. (2022) [51]		✓	YOLOv5, Faster R-CNN, EfficientDet	Not Custom (SeaDronesSee Dataset [6,51])	✓		SAR
Messmer et al. (2024) [40]	✓		YOLOv7, Grad-CAM++	Not Custom [51]		✓	SAR
Borowicz et al. (2019) [5]	✓		CNN-Based Model	Not Custom (WorldView-3 [49], HiDef Aerial [23])	✓		Cetacean protection
Zhang et al. (2023) [57]	✓	✓	YOLOv5, YOLOv8	Not Custom (MOBDrone, SeaDronesSee [8]), [51]	✓		SAR
Paladin et al. (2023) [43]	✓	✓	AI-enhanced MCC	Not Custom (AIS-SART, exactEarth) [25]		✓	SAR
Keymasi et al. (2024) [28]	✓	✓	Modified YOLOv5 Small (YOLOv5s)	Not Custom (PSeg-SSDD [12])	✓		SAR
Leonidas et al. (2021) [29]	✓		AlexNet, VGG16, ResNet, Inception V3 and GoogleNet	MARVEL dataset [20]			Vessel monitoring

3 Methodology

The system includes an Unmanned Aerial Vehicule (UAV), an Unmanned surface Vehicule (USV), or a vessel (with embedded vision sensors) and satellite imagery included in a digital twin simulator. This system is included in a more general path planner that includes collision avoidance and waypoint attraction. The identification of an object on the surface of water is used in the logistic for the maritime transport described in the project [42], while the optimal path planning is described in [13]. Figure 1 shows the overall system for this project, including all data sources and the path planner. This figure is explained in the next sections.

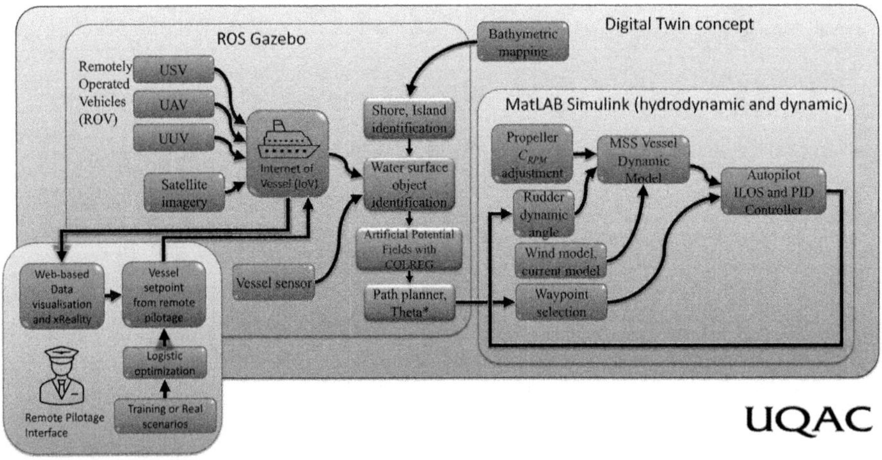

Fig. 1. System architecture applied to logistic for the maritime transport including the remote pilotage and digital twin concept (red box represents the current study, purple boxes represent [42]) and blue boxes are defined in [4]. (Color figure online)

3.1 Simulation Environment for the Digital Twin

The simulation environment, developed using ROS and Gazebo, plays a crucial role in the testing and refining of the SAR system. The environment replicates real maritime conditions and includes features such as realistic water dynamics and various weather scenarios. This setup allows the UAV and USV models to navigate simulated maritime conditions, testing their coordination, detection capabilities, and responses to various operational challenges. The ROS/Gazebo visual representation uses the hydrodynamics of the vessel designed in the MSS library [45] for Simulink Toolbox in MathWorks MatLAB. MSS library uses Integral Line Of Sight (ILOS) guidance law such as described in [55] with (Proportional-Integral-Derivative) with a reference feedforward controller that governs the autopilot system in order to follow a path generated by the Theta* algorithm [11]. This system can find a path according to the artificial potential field (APF) [32] that attracts a human in seawater or buoy (attractive point of interest) or repels the vessel approaching a cetacean [42].

3.2 UAV and USV Models

The SAR system integrates a UAV and a USV, each equipped with sensors to improve detection accuracy. The UAV provides aerial coverage, scanning wide areas from above, while the USV operates on the surface of the water for close-range detection. The system control framework uses ArduPilot SITL for autopilot control of the UAV and USV models. MAVROS serves as the bridge between ROS and ArduPilot, facilitating the exchange of telemetry data, sensor readings, and control commands. This setup allows for flexible command and control of the robotic swarm, with adjustable waypoint management and trajectory algorithms to accommodate varying SAR mission requirements.

Using `rqt`, we present a simplified nodes interconnexion in ROS. `rqt` is a graphical tool in ROS that allows visualization of the communication structure of the system. Figure 2 illustrates the communication graph generated by `rqt`, confirming that sensor information is being correctly transmitted and received across the system. This figure includes nodes for Gazebo simulation, a webcam, two drones (iris and boat), and a tf (transform) node. Topics such as `image_raw`, `camera_info`, `global_position`, `local_ position`, and `home_ position` are used to exchange data between these nodes.

3.3 Object Detection Models

Object detection is essential for identifying rescue targets in SAR missions. This study tests multiple models, including YOLOv8, YOLOv10, and Faster R-CNN (R50-FPN), evaluating their performance based on detection accuracy and computational efficiency. The YOLO model was selected based on the study [36] for one-stage object detection, while Faster R-CNN was selected based on [21] as two-stage object detectors. Faster R-CNN was used in [51], while YOLOv7 was used in [40], both in SAR applications, where the complexity of the environment demands a higher level of detection accuracy, even at the cost of processing speed. By including Faster R-CNN in our model comparison, we aim to explore how well a two-stage detector (Detectron2 framework using Faster R-CNN:R50-FPN) performs against the faster one-stage YOLO models, particularly in scenarios where detection precision is critical.

The models are trained on a custom dataset, with labeled objects such as humans, boats, cetaceans, and buoys, and tested in the simulation environment to assess their effectiveness under various conditions. Table 2 summarizes the comparison of these models, highlighting their respective strengths based on their metrics as explained by Liu et al. (2016) [36] and He et al. (2018) [21].

3.4 Data Preparation and Model Training

Dataset Collection and Annotation. An extensive dataset to train and evaluate object detection models was the main goal of this project phase. A variety of publicly available datasets that were specific to each point of interest, such as humans, boats, and other pertinent things, to guarantee precise and varied representation, were investigated.

The dataset comprises 6,376 images with 28,612 labeled objects, including humans, boats, cetaceans, and buoys [39]. Specifically, the dataset includes 13753 objects labeled

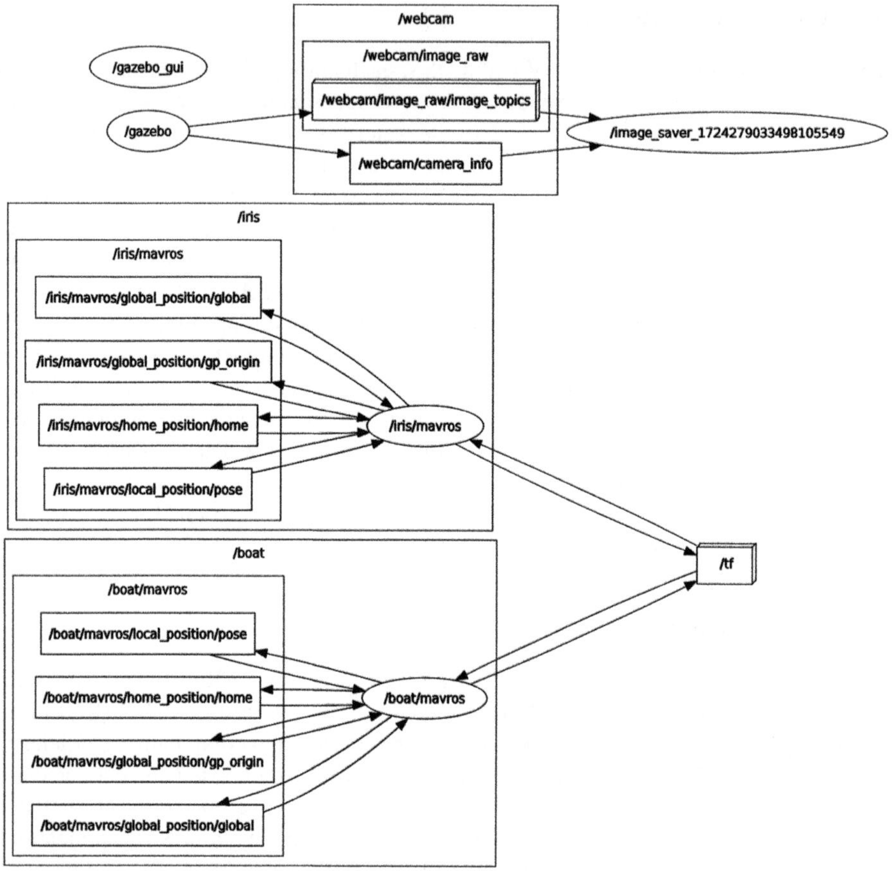

Fig. 2. Simplified ROS graph generated by `rqt`.

Table 2. Comparison of Object Detection Models for SAR Missions.

Model	mAP@0.5 (%)	mAP@0.5:0.95 (%)	FPS	Model Size (MB)
YOLOv8s [36]	81.5	44.9	43.2	143.8
YOLOv8m [36]	91.6	50.2	31.5	143.8
YOLOv10m [36]	92.8	51.3	29.6	173.8
Faster R-CNN (ResNet-50) [21]	42.0	29.2	10	98.6
Faster R-CNN (ResNet-101) [21]	44.1	31.3	8	173.6
Detectron2 (ResNet-50) [22,56]	44.8	31.9	12	104.6
Detectron2 (ResNet-101) [22,56]	46.9	33.9	10	179.6

as humans, 7072 labeled as boats, 5623 labeled as cetaceans and 2164 labeled as buoys. In addition, there are 11 null images, which do not contain objects of interest. Data annotation was performed using the Roboflow framework, with the dataset organized into 91% for training, 5% for validation, and 4% for testing. Figure 3 provides some examples of the data collected for this study.

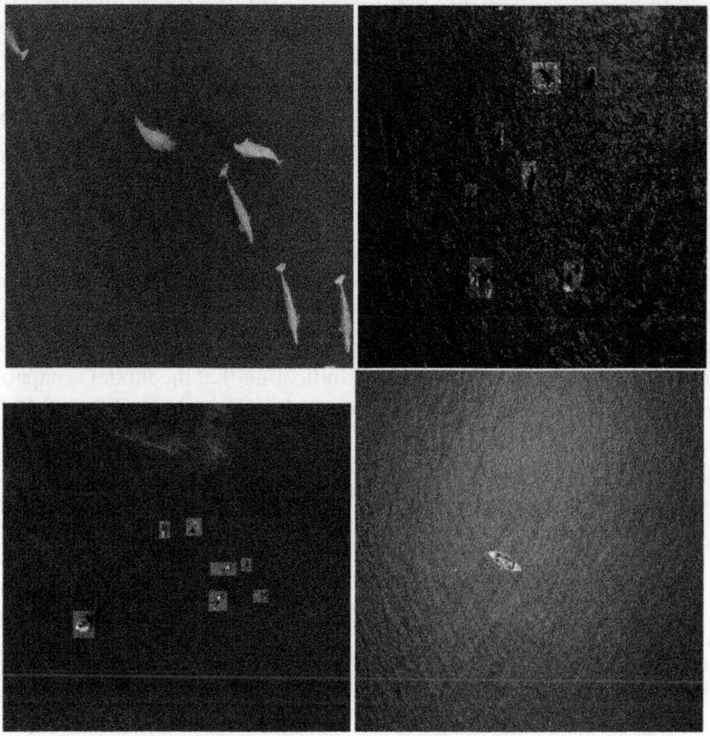

Fig. 3. Image examples from the dataset: a) Beluga using dataset [15], b) human using dataset [2], c) buoy using dataset [1], d) boat using dataset [27,38,47,52].

Data Augmentation and Processing. To enhance model performance, several augmentation techniques were applied, including horizontal and vertical flips, grayscale transformations on 15% of images, brightness adjustments (between -13% and +13%), and the addition of blur (up to 1px) and noise (0.58% of pixels). Preprocessing involved auto-orientation and resizing of images to a uniform 640 × 640 pixels, ensuring consistency across the dataset.

Model Training and Validation. YOLO models were trained on Kaggle's T4 GPU platform, running 100 epochs with a batch size of 64 and a learning rate of 0.05, while Faster R-CNN (R50-FPN) was trained using the Detectron2 framework on an institutional server with 1,140 iterations, a batch size of 16, and a base learning rate of 0.02. Model validation was performed within the simulation environment to evaluate performance in key metrics such as precision, recall, and mAP. The performance of each model was assessed using a validation data set tailored to mimic SAR scenarios, providing information on its suitability for real-time SAR applications.

4 Results and Discussion

This section presents the integration of advanced object detection models, the processes involved in image processing, and the rigorous training of these models. Additionally, it presents an in-depth analysis of the system's performance, providing key insights into its effectiveness and potential for real-world application. The validation process involved evaluating the models on the designated validation dataset, which represented 5% of the total data. We will be presenting the performance metrics for the YOLOv8s, YOLOv8m, YOLOv10m, and Faster R-CNN (R50-FPN) models to evaluate its effectiveness. The selection of these models was influenced by both the quantitative performance metrics provided in the literature (one-stage detection tasks) and the specific demands of the simulation environment suggested.

YOLOv8m model appears to be training effectively. The loss functions are decreasing, as shown in the Figs. 4, suggesting that the model is learning from the data. The evaluation metrics, including precision in Fig. 4(d), recall in Fig. 4(e), and mAP in Fig. 4(i)(j), are also showing improvement, indicating that the model is capable of accurately detecting and classifying objects in the validation set. An APm of 40.7 indicates solid overall performance, and an AP50 of 68.5 suggests good detection of objects with moderate overlap with ground-truth bounding boxes. The precision of 85.3 is also high, which means that the detections predicted by the model are generally correct.

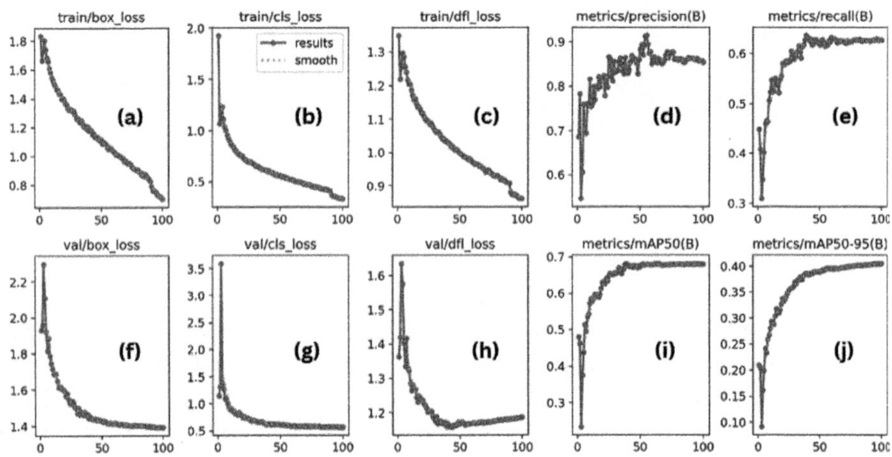

Fig. 4. Training results for yolov8m.

The confusion matrix is shown in Fig. 5 for YOLOv8m. This matrix provides a detailed breakdown of the model's predictions, showing the true positives, false positives, and false negatives. The provided matrix reveals that the YOLOv8m model demonstrates strong performance in object classification, with notable accuracy in distinguishing cetaceans and boats from other categories. However, it exhibits some challenges in differentiating between "buoy" and "human" instances, occasionally misclassifying them.

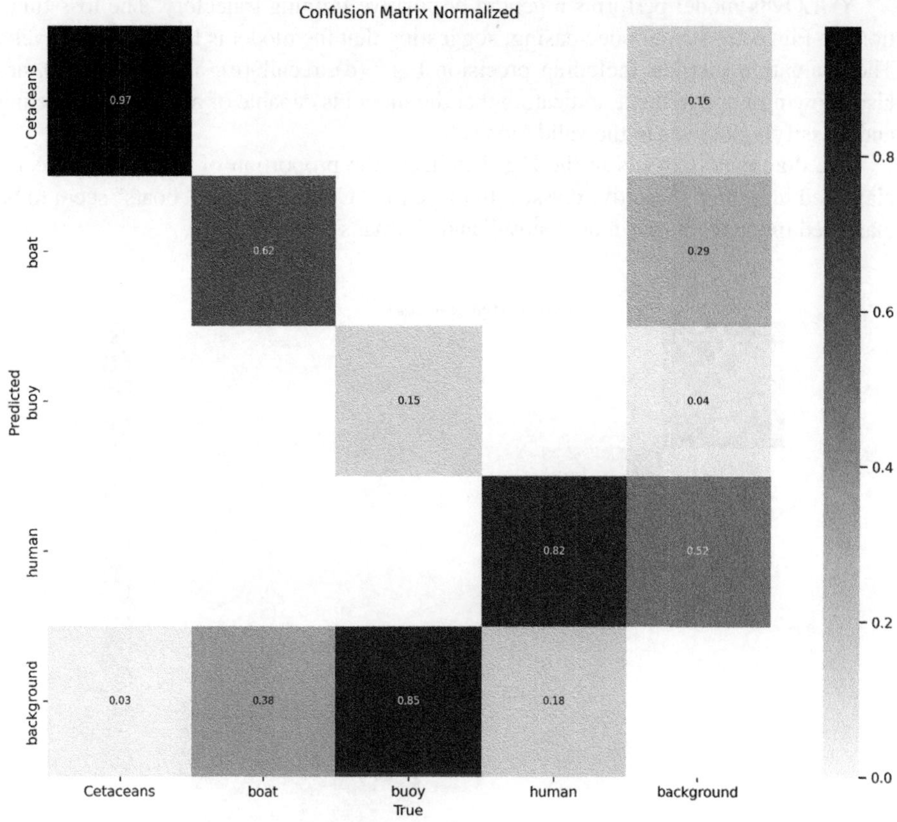

Fig. 5. Confusion matrix normalized for yolov8m.

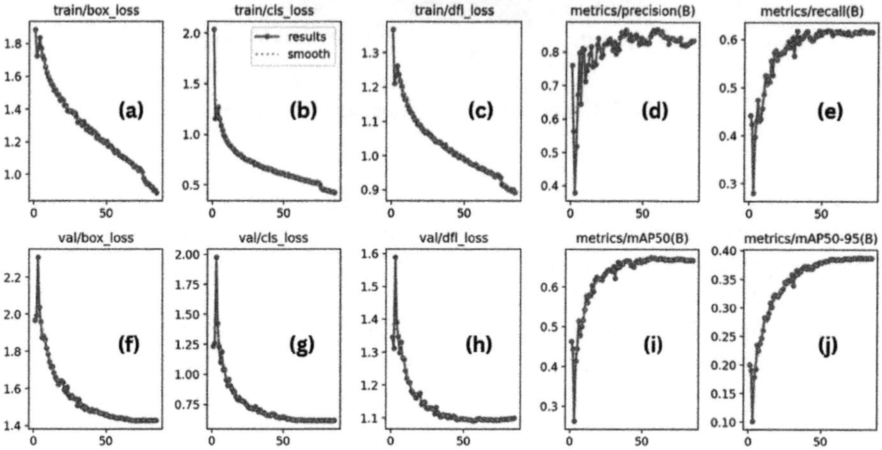

Fig. 6. Training results for yolov8s.

YOLOv8s model performs a generally positive training trajectory. The loss functions in Fig. 6 are steadily decreasing, suggesting that the model is learning effectively. The evaluation metrics, including precision Fig. 6(d), recall6(e), and mAP6(i)(j), are also showing improvement, indicating that the model is capable of accurately detecting and classifying objects in the validation set.

The diagonal elements in the Fig. 7 indicate the proportion of instances correctly classified into their respective classes. In this case, "Cetaceans" and "boats" seem to be classified more accurately than "buoys" and "humans".

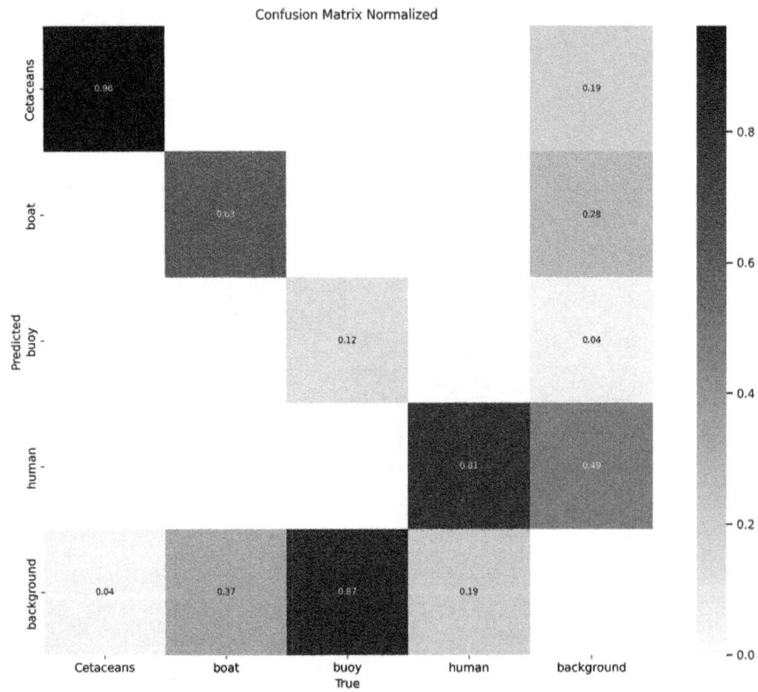

Fig. 7. Confusion matrix normalized for yolov8s.

The Fig. 8 illustrates the decreasing loss curves. These curves show that the model is converging towards an optimal solution. Evaluation metrics like recall and mAP show a general improvement in performance over time, suggesting that the model is becoming more accurate in detecting and classifying objects. The optimizations seem to be having a positive impact, as evidenced by the reduced detection loss in the optimized model.

The diagonal elements represented in the confusion matrix in Fig. 9, which represent correct classifications, are generally strong, suggesting good accuracy for most classes. However, there is notable confusion between "buoy" and "human" instances, indicating potential areas for improvement. The model also exhibits some difficulty in correctly classifying "background" instances.

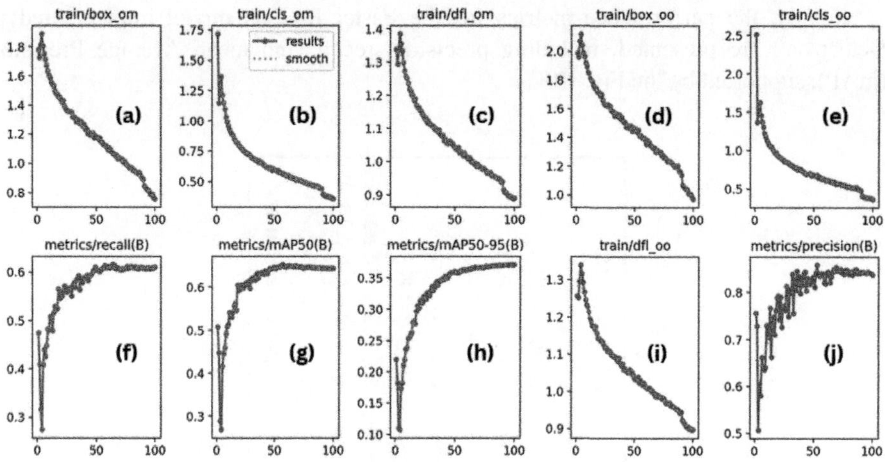

Fig. 8. Training results for yolov10m.

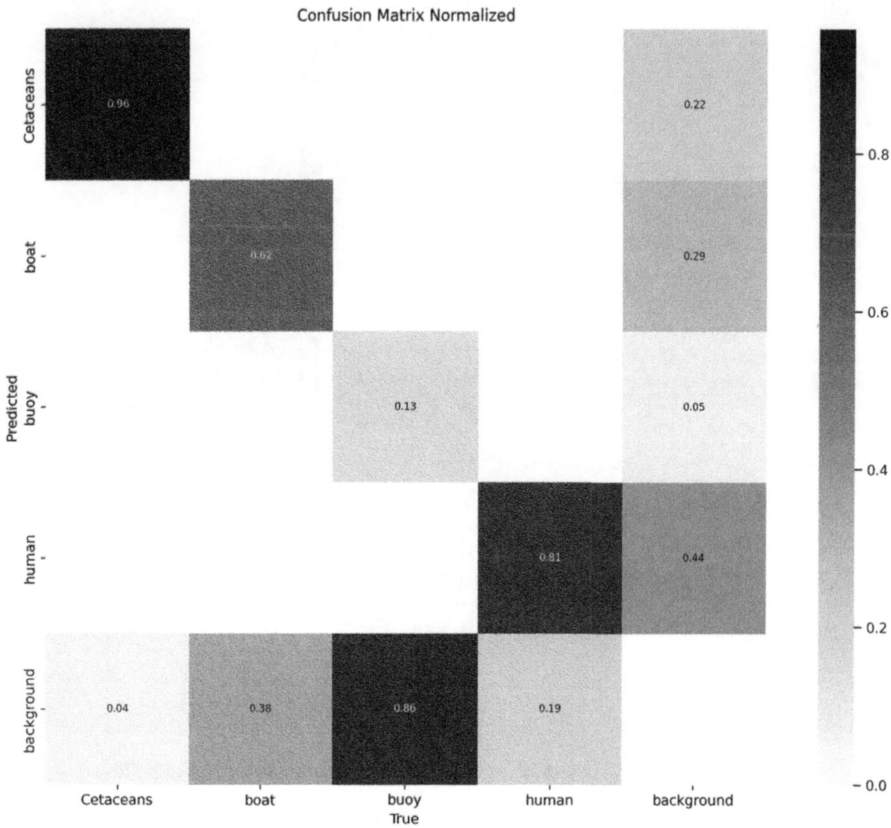

Fig. 9. Confusion matrix normalized for yolov10m.

Finally, the performance metrics for the Faster R-CNN model implemented in Detectron2 are presented, including precision, recall, and mean Average Precision (mAP), supported by the Fig. 10.

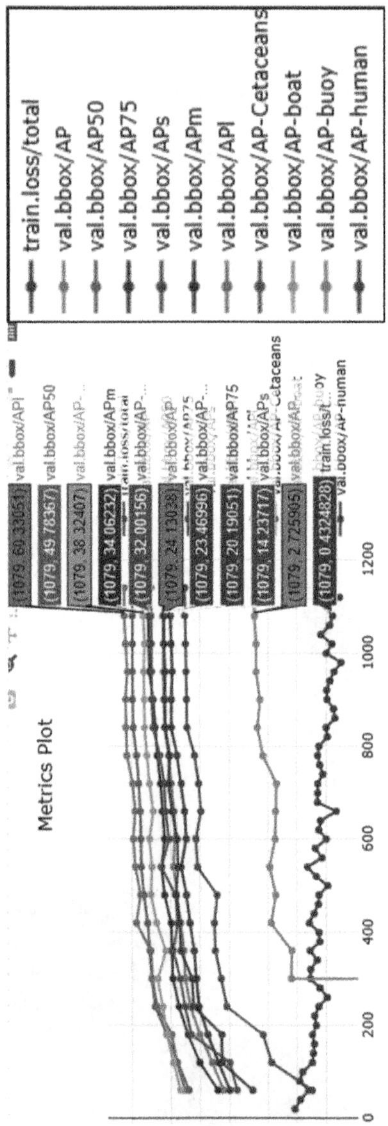

Fig. 10. Performance metrics for the Detectron2 Faster R-CNN (R50-FPN).

In this section, we evaluated the performance of four object detection models: YOLOv8s, YOLOv8m, YOLOv10m, and Faster R-CNN (R50-FPN). The YOLOv8m model achieved the highest mean Average Precision (APm) of 40.7, with an AP50 of 68.5 and precision of 85.3. YOLOv8s followed with an APm of 38.8, AP50 of 67.1, and precision of 84.2. YOLOv10m showed an APm of 37.2, AP50 of 64.4, and precision of 84.3. The Faster R-CNN (R50-FPN) model recorded an APm of 34.06, AP50 of 49.78, and a train loss of 0.432. These metrics highlight the relative strengths and performance of each model in detecting and classifying objects within the simulation environment.

5 Limits of the Study

This study evaluates some algorithms for detecting objects at the water surface. It also suggests an architecture for the implementation of the system. However, this study does not focus on the following points, which should be considered as future works:

1. **Testing or Developing Autonomous Navigation:** The development of different autonomous navigation algorithms for the robotic swarm is outside the scope of this research; however, some recent research suggests some solutions to avoid cetacean [16] and human rescue [48].
2. **Ethical and Regulatory Considerations:** Although the importance of these aspects is acknowledged, they fall outside the scope of this work, which is primarily technical in nature. This paper does not attempt to identify the person at the surface of the water. Moreover, navigation safety uses COLREG rules and path adaptation [17].
3. **Environmental Factors:** Although environmental challenges are considered in simulations (e.g. weather and sea conditions), the study does not take into account the ecological impact of the use of autonomous systems in maritime transportation and SAR operations [44].

By clarifying these limits, the study seeks to contribute to the advancement of SAR technology and the logistics of maritime transport without delving into the development of swarm navigation systems or other areas beyond the technical coordination of UAVs, USVs and detection models.

6 Conclusion

After gathering, organizing and processing the data from the images, we trained and validated a number of object identification models, such as Faster R-CNN (R50-FPN), YOLOv8s, YOLOv8m, and YOLOv10m. The performance of every model was carefully evaluated, offering insightful information about how well they worked in our simulation environment.

The results demonstrated the efficacy of our comprehensive strategy, with YOLOv8m achieving the highest mean Average Precision (APm). One notable flaw discovered during the testing phase was the recognition of buoys, which are critical for navigation and identifying people in seawater. This constraint implies that improving the dataset used to train the detection algorithms could increase performance. Specifically, balancing the dataset and include more buoy objects would likely result in improved detection accuracy and reliability.

Future work could address the detection limitation by augmenting the dataset with more buoy instances to improve accuracy. Additionally, there is significant potential for advancement by integrating autonomous navigation algorithms for the swarm such as those presented in [41]. This would enhance the system's ability to navigate complex environments and interact more dynamically, pushing the boundaries of autonomous robotics capabilities, including autonomous cargo (vessel).

Acknowledgments. Iheb Ben Salah received financial support from MITACS under the Globalink Research Internship Program (international undergraduate training, 12-week internship).

References

1. Eunjae : Plus_human__noboatbuoylabel_to_a dataset (2024). https://universe.roboflow.com/eunjae/plus_human__noboatbuoylabel_to_a. visited on 2024-12-12
2. SARDet : Sardatasetmasar dataset (2024). https://universe.roboflow.com/sardet-u93q0/sardatasetmasar. visited on 2024-12-12
3. Aniceto, A.S., Biuw, M., Lindstrøm, U., Solbø, S.A., Broms, F., Carroll, J.: Monitoring marine mammals using unmanned aerial vehicles: quantifying detection certainty. Ecosphere **9**(3) (2018). https://doi.org/10.1002/ecs2.2122
4. Ardhaoui, M., Otis, M.J.D., Diagne, S.: Indirect vessel velocity control to reduce the impact of underwater noise at cetacean locations. In: 20th International Conference on Automation Science and Engineering (CASE), pp. 1012–1017. IEEE (2024). https://doi.org/10.1109/CASE59546.2024.10711544
5. Borowicz, A., et al.: Aerial-trained deep learning networks for surveying cetaceans from satellite imagery. PLoS ONE **14**(10), e0212532 (2019)
6. Bovcon, B., Muhovič, J., Vranac, D., Mozetič, D., Perš, J., Kristan, M.: Mods–a USV-oriented object detection and obstacle segmentation benchmark. IEEE Transactions on Intelligent Transportation Systems (2021)
7. Burke, C., et al.: Requirements and limitations of thermal drones for effective search and rescue in marine and coastal areas. Drones **3**(4) (2019). https://doi.org/10.3390/drones3040078
8. Cafarelli, D., et al.: MOBDrone: A dataset for person overboard and maritime object detection (2021).https://doi.org/10.48550/arXiv.2203.07973. international Maritime Data Initiative
9. Chen, L., Zhu, J.: Water surface garbage detection based on lightweight YOLOv5. Sci. Rep. **14**(1) (2024). https://doi.org/10.1038/s41598-024-55051-3
10. Cubaynes, H.C., Fretwell, P.T.: Whales from space dataset, an annotated satellite image dataset of whales for training machine learning models. Sci. Data **9**(1) (2022). https://doi.org/10.1038/s41597-022-01377-4
11. Daniel, K., Nash, A., Koenig, S., Felner, A.: Theta*: any-angle path planning on grids. J. Artif. Intell. Res. **39**, 533–579 (2010). https://doi.org/10.1613%2Fjair.2994
12. Dataset Authors: PSeg-SSDD: Pixel-wise segmentation SAR ship detection dataset. https://pseg-ssdd-dataset.org (2023)
13. Deshmukh, Y., Otis, M.J., Diagne, S.: Nautical: navigation aid using u-net and $theta^*$ with integrated collision avoidance and landmarking. In: International conference on Robotic, Computer Vision and Intelligent Systems (ROBOVIS). Springer CCIS (2025)

14. Fan, X., Xiao, D., Li, Q., Gong, R.: Snow-CLOCs: camera-lidar object candidate fusion for 3D object detection in snowy conditions. Sensors **24**(13) (2024). https://doi.org/10.3390/s24134158
15. FAU: Beluga 1080 Dataset (2022). https://universe.roboflow.com/fau-eqjge/beluga_1080. visited on 2024-12-10
16. Gende, S.M., Vose, L., Baken, J., Gabriele, C.M., Preston, R., Noble Hendrix, A.: Active whale avoidance by large ships: components and constraints of a complementary approach to reducing ship strike risk. Front. Marine Sci. **6**(SEP) (2019). https://doi.org/10.3389/fmars.2019.00592
17. Gleeson, J., Dunbabin, M., Ford, J.J.: Colreg scenario classification and compliance evaluation with temporal and multi-vessel awareness for collision avoidance systems. Ocean Eng. **313** (2024). https://doi.org/10.1016/j.oceaneng.2024.119552
18. Gonçalves, L., Damas, B.: Automatic detection of rescue targets in maritime search and rescue missions using UAVs. In: International Conference on Unmanned Aircraft Systems (ICUAS), pp. 1638–1643 (2022). https://doi.org/10.1109/ICUAS54217.2022.9836137
19. Green, K.M., et al.: Gray whale detection in satellite imagery using deep learning. Remote Sens. Ecol. Conserv. **9**(6), 829–840 (2023). https://doi.org/10.1002/rse2.352
20. Gundogdu, E., Solmaz, B., Yücesoy, V., Koç, A.: MARVEL: a large-scale image dataset for maritime vessels. In: Lai, S.-H., Lepetit, V., Nishino, K., Sato, Y. (eds.) ACCV 2016. LNCS, vol. 10115, pp. 165–180. Springer, Cham (2017). https://doi.org/10.1007/978-3-319-54193-8_11
21. He, K., Gkioxari, G., Dollár, P., Girshick, R.: Mask R-CNN (2018). https://arxiv.org/abs/1703.06870, arXiv 1703.06870
22. He, K., Zhang, X., Ren, S., Sun, J.: Deep residual learning for image recognition. In: Proceedings of the IEEE Conference on Computer Vision and Pattern Recognition (CVPR), pp. 770–778 (2016)
23. HiDef Aerial Surveying Ltd.: Hidef aerial whale survey dataset. https://hidefsurveying.co.uk (2022). Accessed: [Insert Date]
24. Hoehner, F., Langenohl, V., Akyol, S., el Moctar, O., Schellin, T.E.: Object detection and tracking in maritime environments in case of person-overboard scenarios: an overview. J. Marine Sci. Eng. **12**(11) (2024). https://doi.org/10.3390/jmse12112038
25. International Maritime Organization (IMO): AIS-SART dataset: Maritime vessel tracking data (2023). https://www.imo.org. Accessed 12 Dec 2024
26. International Organization for Migration: Missing migrants project, migration within the mediterranean (2024). https://missingmigrants.iom.int/region/mediterranean. Accessed 9 Dec 2024
27. ituscrs: trgenelv3 dataset (2024). https://universe.roboflow.com/ituscrs/trgenelv3. visited on 2024-12-11
28. Keymasi, M., Ghozatlou, O., Datcu, M.: Goal-oriented semantic modules for SAR ship detection. In: 2024 International Workshop on the Theory of Computational Sensing and its Applications to Radar, Multimodal Sensing and Imaging (CoSeRa), pp. 16–20. IEEE (2024)
29. Leonidas, L.A., Jie, Y.: Ship classification based on improved convolutional neural network architecture for intelligent transport systems. Information (Switzerland) **12**(8) (2021). https://doi.org/10.3390/info12080302
30. Li, C., Wang, L., Liu, Y., Zhang, S.: Lightweight water surface object detection network for unmanned surface vehicles. Electronics (Switzerland) **13**(15) (2024). https://doi.org/10.3390/electronics13153089
31. Li, C., Wang, L., Liu, Y., Zhang, S.: Lightweight water surface object detection network for unmanned surface vehicles. Electronics **13**(15) (2024). https://doi.org/10.3390/electronics13153089

32. Li, L., Wu, D., Huang, Y., Yuan, Z.M.: A path planning strategy unified with a colregs collision avoidance function based on deep reinforcement learning and artificial potential field. Appl. Ocean Res. **113** (2021). https://doi.org/10.1016/j.apor.2021.102759
33. Li, Z., Ren, H., Yang, X., Wang, D., Sun, J.: LWS-YOLOv7: a lightweight water-surface object-detection model. J. Marine Sci. Eng. **12**(6) (2024). https://doi.org/10.3390/jmse12060861
34. Lin, T.Y., et al.: Microsoft COCO: common objects in context. In: European Conference on Computer Vision, pp. 740–755. Springer (2014)
35. Liu, Q., Chen, H., Zhao, F.: Maritime target detection algorithm based on fusion of visible and infrared images. J. Supercomput. **81**(1) (2025). https://doi.org/10.1007/s11227-024-06509-8
36. Liu, W., et al.: SSD: single shot MultiBox detector, pp. 21–37. Springer (2016). https://doi.org/10.1007/978-3-319-46448-0_2
37. López-Otero, J.: Human migrations in the western mediterranean. Taylor & Francis Group (2024). https://doi.org/10.4324/9781003458494-17
38. Marine ship 3: Ship-aerials-3-cleaned dataset (2023). https://universe.roboflow.com/marine-ship-3/ship-aerials-3-cleaned. visited on 2024-12-10
39. marineenv: Marine_environment1 dataset (2024). https://universe.roboflow.com/marineenv/marine_environment1. visited on 2024-12-10
40. Messmer, M., Kiefer, B., Varga, L.A., Zell, A.: UAV-assisted maritime search and rescue: A holistic approach (2024). https://arxiv.org/abs/2403.14281, arXiv 2403.14281
41. Miao, F., Li, H., Mei, X.: Three-dimensional path planning of UAVs for offshore rescue based on a modified coati optimization algorithm. J. Marine Sci. Eng. **12**(9) (2024). https://doi.org/10.3390/jmse12091676
42. Otis, M.J.D., Deshmukh, Y., Diagne, S.: Vessel optimal trajectory and path adaptation for reducing noise at cetacean location under velocity constraints. In: OCEANS - Halifax, pp. 1–6 (2024). https://doi.org/10.1109/OCEANS55160.2024.10754583
43. Paladin, Z., Fountoulakis, E., Lukšić, Ž., Kapidani, N., Ribar, D., Boustras, G.: Advanced mission critical communication in maritime search and rescue actions. In: 2023 27th International Conference on Information Technology (IT), pp. 1–6. IEEE (2023)
44. Park, S., Lee, H., Kim, D.: Regulatory compliance and operational efficiency in maritime transport: strategies and insights. Transp. Policy **155**, 161–177 (2024). https://doi.org/10.1016/j.tranpol.2024.06.024
45. Perez, T., Smogelif, o., Fossenf, T., Sorensen, A.: An overview of the marine systems simulator (MSS): a Simulink toolbox for marine control systems. Model. Ident. Control **27**(4), 259–275 (2006)
46. Poudel, R., Lima, L., Andrade, F.: A novel framework to evaluate and train object detection models for real-time victims search and rescue at sea with autonomous unmanned aerial systems using high-fidelity dynamic marine simulation environment. In: Winter Conference on Applications of Computer Vision Workshops (WACVW), pp. 239–247 (2023). https://doi.org/10.1109/WACVW58289.2023.00030
47. Shehryar Asim: Ship detection 1 dataset (2022). https://universe.roboflow.com/shehryar-asim/ship-detection-1. visited on 2024-12-11
48. Sruthy, K., et al.: Ocean wings-human identification using drone for sea rescue operations. In: International Conference on E-Mobility, Power Control and Smart Systems: Futuristic Technologies for Sustainable Solutions (ICEMPS). IEEE (2024). https://doi.org/10.1109/ICEMPS60684.2024.10559295
49. Technologies, M.: Worldview-3 satellite imagery dataset. https://www.maxar.com/products/worldview-3 (2022). accessed: [Insert Date]

50. Turgeon, S., Martins, C.C., Bégin-Marchand, C., Chartrand, C., Ménard, N.: Automatic identification system vessel tracking data reports to promote conservation and restoration of the St. Lawrence estuary beluga habitat. Marine Policy **172** (2025). https://doi.org/10.1016/j.marpol.2024.106494
51. Varga, L.A., Kiefer, B., Messmer, M., Zell, A.: SeaDronesSee: a maritime benchmark for detecting humans in open water. In: Winter Conference on Applications of Computer Vision (WACV), pp. 3686–3696. IEEE (2022). https://doi.org/10.1109/WACV51458.2022.00374
52. VTMIT: AI pathways project dataset (2024). https://universe.roboflow.com/vtmit/ai-pathways-project. visited on 2024-12-11
53. Wang, J., Duan, J., Xie, G., Fang, R., Zhu, W., Fu, W.: Sea surface target image enhancement method based on separable reflection and refraction. Optics Laser Technol. **181** (2025).https://doi.org/10.1016/j.optlastec.2024.112012
54. Wen, L., et al.: Method for autonomously identifying people falling into water based on multi-rotor unmanned aerial vehicle (2019). https://www.patentguru.com/CN110321775A, china patent number CN110321775A
55. Wiig, M.S., Pettersen, K.Y., Ruud, E.L.M., Krogstad, T.R.: An integral line-of-sight guidance law with a speed-dependent lookahead distance. In: European Control Conference, pp. 1269–1276 (2018)
56. Wu, Y., Kirillov, A., Massa, F., Lo, W.Y., Girshick, R.: Detectron2. https://github.com/facebookresearch/detectron2 (2019)
57. Zhang, Y., Tao, Q., Yin, Y.: A lightweight man-overboard detection and tracking model using aerial images for maritime search and rescue. Remote Sens. **16**(1), 165 (2023)

A Flexible Output Distribution for Regression-Based Probabilistic Long-Term Human Trajectory Prediction

Ronny Hug(✉), Stefan Becker, Wolfgang Hübner, Michael Arens, and Jürgen Beyerer

Fraunhofer Center for Machine Learning, Fraunhofer IOSB, Karlsruhe, Germany
{ronny.hug,stefan.becker,wolfgang.huebner, michael.arens,juergen.beyerer}@iosb.fraunhofer.de
https://www.iosb.fraunhofer.de/

Abstract. Probabilistic models for sequential data are the basis for a variety of applications concerned with processing timely ordered information. The predominant approach in this domain is given by recurrent neural networks, implementing either a transformative approach (e.g. Variational Autoencoders or Generative Adversarial Networks) or a regression-based approach, i.e. variations of Mixture Density networks (MDN). While these approaches effectively approximate complex probability distributions over full trajectories, their respective output distributions fall short in terms of post-hoc inference capabilities. To overcome this limitation, we extend on an MDN variant, which parameterizes (mixtures of) probabilistic Bézier curves ($\mathcal{N}$-Curves), allowing us to establish a connection to the framework of Gaussian processes. For this, we show that $\mathcal{N}$-Curves are a special case of non-stationary Gaussian processes (denoted as $\mathcal{N}$-GP) and then derive corresponding mean and kernel functions for different modalities. Then, we propose the use of this MDN variant as a data-dependent generator for $\mathcal{N}$-GP prior distributions, resulting in a novel probabilistic trajectory prediction model that inherently supports post-hoc Bayesian inference. We show the advantages granted by this combined prediction model in the context of long-term human trajectory prediction.

Keywords: Probabilistic human trajectory prediction · Mixture density networks · Gaussian processes

1 Introduction

Models of sequential data play an integral role in a range of applications related to representation learning, sequence synthesis and prediction. Thereby, with real-world data often being subject to noise and detection or annotation errors, probabilistic models are favorable. Focusing on long-term human trajectory[1] prediction as an exemplary task, where given a sequence of spatial positions $\mathcal{X}_{\text{obs}} = \{x_1, ..., x_{N_{\text{obs}}}\}$

[1] A trajectory is defined as a sequence of locations, with a velocity profile (implicitly) attached to it.

J. Röning and J. Filipe (Eds.): ROBOVIS 2025, CCIS 2629, pp. 488–509, 2026.
https://doi.org/10.1007/978-3-032-00986-9_31

(the *observation*), a probabilistic trajectory prediction model is tasked to estimate the unknown conditional distribution $p_{fut}(\mathcal{X}_{\text{pred}}|\mathcal{X}_{\text{obs}})$ over the next N_{pred} positions $\mathcal{X}_{\text{pred}} = \{x_{N_{\text{obs}}+1}, ..., x_{N_{\text{obs}}+N_{\text{pred}}}\}$, capturing the multi-modal nature of the task.

Probabilistic trajectory prediction models are commonly based[2] on either Gaussian Processes [44] (e.g. [9,37]) or more prevalently on neural networks either using stochastic weights (Bayesian Neural Networks (*BNN*, [4,6,12])), stochastic input (transformative[3] neural models, primarily conditional Variational Autoencoders (*cVAE*, [7,28,46]), conditional Generative Adversarial Networks (*cGAN*, [15,38,51]) and more recently conditional diffusion models (*cDDPM*, [19,47])), or parameterizing mixture distributions (Mixture Density Networks (*MDN*) [3,17]) combined with recurrent neural networks for handling sequential data in an autoregressive manner.

A crucial characteristic of probabilistic trajectory prediction models is their ability to approximate complex-structured, multi-modal probability distributions. While this is granted to different degrees by relevant models described above, this paper additionally takes a model's post-hoc inference capabilities, defined as the ability to manipulate or re-purpose the output distribution p_{out} after generation, into consideration. This, however, turns out to be a common weak spot in these models. Neural models with stochastic components are capable of approximating complex probability distributions by allowing the generation of samples from p_{fut}, which typically requires computationally expensive Monte Carlo methods. Consequently, these models yield a sample-based output distribution p_{out} given by a set of sample trajectories. This limits post-hoc inference to statistical analyses on generated sample populations. Conversely, MDN-based models are deterministic and map a given input onto the parameters of a sequence of mixture distributions, either directly or through application of a sequential Monte Carlo approach. As a result, these models potentially offer less flexibility in approximating p_{fut}, but are generally more stable and less computationally expensive during training. Further, by directly generating parametric distributions, MDNs provide better support for post-hoc inference. However, challenges in accessing correlations between time steps remain. Figure 1 illustrates the basic prediction problem and the approximation approaches described previously.

Contribution: To address these issues, we present a proof of concept for a novel, more flexible output distribution for probabilistic trajectory prediction models, which retains approximation capabilities while adding post-hoc inference as an inherent feature. To achieve this, we extend on a variation of MDNs proposed by Hug et al. [23], which operates in the domain of parametric curves instead of the data domain. The model was originally designed as an alternative base model in line with the ones listed above and tackles difficulties with multi-modal inference in MDN-based probabilistic sequence models. It allows to infer multiple time steps in a single inference step and is built on a probabilistic extension of Bézier curves ($\mathcal{N}$-Curves), where control points follow

[2] Common base models, e.g. cVAE, cGAN, MDN or cDDPM, as described here, provide the basis for specialized trajectory prediction models, such as [32,34,36,49,50,53], which add modules for processing additional cues, like scene information or social context.

[3] Transformative approaches transform samples of a simple probability distribution (e.g. unit Gaussian) into samples of a more complex probability distribution.

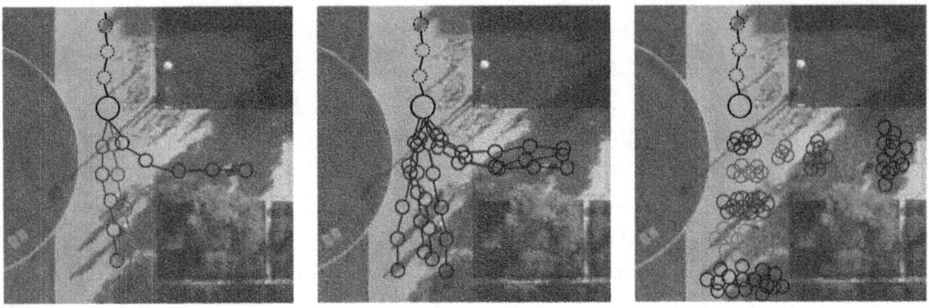

Fig. 1. Schematic of the long-term human trajectory prediction problem and different future trajectory generation approaches. Left: Depicts possible future trajectories given an observation (black). Center: Common cVAE or cGAN approaches generate a set of sample future trajectories in order to provide a sample-based approximate of the unknown conditional distribution. Right: MDN-based approaches often generate predictions in an autoregressive manner, where new sets of samples are sampled from a mixture distribution in each time step.

independent Gaussian distributions, thus passing stochasticity to the curve points. In the context of probabilistic trajectory prediction, the $\mathcal{N}$-MDN generates a sequence of Gaussian mixture probability distributions in terms of a mixture of $\mathcal{N}$-Curves, which resembles p_{out}. Now, using this approach as a starting point, we establish a connection between $\mathcal{N}$-Curves and the framework of Gaussian processes (GPs), which allows us to transform a given $\mathcal{N}$-Curve – based representation of p_{out} into a Gaussian process, enabling post-hoc Bayesian inference on top of the $\mathcal{N}$-MDN. In this setup, the predicted distribution p_{out}, as generated by an $\mathcal{N}$-MDN, is re-purposed to serve as a data-dependent GP prior. To achieve this, we first show that the underlying $\mathcal{N}$-Curves are, in essence, a geometric representation of a special case of Gaussian processes. We denote this $\mathcal{N}$-Curve – induced GP as $\mathcal{N}$-GP in order to reduce ambiguity[4]. Following this, we derive mean and kernel functions for the $\mathcal{N}$-GP considering the multivariate case and present an approach for the multi-modal setting. Ultimately, this allows for a more expressive and flexible probabilistic trajectory prediction model by employing the GP framework for enabling Bayesian posterior inference, with the benefits of a regression-based neural network model for parameter estimation.

In our evaluation, we explore the advantages granted to the base $\mathcal{N}$-MDN by our extension from a practical perspective. Following this, we use our extended model for manipulating predictions generated by the underlying $\mathcal{N}$-MDN by calculating different posterior distributions according to the induced $\mathcal{N}$-GP. For the posterior distributions, we consider two use cases. First, improving the overall prediction performance by calculating the posterior predictive distribution given one or more observed trajectory points. Second, we explore the possibilities of updating the predictions under the presence of new measurements within the predictive time horizon. In our approach, this does not require any additional passes through the $\mathcal{N}$-MDN.

[4] We will use the term $\mathcal{N}$-Curve exclusively to refer to the polynomial curve with variance in its control and curve points and $\mathcal{N}$-GP for referring to the actual Gaussian process, which can be calculated from an $\mathcal{N}$-Curve.

Related Work: Finally, as this work is a derivative of [23], we briefly summarize our main contributions over their work. The main contributions in [23] are given by the concept of $\mathcal{N}$-Curves as a representation of a probability distribution over sequences and the $\mathcal{N}$-MDN neural network as a probabilistic sequence model using those curves as their output. In this paper, we take the concept of $\mathcal{N}$-Curves and extend the theory surrounding them by establishing a link to Gaussian processes, providing a proof of equivalence, and deriving the mean and kernel functions for a GP induced by a given $\mathcal{N}$-Curve (the $\mathcal{N}$-GP) for the univariate, multivariate and multi-modal cases. We further extend their sequence prediction model by re-purposing the $\mathcal{N}$-MDN as a data-dependent generator for $\mathcal{N}$-GP prior distributions, with the goal of enhancing the $\mathcal{N}$-MDN in terms of flexibility and expressiveness. Apart from [23], the work of [27] is worth mentioning in this context, as their approach is building on a similar core idea of deriving a GP from a geometric representation, but with a focus on modeling spatial input using Bézier surfaces. Further, one of their main concerns is given by scalability, which is a frequent issue with Gaussian processes, whereas we have focused on the theoretical foundation of our $\mathcal{N}$-GP in a multivariate and a multi-modal setting. Finally, on a methodological level, they employ an approach based on variational inference for parameter estimation, while we are relying on regression-based MDNs, thus providing an alternative learning strategy.

2 Preliminaries

2.1 Gaussian Processes

A Gaussian process (GP, [44]) is a stochastic process $\{X_t\}_{t \in T}$ with index set T, where the joint distribution of stochastic variables X_{t_i} for an arbitrary, finite subset $\{t_1, ..., t_N\}$ of T is a multivariate Gaussian distribution. Throughout this paper, the index will be interpreted as *time*. The joint distribution is obtained using an explicit mean function $m(t)$ and positive definite covariance function $k(t_i, t_j) = \text{cov}(f(t_i), f(t_j))$, commonly referred to as the kernel of the Gaussian process, and yields a multivariate Gaussian prior probability distribution over function space. Commonly, $m(t) = 0$ is assumed. Given a collection of sample training points X_* of a function $f(t)$, the posterior (predictive) distribution $p(X|X_*)$ over non-observed function values X can be obtained. As such, Gaussian processes provide a well-established model for probabilistic sequence modeling.

2.2 Probabilistic Bézier Curves

Probabilistic Bézier Curves ($\mathcal{N}$-Curves, [23]) are Bézier curves [42] defined by $(L + 1)$ independent d-dimensional Gaussian control points $\mathcal{P} = \{P_0, ..., P_L\}$ with $P_l \sim \mathcal{N}(\boldsymbol{\mu}_l, \boldsymbol{\Sigma}_l)$. Through the curve construction function

$$X_t = B_{\mathcal{N}}(t, \mathcal{P}) = \mathcal{N}(\mu_{\mathcal{P}}(t), \Sigma_{\mathcal{P}}(t)) \tag{1}$$

with

$$\mu_{\mathcal{P}}(t) = \sum_{l=0}^{L} b_{l,L}(t) \boldsymbol{\mu}_l \tag{2}$$

$$\Sigma_{\mathcal{P}}(t) = \sum_{l=0}^{L} (b_{l,L}(t))^2 \boldsymbol{\Sigma}_l, \tag{3}$$

where

$$b_{l,L}(t) = \binom{L}{l} (1-t)^{L-l} t^l \tag{4}$$

are the Bernstein polynomials [33], the stochasticity is passed from the control points to the curve points $X_t \sim \mathcal{N}(\mu_{\mathcal{P}}(t), \Sigma_{\mathcal{P}}(t))$, yielding a sequence of Gaussian distributions $\{X_t\}_{t \in [0,1]}$ along the underlying Bézier curve. Thus, a stochastic process with index set $T = [0, 1]$ can be defined. For representing discrete data, i.e. sequences of length N, a discrete subset of T can be employed for assigning sequence indices to evenly distributed values in $[0, 1]$, yielding

$$T_N = \left\{ \frac{v}{N-1} | v \in \{0, ..., N-1\} \right\} = \{t_1, ..., t_N\}. \tag{5}$$

2.3 Mixture Density Networks

A Mixture Density Network (MDN, [3]) is a feed-forward neural network

$$\Phi(\mathbf{v}) = (\{\pi_k, \boldsymbol{\mu}_k, \boldsymbol{\Sigma}_k\}_{k \in \{1,...,K\}} | \mathbf{v}), \tag{6}$$

that takes an input vector $\mathbf{v}$ and maps it onto the parameters of a d-dimensional, K-component Gaussian mixture distribution. In order to ensure that the MDN generates a valid set of mixture parameters, the partitioned network output

$$\hat{Y} = (\tilde{\pi}_1, ..., \tilde{\pi}_K, \tilde{\boldsymbol{\mu}}_1, ..., \tilde{\boldsymbol{\mu}}_K, \tilde{\boldsymbol{\sigma}}_1, ..., \tilde{\boldsymbol{\sigma}}_K, \tilde{\boldsymbol{\rho}}_1, ..., \tilde{\boldsymbol{\rho}}_K),$$

with

$$\tilde{\pi}_k \in \mathbb{R},\ \tilde{\boldsymbol{\mu}}_k \in \mathbb{R}^d,\ \tilde{\boldsymbol{\sigma}}_k \in \mathbb{R}^d \text{ and } \tilde{\boldsymbol{\rho}}_k \in \mathbb{R}^{\frac{d^2-d}{2}}$$

is further transformed to meet parameter value requirements, i.e.

$$\pi_k = \text{softmax}(\tilde{\pi}_1, ..., \tilde{\pi}_K)_k,$$

such that $\sum_k \pi_k = 1$ and

$$\begin{aligned} \boldsymbol{\mu}_k &= \tilde{\boldsymbol{\mu}}_k \\ \sigma_{k,i} &= f_\sigma(\tilde{\sigma}_{k,i}) > 0\ \forall i \in \{1, ..., d\} \\ \rho_{k,j} &= f_\rho(\tilde{\rho}_{k,j}) \in [-1, 1]\ \forall j \in \left\{1, ..., \frac{d^2-d}{2}\right\}. \end{aligned}$$

Note that the covariance matrices $\boldsymbol{\Sigma}_k$ are calculated from the standard deviations and correlations in order to ensure positive definiteness. Common choices for f_σ are given by the *exponential function* [3], a shifted version of the *Exponential Linear Unit* [8,18] and the *softplus* function [11,14,24]. For f_ρ, an alternative to the originally proposed *tanh* function is given by the *softsign* function [13,24].

For building a probabilistic sequence model using MDNs, a common choice is the Sequence MDN model as proposed by [17]. Here, an MDN is stacked on top of an LSTM [20] network. The recurrent structure is then used for encoding an input sequence as well as for generating predictions one step at a time.

The $\mathcal{N}$-MDN variant: [23] introduced an MDN variant for probabilistic sequence modeling, which avoids the need for Monte Carlo methods when generating multi-modal distributions over sequences by directly parameterizing mixtures of $\mathcal{N}$-Curves, referred to as $\mathcal{N}$-MDN. The model consists of two main components, a recurrent neural network (an LSTM in this case) used as a sequence encoder and an MDN. During training, the $\mathcal{N}$-MDN learns to map a given input sequence onto an $\mathcal{N}$-Curve (mixture) modeling a distribution over target sequences, e.g. subsequent sequence elements in the case of sequence prediction. To achieve this, the $\mathcal{N}$-MDN's LSTM network encodes the input into a vector representation $\mathbf{v}$, which is then passed into the MDN in order to map it onto the parameters of said $\mathcal{N}$-Curve (mixture), i.e. the mixing weights, as well as the mean vectors and covariance matrices of the Gaussian control points.

3 Connecting $\mathcal{N}$-Curve Mixtures to Gaussian Processes

With $\mathcal{N}$-Curves providing a representation for stochastic processes $\{X_t\}_{t\in T}$ comprised of Gaussian random variables $X_t \sim \mathcal{N}(\boldsymbol{\mu}, \boldsymbol{\Sigma})$, we first show that $\mathcal{N}$-Curves are a special case of GPs with an implicit mean and covariance function[5]. Following the definition of GPs [35,44], an $\mathcal{N}$-Curve can be classified as a GP, if for any finite subset $\{t_1, ..., t_N\}$ of T, the joint probability density $p(X_{t_1}, ..., X_{t_N})$ of corresponding random variables is Gaussian. This property is referred to as the *GP property*. We show that this property holds by reformulating the curve construction formula (see Eq. 1) into a linear transformation[6] $\boldsymbol{X} = \mathbf{C} \cdot \boldsymbol{P}$ of the Gaussian control points stacked into a $((L+1) \cdot d \times 1)$ vector $\boldsymbol{P}^\top = \begin{pmatrix} P_0^\top & P_1^\top & \cdots & P_L^\top \end{pmatrix}$ using a $(N \cdot d \times (L+1) \cdot d)$ transformation matrix

$$\mathbf{C} = \begin{pmatrix} \mathbf{B}_{0,L}(t_1) & \dots & \mathbf{B}_{L,L}(t_1) \\ \vdots & \ddots & \vdots \\ \mathbf{B}_{0,L}(t_N) & \dots & \mathbf{B}_{L,L}(t_N) \end{pmatrix} \tag{7}$$

[5] The $\mathcal{N}$-Curve representation does not require an explicit kernel or covariance function, as is the common representation for Gaussian processes, because the correlation between points on the curve emerges from the geometric constraints of the underlying Bézier curve. The curve function itself provides the mean function.

[6] For clarity, multivariate random variables may be written in bold font occasionally.

determined by the Bernstein polynomials, with $\mathbf{B}_{l,L}(t_j) = b_{l,L}(t_j)\mathbf{I}_d$ and $t_j \in T_N$. As $\boldsymbol{P}$ is itself a Gaussian random vector, $\boldsymbol{X}$ and its corresponding probability density $p(\boldsymbol{X}) = p(X_1, ..., X_N)$ are also Gaussian.

As the Gaussians along an $\mathcal{N}$-Curve are correlated through the shared set of curve control points, the mean and kernel functions of the induced GP, denoted as $\mathcal{N}$-GP in the following, can be given explicitly. We first derive the $\mathcal{N}$-GP's mean and kernel functions for the univariate and multivariate cases. Then, we present an approach for defining a multi-modal $\mathcal{N}$-GP, given a mixture of $\mathcal{N}$-Curves. It is worth noting that an $\mathcal{N}$-GP can also be derived from composite $\mathcal{N}$-Curves, based on composite[7] Bézier curves [22].

3.1 $\mathcal{N}$-Curve Gaussian Processes

We first consider univariate GPs, which target scalar-valued functions $f : \mathbb{R} \to \mathbb{R}$, as these on provide the most common use case for GPs and also grant us a simple case for deriving the mean and kernel functions induced by a given $\mathcal{N}$-Curve while also allowing a visual examination of some properties of the $\mathcal{N}$-GP. Here, the stochastic control points P_l are defined by the mean value μ_l and variance σ_l^2. The mean function is equivalent to Eq. 2. Thus, we focus on the kernel $k_{\mathcal{P}}(t_i, t_j)$ for two curve points $X = f(t_i) = \sum_{l=0}^{L} b_{l,L}(t_i)P_l$ and $Y = f(t_j) = \sum_{l=0}^{L} b_{l,L}(t_j)P_l$ at indices t_i and t_j with $t_i, t_j \in [0, 1]$. The respective mean values are given by $\mu_X = \sum_{l=0}^{L} b_{l,L}(t_i)\mu_l$ and $\mu_Y = \sum_{l=0}^{L} b_{l,L}(t_j)\mu_l$. From $k(t_i, t_j) = \mathrm{cov}(f(t_i), f(t_j))$ then follows:

$$
\begin{aligned}
k_{\mathcal{P}}(t_i,t_j) &= \mathbb{E}[(X-\mu_X)(Y-\mu_Y)] \\
&= \mathbb{E}\left[\left(\sum_{l=0}^{L} b_{l,L}(t_i)P_l - \mu_X\right)\left(\sum_{l=0}^{L} b_{l,L}(t_j)P_l - \mu_Y\right)\right] \\
&= \mathbb{E}\left[\sum_{l=0}^{L} b_{l,L}(t_i)b_{l,L}(t_j)P_l^2\right] + \mathbb{E}\left[\sum_{l=0}^{L}\left(\sum_{l'=0,l'\neq l}^{L} b_{l,L}(t_i)b_{l',L}(t_j)P_lP_{l'}\right)\right] \\
&\quad - \underbrace{\mu_Y \sum_{l=0}^{L} b_{l,L}(t_i)\mu_l}_{=\mu_Y\mu_X} - \underbrace{\mu_X \sum_{l=0}^{L} b_{l,L}(t_j)\mu_l}_{=\mu_X\mu_Y} + \mu_X\mu_Y .
\end{aligned}
$$

With $\mathbb{E}[P_i \cdot P_j] = \mathbb{E}[P_i] \cdot \mathbb{E}[P_j]$, which follows from the independence of the control points, and $\mathbb{E}[P_i^2] = \mathrm{Var}[P_i] + (\mathbb{E}[P_i])^2$, we obtain the closed-form solution

$$
\begin{aligned}
k_{\mathcal{P}}(t_i,t_j) &= \sum_{l=0}^{L} b_{l,L}(t_i)b_{l,L}(t_j)(\sigma_l^2 + \mu_l^2) \\
&\quad + \sum_{l=0}^{L}\left(\sum_{l'=0,l'\neq l}^{L} b_{l,L}(t_i)b_{l',L}(t_j)\mu_l\mu_{l'}\right) \\
&\quad - \mu_X\mu_Y ,
\end{aligned} \tag{8}
$$

[7] Oftentimes also referred to as Bézier splines.

where $k_{\mathcal{P}}(t_i, t_j)$ is a positive semi-definite function[8] for any $t_* \in [0,1]$ and arbitrary sets of Gaussian control points with mean values μ_l and variances σ_l.

As a final note, the $\mathcal{N}$-GP is non-stationary, as its kernel depends on the actual values of t_i and t_j. Further, it is non-periodic and its smoothness is controlled by the underlying Bézier curve, i.e. the position and number of control points. As the $\mathcal{N}$-GP is strongly dependent on the given set of control points, it allows for a range of different kernels.

Multivariate Extension: Next, we elevate our univariate $\mathcal{N}$-GP to the multivariate case, where the GP targets a vector-valued function $\mathbf{f}(t)$, which map scalar inputs onto d-dimensional vectors, e.g. $\mathbf{f} : \mathbb{R} \to \mathbb{R}^d$. For this extension, we adopt the approach described in [1], which models matrix-valued random variables using a multivariate Gaussian distribution by employing stacked mean vectors in combination with block partitioned covariance matrices.

Following this, the Gram matrix of a d-variate GP for a finite index subset with $|T_N| = N$ is defined by the $(Nd \times Nd)$ block partitioned matrix

$$\Sigma = \begin{pmatrix} \mathbf{K}_{\mathcal{P}}(t_1, t_1) & \cdots & \mathbf{K}_{\mathcal{P}}(t_1, t_N) \\ \vdots & \ddots & \vdots \\ \mathbf{K}_{\mathcal{P}}(t_N, t_1) & \cdots & \mathbf{K}_{\mathcal{P}}(t_N, t_N) \end{pmatrix} \tag{9}$$

calculated using the matrix-valued kernel $\mathbf{K}_{\mathcal{P}}(t_i, t_j) = \operatorname{cov}(\boldsymbol{X}, \boldsymbol{Y})$. Here, $\boldsymbol{X} = \sum_{l=0}^{L} b_{l,L}(t_i)\boldsymbol{P}_l$ and $\boldsymbol{Y} = \sum_{l=0}^{L} b_{l,L}(t_j)\boldsymbol{P}_l$ are now d-variate Gaussian random variables resulting from the linear combination of d-variate $\mathcal{N}$-Curve control points $\boldsymbol{P}_l$. Thus, the multivariate generalization of Eq. 8 yields a $(d \times d)$ matrix and is given by

$$\begin{aligned} \mathbf{K}_{\mathcal{P}}(t_i, t_j) &= \mathbb{E}[(\boldsymbol{X} - \boldsymbol{\mu}_X)(\boldsymbol{Y} - \boldsymbol{\mu}_Y)^\top] \\ &= \mathbb{E}\left[\boldsymbol{X}\mathbf{Y}^\top\right] - \underbrace{\mathbb{E}\left[\boldsymbol{X}\boldsymbol{\mu}_Y^\top\right]}_{=\boldsymbol{\mu}_X\boldsymbol{\mu}_Y^\top} - \underbrace{\mathbb{E}\left[\boldsymbol{\mu}_X\boldsymbol{Y}^\top\right]}_{=\boldsymbol{\mu}_X\boldsymbol{\mu}_Y^\top} + \boldsymbol{\mu}_X\boldsymbol{\mu}_Y^\top \\ &= \sum_{l=0}^{L} b_{l,L}(t_i)b_{l,L}(t_j)\left(\boldsymbol{\Sigma}_l + \boldsymbol{\mu}_l\boldsymbol{\mu}_l^\top\right) \\ &\quad + \sum_{l=0}^{L}\left(\sum_{l'=0, l'\neq l}^{L} b_{l,L}(t_i)b_{l',L}(t_j)\boldsymbol{\mu}_l\boldsymbol{\mu}_{l'}^\top\right) \\ &\quad - \boldsymbol{\mu}_X\boldsymbol{\mu}_Y^\top. \end{aligned} \tag{10}$$

The $(n \times d)$ mean vector is defined as the concatenation of all mean vectors $\boldsymbol{\mu}_{\mathcal{P}}(t_i)$ (see also Eq. 2) along the underlying Bézier curve, i.e.

$$(\mathbf{m}_{\mathcal{P}}(T_N))^\top = \left((\boldsymbol{\mu}_{\mathcal{P}}(t_1))^\top \cdots (\boldsymbol{\mu}_{\mathcal{P}}(t_N))^\top\right). \tag{11}$$

[8] A positive semi-definiteness proof for the $\mathcal{N}$-GP kernel is provided in appendix 6.

3.2 The Multi-modal Case

With long-term human trajectory prediction being a highly multi-modal problem and GPs as presented before being incapable of modeling such data, we discuss an approach for utilizing $\mathcal{N}$-GPs in a multi-modal setting. A common approach for increasing the expressiveness of a statistical model, e.g. for heteroscedasticity or multi-modality, is to employ a mixture model. Thereby, rather than a single model or distribution, a mixture of which are used with each component in the mixture covering a subset of the data.

Following this and in line with the approach described by [23], which builds on Gaussian mixture models, we define the multi-modal extension of our $\mathcal{N}$-GP as a mixture of K $\mathcal{N}$-GPs

$$\mathcal{MG}(\boldsymbol{\pi}, \{\mathcal{G}_k\}_{k\in\{1,\dots,K\}}) = \sum_{k=1}^{K} \pi_k \mathcal{G}_k(\mathbf{m}_{\mathcal{P}_k}(\cdot), \mathbf{K}_{\mathcal{P}_k}(\cdot,\cdot)), \tag{12}$$

with $\mathcal{N}$-GP components $\mathcal{G}_k$ and the static prior weight distribution $\boldsymbol{\pi} = \{\pi_1, \dots \pi_K\}$ with $\sum_{k=1}^{K} \pi_k = 1$. The mean and kernel functions are determined separately for each GP component according to Eqs. 10 and 11. Given these functions and the weights π, the mixture distribution can be evaluated at a given index.

It is worth noting, that this approach is different from the *mixture of Gaussian process experts* [43,48,52] approach, which extends on the mixture of experts model [26] and is widely used in the context of GPs. The key difference to the Gaussian mixture model approach is evident regarding the mixture's weight distribution, which is a conditional distribution in the mixture of Gaussian process experts approach. Further, mixtures of experts are rather focused on lowering the computational load of a GP model, as less data points have to be considered during inference due to the use of local experts (e.g. [10,30]).

4 Post-Hoc Bayesian Inference for $\mathcal{N}$-Curve Mixture Density Networks

In order to enable GP-based Bayesian inference on top of the regression-based $\mathcal{N}$-MDN model, we propose to use the $\mathcal{N}$-MDN as a data-dependent generator for prior distributions within the GP framework, where the $\mathcal{N}$-MDN is adapted to a given dataset through training[9]. Given an observed trajectory, we achieve this by calculating an $\mathcal{N}$-GP's mean and kernel functions from each corresponding $\mathcal{N}$-Curve output by the $\mathcal{N}$-MDN, yielding a prior for a GP modeling a respective target distribution over future trajectories. Despite the $\mathcal{N}$-MDN being a viable probabilistic trajectory prediction model by itself, the combination of both approaches yields mutual advantages by providing a convenient and stable way of estimating the $\mathcal{N}$-GP's parameters and enhancing the $\mathcal{N}$-MDN's flexibility and expressiveness in an post-hoc manner by creating the possibility of calculating different posterior predictive distributions from the $\mathcal{N}$-MDN's output in light of (new) observations via the induced $\mathcal{N}$-GP.

[9] Training the $\mathcal{N}$-MDN does not involve the $\mathcal{N}$-GP component.

In the following, we first discuss possible real-world use cases of the combined approach (Sect. 4.1). Afterwards, we briefly summarize how the $\mathcal{N}$-MDN network is trained (Sect. 4.2) and how posterior predictive distributions corresponding to the discussed use cases are calculated using our proposed combination of $\mathcal{N}$-MDNs and $\mathcal{N}$-GPs (Sect. 4.3).

4.1 Practical Implications and Use Cases

To put the value of our combined trajectory prediction model into perspective from a practical standpoint, we discuss different use cases that we expect to benefit from the $\mathcal{N}$-GP extension, namely prediction *refinement* and *update*.

Refinement: We first examine the $\mathcal{N}$-GP as a tool for improving the overall prediction performance considering different posterior predictive distributions using different subsets of the observed trajectory. More formally, given an observed trajectory $\{\mathbf{x}_1, ..., \mathbf{x}_{N_{\text{obs}}}\}$, which is processed by the $\mathcal{N}$-MDN yielding the $\mathcal{N}$-GP's prior distribution $p(X_1, ..., X_{N_{\text{obs}}+N_{\text{pred}}})$, a refinement of this initial prediction is given by a posterior predictive distribution

$$p(\{X_1, ..., X_{N_{\text{obs}}+N_{\text{pred}}}\} \setminus \{X_i\}_{i \in \mathcal{I}} | \{\mathbf{x}_i\}_{i \in \mathcal{I}}) \tag{13}$$

with $\mathcal{I} \subseteq \{1, ..., N_{\text{obs}}\}$ giving a subset of the observed trajectory. We expect this refinement to improve the prediction performance, as the original maximum likelihood prediction generated by the $\mathcal{N}$-MDN tends to average out small variations in the data and the refinement procedure adapts the prediction more towards the actual observation in a controlled way. We consider this the most practically relevant use case, as it directly affects the model's accuracy.

Update: Another interesting option opened up by embedding the $\mathcal{N}$-MDN into the GP framework is given by the use case of updating a multi-step prediction under the presence of new data within the predictive time horizon. For this, we calculate a posterior predictive distribution similar to Eq. 13 (refinement), but condition on a new observation within the predictive time horizon instead, i.e. $\mathcal{I} \subseteq \{N_{\text{obs}} + 1, ..., N_{\text{obs}} + N_{\text{pred}}\}$. As trajectory prediction models usually predict several time steps into the future, an easy to calculate and fast to compute update to the prediction under the presence of new data can be valuable. The $\mathcal{N}$-GP enables such updates without the need for additional passes through the underlying neural network. Further, it is unaffected by potentially missing intermediate observations. This is especially valuable, as common trajectory prediction models require complete sequences as input, where such gaps need to be filled with data extracted from the model's own prediction. This can be problematic under the presence of multiple modes in the predicted distribution, making Monte Carlo methods a necessity. In contrast, within the GP framework, missing information between observed data points is naturally interpolated. Following this, when certain requirements are met, our model allows to fill gaps in light of fragmented observations easily. First, a full N_{obs}-step input sequence is required for the underlying $\mathcal{N}$-MDN for generating our prior distribution. Second, the gaps to fill must be within the modeled predictive time horizon.

4.2 Parameter Estimation

In our approach, the $\mathcal{N}$-GP relies on prior distributions generated by an $\mathcal{N}$-MDN, whose parameters are learned from data. Following [23], the $\mathcal{N}$-MDN is trained using a set of M fixed-length trajectories $\mathcal{D} = \{\mathcal{X}_1, ..., \mathcal{X}_M\}$ with $\mathcal{X}_i = \{\mathbf{x}_1^i, ..., \mathbf{x}_N^i\}$, applying the negative log-likelihood loss

$$\mathcal{L} = \frac{1}{M} \sum_{j=1}^{M} - \log \sum_{k=1}^{K} \exp\left\{ \log \pi_k + \sum_{i=1}^{N} \log \left(\mathcal{N}(\mathbf{x}_i^j | \mu_{\mathcal{P}}(t_i), \Sigma_{\mathcal{P}}(t_i)) \right) \right\} \tag{14}$$

in conjunction with a gradient descent policy.

In order to give an illustrative example, training trajectories of length N are split into an observed portion of length N_{obs}, which is used as input for the model, and a to be predicted portion of length N_{pred}, where $N = N_{\text{obs}} + N_{\text{pred}}$. The $\mathcal{N}$-MDN then outputs an $\mathcal{N}$-Curve (mixture), which models full trajectories of length N. This ensures that within the GP framework, we are able to condition on elements within the input trajectory. The negative log-likelihood loss function is calculated given full training trajectories. A schematic of this is depicted in Fig. 2.

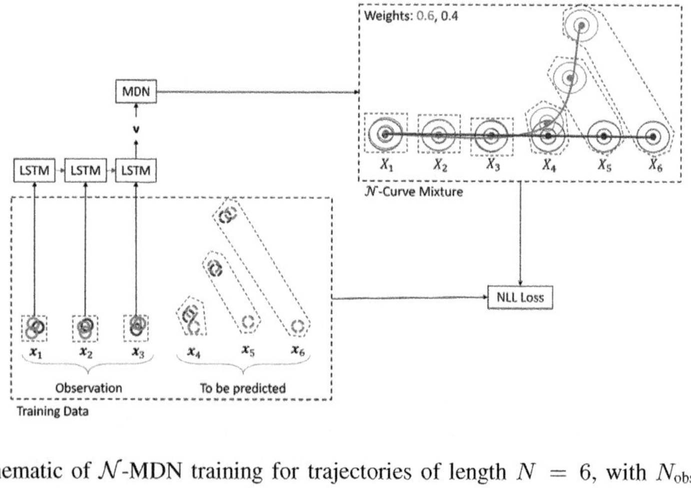

Fig. 2. Schematic of $\mathcal{N}$-MDN training for trajectories of length $N = 6$, with $N_{\text{obs}} = 3$ and $N_{\text{pred}} = 3$.

4.3 Conditional Inference

Finally, we want to give a brief overview of how (conditional) inference works within our combined prediction model, especially with regard to the refinement and update use cases discussed in Sect. 4.1. Given an input sequence, the $\mathcal{N}$-MDN generates an $\mathcal{N}$-Curve mixture, which models the observed as well as possible future trajectories. Using Eqs. 10, 11 and 12, we calculate the $\mathcal{N}$-GP prior $p(X_1, ..., X_N)$ from this mixture, which is a joint K-component Gaussian mixture distribution over all N modeled time steps. Now, for determining a conditional posterior predictive distribution, we first partition the joint prior distribution into a partition containing the N_{obs} time steps to condition on and the remaining N_{pred} time steps

$$\begin{aligned} p(X_1, ..., X_N) &= p(\{X_1, ..., X_{N_{\text{obs}}}\} \cup \{X_{N_{\text{obs}}+1}, ..., X_N\}) \\ &= p(X_A \cup X_B), \end{aligned} \tag{15}$$

with component mean vectors and covariance matrices partitioned as

$$\boldsymbol{\mu}_k = \begin{bmatrix} \boldsymbol{\mu}_{kA} \\ \boldsymbol{\mu}_{kB} \end{bmatrix}, \ \boldsymbol{\Sigma}_k = \begin{bmatrix} \boldsymbol{\Sigma}_{kAA} & \boldsymbol{\Sigma}_{kAB} \\ \boldsymbol{\Sigma}_{kBA} & \boldsymbol{\Sigma}_{kBB} \end{bmatrix}.$$

Following e.g. [5,39,41], the posterior weights, mean vectors and covariance matrices, conditioned on $\mathbf{x}_B$, can then be directly calculated as

$$\begin{aligned} \pi_{kA|B} &= \frac{\pi_k \mathcal{N}(\mathbf{x}_B | \boldsymbol{\mu}_{kB}, \boldsymbol{\Sigma}_{kBB})}{\sum_j \pi_j \mathcal{N}(\mathbf{x}_B | \boldsymbol{\mu}_{jB}, \boldsymbol{\Sigma}_{jBB})} \\ \boldsymbol{\mu}_{kA|B} &= \boldsymbol{\mu}_{kA} + \boldsymbol{\Sigma}_{kAB} \boldsymbol{\Sigma}_{kBB}^{-1} (\mathbf{x}_B - \boldsymbol{\mu}_{kB}) \\ \boldsymbol{\Sigma}_{kA|B} &= \boldsymbol{\Sigma}_{kAA} - \boldsymbol{\Sigma}_{kAB} \boldsymbol{\Sigma}_{kBB}^{-1} \boldsymbol{\Sigma}_{kBA}. \end{aligned} \tag{16}$$

The probability distribution for individual trajectory points at time t can be extracted through marginalization using $X_A = \{X_t\}$, e.g.

$$p(X_A) = \sum_k \pi_k p_k(X_A) = \sum_k \pi_k \mathcal{N}(x_A | \mu_{kAA}, \Sigma_{kAA}).$$

A schematic of the inference scheme for the refinement and update use cases is provided in Fig. 3. In this example, we assume the $\mathcal{N}$-GP to model 6-element trajectories with prior distribution $p(X_1, X_2, X_3, X_4, X_5, X_6)$, where $p(\cdot)$ was calculated from the $\mathcal{N}$-Curve (mixture), output by an $\mathcal{N}$-MDN given an input trajectory $\{\mathbf{x}_1, \mathbf{x}_2, \mathbf{x}_3\}$. As we are now within the GP framework, we can calculate different posterior predictive distributions using observed values from the input trajectory (refinement use case) or values observed after the initial input (update use case). Exemplary posterior distributions can then be given by $p(X_1, X_2, X_4, X_5, X_6 | \mathbf{x}_3)$ or $p(X_1, X_2, X_4, X_6 | \mathbf{x}_3, \mathbf{x}_5)$ for the refinement and update use cases, respectively.

5 Evaluation

In this section we aim to support our proposed combination of $\mathcal{N}$-MDNs with $\mathcal{N}$-GPs in its capabilities of enhancing the $\mathcal{N}$-MDN's flexibility, expressiveness and overall performance, considering the *refinement* and *update* use cases, using standard trajectory prediction benchmarking datasets. It should be noted, that we omit a state-of-the-art comparison of the base $\mathcal{N}$-MDN and focus on an ablation study. The reasons for this are two-fold. On the one hand, the model has been proven viable and competetive on the human trajectory prediction task as a base trajectory prediction model [21,23]. On the other hand, this allows us to keep the evaluation focused on the proposed proof of concept extension for the $\mathcal{N}$-MDN in the context of the use cases discussed in Sect. 4.1.

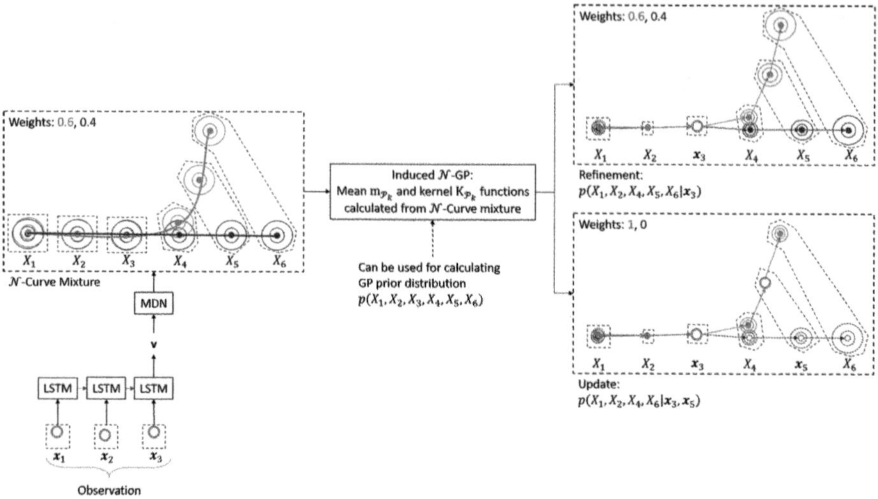

Fig. 3. Schematic of the interplay between the $\mathcal{N}$-MDN and $\mathcal{N}$-GP components with regard to the refinement and update use cases. Green circles indicate trajectory points the predictive posterior is conditioned on.

5.1 Experimental Setup

For the evaluation, we consider scenes from commonly used datasets: *BIWI Walking Pedestrians* ([40], scenes: ETH and Hotel), *Crowds by Example* ([31], scenes: Zara1 and Zara2) and the *Stanford Drone Dataset* ([45], scenes: Bookstore and Hyang). Following common practice, the annotation rate of each dataset is adjusted to 2.5 annotations per second. Further, the evaluation is conducted on trajectories of fixed length $N = N_{\text{obs}} + N_{\text{pred}} = 8 + 12$. We trained one $\mathcal{N}$-MDN independently for each dataset[10] to generate $\mathcal{N}$-Curve mixtures, which model complete trajectories of length $N = 20$, given the first $N_{\text{obs}} = 8$ trajectory points as input to the model. For training, 80% of each dataset are used.

For a quantitative and qualitative evaluation, we are first considering the refinement use case. For each test dataset, the respective $\mathcal{N}$-MDN is used to generate an $\mathcal{N}$-Curve mixture prediction for every test trajectory, yielding initial predictions $p(X_1, ..., X_N)$, i.e. the $\mathcal{N}$-GP prior. These initial predictions are then refined by calculating the posterior distributions

$$p(\{X_1, ..., X_N\} \backslash \{X_{N_{\text{obs}}}\} | \mathbf{x}_{N_{\text{obs}}})$$

and

$$p(\{X_1, ..., X_N\} \backslash \{X_4, X_{N_{\text{obs}}}\} | \mathbf{x}_4, \mathbf{x}_{N_{\text{obs}}}),$$

[10] In this setup, a (probabilistic) trajectory prediction model learns to generate scene-dependent predictions, as the scene structure (e.g. pathways) are captured implicitly.

conditioning on the input's last point $\mathbf{x}_{N_{obs}}$ (*refinement A*) and on $\{\mathbf{x}_4, \mathbf{x}_{N_{obs}}\}$ (*refinement B*), respectively. For more details on how the posterior distributions are obtained, we want to refer the reader to Sect. 4.3. By increasing the number of observed points, we expect the prediction to adapt towards a given sample trajectory. For measuring the performance, we apply the *Average Displacement Error* (ADE, [29]) according to the standard evaluation approach, using a maximum likelihood estimate[11]. As the ADE does not provide an adequate measure for assessing the quality of (multi-modal) probabilistic predictions, we use the *Negative Log-Likelihood* (NLL) in addition to the ADE, which is a common choice for this purpose [2,25]. Both the ADE and the NLL are calculated for the estimate of the observed trajectory, as well as for the time steps to be predicted. For example for refinement B, the marginal distributions

$$p_{\text{obs}}(\{X_1, ..., X_{N_{obs}}\} \backslash \{X_4, X_{N_{obs}}\}) \\ = \int p(\{X_1, ..., X_N\} \backslash \{X_4, X_{N_{obs}}\} | \mathbf{x}_4, \mathbf{x}_{N_{obs}}) d\{X_{N_{obs}+1}, ..., X_N\}$$

and

$$p_{\text{pred}}(X_{N_{obs}+1}, ..., X_N) \\ = \int p(\{X_1, ..., X_N\} \backslash \{X_4, X_{N_{obs}}\} | \mathbf{x}_4, \mathbf{x}_{N_{obs}}) d_{\{}X_1, ..., X_{N_{obs}}\} \backslash \{X_4, X_{N_{obs}}\}$$

are evaluated. As these posteriors are Gaussian mixture distributions, these marginals can analytically be calculated (see Sect. 4.3). Beyond the refinement use case, we are providing a qualitative example for the update use case. Here, the posterior distribution $p(\{X_1, ..., X_N\} \backslash \{X_{N_{obs}}, X_{14}\} | \mathbf{x}_{N_{obs}}, \mathbf{x}_{14})$ is considered.

5.2 Results

The quantitative results for the $\mathcal{N}$-GP – based prediction refinement with respect to the selected performance measures are depicted in Table 1. Overall, an increase in performance can be observed when refining the estimate generated by the $\mathcal{N}$-MDN using 1 and 2 points, respectively. This supports our expectation of an increase in prediction performance through adding GP-based Bayesian inference to the $\mathcal{N}$-MDN. Despite this, however, the results indicate an inconsistent gain in performance comparing both posteriors. Following this, we provide qualitative examples to further investigate these findings.

Two examples highlighting common cases for a positive effect of the refinement on the prediction performance is given in Fig. 4. On the one hand, the refinement can lead to the estimate being pulled closer to the ground truth in the input portion, which expands far into the future prediction. On the other hand, the refinement can lead to the suppression of inadequate mixture components, that were assigned high weights in the prior distribution.

[11] We are using the mean vectors of the marginalized posterior Gaussian mixture distributions for each time step to be considered.

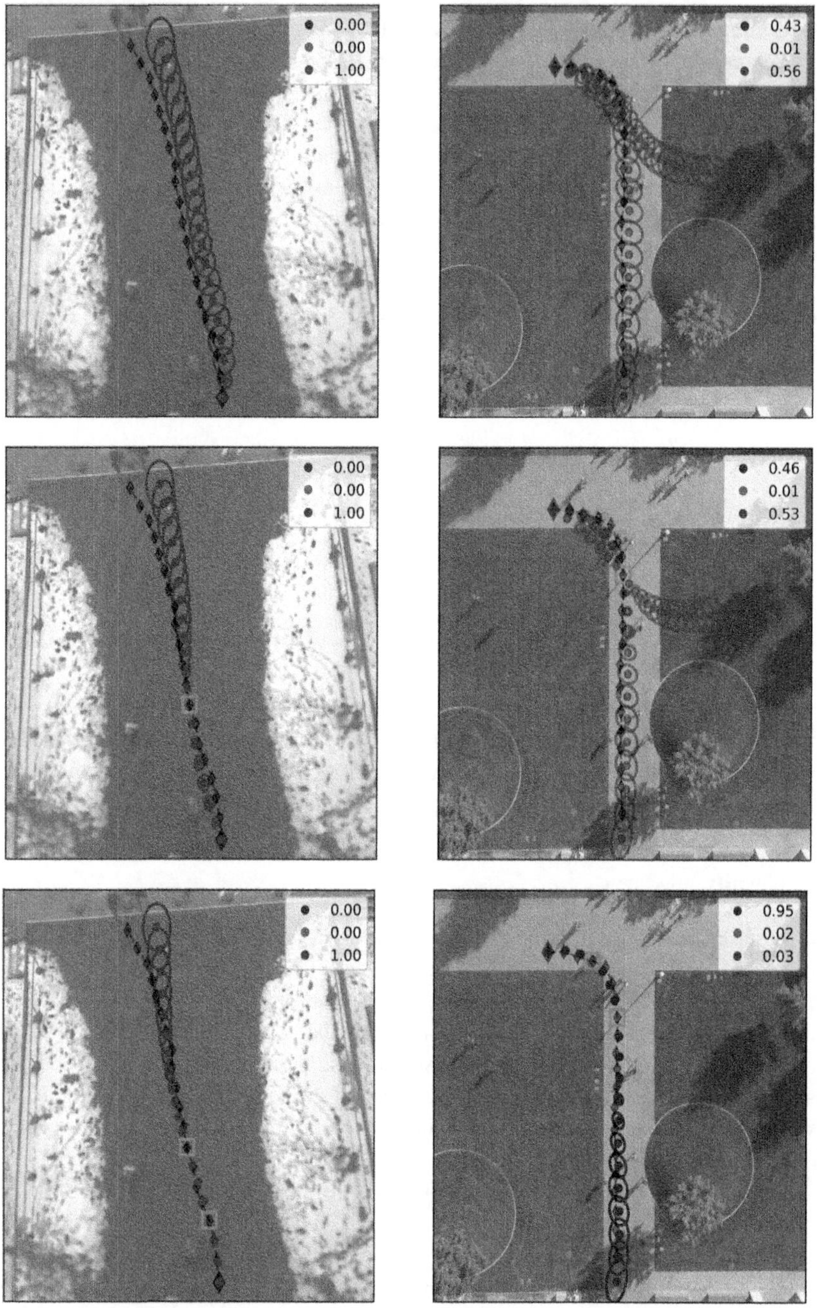

Fig. 4. Examples for improved prediction through conditioning on 1 or 2 points, respectively. Top to bottom: Initial (prior) prediction, refinement A and refinement B. Yellow squares indicate condition points. Ground truth trajectories are depicted in black and start at the bottom (left column) and in the top left (right column). The first 8 trajectory points are input into the $\mathcal{N}$-MDN. (Color figure online)

Table 1. Quantitative results of the initial (prior) prediction as generated by an $\mathcal{N}$-MDN and posterior refinements. Table entries report the estimation error with respect to the input trajectory (p_{obs}, first value) and the trajectory to be predicted (p_{pred}, second value), respectively. ADE errors are reported in pixels. Lower is better for both performance measures.

		Initial Prediction	Refinement A	Refinement B
ETH	ADE	3.85/11.25	3.95/10.12	2.39/10.18
	NLL	6.51/7.58	5.43/7.08	−115.09/1.70
Hotel	ADE	5.69/17.96	4.19/17.07	2.70/16.73
	NLL	6.99/8.20	5.56/7.71	10.63/8.59
Zara1	ADE	4.09/19.10	2.89/17.52	1.63/17.64
	NLL	6.83/8.18	5.27/7.63	−51.93/8.15
Zara2	ADE	2.98/21.38	2.64/20.07	1.69/20.05
	NLL	6.59/8.09	5.08/7.59	−60.95/−1.76
Bookstore	ADE	4.04/17.21	3.65/15.97	2.16/16.29
	NLL	7.46/8.37	5.88/7.76	−11.89/7.63
Hyang	ADE	5.51/36.46	5.01/34.05	3.16/32.18
	NLL	8.21/9.42	6.65/8.86	−49.30/9.05

In some cases it can be observed, that conditioning on 2 points (refinement B) degrades the performance in comparison to using a single point (refinement A). With respect to the NLL, this can be attributed to an increased number of trajectory point variances decreasing or even collapsing. Then, even minor inaccuracies in the mean prediction result in higher NLL values, even if the estimate is closer to the ground truth. Looking at the ADE, the loss in performance can most likely be attributed to the enforced interpolation of the condition points, which sometimes leads to unwanted deformations of the mean prediction. One of the main causes for this is given by the input trajectories commonly being subject to noise. Examples for both of these cases are depicted in Fig. 5. It could be noted, that a common approach for dealing with such problems is given by adding an error term to each observed point [16].

Lastly, we briefly showcase our approach considering the prediction update use case. An example for the posterior distribution given an additional observation within the predictive time horizon is depicted in Fig. 6. While there are initially multiple relevant mixture components (according to their weights), the additional observation leads to the suppression of wrong modes. Here, the new observation occurs several time steps after the last original input. Using the $\mathcal{N}$-GP, the updated prediction can be directly calculated without requiring an additional pass through the $\mathcal{N}$-MDN.

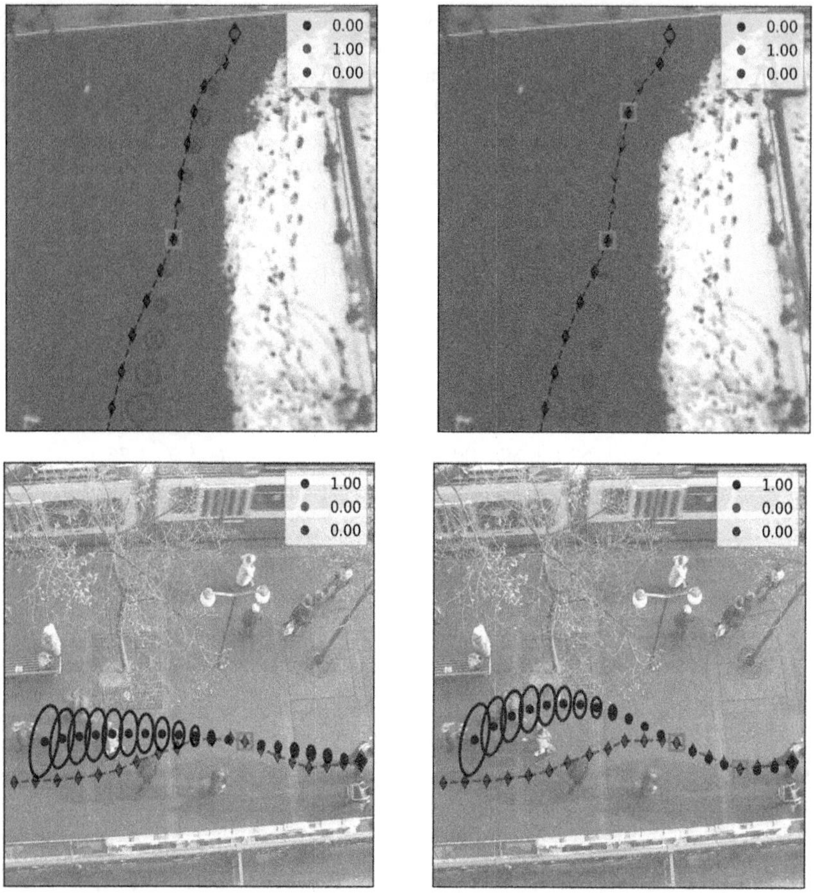

Fig. 5. Cases for refinement leading to degraded prediction performance according to the NLL (1 & 2) and ADE (3 & 4). 1 & 3: refinement A, 2 & 4: refinement B. Yellow squares indicate condition points. Ground truth trajectories are depicted in black and start at the top (left example) and on the right site (right example). The first 8 trajectory points are input into the $\mathcal{N}$-MDN. (Color figure online)

6 Summary and Future Work

In this paper, we presented a novel, flexible output distribution for regression-based probabilistic trajectory prediction, which enables post-hoc Bayesian inference as an inherent feature of the model's output distribution. In our approach, an $\mathcal{N}$-MDN, a variation of MDNs operating in the domain of parametric curves, is embedded in the GP framework as a generator for prior distributions. For this, we first showed that $\mathcal{N}$-Curves, as parameterized by the $\mathcal{N}$-MDN, are a special case of Gaussian processes (denoted as $\mathcal{N}$-GP) and then derived respective mean and kernel functions. Further, we have defined a multi-modal $\mathcal{N}$-GP variant, applicable in the scope of multi-modal long-term human trajectory prediction. In our evaluation, we showed that using the $\mathcal{N}$-

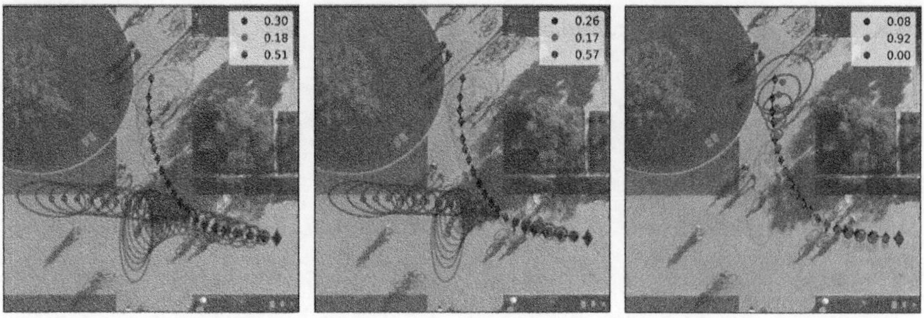

Fig. 6. Example for updating the prediction by an $\mathcal{N}$-MDN using the last observed point and an additional point within the predictive time horizon. Yellow squares indicate condition points. Ground truth is depicted in black.

GP, predictions generated by an $\mathcal{N}$-MDN can be improved by conditioning on different subsets of the original input. Additionally, we looked briefly into practical applications of the approach, focusing on updating predictions generated by the $\mathcal{N}$-MDN in light of new observations within the predictive time horizon. Using our approach, such updates do not require any additional passes through the $\mathcal{N}$-MDN. Further, missing intermediate observations are inherently handled by the $\mathcal{N}$-GP.

This paper focused on long-term human trajectory prediction, a multi-modal yet easily visualizable task, together with two exemplary use-cases benefiting from our proposed approach. Thus, an interesting research direction for future work involves exploring additional capabilities and use-cases enabled by the proposed extension, such as out-of-distribution detection. Furthermore, investigating the scalability of this approach to other domains, particularly those involving higher-dimensional sequence data, could be valuable. Since the approach is based on Bézier curves, which can easily be scaled up to arbitrary dimensions, the scalability is likely more constrained by the Gaussian process component, which requires handling the inversion of large covariance matrices.

APPENDIX

A Positive Semi-Definiteness of the $\mathcal{N} - GP$ Kernel

In this section we provide proof, that the $\mathcal{N}$-GP's kernel function is positive semi-definite, i.e. $k_{\mathcal{P}}(t_i, t_j) \geq 0 \; \forall \; (t_i, t_j)$, with $t_* \in [0, 1]$ and defining Gaussian control points $\mathcal{P} = \{P_0, ..., P_L\}$ with $P_l \sim \mathcal{N}(\mu_l, \sigma_l^2)$. In doing so, we limit the proof to the 1-dimensional case, as it directly translates to the higher-dimensional case as well.

Recalling Eq. 8, the kernel function is defined as

$$k_{\mathcal{P}}(t_i, t_j) = \sum_{l=0}^{L} b_{l,L}(t_i) b_{l,L}(t_j)(\sigma_l^2 + \mu_l^2) + \sum_{l=0}^{L} \left(\sum_{l'=0, l' \neq l}^{L} b_{l,L}(t_i) b_{l',L}(t_j) \mu_l \mu_{l'} \right) - \mu_X \mu_Y,$$

with $\mu_X = \sum_{l=0}^{L} b_{l,L}(t_i)\mu_l$ and $\mu_Y = \sum_{l=0}^{L} b_{l,L}(t_j)\mu_l$. Writing out μ_X and μ_Y and combining superfluous summations yields

$$\sum_{l=0}^{L} b_{l,L}(t_i) b_{l,L}(t_j)(\sigma_l^2 + \mu_l^2) + \sum_{l=0}^{L} \left(\sum_{l'=0, l' \neq l}^{L} b_{l,L}(t_i) b_{l',L}(t_j) \mu_l \mu_{l'} \right) - \mu_X \mu_Y \geq 0$$

$$\sum_{l=0}^{L} b_{l,L}(t_i) b_{l,L}(t_j)(\sigma_l^2 + \mu_l^2) + \underbrace{\sum_{l=0}^{L} \left(\sum_{l'=0, l' \neq l}^{L} b_{l,L}(t_i) b_{l',L}(t_j) \mu_l \mu_{l'} \right) - \sum_{l=0}^{L} \left(\sum_{l'=0}^{L} b_{l,L}(t_i) b_{l',L}(t_j) \mu_l \mu_{l'} \right)}_{= -\sum_{l=0}^{L} b_{l,L}(t_i) b_{l,L}(t_j) \mu_l^2} \geq 0$$

$$\sum_{l=0}^{L} \left(b_{l,L}(t_i) b_{l,L}(t_j) \sigma_l^2 + b_{l,L}(t_i) b_{l,L}(t_j) \mu_l^2 - b_{l,L}(t_i) b_{l,L}(t_j) \mu_l^2 \right) \geq 0$$

$$\sum_{l=0}^{L} b_{l,L}(t_i) b_{l,L}(t_j) \sigma_l^2 \geq 0,$$

which is independent of the control point mean values μ_l and non-negative for any $t_* \in [0, 1]$, due to $b_{l,L}(t_*) \geq 0$ and $\sigma_l^2 > 0$. Thus, $k_{\mathcal{P}}(t_i, t_j)$ is positive semi-definite for any $t_* \in [0, 1]$ and arbitrary sets of Gaussian control points.

References

1. Álvarez, M.A., Rosasco, L., Lawrence, N.D.: Kernels for vector-valued functions: a review. Found. Trends Mach. Learn. **4**(3), 195–266 (2012). https://doi.org/10.1561/2200000036
2. Bhattacharyya, A., Schiele, B., Fritz, M.: Accurate and diverse sampling of sequences based on a "best of many" sample objective. In: Proceedings of the IEEE Conference on Computer Vision and Pattern Recognition, pp. 8485–8493 (2018)
3. Bishop, C.M.: Mixture density networks (1994)
4. Bishop, C.M.: Neural networks for pattern recognition. Oxford university press (1995)
5. Bishop, C.M.: Pattern Recognition and Machine Learning (Information Science and Statistics). Springer-Verlag, New York Inc, Secaucus, NJ, USA (2006)

6. Blundell, C., Cornebise, J., Kavukcuoglu, K., Wierstra, D.: Weight uncertainty in neural network. In: International Conference on Machine Learning, pp. 1613–1622. PMLR (2015)
7. Bowman, S.R., Vilnis, L., Vinyals, O., Dai, A., Jozefowicz, R., Bengio, S.: Generating sentences from a continuous space. In: Proceedings of The 20th SIGNLL Conference on Computational Natural Language Learning, pp. 10–21. Association for Computational Linguistics, Berlin, Germany (2016). https://doi.org/10.18653/v1/K16-1002, https://aclanthology.org/K16-1002
8. Clevert, D.A., Unterthiner, T., Hochreiter, S.: Fast and accurate deep network learning by exponential linear units (ELUs). arXiv preprint arXiv:1511.07289 (2015)
9. Damianou, A., Lawrence, N.: Deep gaussian processes. In: Artificial Intelligence and Statistics, pp. 207–215 (2013)
10. Deisenroth, M., Ng, J.W.: Distributed gaussian processes. In: International Conference on Machine Learning, pp. 1481–1490. PMLR (2015)
11. Dugas, C., Bengio, Y., Bélisle, F., Nadeau, C., Garcia, R.: Incorporating second-order functional knowledge for better option pricing. Adv. Neural Inf. Process. Syst. 472–478 (2001)
12. Gal, Y., Ghahramani, Z.: Dropout as a bayesian approximation: representing model uncertainty in deep learning. In: International Conference on Machine Learning, pp. 1050–1059 (2016)
13. Glorot, X., Bengio, Y.: Understanding the difficulty of training deep feedforward neural networks. In: Proceedings of the Thirteenth International Conference on Artificial Intelligence and Statistics, pp. 249–256. JMLR Workshop and Conference Proceedings (2010)
14. Glorot, X., Bordes, A., Bengio, Y.: Deep sparse rectifier neural networks. In: Proceedings of the Fourteenth International Conference on Artificial Intelligence and Statistics, pp. 315–323. JMLR Workshop and Conference Proceedings (2011)
15. Goodfellow, I.J., et al.: Generative adversarial nets. In: Proceedings of the 27th International Conference on Neural Information Processing Systems - Volume 2, pp. 2672–2680. NIPS'14, MIT Press, Cambridge, MA, USA (2014)
16. Görtler, J., Kehlbeck, R., Deussen, O.: A visual exploration of gaussian processes. Distill **4**(4), e17 (2019)
17. Graves, A.: Generating sequences with recurrent neural networks. arXiv preprint arXiv:1308.0850 (2013)
18. Guillaumes, A.B.: Mixture density networks for distribution and uncertainty estimation (2017)
19. Ho, J., Jain, A., Abbeel, P.: Denoising diffusion probabilistic models. Adv. Neural. Inf. Process. Syst. **33**, 6840–6851 (2020)
20. Hochreiter, S., Schmidhuber, J.: Long short-term memory. Neural Comput. **9**(8), 1735–1780 (1997)
21. Hug, R.: Probabilistic parametric curves for sequence modeling. KIT Scientific Publishing (2022)
22. Hug, R., Becker, S., Hübner, W., Arens, M.: Generating synthetic ground truth distributions for multi-step trajectory prediction using probabilistic composite b\'ezier curves. 6th ICRA Workshop on Long-term Human Motion Prediction (LHMP) (2024). https://motionpredictionicra2024.github.io/
23. Hug, R., Hübner, W., Arens, M.: Introducing probabilistic bézier curves for n-step sequence prediction. In: Proceedings of the AAAI Conference on Artificial Intelligence. vol. 34, pp. 10162–10169 (2020)
24. Iso, H., Wakamiya, S., Aramaki, E.: Density estimation for geolocation via convolutional mixture density network. arXiv preprint arXiv:1705.02750 (2017)
25. Ivanovic, B., Pavone, M.: The trajectron: probabilistic multi-agent trajectory modeling with dynamic spatiotemporal graphs. In: Proceedings of the IEEE/CVF International Conference on Computer Vision, pp. 2375–2384 (2019)

26. Jacobs, R.A., Jordan, M.I., Nowlan, S.J., Hinton, G.E.: Adaptive mixtures of local experts. Neural Comput. **3**(1), 79–87 (1991)
27. Jørgensen, M., Osborne, M.A.: Bézier gaussian processes for tall and wide data. In: Advances in Neural Information Processing Systems (2022)
28. Kingma, D.P., Welling, M.: Auto-encoding variational bayes. In: 2nd International Conference on Learning Representations, ICLR 2014, Banff, AB, Canada, April 14-16, 2014, Conference Track Proceedings (2014). http://arxiv.org/abs/1312.6114
29. Kothari, P., Kreiss, S., Alahi, A.: Human trajectory forecasting in crowds: A deep learning perspective. IEEE Transactions on Intelligent Transportation Systems (2021)
30. Lederer, A., Conejo, A.J.O., Maier, K.A., Xiao, W., Umlauft, J., Hirche, S.: Gaussian process-based real-time learning for safety critical applications. In: International Conference on Machine Learning, pp. 6055–6064. PMLR (2021)
31. Lerner, A., Chrysanthou, Y., Lischinski, D.: Crowds by example. In: Computer graphics forum. vol. 26, pp. 655–664. Wiley Online Library (2007)
32. Liu, M., et al.: LAformer: trajectory prediction for autonomous driving with lane-aware scene constraints. In: Proceedings of the IEEE/CVF Conference on Computer Vision and Pattern Recognition, pp. 2039–2049 (2024)
33. Lorentz, G.G.: Bernstein polynomials. American Mathematical Soc. (2013)
34. Ma, Z., et al.: A pedestrian trajectory prediction method for generative adversarial networks based on scene constraints. Electronics **13**(3), 628 (2024)
35. MacKay, D.J.: Information theory, inference and learning algorithms. Cambridge University Press (2003)
36. Mao, W., Xu, C., Zhu, Q., Chen, S., Wang, Y.: Leapfrog diffusion model for stochastic trajectory prediction. In: Proceedings of the IEEE/CVF Conference on Computer Vision and Pattern Recognition, pp. 5517–5526 (2023)
37. Mattos, C.L.C., Dai, Z., Damianou, A.C., Forth, J., Barreto, G.A., Lawrence, N.D.: Recurrent gaussian processes. In: Bengio, Y., LeCun, Y. (eds.) 4th International Conference on Learning Representations, ICLR 2016, San Juan, Puerto Rico, May 2-4, 2016, Conference Track Proceedings (2016)
38. Mirza, M., Osindero, S.: Conditional generative adversarial nets. arXiv preprint arXiv:1411.1784 (2014)
39. Murphy, K.P.: Probabilistic Machine Learning: An introduction. MIT Press (2022). probml.ai
40. Pellegrini, S., Ess, A., Schindler, K., Van Gool, L.: You'll never walk alone: modeling social behavior for multi-target tracking. In: 2009 IEEE 12th International Conference on Computer Vision, pp. 261–268. IEEE (2009)
41. Petersen, K.B., Pedersen, M.S.: The matrix cookbook. Tech. Univ. Denmark **7**(15), 510 (2008)
42. Prautzsch, H., Boehm, W., Paluszny, M.: Bézier and B-spline techniques. Springer Science & Business Media (2002)
43. Rasmussen, C., Ghahramani, Z.: Infinite mixtures of gaussian process experts. Adv. Neural Inf. Process. Syst. **14** (2001)
44. Rasmussen, C.E., Williams, C.K.I.: Gaussian Processes for Machine Learning. MIT Press, Adaptive computation and machine learning (2006)
45. Robicquet, A., Sadeghian, A., Alahi, A., Savarese, S.: Learning social etiquette: human trajectory understanding in crowded scenes. In: European Conference on Computer Vision, pp. 549–565. Springer (2016)
46. Sohn, K., Lee, H., Yan, X.: Learning structured output representation using deep conditional generative models. Adv. Neural. Inf. Process. Syst. **28**, 3483–3491 (2015)

47. Tashiro, Y., Song, J., Song, Y., Ermon, S.: CSDI: conditional score-based diffusion models for probabilistic time series imputation. Adv. Neural. Inf. Process. Syst. **34**, 24804–24816 (2021)
48. Tresp, V.: Mixtures of gaussian processes. Adv. Neural Inf. Process. Syst. **13** (2000)
49. Wang, K.L., Tsao, L.W., Wu, J.C., Shuai, H.H., Cheng, W.H.: TrajFine: predicted trajectory refinement for pedestrian trajectory forecasting. In: Proceedings of the IEEE/CVF Conference on Computer Vision and Pattern Recognition, pp. 4483–4492 (2024)
50. Wu, X., Wang, T., Cai, Y., Liang, L., Papageorgiou, G.: A multi-stage goal-driven network for pedestrian trajectory prediction. In: 2024 5th International Conference on Computer Vision, Image and Deep Learning (CVIDL), pp. 1039–1046. IEEE (2024)
51. Yu, L., Zhang, W., Wang, J., Yu, Y.: SeqGAN: sequence generative adversarial nets with policy gradient. In: Proceedings of the AAAI Conference on Artificial Intelligence. vol. 31 (2017)
52. Yuan, C., Neubauer, C.: Variational mixture of gaussian process experts. Adv. Neural Inf. Process. Syst. **21** (2008)
53. Zhou, H., Ren, D., Yang, X., Fan, M., Huang, H.: CSR: cascade conditional variational auto encoder with socially-aware regression for pedestrian trajectory prediction. Pattern Recogn. **133**, 109030 (2023)

Is an Object-Centric Representation Beneficial for Robotic Manipulation?

Alexandre Chapin(✉), Emmanuel Dellandréa, and Liming Chen

Ecole Centrale de Lyon, CNRS, INSA Lyon, Université Claude Bernard Lyon 1, Université Lumière Lyon 2, LIRIS, UMR5205, 69130 Ecully, France
{alexandre.chapin,emmanuel.dellandrea,liming.chen}@ec-lyon.fr

Abstract. Object-centric representation (OCR) has recently become a subject of interest in the computer vision community for learning a structured representation of images and videos. It has been several times presented as a potential way to improve data-efficiency and generalization capabilities to learn an agent on downstream tasks. However, most existing work only evaluates such models on scene decomposition, without any notion of reasoning over the learned representation. Robotic manipulation tasks generally involve multi-object environments with potential inter-object interaction. We thus argue that they are a very interesting playground to really evaluate the potential of existing object-centric work. To do so, we create several robotic manipulation tasks in simulated environments involving multiple objects (several distractors, the robot, etc.) and a high-level of randomization (object positions, colors, shapes, background, initial positions, etc.). We then evaluate one classical object-centric method across several generalization scenarios and compare its results against several state-of-the-art hollistic representations. Our results exhibit that existing methods are prone to failure in difficult scenarios involving complex scene structures, whereas object-centric methods help overcome these challenges.

Keywords: Robotics · Object-centric learning · Imitation learning

1 Introduction

Robotic manipulation tasks generally involve a multitude of objects with numerous possible scene arrangements and interaction methods, such as pushing, grabbing, moving, lifting, stacking and more. Several challenges remain to be addressed to enable the deployment of generalizable robots in real-world settings. These challenges include predicting and understanding the dynamics between both seen and unseen objects to successfully complete the required tasks. It is well-known that one of the most crucial aspects of achieving a more efficient and generalizable robotic agent is the ability to effectively handle the representations derived from its sensors [1,21].

In recent years, various studies have explored ways to improve the representations of the environments surrounding robots. For example, through pre-training and time-contrastive learning over human ego-centric datasets [23,24,26], distilling knowledge

J. Röning and J. Filipe (Eds.): ROBOVIS 2025, CCIS 2629, pp. 510–523, 2026.
https://doi.org/10.1007/978-3-032-00986-9_32

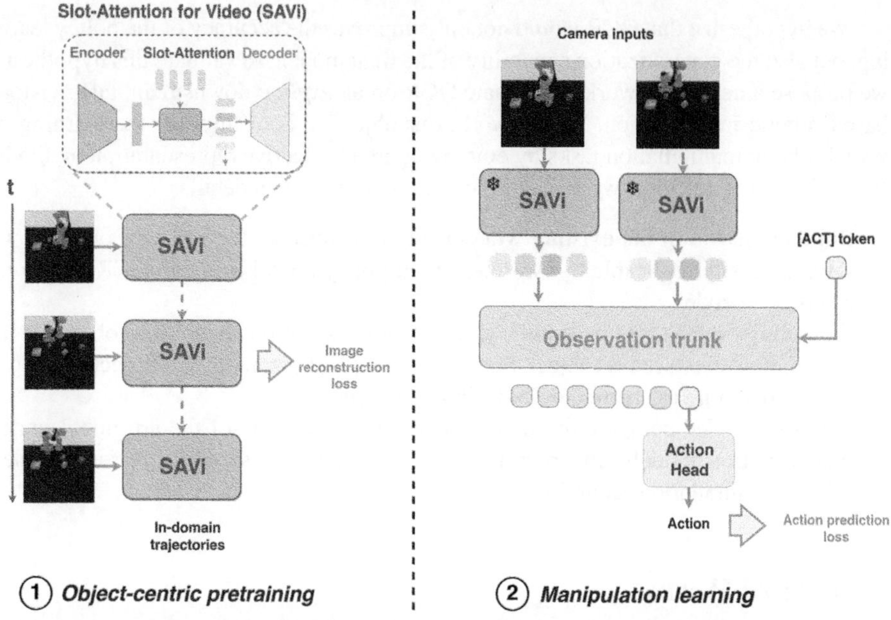

Fig. 1. Overview of the proposed framework. We introduce a new framework to evaluate different representations models for robot manipulation policy learning. Our main objective is to evaluate object-centric representation methods. To do so, the models can be trained following classical scheme through image reconstruction loss on in-domain data. Then, the model can be used as a frozen backbone for manipulation learning: it is used to encode camera inputs from several timesteps before being fed to a transformer models that concatenate all the information into an additional *[ACT]* token. This final token is used as input to an action head in order to predict the next action. The second part of the model is learnt through imitation learning with an action prediction loss.

from pre-trained computer vision (CV) models [31], and leveraging successful learning scheme of the CV field such as masked autoencoding [29]. In [16], an extensive review and evaluation of existing state-of-the-art representation models from CV applied on robotic tasks has been made, and showed that most of existing models can be used "off-the-shelf" for policy learning. However, these approaches often represent the environment as a single global vector, which must account for the wide variety of situations a robot might encounter.

In contrast to these methods, a promising approach has emerged in CV: object-centric representations (OCR). This paradigm treats an image as a set of distinct entities, referred to as *objects*, thereby introducing structure and symbolism into the representation. While the potential of OCR for robotic tasks has been recognized, most studies focus on image decomposition and reconstruction rather than evaluating its impact on robotic applications. Some works have explored how OCR performs in scenarios such as Reinforcement Learning (RL) [13,14,40], but these are typically limited to simple 2D environments or toy tasks [20,36,42].

We hypothesize that OCR would not only improves the accuracy of the policy learning, but also the generalization capability of the final model. To validate this hypothesis, we propose a new framework to evaluate OCR on an *explicit* downstream task: vision-based robotic manipulation. In this work, our objective is to improve the learning of visual robotic manipulation tasks by employing more effective representation methods. In the following sections, we will outline our contributions in details:

- Building on top of the existing works using transformers for behavior cloning, we setup an easily replicable transformer-based policy model using an OCR backbone as vision encoder.
- We build several tasks in simulated environments implying multiple objects with randomness over scenes (object, background, ...) and extract expert trajectories with motion planning to create our **RoboShape** dataset.
- We evaluate and compare our method against several state-of-the-art global image representation models, in order to show the effectiveness of OCR for complex robotic manipulation scenarios.

2 Related Works

2.1 Object-Centric Representation

The learning of an OCR is a prominent and very promising field of research in CV. Early works primarily focused on learning structured image representations through generative modeling [15,19]. Most methods were based on autoencoder architectures, aiming to obtain a structured and disentangled latent space. Later, some studies explored how to explicitely structure this space by decomposing the latent representation into multiple vectors, rather than using a single vector to represent the entire image [3,18,36]. One of the most significant methods in this direction is Slot-Attention [22], known for its simplicity ad efficiency, making it easy to train and deploy. Subsequent papers explored the use of more powerful decoders, such as diffusion models [17,38] and transformer decoders [32], and pre-trained backbones such as DINO [5] to help model learn object representation in more complex, real-world scenarios [30]. Following works extended Slot-Attention to videos by incorporating recurrent neural network or transformer architectures [9,20,33,41].

Recently, some studies have investigated the use of OCR for reinforcement learning (RL) [13,14,36,40], demonstrating their potential to handle multi-entity scenes. In parallel, a transformer-based approach called SlotFormer was developed for next-frame prediction [37], predicting dynamics in the object-centric latent space. This work is particularly promising as it can predict scene dynamics after unsupervised learning. Our work builds upon these advancements by proposing a framework built on top of OCR models to evaluate them in scenarios that require understanding the notion of objects.

2.2 Vision Based Imitation Learning

Imitation learning (IL) is a paradigm that allows robots to learn from expert demonstrations. One of the most prominent and simple implementations of IL is Behavior cloning (BC), which can be viewed as a form of *supervised learning*. It consists of mapping observation data to actions. BC has been successful in teaching a wide range of tasks (e.g., grasping, pick and place, etc.) from low-dimensional states, demonstrating the generalizable properties of agents trained on sufficient data [2,7]. Most of the work in BC has focused on creating new architectures for learning policy, ranging from simple MLPs to transformers [2,8], diffusion models [6] and even combinations of transformers and diffusion models [35]. Some recent studies have explored the use of object-centric representations to learn behaviors, showing promising results on toy scenarios [14]. In [4], it was demonstrated that pre-trained models like DINO [5] can provide strong generalization capabilities, even surpassing models specifically designed for robotic manipulation [23,26]. In [28], an object-centric representation was extracted from DINOv2 [27], showing that such representations not only improved the success rate of robotic manipulation over the original models but also matched the performance of state-of-the-art pre-trained robotic representation models. More recently, [31] combined several recent state-of-the-art CV foundation models with knowledge distillation. Their final model demonstrated impressive performance across several behavior cloning benchmarks.

In this work, we focused on developing a simple policy architecture on top of existing OCR models, which we compare with current methods for representation learning.

3 Method

3.1 Preliminaries

Imitation-Learning. Our aim is to learn a robotic policy capable of solving a task using vision. The robot agent receives as input a sequence of observations $(o_0, o_1, ..., o_t)$. These observations are processed by an encoder model to produce a sequence of states $(s_0, s_1, ..., s_t) = f(o_0, o_1, ..., o_t)$. Based on a fixed-horizon history H, the policy generates an action distribution $\pi(.|\{s_t\}_{t=0}^{H})$ from which the action a_{H+1} is sampled and applied to the robot. The entire model can be trained end-to-end or in two stages : first, pre-training the vision component on out-of-domain data, followed by freezing it for policy learning.

Slot-Attention for Video (SAVi). One of the most prominent object-centric models for video decomposition is Slot-Attention for Video [9,20]. The model consises of an encoder $f(o_t) = h_t$, typically a convolutional neural network (CNN), which processes the input image before passing it to the Slot-Attention module [22]. The Slot-Attention module clusters features into a slot representation : $SA(h_t) = \mathcal{S}_t = \{s^1, ..., s^K\} \in \mathbb{R}^{K \times D}$ where K is the number of slots and D is the slot size. Next, a predictor model, generally a transformer, is applied to the slots to capture temporal dynamics by propagating information between slots across timesteps: $p(\mathcal{S}_t, \mathcal{S}_{t+1}, ..., \mathcal{S}_{t+h})$, where h is the temporal horizon. Finally, a decoder attempts to reconstruct the input image from the slot representation : $d(\mathcal{S}_t) = \tilde{o}_t$.

3.2 Object-Centric Transformer Policy

Architecture. An overview of our model is shown in Fig. 1, it is composed of three components: an image encoder handling the camera inputs, a transformer-based observation trunk, concatenating the informations from the observations, and finally an action head making the final decision choice.

Encoder: Our image encoder is the video object-centric model SAVi [20]. It consists of a small CNN, which is a stack of five convolutional layers with ReLU activation, concatenated with positional encoding. The resulting feature grid is flattened before being passed to the Slot-Attention process. In the Slot-Attention process, each slot is initialized as a random vector and iteratively cross-attended with the output features from the CNN. Unlike classical cross-attention, renormalization is performed over the queries instead of the keys. Each frame of the input video is encoded independently by the CNN, and the first frame is further processed by the Slot-Attention module. The output slots from this process are passed through a transformer model (predictor) and are then used as initialization slots for the subsequent frame. This step allows the model to maintain a memory of the slots over the course of the video.

Observation Trunk: To effectively handle the multiple vectors extracted from object-centric representations, we adopted the architecture proposed by [12], which uses a transformer-based observation trunk. This approach allows for a more sophisticated integration of all information into a single vector, avoiding the limitations of traditional methods. Indeed, existing works often rely on a MLP head as a bottleneck before the action head. However, such a structure is not well-suited for object-centric representations.

The transformer takes as input the history of representation of the last H frames $(S_{t-H}, ..., S_t)$ with $S_t = \{s^1, ..., s^K\} \in \mathbb{R}^{K \times D}$ and an additional learnable action token $[ACT]$. The purpose of the action token is to aggregate the information from the history of slots in order to then perform the prediction.

Action Head: After a forward pass, the $[ACT]$ is isolated to predict the next action a_t through the action head. The actions are composed of 7 dimensions corresponding of the 6D relative pose of the end-effector (x, y, z, r_x, r_y, r_z) and one for the gripper state $\in [-1, 1]$ (close or open). In our experiments, we use a Gaussian-Mixture Model (GMM) head, as it is done in several recent works [25,43], in order to handle the multi-modality of the encountered environments.

Training. The training pipeline of our model is divided in two parts: a vision pre-training phase and a behavior learning phase.

During the pre-training phase, the model is trained on in-domain data (the same data used for the behavior learning phase). Following the SAVi training scheme, the model processes a short input video, decomposes each frame into slots, and then reconstructs the input video from these slots. The model is learned end-to-end with an image reconstruction loss (MSE loss) and permits to obtain a good decomposition of objects over the dataset.

In the behavior learning phase, the representation model is frozen and used to extract slot representation from the input frames. These slot representations condition the prediction of the next action. To optimize the policy model, a negative log-likelihood loss (NLL) is applied to the predicted action distribution, comparing it to the target action.

4 Experiments

4.1 Experimental Setup

In order to validate our model against existing methods, we designed several multi-object robotic manipulation tasks using Maniskill [34], an open-source robotic framework built upon the SAPIEN environment [39]. In our experiments, we aim to address the following questions: 1) Can an OCR solve visual-based robotic manipulation ? 2) Can an OCR generalize better than classical global representation methods to unseen scenes, distractors, or colors?

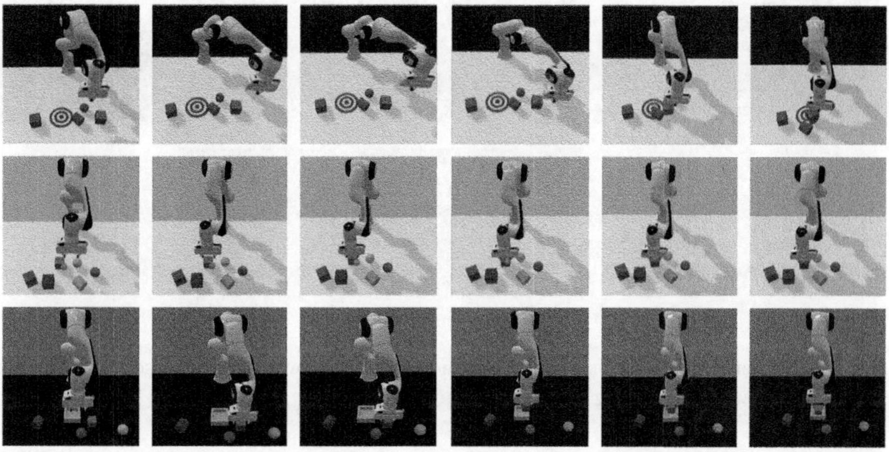

Fig. 2. Example rollout of the tasks. Top row: *Push cube to target*; Middle row: *Pick cube*; Bottom row: *Place cube in bin.*

Tasks Definition. The models are trained on a new dataset we created, called **RoboShape**, composed of 3 different tasks with an increasing level of difficulty as shown in Fig. 2.

- Task 1: *Push cube to target*; the goal is to push the red cube to the target.
- Task 2: *Pick cube*; the goal is to pick up the red cube, and place it to a pre-determined position.
- Task 3: *Place cube in bin*; the goal is to pick up the red cube and place it into the green bin.

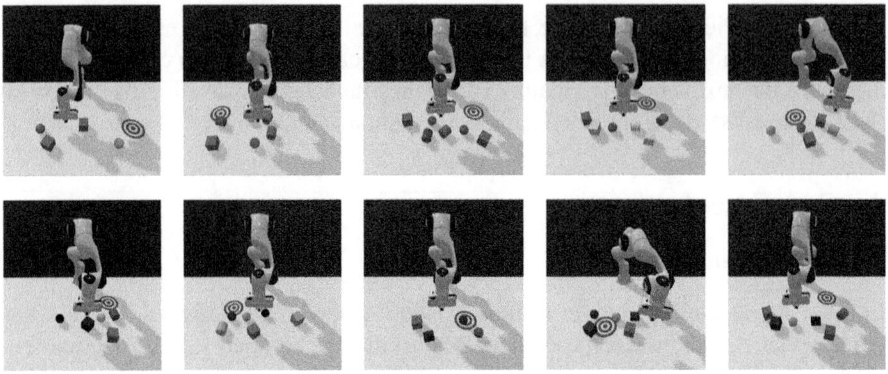

Fig. 3. L1 generalization - Unseen distractor colors Top row: distractor colors seen during training; Bottom row: unseen distractor colors.

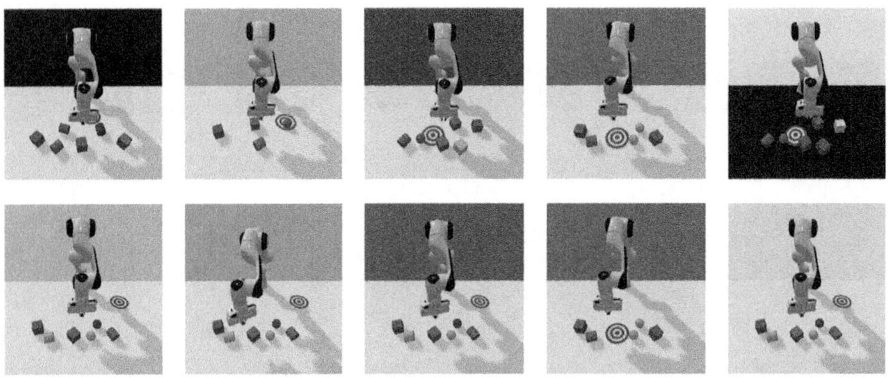

Fig. 4. L2 generalization - Unseen background colors Top row: background seen during training; Bottom row: unseen background colors.

Each task is a table-top manipulation task performed with a Franka robot using a single view positioned in front of the robot. We do not use proprioceptive information such as end-effector pose or joint positions. Using oracle information, we built a dataset of expert trajectories by collecting 2000 expert trajectories for each task.

At each reset of the environment, several randomization processes are applied: target and distractor positions, distractor shapes and colors, background and table color and the robot's initial position. All randomization process can be observed on Figs. 3, 4 and 5. The colors of the distractors are defined as [●, ●, ●, ●, ●, ●, ●], as shown on first row of Fig. 3. Those of the background are defined as [●, ●, ●, ●, ●], as shown on first row of Fig. 4.

Given the high level of randomization, especially on the target positions, the policy needs to understand high-level concepts in order to solve the tasks such as "what are the objects I need to interact with ?", "where should I move the objects ?".

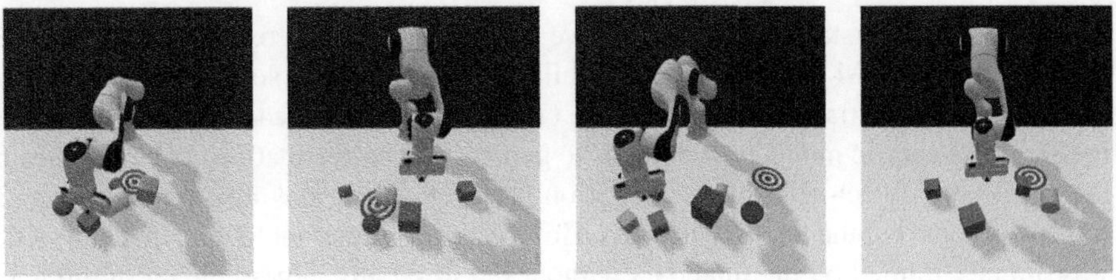

Fig. 5. L3 generalization - Unseen distractor sizes the distractors have a random size and can have smaller or bigger sizes than seen during training.

Evaluation Process. In order to test the generalization capabilities of the different representations, we define 3 levels of generalization:

- (L1) *unseen distractor colors*
- (L2) *unseen background colors*
- (L3) *novel distractor sizes*

The unseen distractors colors are randomly sampled from the following set: [●, ●, ●, ●, ●, ●, ●] while the unseen set of the background is [●, ●, ●, ●, ●]. The table color is randomized between black and white.

The metric we use for evaluation is the mean success rate over 100 different rollouts, with a new seed for each rollout. We repeat the experiment 3 times (300 trajectories) to compute then mean and standard deviation, which are presented in the following tables.

Baselines. As we aim to evaluate whether the structure provided by an object-centric representation is beneficial for learning downstream robotic tasks, we decided to use two global reprsentation models as baselines: one classical CV model and one robotic pre-trained representation. Specifically, we use the pre-trained vision transformer (ViT) version of DINO [5] and the R3M [26] model. For the object-centric model, we tested the original version of SAVi [20]. All models are frozen during policy learning.

4.2 Quantitative Results

In the following, we refer to the policy models by the encoder used in their behavior learning process: R3M, DINO or SAVi.

In the task *Push Cube to target* presented in Table 1, the pre-trained representation of R3M performs the best. The task is relatively simple, as the primary requirement is to understand the relative position of the cube to the target in order to push or pull it to the correct target spot. The DINO model fails to perform any successful rollouts. We hypothesize that, even though the task is simple, the representation model may easily overfit to the background or the table, as it dominates the input observation. R3M overcomes this issue by learning dynamic information through its time-contrastive learning, enabling it to use this knowledge to complete the task. The object-centric model SAVi is able to perform the task but with a lower success-rate than R3M.

To better understand these results, we visualized the different rollouts produced by the models: R3M demonstrates the ability to recover from suboptimal trajectories where the robot initially fails to push the cube to the target, a capability not observed in the object-centric model, which tends to get stuck in such situations. We hypothesize that while the object-centric representation is beneficial, it may also require dynamic information during the learning process. However, it is important to note that our model was directly trained on the final data without requiring any large-scale pre-training on out-of-domain data and operates with a significantly smaller scale (approximately 25 times fewer parameters). This suggests that larger pre-training and a more complex loss function could potentially yield even better results.

We also observe an interesting trend in the *L1* scenario: R3M experiences a significant drop in success rate (approximately 60%). This scenario introduces distractor colors unseen during training. In contrast, the object-centric method is notably robust in this scenario, with only a 14% drop in success rate. Since the encoder segments the objects in the scene into separate slots, it can isolate the object of interest to complete the task while avoiding reliance on "noisy" information. A similar trend is observed in other generalization scenarios: the object-centric method consistently demonstrates robustness to out-of-distribution scenarios, experiencing relatively smaller performance drops compared to R3M.

Table 1. Success rate of *Push Cube to target* task over the different generalization scenarios.

	DINO	R3M	SAVi
	0.	**0.88** $\pm$ 0.07	0.69 $\pm$ 0.06
L1	0.	0.26 $\pm$ 0.06	**0.55** $\pm$ 0.02
L2	0.	**0.70** $\pm$ 0.01	0.60 $\pm$ 0.04
L3	0.	**0.76** $\pm$ 0.01	0.56 $\pm$ 0.08

The task *Pick cube*, presented in Table 2, is more complex as it requires the model to grasp the red cube and position it at a specific relative location above. This task demands greater precision and reasoning to identify the correct shape in the scene and place it in the correct position.

The results in the Table 2 show that the object-centric model outperforms the other models. As expected, the DINO model is unable to perform this task, similar to the previous one. Surprisingly, R3M also fails in this task, but not as we expected. While R3M is able to grasp the cube in most rollouts, the single front-view input and lack of additional information make it difficult for the model to correctly position the cube. As a result, it often releases the cube in the wrong place, leading to failure in most cases. Although the dynamic information encoded in R3M helps the model approach and grasp the cube, it is insufficient for accurately placing the cube in space, as no visual cue for the target position is provided.

The object-centric model successfully performs the task, with only a small drop in performance compared to the first task. Notably, it is the only model capable of completing this task. Furthermore, the object-centric model demonstrates robustness across different generalization scenarios, with an approximate performance drop of just 10% per scenario.

Table 2. Success rate of *Pick cube* task over the different generalization scenarios.

	DINO	R3M	SAVi
	0.	0.	**0.56** $\pm$ 0.01
L1	0.	0.	**0.44** $\pm$ 0.04
L2	0.	0.	**0.48** $\pm$ 0.07
L3	0.	0.	**0.51** $\pm$ 0.02

For the task *Place cube in bin*, none of the models are able to achieve a positive success rate. The task requires the model to first grasp the cube, place it on top of a box and realease it. The model must understand which cube to grab, identify the target position, and determine how to move from one to the other.

Interestingly, both the R3M and SAVi models fail, yet they are able to grasp the cube and move it toward the box. However, the R3M model is unable to drop the cube inside the box, and instead, it falls next to it. This suggests a need for better spatial understanding. The SAVi-based model, on the other hand, is able to position itself directly above the box but do not drop the cube. We hypothesize that this is due to the uncertainty introduced by the single-view input. In many cases, the model appears to perceive the cube as already inside the box, as illustrated in Fig. 6. We believe that using a mounted camera view would resolve this issue.

Fig. 6. Failure case in the last task: the robot is blocked on top of the green box and do not realease the cube. Left: Input observation; Right : Model reconstruction.

Finally, the Fig. 7 provides an overall comparison of the mean success rate across all scenarios in the different tasks for each model. Since the DINO and R3M models are unable to perform the second and third tasks of our benchmark, they overall underperform compared to the object-centric alternative, which demonstrates robustness across different generalization levels with only small drops in performance.

The underperformance of R3M in the *L1* scenario suggests the need to further explore further this direction: how robust are global representation models to unseen distractors ?

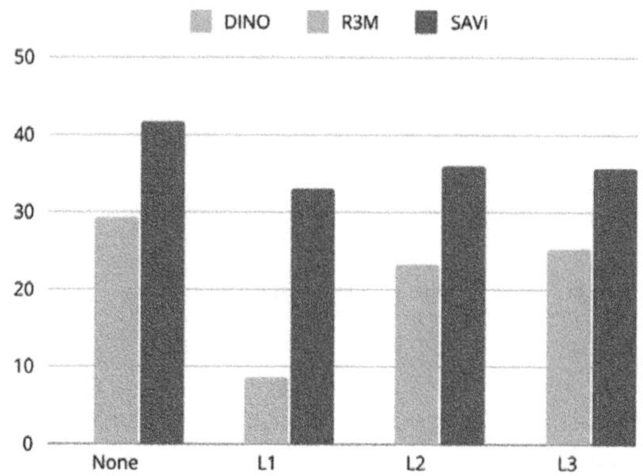

Fig. 7. Overall success rate: mean success rate over the 3 tasks on the different generalization scenarios.

4.3 Qualitative Results

For validation purposes, we visualize the reconstruction of the predicted next slot by the object-centric model during behavior learning, comparing it to the rollout obtained in the real environment with the predicted actions. Figure 8 shows the decomposition for five different rollouts. It demonstrates that the model accurately splits the input observation into distinct parts: the background, the robot, and the various objects in

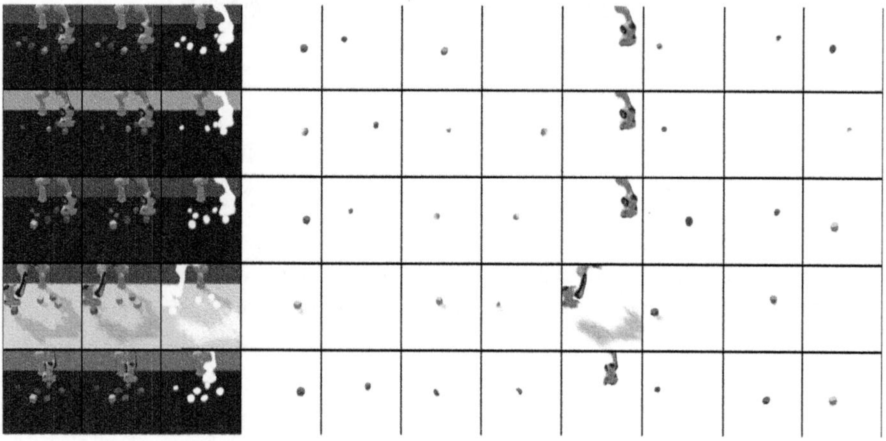

Fig. 8. Object decomposition on rollout From left to right : input image, full reconstruction, slot decomposition.

the scene. By leveraging this pre-trained model, future exploration could focus on the concept of world models [10, 11], enabling "learning within an imagined world."

5 Conclusion

We introduced a new simple framework which combines behavior cloning with object-centric representations. To validate the effectiveness of our approach compared to existing global representation methods, we propose three new challenging robotic tasks that feature increasing levels of difficulty and varying degrees of generalization for each task. Despite a limited model size and data scale, our method achieves success in complex tasks where state-of-the-art computer vision and vision-based robotic models fail.

Furthermore, we demonstrate that object-centric methods can mitigate the effects of out-of-distribution scenarios, such as handling new distractors. This highlights the potential of object-centric representation methods as a promising direction for advancing the generalization of robotic manipulation learning. We hope this work inspires others to explore the use of object-centric representations in robotics.

Limitations and Future Works. Our work is currently limited to simulation settings involving relatively simple tasks. We plan to extend this research by exploring more complex environments with objects from everyday life.

Additionally, we aim to scale our method to real-world applications by pretraining our object-centric approach on existing large-scale robotic datasets [7], leveraging recent state-of-the-art object-centric methods [41]. Finally, we seek to have a deeper understanding of how different representations influence learning by conducting comparisons with a broader range of methods, including both object-centric and global approaches.

Acknowledgments. This work was in part supported by the French national program of investment of the futur and the regions through the PSPC FAIR Waste project, as well as the French Research Agency, l'Agence Nationale de Recherche (ANR), through the projects Chiron (ANR-20-IADJ-0001-01), Aristotle (ANR-21-FAI1-0009-01), and Astérix (ANR-23-EDIA-0002-001).

References

1. Bengio, Y., Courville, A., Vincent, P.: Representation learning: A review and new perspectives (2014). https://arxiv.org/abs/1206.5538
2. Brohan, A., et al.: Rt-1: Robotics transformer for real-world control at scale (2023). https://arxiv.org/abs/2212.06817
3. Burgess, C.P., et al.: MONET: Unsupervised scene decomposition and representation (2019). https://arxiv.org/abs/1901.11390
4. Burns, K., Witzel, Z., Hamid, J.I., Yu, T., Finn, C., Hausman, K.: What makes pre-trained visual representations successful for robust manipulation? (2023). https://arxiv.org/abs/2312.12444
5. Caron, M., et al.: Emerging properties in self-supervised vision transformers (2021). https://arxiv.org/abs/2104.14294

6. Chi, C., et al.: Diffusion policy: Visuomotor policy learning via action diffusion (2024). https://arxiv.org/abs/2303.04137
7. Collaboration, E., O'Neill, A., et al.: Open x-embodiment: Robotic learning datasets and rt-x models (2024). https://arxiv.org/abs/2310.08864
8. Dalal, M., Mandlekar, A., Garrett, C., Handa, A., Salakhutdinov, R., Fox, D.: Imitating task and motion planning with visuomotor transformers (2023)
9. Elsayed, G.F., et al.: SAVi++: Towards end-to-end object-centric learning from real-world videos (2022)
10. Ha, D., Schmidhuber, J.: World models (2018). https://doi.org/10.5281/ZENODO.1207631, https://zenodo.org/record/1207631
11. Hafner, D., Lillicrap, T., Ba, J., Norouzi, M.: Dream to control: Learning behaviors by latent imagination (2020). https://arxiv.org/abs/1912.01603
12. Haldar, S., Peng, Z., Pinto, L.: BAKU: An efficient transformer for multi-task policy learning (2024). https://arxiv.org/abs/2406.07539
13. Haramati, D., Daniel, T., Tamar, A.: Entity-centric reinforcement learning for object manipulation from pixels (2024). https://arxiv.org/abs/2404.01220
14. Heravi, N., et al.: Visuomotor control in multi-object scenes using object-aware representations (2023). https://arxiv.org/abs/2205.06333
15. Higgins, I., et al.: beta-VAE: learning basic visual concepts with a constrained variational framework. In: International Conference on Learning Representations (2017). https://openreview.net/forum?id=Sy2fzU9gl
16. Hu, Y., Wang, R., Li, L.E., Gao, Y.: For pre-trained vision models in motor control, not all policy learning methods are created equal (2023). https://arxiv.org/abs/2304.04591
17. Jiang, J., Deng, F., Singh, G., Ahn, S.: Object-centric slot diffusion (2023). https://arxiv.org/abs/2303.10834
18. Kabra, R., et al.: SIMONe: View-invariant, temporally-abstracted object representations via unsupervised video decomposition (2021). https://arxiv.org/abs/2106.03849
19. Kingma, D.P., Welling, M.: Auto-encoding variational bayes (2022). https://arxiv.org/abs/1312.6114
20. Kipf, T., et al.: Conditional object-centric learning from video (2022). https://arxiv.org/abs/2111.12594
21. Kroemer, O., Niekum, S., Konidaris, G.: A review of robot learning for manipulation: Challenges, representations, and algorithms (2020). https://arxiv.org/abs/1907.03146
22. Locatello, F., et al.: Object-centric learning with slot attention (2020). https://arxiv.org/abs/2006.15055
23. Ma, Y.J., et al.: VIP: Towards universal visual reward and representation via value-implicit pre-training (2023). https://arxiv.org/abs/2210.00030
24. Majumdar, A., et al.: Where are we in the search for an artificial visual cortex for embodied intelligence? (2024). https://arxiv.org/abs/2303.18240
25. Mandlekar, A., et al.: What matters in learning from offline human demonstrations for robot manipulation (2021). https://arxiv.org/abs/2108.03298
26. Nair, S., Rajeswaran, A., Kumar, V., Finn, C., Gupta, A.: R3M: A universal visual representation for robot manipulation (2022). https://arxiv.org/abs/2203.12601
27. Oquab, M., et al.: DINOv2: Learning robust visual features without supervision (2024). https://arxiv.org/abs/2304.07193
28. Qian, J., Panagopoulos, A., Jayaraman, D.: Recasting generic pretrained vision transformers as object-centric scene encoders for manipulation policies. arXiv preprint arXiv:2405.15916 (2024)
29. Radosavovic, I., Xiao, T., James, S., Abbeel, P., Malik, J., Darrell, T.: Real-world robot learning with masked visual pre-training (2022). https://arxiv.org/abs/2210.03109

30. Seitzer, M., et al.: Bridging the gap to real-world object-centric learning (2023). https://arxiv.org/abs/2209.14860
31. Shang, J., et al.: Theia: Distilling diverse vision foundation models for robot learning (2024). https://arxiv.org/abs/2407.20179
32. Singh, G., Deng, F., Ahn, S.: Illiterate DALL-E learns to compose (2022). https://arxiv.org/abs/2110.11405
33. Singh, G., Wu, Y.F., Ahn, S.: Simple unsupervised object-centric learning for complex and naturalistic videos (2022). https://arxiv.org/abs/2205.14065
34. Tao, S., et al.: ManiSkill3: GPU parallelized robotics simulation and rendering for generalizable embodied AI (2024). https://arxiv.org/abs/2410.00425
35. Team, O.M., et al.: Octo: An open-source generalist robot policy (2024). https://arxiv.org/abs/2405.12213
36. Watters, N., Matthey, L., Bosnjak, M., Burgess, C.P., Lerchner, A.: COBRA: Data-efficient model-based RL through unsupervised object discovery and curiosity-driven exploration (2019). https://arxiv.org/abs/1905.09275
37. Wu, Z., Dvornik, N., Greff, K., Kipf, T., Garg, A.: SlotFormer: Unsupervised visual dynamics simulation with object-centric models (2023). https://arxiv.org/abs/2210.05861
38. Wu, Z., Hu, J., Lu, W., Gilitschenski, I., Garg, A.: SlotDiffusion: Object-centric generative modeling with diffusion models (2023). https://arxiv.org/abs/2305.11281
39. Xiang, F., et al.: SAPIEN: a simulated part-based interactive environment. In: The IEEE Conference on Computer Vision and Pattern Recognition (CVPR) (2020)
40. Yoon, J., Wu, Y.F., Bae, H., Ahn, S.: An investigation into pre-training object-centric representations for reinforcement learning (2023). https://arxiv.org/abs/2302.04419
41. Zadaianchuk, A., Seitzer, M., Martius, G.: Object-centric learning for real-world videos by predicting temporal feature similarities (2023). https://arxiv.org/abs/2306.04829
42. Zhang, C., Gupta, A., Zisserman, A.: Is an object-centric video representation beneficial for transfer? (2022). https://arxiv.org/abs/2207.10075
43. Zhu, Y., Joshi, A., Stone, P., Zhu, Y.: VIOLA: Imitation learning for vision-based manipulation with object proposal priors (2023). https://arxiv.org/abs/2210.11339

Outdoor Robot Geo-Localization Using Vision Technics

Hasinarivo Marie Berthis Ramanana[1(✉)], Jean-Pierre Jessel[2], Tahiry Filamatra Andriamarozakaniaina[1], and Hagamalala Santatra Bernardin[1]

[1] MISA - MIT, Université d'Antananarivo, Antananarivo, Madagascar
hasram006@gmail.com
[2] IRIT, Université Paul Sabatier Toulouse, Toulouse, France
jessel@irit.fr

Abstract. Outdoor geolocation generally relies on the smartphone's GPS (Global Positioning System) for positioning. However, GPS encounters difficulties when the sky is cloudy or in dense urban areas between tall buildings. This article proposes an alternative method of geolocation in the event of GPS unavailability or failure, using vision to locate oneself. The method is based on a neural network model based on MobileNet, followed by regression and logo detection using YOLO to help the user locate. We will compare our method with that used by Nilwong et al., AlexNet and ResNet50. The datasets used are images captured on a campus with a smartphone and used to train the model. The results are obtained using an Android application, which compares the predicted position from the input images with the actual position measured by GPS in good conditions (clear sky). The results show that our model can replace GPS for locating a pedestrian in an urban environment.

Keywords: Outdoor localization · MobileNet · Regression · YOLOv10 · GPS

1 Introduction

Whether you're a tourist or a resident, you may encounter the challenge of finding your way to a specific location [6]. Navigation in urban environments is becoming increasingly important with advances in mobile technology. These advances include navigation applications on smartphones, such as Google Maps, Maps.me, and Here WeGo [8,10,16]. However, there are also other navigation applications designed for specific, well-defined locations, such as apps for campus navigation [13] or indoor navigation like in [12,20,25].

Global Navigation Satellite System or GNSS is the most used technology in the domain of outdoor localization. Among the GNSS we find Galileo (EU) [5], Global Positioning System or GPS (USA) [9], GLONASS (Russia) [7] and BeiDou (China) [4]. These systems are essential for a variety of applications, including navigation, mapping, and tracking. Under optimal conditions, GPS systems are accurate to within 3 to 5 m [2]. However, their accuracy and performance can be degraded by a number of factors. Poor reception of signals from satellites remains the primary cause of reduced GNSS effectiveness. This can be due to a hardware failure in the receiver or to cloudy skies or the presence of several buildings or trees that can block the signals [19].

J. Röning and J. Filipe (Eds.): ROBOVIS 2025, CCIS 2629, pp. 524–534, 2026.
https://doi.org/10.1007/978-3-032-00986-9_33

It is important to note that the integration of signals from the four Global Navigation Satellite System (GNSS) constellations (GPS, Galileo, GLONASS, and BeiDou) can enhance overall positioning accuracy; however, this integration does not fully resolve urban GPS error issues. The primary causes of GPS errors in urban environments are phenomena such as multipath (signal reflections from buildings), occlusions (loss of direct line-of-sight to satellites), and geometric dilution of precision (suboptimal satellite configuration). Even with the incorporation of signals from all four GNSS constellations, these challenges persist if satellites are not directly visible or if signals experience significant interference. The problem of GNSS unavailability has given rise to a new area of research, image-based localization. Several research projects have been carried out in this area. In [3], for example, the authors use an image database to correct GPS errors. They estimate the camera position by 3D reconstruction of descriptors from SIFT (Scale-Invariant Feature Transform) [14]. Other authors, as in [21], prefer to calculate the cross-ratio of windows on building facades to find their way around dense urban environments. This technique is specific to environments with several buildings that have many windows. However, their method is flawed if the aspect ratios of different buildings have the same value. This is highly likely with the standardization of building windows.

As machine learning and deep learning methods gain popularity, many authors are exploring solutions to the GPS problem using variations of these approaches. In [15], authors present an algorithm that first extracts self-similarity matrix features to represent the image, effectively capturing the user's spatio-temporal information. Then, image retrieval is performed using trained multitask classifiers to identify the scene's location and orientation. Jabborov et al. [11] apply the SIFT method to detect corresponding points and to minimize re-projection errors for a given pair of images, the LevenbergâĂŞMarquardt optimization method is used. [28] use a multi-sensor approach followed by RANSAC to remove outliers. Nilwong et al. [3] propose a GPS-free localization: (1) Faster Regional-Convolutional Neural Network or Faster R-CNN to capture landmarks [23] followed by a training phase based on Feed Forward Neural Network or FFNN to determine the location coordinates of mobile robot and the compass orientations. (2) image-based localization using Convolutional Neural Network. The principle of the first method by Nilwong et al. is to detect specific markers and signs in the terrain (such as road signs, nameplates, etc.) by using Faster R-CNN. Coordinates of the bounding boxes, labels and scores of the detected objects will be used as input to a feed forward neural network to predict the longitude, latitude and angles of objects. For the second method, they use the entire image with 320×240 pixels as input to a convolutional neural network. At the end, a dense layer is used with regression to predict latitude, longitude and angles. In the remainder of this article, the method of Nilwong et al. will be considered and compared with our method, as it is the closest to ours.

This article proposes a method for locating yourself if your GPS is absent or nonfunctional. To do this, we propose a vision-based localization method. Inspired by [3], our approach tries to combine the natural human locating technique of finding landmarks and signs in the surrounding area. We'll be using landmarks such as logos and road signs. We use YOLOv10 (You Only Look At Once version 10) [22,23] for detecting interesting landmarks in images. We are also going to propose another location method based on MobileNet [17]. We will compare our method with Nilwong et al.'s one, AlexNet [1] and ResNet50 [24].

Our paper is organised as follows: first, we present our two localisation methods. Next, we describe the experimental tests we carried out with the data we used and the results obtained. We end with a conclusion.

2 Proposed Method

The application we have developed is a user location application in the event of GNSS not being available. Users need to be able to find their way around their environment even if GPS data is not available on their smartphone, whether for hardware or environmental reasons (an environment cluttered with buildings, which reduces the strength of GPS signals, or the reflection of signals in building windows). This is why we are proposing a vision-based localization application.

This localization method uses images taken by the smartphone's camera to geolocate. We can therefore distinguish between two geolocation methods: one that detects landmarks and signals in the external environment and another that uses the camera images to predict its position: latitude, longitude, azimuth angles, pitch and roll. Figure 1 shows the activity diagram for our application

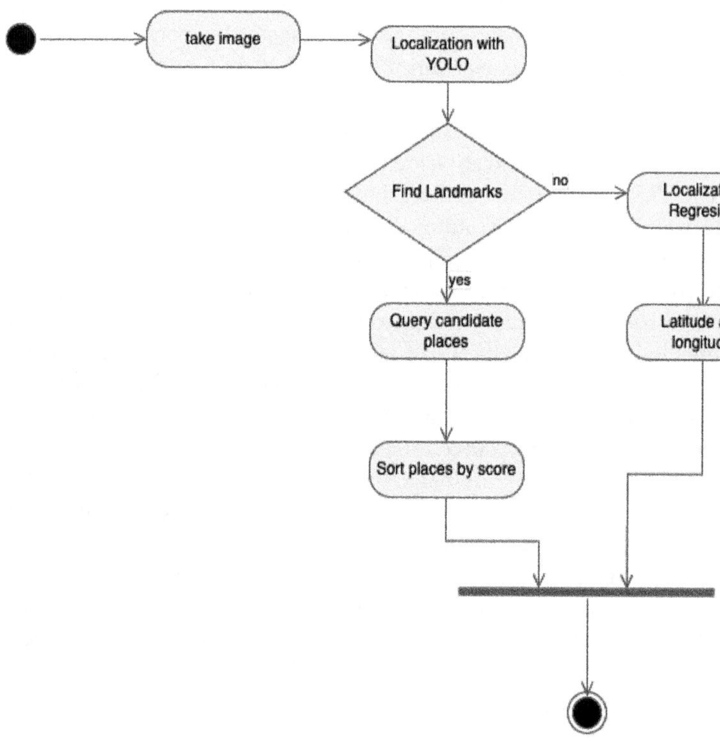

Fig. 1. Our activity diagram.

2.1 Image-Based Localization by Regression

Our approach for this first type of localization is to extract features from an image and predict the position of the user who took the image. Image-based localization is one of the research area of Sattler. In one of his paper, [26] uses SIFT in order to extract images features and save relevant images descriptors in a bag of words. Query are performing in the dictionnary. This approach is reliable but suffers from scalability.

Thus, we use the power of deep learning approach to solve the scalability problem in image-based localization. For this purpose, we tested several deep learning models and selected the one that best fits our requirements which is based on error minimization during localization. We have four candidates, namely: AlexNet, MobileNet, ResNet50 and Nilwong's model. The comparative result of our work is shown in result section of this paper.

2.2 Localization by Landmarks and Signs Detection

The second localization approach that we propose detects landmarks and signs in the same way as a human being to locate itself. For this we have opted for YOLOv10. The choice of YOLOv10 over Faster R-CNN or SSD (Single Shot Detection) is explained by the results of research in [27]. It turns out that for an application requiring speed of performance to prioritise the user experience and not minimise the precision and efficiency of the model, YOLOv10 is the best choice.

3 Experiments

3.1 Experiments for Image Based Localization Using Regression

Datasets. We have developed a mobile application to collect the data needed for our application. We need a collection of images. Each of these images will be associated with the position of the smartphone when the photo was taken (latitude and longitude position) and the angles (azimuth, pitch and roll) of the smartphone's camera when each photo was taken. The positions are taken from the smartphone's GPS data and the angles are obtained from the smartphone's accelerometers. In total, we collected 1,123 photos on a university campus. In order to have a good representation of the data, we have normalised the longitudes, latitudes, azimuth angles, pitch angles and roll angles of our dataset. To do this, we used the z-score normalisation, given by the following formula:

$$z = \frac{x - \mu}{\sigma} \tag{1}$$

With:

- z: the normalized value,
- x: value to be normalized,
- μ: the mean of the values of the variable x,
- σ: the standard deviation of the values of the variable x.

Methodology. In the literature, the method of Nilwong et al. [3] is the one that comes closest to our research. We wanted to find other methods that could improve the results of the Nilwong et al. method. We took MobileNet, AlexNet and RestNet50 to compare with the Nilwong et al. method. We then developed a mobile application to acquire the images taken by the smartphone camera along with the position, latitude, longitude, azimuth angle, pitch and roll data for each image. This data is saved in a csv file with the name of the corresponding image. In total, we collected 70 images for the test.

As the size of a model depends on its number of parameters, we want to have a model that is the most accurate (gives us a reliable value of latitude and longitude predictions) and lighter in terms of size or parameters.

Our problem can be described as follows: for each model f_θ^k where $k \in \{1, 2, 3, 4\}$, we want to minimize three objectives:

- Prediction error $\mathcal{L}_{\text{perf}}$: As this is a regression problem, we calculate the Mean Absolute Errors, which can be written as:

$$MAE = \frac{1}{n}\sum_{i=1}^{n} |y_i - \hat{y}_i| \tag{2}$$

  Thus, our first objective is

$$\mathcal{L}_{\text{perf}}(\theta) = \frac{1}{N}\sum_{i=1}^{N} (|\hat{y}_{\text{lat},i} - y_{\text{lat},i}| + |\hat{y}_{\text{lon},i} - y_{\text{lon},i}|) \tag{3}$$

- Model size: that can be represented by the number of parameters (P) or memory size (M) of the model f_θ^k. In our experiments, we take the memory size (M). This gives our second objective:

$$\mathcal{L}_{\text{size}}(\theta) = M \tag{4}$$

- We can make the same test using the geodesic distance. The geodesic distance between two points $(\hat{y}_{lat}, \hat{y}_{long})$ and (y_{lat}, y_{long}) is calculated using the Haversine formula:

$$d(\hat{y}_i, y_i) = 2R.arcsin(\sqrt{sin^2(\frac{\Delta\phi}{2}) + cos(\phi_1).cos(\phi_2).sin^2(\frac{\Delta\lambda}{2})}) \tag{5}$$

  With :
  - R is the radius of the earth, which measures approximately 6371km
  - $\Delta\phi = \hat{y}_{\text{lat}} - y_{\text{lat}}$
  - $\Delta\lambda = \hat{y}_{\text{long}} - y_{\text{long}}$
  - ϕ_1 et ϕ_2 are the latitudes in radians,

  Based on the geodesic distance, we have our third objective, which is:

$$\mathcal{L}_{\text{geo}}(\theta) = \frac{1}{n}\sum_{i=1}^{n} d(\hat{y}_i, y_i) \tag{6}$$

To quantitatively compare the models, we can combine these three objectives into a composite function using weighting coefficients $\lambda_1, \lambda_2, \lambda_3 \in [0, 1]$ and $\lambda_1 + \lambda_2 + \lambda_3 = 1$

to balance accuracy and efficiency. But before combining all objectives, we normalize them to the same scale between 0 and 1:

$$\mathcal{L}(\theta) = \lambda_1.\frac{\mathcal{L}_{\text{perf}}(\theta)}{\max\mathcal{L}_{\text{perf}}} + \lambda_2.\frac{\mathcal{L}_{\text{size}}(\theta)}{\max\mathcal{L}_{\text{size}}} + \lambda_3.\frac{\mathcal{L}_{\text{geo}}(\theta)}{\max\mathcal{L}_{\text{geo}}} \quad (7)$$

As we want to prioritize the geodesic objective, we take $\lambda_1 = 0.2, \lambda_2 = 0.2$ and $\lambda_3 = 0.6$.

3.2 Experiments for Signs and Logo Detections

Datasets. As datasets, we took images of the university campus. The images are made up of the logos of various departments, pharmacies, restaurants and banking groups. Our dataset therefore has six classes. In total, there are 201 images.

Training. Our model's training is made on google colab, with 100 epochs and by resizing the images in 640×640.

4 Results

4.1 Results for Image-Based Localization Using Regression

The Table 1 summarize results for image-based localization using regression. We can see that the MobileNet-based model is more accurate for geolocation with an average error of 58.64 m, which is acceptable for non-critical pedestrian geolocation applications. With this distance, we can see a building from a distance without any problem.

As we're using the model for a mobile application, it's best if it's lightweight to avoid consuming a lot of resources. In the Table 1, we can see that MobileNet meets our criterion. The ResNet model and the Nilwong model are respectively 6 times and 27 times heavier than MobileNet.

Table 1. MAE values for each model.

Model	MAE	Params(Size)	Geodesic dist	$\mathcal{L}(\theta)$
Nilwong's model	0.4354	108,702,497 (414.67 MB)	90,79 m	0.924
MobileNet	0.2621	**4,019,921 (15.33 MB)**	**58,64 m**	**0.494**
ResNet50	0.2948	25,142,289 (95.91 MB)	77.07 m	0.604
AlexNet	**0.2016**	174,905,489 (667.21 MB)	78.91 m	0.651

In Fig. 2, the actual latitude and longitude data from the test are shown in red. The latitude and longitude values predicted by MobileNet are in orange, those predicted by ResNet50 are in green and those predicted by the Nilwong et al. model are in blue. The figure shows that the values closest to the real values are those of the MobileNet model (Fig. 3).

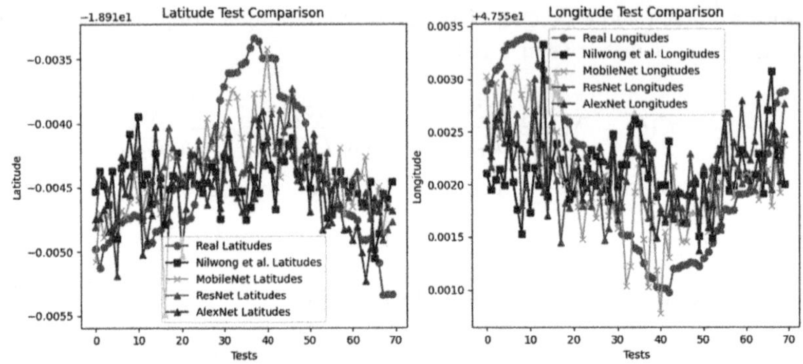

Fig. 2. Comparison of latitude and longitude values according to the models used. We can see that MobileNet is the closest to the actual values. (Color figure online)

4.2 Result for the Localization of Landmarks

We used several metrics to measure the performance of our sign detection model. Here are the values of these metrics after our test:

Precision (0.97707 ou 97.71%). This is the proportion of correct positive predictions among all the positive predictions made by the model.

$$P = \frac{TP}{TP + FP} \tag{8}$$

With TP: True Positives or correct prediction and TF: False Positives or incorrect predictions The accuracy value of 97.71% indicates that, of all the images or classes predicted as positive by the model, a large majority are correct.

Recall (1 ou 100%). This is the proportion of correctly identified objects or classes out of all the objects or classes actually present.

$$R = \frac{TP}{TP + FN} \tag{9}$$

With : FN (False Negatives) A recall of 100% means that the model has identified all the objects or classes present in the test data.

mAP@50 (0.995 ou 99.5%). This is the average of the accuracies obtained for different recall thresholds, with an IoU threshold set at 50% (Intersection over Union). It gives an overall assessment of the model's ability to detect objects correctly. A high mAP@50 (99.5%) indicates that the model is very good at detecting or classifying objects at a low IoU threshold. Our model is excellent at identifying whether an object is present in an image.

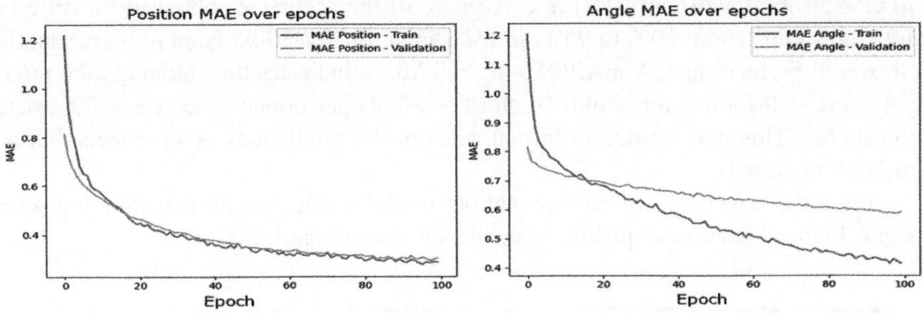

(a) Position and angle MAE over epochs for MobileNet

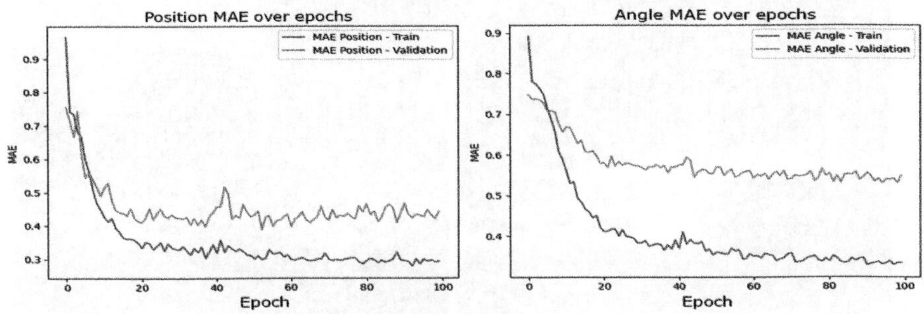

(b) Position and angle MAE over epochs for Nilwong's model

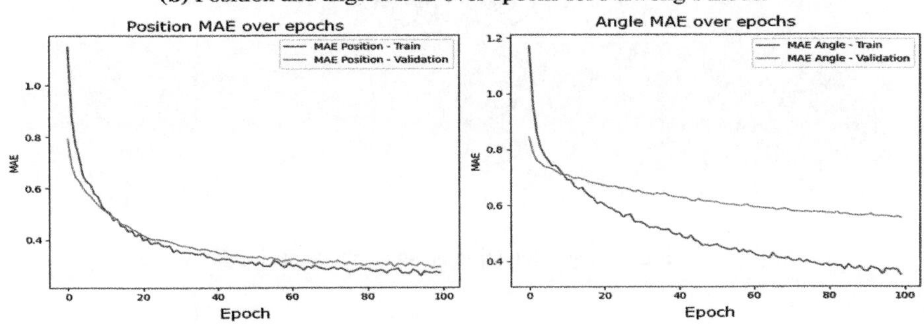

(c) Position and angle MAE over epochs for ResNet50

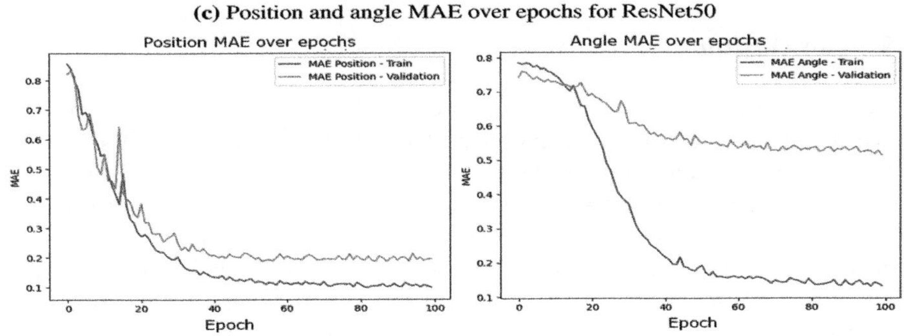

(d) Position and angle MAE over epochs for AlexNet

Fig. 3. MAE comparison over epochs for each model.

mAP@50-95 (0.7701 ou 77.01%). Average of the accuracies obtained for different IoU thresholds (from 50% to 95%, in 5% steps). mAP@50-95 is more representative of overall performance. A mAP@50-95 of 77.01% indicates that, although the model performs well for low thresholds (such as 50%), its performance decreases for stricter thresholds. This may be due to inaccuracies in the predictions or to objects that are difficult to classify.

From these metrics, we can say that our model is effective for detecting logos and signs. Figure 4 shows the qualitative results on smartphones.

Fig. 4. Logo Detection on smartphone device.

5 Conclusion

We proposed a new method for image-based localization using two approaches. The first detects signs and logos in images captured by a camera using YOLOv10. The second employs a regression model based on MobileNet to predict the latitude, longitude, and orientation of the user's camera. Our regression model is compared with Nilwong's method, AlexNet, and ResNet50. The experiments show that our proposed method quantitatively outperforms Nilwong's approach and is lighter than the others so, it is suitable for mobile applications and for robots. With these results, we estimate the robot's position with six degrees of freedom (6-DoF).

In future, we will include additional signs and logos to improve image detection and we will test the image-based regression approach over a larger area in urban environments. In addition, it would be interesting to combine the accuracy of SIFT descriptors with the speed of deep learning approaches and compare the results with the Mobilenet model.

Acknowledgments. We thank everyone who contributed to the completion of this paper.

Disclosure of Interests. The authors have no competing interests to declare relevant to this article's content.

References

1. Krizhevsky, A., Sutskever, I., Hinton, G.E.: ImageNet classification with deep convolutional neural networks. In: Communications of the ACM, vol. 60, no. 6, 24 mai 2017, pp. 84–90 (2017). https://doi.org/10.1145/3065386
2. Aravind, A., Ashwin, V., Chandeep, S., Yasaswi, P., Gandhiraj, R., Sundaram, G: Enhancing GPS position estimation using multi-sensor fusion and error-state extended Kalman filter. In: International Conference on Distributed Computing, VLSI, Electrical Circuits and Robotics (DISCOVER), pp. 201–206 (2022)
3. Arth, C., Klopschitz, M., Reitmayr, G., Schmalstieg, D. : Real-time self-localization from panoramic images on mobile devices. In: 10th IEEE International Symposium on Mixed and Augmented Reality (2011)
4. Beidou Homepage. http://en.beidou.gov.cn. Accessed 08 Dec 2024
5. Galileo Homepage. https://galileognss.eu. Accessed 08 Dec 2024
6. Garcia-Lopez, E., Garcia-Cabot, A., De Marcos, L., Teixeira, A.: An experiment to discover usability guidelines for designing mobile tourist apps. Wirel. Commun. Mob. Comput. (2021). https://doi.org/10.1155/2021/2824632
7. GLONASS Homepage. https://glonass-iac.ru/en/. Accessed 08 Dec 2024
8. Google Maps Homepage. https://www.google.com/maps. Accessed 08 Dec 2024
9. GPS Homepage. https://www.gps.gov/. Accessed 08 Dec 2024
10. Here Wego Homepage. https://wego.here.com/. Accessed 08 Dec 2024
11. Jabborov, F., Cho, J.: Image-based camera localization algorithm for smartphone cameras based on reference objects. Wireless Pers. Commun. **114**(3), 2511–2527 (2020). https://doi.org/10.1007/s11277-020-07487-9
12. Landau, Y., Ben-Moshe, B.: STEPS: An Indoor Navigation Framework for Mobile Devices. Sensors, Basel, Switzerland (2020). https://doi.org/10.3390/s20143929
13. Lokhande, J., et al.: Campus Navigation using Augmented Reality and Virtual Reality. International Journal For Multidisciplinary Research (2024). https://doi.org/10.36948/ijfmr.2024.v06i03.19504
14. Lowe, D. G.:Object recognition from local scale-invariant features. In: IEEE Proceedings of the Seventh IEEE International Conference on Computer Vision, vol. 2, pp. 1150—1157 (1999). https://doi.org/10.1109/iccv.1999.790410
15. Lu, G., Yan, Y., Sebe, N., Kambhamettu, C. : Indoor localization via multi-view images and videos. Comput. Vis. Image Understanding 145–160 (2017)
16. Maps.me Homepage. https://maps.me/. Accessed 08 Dec 2024
17. Howard, A.G., et al.: MobileNets: Efficient Convolutional Neural Networks for Mobile Vision Applications (2017)
18. Nilwong, S., Hossain, D., Kaneko, S., Capi, G.: Deep learning-based landmark detection for mobile robot outdoor localization. Machines (2019). https://doi.org/10.3390/MACHINES7020025

19. Oxley, A.: Uncertainties in GPS Positioning: A Mathematical Discourse. 1st Edition, Elsevier, pp. 99—114 (2017)
20. Potorti, F., Palumbo, F., Crivello, A.: Sensors and Sensing Technologies for Indoor Positioning and Indoor Navigation. Sensors, Basel, Switzerland (2020). https://doi.org/10.3390/s20205924
21. Ramamana, H., Rahajaniaina, A., Jessel, J.-P.: Image based-localization on mobile devices using geometric features of buildings. In: GEOPROCESSING, Venise, Italy, pp. 58–62 (2016)
22. Redmon, J., Divvala, S., Girshick, R., Farhadi, A.: You Only Look Once: Unified, Real-Time Object Detection (2015)
23. Ren, S., He, K., Girshick, R., Sun, J.: Faster R-CNN: Towards Real-Time Object Detection with Region Proposal Networks (2015)
24. He, K., Zhang, X., Ren, S., Sun, J.: Deep Residual Learning for Image Recognition (2015)
25. Ruotsalainen, L., Morrison, A., Mäkelä, M., Rantanen, J., and Sokolova, N.: Improving computer vision-based perception for collaborative indoor navigation. IEEE Sens. J. 4816–4826 (2022). https://doi.org/10.1109/jsen.2021.3106257
26. Sattler, B.L., Kobbelt, L.: Fast image-based localization using direct 2D-to-3D matching. In: ICCV (2011)
27. Wang, A., et al.: YOLOv10: Real-Time End-to-End Object Detection (2024). https://doi.org/10.48550/arXiv.2405.14458
28. Yan, S., et al.: Long-term visual localization with mobile sensors. In: 2023 IEEE/CVF Conference on Computer Vision and Pattern Recognition, CVPR, pp. 17245–17255 (2023). https://doi.org/10.1109/CVPR52729.2023.01654

Improving Stability and Precision of Bird Tracking in Stereo Vision Systems

Grzegorz Madejski[1(✉)], Aleksy Stocki[1], Dawid Gradolewski[1], Włodzimierz Kaoka[1], and Wlodek J. Kulesza[2]

[1] Bioseco S. A., Budowlanych 68, 80-298 Gdansk, Poland
{grzegorz.madejski,aleksy.stocki,dawid.gradolewski, wlodzimierz.kaoka}@bioseco.com

[2] Department of Mathematics and Natural Sciences, Blekinge Institute of Technology, 371 79 Karlskrona, Sweden
wlodek.kulesza@bth.se

Abstract. Wind energy offers a sustainable solution to reduce carbon emissions but presents risks to bird populations, particularly through potential collisions with turbine blades. The Bird Protection System, BPS, employing stereo vision, aims to mitigate these risks by detecting and tracking birds and estimating their distance from turbines. The precision of distance estimation remains challenging due to quantization uncertainty and environmental factors such as lighting, background complexity, and asynchronous camera frames, which can lead to unstable and imprecise measurements. This paper explores methods to enhance the accuracy and reliability of bird tracking systems by addressing one of the key technical challenges: precise disparity estimation. We investigate three methods: based on the detected object's bounding box center, the object's center of gravity, and the image alignment technique that uses cross-correlation. The methods use an object's image extracted from the background and resized to ensure a subpixel refinement. Our findings show that the center of gravity and cross-correlation methods with resizing significantly enhance tracking stability and precision, and the former is also computationally efficient, rendering it useful for real-time applications, such as BPS.

Keywords: Autonomous System · Bird Protection · Computer Vision · Disparity · Image Alignment · Image Processing · Stereo-Vision · Wind Farms

1 Introduction

Modern surveillance systems autonomously monitor wide industry areas utilizing heterogeneous data driven by distributed sensor networks [11]. One of the recently developing applications is the Bird Protection System (BPS) [21], which allows the sustainable development of wind energy concerning biodiversity [13,22] or increases the safety of air traffic operations [7]. Long-base stereovision systems

J. Röning and J. Filipe (Eds.): ROBOVIS 2025, CCIS 2629, pp. 535–556, 2026.
https://doi.org/10.1007/978-3-032-00986-9_34

can spot and track birds in an extensive range of kilometers [1], allowing turbines to shut down only when a risk factor reaches certain safety level [20].

The desired reaction radius of BPS needed for stopping the turbine (r_{stop}) results simply from the birds' speed (v_{bird}), turbine's rotor radius (r_{rotor}), the time needed for the turbine to be stopped (t_{stop}), and BPS latency ($t_{latency}$), see Fig. 1. Depending on the size of the wind turbine and manufacturer, the time needed to slow down the rotor blades along with the BPS latency is between 15 s and 30 s [2]. The average bird speed depends on particular species' capabilities, and, for Red Kite, is assumed to be 8 m/s [24]. This leads to an extensive turbine stop radius interval of 300 m to 500 m. Strobe or sound deterrent methods can be used as a supplementary prevention method with a radius r_{deter}.

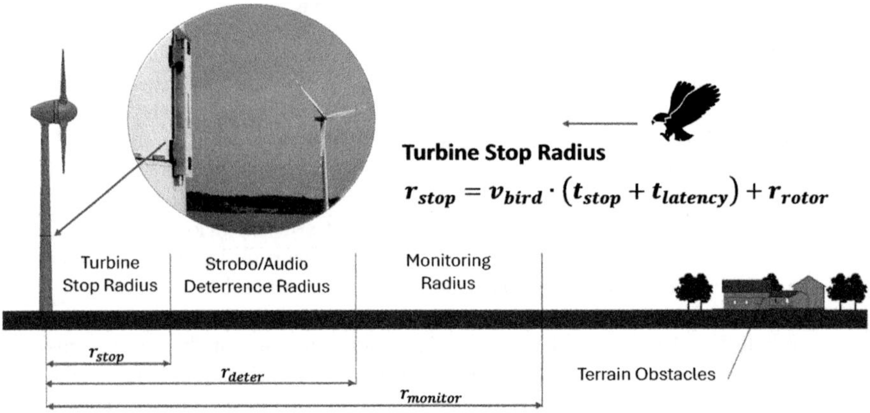

Fig. 1. Topology of different zones defined for a Bird Protection System (BPS) developed by Bioseco.

The distance at the stereo-vision system is calculated by differences in the object projections at two cameras. In the case of BPS with a vertical base line, we have an up camera (Camera Up) and a down camera (Camera Down) of a detection module; see Fig 2, [12,13,22]. To reduce the computational complexity, the object identification algorithm is based on motion detection. This allows us to calculate the distance from the disparity in image object center coordinates ($y_U - y_D$) or with the use of image correlation method, depicted as green boxes at Fig. 2. The distance is used for object localization and tracking in a 3D space, and then a decision for a collision prevention action is made.

However, precise distance measurement is challenging due to the camera's resolution and the changeable outdoor environment, which is affected by light changes, rapid object movement, and camera parameter variations. The uncertainty in distance measurement could be at a level of hundreds of meters [13]. The precise and repeatable distance measurement plays a core role in BPS control since measurement errors could lead to unnecessary turbine shutdowns, resulting in profit losses.

The state-of-the-art BPS system utilizes techniques and methods to stabilize positioning and disparity estimation over time to improve the measurements' reliability. The paper aims to review some techniques and evaluate their adaptability and usability in a real-time application.

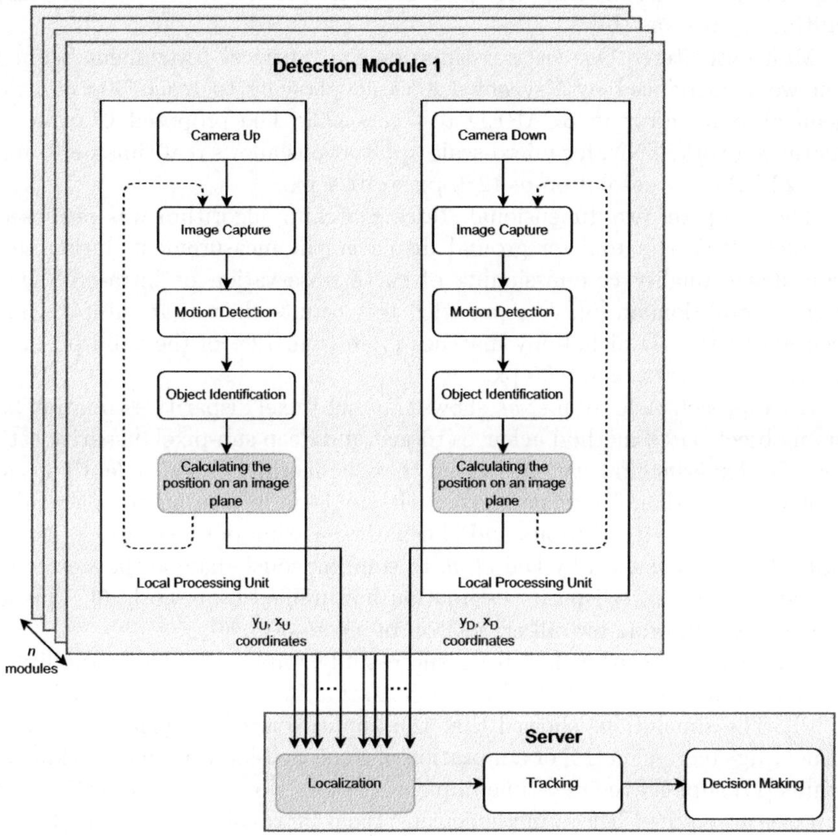

Fig. 2. The flowchart of the data processing of Bird Protection System.

2 Review of Related Works

The stability and precision of the disparity estimation have become a main research problem for many scientists and research groups working on the applications of a stereo-vision-based technology in various fields of industry and science. Conventional disparity calculation relies on estimating the object's geometric center at each of the image planes [12,13]. This low computational complexity approach allows bird localization at wind farms [13]; however, stability improvement is required for accurate risk assessment [20].

The distance measurement stability could be improved with the sub-pixel method as reported in [8,9,16]. These studies show that large-scale 3D reconstruction can benefit significantly from sub-pixel refinements. However, they do not deal with real-time implementation challenges. One of the attempts was made by Jiang, Qu, and Li, who reduced the stair-casing effect in disparity maps by estimating the disparity planes. Their solution accelerates the computing time by 600 ms [16].

Multitask Stereo Disparity Estimation and Surgical Instrument Segmentation were introduced by Psychogyios *et al.* allowing to reach 3.18 mm depth mean absolute error in SCARED test sets [23]. The proposed Convolutional Neural Network, CNN, for micro-scale applications allows real-time performance with 22 FPS at a resolution of 1280 px $\times$ 1024 px.

The sub-pixel two-dimensional stereo matching algorithm was proposed by Cournet *et al.* as a tool for ground displacement measurement during the in-orbit image quality commissioning of earth observation or intra-oral scanner in the dental domain [5]. The provided test results show that sub-pixel match accuracy in the 1D dichotomy matches more than 72% of the valid pixels with an accuracy higher than 0.05 px.

An approach of Jo-Jiun *et al.* shows that sub-pixel disparity estimation based on an object-based method achieves robust and deep sub-pixel disparity estimation. The experimental system showed that the method provides depth measurement with less than 5% relative error within 150 m in continuous space [4].

Stereo Super-Resolution and Disparity Estimation Feedback Network (SSRDE-FNe) was used by Dai *et al.* to simultaneously handle the stereo image super-resolution and disparity estimation in a unified framework [6]. This leads to a synergy allowing overall error drop by up to 3 px [6].

A tracking algorithm has been successfully implemented for stability performance improvement of an object localization in a long-base stereovision [14, 17,19]. The simulations showed that the application of blueprint to linear and kernel ridge regression [14] or adaptation of some well-known radar tracking algorithms [17] support the real-time implementation. However, quantitative validation is still required before implementing them in a real environment [17].

Tracking methods have also been successfully implemented for small baseline applications like robot navigation. It was shown that the Kernelized Correlation Filter (KCF) used to track the moving object improves an average accuracy of distance estimation of over 95% in the range from 88 cm to 300 cm when the baseline is 151 mm [16].

Hsu and Wang proposed a measurement procedure composed of detection, segmentation, and distance calculation capable of proximity sensing with an error less than 5% [15]. As the authors admit, the drawback is the algorithm's susceptibility to light changes.

This paper considers three techniques that are easy to implement and are supported by programming libraries, such as OpenCV. The first technique involves using the center of the bounding box of segmented objects and calculating disparity as a difference between the centers in x or y coordinates [3]. This method, while computationally efficient, is sensitive to object orientation and scale variations. A more robust approach utilizes the weighted centroid (center of gravity) of the object's image representation, calculated using image moments [10]. Finally, cross-correlation-based methods provide a more accurate but computationally intensive solution [18]. These methods find applications in various fields, including robotic navigation, object tracking, and 3D scene reconstruction [25].

3 Problem Statement and Research Objectives

For bird-turbine collision risk assessment, it is essential to estimate the 3D localization of the bird accurately, which is also crucial for speed estimation and plays a crucial role in risk analysis. The localization accuracy improvement methods of the stereo vision system are addressed in this research. Tracking small objects, such as birds at long ranges, is challenging not only because of the size of the object at a long distance but also because of the object's dynamics. Two issues need to be considered: The first one is a method's quantization error, which is a non-linear function of distance and can be significant at long distances. Another problem is the changing shapes of the flying birds in images, which can vary on each stereo camera, too.

The first research problem would be to find out what measures are suitable for evaluating the stability and precision of the bird image disparity on two cameras, which is used to estimate the distance to the detected object.

To evaluate the methods' quality, we propose four measures of disparity signal in the time domain: mean absolute error, percentage mean absolute error, variance of standard deviation, and average absolute change. The combined measures ensure a comprehensive evaluation of the signal's properties.

The second research problem of this paper is the evaluation quality of three methods: bounding box center method, center of gravity method, or cross-correlation image alignment.

Based on our experiences, we assume that the bounding box centers method, which is the simplest, can result in worse evaluation scores. The weighted centers method, which includes pixel intensity, can give better scores. Then, we assume that the cross-correlation image alignment, which also takes object shape into consideration, will result in the best evaluation scores.

The third research problem is to evaluate to which degree image resizing can reduce the quantization error and improve the stability of the disparity signal over time for the tested methods.

We hypothesize that resizing applied in bounding box centers and cross-correlation image alignment, should reduce the quantization error and improve stability, as they are strongly affected by resolution. However, the center of gravity method will not be significantly affected by resizing because it anyway has sub-pixel accuracy due to weighted multiplication, addition, and division operations.

The main contribution of this research is to model and implement the proposed methods to evaluate their ability to improve the stability and accuracy of

3D localization of moving objects. The evaluation is done on real data collected by BPS at wind farms in different weather and light conditions.

The novelty of the research comes from finding, through a heuristic manner, a configuration of state-of-the-art methods for dynamic disparity calculation that improve its stability and resolution in real-time application. This study gives new insights into the efficient methods for long-range moving object 3D localization, which has not been implemented on real-life data, and evaluation using various stability and noisiness measures.

4 Modeling of Improvement Methods

We aim to improve the stability and precision of the Disparity Estimation Method (DCM) of the BPS stereo system. The improvement can be evaluated by comparing their results with the original method based on bounding box centers. The first method computes the center of gravity of the object, as is described in Sect. 4.3. The second one aligns images from stereo cameras to maximize the cross-correlation of two images; see Sect. 4.4. Finally, we evaluate both techniques for a set of different resize factors $r = 1, 2, 5$, using signal stability measures presented in Sect. 5.1. Each of the methods is preceded by the same pre-processing stages consisting of background subtraction and contouring described in the following subsection.

4.1 Preprocessing Stages: Background Subtraction and Contour Detection

The BPS system is based on extracting and isolating a flying bird from an image using a combination of background subtraction and contour detection as described in [11]. In this study, the approach is simulated using image frames containing the bird as foreground frames and segments of the same image or nearby frames that do not contain the bird as background frames. The background is reconstructed and subtracted to isolate the moving bird. The bird's contour is detected, and anything outside is considered as a background and is removed i.e. set as white. The bird is then blurred to remove any noise. A bounding box is additionally calculated for the contour to estimate the bird's position and center. The process is visualized on an example image in Fig. 3.

Then, the miniature with removed background is resized with three different factors, i.e. $r = 1, 2, 5$. The resizing is performed with bilinear interpolation. To reduce noise and smoothen the image, a Gaussian blur is applied with a kernel size proportional to the resizing factor defined as: $k = 2 \cdot r + 1$.

After the preprocessing, a miniature image of a bird is provided, resized with a given factor, the background is removed, and the image is blurred. Additionally, the contour and the contour's bounding box are estimated.

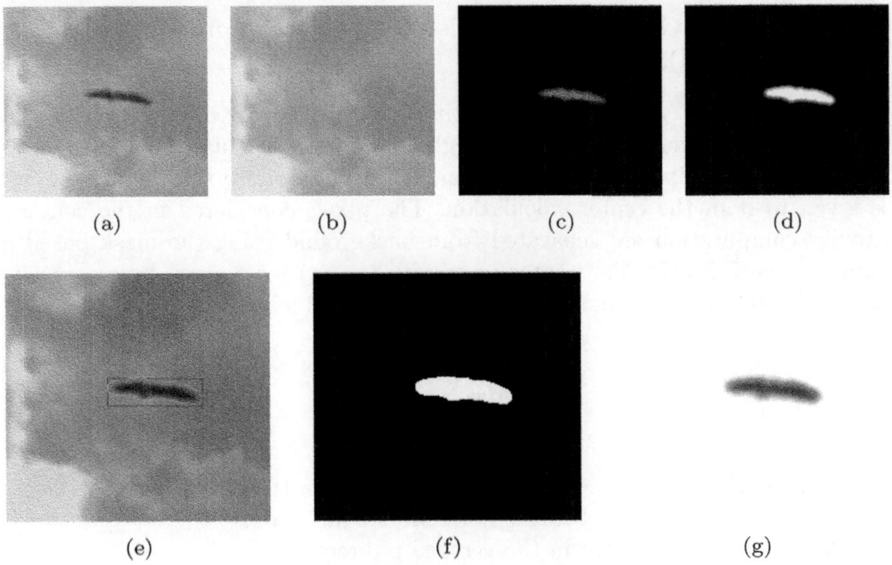

Fig. 3. Illustration of preprocessing stages: (a) Original segment resized, (b) Background extracted, (c) Bird/background difference, (d) Difference with threshold and blur, (e) Contour and bounding box, (f) Mask based on contour, (g) Mask applied to original image and blur.

4.2 Bounding Box Based Disparity Calculation Method (BB-DCM)

Assume a miniature of size 100×100 with the object's representation is centered around a point (x, y) in the pixel coordinate system of the whole image. Following the preprocessing steps, the miniature is resized by a factor r and contains an object with a bounding box with coordinates (x_b, y_b) of the top-left corner in resized miniature and width w and height h of the rectangle. The center of the box (c_x, c_y) is calculated using the formula:

$$c_x = x_b + \text{round}\left(\frac{w}{2}\right), \quad c_y = y_b + \text{round}\left(\frac{h}{2}\right). \tag{1}$$

Then (c_x, c_y) is translated to pixel coordinates of the whole image in original resolution:

$$c'_x = x - 50 + c_x/r, \quad c'_y = y - 50 + c_y/r. \tag{2}$$

The disparity is then calculated using c'_y from two miniatures:

$$y_{\text{diff}} = c'_{y\_\text{top}} - c'_{y\_\text{bottom}}. \tag{3}$$

This method's weakness is that it does not take pixel intensities of the bird image or its shape, but its advantage is simplicity and ease of computation.

4.3 Center of Gravity Based Disparity Calculation Method (CG-DCM)

The second, more complex method estimates the disparity using center of gravity, or center of mass, which is a weighted centroid calculated based on pixel coordinates and pixel intensity. The darker the color of a pixel, the more weight is given to it in the center calculation. The pixels considered in the center of gravity computation are separated from background using the mask based on contour, see Fig. 3(f). The center of gravity (x_c, y_c) for a given binary mask is calculated using image moments, which are defined as follows:

$$x_c = \frac{M_{10}}{M_{00}}, \quad y_c = \frac{M_{01}}{M_{00}}, \tag{4}$$

where

- M_{00}: zeroth-order moment (area or total mass of the binary mask).
- M_{10}: first-order moment in the horizontal x direction.
- M_{01}: first-order moment in the vertical y direction.

These moments are computed as follows:

$$M_{pq} = \sum_x \sum_y x^p y^q I(x, y), \tag{5}$$

where $I(x, y)$ is the pixel intensity at coordinates (x, y) in the binary image, and p and q represent the powers for the horizontal and vertical components, respectively.

The zeroth-order moment M_{00} represents the total number of pixels, *mass* in the binary mask, while the first-order moments M_{10} and M_{01} are weighted sums of the pixel coordinates. Dividing the first-order moments by the zeroth-order moment gives the coordinates of the centroid (x_c, y_c), which represents the center of gravity of the object. For each pair of top and bottom images, the disparity is calculated the same way as in BB-DCM method using (2, 3).

4.4 Image Alignment with Cross-Correlation (CCIA-DCM)

The third method searches for a shift vector defined as:

$$v_{\text{align}} = [v_x, v_y], \tag{6}$$

which aligns one of the miniatures, e.g., the bottom one, to best match the pattern on the top one. The alignment is performed on the bird miniatures resized and with the background removed i.e. set as white. The bounding box around the bird from the top miniature is the area where the alignment is measured. The bottom miniature is shifted to the best-matched pixel in the box. This study uses cross-correlation to quantify the similarity between two images. The normalized cross-correlation, which is used in this study, is defined as:

$$C(v_x, v_y) = \frac{\sum_{i,j} (I_1(i,j) \cdot I_2(i + v_x, j + v_y))}{\sqrt{\sum_{i,j} I_1(i,j)^2 \cdot \sum_{i,j} I_2(i + v_x, j + v_y)^2}}, \tag{7}$$

where:

- $C(v_x, v_y)$ is the correlation value for a given shift (v_x, v_y),
- $I_1(i, j)$ and $I_2(i, j)$ are the intensity values of pixel (i, j) in the first and second images, respectively,
- v_x, v_y represents the horizontal and vertical shifts of the shift vector v_{align} applied to the second image.

The goal is to find v_{align} that maximizes $C(v_x, v_y)$, indicating the best alignment between the two images; see an example in Fig. 4.

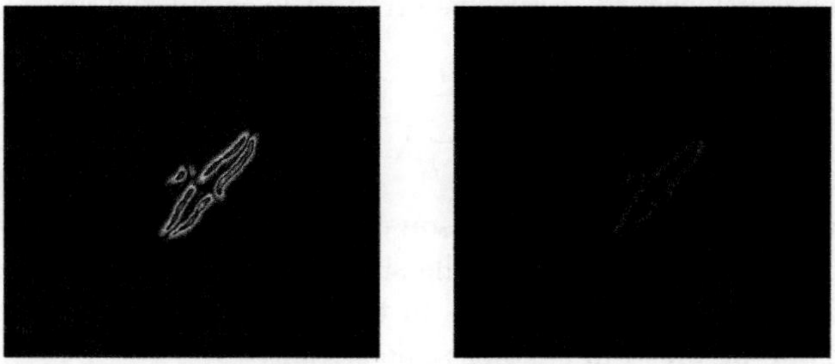

Fig. 4. Pixel intensity difference map for miniatures overlapped without correction, on the left, and with cross-correlation alignment on the right.

This method applies an iterative coarse-to-fine search. First, the best shift vector is found using resize factor 5 px jumps. Then, around the found shift vector, the search is done for fine 1 px jumps. This double-stage search is crucial for resized images with a larger search scope.

5 Method Evaluation

In this section, we test the methods from the previous chapter for their precision and stability. First, in Sect. 5.1, we define the measures suitable for such a task. Next, in Sect. 5.2, we present the data used for evaluation: four bird tracks. Then, in Sect. 5.3, we present and interpret the results. Finally, in Sect. 5.4, we test how the methods might affect distance measurements around wind turbines.

5.1 Evaluation Measures

A set of evaluation measures is employed to assess the quality and noisiness of disparity signals. These measures provide insights into different aspects of the signal, including smoothness, variability, and noise. In the following section, we describe the measures in detail.

Mean Absolute Error (MAE) quantifies the average absolute difference between the original signal and its smoothed version. The smoothed version is computed using the *Savitzky-Golay filter*, which applies a polynomial fit over a sliding window of size 11 to preserve local trends while reducing noise. The formula for MAE is:

$$MAE = \frac{1}{M}\sum_{i=1}^{M}|y_i - \hat{y}_i| \tag{8}$$

where y_i is the sample, $\hat{y}_i$ is the smoothed sample, M and is the total number of samples. A higher MAE indicates larger deviations from smoothness, which may be caused by noise, fluctuations, or structural inconsistencies in the signal.

Percentage Mean Absolute Error (pMAE) extends the concept of MAE by expressing the deviations as a percentage of the smoothed values, providing a scale-independent measure of relative error. It is calculated as:

$$pMAE = \frac{1}{M}\sum_{i=1}^{M}\left(\frac{|y_i - \hat{y}_i|}{|\hat{y}_i|}\right) \times 100\% \tag{9}$$

This measure allows for the comparison of signals with varying magnitudes and highlights relative deviations from the smoothed version. A higher $pMAE$ suggests significant relative fluctuations in the signal, often due to localized noise or variations pronounced in smaller-scale signals.

Average Absolute Change (AAC) quantifies the average magnitude of changes between consecutive samples and is calculated as:

$$AAC = \frac{1}{M-1}\sum_{i=1}^{M-1}|y_{i+1} - y_i| \tag{10}$$

where y_i is the signal at the ith sample and M is the total number of samples. This measure highlights local variability in the signal, focusing on changes between adjacent points without considering the directionality of the changes.

Standard Deviation of the Derivative (σ_d) evaluates the spread or variability in the rate of change of the signal, providing insights into the consistency of the signal's dynamics and is defined as:

$$\sigma_d = \sqrt{\frac{1}{M-1}\sum_{i=1}^{M-1}\left(\frac{y_{i+1} - y_i}{t_{i+1} - t_i} - \mu_d\right)^2} \tag{11}$$

where t_i, t_{i+1} is sampling times and μ_d is the mean of derivative. A high σ_d indicates large fluctuations in the signal's rate of change, which may reflect erratic or noisy behaviour, while a low value means smoother dynamics.

Analysis of the Measures. Using the multiple measures ensures a comprehensive evaluation of the signal's properties, as each measure captures a distinct aspect of variability or noisiness:

- *MAE* and *pMAE* assess the overall deviation from a smoothed baseline. However, *pMAE* normalizes these deviations by the magnitude of the smoothed values, making it more sensitive to relative changes in smaller-scale signals. A signal with small deviations but large relative errors could have a low *MAE* and a high *pMAE*.
- *AAC* highlights local variability between consecutive samples and is well-suited for identifying frequent small changes. It can differ significantly from *MAE* in signals where local oscillations occur without substantial overall deviation from the smoothed baseline.
- Standard deviation of the derivative, σ_d, provides insight into the rate of change with respect to time.

These measures produce differing results based on signal characteristics. For instance, a slowly drifting signal with small oscillations may have low *AAC* but high *MAE*, while a rapidly oscillating signal with low amplitude relative to the smoothed version may exhibit high *AAC* but low *pMAE*. Combining these metrics provides a robust assessment, enabling a nuanced analysis of signal variability and noise.

5.2 Source Data

Bird flight tracks involving numerical and visual data are considered in this research. The data were generated by BPS in March 2023 on a Wind Farm in central Germany. The video footage of the bird's flights is processed with a frequency of 16 FPS, and several components are extracted from each processed frame; these are:

- The pixel coordinates (x_{bottom}, y_{bottom}) of an estimated object's center, given as integer numbers, from the bottom camera in a stereo vision camera pair;
- The pixel coordinates (x_{top}, y_{top}) of an estimated object's center, given as integer numbers, from the top camera in a stereo vision camera pair;
- Two grayscale image segments centred around the object's center cropped to the size of 100 px $\times$100 px;
- The date and exact time t of the miniature pair generation. Both the coordinates and miniatures can be viewed as a time-domain series.

For methods evaluation, four bird flight tracks were selected from the dataset. The flights were viewed by different camera sets in slightly different weather conditions, see Fig. 5. The first flight, denoted as *Track 267f8-m9-t0*, happened on 17.03.2023, where a soaring bird of prey is clearly visible on a clear background, and its shape, tail and wings can be recognized. The label *Track 18c39-m6-t0* marks a bird flight on 22.03.2023 with a similar bird but a slightly more cloudy background. The *Track 338df-m8-t0* on 22.03.2023 includes a bird flying at a larger distance and on a very cloudy day. Finally, *Track 5ffa7-m6-t2* collected on 17.03.2023 depicts a bird that maintains a horizontal position.

Note that the datasets contain images in grayscale, which depict birds seen at a considerable distance as dark spots. This low variability of data is typical for long-range monitoring systems. However, a bigger dataset will be considered in future research that will also take images with better quality.

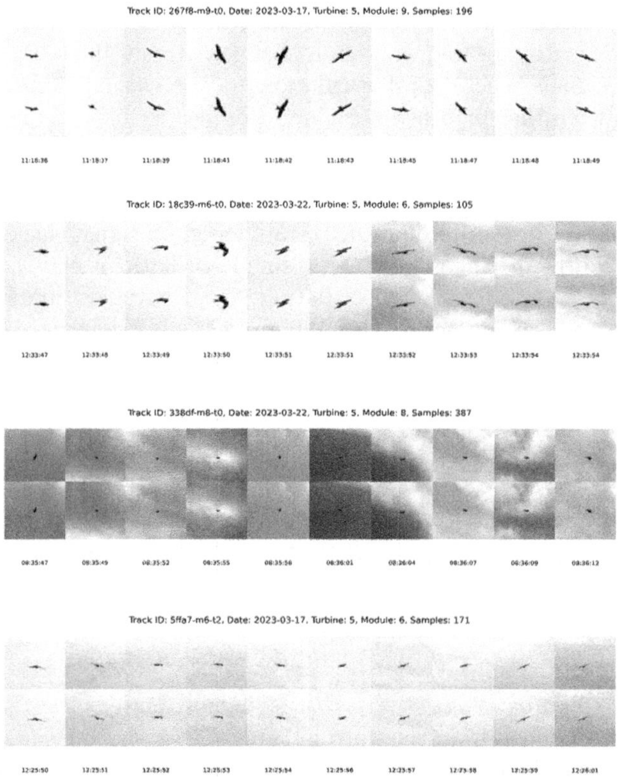

Fig. 5. A selection of image segments from various tracks (from top to bottom): *Track 267f8-m9-t0*, *Track 18c39-m6-t0*, *Track 338df-m8-t0*, and *Track 5ffa7-m6-t2*.

5.3 Evaluation Results and Discussion

The four measures introduced in Sect. 5.1 were applied to the four tracks presented in Sect. 5.2.

The results are presented in the form of Tables 1a, 1b, 1c, and 1d. The tables were additionally colored in linear scale to highlight the performance of methods, with red color marking the score whose normalized value was the highest (> 0.9)

and considered the worst, and shades of green marking with the lowest, best scores (< 0.1). The methods names, i.e. BB-DCM, CG-DCM, and CIAA-DCM, were additionally marked with the resize factor used with them $r = 1, 2, 5$, resulting in 9 evaluated cases.

Table 2 aggregates the scores for all tracks. The measures of individual tracks were taken, and a weighted mean was calculated using the formula

$$Measure_{\mu} = \frac{1}{w_1 + w_2 + w_3 + w_4} \sum_{track=1}^{4} Measure_{track} \cdot w_{track} \tag{12}$$

where the weights $w_1, w_2, w_3, w_4 \in (0, 1]$ of the four tracks are the numbers of their samples divided by the number of samples of the longest track. This table gives insight into the general performance of the tested methods across different tracks.

The results in all the mentioned tables indicate that the basic bounding box method with no resizing, i.e. BB-DCM-1, performs the worst. For this method, neither image resizing nor yield very good results compared to other methods. CG-DCM performs well, especially with resizing by a factor of 2 or 5. The CCIA-DCM also shows good scores, especially for resize factor 5.

Table 1. Evaluation of DCMs for the four studied tracks.

(a) Track 267f8-m9-t0.

Method	MAE [px]	$pMAE$ [%]	σ_d [px/s]	AAC [px]
BB-DCM-1	1.000 0.33	1.000 1.35	1.000 0.63	1.000 0.38
BB-DCM-2	0.519 0.20	0.505 0.81	0.419 0.38	0.586 0.26
BB-DCM-5	0.222 0.12	0.220 0.50	0.140 0.26	0.276 0.17
CG-DCM-1	0.074 0.08	0.055 0.32	0.023 0.21	0.103 0.12
CG-DCM-2	0.037 0.07	0.018 0.28	0.000 0.20	0.034 0.10
CG-DCM-5	0.000 0.06	0.000 0.26	0.000 0.20	0.034 0.10
CCIA-DCM-1	0.259 0.13	0.275 0.56	0.279 0.32	0.034 0.10
CCIA-DCM-2	0.185 0.11	0.165 0.44	0.116 0.25	0.000 0.09
CCIA-DCM-5	0.074 0.08	0.055 0.32	0.023 0.21	0.000 0.09

(b) Track 18c39-m6-t0.

Method	MAE [px]	$pMAE$ [%]	σ_d [px/s]	AAC [px]
BB-DCM-1	1.000 0.64	1.000 1.91	0.949 1.43	1.000 0.83
BB-DCM-2	0.656 0.53	0.642 1.57	1.000 1.46	0.949 0.81
BB-DCM-5	0.750 0.56	0.747 1.67	0.898 1.4	1.000 0.83
CG-DCM-1	0.094 0.35	0.095 1.05	0.034 0.89	0.179 0.51
CG-DCM-2	0.063 0.34	0.084 1.04	0.034 0.89	0.154 0.50
CG-DCM-5	0.063 0.34	0.074 1.03	0.017 0.88	0.154 0.50
CCIA-DCM-1	0.375 0.44	0.400 1.34	0.136 0.95	0.026 0.45
CCIA-DCM-2	0.094 0.35	0.126 1.08	0.017 0.88	0.000 0.44
CCIA-DCM-5	0.000 0.32	0.000 0.96	0.000 0.87	0.026 0.45

(c) Track 338df-m8-t0.

Method	MAE [px]	$pMAE$ [%]	σ_d [px/s]	AAC [px]
BB-DCM-1	1.000 0.42	1.000 4.53	1.000 0.86	1.000 0.57
BB-DCM-2	0.333 0.26	0.339 2.85	0.303 0.63	0.387 0.38
BB-DCM-5	0.208 0.23	0.185 2.46	0.242 0.61	0.290 0.35
CG-DCM-1	0.208 0.23	0.193 2.48	0.121 0.57	0.323 0.36
CG-DCM-2	0.042 0.19	0.008 2.01	0.000 0.53	0.097 0.29
CG-DCM-5	0.000 0.18	0.000 1.99	0.000 0.53	0.097 0.29
CCIA-DCM-1	0.375 0.27	0.346 2.87	0.545 0.71	0.226 0.33
CCIA-DCM-2	0.125 0.21	0.114 2.28	0.061 0.55	0.000 0.26
CCIA-DCM-5	0.042 0.19	0.028 2.06	0.000 0.53	0.032 0.27

(d) Track 5ffa7-a6-t2.

Method	MAE [px]	$pMAE$ [%]	σ_d [px/s]	AAC [px]
BB-DCM-1	1.000 0.42	1.000 3.34	1.000 0.99	1.000 0.55
BB-DCM-2	0.517 0.28	0.480 2.15	0.469 0.65	0.487 0.35
BB-DCM-5	0.414 0.25	0.410 1.99	0.625 0.75	0.487 0.35
CG-DCM-1	0.138 0.17	0.153 1.4	0.109 0.42	0.205 0.24
CG-DCM-2	0.034 0.14	0.013 1.08	0.000 0.35	0.051 0.18
CG-DCM-5	0.000 0.13	0.000 1.05	0.000 0.35	0.000 0.16
CCIA-DCM-1	0.379 0.24	0.367 1.89	0.297 0.54	0.231 0.25
CCIA-DCM-2	0.034 0.14	0.035 1.13	0.047 0.38	0.000 0.16
CCIA-DCM-5	0.034 0.14	0.013 1.08	0.000 0.35	0.000 0.16

Table 2. Evaluation of DCMs for all tracks. The weighted mean of the previous tables was taken into account with the track confidence level based on length as weight.

Method-Resize	MAE [px]	$pMAE$ [%]	σ_d [px/s]	AAC [px]
BB-DCM-1	1.000 0.43	1.000 3.25	1.000 0.90	1.000 0.55
BB-DCM-2	0.444 0.28	0.408 2.09	0.500 0.68	0.545 0.40
BB-DCM-5	0.333 0.25	0.270 1.82	0.432 0.65	0.455 0.37
CG-DCM-1	0.148 0.20	0.158 1.6	0.091 0.5	0.242 0.30
CG-DCM-2	0.037 0.17	0.010 1.31	0.000 0.46	0.091 0.25
CG-DCM-5	0.000 0.16	0.000 1.29	0.000 0.46	0.091 0.25
CCIA-DCM-1	0.333 0.25	0.342 1.96	0.364 0.62	0.182 0.28
CCIA-DCM-2	0.111 0.19	0.097 1.48	0.068 0.49	0.000 0.22
CCIA-DCM-5	0.037 0.17	0.020 1.33	0.000 0.46	0.030 0.23

Linear charts that contain disparity calculated over time were produced and are shown in Figs. 6, 7, 8, 9. The BB-, CG- and CCIA-DCM are separately plotted on three diagrams to ensure clarity. The results of BB-DCM-1 are added to each plot for comparison.

The plots indicate that BB-DCM produces the most noisy disparity signal, with occasional spikes deviating from surrounding values by up to 5 px. This can be clearly seen in Track 18c39-m6-t0 after the timestamp 12:33:53. This situation happened due to the bird's contour missing one wing, probably due to obstructed visibility or an error in simulated background extraction. On the other hand, CG-DCM shows good stability and produces smooth curves, confirming the hypothesis that CG-DCM is resistant to quantization effects. The CCIA-DCM is characterized by good stability, but the quantization error is visible compared to CG-DCM. These methods are more resistant to noises affecting birds' images.

The presented data show that CG-DCM-2, CG-DCM-5 and CCIA-DCM-5 are the most robust methods in light of the four measures, which confirms our hypothesis that these techniques would yield better results than BB-DCM. However, the CCIA-DCM-5 is not better than CG-DCM-5 in light of most of the measures.

Another important property of the tested methods is their computational complexity. BB-DCM and CG-DCM methods perform only a few simple operations on an image to calculate the centers, but CIAA-DCM needs to find the best shift vector iteratively. Simple performance time measurements for CCIA-DCM-5 and CG-DCM-5 show that their average running time for one image was 953 ms and 0.5 ms, respectively, i.e. that the second one is almost 1000 times faster without compromising other quality measures.

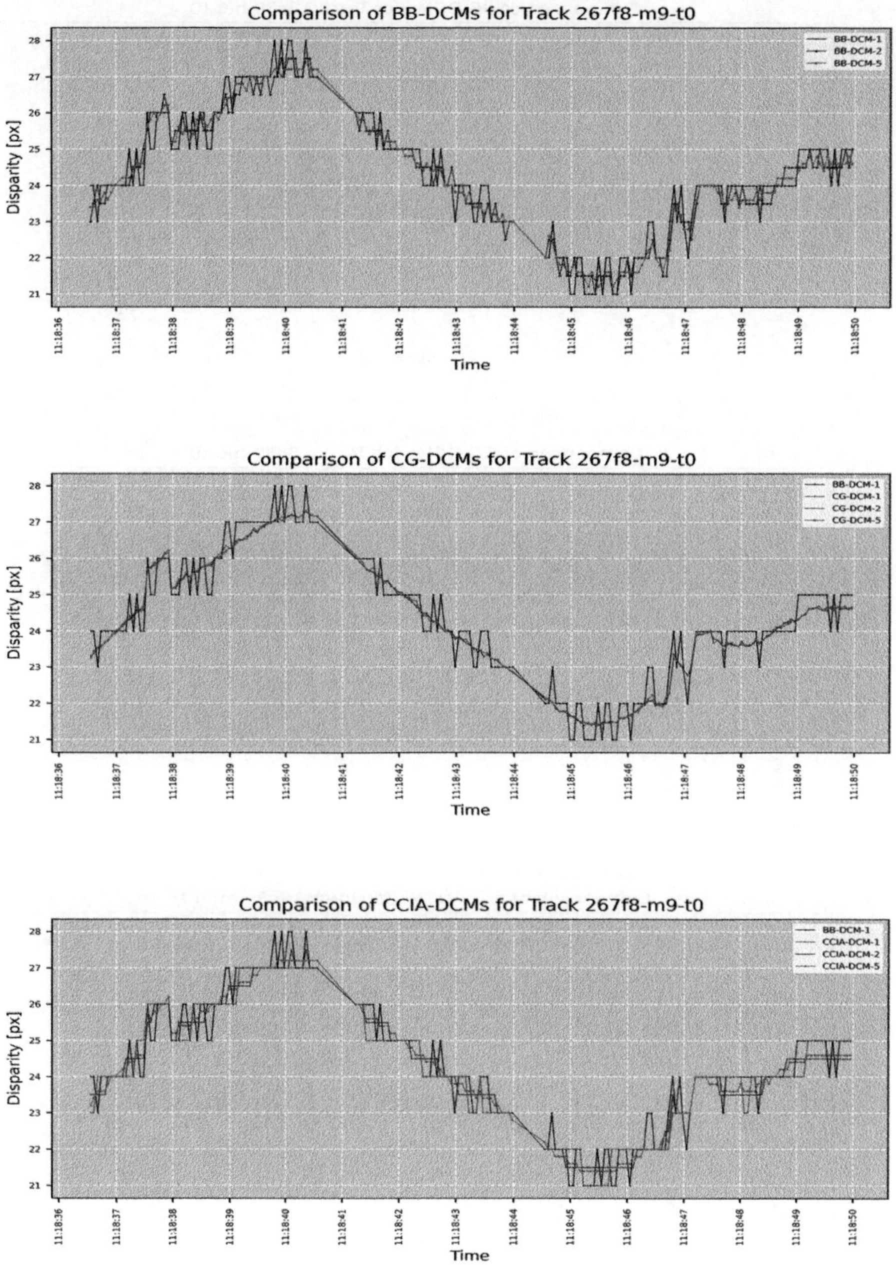

Fig. 6. Disparity calculation over time for Track 267f8-m9-t0 using different methods. Resize factors (1, 2, 5) were included in the method's name.

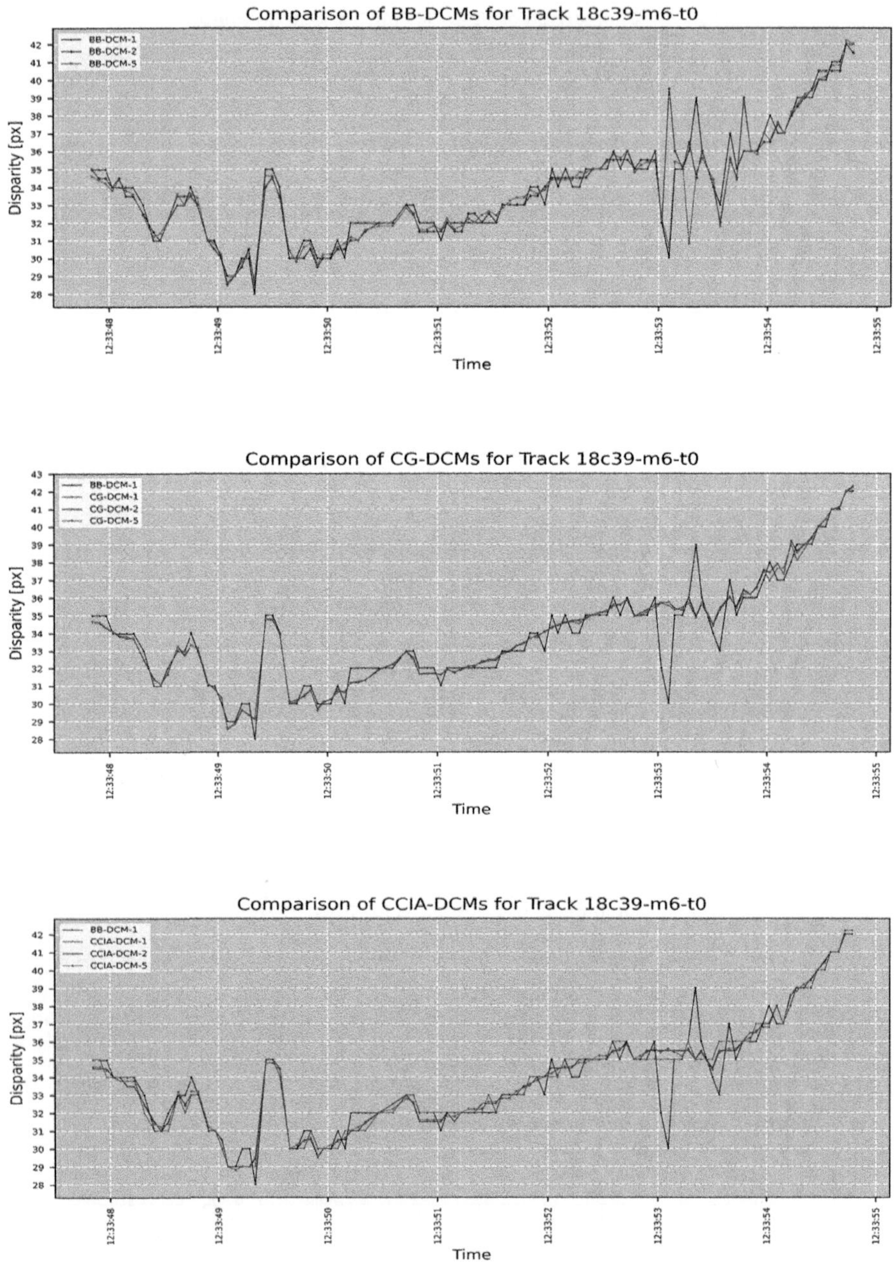

Fig. 7. Disparity calculation over time for Track 18c39-m6-t0 using different methods. Resize factors (1, 2, 5) are included in the method's names.

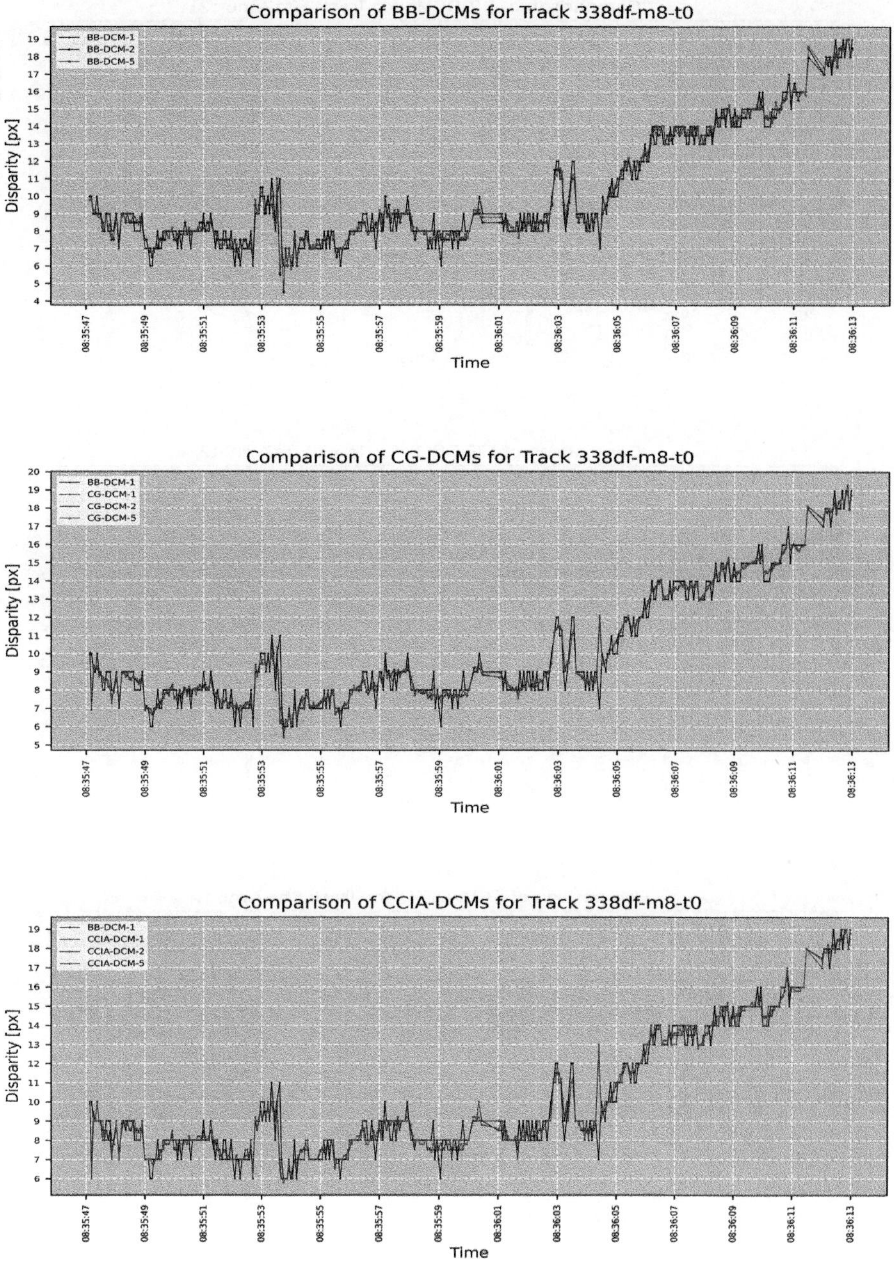

Fig. 8. Disparity calculation over time for Track 338df-m8-t0 using different methods. Resize factors (1, 2, 5) are included in the method's names.

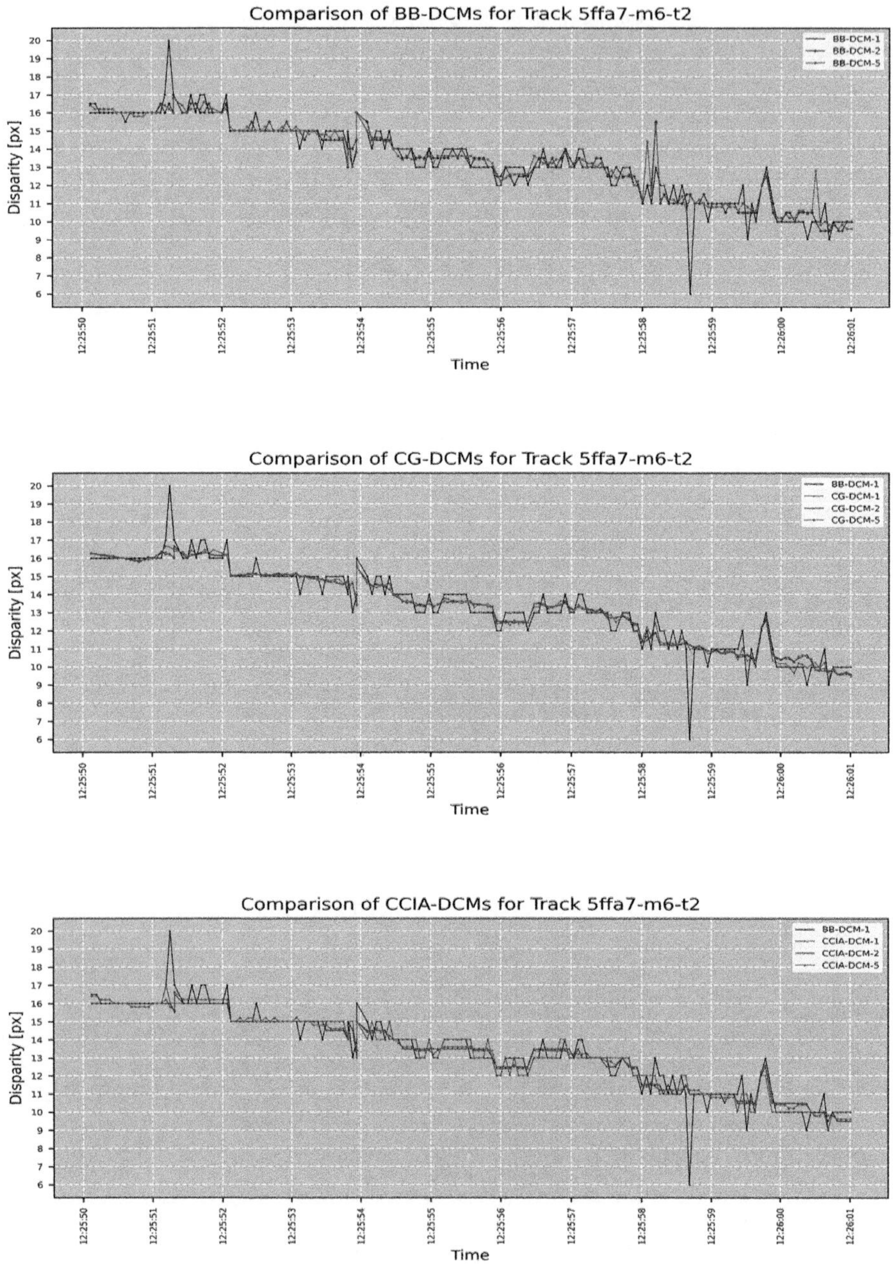

Fig. 9. Disparity calculation over time for Track 5ffa7-m6-t2 using different methods. Resize factors (1, 2, 5) are included in the method's names.

5.4 Methods' Impact on Distance Estimation

Since the variable that matters most in the bird monitoring and collision prevention system is the distance from the wind turbine, this section translates the disparity studied in previous sections to distance, gives a simple visualization and analyzes distance differences between studied methods.

We assume that the reader is familiar with basics of epipolar geometry, otherwise please consult [26]. The stereo vision cameras admit the pin-hole model and are well aligned and calibrated. To show how the presented methods affect distance estimation, we recall some basic formulas.

For the given camera parameters: resolution 3200 px $\times$ 2400 px; the field of view $42.9° \times 32.8°$; focal lengths $f_x \approx 4072$ px, $f_y \approx 4077$ px; the principal point c_x, c_y marking the center of the image and baseline $B = 1$ m between two cameras, we are able to calculate real-world coordinates of the object, relative to the camera pair:

$$X = \frac{(x - c_x) \cdot Z}{f_x}, \tag{13}$$

$$Y = \frac{(y - c_y) \cdot Z}{f_y}, \tag{14}$$

$$Z = \frac{f_y \cdot B}{y_{\text{diff}}}. \tag{15}$$

Since our focus is on long distance, it is beneficial to represent the object in spherical coordinates:

$$(\theta, \phi, D) = \left(\arctan 2(Y, X), \arccos\left(\frac{Z}{\sqrt{X^2 + Y^2 + Z^2}}\right), \sqrt{X^2 + Y^2 + Z^2}\right) \tag{16}$$

with azimuthal angle θ, polar angle ϕ and the Euclidean distance to the object D.

In Fig. 10, four circular diagrams are presented plotting (θ, D) for BB-DCM-1 and CCIA-DCM-5. The figures show that due to the quantization phenomena, the relative distance estimation uncertainty is higher for birds flying further from the turbine. We see that for a bird flying within a 200 m distance, see Fig. 10c and 10d, the measurement uncertainty is around 10 m, i.e. 5%. For a bird flying at an average distance of around 450 m, the uncertainty grows to around 100 m, i.e. 22%; see Fig. 10b.

As was mentioned in the introduction section, this is a distance that can be considered as a turbine stop radius. If the estimation uncertainty is high, it might negatively impact bird-turbine collision risk assessment models [20].

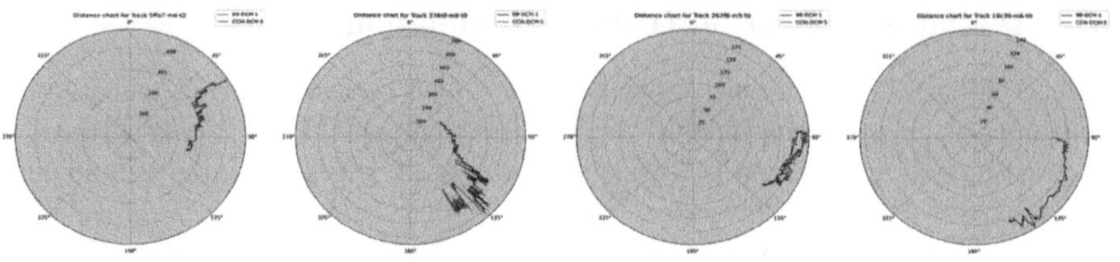

(a) Visualization of Track 5ffa7-m6-t2. (b) Visualization of Track 338df-m8-t0. (c) Visualization of Track 267f8-m9-t0. (d) Visualization of Track 18c39-m6-t0.

Fig. 10. Visualizations of the four tracks with respect to bird's distance D from the wind turbine and horizontal angle θ.

6 Conclusions and Future Work

This paper addresses the need for 3D monitoring of the birds around wind turbines in a stable and precise way using a stereovision system with pairs of cameras. The key challenge is to assess the bird's distance from the wind turbine and to improve its precision and stability; a robust method for disparity estimation needs to be found.

Three methods are studied in this paper: the bounding box method (BB-DCM), the center of gravity method (CG-DCM) and the cross-correlation image alignment method (CCIA-DCM). Resizing the images to greater resolutions by a factor of 2 and 5 is also considered.

The comprehensive evaluation provided insights into their strengths and limitations. Of all the methods, the CG-DCM with resize factor 2 and 5, and CIAA-DCM with factor 5 are confirmed to be the best, with most of their scores being in the top 10% on the normalized values scale. However, only CG-DCM is efficient enough in terms of running time to be considered a good candidate for real-time systems.

As was highlighted, the paper's aim is to review disparity estimation methods and evaluate their usability in a real-time application. The most suitable solution in terms of stability, precision and time complexity is the CG-DCM method with a resize factor of 2 or 5.

In the future, additional testing on other tracks can be conducted, and the method may be adjusted in terms of hyper parameters such as blurring kernels, resize factors and thresholds. After the tuning, it can be implemented in the BPS system to enhance bird monitoring.

Acknowledgement. This research was funded by The National Centre for Research and Development of Poland grant number POIR.01.02.00-00-0247/17. Project title: 'Realization of R&D works leading to the implementation of a new solution - MULTIREJESTRATOR PLUS for monitoring and control of the power system in terms of operational efficiency, the life span extending and optimizing the impact on the surrounding wind farms'.

Disclosure of Interests. The authors have no competing interests to declare that are relevant to the content of this article.

References

1. KNE - Detektionssysteme zur ereignisbezogenen Abschaltung von Windenergieanlagen zum Schutz von tagaktiven Brutvögeln - Kompetenzzentrum Naturschutz und Energiewende (2024). https://www.naturschutz-energiewende.de/publikationen/. Accessed 10 Nov 2024
2. Valorisation scientifique : publications - Projet Mape (2024). https://mape.cnrs.fr/autres-telechargements/publications-valorisation-scientifique. Accessed 18 Nov 2024
3. Bradski, G.: Learning OpenCV: computer vision with the OpenCV library. O'REILLY Google Schola **2**, 334–352 (2008)
4. Chen, L.D., Yu, J.J., Cheng, W.H., Huang, C.T.: Sub-pixel disparity estimation in continuous space. In: 2015 IEEE International Conference on Consumer Electronics - Taiwan, pp. 06–08. IEEE. https://doi.org/10.1109/ICCE-TW.2015.7216807
5. Cournet, M., et al.: 2D sub-pixel disparity measurement using QPEC/Medicis. Int. Arch. Photogrammetry Remote Sens. Spatial Inf. Sci. **XLI-B1**, 291–298 (2016). https://doi.org/10.5194/isprs-archives-XLI-B1-291-2016
6. Dai, Q., Li, J., Yi, Q., Fang, F., Zhang, G.: Feedback Network for Mutually Boosted Stereo Image Super-Resolution and Disparity Estimation. arXiv (2021). https://doi.org/10.48550/arXiv.2106.00985
7. Dziak, D., et al.: Airport wildlife hazard management system - a sensor fusion approach. Elektronika ir Elektrotechnika **28**(3), 45–53 (2022). https://www.diva-portal.org/smash/record.jsf?pid=diva2%3A1687227&dswid=-3207
8. Gehrig, S., Franke, U.: Improving stereo sub-pixel accuracy for long range stereo, pp. 1–7 (2007). https://doi.org/10.1109/ICCV.2007.4409212
9. Gehrig, S.K., Badino, H., Franke, U.: Improving sub-pixel accuracy for long range stereo. Comput. Vision Image Understanding **116**(1), 16–24 (2012). https://doi.org/10.1016/j.cviu.2011.07.008
10. Gonzalez, R.C.: Digital image processing. Pearson education India (2009)
11. Gradolewski, D.: Sensors and Algorithms in Industry 4.0 : Security and Health Preservation Applications. Ph.D. thesis, Blekinge Tekniska Högskola (2021). https://www.diva-portal.org/smash/record.jsf?pid=diva2%3A1553796&dswid=-3720
12. Gradolewski, D., Dziak, D., Kaniecki, D., Jaworski, A., Skakuj, M., Kulesza, W.J.: A runway safety system based on vertically oriented stereovision. Sensors **21**(4), 1464 (2021). https://doi.org/10.3390/s21041464
13. Gradolewski, D., et al.: Comprehensive bird preservation at wind farms. Sensors **21**(1), 267 (2021). https://doi.org/10.3390/s21010267
14. Henriques, J.F., Caseiro, R., Martins, P., Batista, J.: High-Speed Tracking with Kernelized Correlation Filters. arXiv (2014). https://doi.org/10.1109/TPAMI.2014.2345390
15. Hsu, T.S., Wang, T.C.: An improvement stereo vision images processing for object distance measurement. Int. J. Autom. Smart Technol. (2015). https://www.semanticscholar.org/paper/An-Improvement-Stereo-Vision-Images-Processing-for-Hsu-Wang/e4da0993bcb064a8ea2936a8b405a5fe16768ef3

16. Jiang, N., Qu, Y., Li, Y.: Fast sub-pixel accuracy stereo image matching based on disparity plane. In: Proceedings Volume 9622, 2015 International Conference on Optical Instruments and Technology: Optoelectronic Imaging and Processing Technology, vol. 9622, pp. 362–370. SPIE (2015). https://doi.org/10.1117/12.2193512
17. Krenc, K., Gradolewski, D., Dziak, D., Kawalec, A.: Application of radar solutions for the purpose of bird tracking systems based on video observation. Sensors **22**(10), 3660 (2022). https://doi.org/10.3390/s22103660
18. Lewis, J.P., et al.: Fast template matching. In: Vision interface. vol. 95, pp. 15–19. Quebec City, QC, Canada (1995)
19. Lim, Y.C., Lee, C.H., Kwon, S., Jung, W.Y.: Distance estimation algorithm for both long and short ranges based on stereo vision system. In: 2008 IEEE Intelligent Vehicles Symposium, pp. 04–06. IEEE. https://doi.org/10.1109/IVS.2008.4621190
20. Madejski, G., Tkaczyk, R., Gradolewski, D., Dziak, D., Kulesza, W.: Risk assessment of bird collisions with a wind turbine based on flight parameters. Elektronika ir Elektrotechnika **30**(4), 4–10 (2024). https://www.diva-portal.org/smash/record.jsf?pid=diva2%3A1906894&dswid=-6584
21. Marcoň, P., et al.: A system using artificial intelligence to detect and scare bird flocks in the protection of ripening fruit. Sensors **21**(12), 4244 (2021). https://doi.org/10.3390/s21124244
22. McClure, C.J.W., Martinson, L., Allison, T.D.: Automated monitoring for birds in flight: proof of concept with eagles at a wind power facility. Biol. Conserv. **224**, 26–33 (2018). https://doi.org/10.1016/j.biocon.2018.04.041
23. Psychogyios, D., Mazomenos, E., Vasconcelos, F., Stoyanov, D.: MSDESIS: multitask stereo disparity estimation and surgical instrument segmentation. IEEE Trans. Med. Imaging **41**(11), 3218–3230 (2022). https://doi.org/10.1109/TMI.2022.3181229
24. Stark, H., Früh, D.: Endbericht Raumnutzungsanalyse Großvögel im Windpark Osterburg. Auftraggeber: FEFA (2020). www.landkreis-helmstedt.de/downloads/datei/
25. Szeliski, R.: Computer vision: algorithms and applications. Springer Nature (2022)
26. Xu, G., Zhang, Z.: Epipolar geometry in stereo, motion and object recognition: a unified approach, vol. 6. Springer Science & Business Media (2013)

Author Index

A
AI-Hamadi, Ayoub 312
Akram, Waseem 103
Al-Hamadi, Ayoub 28, 74, 164
Al-Tawil, Basheer 74
Andriamarozakaniaina, Tahiry Filamatra 524
Ardhaoui, Mahassen 469
Arens, Michael 488
Arik, Sabri 265

B
Ballesteros-Jerez, Javier 148
Bani Milhim, Alaeddin 294
Becker, Stefan 488
Ben Salah, Iheb 469
Bernardin, Hagamalala Santatra 524
Beyerer, Jürgen 488
Burgdorf, Simon-Johannes 15

C
Castillo-Cara, Manuel 148
Cech, Jan 1
Chapin, Alexandre 510
Chen, Liming 454, 510
Coleman, Sonya 364
Cunningham, Colton 294

D
Dellandréa, Emmanuel 454, 510
Deshmukh, Yashwardhan 433
Deveza, William Kyle 228
Dhungana, Hariom 383
Diagne, Salick 433
Din, Muhayy Ud 103
Dinges, Laslo 164

E
Engelhardt, Helmut 348

F
Farid, Ali Moltajaei 193
Faydasicok, Ozlem 265
Franke, Jörg 348
Frese, Udo 208
Fujii, Noeko 328

G
García-Varea, Ismael 148
Gradolewski, Dawid 535
Grard, Matthieu 454

H
Hanis, Tomas 1
Hartl-Nesic, Christian 275
Hashimoto, Manabu 130
Hasselbring, Arne 208
Hempel, Thorsten 28, 74
Hübner, Wolfgang 488
Hug, Ronny 488
Hussain, Irfan 103
Hyashi, Kota 115

I
Ibarra, Joseph Bryan 228

J
Jahoda, Petr 1
Jatzkowski, Inga 414
Jessel, Jean-Pierre 524
Jung, Magnus 74, 164, 312

K
Kalenberg, Matthias 348
Kaoka, Włodzimierz 535
Karim, Md Rezwanul 15
Kerr, Dermot 364
Knoop, Niklas 414
Kulesza, Wlodek J. 535

J. Röning and J. Filipe (Eds.): ROBOVIS 2025, CCIS 2629, pp. 557–558, 2026.
https://doi.org/10.1007/978-3-032-00986-9

L
Latha, Abhishek V. 92
Loianno, Giuseppe 250

M
Madejski, Grzegorz 535
Marcus, Richard 414
Martin, Sina 348
Martínez-Gómez, Jesus 148
Merabet, Adel 92
Michiels, Nick 44
Morillo, Paulina 182
Mouhoub, Malek 193

N
Nguyen, The Leo 294
Nienaber, Sören 164

O
Olszewska, J. I. 397
Omori, Motonobu 115
Ormaza, Jesús 182
Orozco-Barbosa, Luis 148
Otis, Martin J.-D. 433, 469

P
Páez-Ubieta, Ignacio de Loyola 63
Puente, Santiago T. 63
Put, Jeroen 44

Q
Quinn, Justin 364

R
Rahem, Remy 469
Rahimipour, Mohammad 92
Ramanana, Hasinarivo Marie Berthis 524
Reeth, Frank Van 44

S
Sakai, Tetsuya 328
Schulz, Paul 28
Sebeto, Paolo 275
Sejera, Marloun 228
Seneviratne, Lakmal 103
Shino, Motoki 115
Shuvo, Md Golam Rabby 364
Stamminger, Marc 414
Stocki, Aleksy 535
Suzuki, Takahiro 130
Svancar, Jan 1

T
Thurow, Kerstin 15

V
Vallejo-Huanga, Diego 182
Vanhele, Bram 44
Velasco-Sánchez, Edison P. 63
Vincze, Markus 275
Vogel, Christian 414

W
Wachsmuth, Sven 74, 312
Wang, Huibin 164
Weber, Amadeus 312
Weibel, Jean-Baptiste 275

Y
Yang, Qiaoyue 74, 312
Yang, Rui 454
Yoshitake, Hiroshi 115

Z
Zhou, Yang 250
Zoomers, Brent 44

GPSR Compliance

The European Union's (EU) General Product Safety Regulation (GPSR) is a set of rules that requires consumer products to be safe and our obligations to ensure this.

If you have any concerns about our products, you can contact us on ProductSafety@springernature.com

In case Publisher is established outside the EU, the EU authorized representative is:

Springer Nature Customer Service Center GmbH
Europaplatz 3
69115 Heidelberg, Germany

Batch number: 09013048

Printed by Printforce, the Netherlands